TRISTANISSIMO

TRISTANISSIMO

The Authorized Biography of Heroic Tenor Lauritz Melchior

SHIRLEE EMMONS

Foreword by
Birgit Nilsson

SCHIRMER BOOKS
A Division of Macmillan, Inc.
NEW YORK
Collier Macmillan Publishers
LONDON

Schirmer Books
A Division of Macmillan, Inc.
866 Third Avenue, New York, N.Y. 10022

Collier Macmillan Canada, Inc.

Library of Congress Catalog Card Number: 89-10938

Printed in the United States of America

printing number
1 2 3 4 5 6 7 8 9 10

Library of Congress Cataloging-in-Publication Data

Emmons, Shirlee.
   Tristanissimo: the authorized biography of heroic tenor Lauritz Melchior/Shirlee Emmons:
foreword by Birgit Nilsson.
      p.   cm.
   Includes bibiliograhical references and discography.
   ISBN 0-02-873060-7
   1. Melchior, Lauritz. 2. Singers—Biography. I Title.
ML420.M352E4 1990
782.1'092—dc20
[B]

                                                                                      89-10938
                                                                                         CIP
                                                                                          MN

For Rollin and Hilary

who never once in seven years protested
my abdication of wifely and motherly duties

Contents

Foreword by Birgit Nilsson   ix
Preface   xi
Acknowledgments   xv

CHAPTER 1 • Da Capo: "En Københavner Dreng" (1890–1905)   1

CHAPTER 2 • Training as a Baritone (1905–1916)   6

CHAPTER 3 • Metamorphosis: Baritone into Tenor (1916–1922)   12

CHAPTER 4 • A Bayreuth Beginning (1923–1924)   29

CHAPTER 5 • From Bayreuth to the World (1924–1927)   45

CHAPTER 6 • The Metropolitan Debut (1926–1927)   63

CHAPTER 7 • Learning Tristan (1927–1930)   78

CHAPTER 8 • Tristanissimo (1929–1931)   95

CHAPTER 9 • The Wagnerian Ensemble at the Met (1931–1935)   112

CHAPTER 10 • The Golden Years (1935–1939)   133

CHAPTER 11 • Hitler Interferes (1939–1941)   167

CHAPTER 12 • Another Legendary Partnership: Melchior and Traubel
(1941–1946)   186

CHAPTER 13 • From Opera Star to Movie Star (1943–1946)   207

CHAPTER 14 • The Hottest Dane Since Beowulf (1946–1949)   226

CHAPTER 15 • A Dream Unrealized (1949–1950)   249

CHAPTER 16 • Vacation from Valhalla (1950–1959)   271

CHAPTER 17 • Melchior and the Heldentenor Crisis (1960–1972)   291

CHAPTER 18 • "Leb' wohl, mein Held" (1973–1974)   323

Notes   333
Sources   405
Bibliography   407
Lauritz Melchior's Roles   411
Discography by Hans Hansen   417
Index   452

Illustrations follow pages 110 and 238

Foreword

"I'm sorry I missed the train," said Lauritz Melchior to me when we met. "What a wonderful couple we would have made!"

Mutual friends had taken me to Melchior's hotel suite, where he and I were to be introduced to each other. The very prospect of our meeting had so overawed me that I kept asking myself, "What should *I* say?" While I had always heard so much about Melchior, how all-embracing and irresistible his personality, how unaffected and genial his manner, I was not really prepared for the physical effect of the man himself. There he stood just inside the door, tall and broad-chested, so very attractive and masculine that my heart actually began to flutter. Immediately very friendly, he clasped me in his arms as he said hello. When I then shyly retreated a bit, he said, "Come here," and put out one arm shoulder-high. Because I am not as tall as I look on stage, I stood precisely under his arm. "It just fits," he beamed. "We would have been fine together."

After a most pleasant conversation, he invited me to have dinner at his favorite restaurant. I was thrilled to accept his invitation, but insisted upon changing into clothes more suitable for such a stellar occasion. At the Copenhagen restaurant, I witnessed what I had previously only been told about: Melchior's great pleasure in being a host. Although there was an immense smorgasbord, he ordered even more delicious Scandinavian dishes to tempt me. He of course had his aquavit and his beer, as is the Scandinavian custom. Despite the profusion of wonderful dishes before us, he absolutely astonished me by eating piece after piece of pumpernickel bread spread with goose fat, covered with an onion slice, then peppered and salted—another old custom, I believe. My stomach had difficulty adjusting to the sight. Surely, I thought, this was not a healthy thing for a man who was no youngster any longer. But he just kept eating his dangerous concoction and saying, "This is delicious!"

That entire night was a sleepless one for me, for it was impossible to stop thinking about our meeting. I had been completely captivated by the man.

Living up to his reputation—not only as a superb raconteur but also as a prankster—Melchior had told me a very funny story. It was about Frida Leider, a singer whom he really loved. They were singing a joint concert in Philadelphia. Frida's solo group started with Brahms's "Auf dem Kirchhofe," which is so sad a song that Melchior thought he should cheer up the audience. Seeing a bicycle backstage, he took it out and rode it behind her back while she was singing. The public burst out laughing at the sight, and poor Frida Leider could not understand what was going on. Indeed, Melchior never did admit to her the truth about his mischievous deed.

What a wonderful sense of humor the Danes have. I really envy them because they know how to live and they take life much easier than we in

Sweden. Tomorrow is another day, they say. That is their way. Melchior knew how to enjoy himself and took everything as it came. He was a real man, a real Viking, exactly as one thinks a Viking ought to be.

And he even had something from Denmark in his voice, a typically Danish timbre, I think. Hearing his singing only in recordings, I had always thought that his voice was so virile. Then, when I saw the man in person, I thought, "It fits," even as he had said to me.

His voice was wonderful, so very, very beautiful, and with a darkness that there should be in a Wagnerian tenor. He had something indefinable in the voice. One was absolutely taken with it. I cannot explain it except by saying that it was sexy, for it had so much masculinity. When I think how long he sang, it is unbelievable to me, but seeing that man, so tall and big, you knew he must have had the stamina for three.

I come from the south of Sweden, which belonged to Denmark 300 years ago. Once when I was introduced before a concert in Copenhagen, the director said, "Sweden can keep that territory, but we want Birgit back." Perhaps if history had been different, I might have been able to sing with Melchior. I really would have loved that. Melchior himself said, "Poor Birgit Nilsson. She has no playmate for her Isolde and her Brünnhilde." Many others have lamented the bad timing that kept us from singing Wagner together, saying, "If only you had sung with Melchior," but I am the one who regrets it the most. To have *such* a playmate would have been a fantastic experience.

Birgit Nilsson

Preface

The Danish singer Lauritz Melchior (1890–1973) sang leading Wagnerian roles at the Bayreuth Festival from 1924 through 1931, at London's Covent Garden from 1924 through 1939, and enjoyed a career as reigning Heldentenor at the Metropolitan Opera spanning the years from 1926 through 1950. Melchior was unquestionably the greatest heroic tenor of his time. Critically regarded throughout the world as vocally unexcelled—even to this day—he may very well prove to be the greatest Heldentenor of all time. Indeed, he has become the standard by which other candidates are now measured: Forty years after his last performance, seventeen years after his death, the world still actively awaits "another Melchior." Each time a status report is issued on the international supply of operatic singers, new voices are exhaustively compared to earlier artists, but no such elaborate comparisons are made in the heroic tenor category. Invariably, music critics, such as radio commentator and critic George Jellinek, make simple statements: "The more tenors I hear in Wagnerian repertoire the more I am convinced that Melchior will never be equaled, let alone surpassed." British music historian Michael Scott writes that "when nature created Lauritz Melchior she broke the mold and having done so threw it away. . . . To this day he has had no successor."

The standards Melchior set in the cruel Heldentenor repertoire were primarily vocal: a power that for music critic Peter G. Davis "[defied] the laws of nature"; a capacity for beautiful lyricism, rare in a voice possessing such strength and thrust; a ringing tone that was not diminished, as is usual, by vicissitudes of range; a superbly skillful and dramatic declamation of text; a limitless physical stamina that enabled him to sing with lavish intensity and fervor to the age of 70 and to cancel only three times in a total of 515 Metropolitan Opera performances. These facets of his art garnered him an imposing international group of admirers, some of whom heard him only on record many years after he stopped singing. The astonishing ease and absolute security with which he sang those exigent Wagnerian roles have made him a legend.

Lauritz Melchior was not only a "Wagnerian tenor supreme" (as British music critic John Steane called him), justly revered for his vocal superiority. He was also, literally, a towering and imposing figure, a fascinating man with a larger-than-life personality and a generous, kindhearted, as well as trusting, nature. John Steane even taxes his "jovial, easy-going humanity" with "perhaps [costing] him something in artistic stature and respect." Indeed, Melchior's high-profile "physical bulk, appetite, thirst, joking, and buffoonery" caused him to be "to some degree taken for granted" as an artist.

It is clear that vocal and physical endowment, technical skills, and character must mesh to produce a singing legend, but there is in Melchior's case the added element of his Danish heritage. It pervaded the tenor's life from its outset to its conclusion and, as we shall see, totally shaped his personality. Those characteristically Danish qualities, such as a genial hedonism, dedication to hospitality and friendship, cheerfulness and generosity, deep patriotism, a vigilant preoccupation with the quality of food and drink, and, not least, a love of music and singing, were to be found in Melchior's personality throughout his life. Above all, Melchior was graced with a first-rate sense of humor that often erupted in a penchant for practical jokes and enabled him both to invent some very funny one-line ripostes on the spur of the moment and to play the clown without inhibitions. Although these qualities were not publicly evident in the beginning of his career, they later made it possible for him to become a fine comedian in movies and radio, and, coincidentally, to sway the American public of the 1940s and 1950s from its ingrained belief that opera singers were highly dignified, exalted, and unfriendly creatures who sang pretentious music that the ordinary person could never understand. He converted large numbers of Americans into opera enthusiasts. Americans and Europeans alike appreciated his no-nonsense attitude—he sang whenever he was supposed to, without fussing over circumstances or surroundings—and they treasured his oft-repeated comment, "I never let singing interfere with living."

His deep conviction that there was only one way to deliver the Wagnerian roles—the way he was taught at Bayreuth by Cosima and Siegfried Wagner (the composer's widow and son) and by his coach Karl Kittel—left him vulnerable to attacks against what some perceived as his complacency and laziness. Having worked diligently to perfect his Wagnerian roles according to the "Bayreuth tradition," as Cosima and Siegfried perceived it, he then refused to change artistically. Outside of his singing responsibilities, his life was a convivial one: he delighted in entertaining friends, colleagues, and fellow Royal Danish Guards. In addition, he was devoted to hunting, one of his great passions. His love for nature, wilderness areas, and the outdoor life was genuine, instilled at an early age by his father. By the last quarter of his life, his leisure time was spent preparing for, enjoying, or returning from hunting.

Although he was from an educated and cultivated family, their financial reverses made struggle for success an inevitable fact of his artistic life. He did enjoy, however, phenomenal luck. At the critical moment someone always appeared to propel him along his path. Kristine Jensen, the Melchior family housekeeper, made a small fortune writing cookbooks and lavished the proceeds upon her charge, making early voice and drama lessons possible. The British writer and opera dilettante Hugh Walpole took it upon himself to finance further studies, support Lauritz's family, and launch an international career. Queen Alexandra of England, born a Danish princess, unquestionably aided his early career in Britain. His second wife devoted her entire life to his well-being and his career. She even set herself to learn the methods (admirable or not) of the newly invented "personal" public relations of the 1930s, and became so expert at it that *Melchior* was eventually a household word in an era when the fame of serious singers was more or less confined to opera aficionados.

Like most voice teachers, and perhaps some critics, I find that it is virtually impossible to explain the complicated neurological, physiological, and psychological processes going on in the minds and bodies of singers that produce their vocal prowess. It is tempting to work backwards from the audible result, but such deductions often lead to regrettable misconceptions. It is for this reason that voice teachers find it presumptuous to assume that their conclusions are the only valid ones. Especially unbecoming are guesses (however educated) about a phenomenon like Melchior. I have made a strenuous effort to reserve my own technical comments to areas well within my teaching and singing experience, and I have relied instead on the observations of voice teacher and writer Conrad L. Osborne, which are almost without exception accepted as the most knowledgeable. I also include Melchior's own views on vocal technique, although his statements on this subject are quite limited. The late eminent voice scientist Berton Coffin has wisely suggested that Melchior may have feared discussing his vocal technique lest it be rendered too cerebral, too conscious, and thus lead to an inadvertent diminution of his physical control.

Bringing the life and art of Laurtiz Melchior to the reader, I have been allowed to view without restrictions the Melchior family's collection of papers, diaries, and correspondence. Among these sources is a diary that, judging from the changes in handwriting and colors of ink, Melchior began somewhere around the 1920s, at which time he went back and filled in dates and events from his childhood. He continued to keep it up to date until 1945. A personal manuscript was handwritten by Melchior and, according to family belief, had been started in 1946. It covers the years from 1907 through 1950. These two sources are written in Danish, have never been published, and have been translated for my use in this biography by Inga Hulgaard. Over fifty scrapbooks kept by Lauritz and Kleinchen Melchior contain press clippings and special-interest materials dating from 1918 to 1973. They are housed in the Lauritz Melchior Memorial Room at Dana College in Blair, Nebraska. Melchior kept a fanatically accurate account of all his performances and fees, casts and conductors, in a special account book that I have taken as the basis for my appendix listing his roles. The family history book, or *Stambog*, contains all the births and deaths of family members—these were recorded first by Melchior's father, then by Melchior himself, and are now kept up to date by his son, Ib Melchior. I have also taken much material from the two remaining diaries of Melchior's second wife, handwritten in German, and translated by Inga Hulgaard.

Melchior prided himself upon his ability as a raconteur, telling and retelling the major stories of his life, seemingly relishing the most humorous ones. Whenever possible, I have preferred to use the versions as told to family and friends by Melchior in person, rather than those that appeared in print.

In the course of writing this book, I have come to feel more than respect, more than the honest affection I accorded Lauritz Melchior during our professional relationship. Knowing all the facts that illuminate the admirable as well as the less praiseworthy facets of his life has led me to a poignant conclusion, recently confirmed for me by Lauritz's daughter-in-law, Cleo Melchior, whose professional name is Cleo Baldon. In his declining years, spurred perhaps by the failure of his third marriage, an uncharacteristically philosophical Melchior confided to her, "How wonderful it must be to know whom to trust. I have never been able to do that. So I decided that I would trust everyone." Clearly, he had decided upon self-delusion as the most comfortable way of life. A theme of crucial significance to him throughout his life was his fear of loneliness and his hunger for unreserved love and affection from those closest to him.

Perhaps one of the most conspicuous failings of Melchior's life was his neglected relationship with his two children and what he allowed to happen to them as a result of his absolute trust in his second wife. Nevertheless, this desire to be at peace about human relationships did solve the problem faced by all singers, that of how not to become a monster in the quest for success. Melchior never turned into a "divo." He was able to be unfailingly jovial, kind, generous, and comradely, and for this he was loved.

Acknowledgments

I am deeply indebted to Marianne Tegner, Lauritz Melchior's last personal secretary, for introducing me to the Melchior family, for helping me with unabating energy in every conceivable way to reap the most benefit from my first visit to Copenhagen, for offering me materials in her possession that related to Melchior, for opening paths to other persons in Melchior's later life, and for her unflagging interest in my project over seven years.

A great debt of gratitude is owed to Ib and Cleo Melchior who not only trusted me with the diaries, family papers, and photos, and tolerated with unflagging grace and candor my very personal questions concerning their feelings about Lauritz—thus making it possible for me to write this family-authorized biography—but generously offered me both their friendship and the bounteous hospitality of their home.

To Birte Melchior, my thanks for being so forthcoming about family history, candid about her own feelings, and generously sharing her personal materials.

Finally, this book was read and much improved by the criticisms of Ib and Cleo Melchior and Marianne Tegner.

It would have been impossible to write *Tristanissimo* without the immeasurable help of three people: Inga Hulgaard, who acted as an editorial assistant, translated all Danish and German materials, and took upon her capable shoulders many of my research problems; Andrea Matthews, who spent untold selfless hours away from her singing in order to rescue me from the difficulties of editing my own work in progress; and my editor, Robert Axelrod, who made it possible for me to change this manuscript from a less professional, although loving, account of Lauritz Melchior's life into a reasonably literate biography.

I am most grateful to two Danish gentlemen, Knud Hegermann-Lindencrone and Andreas Damgaard, for viewing this project as their own, indefatigably searching out related materials, helping in every imaginable way throughout the many years required to bring the book to a conclusion. To another Danish gentleman, Hans Hansen, my gratitude for his aid. Not only did he allow me to include his fine discography, but he unselfishly shared many materials that his own research had unearthed.

To my friend Stanley Sonntag, a passionate Wagnerite whose knowledge of that composer is encyclopedic, for his unstinting cooperation in all ways, and to Robert Fitz, who lent his editorial and management skills at the inception of this project, I give my thanks.

Many thanks to Robert Tuggle, head archivist of the Metropolitan Opera Archives, and Kenneth Schlesinger, his assistant, who suffered my intrusive presence for months, helped me to locate materials in their collection, and offered invaluable advice on avenues of further research.

To my colleagues of the American Academy of Teachers of Singing, thanks are due for allowing me to seek their professional advice rather too often, and especially to the late Berton Coffin for encouraging this project and for contributing his technical vocal expertise as well as his memories of Lauritz Melchior.

To my dear friend of many years John Wustman, who never in seven years ceased asking how he could be of help, who encouraged me in the beginning of this project, sustained my spirits during the many rewritings, and at the end, by means of his own respected position in the musical world, made the impossible possible, I must make known my deep gratitude for his active part in this entire endeavor.

For the courteous and prompt response to my questions, I owe my gratitude to Gunther Kossodo, Wagner expert and lecturer, Erik Østby of the Kirsten Flagstad Museum, and Günther Fischer of the Bayreuth Museum, as well as to Professor Tage Kaarsted, Danish historiographer of the Orders of Chivalry, for his generosity in tracing needed information. To the Danish photographer from Nordisk Pressefoto, Poul Petersen, my thanks for allowing me to use his picture.

The late Lela Neve, a most unusual woman, transformed herself from a stranger to a friend and most able assistant in a mere seven days that I spent at Dana College researching the Lauritz Melchior Memorial Room. Led by her pride in a fellow Dane, she involved herself with utmost generosity in the Melchior biography even when in the throes of a life-threatening illness. I can but inscribe my deep appreciation to her and to the members of her family. To the other librarians of Dana College (Jo Ann Hohensee, Sharon Jensen, and Caroline Schoneweis) for their hospitality, cooperation, and tireless interest during my sojourn in Blair, Nebraska; to Lewis Daniels of the Westbrook, Connecticut, Public Library for his ungrudging help through many summers; and to Helen Lightener of the New York Singing Teachers Association, for teaching me her research skills, I am most indebted.

To all my students I offer my untold thanks for their understanding and support through these seven years. I am especially indebted to Susan May for taking from me the burden of the index and some translations, to Sarah Young and Valerie McMorris for helping with the research duties, to Julie Kroloff for making it possible for me to meet my deadlines by contributing a laser printing of the many drafts, and to Marcia Early for her help with the proofreading.

For those whose names are not here recorded, I beg forgiveness and offer my gratitude.

TRISTANISSIMO

CHAPTER 1

Da Capo: "En København-dreng"

(1890–1905)

As a world-famous tenor, Lauritz Melchior had announced at the onset of every interview, whether in Peru or New York City: "I was a Copenhagen lad." To Melchior this little phrase was the simplest and most direct explanation not only of his origins but of his character: To have been born a Dane was to be liberally endowed with friendliness, helpfulness, and a gift for extending hospitality; to have grown up in Denmark was to grow up literate, broad-minded, and patriotic; to have been born in Copenhagen, the city of laughter, was to inherit the proper ingredients for living—sociability, humor, and the enjoyment of food and song.

By 1890, the year of Lauritz Melchior's birth, Jørgen Conradt Melchior and his wife, born Julie Sofie Møller, were already the parents of four children: three girls, Bodil, Ellen Marie, and Agnes, and a boy, Henrik Emil. (Another son, Knud, had died of pneumonia in his first year.) On March 20, the couple's sixth child was born, Lauritz Lebrecht Hommel Melchior, named for his godfather, Professor Lauritz Lebrecht Hommel, a professional associate of Jørgen's.

The Melchior household was situated not far from the center of the city, Town Hall Square. A left turn from the square takes you to the main entrance of Tivoli Gardens, that jewel of entertainment. This carnival of merrymaking, with its colored lights, sidewalk restaurants, merry-go-grounds, fireworks displays, concerts and ballet, was a treasured part of Lauritz Melchior's childhood. The liveliness of its offerings exactly matched his exuberant personality.

A right turn from Town Hall Square, away from Tivoli, reveals a scene very much changed from the one Melchior knew as a child. The series of streets running east have been transformed into a pedestrian mall, now collectively known as Strøget, the Fifth Avenue or Bond Street of Copenhagen. At the end of Frederiksberggade, the first street of the series, there is a double square. The north half, Gammeltorv, boasts a splendid fountain where, every

1

year on the monarch's birthday, children gather to watch jets of water make golden apples dance.

Turning left beyond the Gammeltorv fountain, you find yourself in Nørregade, the street on which the Melchior apartment was located. Almost immediately on your right is Copenhagen's Lutheran cathedral, Vor Frue Kirke, the Melchior family's neighborhood church at the time when Lauritz was christened in 1904. Next on the right is the University of Copenhagen. On the left, just beyond the dark-red brick of St. Peter's Church and down the gentle curve of Nørregade, you can see twin four-story buildings, Nørregade 31 and 33. Lauritz's father, Jørgen Melchior, inherited these buildings along with Melchior's Borger- og Realskole, a private school founded in 1839 by his father Henrik Emil. The once-rebuilt school building, which stood behind the apartment houses, was torn down after the school closed in 1908. The graduates, the "Melchiorianer," although reduced in numbers, still met for annual reunions during Lauritz's lifetime.

As the meticulously kept *Stambog* (family history book) reveals, the Melchiors had been Lutheran ministers, doctors, and teachers since the seventeenth century. Young Jørgen had commenced the study of medicine, but, despite his deep-rooted interest in science, was soon asked to forgo it and to take over the school for the good of the family. The study of mathematics and natural history would be far more useful for a schoolmaster. By the time Lauritz was born, Jørgen, as owner and co-principal (with Lauritz's namesake, Lauritz Lebrecht Hommel), had built Melchior's Borger- og Realskole into a thriving school. Six hundred lively pupils were stuffed into the six-story building and many more waited for the opportunity to be educated there.

Not quite six feet tall, with dark hair and beard, Jørgen Melchior had wooed and won his beautiful second cousin Julie. She was a small-boned, happy-natured blonde (from whom Lauritz inherited his blue eyes), whose lovely soprano voice was not the least of her attractions for music-loving Jørgen. The couple was often invited out and told to "bring music." At home for their own pleasure they played and sang Schubert and Mendelssohn duets.

In April 1890, less than a month after the birth of Lauritz, the happiness of their close-knit family was rent by the death of the thirty-nine-year-old mother. "It caused immense sorrow to my father and to all friends of the household," wrote Lauritz. Soon after the May 16 baptism, Jørgen, despairing, sent his newborn son, who looked so like his mother, to be cared for by his sister and her minister husband. By the fall of 1890, Jørgen recognized that managing the house and taking charge of three other children was simply too much for thirteen-year-old Bodil. So it was that Lauritz, when he was eighteen months old (a very big baby, said Bodil), was brought back to a home presided over by the new, 32-year-old housekeeper, Kristine Jensen.

Lauritz and his sister Ellen Marie, eleven years his senior, were inseparable from the moment the little boy returned to the family home. For the next few years, Ellen Marie doted upon her baby brother, and often told him what a fine singer he was. Sadly, she died in 1893; "Auntie" Jensen stepped in to care for "Lalle Menkør" (as three-year-old Lauritz, unable to pronounce his name, called himself).

Lalle, who could not remember his mother, enjoyed being fussed over by Miss Jensen and basked in being the center of everyone's attention. His puppylike nature—content, trusting, and expectant of good fortune—kept him from becoming truly spoiled. At first sight "Auntie" Jensen had promptly fallen in love with the baby. "She loved me and spoiled me," recalled Lauritz. So began her seventeen-year supervision of Lauritz, marked by a total dedication to his well-being. Until her death in 1923, her active concern for Lauritz never faltered. With her succor, her advice, and her financial help, it was she who made possible his ultimate artistic development.

Lalle thought Frøken Jensen had to be the best cook in Copenhagen, and as her famous cookbooks are available to this day, evidently other Danes agreed. *Frøken Jensens Kogebog* (Miss Jensen's Cookbook) still enjoys a lively sale in Danish bookstores, and is the traditional Danish bridal gift.

At the age of six, Lauritz began his education at the Melchior School. He describes his father as "half a father and half a school teacher. He was always very kind and loving, but there was always a certain distance between him and me. This distance was . . . reduced gradually as I grew up, and I think that . . . he could not get over the fact that my birth caused his young wife's death much too early."

In school Lalle showed a good ear for languages and a fair vocabulary in the major ones, German and French, but such a distaste for grammar and spelling that Principal Jørgen held him back in the eighth grade. Friends in Copenhagen even now attest that "Lauritz could never spell, not even in Danish." Inattentive to such niceties, he actually allowed his second wife's name to be misspelled on her granite tombstone.

Lauritz's sister Agnes was blind, and, as her escort, Lauritz gained experiences useful to a future singer. For example, he accompanied "Agge" to the Royal Theater, where students from the Institute for the Blind were permitted to hear performances from the long, narrow room situated underneath the stage on either side of the prompter's box. The young people called it "getting into the hole." Seated on wooden benches with their backs to the thin wood wall that separated them from the orchestra itself, their knees touched the wall in front of them, leaving whitewash marks that indicated that they "had been to the theater." Sometimes Lauritz would sneak out of the pit and watch the performance surreptitiously from the wings. Many years later he explained to Rose Heylbut of *Etude* what he had learned:

> Down there, where the acoustics were unsurpassed, we "watched" plays and ballets and heard operas. . . . We were forced to . . . feel the art coming to us as the blind did. . . . I learned how important it is for the artist never to lose tension or the character of his part. The power of the voice is enormous. . . . It is impossible to overstress the value of learning by observing and listening to what went on upon the boards overhead. I learned what to do and what not to do by the effects . . . later analyzing them and applying the results of my analyses.

In many respects Lauritz Melchior's eventual success evolved from his family's financial plight, which was due to the new public schools that were eating into the enrollment of Melchior School. Music, which had departed their home since the death of their mother, returned with the arrival of a single lady border, Thora Lunddahl, who was a singing teacher. (Later Lauritz realized that it was Miss Jensen, turning her overwhelming energy to the fiscal problems of the Melchior family, who had arranged for Miss Lunddahl to move in as a paying boarder.) Ten-year-old Lalle was envious of Bodil and Agnes when they were closeted in the morning room with Miss Lunddahl for their singing lessons. The whole family was musical, and as Bodil recollected, father Jørgen possessed "one of the most beautiful baritone voices I ever heard." Jørgen Melchior's musical genes had descended through the Melchior side of the family, and singing was a lifelong pleasure. Musical evenings, once again a staple of the Melchior family life, "probably played a great part in the . . . love of singing which was planted in my mind during those young years," said Lauritz.

By the age of fourteen Lauritz looked the bass he considered himself. Basses are typically tall and spare of frame, and Lauritz, six-foot-three-and-a-half-inches tall, was thin as a telephone pole, with an equally straight posture, altogether a good-looking boy. Moreover, the girls he met at Tivoli judged him to be, he said, "the best dancer in Copenhagen," and, Bodil added, "he was a dandy, wore silk stockings, carried a cane, was a real ladykiller." In October of 1904 he was confirmed in Vor Frue Kirke, and in 1905, at the age of fifteen, he took his final ninth-grade exams at the Melchior School.

Like all graduates, he thought constantly about what he was going to do with his life. Because his father had longed to be a doctor, Lauritz had "medicine in [his] blood." Initially he toyed with the thought of becoming a doctor, "the idea of being able to help cure people and make them happy," but he was put off by the stringent academic requirements. The thought of enduring many more years of hated schooling forced him to conclude that singing was really his first love, although, as sister Bodil recollected, "It was a little bit of a disappointment to father that none of my brothers wanted to go to the university." Jørgen, always practical, tried to reason with Lauritz: Just as many years as would be needed for medical school, or more, would be needed to become a singer. One could not simply embark on a career; rigorous study and discipline were needed to become a fine singer. Of course, Lauritz didn't listen. "When the time came to choose . . . between medicine and singing, I took the easier and more comfortable choice of becoming a singer."

CHAPTER 2

Training as a Baritone
(1905–1916)

At the turn of the century, the vocational training offered by the public schools had made great inroads into the enrollment of the Melchior's Borger-og Realskole, and by 1908 it would be forced to close its doors. In their straitened circumstances, it was again Kristine Jensen who came to the rescue, making it possible for Henrik Emil to study painting in Paris and helping Lauritz and his father both financially and socially. "Tante [Jensen] . . . loved to invite my father and me to go with her, especially to premieres," Melchior remembered, "and then afterwards we would always go to restaurants and have open-faced sandwiches. These were very festive evenings for me."

Jørgen Melchior, unable to shoulder his son's financial burdens, counseled Lauritz to "choose a trade that has something to do with music. If you are not a success, you will have something to fall back on." Lauritz was pleased to mark his transition from schoolboy to independent working man. Helped by his father's musical connections, he worked first as a junior clerk in a music store, where he sang new songs for the customers, then briefly as a photographer's assistant, and finally as a shipping clerk for an instrument company. Although the many hours of work tended to interfere with the happy existence he had enjoyed previously, the time outside work was spent mainly in musical pursuits. Lauritz and a group of instrumental and singer friends joined in twice-monthly musical fetes held by their group, The Music Club. Soon he was admitted (as a first bass) into the best male choir in the city, the Bel Canto Choir, to whose meetings fellow member Jørgen Melchior accompanied him.

Although his later publicity was rife with highly romanticized tales of beginning singing lessons, in his personal diary Melchior described the circumstances matter of factly:

> At last, after all these trials and tribulations of selling instruments, etc., in the month of October, 1908, Far [Father] and I and Miss Jensen went

to the singing teacher Poul Bang to evaluate my abilities for a singing career. He found me "promising" and therefore I began my life career as a singer.

A majority of evidence points to Tante Jensen as the person who made this possible, for Melchior made a subsequent oblique reference to work, interest, and money given by her, adding that

> if she had not existed, I do not think that my father with his substantial financial worries could have carried me through my training, because it costs a lot of money, and if one has to learn well, one has to go to the best teachers, who are notoriously not the least expensive ones. . . . Tante did not really have an ear for music, but since she heard a lot of music at our home, she realized what my ability and my future were as a singer, and from the moment she realized that, she threw herself with her unique energy into the task of making me a singer of international status.

Voice teacher Poul Bang's opinion that, in spite of the "promise" shown by young Melchior, it would take many years to develop him as a good baritone made Lauritz determined to show the experts. It wouldn't take *him* more than a few months!

> At that time I had a light baritone voice and Poul Bang was a very astute teacher and reasonable, and he gave great importance to using the head resonance in the voice as well as the breathing—two factors that in my opinion are the fundamentals in teaching singing. I sang with him twice a week for half an hour, often longer. Later on some of his pupils used to meet with him in the evening and sing excerpts from various operas. That was outside the paid singing hours.

Melchior recorded very little of what he thought about vocal technique. To him, there seemed to be no need to write these things down; they were self-evident. Only when he was prodded to explain for the benefit of others did he do so. Accordingly, much later, when his voice was completely settled in the Heldentenor *Fach*,* Melchior clarified one vocal priority to Rose Heylbut, who adopted as the title of her article one of his favorite phrases for describing the gift of artistry, "A Little Touch of God's Finger":

> The basic thing of all singing is the control of the breath, and by breath

---

Fach means vocal category: e.g., lyric soprano, dramatic mezzo, basso cantante. The *Heldentenor Fach* demands a tenor voice of large size, exceptional stamina, and more strength in the lower register than other tenors can summon. This voice often evolves, with maturity, from a high baritone voice. Indeed, it could be characterized as a tenor/baritone. Wagner wrote his tenor roles almost exclusively for this voice, but there are roles in other operas that demand such skills: Beethoven's Florestan (*Fidelio*), Verdi's Otello and Radamès (*Aïda*).

control I mean more than diaphragmatic breathing. I included in the term control of the breath after it has been taken, its budgeting, its resonance, its position in the resonance chambers so that it is not too far forward and not too far back, the management of the mouth and the palate. It is here that the guidance of a good teacher is essential, but the best teacher . . . cannot perfect the task alone.

There has been a common misperception that Melchior had assigned little importance to the dramatic responsibilities of a singing artist and had spent little time trying to perfect himself in those skills. In point of fact his work on diction and acting of roles began early, and it continued to be of paramount significance to him. Auntie Jensen agreed with Jørgen that theatrical training was important ("your words and your emotions must be understandable," he said) and financed four years of twice-a-week studies in diction and acting, beginning in 1909, with Peter Jerndorff, a Melchior School alumnus and a very well-known, treasured actor at the Royal Theater in Copenhagen, famous for his beautiful diction. Soon Millie Walbom, a beautiful Music Club comrade (with whom Lauritz was then in unrequited love), told him about the opera school that her mother had opened with Peter Gradman. Jørgen encouraged Lauritz to join the school, hoping it might lead his son to the Royal Opera.

"Uncle Peter" was a Wagnerite. It was from him that Lauritz first heard about Bayreuth and its great singers: "He was the first one to lead me into the Wagner repertoire later on, when my voice had developed into a Heldentenor. He did so with great interest and understanding. I can thank him for a great part of the love that I feel for the art of this great master."

At the time of his "unofficial" debut at the school, February 15, 1911, Lauritz's voice was displaying new possibilities. "My voice had developed more and more top, even if the top was still somewhat thin." It was in one of the opera school's public performances that Melchior first stepped on stage; he played Antonio, the gardener, in Mozart's *Le Nozze di Figaro*. Gradman later told fellow Danish Wagner enthusiast Knud Hegermann-Lindencrone that Melchior "would absolutely have sung the count's part, but we really thought it was too dignified a role for a young fellow of twenty."

All who knew him well agreed that Melchior cared about only three things outside of singing: hunting, eating and drinking, and the Royal Danish Guard. Melchior was inducted into the Guard as #686 on May 26, 1911. He always claimed that he had looked forward to being a soldier, implying that he loved every second of his compulsory service, but he actually spent precious little time at the soldier's life. The Royal Theater wrote granting an audition for the Royal Opera School, and Frøken (Miss) Jensen again took care of Lauritz's problems by paying a 600-kroner fee so that he could be "ransomed at the end of September," as he wrote. (His second stint of "active" duty with the Guard in 1915 was to go on for only two months; his third and last assignment in 1917 extended to three months.)

Gradman, Bang, and Jerndorff welcomed Lauritz back to his studies, and he was convinced that his diligence would be rewarded with a good audition at the Royal Opera. On May 14 he sang Germont's aria from *La Traviata* and the "Toreador Song" from *Carmen*, two high and difficult baritone arias, for the auditioners. Finally, on July 1, the Royal Opera School's letter informed him that he was to be one of the four baritones accepted in its apprentice program, where he would study singing, drama, and ballet. His roles were to be Amonasro (*Aïda*), Valentin (*Faust*), Marcello (*La Bohème*), and Wolfram (*Tannhäuser*).

Now that he had graduated from the workshop level, his needs were twofold: money and onstage experience. Two months later, an opportunity for both came Lauritz's way. Mme. Willi Zwicki, an operetta singer, decided to make a career change and formed an opera company so she might debut as Violetta in *La Traviata*. A roster of supporting singers notable for its miscasting was rounded up: handsome Alfredo was actually fat and fiftyish; his "father" was Lauritz Melchior, spare, gangling, and unmistakably (despite a gray wig and a huge beard) a youth of twenty-two. Nonetheless, the Royal Opera saw this as a fine chance for their young hopeful to acquire stage knowledge and gave him leave to tour with the Zwicki and Stagel Company. For years after, Lauritz gleefully recited from memory his first review: "The only outstanding aspect of the portrayal of Germont, Senior, by Lauritz Melchior was the singer's beard, which made him look like the dog-headed man from Circus Barnum."

In the *Traviata* cast was a lovely dark blonde with brown eyes and a beautiful smile, whom Mme. Zwicki had persuaded to sing the role of Annina, Violetta's maid; soon after meeting her, Lauritz was consumed with his first all-absorbing romantic passion. Previously, said his sister Bodil, he had taken for granted that women would become infatuated with him, but now it was he who had fallen in love—and "at first glance." Her name was Inger Holst-Rasmussen, and she was not only a mature woman (divorced from Mr. Holst-Rasmussen after a brief marriage), but the daughter of the legendary Ludvig Nathansen, a famed matinee idol of the Danish theater who had killed for love and passion. Thus her attraction for Lauritz was further enhanced by her membership in that world of the theater to which he now knew himself dedicated. Inger's actor-father had lived a life that was as overcharged in private as on the stage. He had divorced his first wife, Inger's mother, and, in 1907, he shot his second wife, and then himself. She survived; he did not. This flamboyant scandal did not endear Inger to the staid Melchior family, whose enthusiasm for the love affair was already dimmed by her divorce, and they looked down upon this family of actors and singers, despite their professional success. Lauritz and Inger were but 22 and 23 years old respectively. The tour had begun in September 1912, and by October 8 they had announced their engagement.

Inger felt they should wait to be married until Lauritz could find regular employment. Happy-go-lucky Lauritz, for his part, found it astonishing that people should worry about financial security. At this point, he was not concerned about his lack of substantial income. His mind was totally occupied by his work. Nevertheless, to set his lovely finacée's mind at rest, he searched out singing jobs here and there after their return from the Zwicki tour, while resuming his studies at the Royal Opera School.

Attempting to assume more financial responsibility, Lauritz sang at many funerals, at which a "fat corpse" yielded 100 kroner, although a "lean corpse" was worth only 25. One day at Assistens Kirkegaard, the cemetery, a fat corpse funeral provided a tale Lauritz loved to recount. While singing, he looked out over the mourners, puzzled by the handkerchiefs they had stuffed into their mouths and the tears flowing down their cheeks. Later he discovered that the tears were barely concealed laughter. The title of his song, "An Angel has Touched Your Forehead" by Lange-Müller, had a particular significance. The departed was a bar-owner who had been fatally hit over the head with a beer bottle by one of his customers.

In March 1913, the Royal Opera's lyric baritone left Copenhagen for the Berlin Städtische Oper, and Lauritz inherited his role, Silvio in Leoncavallo's *Pagliacci*, in which he made his Royal Opera debut on the evening of April 2, 1913. He had eagerly anticipated recognition of his fine acting, and was disappointed when the notice called him only "promising," (although seven years later a local newspaper would remark about his "extraordinary aptitude for characterization in the role of Silvio"). Lilly Lamprecht, his Nedda, found him "brilliant, for he had a very beautiful voice, the so-called tenor-baritone, which was . . . warmer than most tenors' voices are, or become." Another friend declared Melchior's voice to be "the most wonderful baritone. . . . I found it more beautiful than his tenor voice ever was." When Lauritz sang as a baritone, recalled his sister Bodil, "It was as if one heard his father's voice." Still, Lauritz passed his final auditions and, on July 1, 1914, was formally engaged by the Royal Opera under a three-year contract.

Inger was thrilled at the permanence suggested by the Opera's commitment and became convinced of Lauritz's ability to maintain a family life despite his precarious calling. As soon as he was released from his second tour of duty with the Guard, they were married in Copenhagen's Slotskirken

(Castle Church) on November 2. Melchior's lusty temperament, love of ceremony, and appetite for music, food, and drink must surely have been
satisfied by the marvelous wedding. His Royal Opera colleagues sang as a
choir, and a twenty-four piece orchestra played during the ceremony. A
lavish reception offered the guests an opportunity for typical Danish con-
viviality. As custom dictated, each time a guest picked up the glass and said
"*Skål,*" looking directly into the eyes of the happy couple, everyone else at
the table was honor-bound to raise his glass and echo the toast. A traditional
wedding cake—the *kransekage*—with its layers of marzipan wreaths that diminished in size as they rose to the top, ornamented with chocolate butterflies
soaring from slender wires, crowned the meal. Afterward the newlyweds
returned to their little three-room apartment with its furniture borrowed
from the flat above Melchior's School. As Lauritz's daughter wrote in 1970,
"Inger's dream of a cozy home and a loving, understanding husband . . .
were fulfilled, and she believed that it was going to last."

CHAPTER 3

Metamorphosis: Baritone Into Tenor

(1916–1922)

Peter Gradman engaged Melchior, now twenty-six, for another Swedish tour in the spring of 1916. In Verdi's *Il Trovatore* he was to sing the Count di Luna, and Inger the tiny role of Inez. For Azucena, Gradman had engaged Sarah Cahier, known to the company as Mme. Charles Cahier. An American contralto formerly of the Metropolitan Opera, she had originally studied in Paris with Jean de Reszke.

One evening Mme. Cahier witnessed a strange and portentous scene. The company's Leonora, increasingly fearful of her high C at the end of the duet with di Luna, had convinced herself that she could not manage it that night. Trying to calm her, Lauritz suggested that she might feel better if they switched notes. Leonora was very relieved, and di Luna interpolated an effortless high C. After the performance Cahier spoke privately to her young colleague: "But you are not a baritone! I think that you are a tenor with the lid on. A Heldentenor probably."

While Cahier persisted in advising Melchior to train in Germany as a Heldentenor, he was consumed with the practical problems posed by her suggestion. How could he go to Germany when, despite Denmark's neutrality, the war was still going on? Not only did he have a wife to support, but, since he and Inger were expecting their first child in September, it was not financially feasible to give up his earning power as a performer in order to start vocal studies once again. Most of his musical advisors were in agreement with Cahier about Germany, but Inger "could not understand that he was not satisfied with what satisfied her." She thought they could begin to live "and have wonderful time" now that Lauritz had a contracted position with the Royal Opera. To her it did not really matter whether he was a baritone or a tenor.

In the absence of a decision, the strong-willed Cahier took charge. She extolled Melchior's talents before the Directors of the Royal Opera in Co-penhagen, declaring him to be a potential heroic tenor, and charged them with the responsibility of ensuring his proper artistic development. To their credit, the administration of the Royal Opera took her advice and rewrote Melchior's contract to include an extra 1,000-kroner stipend. After another short assignment to the Royal Guard, and a few months before the birth of his son Ib Jørgen, Melchior began his lessons with the great Kammersanger* Vilhelm Herold. Herold had been Lauritz's idol from the time the tenor used to bring a bag of oranges to his blind audience sitting beneath the Royal Opera stage. Herold was a true singing actor who had sung abroad as well as in Denmark before his retirement in 1915. In his recordings one can hear a certain tonal and stylistic similarity with his famous student Melchior. Generously, Herold gave Lauritz lessons for a year gratis, so that he might use the Royal Opera's stipend for his family expenses. "He did for me the transition, the work that has to be done to change a baritone into a tenor." The young singer commenced his lessons as a tenor on June 1, 1917.

There is a certain type of voice that might accurately be labeled in two ways: either as a tenor with an exceptionally powerful bottom range or as a baritone with exceptionally easy high notes. (Many Verdi baritones, for example, can sing a high C, although they are not called upon to execute it in public.) History does show us an impressive list of fine tenors who began their singing careers as baritones, including Jean de Reszke, Giovanni Zenatello, and, in our own time, Carlo Bergonzi, Set Svanholm, and Plácido Domingo. All exhibit a brilliance, a fullness in their upper tones, traceable to the baritonal quality. Distinguishing between a baritone and a tenor is made more difficult within the Wagnerian repertoire, which, for all practical purposes of the heroic tenor roles, demands a voice that can manage to be a "tenor/baritone." Julius Hey, Richard Wagner's preferred vocal coach, insisted that a Hel-dentenor developed from a "low tenor," is not "an original talent" but "the result of a rather long development." Gustav Mahler, conducting a Vienna performance of *Tristan und Isolde*, bade his Tristan: "Before the love potion sing like a baritone, afterwards, as a tenor." A voice that can straddle the line of demarcation is most valuable in Wagnerian and heavy Italian roles.

*This Danish word (and the Swedish *hovsångere*) has the same literal meaning— "Singer to the Court"—and the same significance as its German counterpart, *Kam-mersänger*, or *Kammersängerin*, the female equivalent. Originally granted by royalty, it is now given by the state or city. In Vienna as elsewhere this traditional honorific was not abandoned even when the "Court" Theater became, with the end of the monarchy and the advent of the Austrian Republic, the "State" Theater. (Sohlmans, p. 13)

About these early months of study as a tenor, which are of such interest to us, Melchior was always rather vague and noncommittal. In fact, he spoke very little about the beginning of this transition from baritone to tenor, saying simply that "only with a solid technical background can a baritone voice be developed to include a high register," or that

> there is a big hole between the high notes of the baritone and . . . [those of] the tenor, so the first thing to do, when the right material for a Heldentenor exists, is to "grind down" the voice. There are not so many born tenors who can become Heldentenors, because they lack . . . the solid low notes [of the born baritones]. [Born] tenors press down [to get these notes].

His conviction that a Heldentenor could never be found among lighter-voiced lyric tenors, who lack lower register strength, later became well-known. Equally often, however, he pointed to those Wagnerian roles (as well as Beethoven's Florestan, and Verdi's Radamès and Otello) that contain both lyrical and heroic sections to illustrate that a Heldentenor must also be able to sing lyrically. One of Melchior's last accompanists, Leonard Eisner, recalls that "Melchior believed it was almost mandatory for a real Heldentenor to have been a baritone first. He considered it a logical sequence." "The Heldentenor voice is one that goes up with age," Melchior said in 1944.

> If you start as a real tenor and try to do heroic roles, you bring the voice down instead of up. The high notes begin to disappear. It's different if you begin as a high baritone. That way you can easily build up your high notes. You have only to make the middle high of the voice a little lighter. Then you put the top notes on it.

Vilhelm Herold's intention was that Lauritz should make his tenor debut at the Royal Opera as Lohengrin, a role suitable for a *jugendlicher* (youthful) Heldentenor, and the Wagnerian role for which he himself was best known. However, in the spring of 1918 the Royal Opera engaged a foreign singer to do Lohengrin. According to Melchior, when Herold learned of this, he "exploded, and from experience, I can imagine what he said to the management. He and I worked like horses to prepare for my debut." Herold had a different view of their work, which he later related to Danish singer Holger Boland:

> I helped him a little . . . but I could not do much about the voice. It was almost rather inborn: a big, impressive voice with this little cheap hammer-vibrato that cannot be changed. His stage talent was not nearly as impressive as the voice, but then it was big enough for him to secure a career in the big wide world as a Wagner tenor.

Boland's sage postscript was "You should not ask one great singer about another one."

The opera Herold then selected for Melchior's debut was *Tannhäuser*, which Lauritz viewed with some apprehension. Learning the role in two months was a Herculean task. But, as Lauritz said, "Life does not give you roasted doves flying about; you have to work and work hard." Although he always said that he was not overly fond of the role of Tannhäuser, he understood its masterful quality:

> Speaking of emotional effects that can be re-created through the music, nothing in all Wagner—for the tenor at least—eclipses the last act of *Tannhäuser*. This is a long and difficult role, but Wagner's inspiration in the last act seems to invigorate the singer, that is, if he's been conserving his energies for the singing of the role. . . . You cannot stay up and carouse all the night before and expect to do justice to a Wagnerian part.

In a costume paid for by his brother, the 28-year-old Lauritz Melchior made his Wagnerian debut as a young-looking Tannhäuser at the Royal Opera on October 8, 1918, one month before the end of World War I. Herold's personal opinion about the role ("Tannhäuser is first of all a poetic dreamer, who does not care for this world") had persuaded his student to give a very lyrical performance. A Danish reviewer found the young singer's first essay at singing Wagner not markedly exciting, though promising:

> His voice already seems to have the right trumpeting sound on the high notes, and probably, as time goes by—he is still so young—it will acquire more. At any rate it rings beautifully, is fresh and healthy and is treated with a pleasant culture and musical understanding. Even if his somewhat youthful slight figure cannot yet fill and form the natural center of the opera, his dramatic contribution is so talented that one does not miss anything essential, if one bears in mind that it is a new man in this demanding role.

Even though the review was reasonably good, following this single performance the Directors of the Royal Opera made the decision that Melchior was to be given neither another *Tannhäuser* performance nor a chance to do Lohengrin. He returned to his studies with Herold, learning the role of Heinrich, a *comprimario* (secondary) tenor role in *Tannhäuser*. Now fully aware of how much he had yet to learn, he contentedly sang his little part. When the celebrated Heldentenor Leo Slezak arrived to sing *Tannhäuser* in German, Melchior, singing in Danish along with the rest of the cast, learned for himself what Gradman had told him: how much more correct Wagner sounded in the German language. His admiration for Slezak's beautiful voice and storytelling ability was boundless.

Melchior sang other comprimario roles in Danish, including the tenor role of Prince Ottokar in von Weber's *Der Freischütz*, and the half-baritone, half-tenor role of Faninal in Richard Strauss's *Der Rosenkavalier*. Strauss himself, in attendance as conductor, was full of praise for Melchior, who sang the role—from its very high range down to its very low notes—exactly as the composer wished it to be sung. Clearly, his was a voice made to sing those roles that lay across the tenor and baritone ranges.

By any standards, the number of persons who appeared in Lauritz Melchior's life at the opportune moment, prepared to aid and succor him in his quest to become a professional singer, is impressive. The list began with Kristine Jensen and continued through Peter Gradman, Sarah Cahier, and Vilhelm Herold. In 1919, a kind friend, fellow Freemason, and Instrument Maker to the Royal Court, Aage Cornelius Knudsen, knowing the unhealthy state of the Melchior family finances, invited Lauritz and Inger to have a July vacation in London at his expense, while investigating the singing opportunities in England. Melchior accepted on the spot—only to find that Inger did not share his enthusiasm for the vacation. Unable to understand, and possibly lacking the insight to imagine that she might be embarrassed by her inability to speak any language but Danish, Lauritz sailed off with the Knudsen family.

What Lauritz called his "second big luck" of this year happened in characteristic fashion: In the men's room at the Savoy Hotel he absent-mindedly whistled a Danish song as he washed his hands. A stranger who was walking past him stopped and exclaimed, "I know that tune. Are you by any chance Danish?"

The gentlemen was, it turned out, a son of Christensen, the owner of the big Aarhus coal company. Wanting to be Melchior's host in London, he offered to install him in his beautiful suite at the Savoy, to put a Rolls-Royce and a butler at Lauritz's service, and to give him both a living allowance and an expense account for all hotel charges. A true Dane with a pleasure-oriented approach to living, he urged Lauritz to live in the grand manner as a great singer should. The next day Christensen left on a trip and Melchior moved into this new friend's beautiful suite, the promised butler and chauffeur attending his every wish.

Lauritz's normal inclination toward hedonism allowed him to follow the instructions given by his countryman. As he recollected, "I lived like a small prince." Perhaps it was during this interlude at the Savoy that he began to acquire his undeniable taste for the grand style. He entertained often in Christensen's well-appointed suite and was entertained at others' homes, where he met the young artistic people of England as well as the fashionable dilettantes. It was in such surroundings that he was introduced to Sir Henry Wood, founder and conductor of the Promenade Concerts.

Sir Henry, born in 1869, had made his first visit to Bayreuth in 1886 and was a champion of Wagner. The inaugural Promenade Concert was given on August 10, 1895. During World War I the Proms ran uninterruptedly, Wood ignoring the threat posed by the Zeppelin visits. "Through the 1920s and 1930s Wood, as punctual as Big Ben and as safe as the Bank of England, was there," wrote pianist Gerald Moore. After a short hiatus in 1939, prompted by a fear of air raids, the Proms would resume in 1940, Sir Henry still presiding, until a June 10, 1941 attack by the Luftwaffe would bring down Queen's Hall and temporarily terminate the tradition.

Lauritz sang for Sir Henry and for William Boosey, managing director of Chappell and Company, an important music publishing firm that sponsored the Prom concerts. The two gentlemen engaged him unofficially for some concerts during the following season. Lauritz, having enormously enjoyed his visit and new acquaintances, sailed back home.

In Copenhagen Melchior was greeted with wonderful news: The Opera Comique of Christiania (later named Oslo) wished to engage him for three performances of *Tannhäuser* between August 29 and September 3, 1919. He felt a great personal satisfaction that someone—if not the Royal Opera— approved his work as a Heldentenor. Alone (Inger had declined for health reasons to accompany him) he went off to Norway to sing his second performance as a Heldentenor. Some years later Kirsten Flagstad, who had been in that audience, told writer Louis Biancolli of hearing Melchior for the first time in Oslo as Tannhäuser. For his part, Melchior was flattered that Kirsten Flagstad had remembered, however faultily, the three performances (she had recalled two as being done by Slezak and one by Melchior). He relished being confused with Slezak for, in fact, Melchior himself had sung all three performances.

Upon returning from Oslo, having not been invited to return, Lauritz tried to persuade Inger that they should go to London to live, where he had the promise of an engagement with the Promenade Concerts. He felt strongly that the Danish Royal Opera would not give him opportunities for advancement. Inger remained pragmatic, reminding him that the Royal Opera did not think much of him as a Heldentenor. She persuaded him to be resigned, temporarily, to the realities of his situation. Interspersed with his singing— sometimes as a baritone, sometimes as a tenor—for the Royal Opera, he busied himself learning new roles.

Perhaps it was Richard Strauss's unqualified praise for Melchior's singing of Faninal the previous season that prompted the administration to give Melchior another chance as a leading tenor, but their choice was, curiously, the role of Samson in Saint-Saëns's opera *Samson et Dalila*. In this May 3, 1920, performance the young tenor was undone not by his inexperience, but by his physical strength. By wrestling the columns of the temple to the floor, breaking most of the scenery as well as the back stairs, he cost the management several thousand kroner in set renovations and stage repairs. Despite the destruction, one Copenhagen paper averred that he "lacked the grand opera style," and was somehow unable to convince the audience that Samson was a "tower of strength." Another believed, to the contrary, that he performed "with great force and authority." As to his vocal development, two Danish critics found gains in volume, pianissimo singing, and confidence, although his high notes were "strangely uneven. . . . One is always a little uneasy about these barytons [sic] becoming tenors." He was to sing later in life only one more (and much less destructive) performance of this role on the radio in the United States.

By June 1920 Melchior was restored to his naturally ebullient and confident self, ready for new experiences. Certainly there could be no doubt about the opportunities awaiting him in London. With or without Inger he would go. As it turned out, it was to be without her. Well into her second pregnancy and almost disabled by her heart problems, she decided not to accompany him on what she realistically deemed a wild goose chase. Inger was fearful, says their daughter Birte, and her doctor had advised against a second pregnancy for a woman with such a bad heart. Nevertheless, Lauritz disapproved of his son Ib being an only child and was optimistic about the outcome of this pregnancy. As Birte recollected years later,

> My father was *such* a selfish person. He thought she should do what *he* wanted. She was happy with her family in Denmark and didn't understand why he wanted to go abroad. She was not able to see that his voice belonged to the world.

The fear of spending his small hoard of money too swiftly was never absent from Lauritz's mind. His first task in London was to locate an inexpensive place to live. In a boarding house on King's Road, he found a furnished room that was far down the scale from the Savoy as an accommodation. One young executive from The Gramophone Company, Fred Gaisberg, remembered Melchior at this time haunting the back door of Covent Garden waiting for an audition as a baritone. "He found the going hard in those days and certainly looked it." Lauritz's luck turned when he met a fellow Dane, Olaf Trost, who was an engineer employed by Guglielmo Marconi, inventor of the wireless telegraph. After hearing Melchior sing at St. Clement Danes, Marconi wanted Lauritz to help him with an experiment to determine at what distance and how clearly one could hear a radio-transmitted voice. Nellie Melba had been the first woman to try it and now Lauritz would be the first male singer to be heard on the new, larger network.

Clad in his wedding suit, Melchior appeared on July 30 at Chelmsford near London, where Marconi's experimental transmitter was located in an unused army barrack. The microphone was a plain, upright telephone whose enlarged mouthpiece was held in a vertical position by tying a police rubber truncheon to it. A huge paper cone enclosed the grand piano. Lauritz, singing in German, French, English, Swedish, Norwegian, and Danish, was heard in Canada, Russia, Italy, and the United States. This radio broadcast was the first to be recorded on a cylinder, as Melchior described in his 1938–1939 press book:

> I stepped up to the funnel. The pianist began and I started to sing 3,500 kilometers out over the world. What a strange and empty feeling to sing for this huge invisible audience. I sang as if my life depended on it. The knowledge of the distance really scared me and before I knew it, it was over. And I just had time to shout "Farewell" to my wife who I knew was sitting at the other end of the wire. And then it was all over and I got my pen out and ceremoniously wrote my name on the drum which then was sent into the Marconi Museum. My song has been forgotten, but that drum is still there. . . . At the Marconi house in London they had placed the earpiece from a telephone in the horn of a dictaphone, and this one, together with the cylinders, were given to me as a memento. Unfortunately they were lost during the Second World War.

Perhaps because of Lauritz's newfound eminence, Sir Henry Wood declared himself pleased to hear the young Dane again, and Lauritz's fortunes took an upturn when the conductor again promised to use him in a September Promenade Concert in Queen's Hall. At his very first symphonic appearance, on September 6, 1920, Melchior included in his presentation arias from *Tannhäuser, Lohengrin*, and *Samson et Dalila*. The public applauded enthusiastically and almost all the reviews were uniformly good. Sir Henry wrote that "his manly appearance appealed almost as much as his voice."

The fall of 1920 was a very important time for Melchior. He was introduced to the British author Hugh Walpole, who generously invited him to live in his house, and introduced him to his immense social and artistic circle. Walpole, a Wagnerite, had heard Melchior at the Prom Concert, and he sent an approving letter to the young singer afterward, writing that he had taken the *London Times* to task for printing the single less-than-laudatory review of the Danish tenor. Amiable Lauritz, not recognizing Walpole's name, simply basked in the compliments of a British citizen without making very much of it. Walpole inscribed in his journal at the time that "the joy of the evening was a Danish tenor, Melchior—quite superb. Just the voice for me."

Lauritz had become friendly with several literary enthusiasts during his elegant sojourn at the Savoy. One month after his Prom Concert, one of them invited him to attend a soirée at which Walpole was to speak. Dumbfounded when Lauritz blithely identified Walpole as his correspondent, his "intimate friend" Marjorie listed Walpole's accomplishments: Only six years Melchior's senior, he had published twelve novels, a book of short stories, and a critical study of Joseph Conrad's work; was a Commander of the Order of the British Empire; had already completed his first lecture tour of America; and regularly wrote book columns for six different literary journals.

At the completion of the lecture, which revealed Walpole's unceasing energy and great personal charm, Lauritz's friend presented him to the author. Walpole was scandalized to hear where the young singer was living and immediately invited Lauritz to save his money by coming to live at his house near Regent's Park, where he could have the entire top floor for himself. Lauritz's assent changed the rest of his life.

Soon after their meeting at the Pen Club, Walpole depicted Melchior in his journal as "a great child, but very simple, most modest, with a splendid sense of humor." It is revealing that he used the word "child." Walpole's biographer portrays the writer himself as having a "great deal of the child in his nature." Like most people, Walpole found others attractive to the degree that they possessed his own traits—in this case, those that made him such a gay and enchanting companion himself. (In later years Melchior too was aptly characterized as "six parts child and four parts living artist.") We have seen that Melchior, like the man who would become his patron, was impetuous, generous, often indiscreet, and desirous of affection, but most of all, appreciative of the little things of life. Describing why he admired another friend, Walpole once wrote, "He had the actual consciousness of his happiness at the instant he was experiencing it. This is perhaps one of the rarest gifts given to human beings." It is probable that his liking for the Dane was based upon Melchior's cheerfulness, his lack of pretension, his sense of humor, his love of pranks, and his enjoyment of simple pleasures. A German quotation chosen by Walpole's biographer illuminates not only the nature of Walpole but also of Melchior: "He loved every dog and wished himself to be loved by every dog."

Having convinced himself of the worth of this young Danish tenor, Walpole set to work at once to introduce Melchior to his social circle. Among his friends were persons of utterly diverse backgrounds: Queen Mary, Charlie Chaplin, Mary Pickford, Gene Tunney, and Ernest Hemingway. "Melchior is indeed turning my life upside down, and jolly glad I am," wrote Walpole.

Next came the literary circle: Eliot, Arnold Bennett, and Galsworthy. The three Sitwells were also introduced to Melchior at 24 York Terrace. In Walpole's large Georgian house Melchior also hobnobbed with Britain's most talented actors and actresses: Beatrice Lillie, then just commencing her career;

the already well-established Edmund Gwenn; and young Charles Laughton (who would later appear with Edward G. Robinson in the 1928 dramatization of one of Walpole's novels, *Portrait of a Man with Red Hair*).

Lauritz had been drawn back to Denmark for the November christening of his new daughter Birte, who was born on September 10, and by the necessity to go over his contract with the Royal Opera. A few concerts scheduled in Copenhagen and some performances in the provinces were expected to extend his stay through February 1921. On January 14, he sang—as a tenor—for the first time ever before the Danish Royal Court.

At the end of January Walpole sailed from Harwich, England, to Copenhagen, where he installed himself at the prestigious Hotel d'Angleterre for a month. As godfather to Melchior's new daughter Birte, Walpole was now virtually a member of the family. He zealously attended all of Melchior's performances—concerts, opera, even funerals. He was present to hear Lauritz sing his last regular Royal Opera performances as Canio in *Pagliacci* on February 20. Again he stated his unshakable belief that his young protégé (whom he had affectionately nicknamed David) could become a great singer, given the chance. "The true quality of his voice, which is most remarkable, doesn't seem truly understood here. I see no one who really appreciates it. However they will one day."

Thus convinced, Walpole laid before Melchior a plan: not only would he pay for Lauritz's lessons and living expenses, but he would support Lauritz's family while he studied. All this he would do, said the Englishman, because he realized that Melchior's career would not move forward if he stayed in Copenhagen. Hearing this extraordinary offer, Inger left it to her husband to make his own decision. She felt confident that she would soon be able to travel to England if Lauritz would come home to fetch her in August. On February 22, 1921, he and Walpole boarded a boat for England, convinced that this was the beginning of an international career.

Surely Melchior was torn by his conflicting loyalties. On the one hand he was attracted to the Walpole plan, and not only because it would solve his financial worries. More significantly, it meant that someone believed so strongly in his potential as a singer that he was willing to underwrite a career as well as the support of a family while that career was started. For the first time Melchior did not have to bear alone the entire burden of sustaining the faith in his own abilities. Only a year ago he was living in a cheap boarding house, fearful of running out of funds; now he was comfortably supported by Walpole. Still, he continued to worry. Was he really prepared to live up to such grandiose expectations? Was he strong enough or sufficiently secure in his technical skills? Was he temperamentally suited to make the most of his help? Was he truly worthy of Walpole's faith?

With great appetite Walpole undertook to launch his protégé's career, his first task being to find management. Only the very best would do—the firm of Ibbs and Tillett. Tillett immediately demonstrated his proficiency. He was highly distressed that Melchior had sung Chappell's popular songs at the Promenade Concerts the previous September. The only correct way to build a concert career in London was, he explained, to begin with a formal concert. Walpole had his own opinions about the program, of course. He disagreed with the excessive formality planned by Tillett. Knowing the London audience well, he wanted something titillatingly different.

Melchior solved the problem. He suggested Wennerberg's "Gluntarne," the very songs he and his family had sung during their at-home musical evenings. He had already sung them publicly in a 1916 tour of Denmark and Sweden together with his friend Holger Hansen, a bass from the Royal Opera. These Swedish folk and parlor songs, he felt, would appeal to the educated listeners and ordinary audience members as well because of their simple, honest melodies and words. Walpole embraced the idea wholeheartedly. He could see it now: Two strapping Scandinavians would sing repertoire sufficiently formal to appease the London critics and, at the same time, tuneful and unusual enough to please a British audience.

Tillett was persuaded and Walpole was in his element. Wigmore Hall was rented for April 6. Lauritz was horrified at the mounting expenses that were being met entirely by Hugh Walpole. He was undergoing an education in the costs of a singing career. Clearly, a singer had to have "a Croesus of his very own," he confided to his diary. He worried whether he could make a success that would justify the expenditure of all this money. Nevertheless, he was so convinced that he was on the right path that he resigned from the Royal Danish Opera two weeks before the concert, on March 1, 1921.

The concert was an unconditional success. (One reason was that the *Gluntarne* songs and duets were written for baritone and bass, with E as the highest note in the upper part. Strictly speaking, Melchior was not debuting as a tenor.) For two completely unknown young singers to sell out a London concert was unheard of, but Walpole made it happen. The *Times* sent a different critic, and this time the reviews were favorable, so much so that a second concert was arranged for June 8. To himself, however, Lauritz acknowledged that he and Holger never reached the level of musicality and humor that his father and Uncle Bøchman had achieved, with Miss Lunddahl at the piano, during those inspiring evenings at home.

The large circle of people who helped Melchior achieve his stardom may very well have included Queen Alexandra of England, the Queen Mother.

As Princess of Wales, Alexandra had taken a great interest in the affairs of Covent Garden Opera, initiating and sustaining Nellie Melba's position as leading artist there. To conjecture that she may have done as much to further her countryman's career in England is difficult to resist. Walpole had arranged for Lauritz to sing on June 13 for Queen Alexandra at Marlborough House. The Queen Mother's sister, Empress Maria Feodorovna (Dagmar) of Russia was also present. "They were two beautiful and fine elderly ladies. Alexandra was very deaf, but she was so vain that she did not want to use an ear trumpet, and I do not think that she heard very much of what I sang," Lauritz noted. After performing, Lauritz was presented to Alexandra. He asked her a mischievous question inspired by an episode from his boyhood. (At the age of six, after singing a soprano solo one Sunday with other Melchiorianer at Copenhagen's "English Church," Lauritz had been called down by Princess Alexandra, who gave him a kiss.) "Does Your Highness recall the time she kissed me?" he now asked her at Marlborough House. Queen Alexandra took him up to her small private study for a long gossip about Denmark, at the close of which she presented him with a diamond-emblazoned tiepin as a memento.

Lauritz returned to Copenhagen in August to find Inger under the constant care of the nurse. He persuaded Inger to come back with him to England, where she remained for one month. It was not a happy time for either of them. London did not please her, and she didn't care much for Lauritz's friends. Her poor health exacerbated her homesickness, and in the end she packed and returned home to her beloved children.

Walpole, the neophyte musical-career builder, had begun to see clearly the error of his ways. Neither "royals" nor society figures could further the making of Melchior's voice into a first-class Heldentenor. A good voice teacher was crucial. He had chosen, after soliciting advice from friends, a lieder and oratorio singer-turned-teacher, Raymond von zur Mühlen, who had been a student of Julius Stockhausen (teacher of Dietrich Fischer-Dieskau). Melchior, however, had found von zur Mühlen's thick German accent impossible to comprehend, the more so as it filtered through a luxuriant beard. He retained very little of von zur Mühlen's instruction, leaving after a few months.

The act of finding the next voice teacher followed the same pattern: Lauritz allowed Walpole to make the decision. Rather characteristically, Walpole turned his attention to Victor Beigel, a man whose position in the musical world paralleled Walpole's in the world of letters. A bon vivant, Beigel moved in the most elevated musical and social circles, and was consequently the most fashionable voice teacher in the city. At opening nights at Covent Garden socialites asked his opinions and passed them off as their own (as on the occasion of Lotte Lehmann's 1924 debut as the Marschallin in Strauss's *Rosenkavalier*, when her success was so great that "there was no need to discover whether she had the cachet of Victor Beigel's approval"). His technical methods were probably learned from Jean de Reszke and von zur Mühlen, for he had formerly worked as accompanist to both singers. His linguistic skills had made him a welcome guest at musical parties where his specialty was to accompany himself and sing Fiakerlieder with the authentic accent and dialect of a Viennese cabby, an ability that Lauritz admired enormously. Learning that Beigel's studio was already quite full, Walpole began his campaign by inviting Beigel to an elaborate party at York Terrace. Then Walpole put his famous charm and his equally famous connections to work, and persuaded this socially prominent teacher to hear Lauritz.

On November 22, 1921, Lauritz presented himself at Beigel's Little Venice home to audition on the dot of five. A secretary led the previous student out and ushered Lauritz in at the same time, adhering firmly to Beigel's rigorous schedule. A little, fat, jolly Viennese with a "big gray Schnurrbart [mustache]" and a shaven head, Beigel wasted no time with amenities, but brusquely asked what Melchior would sing for him.

Hearing that Melchior wanted to sing the Rome Narrative from *Tannhäuser*, but in Danish rather than German, Beigel affected a loud, theatrical groan.

After hearing the tenor, Beigel informed Lauritz that if it was true that he was not an idiot, the possibilities were limitless.* ("He said to me that if I wanted to become really skilled and would be willing to work well, then I could become a Wagnerian Caruso.") When this statement was met with silence, Beigel inquired with his ready irony, "You *have* heard of Enrico Caruso?"

Finally Lauritz answered: "Yes, in August when he died."

When Beigel heard the secretary thumping on the door, he issued some rapid orders: He didn't want Lauritz to sing anything at all until *he* told him to do so. No opera, no concerts, nothing. There was an enormous amount to learn.

Before Lauritz could protest, the secretary came in, escorted him out, and intoned majestically the hour for his first lesson. Melchior's diary entry regarding this audition contained nothing about vocal methods, saying only that "Victor Beigel costs one £ for a half-hour lesson. So far I am taking twelve hours. He seems a fine and clever voice teacher." In 1970 he added, "What he taught me is what I have become a singer on, and I can still sing."

---

*Later in life Melchior, when asked how one became a Heldentenor, would frequently say, "First you must not be an idiot," recalling Beigel's phrase. Another of his favorite maxims, "Do not sing on the principal; just use the interest," was also borrowed from Beigel, who was in all likelihood quoting his former mentor, Jean de Reszke, whose motto it was.

Both Lauritz and his patron were behaving characteristically, Melchior by allowing himself to be acted upon by another strong individual, and Walpole by seeking approval for his protégé from a teacher whose opinion was deferred to by society figures and the musical establishment. When Beigel accepted Lauritz, Walpole was pleased with himself. He had discovered a talented singer; he had foreseen the likelihood of success; he had found a voice teacher for his protégé; and that famous teacher had concurred with his evaluation of Melchior's potential.

On December 3 Melchior arrived at the appointed hour. Before the first lesson began he found the courage to tell Beigel two difficult things: He had a contract to sing two concerts the following week with the Scottish Orchestra, Sir Landon Ronald conducting (considering Walpole's influential connections in Scotland it can be inferred that he obtained this engagement for Lauritz). Worse yet—and for this there was no professional excuse—he must return to Copenhagen to spend Christmas with his family. As expected, Beigel exploded and interspersed his shouting with many loud groans, saying that Lauritz was throwing away valuable time.

The Dane returned to Copenhagen late in December. No sooner had he found the right words to explain to his family, his father, and Frøken Jensen that he was not allowed to sing in public at the present time than, on his second day at home, the Royal Theater called. Peter Cornelius, their Tannhäuser, was sick. They asked whether Lauritz would sing the role for them that very evening. Although he had not sung through *Tannhäuser* for three years, Melchior agreed, against the specific interdiction of Beigel. On December 18, 1921, he happily sang his first guest appearance with the Danish Royal Opera, on six hours' notice. Lauritz's faltering confidence in his abilities rose at last when, for the first time in his singing life, hometown music fans gave him unstinting approval, eight curtain calls. The Royal Opera rewarded his cooperation and splendid performance as Tannhäuser with another performance ten days later—Canio in *Pagliacci*. Success followed upon success. Invited by King Christian, he sang at Amalienborg Palace the following week, on January 3, 1922.

The guilty secret of these forbidden performances must have been nicely concealed, for upon arrival in London, after crossing on a coal boat arranged by Christensen, Lauritz was permitted to return to his lessons. He, in turn, refused all engagements (except for a February appearance at No. 10 Downing Street for Prime Minister David Lloyd George's soirée for the royal family, which Walpole persuaded Beigel to condone) and concentrated on study. Beigel agreed to give Lauritz three lessons a week until the autumn. Two-thirds of his fee was to be paid by Walpole and the remainder by Melchior, who was proud to contribute the small amount of money from his secret singing engagements. The Walpole-Beigel plan had as its goal to turn Lauritz Melchior into the greatest Wagnerian tenor in the world. Lauritz later said, "Beigel taught me a solid singing technique. Especially breathing was outstanding. The knowledge that was imprinted on me has caused my vocal material to maintain itself so long."

In February 1922 Victor Beigel unexpectedly declared Melchior ready to be instructed in the tradition of Wagnerian repertoire. He arranged with Dr. Franz Schalk, co-director with Richard Strauss of the Vienna Staatsoper at the time, for an audition in early March. This sudden abandonment of Beigel's initial pronouncements about Melchior's youth and inexperience as a heroic tenor and his edict against singing in public occurred after a study period of not more than two months. Either Melchior had been a very quick study or Beigel overestimated the amount of vocal work to be completed. Walpole did not falter in his role as mentor. Consumed with anxiety about what the eminent Dr. Schalk might think of his protégé, he accompanied Lauritz to Vienna. Sometime after March 14 he sang for Dr. Schalk, from the stage of the Vienna Opera House, Siegmund's "Winterstürme," learned in German with Beigel, as well as the Lohengrin aria and Canio's aria in Danish. Dr. Schalk's diagnosis was that Melchior was not really ready to sing as a Wagnerian tenor and needed more study—he especially needed to work on his atrocious German. Although he wasn't sure that she would accept the young singer, Schalk recommended the eminent Kammersängerin, Anna Bahr-Mildenburg, who had sung Kundry and Ortrud at Bayreuth, acted as stage director at the Munich Opera, and who, Gustav Mahler had said, "understood how to turn the spirit of the role . . . into sound." By the end of March Walpole had convinced Bahr-Mildenburg to hear Lauritz at her home, where he sang two arias for her. She agreed to teach him a series of Wagnerian roles, but emphasized that this effort would demand a year of work at the very least. At the end of that time she expected "the world to be at [his] feet."

It was back to London and his studies for Lauritz at the beginning of April, while Walpole traveled on. In May Walpole returned to London, made sure that his protégé was taking German lessons and was working with Beigel, and left again for an ever-continuing round of visits to country houses of the highborn. Again the period of study was shortened, this time by Beigel's departure for his summer vacation. Lauritz took advantage of the hiatus and returned to Copenhagen for a three-month visit to his family, the longest in several years.

In the midst of the happy family vacation (Birte often refers to Ib and herself as having been "vacation-time children") on the island of Amager in the Øresund Strait, Lauritz was dispirited and tormented by worry. Torn between love and ambition, he hated the constant worry about money, hated living in foreign countries without his loved ones, hated being pulled in different directions by each person he knew, hated being a 32-year-old man still preparing for a nebulous career that was yet to come. "[Inger] objected strongly to my desire to enter an international career," but Lauritz was determined not to admit defeat by moving back to Copenhagen. He wanted Inger to spend the coming year in Munich with him, but it was difficult to convince his suffering wife that he loved her as much as he loved singing on stage. Why could he not be content with a successful career in Copenhagen? she asked. Lauritz insisted that his potential was worth these present sacrifices. Inside he had a half-formed feeling that he should be singing now, but he didn't know how to go about it. There were no models for how to start an international career; he had to put his faith in Beigel and Walpole. Yet he began to fear that if he didn't justify himself quickly, the family would not survive.

The couple's increasingly frequent arguments about his career drove Lauritz to leave for Munich a month early. He intended to find an apartment, to acquaint himself with the city, and to hear a lot of German spoken before his vocal instruction began on October 2.

The character of a creative person is often marked by qualities not very admirable in themselves, such as a selective selfishness and a singleminded vision of future achievement. With his determination to go to Munich, Lauritz showed that his talent as a singer was matched, as it must be in an artist, by his ability to surmount obstacles and, when necessary, to place his own needs above others'. Living alone in Munich, Lauritz had to face a new set of artistic and personal challenges.

At least his English income kept him well off in Weimar Germany's outrageously high inflation. He could afford an elegantly furnished apartment in the Pension Toussaint on Briennerstrasse, in the nicest part of the city. When he learned that Richard Wagner himself had lived at Number 21 on the same street in 1864, he felt that forces of destiny were at work. Lauritz took great delight in exploring Munich. It was here that he formed a liking for Lederhosen, those leather shorts held up by embroidered suspenders. The rest of his life he was to prefer for informal occasions this soft and flexible garb of the men of Bavaria, topped off by a Tyrolean hat.

During his hours away from studying, he must have found time to visit a Munich cabaret, for it was in such a setting that, sometime before October 22, Lauritz met a very pretty, rather plump, eighteen-year-old girl called Anny (named Maria Anna Katharina) Hacker who worked in films. At their first meeting, Lauritz dubbed Anny "Kleinchen" ("little little-one") because she was so short, a full 12½ inches shorter than he. According to the story

Lauritz later told to his daughter-in-law, he spent an enjoyable evening at the cabaret with a group that included Kleinchen and afterward he invited them all over to his place. In order to enter the foyer, they were obliged to skirt several high stacks of wine cases. (Lauritz had found a bargain.) Lauritz asked Kleinchen if she could guess what he did for a living. "I think so," she replied. "You sell wine, don't you?"

When he corrected her impression—he was an opera singer determined to become a Heldentenor—she was puzzled. She knew nothing about serious music. What was a Heldentenor? That very first evening, according to Lauritz, he not only explained what a Heldentenor was but also told Kleinchen that he was a married man with two children, and that he and Inger were now separated. The attraction between tenor and actress was galvanic. Kleinchen, wrote Lauritz, was content that her new film would call her away from Munich and keep her busy, because her dreams of marriage did not include a liaison with a married man, nor with a struggling artist. (It is the belief of Melchior's children as well as many others who knew her, however, that Kleinchen deliberately set her cap for this young man who lived alone and far away from his family.)

Beginning in October, Lauritz started to learn his first complete role in German—Siegmund in *Die Walküre*—with Bahr-Mildenburg as his coach. Inger arrived to visit Lauritz in Munich as they had planned in Copenhagen, but on November 18 she was called back to Copenhagen, where her mother was dying. Lauritz asked his "intimate friend" Kleinchen to accompany her to the ferry.

On February 7, 1923, Kristine Jensen died. It was she "who had watched over me like a mother," Melchior recollected, and "who had in every way dedicated work, interest, and money in order to make me a famous singer." Ironically, at about the same time, Mme. Bahr-Mildenburg told him that his progress was such that she could now recommend him to audition at Bayreuth. In two months he would sing for Cosima Wagner and her son Siegfried. (As in his work with Beigel, his progress must have been remarkably rapid.) Still Lauritz complained that he needed some performance feedback before he auditioned for the Wagners. Finally winning Bahr-Mildenburg's approval, Lauritz scheduled a concert in Munich's Odeon Hall and engaged the composer Richard Trunk as an accompanist. The success that this April 26 concert enjoyed was the catalyst for a telegram from Siegfried Wagner. Melchior had been summoned to Bayreuth.

CHAPTER 4

A Bayreuth Beginning

(1923–1924)

Once Bayreuth was just a sleepy little Franconian town near Nuremberg. Yet beginning with the first Wagner festival held there in 1876, Bayreuth became, and has continued to be for more than a century, a symbol of the art and philosophy of Richard Wagner. So, too, Bayreuth became synonymous with the various interpretations of Wagner's aesthetics, first established by the Master himself, then preserved by his widow, and finally developed by his son, his daughter-in-law, and his grandsons, in succession. Bayreuth's prestige issued directly from the operatic festivals themselves; indirectly, the immense influence of the "Bayreuth tradition" has been exerted by artists who, after being trained there, disseminated their views throughout the international musical community.

Lauritz hesitated outside Bayreuth's sumptuous Villa Wahnfried, not knowing what to make of the elaborate frescoes and mottoes (such as the carved door panels featuring the letter W) adorning the facade of Richard Wagner's home. For him, the name "Bayreuth" invoked a storm of contradictory emotions. An invitation to present himself at this hallowed place for an audition before Siegfried Wagner was as intimidating as it was encouraging. Acceptance at Bayreuth would be tantamount to worldwide approval of his abilities, but to fail at Bayreuth would call a halt to his ambitions for an international career as a Heldentenor. Lauritz's belief in his own worth as a singer was about to be tested in the highest Wagnerian court. Effectively, there could be no reprieve elsewhere from a bad verdict handed down by the Wagner family. Yet Bahr-Mildenburg had told him of the extraordinary care with which Bayreuth artists were chosen and of the meticulous preparation they were given, down to the smallest detail. Perhaps she had also shared with him the inspirational words written to her by Mahler just before her own Bayreuth audition: "Soon you will stand in the room where one of the most magnificent spirits who ever walked among human beings ruled. This feeling must lift you beyond any timidity that might overcome you.

. . . Just think of this: HE would have been satisfied with you, for he looks into your heart and knows all that you can and will do." Lauritz longed for the opportunity to learn the tradition as Wagner himself had created it and as Bayreuth had nurtured it.

Feeling rather ill-at-ease in these opulent surroundings and a bit over-whelmed by the significance of the occasion, he rang the doorbell. When the old butler opened the door, not a sound disturbed the silence within the house. He was led to a room called "The Hall," which contained only a grand piano and a few chairs. This huge room with its flagstone floor had accommodated the piano rehearsals of every great Bayreuth artist since 1876. There by the piano, prepared to accompany him, stood Professor Karl Kittel, a Viennese who had come to Bayreuth in 1904 via Graz and Hamburg and who had served as chief coach of the festival since 1912. Awaiting him, Lauritz also found Siegfried Wagner, only son of the great Richard Wagner. Because Wagner's widow had ceded her authority to her son, Siegfried Wag-ner now had complete charge of the coming festivals, slated for resumption in 1924 after the hiatus forced by World War I. Siegfried was clad in what Lauritz later realized was his invariable, idiosyncratic garb, knee breeches and yellow stockings. The young tenor noted Siegfried's distinctive eyes, of palest blue, which looked almost disembodied.

Lauritz had elected to sing "The Rome Narrative" from *Tannhäuser* and "Winterstürme" from *Die Walküre*. This would be his first essay at singing Tannhäuser in German, and Siegfried Wagner, seated in one of the two easy chairs, was the first to hear it. Melchior positioned himself by the huge Ibach piano and commenced the first aria. At the conclusion of the singing, Wagner said nothing, but simply arose. He climbed the narrow stairway just inside the door up to the third-floor gallery. As his eyes followed Siegfried up the stairs, Lauritz noticed the extreme height of The Hall. It extended beyond a gallery to the top of the house and was illuminated by a skylight on the roof. Melchior and Kittel waited in the enveloping silence.

When Siegfried descended, he said, "Mother has complimented you. She likes your singing." Only then did Lauritz look up to see that Cosima Wagner had been in the balcony the entire time, as he wrote years later, like a "motionless, white apparition." Siegfried engaged him "on the spot to sing two of the leading roles in the coming festivals, Siegmund in *Die Walküre* and the title role in *Parsifal*." Cosima's approval was, without a doubt, of paramount importance. Daughter of Franz Liszt, she married first Hans von Bülow, a conductor of great repute who was much admired by Richard Wagner. Leaving her husband, she had lived with Wagner for some years before they were able to marry. She had dedicated herself to the furthering of her new husband's career, and, after his death, to the preservation of his work.

At this moment, then, Melchior had the approval of the most important people in the Wagnerian world: Cosima and Siegfried Wagner had officially sanctioned his skills as an artist. Lauritz hastened to thank both Professor

Kittel and Siegfried. Intending to express his gratitude to Frau Cosima, too, he looked up to the gallery, but there was no one there. She had gone, leaving the details to her son. Although the way it had turned out was far beyond his original hopes, Lauritz feared that it was all too good to be true. Could things go that easily? Might the Wagners not later discover some flaws in him and regret their choice? Despite his worries, he sent Walpole a telegram outlining the new developments.

Already engaged for 1924, he submitted happily to the yoke of the "Bayreuth tradition." "I stayed on in Bayreuth for a month to study these roles and learn the real Wagner style," wrote Lauritz. His days in Bayreuth soon settled into a pattern. Lessons with Professor Kittel, "a very delightful and pleasant man," were held for three to five hours each day. Kittel, responsible for inculcating the artists with Bayreuth style and presentation, was generally acknowledged to be as thorough in his understanding of Wagner's music as the family itself. "What he taught me about my Wagner roles has stayed with me always," wrote Lauritz. Later, in 1932, he passed on his coach's remarks about Wagnerian style in a speech to the New York Wagner Society:"In the works of Richard Wagner melody is, always has been, and always must be the life blood of the drama. Complete integration of dramatic impulses with musical expression forms the basis of the Bayreuth style."

Although it cannot be documented, Bahr-Mildenburg surely had prepared her gifted student in much the same way as she had been schooled by Gustav Mahler. Now Karl Kittel, kind, and thorough as well, used Richard Wagner's orderly method of rehearsal with Melchior, first reading "the whole part through with me to give me a picture of the character and the person I had to portray as well as his relationship to the other characters in the opera," then making phrase-by-phrase corrections. At various points during their work, Kittel and his young charge would present themselves at Wahnfried for the Wagners' approval. Frau Cosima would silently take her accustomed place in the gallery. Often Siegfried would sit near the piano, from which position he could make suggestions as Melchior sang. Now and then Siegfried, alerted by a tiny "sign from 'Mama'" in the balcony, would dutifully ascend. Returning to the artists below, he would convey Cosima's specific criticisms: "Mother wants me to explain about this section." In this fashion the fledgling Heldentenor came to understand how to interact with the orchestra and other singers, how to make meaning evident by his expression even during the long periods when not actually singing, when to give his all, and when to hold back. In sum, he learned how to listen as well as how to sing.

Sometimes the budding Heldentenor had the uncomfortable feeling that he was the only person in Bayreuth who had to be taught the "Bayreuth

Tradition." He felt stuffed with rhythms and notes and admonitions and traditions. Even Daniela, daughter of Cosima by Hans von Bülow, was preoccupied with protection of Wagnerian traditions, and lectured Lauritz about his duty to provide visual expression for every melodic phrase of her stepfather's aria-less, recitative-like music. Through it all Lauritz was eager and diligent, for he saw Cosima and Siegfried as the staunch protectors of Richard Wagner's purity of purpose.

Following Richard Wagner's death in 1883, Cosima Wagner took over the stewardship of Bayreuth, established by Richard Wagner's mentor, King Ludwig of Bavaria. Cosima Wagner regarded herself as the sole conduit of the true faith from the Master himself to the participants in the festival, and resisted all change. "Frau Cosima stressed that Bayreuth was a consecrated place and not at hand for experiments," wrote Lauritz. Although he would have been horrified to hear it, his view of her importance was not universally accepted. George Bernard Shaw, a passionate Wagnerite, saw her role as nothing more than "chief remembrancer."

What was she remembering? Richard Wagner believed that the theater was the center of popular culture, unlimited in its power. Yet, he believed, the corruption he found before and behind the scene served not art, but money. He was repelled by the empty striving after outward effect in the operatic music of the day. Music, the means of expression, had been transformed into the sole aim of opera, while the drama, the true aim, had been neglected for the sake of musical forms. In dissolution, opera had sunk to the level of a mere pastime. His Reformation would one again unite the arts into music-dramas that would become for future generations what the Greek drama had been for the Ancients. His innovative *Zukunftsmusik* (Music of the Future) solved the problem of unifying music and works by means of leitmotifs, small melodic figures or harmonic progressions that illustrated situations, personages, objects, places, feelings, and ideas. As the librettist as well as the composer of his works, Wagner's vocal melodies, couched in recitative-like narration, issued from his poems and were supported by the orchestra. In Bayreuth he was finally provided with an ideal theater in which to produce his music-dramas, and a community in which artists could concentrate on their training in Wagnerian principles. In such an atmosphere, each artist could devote himself exclusively to the proper interpretation of Richard Wagner's art and philosophy.

When Cosima became director of the festival, it was immediately clear that she saw herself as her husband's official conservator. "*We* are preserving the pure ideals," she declared. "*We* know the Master's artistic philosophy." Yet Wagner himself had planned future alterations, and Cosima had actually witnessed firsthand only the "superb *Tristan* conducted by von Bülow, one good *Meistersinger*, one experimental *Ring*, and one incompletely realized *Parsifal*." Most historians agree that "what began as a general artistic principle had been brought down to the level of a recipe."

Cosima was criticized then as now. Even Bayreuth artists put the lie to her pretensions. Conductor Felix Mottl noted that Cosima, while insisting on strict observance of her husband's scores, actually made changes in the *Tristan* score, lowered some dynamics, deleted some string complements, and eliminated a cymbal crash. A Rhinemaiden under Wagner himself, the famous soprano Lilli Lehmann (who was later renowned as a voice teacher) was an equally vociferous critic. She praised Cosima's intellect, but added that Cosima had no heart: "The Master [had] allowed everybody to express his own . . . individuality," whereas in Cosima's Bayreuth the only chance for peaceful coexistence lay in total submission to Cosima's will. Anna Bahr-Mildenburg, too, understood that Cosima, by imposing upon the singer the very actions that ought to give life to the character, in fact often destroyed spontaneity. Surely she had inculcated Cosima's principles in her student Melchior, although she often expressed her worry that "not all could see beyond the drill to the inner intention."

Sadly, all the energy expended on the task of repeating the "tradition" had, by 1914, led only to mechanical precision and a loss of vitality. After the war, when Siegfried was put in charge, those changes that he dared to make were much-criticized. But Lauritz, devotedly working to absorb the Bayreuth ideal, knew nothing of those who spoke ill of either Cosima or Siegfried. (As late as 1970 he still proudly recalled that he "was the last singer to whom she ever devoted time.") He was naively enthusiastic and studiously receptive to all Cosima's suggestions although they came to him secondhand. "I never spoke one word directly with the old lady, but I received a bow of her head and a movement of her hand as from the pope."

Lauritz and the other Bayreuth artists really liked "Fidi," as Siegfried Wagner was called. Unlike his mother and his wife Winifred, Siegfried was approachable as a human being, warmhearted and modest, more tolerant, and more liberal than either Richard or Cosima Wagner. Winifred had been born in England, placed in an orphanage when her parents died, and adopted by Karl Klindworth, the piano arranger of Wagner's works, who took the young girl to Bayreuth in 1914. Forty-year-old Siegfried Wagner promptly fell in love with the "bewitchingly charming" girl with "a beautiful face" and a "clean-cut profile." Within a year they were married. Winifred emulated her mother-in-law in all things, even in Cosima's bizarre hatred of Jews, absorbed at her husband's side.

One afternoon in Siegfried's office at Wahnfried, Melchior looked out the window to see an outlandish group of young and middle-aged men wearing armbands emblazoned with swastikas entering the courtyard in two ranks. As a small man in an overcoat entered the garden and approached the house the men all came to attention, shooting their arms into the air in a strange gesture. Curious, Melchior asked Siegfried who they were. Police? Extras? If so, why were they rehearsing in the Wahnfried garden? No, he was told, they were neither. They were some of Winifred's new friends. The short one, said Fidi with a shrug, was a Herr Hitler, but he quickly pulled the curtains tight. "Siegfried was not very Nazi. It was mostly she," Lauritz recalled.

In Bayreuth, Lauritz, as usual, made friends with the nearest children, in this case, the four youngest Wagners—Friedelind, Wolfgang, Wieland, and Verena Wagner. He was a willing audience for their performances in the Wahnfried garden, where they dressed in miniature Wagnerian costumes (made for them by Aunt Daniela, Bayreuth's designer) as Fricka, Wotan, Siegfried, Brünnhilde, complete with spears, shields and war cries. Their own versions of the Wagnerian music drama and their wheelbarrow tours of Wahnfried netted many pfennigs from their friend Lauritz and the charmed tourists. Lauritz was known to prefer "the congenial and natural society of children."

Melchior's simple, uncomplicated nature might well have pleased Wagner, especially in the role of Siegfried. Wagner had lectured another tenor about playing this part: "Your entire way of looking at life is too ponderous and colored too dark. You must become more gay and sunny." He had continued with advice that Melchior later passed on almost verbatim to a young tenor in 1965: "Don't think that your way of life and your way of acting are separate entities and that one has nothing to do with the other."

For six weeks Melchior's education in Wagner's music had continued daily—the historical evolution, the musical style, the dramatic principles— and, luckily, his teachers were Bayreuth's best. Yet, despite the monumental importance that most of the world ascribed to the works produced by Wagner, there were problems. Wagner had been constantly plagued by the difficulty of finding actors who were also singers, singers who possessed sufficient stamina to sing the parts he had written, especially those for tenor. In 1876 he wrote in a letter to a colleague, "I must constantly go back and ask myself how I got the idea to write all the emotionally important leading roles of all my works for the tenor voice." On the other hand, he artlessly expected the fearful vocal difficulties of his music to disappear once the singer had the true sympathy for the drama which he demanded. Pragmatically speaking, it cannot be denied that singing a major Wagnerian role demands a robust and sturdy body, not least because the Wagnerian orchestra emits a richness of sound that mandates singers with enormous and powerful voices to sing over it. Someone had to teach Melchior to pace his delivery so that his voice would not be incapacitated at the end of the drama, and the task was assumed by Karl Kittel. Obviously Melchior was well-equipped by nature for this contest of strength. He was endowed with an immense physique, boundless vitality, and great vocal endurance. He often argued with those who claimed "that Wagner cannot be sung without shouting and that singing of Wagner's music ruins the voice in a short time." Indeed, he maintained: "You should sing Wagner exactly as you always sing, but you should follow the ways the Master shows you so your voice never gets into a fight with the great heavy orchestration, and you should never try to sing over the orchestra when you are not supposed to."

To Wagner one of the most important attributes of a singer was his appearance: "How can the spectator receive an impression of the courageous Tannhäuser or the idealistic Lohengrin if these roles are incorporated in singers of small, thickset stature, with a fat head [and] without a neck?" Tall, well-built, and broad-chested, Melchior looked the part of Wagner's super-tenor creations. By 1920 he had begun to put on weight and pictures from this year showed him to be decidedly burly. His physical strength was evident, and even his lack of vocalizing pointed to his vocal strength. Melchior often did not sing so much as a single note before appearing on stage. By 1950 his "warming up" consisted of drinking a bottle of Carlsberg beer, clearing his throat a bit and heading for the stage, altogether ready to perform.*

Melchior's heroic build was made to order for his Wagnerian roles, as was his natural facility for coloring the voice to respond flexibly to the dramatic situation, another criterion of Wagner's. The importance with which Wagner imbued the drama in opera does not mean, however, that he minimized beauty of tone. Vigorous declamation achieved at the cost of intonation or healthy tone production was unacceptable, and he would not have condoned what is termed the "Bayreuth bark." He treasured the rounded tone, the sustained legato vocal line, a supported *piano*—trademarks of an Italianate vocalism that Melchior produced in abundance.

What Richard Wagner wanted in a singer had turned out to be exactly what Lauritz Melchior was. Despite the rigorously detailed training he received in Bayreuth, it might be argued that he was actually more an embodiment of Wagner's wishes than of Cosima's and Siegfried's directions. In fact, Lauritz's success could increasingly be credited to his innate talent rather than to Hugh Walpole's expert society maneuvering.

When Hugh Walpole arrived in Bayreuth, he confided to Melchior the grand strategy he and Tillett had worked out for the future. Lauritz would

---

*My own lengthy warm-up always annoyed Melchior inordinately. It was this that had made him decide that I was "just like Kirsten Flagstad." I had been speechless with delight until I found out what he really meant.

study another year with Bahr-Mildenburg, subsidized by £800 from the English serial rights to Walpole's novel *Portrait of a Man with Red Hair*. In the spring Covent Garden was planning the first German season since the war, and Hugh had his eye on *Die Walküre* as an opportunity for Lauritz. To that end, Lauritz would sing several concerts in England during the summer to keep his name before the British public and their "royals."

Upon return to Munich in October, Lauritz's lessons with Anna Bahr-Mildenburg were resumed until November 6, when he set off to Berlin. Rehearsals were scheduled for a concert with the Blüthner Orchestra that Walpole had arranged at the Staatsoper with Germany's most eminent Wagnerian soprano, Frida Leider, under the baton of Leo Blech, one of Germany's most distinguished Wagnerian conductors. The enormous expenditure of British pounds that this would require did not faze Walpole; after all, the already low exchange rate of the German mark was falling even lower. The program included the "Prize Song" from *Die Meistersinger*, the prayer from *Rienzi*, and the first act of *Walküre* with Frida Leider. Although he had never sung this music in public before, Lauritz felt ready: there had to be a first time sometime.

Leo Blech was a revelation to the young Melchior. His methods, his skills, his understanding of singers, and his musicianship, were all on a level far above anything Lauritz had encountered previously or was ever to find again. "Of all the conductors with whom I have worked all over the world," he wrote in 1967, "no one was greater as an opera conductor than Leo Blech. . . . He was like a father to me and I shall always be thankful to him for what I achieved through my long artistic life."

Most singers liked Blech. Because his memory for previous vocal faults or successes was so good, his rehearsals were very efficient. On the other hand, because all facets of the singers' skills were so apparent to him, he was not averse to discussing vocal or musical problems openly during rehearsals, sometimes in an embarrassingly candid fashion. Yet, said Leider, he was of great help when a singer he respected wasn't in top form, although those singers he did not like were apt to find any errors they made mercilessly revealed to the audience.

The lucky Lauritz Melchior experienced none of the pitfalls of working with Blech. Had Blech dismissed as unimportant this thirty-three-year-old Dane with shaky rhythmic skills, supported by a wealthy British patron, it would have been understandable. However, he responded to Melchior's sunny disposition and naive earnestness as others did. Blech simply liked him.

The November 8 concert in Berlin was a signal event for young Melchior. He was thrilled to sing with Frida Leider, whose vocal and personal beauty moved him deeply, whose artistic equal he had never encountered, and to be so enthusiastically approved as her singing partner by the knowledgeable Berlin public. Literally leaving while his Berlin debut audience was still cheering, Melchior dashed to catch the night train to Munich for two concerts that Siegfried Wagner had offered him, expecting to sleep en route. It was, however, the night of the Beer Hall Putsch in Munich, as he wrote in his manuscript:

> I left Berlin by train, but when we reached the Bavarian border we learned that the Hitler Movement had started a revolt in Bavaria, and that the train would go no farther than the town of Plauen. This was a bad predicament for me, but after negotiations with the train conductor, the locomotive engineer and the train guard, these gentlemen agreed to take me along in their automobile, in which they intended to try to reach the town of Hof in Bavaria, and from there to München, where they all had their homes about which they were deeply concerned. On the way we were often stopped by the revolutionary troops. Each time a couple of armed men stood on the running board and accompanied us through the next roadblock to the next guards. When we finally arrived in Hof, our engineer found a single locomotive with the steam going. We were all loaded onto this engine, I with my suitcase and everything, whereupon we steamed off to München. It was a windy trip for a tenor, and at my arrival I was missing my hat; on the way it had decided to take wings.

When Lauritz left his new friends to seek out Siegfried in his hotel suite, he found Siegfried and Winifred hanging out the windows to watch Hitler's storm troopers marching, General Ludendorff and Hitler leading. Siegfried, who had been horrified to see the general fired upon by the Bavarian police, greeted Lauritz and related how the revolution hadn't turned out quite as Hitler had hoped. Due to the events of November 9 and 10, the two Wagner concerts were postponed.

A few days after Hitler's march on Munich had failed, Siegfried Wagner announced that a new tenor, Lauritz Melchior, had been engaged for the next Bayreuth season. Now an avalanche of offers for every sort of singing engagement showered down on the new Heldentenor who was anointed by Siegfried and Cosima Wagner. Opera intendants, agents, and recording company executives all scurried to secure his participation in their projects: Siegmund in Coburg, Magdeburg, and Braunschweig, Parsifal in Chemnitz and Breslau.

The concert with Siegfried Wagner, which finally took place on December 15, was not a *succès fou*. Although Lauritz was flattered to be included in any concert conducted by a member of the Wagner family, Siegfried suffered by the unavoidable comparison with Leo Blech. In addition, Siegfried's penchant for slow tempi exposed for the first time (but not the last) Melchior's inability to execute such tempi accurately. Had Lauritz been complacent, the little framed note in Wagner's handwriting that hung in the hallway to the stage at the Festspielhaus should have reminded him: "*Achtung auf die kleinen Noten; die grossen kommen von selbst!* (Take care of the little notes, the big ones will take care of themselves!)"

In a very short time the new Heldentenor became infamous in conducting circles. Accompanists and conductors who were closely associated with the tenor agree that his rhythmic memory was faulty. In addition, he had real difficulty keeping a tempo. During passages depicting any compelling emotion, he would rush forward and invariably get ahead of the beat, as in the recording of a 1941 Metropolitan Opera *Tannhäuser* broadcast. In Act I, each time Melchior took the harp from Venus and passionately sang his praises of love and the delights of her kingdom, he outran the actual harpist and the conductor, who were vainly attempting to stay with him.

It is difficult to avoid the conclusion that Melchior's rhythmic and tempo faults were irremediable. Anna Bahr-Mildenburg was devoted to Gustav Mahler's high standards regarding rhythmic accuracy and has lovingly described them at great length: "Indifference, carelessness, comfortableness could not be accepted. . . . Correctness is the soul of an artistic performance. . . . He taught me to attribute to every rest exactly the same importance as to sung notes. . . . The smallest note values were to him means of expression." Surely she made every effort to inculcate Melchior with these principles, but perhaps to little avail. Melchior's shortcoming was not universally condemned. Henry Pleasants, for one, realized that Melchior was not the only sinner; "but then, a nice sense of rhythm has rarely been a tenor virtue." Other tenors, revered for their musicianship, possessed the same qualities for which Melchior was roundly chastized by critics. British record and television producer John Culshaw's description of making a recording with Heldentenor Wolfgang Windgassen furnishes an example: "[Windgassen] had, and still has, a rather endearing habit—execrable to conductors—of 'running ahead of the beat' . . . I only once remember him managing to get behind the beat, at which moment Solti warmly congratulated him." Melchior, too, slighted beats and notes, and he raced ahead—but only, said he, when "a real maestro" was not on the podium. Whatever his rationalization, however, most conductors did agree that in terms of tempo, it was virtually impossible to restrain him.

Now events were moving rapidly. Lauritz Melchior was no longer an unknown, struggling tyro, but an artist whose engagements were booked a year in advance. One such engagement, a concert tour of German commencing in October of 1924, was, as Lauritz himself recognized, his big chance. If he did not prove himself during the next few months, the opportunity would pass him by.

Between engagements, he continued to work very hard with Bahr-Mildenburg. (Melchior spent a great deal of time at this stage of his career mastering the roles "exactly as he wanted them." Later, understandably, he would be "disinclined to change anything," particularly when changes were requested by those whose credentials he did not find authoritative.) In retrospect, he considered "the year 1924 . . . the beginning of [my] international singing career. . . . Like a real Meistersinger, I started that year with a recital in the old Meistersinger Church in Nuremberg. . . . The atmosphere of those surroundings was elevating to a singer's mind, and I think that I was inspired that evening."

This appearance netted an opera engagement in that city for late April 1924, where he managed the feat of singing both Turiddu in *Cavalleria Rusticana* and Canio in *Pagliacci*. In mid-April Lauritz joined Hugh Walpole and his mother in Venice. Hugh had welcome news: Lauritz was engaged to sing Siegmund at Covent Garden in May. Indeed, Melchior's debut would be under the baton of the renowned Bruno Walter. (No one told Walter, however, that he would have a Siegmund who had never sung the role in public.)

In August 1923 Lauritz had returned to Copenhagen for a family visit. Now that the Wagners had placed their imprimatur upon him, he and Inger could be together only if she moved to Germany. He was lonely, but Inger was adamant: She did not want her children to go to school in Germany; she hated Germans, and feared dying in a foreign country. Their discussions resulted in a formal separation (although Lauritz had told Kleinchen at their 1922 meeting that he and his wife were already separated).

Subsequently, the otherwise all-inclusive publicity describing Melchior's life virtually expunged Inger's existence, and her side of this story has never been heard. Of those who could impart it to us, only Eva Andersen, Inger's niece, is still living. She tells us that Inger loved Lauritz very much, and often confided in her young niece. Inger's troubles with Lauritz "contributed to her bad health," Andersen reveals, and she "really died of a broken heart."

Very likely Inger found in the career of an actor and singer no such fascination as do outsiders to the profession. Inger valued a normal home life over the seeming romance of the performer's life. Her actor-father's infatuation with a younger woman, resulting in a messy divorce and much heartache for Inger's mother, had been followed by the incredible publicity surrounding the shooting of his second wife and his own suicide. It was hardly surprising that Inger longed for calm and order in her life: The turmoil of travel, the effort of speaking new languages, the dependence upon strangers for medical help, life in hotels, the hazardous livelihood of singing—all were simply beyond her stamina.

Lauritz and Kleinchen, meanwhile, had greatly strengthened their relationship by the time of his departure for London. Her father, trying to talk some sense into his daughter, reminded her that she, thirteen years younger than Lauritz, was already ensconced in her career, while he was still learning his skills. Kleinchen agreed with her father's point, of course, but then neither she nor her parents had ever heard an opera or been to a concert. How could they tell if Lauritz Melchior was talented, and whether his future held any promise? Lauritz tried to reassure the Hacker family by inviting them all to come to Bayreuth that summer where they could judge for themselves. Content with their acceptance of his invitation, he then left for London.

Covent Garden, like Bayreuth, was doing a German season for the first time since the beginning of World War I. It is notable that Lauritz Melchior shared the season with the veteran Jacques Urlus (who was "competent, if not thrilling" at this stage of his career), now generally agreed to be the greatest Heldentenor between Jean de Reszke and Melchior.

Melchior arrived on May 6, 1924, and as he wrote, "eight days ahead of time in order to get my rehearsals with Bruno Walter. . . . I showed up every day at the opera house, but no rehearsals were scheduled." In four days a new production of *Rosenkavalier* was to premiere; the opera had not been done in England since Beecham conducted it in 1913. Several rehearsals had been held, assisted by Richard Strauss, who had arrived in London to oversee, but things were not going well. Each morning Melchior was promised a rehearsal the next day, only to have it canceled again. *Walküre* had to take a back seat until the premiere of *Rosenkavalier*, in which Lotte Lehmann played the Marschallin.

On the morning of May 14, the day of the *Walküre* performance, Lauritz spent the entire morning trying to speak to Bruno Walter at Covent Garden. With each passing hour he dreaded more the task of informing Dr. Walter that he was doing the role of Siegmund for the first time. (What was going to be even harder was to admit that he had never seen the entire opera.) Finally, when he had Walter on the phone, he introduced himself and explained why he might need some help from the conductor that evening. There was probably not all that much to worry about, Lauritz said, since he had sung a concert version of Act I in Berlin with Frida Leider. Moreover, he had *heard* the entire opera. "[Walter] nearly had a stroke, but as it was impossible to get another Siegmund, he had to swallow the bitter pill and let me sing the role without rehearsal, hoping that fortune would favor the brave!"

Why did Covent Garden not research Melchior's artistic experience a little more seriously and inform Bruno Walter? The Covent Garden scouts had heard of Melchior, probably from master strategist Hugh Walpole, and the sponsoring syndicate was willing to put up with any imperfections that might accompany his lack of experience in the great roles because of his engagement by Siegfried Wagner and the usual dearth of Wagnerian tenors. Perhaps it also had something to do with the size of Melchior's fee—a mere £40.

In the narrow Wagnerian world of the time, new productions of the music-dramas were virtually nonexistent. The gestures, stage blocking, and general style adopted by Bayreuth-trained artists were universally imitated. For the most part, outside of Bayreuth there were few or no rehearsals because the opera administrations could rely on the singers to know the blocking and stage conventions. Today's nostalgia for the Golden Age is probably misplaced. Those singers who lived during that era and actually viewed these performances tell us that it was a system that relied more on survival of the fittest than on study or preparation. After what we would today call minimal study, the singer of apparent talent was thrown on stage. If he survived, he had a career; if not, he passed from sight. This *Walküre* performance was Melchior's survival test, his first German performance of a Wagnerian music-drama in a major opera house, and his first experience with an international cast.

Göta Ljungberg, whose "vocal manner always promised to produce a better sound than it did," was cast as Sieglinde. Maria Olczewska, possessor of "the most beautiful female voice in the company" and "an actress of greatest intelligence," was to appear as Fricka, with Friedrich Schorr as Wotan. Lauritz's new friend Frida Leider, making her London debut as Brünnhilde, was the only performer that evening who knew that this *Walküre* was Melchior's debut. She was very nervous, but her worries paled before those of Bruno Walter. Bitterly, he braced himself for the inevitable calamity.

Melchior thought that "the performance went rather well; I just made a mistake in the text of the 'Todesverkündigung.'" There, trying to remember where to stand, he asked Brünnhilde the second of two questions first. "In her nervousness she answered the wrong question instead of staying in the correct place in the music, and this caused a slight confusion, but so slight that few people noticed it, even among the critics."

Walter had not a word to say to Melchior, friendly or otherwise, but some reviewers found the young tenor very promising. The *Times* called his Siegmund "uneven," and chided him because he had "conceived the wrong tempo for the sword song, though he was not allowed to adopt it." Schorr was praised for his "tremendous and dramatic voice," while Leider "caused critics to exhaust their vocabulary of superlatives."

Meanwhile, Hugh Walpole took issue with the impossible ten-year-old Siegmund costume, and asked a friend, Charles Ricketts, to design a costume worthy of "Melchior of Bayreuth" in time for the second performance. Melchior remembered:

> The famous English designer and painter created a costume for me that rather made me look like a mixture of a Viking and an Indian Chief on the warpath. I had red hair, two long braids with ribbons braided into them, hanging all the way down to my stomach, long trousers, also wound with ribbons. I must indeed have looked beautiful. Unfortunately, there exists no picture of me in this costume, for it was the first and only time I wore it.

Grateful that the conductor that evening was not Bruno Walter (what a fuss he would have made over *this* Siegmund), Melchior made his entrance. Before they recognized this bizarre stranger as Melchior, his colleagues believed they were saddled with yet another Siegmund. They were forced to glue their eyes upon the conductor, Karl Alwin, for the laughter from the audience obliterated the sound of the orchestra. Lauritz was the talk of London town for weeks to come. "Very good publicity," Walpole decreed, not at all chagrined.

Once the strain of the first *Walküre* was over, Frida Leider and Melchior had rejoiced in the unusually splendid weather and in the excitement that attended a Covent Garden spring season. Before the war, opera in London had always been a social event as well as a musical one, and this season, which offered German opera for the first time since the war, was especially interesting to the British. English society was slowly returning to its prewar customs, and though many wartime austerities were still in force, there was much to interest the foreign singers. Lauritz and his British friends showed Frida everything worth seeing and hearing in London. Afternoons they toured the British Empire Exhibition. Evenings they went to a big revue or to dine at the Savoy, where everyone congregated before and after the opera. It was here in London during the 1924 German season at Covent Garden that Melchior and Frida Leider cemented their friendship. "To this day I feel bound to him and his wife by a deep and true friendship that has held steadfast through all the confusions of the age we live in," wrote Leider.

Having acquired a new knowledge of Wagnerian lore from this performance, Lauritz decided that "Siegmund is very depressed because everything goes wrong. He was born under a bad star." Although "it is not really suitable for a high baritone, and it is not really comfortable for most tenors," Lauritz realized that most heroic tenors learn *Die Walküre* first because Siegmund is the shortest role, it has the lowest tessitura, and is a good test of a tenor's vocal "foundation." As he later explained:

> You must have a good natural low register to build high tones. You can't put a skyscraper on sand. In Wagner you must go up to a high C, but is has to be supported with a solid base. What most often happens is that tenors press down their voices to get through the heavy Wagnerian orchestration. After a time they lose their high notes and their voices. . . . The heroic tenor must learn to conserve his energy. It's like a horse race; if you try to lead the field the whole time, you'll never make the finish.

Even later, Melchior often alluded to that all-important "foundation," as he did in April 1964: "One must have the granite foundation of the baritone voice. . . . Then the baritone's top three notes, E, F, and G, must be filed down to match his lower notes. . . . Then he must add three top notes, A, B, and C."

Few of Melchior's colleagues ever publicly ventured a technical opinion about his singing. Danish baritone Mogens Wedel, however, added to Melchior's own deceptively simplistic description when he noted a few pertinent technical details after singing with Melchior at his very last Wagnerian performance in 1960:

> With some astonishment, I ascertained how early Melchior started to cover*—a technical phenomenon, which we all know and simply have to learn in order to survive. Already at the tone F-sharp Lauritz started to calculate his covering process. In the cases of many people who round off so early, normally nothing much is produced on the extreme high notes. Here Lauritz proved himself to be unique sound-wise. He became better and better the higher he went.

Another Danish singer, Ulrik Cold, former general manager of the Danish Royal Opera (Sarastro in Bergman's *Magic Flute* film), also speaks openly about the vocalism of Lauritz Melchior, which he compares favorably with Flagstad's and Caruso's. At the same time, he stresses that all three abstained from taking the easy way, supporting fortes and pianos equally fully, and therefore matching a big orchestra "with their naked voices alone . . . no artificial darkening or muting . . . all resonances used to the fullest extent [giving] a compact, intense sound . . . that makes the voice shine."

For good reason, Conrad L. Osborne has long been the music community's most respected writer on the subject of great Wagner singing:

---

*To "cover" is to make a technical transition into a mixed tone containing a large proportion of head voice, so as to be able to sing high notes without either reverting to falsetto or relying on brute-strength bellowing in chest voice. (For a fuller explanation, see Vennard, pp. 151–154, 250.)

Good singing in Wagner bears an uncanny resemblance to good singing in the writing of any other composer for the lyric stage. It partakes of exact intonation, identifiable vowel formation, the ability to swell and withdraw the voice, continuity and sustainment provided by a true vocal legato, and the sense of natural movement furnished by a free vibrato. . . . I lay particular emphasis on legato and vibrato because these qualities are virtually absent in the work of numerous Wagnerians, many of whom are downright famous.

It is the concepts discussed by Osborne that most satisfactorily explain Melchior's superiority. Except at the very end of his singing life (when a long career of executing the most demanding repertoire known to the tenor voice had somewhat thickened the vocal texture, had rendered a true *mezza voce* [half voice] difficult, and had required some real constriction of high notes), Melchior's singing suffered no substantial change throughout his career.

To manage both an unceasingly exciting, brilliant tone and an extraordinary vocal vigor during the early stages of a career is not unprecedented, but Melchior actually maintained that same consistency of resonance and that identical level of vocal stamina undiminished for three decades. The hallmark of his singing—that heroic ring—was, in my opinion, the result of his ability to maintain the very core of resonance on every note in his range. This he managed to do even while responding to the changing demands of vowel, dynamic, and pitch. The baritone/tenor range of Wagnerian music (which requires endless fatiguing climaxes in that treacherous area from D to F#, and heavy singing in the lower range) could not seduce Melchior from his uncannily accurate vocal balance into the usual Wagnerian faults—bellowing, barking, and overly covered or dangerously opened high notes.

Melchior survived because he sang superbly. Moreover, while a model of technical virtuosity, the tenor had "genuine passion and conviction," said Osborne, and a "truly musical variety of dramatic inflection" in his interpretations, which were not "less dramatic [but] simply more subtle, less pretentious, and less gimmicky."

When supplying his own interpretation of his technical means in later years, Melchior was invariably overly-simplistic (attempting, some say, to make it appear that he didn't really work at it): "I rarely think [about] technique; I sing my feelings."

CHAPTER 5

From Bayreuth to the World

(1924–1927)

The Festspielhaus was alive with workmen as Lauritz returned to Bayreuth on May 16, 1924. To prepare for the upcoming festival, Siegfried Wagner extended the area backstage to accommodate the immense pre-1914 sets still in use. The theater, built over a period of four years, had been the largest freestanding timber-framed building ever constructed, and Richard Wagner had insisted on its spare and simple design. The machinery and stage fittings were necessarily elaborate. Their expense was not an issue, for he was determined to have a theatre that could manage the dramatic elements in his score. Wagner had replaced the usual side boxes with a series of proscenium arches that lined the side walls, directing the wandering eyes of the audience toward the stage. Sixteen hundred and fifty creaky cane-bottomed seats were set in thirty ascending rows with no center aisle, another of Richard Wagner's innovations. In 1924, this efficient seating system was still exactly as he had designed it. Sight lines were equally good from all seats, although one was said to hear best from the center of rows four through eight. The orchestra was hidden from the audience's view in a sunken pit below the stage, whose depth was as great as the auditorium was high. The superb acoustics (designed to please Wagner's ear) with a reverberation period of no less than ten seconds, were originally tested by a group of soldiers called in from the nearby garrison. (Characteristically, Wagner pronounced them the best audience ever seen because they sat quietly and knew that they were ignorant.) To this day, the Festspielhaus crowns the hill over the Baroque country town of Bayreuth, gently framed by Franconian pine woods, meadows, and hills.

When he wasn't rehearsing or hobnobbing with the local royalty, Lauritz Melchior hung around the Festspielhaus like a stagedoor Johnny. As enthusiastic as a small boy, he was entranced with the mechanical details of the apparatus that made the Rhinemaidens appear to swim. He noted that they had more stage rehearsal than anyone else, and for good reason. The mechanism that whirled the Rhinemaidens up and down and around along the "rocky riverbed" was reminiscent of a Rube Goldberg contraption. Strapped uncomfortably into their harnesses, suspended and rocked by a tangle of pulleys, ropes, and wires, they were at the mercy of the stagehands who operated the machinery, cued by assistant conductors. The poor maidens were forced to ride this wave machine for hours every day. Lauritz, with his reverence for food, found it particularly sad that the wretched maidens could hardly sing their parts without becoming seasick and losing their lunch.

Lauritz had begun to take in stride the constant observation by Cosima, the pale figure up in the Wahnfried gallery, as, down below, he thoroughly worked his two roles, Siegmund and Parsifal. Kittel continued to drill Lauritz in Wagnerian tenets: first, total command of the musical line; then, clarity of the words and use of the consonants for characterization; finally, details of acting and expression. (When the rehearsals were moved from Wahnfried to the Festspielhaus, Cosima, frail and almost blind, demonstrated her approval of the tenor by demanding to be driven to the theater to see how his dress rehearsal went—an event so unusual as to be documented by both Lauritz and historians—although even there she would maintain her distance in the second-floor family box.)

It is widely known that Cosima regarded the eyes as "the mirror of the soul," but it is perhaps less often mentioned that Cosima required her codified eye movements to be *rehearsed* by the Bayreuth singers. Under the guidance of Siegfried and Kittel they mastered the positions: (1) lids covering a major portion of the eyes, which gazed onto the stage floor about five yards in front of the performer; (2) eyes exposed normally, with the gaze raised to eye level; and (3) eyelids drawn up as the eyes widened in an expression of recognition, longing, or fatigue.

Cosima had also subdued every gesture and prohibited unnecessary going and coming. Her watchword for acting was *Ruhe* (stillness): "A certain well-meaning realism is quite out of place, whereas a static pose, which may . . . be regarded as the shell in which the emotion portrayed by the orchestra lies hidden, is at least harmless." Actually, when Cosima was in charge she spent far less time on the music than on the words and their dramatic effect. Clearly Melchior's style of acting (later found wanting by many critics) grew from his single-minded desire to perform and preserve Wagnerian style as imparted by Richard Wagner's widow and son. So steeped in the Stanislavsky "method" are we now that we view Cosima's planned eye movements and gestures with contempt. Yet even Maria Callas, a much later and very different artist, made use of such *plastique*. Stage director Luchino Visconti admits that Callas's thrilling gestures were perfected by systematically borrowing from both the French *tragédiennes* and Greek drama.

Many critics took exception to Cosima's work as a director, particularly as she disdained the use of the new acting principles and new production ideas being formulated by adventuresome scenic designers such as Adolphe Appia. As a result, singers were not freed from the need to react overtly to the musical accompaniment until Wagner's grandsons were directing the festival. Both Bahr-Mildenburg and Lilli Lehmann recognized that one had either to accept a forced copy of the outward form, or to go past simple imitation of Cosima's movements and make them one's own, for which "many singers had neither the aptitude nor the good will nor the earnestness. It was, after all, so easy to give nothing of one's own, to submit simply to the yoke."

In Melchior's later explanation to the New York Wagner Society one sees that he was content to learn his Wagnerian acting in the prescribed fashion:

> How necessary it is that the singer knows the Wagner tradition. The power of doing the right thing with the right gesture at the right moment, supported by the music, gives life and soul to everything. . . . The first thing you have to do is to learn to follow the advice the Master himself has given. Many of these are printed in the piano scores. And do not try to make Wagner "better." It is impossible. In Bayreuth, of course, you were able to get even more of the original advice and instructions from the Master, which were kept and recorded during the years in which he himself was directing the rehearsals. In order never to forget these, I myself kept a little book. In that book I wrote all these instructions and directions as we went along in the study of the part. Then I marked them with a number in my score. Every time I wanted to see the intentions and instructions of the Master, I checked that number in my score and compared it with my notes in my little book.

In his personal manuscript Melchior articulated more specifically the nature of his dramatic intentions, as learned in Bayreuth, citing several situations from *Walküre*, Act I, beginning with Siegmund's collapse in front of the fireplace. After Sieglinde brings the water he requested, and he drinks, "you can hear how the music paints that action. . . . Siegmund drinks once, then he takes a breath; then he drinks a third time, and then there is a long look at Sieglinde. It is . . . necessary for them both to look at each other, spellbound and motionless, for the moment to pay off."

Somewhat sarcastically, Melchior registers his objections to the contemporary practice of inserting ordinary routine actions into operatic sequences in order to preserve realism: "If Sieglinde thought she ought to behave like a good housewife by looking after domestic chores, walking around and perhaps turning her back to Siegmund just when he should look deeply into her eyes, the whole situation is ruined." When he sang Act I of *Walküre* for the last time in 1960, Melchior was still insisting upon this spellbound look. Mogens Wedel, who sang Hunding that evening, had this rehearsal story to tell, which points up Melchior's still-active observance of Bayreuth traditions:

> Normally such piano rehearsals take place in a very matter-of-fact atmosphere, but Lauritz already felt as if he were on stage. At the beautiful lyric cello solo at the beginning of the act, he said [to Dorothy Larsen,

the Sieglinde], "May I have your glance, Dorothy?" Although [she] asserted that it should really not be necessary during rehearsals, there was no way to escape it. Melchior got his warm glance from Dorothy, and then he was satisfied.

Another example Melchior gives of the instructions contained in his little black book concerns the moment when Siegmund must decide whether to leave or to stay, as Sieglinde has asked.

He stops for a moment, looks at her, then thinks, "Shall I leave?" Then he looks upon her again and makes his decision—he'll stay. . . . All that must be plainly shown by the singer in his acting and must follow the music. *Then* he walks to the front of the stage and sings his decision. Again there is a very long look exchanged wherein you must feel the growing love between the two, a moment that seems certain to end with them throwing themselves into each other's arms. But it is broken by a noise outside announcing the return of Hunding. If this deep under-current of love is not strongly felt by the artist in that situation and shown by him, if it were broken by silly, unnecessary small gestures, inattention or restlessness, the audience would feel an empty spot in the dramatic action.

While stressing his belief that, although "the power of the voice is enormous," the singer "must try not only to sing his part but to give it flesh and blood and soul," Melchior also insists that one "cannot act" those Wagner characters that are gods. Therefore, "you must be a true instrument of tradition and let the music and its power help you."

Lauritz stayed with a family right at the *Festspielhügel* (festival hill), conveniently across from the theater, where piano rehearsals, orchestra rehearsals and stage rehearsals filled his day. The pleasure he took in his busy days is evident in his description of how he "breathed in the old times handed down by Richard Wagner himself and kept alive by his widow, Cosima, and his son, Siegfried, whom we artists affectionately called 'Junior Meister,' and by his daughters and stepdaughters, who knew and loved the great Master." The stage rehearsals with Siegfried Wagner gave Melchior an opportunity to appraise Siegfried's real vocation: directing. Conducting and composing were simply not young Wagner's forte, concluded Lauritz, but at directing he was inspired.

Even amid the chaos of preparation, Siegfried Wagner paid some attention to building the reputation of his young Heldentenor. He arranged another paid appearance at the palace of Coburg, where Ferdinand, the former king of Bulgaria, was visiting. Ferdinand, a true Wagnerite, presented Lauritz with a ruby and diamond tiepin. Ferdinand was also present on July 5, when, some two weeks before he was to portray the knight Parsifal on the Bayreuth stage, Lauritz was knighted in earnest by the Duke of Saxe Coburg-Gotha. The awe-inspiring, medieval ceremony, which Kleinchen and her parents also attended, raised him to the second rank of the Order of Saxe Coburg-Gotha. Not unduly awed by duke or decoration, Kleinchen said with splendid indignation, "*Second* class?!" By June 1925, however, he would be elevated to the Carl Eduard Medal, First Class, for his "outstanding achievements," which must surely have gratified Kleinchen.

Hugh Walpole arrived in Bayreuth only a few days before Lauritz's debut on July 23, 1924, having been delayed by his attendance at the Olympic games in Paris. As always, Hugh was alternately amused and put off by the antics of the opera crowd. The strains of this six-week visit to Bayreuth, however, were not solely traceable to Winnie (as he now called her) Wagner's cloying attentions, nor her invitations to intimate little dinner parties with General Ludendorff and the former king, Ferdinand. Rather, his usual *joie de vivre* was undermined by an intense jealousy of Kleinchen; he reproached "David" bitterly for what he perceived to be the loss of their friendship. Their many arguments culminated on the morning of July 16. This quarrel ended with Hugh promising to "pull myself round and adopt the young woman." Beginning the very next morning, when the three drank a toast to one another, harmony was restored and a friendship *á trois* was firmly cemented. By 1925, as Walpole arrived for his annual Bayreuth visit, he would have accepted the fact that his "perfect friendship" with Lauritz had passed its zenith, and that Kleinchen was "all heart, love, and unselfishness to those she cares for." His perception was unwittingly prophetic: In years to come, Kleinchen's exclusive loyalty would yield unpleasant, even tragic consequences.

The imminence of Lauritz's debut gave rise to doubts in Kleinchen's mind. Lauritz understood her questions about the presence of newspaper people at the debut. It indicated her need for outside reassurance of his worthiness as a singer (and therefore as a suitor for her hand). Yes, he said, critics from all over the world would indeed be reporting on his debut. Distressed also at the prospect of her first opera being one that required her and her parents to sit still through a four-hour ordeal (Mark Twain had found it "almost too much for the money"), Kleinchen could not manage to focus her attention upon the music-drama before the performance.

Despite her apprehensions about Lauritz's debut and the length of the opera, Kleinchen and her parents did enjoy the leisurely twenty-minute walk up the promenade leading to the Festspielhaus. On the way up the hill they heard the first flourish of the brass, announcing the impending performance. After buying a program, the neophyte operagoers easily found their seats, for each ticket efficiently directed its holder to the door closest to the seat's row. Kleinchen could see the building's interior was beautiful, symmetrical, and simple, with no conspicuous colors and no superfluous decoration. Though the original gas lights had been converted to electric power in 1888, the auditorium was only softly lit. A subdued instrumental humming came from under the stage but did not disturb. (It was so hot that the conveniently hidden orchestra had stripped to shorts.) Again came the trumpet fanfare. All the lights went out at precisely 4 P.M. The pre-curtain darkness in the Festspielhaus was more profound than any she had experienced in a theater. The audience subsided into complete silence. When the curtain opened, the stage seemed to be a beautifully illuminated, three-dimensional postcard. Some conventions of Wagnerian opera seemed strange—the lack of applause after Act I; the rapt concentration of the audience, who were petrified in positions assumed at the beginning of the act; and the lengthy dinner inter-mission (a welcome rest, however). Later Kleinchen and her parents agreed that while the performance had seemed interminable, they had acquitted themselves admirably.

Kleinchen herself had listened very carefully and now impatiently awaited the reviews, knowing that her future depended upon Lauritz's ac-ceptance by the critics. On July 24, the day after the debut, she and Lauritz scanned the Nuremberg papers feverishly for the official Bayreuth reviews. In the very last line of one of the critiques they spied two sentences they would remember for years: "A tenor by the name of Lauritz Melchior made his debut in the title role. There is no reason to repeat his name, for nothing will ever be heard of him again." Comparing Melchior's Parsifal and Sieg-mund (sung three days later) against another tenor's stylish but vocally flawed Siegfried, the Berlin critic said:

> Perhaps reversed was the situation with Lauritz Melchior, whose high vocal quality stands unquestionable, but who has much to learn styl-istically and in his command of the German language before he may be numbered among the great Wagner singers.

Lauritz's own evaluation was as follows:

> My *Parsifal* was not all recognizable from the performance at dress rehearsal. I can only tell you that both strangers and my artist colleagues, all with tears in their eyes, congratulated me. . . . I am happy, so happy! I only hope the Siegmund goes as well; then a big battle has been won.

Walpole, an eyewitness and a knowledgeable opera lover, although not unprejudiced, states in his journal: "Never have I heard such singing. . . .

Everyone in the boxes near me was crying." On his farewell visit to Wahn-fried he caught a last glimpse of Cosima in the gallery, "a bent, white-haired old woman in a yellow bedgown talking in a most vigorous manner, and about David, too." For their part, Siegfried and Cosima—she always referred to Lauritz Melchior as "the greatest Parsifal"—praised his portrayal despite his still rather thin high notes (a problem that Lauritz himself mentioned at the beginning of his tenor studies): "It is preferable to have them frail and to better them later on, than to force the voice and then spoil it after a few years screaming, as most of our Parsifals do." Despite Lauritz's mixed reviews Siegfried Wagner did engage him for the following summer's festival. This, more than anything else, convinced Kleinchen's father, Karl Hacker, that as a rising singer Melchior might be able to support a wife in proper style.

Doubtless his contract for the 1925 Bayreuth Festival garnered two other engagements, singing Parsifal and Siegmund at Berlin's Staatsoper and the Deutches Opernhaus in Charlottenburg. These guest appearances took place during breaks in his first tour of Germany and Czechoslovakia (five opera performances and 26 concerts with Richard Trunk at the piano). Directly after this, Lauritz returned in January to his studies—and Kleinchen—in Munich, where Anna Bahr-Mildenburg taught him new roles: the young Siegfried and the Paris version of *Tannhäuser*. The Kammersängerin had insisted upon this *Tannhäuser* because many opera houses preferred the Paris to the Dresden version he had been singing previously. As for Siegfried, Lauritz was soon aware that it was not only one of the two most formidable Wagnerian tenor parts, but also the longest he would have to learn.

From his struggle with this demanding role he came to a conclusion that he later shared with journalist Alan Rich: "A real . . . Siegfried cannot come out of the tenor ranks. It must be a high baritone with plenty of power." Certainly in 1925 Melchior began to be more knowledgeable about the Fach for which his endowments had fitted him, as he related later (quoting again Beigel's phrase "you need not to be an idiot," which Beigel had borrowed from Jean de Reszke):

> [To be a Heldentenor you need] first of all, not to be an idiot. And next, to have the right sort of material—a little darker-colored voice than the ordinary Italian lyric tenor. A baritone quality points the way to the dramatic or heroic Wagnerian tenor, the so-called *Schwererheld* [sic] [a heavy hero]—Siegfried, Tristan, Tannhäuser. The lighter *Held* is Lohengrin and Walther. Most [of these roles] are very long, and the voice is not used as in an Italian opera, where there are arias and you sing only a melody with the orchestra underneath—um-pah-pah, um-pah-pah. In Wagner you are part of the orchestra and there are no breaks for applause after arias. The big climax always comes at the end of the opera.

Back in Bayreuth in June of 1925, Lauritz spent his time going very thoroughly through his two original Wagnerian roles—Siegmund and Parsifal. In a June 23 letter to Kleinchen, Lauritz described his busy rehearsal schedule and told how he had added—of his own volition—attendance at the *Siegfried* rehearsals for the other tenor, who gave Lauritz "many tips." The company's anxiety level, which had been excessively high during the previous summer due to the new and untried management and the resumption of the festival after a ten-year hiatus, was now back to normal. Camaraderie among the artists was complete. Almost every evening saw them troop into Die Eule for dinner, Siegfried Wagner leading the way with great good humor, Lauritz enjoying every moment, as he said:

> The time of rehearsal was unforgettable. It was an adventure just to be together with these people, and to have comradeship in the pleasant evenings . . . heightened by foaming steins of beer. . . . Yes, it was truly a . . . splendid, very non-political time . . . in Bayreuth. We all were deeply happy in this world with Siegfried as our good shepherd.

The only holdout from the general companionship of the musicians and singers was Dr. Karl Muck, who had been at Bayreuth as conductor of *Parsifal* since 1901. He was a violent and harsh disciplinarian to the singers and orchestra members alike, and had displayed his "contempt for the human race" in Boston as well, while conductor of the Boston Symphony. Fortunately Michael Balling, an experienced Bayreuth conductor, and the conductor for Melchior's *Walküre* and the rest of the *Ring*, was more well-liked by the artists.

Lauritz's reviews this summer were approving, but contained some reservations. A German critic, referring to a vocal weakness that the American critics chose not to mention for some reason, wrote: "Parsifal was Lauritz Melchior who is at his best . . . where the brilliance of his baritonal tenor may speak. But this is exactly it: the uniform color of voice is yet to be acquired."

Adolf Hitler, after serving his year in jail for the 1923 Putsch, had quietly returned to Bayreuth, where he lived at Wahnfried with the Wagners. He and his followers, still sporting their black armbands, stayed out of the public eye, planning the reorganization of the Nazi party. "Winnie" Wagner complained to Walpole incessantly: The Rhinemaidens were being troublesome; the *Parsifal* scenery persisted in sticking; her husband's health worried her; and she was concerned for the future of the festival should Siegfried die. Furthermore, though she fervently supported Adolf Hitler, she feared that the presence of an ex-convict with them in Bayreuth would bring discredit to the Wagner family. She asked "Wolf," as she and her children were encouraged to call Hitler, to arrive at the Festspielhaus only after dark and to sit well back in the Wagner box. From this vantage point Hitler listened to Melchior sing Parsifal, his face wet with tears.

Lauritz asserted in his personal manuscript that Kleinchen and her mother insisted his duty lay in a rapprochement with Inger. Melchior's son and daughter, however, are convinced that any demand on Kleinchen's part for a reconciliation between Lauritz and Inger was strictly pro forma. Despite his protestations of their innocence, the correspondence between Lauritz and Kleinchen shows the romance to be in an advanced stage, and clearly far from platonic.

Kleinchen saved 19 postcards from Lauritz dated May through December of 1924. Common to them all was a distinct Bavarian flavor and incredibly poor spelling, an incapacity that was by no means limited to the German language or his erratic way with umlauts: "*Büsse, bin ich immer dein* [Kisses, I am forever yours]." "*Ich kysse dich in Gedanken mit* [I kiss you in my thoughts]." "*Ich sende dir al meine Liebe* [I send you all my love]." This last was signed ingenuously "*dein Grossman* [your Big Man]." One was actually addressed to "Frau Maria Melchior" in "*Vienna, Ostria*," and the salutations varied from "*Liebling* [darling]" to "*Meine Schazele* [my sweetheart]."

At the same time that he was writing these love notes to Kleinchen, he was also persuading Inger to meet him in Berlin during November 1924, when he would be singing Parsifal at the Städtische Oper during a break in his concert tour. Lauritz's personal manuscript reports the details of his reunion with his wife in this fashion: Inger arrived in Berlin but a few hours before her husband's November 19 performance. They made plans to meet backstage after the performance. When asked what she thought of the opera, Inger confessed that she had gone to a revue instead. To Lauritz this was the last straw. His wife had no thoughts for opera or for her husband the opera singer. It seemed time to admit defeat and obtain a divorce. Inger agreed and went back to Copenhagen.

In the middle of December 1924, after finishing his Berlin appearances, Lauritz himself returned to Denmark for a long visit with his children and to celebrate his father's birthday. Serious but calm discussions about the impending divorce were also on the January 1925 agenda. The settlement was a reasonably generous amount, says niece Eva Andersen, but the children, who were living on this allowance, declare that it was barely sufficient, given the substantial medical and nursing expenses incurred by Inger's illness. At this time Lauritz informed Inger that he had made plans to marry a German girl after the divorce. Surely Inger must have realized, if only belatedly, that this was the same young girl who escorted her to the ferry in 1922. Birte remembers her mother crying uncontrollably over her childish questions about the divorce, while brother Ib tried to help his younger sister comprehend what had happened.

Only three months later, the death of Lauritz's father, at eighty, necessitated another trip to Copenhagen. Among his father's effects was the 286-page document that Jørgen had written during the last year of his life, *Memories, Especially of Singing and Music.* Reading through this manuscript, Lauritz understood how his father had been able to give him sensible advice about a singing career, and how his family's vivid musical life had ultimately yielded a professional singer.

After his father's death in April 1925, Lauritz (although technically still married) formally requested permission from Karl Hacker to marry his daughter. Hacker was presumably either so fond of Lauritz or so led by the women in the family, that, while a staunch and devout Catholic, he agreed. When Karl and Mutti announced the "engagement" in their home in Mühldorf on April 10, Lauritz was happier than he had been in a long time.

Lauritz and Inger Melchior were divorced on May 23, 1925. Three days later Lauritz, clad in his new white trousers, and Kleinchen, in a perky red-and-white-striped dress, were married in Copenhagen's Rådhus (Town Hall) with two ceremonies. The German-speaking bride was disturbed that she didn't understand the Danish ceremony, and considered herself "married" only after they went through another one in German.

Kleinchen, who soon was working very hard at a film project in Vienna, traveled to Bayreuth on her few days off to tell her new husband that being separated from him made her too unhappy. She would leave the movies once she had completed her present project, she announced, for she could not be a married woman living alone.

During these few days together in Bayreuth, Lauritz, again displaying his disarming naivete, sought out an interest or hobby that they could share in their married life. Significantly, music was not considered. Instead, the couple tried hunting, but the undisguised misery that Kleinchen went through on this first joint expedition put an end to that dream. "Togetherness" was not to be found this way.

Lauritz then turned to bridge-playing. He mistakenly considered himself very good at the game, and he enlisted two fine players—Friedrich Schorr and his wife, Anna—to help teach Kleinchen. She showed little enthusiasm for the game, and when they lost consistently, it was depressing to Lauritz, who always wanted in the worst way to win. Kleinchen was forced into retirement for her ineptitude. Others who were pressed into service as his partners in the ensuing years attest to the lengths to which Lauritz would go to win a card game.

Although Melchior's aversion to losing at cards was firmly engrained, he remained an honorable gentlemen in spite of it. His friend Karl Laufkötter says that "he would not stop before he was on the winning side, even when the game lasted until the early morning hours." In 1942 he almost missed the flight to Mexico City, where he was to start a concert tour, because he was losing the card game. "He was the worst serious bridge player I've ever run across. His passion for the game was matched only by his vast ineptitude," said a bridge expert, whose affectionately respectful words help us to measure the extent of Melchior's love for that game, his lack of expertise, and his honesty:

His ambition was as pathetic as it was heroic. . . . Melchior exemplified [the] . . . description of a true amateur. The word *amateur* comes from the Latin: a lover. [Melchior's] endearing ambition was to win a game or tournament, to attain even the lowest rung of masterdom in bridge. But, with his usual rugged honesty, he refused to adopt the shoddy practice of some; that is, he never hired an expert as a partner to win master's points for him by letting him play most of the hands. Thus he won the respect of those inside the coterie who had nothing but amused contempt for spurious masters who bought their way in.

Eventually his name was immortalized in the first edition of the official encyclopedia of bridge, a book listing all championship titles and records in the game. He had finally broken a bridge record! He had entered a tournament and achieved the lowest score ever recorded by the American Contract Bridge League—thirteen percent.

Kleinchen herself scarcely suffered at being banished from the bridge table, writing cheerfully in her diary about one such game. "My wonderful husband gave himself before and after the concert to playing bridge, and lost (as always). . . . [Helga and I] ate more than we talked." Kleinchen's diaries consistently dwell on details of the food the couple consumed (great quantities, and of increasingly higher quality). At this time she still didn't worry too much about Lauritz's weight, though it was visibly increasing in each photograph. The pattern for their future life was being set. A constant stream of invitations came from titled and untitled socialites, many of which were accepted for financial reasons. After evening performances or rehearsals, parties lasted into the early morning hours, Kleinchen assessing them according to the quality of their caviar and champagne, a subject on which she was fast becoming an expert.

It must have been with a certain sense of relief that Lauritz handed over his business affairs to Kleinchen. During his marriage to Inger he had been given the unpleasant taste of assuming total responsibility for himself and his family, earning a living as he made the difficult transition to tenor while learning new roles and improving his musical skills. Inger, too often ill, could not be of substantial help to him. Furthermore, yearning for her husband's company at home, she had often expressed concern about his absence from Denmark. Kleinchen, however, was happy to accompany him wherever the career led, and took over the onerous details of their married life. Lauritz began to lean on her.

On one of his Berlin visits Walpole not only observed Lauritz's successes, but also how taken with Kleinchen were the men at the many parties they attended. Kleinchen's diary reveals her philosophy about these little situations: "I am . . . happy when a man adores me who can be useful for Lauritz. A woman can really help a lot by smiling a little." Walpole must have sensed that his own help was no longer so important for Lauritz's success. His able social maneuvering, so necessary to an artist's life, had been outmoded; Kleinchen could manage as well as he. "Well, I've done my part," he wrote.

Melchior's fame was increasing and engagements were picking up. Berlin Städtische Oper had contracted him for a return engagement from September 1925 to January 1926, and both the guaranteed number of performances and the fee were excellent. A contract was written with an American recording company, Brunswick Gramophone Company—Kleinchen could hardly believe that her husband would be paid $1,000 for four simple songs—and New York's Metropolitan Opera wanted him in February 1926 at the close of his Berlin performances. (Lauritz's only other contact with an American company had been an audition for Spangler of the Chicago Opera in Paris during July 1921, when he had been judged "too inexperienced.")

There had been considerable jockeying over Lauritz's first contract with the Metropolitan Opera. The extensive mail and cable traffic between the Met's managing director, Giulio Gatti-Casazza, and two Berlin agents is illuminating. On October 9, 1924, Norbert Salter, one of the two agents, had written Gatti, "I have heard in this time the tenor Lauritz Melchior. He pleased excellently. I regret much that you could not have heard him." On October 14, Gatti replied coldly, "I also have heard that the tenor Lauritz Melchior sang Siegmund at London the last summer and he left an impression rather bad."

The subject of the new tenor appeared to be closed, but in November Salter had some kind of run-in with the police that caused his agency to be deprived of its license. Thereupon the Metropolitan transferred its business to the Wolff Agency of Berlin, where Erich Simon was in charge of singers. Gatti was clearly entertaining once again the notion of engaging Melchior for New York, for he took up his case with Simon.

Melchior's first contract with the Metropolitan Opera was dated March of 1925. It called for six appearances each year for five years, each performance "cachet" (as the Metropolitan paybook called it) to be $600 the first year, increasing by $50 increments each year. In an April 22 letter to Gatti, referring to the arrival of the contracts for Melchior, Simon reported that Melchior was exceedingly disturbed to see the roles of Loge and Tristan written into the agreement, that he declared his willingness to study these roles and to have them ready as soon as possible, but wished to wait for Artur Bodanzky's visit to Berlin before signing. (Bodanzky was the Metropolitan's German-wing conductor, whom the company hired because of the fine impression he made when he introduced London to the operas *Die Fledermaus* and *Parsifal* in 1914.)

On May 2 Gatti cabled Bodanzky:

> VERY MUCH SURPRISED TO RECEIVE LETTER FROM SIMON SAYING MELCHIOR DOES NOT GUARANTEE TRISTAN NOR LOGE FOR NEXT SEASON STOP PLEASE SEE THAT AT LEAST TRISTAN BE INCLUDED IN HIS REPERTOIRE REGARDS.

Bodanzky cabled Edward Ziegler (Gatti's assistant) on May 5:

> MELCHIOR READY TO SING WITHOUT ANY REHEARSAL TANNHAUSER PARSIFAL SIEGMUND AND BOTH SIEGFRIEDS STOP TRISTAN PREPARING BUT WILL NOT BE READY TO SING COMING SEASON LOGE OUT OF QUESTION SHALL HEAR MELCHIOR SING WEDNESDAY CABLE AGAIN.

In the light of later events, one should note especially the optimistic comment that Melchior would perform "without any rehearsal." As promised, on May 7 Bodanzky reported to Gatti on the audition in his idiosyncratic but serviceable Italian:

> SENTITO MELCHIOR IMPRESSIONE EXCELLENTE [sic] BELLISSIMA VOCE APPARENCA [sic] SPLENDIDA SALUTI. (HEARD MELCHIOR EXCELLENT IMPRESSION MOST BEAUTIFUL VOICE SPLENDID APPEARANCE REGARDS.)

Clearly the matter of Melchior's engagement was not allowed to go forward until Bodanzky's seal of approval arrived, for the contract drawn up in March was finally validated in May, listing Tannhäuser, Parsifal, Siegmund, and Siegfried as his roles.

It was on October 21, 1925, with the Städtische Oper of Berlin, that Melchior sang his first *Tannhäuser* in German, Paul Dessay conducting. His reception was sober but warm; Lauritz, however, had occasion to be grateful for any restraint on the audience's part when they saw the costume. Not yet owning his own, Lauritz had solicited suggestions from Siegfried Wagner, who took him to a designer friend named Franz Stassen. As Lauritz later wrote:

> Those who saw this performance will surely never forget my costume. . . . It was fantastically expensive. When I saw it the first time I expressed my doubts, but I was told by the designer: "My dear fellow, don't forget that Tannhäuser is a kind of love God." I rather thought I

looked more like the King of Hearts. The entire costume, made of blue satin, was appliqued with red velvet hearts! The audience didn't have much understanding of Mr. Stassen's idea; they greeted my entrance in the second act with great hilarity. It was the first and last time I had the pleasure of wearing this costume . . . but I had to sing many Tannhäusers before all those velvet hearts were paid for.

In future years Kleinchen would insist on approving his costumes. When she did not, disaster usually befell Lauritz, as in Copenhagen when he entered as Siegmund, bewigged in abundant yellow curls and dressed in what seemed to be a type of pink lingerie, topped by a fur loincloth. The audience, greatly amused, thought he looked "like a happy giant baby," according to Danish singer Holger Boland.

By the second of the three scheduled *Tannhäuser* performances, Kleinchen, who was beginning to sound more knowledgeable, reported that *Tannhäuser* was very good, the "best so far. The text over the harp was diligently handled. The main thing is that he did not weaken the Venuslieder thereby." Lauritz was now studying regularly with Ernst Grenzebach, a respected Berlin voice teacher recommended by Victor Beigel. Perhaps Grenzebach had something to do with the improvement. It is said that he concerned himself as a teacher only with vocal technique. Others who had studied with Grenzebach included Max Lorenz, Alexander Kipnis, Herbert Janssen (a great Wagnerian baritone who sang with Melchior all over the world), and Maria Ivogün, teacher of Elisabeth Schwarzkopf. Grenzebach himself had studied with Cotogni, who had taught the great Jean de Reszke, and with Rosati, teacher of Gigli. Then, for unspecified reasons, Lauritz worked with another "very helpful" Berlin voice teacher named Freitag Frey from November until January 1926.

After the *Tannhäuser* performances, Lauritz's attention immediately turned to preparation for the next big test: his debut as young Siegfried, another role demanded by his Metropolitan contract. He was in awe of this longest Wagnerian role. Siegfried is double the length of Verdi's *Otello*, 2,000 notes longer than Tristan and seven times the length of Canio in *Pagliacci*. The prospect of six hours of continuous, full-volume singing bothered him little; what gave him pause was the crucial scene from the last act, the most difficult test of a Heldentenor.

If chasing bears, killing dragons, and fighting Wotan were not enough to tire poor Siegfried, his music in Act I contains primarily heavy declamatory singing. "The Forging Song" is in fact so punishing that most Heldentenors must find a way to sing it with seeming lavishness of tone, while in reality conserving their energy and voice as much as possible. Then Siegfried must be able to bring his voice down to the quiet and lyricism of Act II, an equally demanding task. By Act III, the 35-minute duet with Brünnhilde (who is energized by her sleep during Acts I and II) looms as an almost impossible undertaking. To commence this act seemingly as fresh-voiced as Brünnhilde and then to survive it, still able to sing, is a triumph of vocal strength and technique. Melchior was able to sing Act I's "Forging Song" without restraining or husbanding the brilliance of his tone, which made possible an electrifyingly accurate and energetic delivery of its marcato requirements. Furthermore, he could then manage the lighter singing in Act II, and arrive finally at Act III with tone and stamina in reserve.

Along with vocal exigencies, the drama of *Siegfried* presented its own kind of problems, which Melchior delineated in an unfinished note that he later incorporated into his personal manuscript:

> It is the story of a youth and his development from a young boy without fear to a man who knows fear. Siegfried is supposed to be a boy of sixteen–eighteen and it is, of course, impossible for a singer who is portraying him to look that age and also possess the knowledge and experience, the voice and the stamina to sing the part. Therefore in the first two acts of the opera the singer must try to get as much youthful feeling as possible into his voice and try as best he can to give the appearance of youth in makeup and acting without becoming ridiculous.

Melchior also pointed out a humorous distinction between the younger and elder Siegfried: "The young Siegfried knows nothing of love, but Brünnhilde, I hope, teaches him a little about it."

Some of those who later wrote about Melchior's ungainly body appearing slightly ridiculous in the role seemed never able to perceive, as did Melchior, that the demands of the role were almost mutually exclusive. "Unmatchable expectations," critic John Rockwell realistically called them later. "A Wagnerian L'il Abner" was the expression used by Jon Vickers. the great Canadian tenor. Melchior himself made his peace with the fact that a man who could sing the role with ease was not likely to play the reckless, fearless youth convincingly.

Although a first performance of Siegfried should instill caution in a tenor's offstage behavior, the Melchior physique allowed him to survive a punishing, if foolishly crowded, schedule in the ten days before his November 25 *Siegfried* debut in Magdeburg. He went to five parties, none of which brought him home before 2:30, sang other opera performances, a benefit in Berlin, two concerts elsewhere, and traveled to Magdeburg, where he arrived at 4:00 A.M., on November 24. After five hours of sleep, he rehearsed *once* with conductor Max von Schillings, actually went to another party the night before *Siegfried*, and still managed to acquit himself well.

Melchior had prepared for his first Siegfried in the customary manner, at the piano with Mme. Bahr-Mildenburg. (These 1925 studies were Melchior's last with Bahr-Mildenburg, who always spoke of Melchior as the greatest exemplar of her teaching.) Never had he sung it with other singers and never with an orchestra, but he and Kleinchen did practice the text on those odd evenings when they stayed home. Frida Leider, to whom fell the precarious honor of portraying young Siegfried's first love, had learned her lesson in London. How could one yield to panic when in the presence of the calm young Heldentenor, so quietly sure of himself? Kleinchen was nervous enough for both singers, and kept busy by acting as a back-up prompter. It was just as well that she did, for Lauritz, because of Kleinchen's relentless drilling on the Danish meaning of every German word in the score, occasionally slipped into his own language to express the same thoughts. (Some blame for his rhythmic errors can also be laid to his consequent ability to switch words and rhythms while maintaining the general sense of the libretto.) Nonetheless, he sailed through the difficult role with energy to spare. Kleinchen wrote about it in her diary:

> Lauritz's first Siegfried! And so good; he had a giant success! He was called in front of the curtain perhaps fifteen–twenty times. We are now delighted that the first Siegfried is done. I was with him the entire evening on stage and prompted. . . . And how my Schatzi can control himself, unbelievable! Nobody felt his stagefright, as he a foreigner for the first time sang Siegfried in German. Outwardly, also towards me, the greatest calm, inwardly probably tense and nervous. I was terribly nervous, but did not blink an eyelash; only bled in torrents from my nose when the curtain went up. . . . Thank God everything went fabulously well, and the reviews were overwhelming, wonderful. Very wise that the first Siegfried was not in Berlin!

The next day (after breakfast in bed featuring caviar) was a day of rest, followed that night by a party that lasted until 5:00 A.M. Melchior again managed the role splendidly some weeks later with a new cast and Bruno Walter conducting. Walter was "very enthusiastic," said Kleinchen.

Melchior's Berlin success probably precipitated an invitation to sing Siegmund and Tannhäuser (the Dresden version) in Vienna. Of his debut there in December 1925, he made this assessment: "I was not a sensation there, but it went quite well. I have never ever felt good in that opera house. Already then I felt ill at ease at the dishonest atmosphere, smiling and kind on the surface, but ready to put a knife in your back when you turned around."

Kleinchen and Lauritz spent ten days in London during January as guests of Hugh Walpole. Walpole was infinitely hospitable, hosting parties, theater visits, and sightseeing expeditions (during which Kleinchen was shocked to find Covent Garden "a dirty theater from the outside, in a terrible neighborhood"). Lauritz and Victor Beigel worked daily, concentrating on putting together a concert program—songs by Schubert, Schumann, Wolf, Brahms, and his friend Richard Trunk—for his first American tour. Eighteen concerts in thirteen days had been booked by the American manager Arthur Judson on the strength of Melchior's European reputation. It was Kleinchen, normally the more frugal one, who proposed that Beigel accompany them to America, and her husband was, she said, "crazy happy" with the idea. Not being totally secure about his technique, he had feared being without a teacher for three months in New York.

The Melchiors and Beigel (accompanied by his valet) took the boat train to Southhampton. Aboard the ship, the young and newly sophisticated Kleinchen was thrilled by her first experience with the crowds of people waving, the tugboats nudging the great ship into the open sea, the music playing, even the flocks of seagulls circling the *Aquitania* as it embarked for America on January 20, 1926. She carefully and naively inscribed in her diary all details of the seven-course dinners and the quality of the food on board, but by the third day she had trained their table steward to bring a quarter-pound of caviar for each meal. While Lauritz played nonstop bridge in the salon, Kleinchen walked the deck with Beigel, who graciously tutored her in English. On arrival in New York on January 28, she was enchanted with the city: "Our first view of New York was indescribable. It was lying in front of us in the fog. The skyscrapers broke through. . . . Never in my life shall I forget that." The press were waiting en masse to photograph the new Metropolitan Opera tenor and his movie-actress wife.

While Beigel and his valet taxied to the Waldorf, Kleinchen and Lauritz went to a more modest hotel. Kleinchen was shocked at the bare room, which cost the enormous sum of eight dollars daily, and she found the food and laundry prices in America unbelievably high. Lauritz also came to bemoan the inordinate expense of keeping Beigel in America with him, although, as it turned out, it was thanks to Beigel's social network that the Melchiors were taken up by "the right people" from the start. On their very first trip to New York they were attending parties in the company of such opera lovers and Metropolitan boxholders as Otto Kahn, the Lewissohns, and the Guggenheims, whose approval and friendship would certainly ease along his American career.

Lauritz and Beigel worked fruitfully together almost daily. Kleinchen enjoyed "the nice good humor Victor brings with him," and assiduously continued her English lessons. "A genius with languages," according to Birte, Kleinchen had decided not to be "so stupid as the other German artist-wives who have been here for years and still cannot speak a sentence." Beigel and the Melchiors ate together, attended parties together, and became so close that, on February 1, they celebrated the changing of their mutual form of address from the formal "Sie" to the informal "du."

Lauritz had not been told what his debut role was to be. Upon signing the contract, Melchior had written to Giulio Gatti-Casazza asking for Siegmund as his debut role, *Walküre* being the opera he knew best, but there was no answer. Judging from Gatti's correspondence with others, only requests of singers far more important than Melchior were honored.

A singer would like to debut in a role for which he is ideally suited, physically and vocally. Other factors also come into consideration, as in Melchior's case: Tannhäuser was problematical because of the newness of the Paris version; Siegfried was not routined* sufficiently; Parsifal was not enough of a spectacle role for a debut; and finally, Melchior simply knew Siegmund the best. The debut artist should be at ease in his role so that he can afford to divert some of his concentration toward such things as the acoustical problems presented by a new house. Administrators often do not have the expertise to make this important debut decision. Also, their minds are focused on their own problems, such as casting a role in the most convenient or least expensive way, or choosing an opera that the ticket-buying public supports more strongly. In many cases the singer himself is in a quandary as to which role would be best, because his future literally hangs on the decision.

A singer's debut role in a new house is always important, but when the debut is for the Metropolitan Opera—not only one of the most prestigious houses in the world, but the greatest international opera house in the United States—the choice of role is crucial. Even when the artist is of such renown that he is allowed to choose the debut vehicle himself (and Lauritz did not have that privilege), he often has trouble deciding because the stakes are so exceedingly high. The reviews of such a performance can color a reputation for several years to come; a career can be furthered by good critiques, but it can also be brought to a complete halt by bad ones.

Poised on the threshold of an American debut, the question of which role it was to be filled Melchior with anxiety.

---

*"Routining" is a standard term used by singers to describe the system of repetition by which they make automatic the forty-some vocal, dramatic, and musical controls that they must balance at any one moment in a staged performance.

CHAPTER 6

The Metropolitan Debut

(1926–1927)

The very first morning after his arrival in New York, Lauritz announced his presence with a phone call to the Metropolitan Opera, asking when he should "show up at the opera house." Thoroughly preoccupied with worries about his debut role, he nevertheless phrased the question in his own characteristically informal manner, rather than with the self-importance generally adopted by a *primo tenore*. He was, as he remembered later, "granted an audience with Gatti-Casazza," the bearded and elderly Italian general manager of the Metropolitan Opera.

> Our conversation took place in English, which he could understand and speak when he wanted to, but if something was unpleasant to him, he pushed a small button on his desk, and in came a secretary, Mr. Villa, or the assisting manager, Edvard [sic] Ziegler, and he continued the conversation in Italian with an interpreter. He liked to place both thumbs in the armholes of his vest, to sit with his legs on top of his writing desk, to stick his finger in his nose, and to chew on a toothpick; he was an unusually gifted businessman and understood the art of handling artists, toward whom he could be extremely kind and pleasant, but also brutal and cold. Edvard Ziegler, who was German-American, was the one with whom one negotiated about the daily problems. When one shook hands with him, one had the feeling that they must be made from jelly. When everything went according to his wish, he was kindness itself, but at the moment that something went against his opinion, he changed into a statue of stone, and the audience came to a very quick close.

The disappointment with which Melchior learned of the role (he would sing Tannhäuser on February 17) was tempered by the knowledge that he was scheduled to sing Siegmund the week after his debut. The latter performance, moreover, would not be in New York but in Philadelphia. After more conferences with Gatti, Ziegler, and Arthur Judson, all of whom confirmed that everything about his future in America depended upon the success of his debut, Lauritz was reconciled to their choice of Tannhäuser as the more impressive role (although more perilous in practical terms due to his lack of familiarity with the Paris version, the comparative newness of the German text, and the absence of orchestra rehearsals that might have given him musical confidence with the new conductor as well as practical command of the unknown stage and sets).

Of all the international opera houses, rehearsal practice at the Metropolitan Opera was quite possibly the worst. Certainly in the German wing a singer hired by the Metropolitan was expected to be completely in command of his role. He was to be at ease with, and routined in, a stock staging that emulated (if it did not slavishly copy) the staging adopted at Bayreuth. The slapdash and execrable rehearsal methods of the Metropolitan Opera Company at that time could hardly have been expected to produce anything like the performances that Melchior achieved in Bayreuth, where seriousness of purpose and attention to detail prevailed. During the 1927 Bayreuth season, for example, there would be 47 stage rehearsals with orchestra, technical and musical, and over 500 piano rehearsals with singers. Of course, standards were very casual *everywhere* outside Bayreuth. Even in Germany Frida Leider had sung her first Venus with no dramatic rehearsal at all and her first Brünnhilde without a full rehearsal. But Melchior had now acquired some experience with opera houses other than Bayreuth, and none of them had included as part of their requirements for engagement that Melchior be ready to perform "without rehearsal" (as did Gatti and Bodanzky).

It was simply a matter of money: Gatti was expected to return a profit to the shareholders at the end of each season. Profit was made with every hour of rehearsal saved. Conductor Artur Bodanzky's contract, for example, specified payment of $100 for each hour of rehearsal in excess of the first 14 hours each year. In addition, there were few new productions, and an operatic stage director was more an efficient traffic director than a molder of emotional and acting values. This situation allowed Gatti to mandate that Melchior perform without rehearsal as a condition of his engagement with the Met.

Even when a rehearsal was truly necessary, the mean accommodations afforded the Met artists by architect Josiah Cleaveland Cady made it nearly impossible to hold it anywhere but on the stage itself. In 1883 Cady had designed his building to be the largest, rather than the most well-appointed or efficient, American theater. A rehearsal space for singers simply never occurred to anyone, not to the multimillionaire boxholders of the Met, nor to the members of the board.

Lauritz dutifully presented himself at the Met for his first rehearsal only to find that it was being held in the ladies' dressing room. Most piano rehearsals took place there, he was told, for lack of another space. He thought it even more curious to encounter within the ladies' dressing room neither the conductor nor his assistant, but rather a pianist, a chorus master, and a group of people who proved to be not the singers but their stand-ins. The chorus master soon enlightened him: Artur Bodanzky, his conductor for *Tannhäuser*, was the only German-wing conductor at the Met. Bodanzky, as Melchior later described him, was "a tall, lean . . . gentleman with a giant nose. . . . Since at the Met he never conducted anything but Wagner operas, it gradually became such routine to him that the poetry and inspiration suffered. He would rather have a bad voice sing a role when the singer sang without pitch or rhythm mistakes than a good voice with a little liberty musically." Bodanzky and Melchior would probably not rehearse before the curtain rose on *Tannhäuser*, because Bodanzky never came to piano rehearsals. If there were any orchestra rehearsals at all, they were conducted by his assistant, Karl Riedel. Melchior thus learned of a Metropolitan tradition: The conductor and the leading singers wasted neither their time nor their energy on rehearsals. In later years the tenor would be universally denounced for continuing the practice.

Repeatedly, Melchior was the only singer to present himself for rehearsals. Indeed, management conceded to Lauritz exactly twenty minutes for his orchestra dress rehearsal on February 11. It consisted of the "Venusberg Scene" on a stage without sets, with Venus, played by Karin Branzell. Although Kleinchen detected an understandable nervousness in her husband's singing voice, Lauritz himself noted that Branzell "was a great artist and a calming influence on me."

In addition to Branzell as Venus, beauteous Maria Jeritza was to appear as Elisabeth, Michael Bohnen as the Landgraf, and Lauritz's new friend Friedrich Schorr as Wolfram. Bohnen, Melchior wrote, was "one of the greatest singer-actors the world has seen."

> He was just as excellent as Chaliapin, but then he was just as capricious. One night he could sing a role so that the audience went completely wild from enthusiasm, and another night he would mumble the role and be completely impossible. One never knew . . . what he would look like in a role that evening; he changed his makeup to suit his whim. Once he sang Wotan with short hair, a patch over his eye, and a small mustache, and he juggled his spear like a bon vivant with his cane, rolling it around in his fingers. . . . Once in *Parsifal* at the Met, where he sang Gurnemanz with me, where I faint before the Good Friday scene and the washing of my feet, he took me quietly under his arm, like one takes a parcel, head one way and legs the other, and then he carried me over to the tree stump on which I was to sit.

Jeritza was reputed to have an aversion to all tenors. Lauritz was intrigued by the prospect of appearing with this "gorgeous-looking and -singing Elisabeth," but she was to remain one of his few soprano partners with whom he never became friendly. (It was said that when Jeritza performed the famous dance in *Salome*, it was next to impossible to prevent her from shedding the seventh and last veil. Having heard that she sang "Vissi d'arte" [from *Tosca*] lying prone and the "Séguidille" [from *Carmen*] lying flat on her back, Lauritz looked forward to observing at first hand her choice of position for Elisabeth's "Dich teure Halle.") "Many are the stories of fights on and outside the stage between her, conductors, singers. On this occasion our cooperation went very well," Lauritz wrote. He was lucky not to have a personality clash with Jeritza to complicate his already precarious debut. During one Met performance, feeling abused by Beniamino Gigli, she had walked to the very edge of the stage apron and complained petulantly to an astonished audience that "Mr. Gigli is not nice to me." At the time Melchior began singing at the Met, Jeritza was box-office queen. She received $2,700 per performance, an astounding figure for the time, and a fee that neither Melchior nor Gigli ever matched. Yet Kleinchen, having seen Jeritza in *Fedora* this year, had concluded that the opera was boring and "she was not good either."

One of the most commonly followed, although unwritten, principles of the operatic world at this time was the survival of the fittest. A singer was put on the stage after some study to see how he did. If he survived vocally and had some sort of dramatic flair, he was kept; otherwise, he was not. Lauritz's Met debut experience largely followed this Darwinian principle. His Wednesday matinee debut would be not only his first performance of the Paris version of *Tannhäuser* (prepared almost entirely with piano rehearsal only), but only his third performance of this opera in German, and his first performance of any opera with Bodanzky (without any rehearsal). None of these circumstances were in his favor, and yet everything depended upon his survival as one of "the fittest."

On February 17, Beigel came at ten for breakfast and a warm-up (which is interesting in view of Melchior's later disdainful attitude toward "warming up"). At eleven Lauritz went to the opera house to be made up and to try on the Met's own costume, as his was delayed in transit (this was yet another annoyance that threatened his composure). Still, approaching the Metropolitan Lauritz was thrilled to see a vast crowd of people lined up before the box office, held in check by mounted police. "I threw out my chest as I elbowed my way through the crowd that was pressing in to witness the birth of a new star in the firmament of tenors," he recollected. Finally costumed and made up, he went up to the stage, where inexplicable, loud hammering noises were coming from, mingling evilly with the chaos that reigned within. He peeked through the curtains at the auditorium. To his surprise it was empty. When he asked one of the stagehands why, in view of the long line of people outside, the house wasn't full, the man explained that the crowd was awaiting not his debut, but the debut that evening of the eighteen-year-old American soprano Marion Talley as Gilda in *Rigoletto*. The pounding in question was caused by the Associated Press, who was installing a telegraph line so that Talley's father, a telegraph operator, could send his own version of his daughter's debut back home to Kansas City. The publicity had been so overwhelming that critic Pitt Sanborn was moved to write: "To parallel at all the Talley debut one would have to go back to the birth of Venus or Eve."

Kleinchen arrived at one for the debut matinee and "shook like ash-tree leaves." Lauritz, she was astounded to see, "might have felt the same way, only he [could] control himself fabulously." She sat in Box 3 with people from Bayreuth as well as the Cahiers (who were in America at the time for Sarah Cahier's appearance in Stravinsky's "Les Noces" with Stokowski and the Philadelphia Orchestra). When the curtain rose, Lauritz tried to get a look at the famous Artur Bodanzky. He was unsuccessful, however, because a scrim had been lowered between the stage and the pit. As a result of that scrim, Melchior could neither hear the orchestra very well nor see Bodanzky very clearly. When the time came to sing, he sang, although the continuing incessant (and off-the-beat) hammering that made the orchestra almost inaudible also unsettled his pitch and tempo.

Kleinchen had her own impressions of the debut: "He had the audience at once and his Rome narration he sang as he has never done it before." Regarding herself as a member of the theater community, she could not resist adding that "I was very disappointed in Jeritza as Elisabeth. She does not play; she only thinks of her clothes and of her looks." As for Marion Talley's success that evening (she was received more positively than the male debutant of the day), it affronted Kleinchen. She concluded that Talley was still "like a student with a good voice, without temperament, unfinished," and sniffed that America was just inartistic enough to "make such a fuss about a little stupid girl who has no ideas about art."

American critics' expectations for the singing of a Heldentenor were nicely defined by the sensibilities of Edward Cushing of the *Brooklyn Eagle*, who, reporting from the Bayreuth Festival of 1925, had declared that Melchior had given him and other Americans "the thrill of authentic discovery." The young Dane, he continued, was the last in a line of dramatically graceless tenors that included Rudolf Laubenthal and Kurt Taucher. Over these gentlemen, however, Melchior had "one estimable advantage–he can sing." (Cushing's delight is understandable when one considers George Bernard Shaw's cutting description of a typical Heldentenor of his day, who "gasped his way from note to note producing effects which had exactly the same relation to Wagner's shapely phrases as a heap of broken glass does to a crystal goblet.") Because Shaw's description was that of the standard 1925 tenor fare in the United States as well, Cushing had reminded his readers that Melchior was the first good Wagnerian tenor to be acquired by the Metropolitan Opera since before the war, declaring that he was "a great Wagnerian tenor. . . . His Parsifal . . . [was] indisputably fine, made so by a voice so powerful, of such range and flexibility, of such suggestive expressiveness that at first impact one does not stop to consider that singing, however fine, is only a part of the operatic artist's job."

Thus had Melchior's Bayreuth reputation preceded his New York debut, with the result that most New York reviewers expressed their determination to await further performances to assay the new Heldentenor's abilities. Lauritz always maintained that he improved when the scrim went up and the hammering finally ceased, and the reviews seemed to agree in principle. His *mezza voce* skill was a cause for rejoicing but his apparent rhythmic weakness was deprecated. His stage presence was judged to be awkward, but his singing was a feat not witnessed in a long time at the Metropolitan.

New York Times critic Olin Downes pointed out that there was "no denying that the music of Tannhäuser seemed . . . high for him," but that the narrative of the last act [when the scrim was removed] was "impressively delivered. Here its singing had a quality and a freedom not apparent before." W. J. Henderson of the *Sun*, too, felt that Melchior had come into his own during the last act, where "warmth and fervor crept into his work. A touch of velvet softened the edges of his voice and his whole interpretation increased in stature, dramatic conviction and profundity of feeling. . . . He is probably capable of greater things than were brought forward yesterday." *New York Herald Tribune* critic Lawrence Gilman described Melchior as "an improved variety of that disheartening species, the Wagner tenor." Melchior had "genuine power," Gilman continued, but he "lacked a natural instinct for the stage. When Mr. Melchior does not imagine that he is a tenor tuba—when he sings *mezza voce*—he dispenses a tone that is often pleasurable." Although "his feeling for rhythm seems insecure," he was, nevertheless, "not unlikely to prove an asset to the Met."

In the light of Richard Wagner's own phrases from his essay "On performing *Tannhäuser*," we might conjecture that Melchior's rhythmic inconsistency was something originally taught him in Bayreuth. After all, while Wagner urged singers to execute "recitative passages in strict values for notes and bars," and to sing the recitative passages in a tempo "corresponding to the sense of the words," he also recommended that they adopt "an almost entire abandonment of the rigor of the musical beat," giving "freest play to . . . natural sensibility, even to the physical necessities of . . . breath in agitated phrases. The conductor will then have only to follow the singer to keep untorn the bond that binds the vocal rendering with the orchestral accompaniment." Lilli Lehmann provided further proof of Wagner's attitude: When asked about keeping a strict beat by solo artists, the Master responded, "That is your business; do it as you like."

Edward Cushing also came to the common conclusion that Melchior had not done himself "entire justice" on this occasion, since he had for two acts "displayed faults common to German tenors, disregarding the pitch, producing pinched tones and a forte like the rattle of a machine gun." However,

in the last act he recovered and sang with notable success the narrative. . . . His is a naturally beautiful voice, warm and rich in its lower register, capable of an almost ravishing mezzo-voce [sic] and colored with a scrupulous regard for dramatic point. On the other hand, Mr. Melchior is by no means a persuasive actor. He is awkward and inchoate in gesture, mammoth in bulk, and heavy in movement. . . . [Still,] he can sing. And we have not for so long made the acquaintance of a Wagnerian tenor who can accomplish this necessary feat that Mr. Melchior deserves a hearty welcome.

A critic's conclusions about the performance of an artist may not indicate how the audience in fact received the artist, and it is quite possible for an artist to receive a tumultuous ovation that is never mentioned in the press. Everybody had warned the Melchiors that "it is always so here in the beginning." Nevertheless they could not banish their dejection at the first reviews, being, said Kleinchen, "annoyed [that the reviews] were not as good as the success."

Melchior, criticized as often as any other tenor for singing Tannhäuser badly until the "Rome Narrative," had the answer: It was built into the part. "It is difficult to start off so excited. You are not warmed up . . . to sing that way. But you learn to prepare yourself. By the Rome Narrative you can really do something vocally, color your voice, put some human feeling into it. Before that Tannhäuser has no real feelings—just excitement." Melchior felt that the difficulty of Tannhäuser lay in "portraying his craziness, a man who jumps from one extreme to another, from carnal love to the worship of God. There is no bridge between. One second he sings like this, next he sings like that."

In recent years *Tannhäuser*, no longer even among the fifty most performed operas, has come to be one of the least performed of Wagner's major works. At one time (in Europe and in pre–Rudolf Bing America), however, it was often, along with *Lohengrin*, among the ten most repeated operas. Owen Lee, for one, accounts for the eclipse by citing the passing of Melchior, who "sang the fiercely demanding role so that the catch was at our throats not his."

A new critique on February 21 by W. J. Henderson (regarded as a very astute judge of vocal abilities and an accurate journalist) provided some welcome laughs. Henderson announced that he was surprised that *Die Walküre*, performed the previous day, had been so poor because Melchior's Tannhäuser had seemed so very promising. Nevertheless, in his opinion the Danish tenor's performance as Siegmund had been "literally worthless." As it had actually been Rudolf Laubenthal who sang Siegmund that day, the Melchiors were, in one sense, vastly entertained by Henderson's reporting; Kleinchen, however, found it "an insolence." Although some newspaper accounts, said Kleinchen, annoyed Bodanzky by saying he could learn something about tempos from Melchior, the two men companionably played cutthroat bridge all the way to and from the actual first Siegmund in Philadelphia.

Melchior was privileged to sing his first New York Siegfried on March 10, with contralto Ernestine Schumann-Heink (then in her 70s) in the role of Erda. Brünnhilde was sung by Nanny Larsén-Todsen, who had debuted at the Met in 1925 as Brünnhilde, and was regarded in New York as one who sang intelligently, but with a hard voice. *Siegfried* continued the Metropolitan pattern: It was so underrehearsed that before Act III Melchior was forced to ask how and where to go on stage to find the "mountain top" where Brünnhilde lay sleeping, so as to wake her with the stipulated kiss. He had been confined to his bed for an entire week with severe influenza, thereby missing two performances. Although accustomed to performing despite a handicap whenever humanly possible, this time he was hampered by a temperature of well over 100 degrees. He permitted a slip to be inserted in the program: "Mr. Lauritz Melchior who is singing the cycle role in this afternoon's performance of *Siegfried* is recovering from a severe illness. The indulgence of the audience is asked in his behalf." He was, in fact, to cancel only once more during his entire Metropolitan career. (Even at the age of 22 he had been virtually indestructible, as on the day of his Royal Opera audition when, despite a high fever and cold, he sang well enough to be awarded an apprenticeship. In later years at the Met, stricken with a swollen polyp in his throat, he discovered that he could sing if he held his head to the side and actually sang the opera this way, start to finish.) Persistent attacks, ranging from mild but bothersome catarrh to influenza, were, in 1930, finally traced to chronic infection of the tonsils. After they were removed, Lauritz's ability to rise above vocal or physical infirmities grew with his career, and was eventually all but unbelievable, especially for a Wagnerian tenor. His amazing physical fortitude allowed him to assemble an unparalleled record for the least number of cancellations.

By the end of his first season then, under difficult conditions, Melchior had unveiled his complete Wagnerian repertoire—Tannhäuser, Siegfried, Siegmund, and finally Parsifal (on Good Friday). Kleinchen, with amusing presumption, found "the *Parsifal* sets and the chorus . . . below any passable standard. . . . Every provincial theater has better ones." Of Melchior's (Cosima-inspired) Parsifal, Henderson complained, "[He] seems devoted to the utmost economy and simplicity of attire in Wagner's music dramas. He gave a creditable and often moving portrayal of the title role. . . . Parsifal in Act III achieved a dignity and a depth of emotional force."

Melchior himself had special feelings about *Parsifal*, believing it to be "an interesting opera, but not absolutely human."

> Parsifal is a short role, but as a character, he is not convincing . . . in the beginning or at the end. . . . There is the moment when the Flower Maidens . . . try to seduce him, and he is really too young. Then Kundry comes and by her kiss [he] must wake up in one second to be a grown man, remembering all [he has] seen. [He cries] out, "Amfortas!" That is the great moment. From there on [he goes] over to religion, to God.

Parsifal is not human; there exists no Parsifal. No man can be God. Only when he changes from childhood to manhood is Parsifal real.

At another time he elaborated, saying, "Parsifal is the embodiment of the spirit of God, of what is right on this earth, the Savior of the world. It is a sort of Oberammergau play, which I feel should not be given except at Easter."

His operatic reviews brought Melchior an invitation to give a concert in New York. Kleinchen and he conferred. It was a dubious honor, a New York concert being far more expensive to mount than one in London, but Kleinchen determined that they should go ahead. New York knew Lauritz only as an opera artist, and this occasion would allow him to reveal his skills as a concert singer. Good reviews from this recital might well shore up the mixed reviews from his operatic appearances, making Lauritz Melchior more in demand for concerts, where the real money was to be made.

Aeolian Hall was rented for March 30 and Walter Golde hired as accompanist. The program included Strauss, Schubert, Griffes, Ireland, and Sibelius and other Scandinavian composers. Preparations included attending Alexander Kipnis's concert (by way of reconnaissance) and singing through the program twice for Sarah Cahier (Beigel had left by this time). Kleinchen admitted that they "were anxious, for we knew how much depended on the concert. I sat upstairs in a box with Mrs. Schorr and Cahier. . . . Lauritz sang like a young god and had storms of ovations that he deserved."

Henderson concurred with Kleinchen's evaluation. A scant six weeks after the *Tannhäuser* debut, he wholeheartedly approved of Melchior.

It would be cataloguing most of the essentials of song interpretation to go into details in describing Mr. Melchior's art as revealed last night. There was beauty and quality throughout the scale. There was an unusual and extremely finished use of head tones, which added immensely to the delicacy and polish of a style distinguished by fastidious choice in the means of expression. There was an exquisite sense of the melodic line and an admirable justice of phrasing. Indeed, in the artistic structure of the phrasing one perceived the mastery of a singer who was able to spin the tone through long and sustained utterances with confidence born of technical certainty and with a conviction of the purpose of the composer. . . . Such a lieder singer should be able to make a brilliant concert career in this country and establish for himself a celebrity such as he has acquired in England as well as on the continent.

Suddenly Lauritz enjoyed real success, ironically, more as a singer of songs than as an operatic artist. The Melchiors rejoiced because "better reviews one cannot wish for." A combination of the wonderful review by Henderson and the magical phrase, "of the Metropolitan Opera" had given Lauritz new stature, as measured by the recording for Brunswick and another Covent Garden engagement.

The Melchiors, traveling with the Cahiers, arrived in London ahead of schedule. This 1926 engagement was the first in London since Lauritz's sketchy rendition of *Die Walküre* two years before. Covent Garden had made no overtures to Melchior in 1925; now not only had they engaged him to do Siegmund and Siegfried during May, but the scheduled conductor was once more Bruno Walter. Presumably he also had forgiven the tenor by this time, reassured by the Berlin *Siegfried* Melchior had sung for him in 1925.

For his part, Lauritz respected Dr. Walter, but found him wanting, especially in comparison with his touchstone of conductors, Leo Blech: Dr. Walter was "not helpful" to his singers, but "continually criticized them behind their backs." Walter's sentiments are not known, but an amusing story told by Robert Tuggle provides a clue. In rapidly intensifying despair of confining Melchior to the printed rhythms and tempos, Walter once shouted from the pit: "Melchior! My left hand is exclusively yours!"

When Maria Jeritza and Lauritz Melchior met in London for the 1926 *Walküre* performances, it was for the first time since his New York debut, when everything had gone well between them. Perhaps Jeritza concluded that Lauritz's reception by the audience was warmer than hers, for during the first intermission she approached him, asking that they go down to the stage to rehearse Sieglinde's swoon into his arms before the "Todesverkündigung." Her instructions were most particular. She would throw herself backwards and to the left. Lauritz was to catch her before she hit the floor and lift up her garment with his free hand so that the audience would not be cheated of the sight of her shapely legs while she lay on the ground. Lauritz wondered why such a detailed rehearsal was necessary. Warned of her tricks by his colleagues, when it came time for the scene, he was on his guard. As he suspected, once onstage Mme. Jeritza swooned to the right, probably trying to make Lauritz appear awkward and to create sympathy for herself. Lauritz, however, did not allow her beautiful body to fall to the floor. He seized her right arm in a steely grip, holding her upright until he could sit down. When she could finally lie on the floor, she complained loudly, under cover of the orchestra, about his grip and the discomfort of her position against one of his knees. The discussion raged during the entire passage before Brünnhilde entered, at which point Lauritz had to ask her to be quiet so that he might sing. For the curtain call she came on late—and crying—but the audience did not respond. Lauritz took some satisfaction in noticing the five black and blue marks that remained on her comely arm for a long time. Critics found Lauritz "improved as an artist," and Jeritza "not particularly well-suited to Wagner." Ernest Newman went farther in his disapproval: "I have no objection to seeing *Thaïs*, but I prefer it to be to the accompaniment of Massenet's music. . . . Throughout the love duet, she was apparently vamping the young man."

During the fall of 1926, Melchior really began to make a name for himself in Germany, thanks to his Bayreuth appearances, his radio broadcasts from Berlin, Hamburg, and Frankfurt, and his concert tours. He was consistently well received by the German public and his fame grew rapidly. On August 28, after a healthy and productive summer, Melchior made his debut at the Stadttheater of Hamburg, singing Siegmund, after which he was invited back to sing *Lohengrin* in October.

In September, during the tenor's second tour through Germany, he learned that some of his American concerts would be shared with the Hungarian violinist, Joseph Szigeti. A veritable recluse by Melchior's standards, Szigeti could not have been more antithetical in personality from the outgoing and happy-go-lucky Dane. Also, in their shared love of *méchanterie* Lauritz and Kleinchen were never respecters of artistic dignity. The circumstances seem to suggest that Szigeti was the shy and retiring violinist upon whom they played this practical joke: they contrived to substitute a five-dollar violin for Szigeti's treasured instrument, which Kleinchen proceeded to drop and Lauritz to step on, both bursting into gales of laughter as Szigeti's face blanched.

The Melchiors had planned this American tour of 27 concerts, which began in October and extended, sporadically, through March 1927, so that they could be in New York for Christmas, where Hugh Walpole, in the midst of his own highly successful tour of America, joined them. During the 1926–1927 season Melchior's participation at the Metropolitan was limited to two performances, in February and April. Of Parsifal, Henderson wrote: "The singer imparted a fine manly strength and a just conception of the part which was at once powerful, interesting, and frequently poetical." The *Times* was pleased: "It has the stamp of authoritative and experienced interpretation." Siegmund elicited two left-handed compliments. The *Brooklyn Eagle* thought it "unfortunate that . . . the most musical voice of any Wagnerian tenor . . . [should be paired with a body] that bears a disturbing physical resemblance to Babe Ruth." The *World* dryly noted that "his bounce upon the table to grasp the sword shook the proscenium arch."

Melchior sang another New York recital on January 25, 1927. With this concert he solidified his reputation for being a great recitalist. American critics gave the tenor powerfully affirmative reviews. The voice itself was called "manly and beautiful," "of unusual beauty, with clear and pleasing top notes and a . . . fluent and robust . . . low register." His interpretations were "convincing and emotionally contagious," supported by "musicianly judgment and intelligence." Pitt Sanborn paid the tenor a fine compliment, saying that his "voice rang out rich and free, and high notes poured forth with an ease, a fullness and a splendor of sonority not equalled here by any man labeled tenor since the later prime of Caruso." In St. Louis his concert was called "a great evening of song," by a "grandly gifted man," a "veritable god of song."

His great success notwithstanding, Melchior later astutely assessed his early operatic problems as stemming from the difficulty of studying enough when "success came too fast": "It was really a big handicap. I was singing leading roles at Bayreuth and Covent Garden and the Met before I had enough experience as a tenor. I had to work very hard to make up for that." Even Kleinchen admitted in her diary that Lauritz deserved some of the blame for the fact that the reviews were but reasonably favorable: "If only he knew about eight roles as well as he knows his Parsifal and Siegmund." (Clearly, those roles he had learned in Bayreuth were the most secure.) Talks with Gatti, Ziegler, and Bodanzky revealed some reservations on their part also, as they procrastinated about next year's contract.

Kleinchen's considerable take-charge abilities began to reveal themselves about the time of Melchior's debut in America. By the 1940s, she was a legend in show business, many professionals outside opera having heard of her before they knew who her husband was. After Lauritz's New York debut she came to certain business conclusions: Their livelihood depended on the skills of her husband; those skills, in turn, depended to a large degree upon his health, vocal and physical. Therefore she extracted a promise from Lauritz, the bon vivant, to spend this summer's vacation from Bayreuth—every third year the Festspiel was in abeyance—working on his technique.

The month of July they spent as guests of the Cahiers at Helgerum, their palace in Sweden. Lauritz later described for his press book the work he and Mme. Cahier had done together as "lightening my middle range." To sweeten the chores demanded of her artist-husband, Kleinchen then invited Beigel to join them for a working vacation in Bavaria. In addition to swimming and hunting, card-playing, beer-drinking, and lots of eating clearly figured largely in Lauritz's plans. Some of their best friends were also invited: fellow Heldentenor Fritz Wolff, his wife "Clairchen"; Ivar Andresen, a Norwegian bass, and his wife. That the Melchiors' guests were avid and expert card players was no coincidence. (Other games seem to have been a part of the entertainment that summer, as Claire Wolff laughingly reminded Lauritz in 1970 when he and his son Ib paid her a visit: "Do you remember, Lauritz, how we returned to Fritz and Kleinchen with my panties hanging from the car aerial and how we all laughed?")

Kleinchen the businesswoman was concerned that Lauritz's fee was only $600 for each of the two 1927 Metropolitan performances. It was obvious to her that Wagner was not the most popular wing of the opera. Not only did the public flock to hear the romantic Italian operas, but the greatest stars were the singers of the Italian wing. The Atwater Kent Radio Hour, for example, persisted in hiring Bonelli, Tibbett, Jagel, and Ruffo, but they never asked the Metropolitan for Melchior, nor did the Met put his name forward. Not only in New York but internationally, artists of the German wing were never paid as handsomely as those of the Italian.

Clearly, it would be difficult for a singer to succeed in America without a Metropolitan contract, but Kleinchen's analysis went further: the Metropolitan did not yet have a vested interest in Lauritz. She determined to give them one. This resolve marked Kleinchen's assumption in earnest of her new responsibilities.

Thus, in 1926 as thereafter, Kleinchen had her financial ear to the ground. She was disturbed to hear that Beniamino Gigli, the successor to Caruso, and Feodor Chaliapin, the great Russian basso, were the highest paid Metropolitan artists. (Actually her information was somewhat misleading. The Met payroll accounts show that Chaliapin was paid $3,000 per performance—$3,500 in Philadelphia—and Gigli averaged about $2,000 a performance, being paid a monthly sum.)

Kleinchen began to assess the competition. Lauritz was, to the day, the same age as Gigli. How far behind the Italian tenor was the Heldentenor? The results of her investigation left her quite dissatisfied. Gigli had already been at the Metropolitan for five years when Melchior first arrived. He had participated this year in 38 performances of 13 different roles. Kleinchen's sources set his total yearly income at over $100,000, probably roughly accurate, considering the Met's contribution alone.

In the German wing, Melchior appeared to be behind by any standard of comparison. Curt Taucher had joined the opera company in 1922 and Rudolf Laubenthal in 1923. This season Taucher sang twelve performances, Laubenthal nineteen, and Melchior only two—very depressing figures. Kleinchen's suspicions were well founded. The Met paybook shows Laubenthal's and Taucher's performance "cachets" as $800. Kirchhoff earned the same as Melchior ($600) but fared better because of a guarantee of ten performances. (On the other hand, Friedrich Schorr, that splendid baritone, received a seasonal salary of $11,000, about $150 a performance.)

Charles O'Connell, who knew the Melchiors well in his professional capacity first as artistic director for RCA, and then for CBS, offered further insights about the Melchiors as a couple: Lauritz and Kleinchen were "a piquant combination," she so feminine and he so masculine; she so diminutive and effervescent; he a "cetacean bulk with no extraordinary attractiveness."

He had "a lumbering, honest, simple mind," whereas Kleinchen's was "quick, serpentine, and devious." Indeed, those who were to run afoul of her in business dealings were quickly and effectively put in their place. Like O'Connell, some found the celebrated charm a little hard to believe, remarking that a con man is expected to be charming. Melchior accompanist Leonard Eisner, privy to some revealing scenes *en famille*, says that Kleinchen was "an ironclad lady. There was nothing soft about her. For all her prettiness, not really feminine."

With an occasional exception, however, most people agreed that Kleinchen was superbly feminine, adorably tiny, beautiful, vivacious, witty, and very, very charming. Virtually everyone recognized the woman of steel concealed within this attractive exterior and some admired that, too. "I was devoted to her. She was one of the great women I encountered in my life," said Alma Strasfogel, wife of the conductor Ignace Strasfogel. Melchior's two publicists, first Constance Hope and later Betty Smith, also became Kleinchen's genuinely loving friends. At odds with her facade of frail womanliness was Kleinchen's sincere interest in the financial market and her genuine flair for business, which began to surface in 1926. To the Strasfogels Kleinchen confided much later that during their visits to Buckingham Palace in the 1930s, while Lauritz was busy at the buffet table and bar or chatting with the princesses Marie Louise and Helena Victoria, she would corner the head of the Bank of England, also a favorite at the palace, and absorb what he had to say about investments. She was said to boast of a well-placed financial advisor in every country; her advisor in France was rumored to be a Rothschild.

Kleinchen's own assessment of her position was probably the most accurate: "In every family there is a strong and a weak member. I am really the husband. He does the singing and I do everything else."

In March 1927 the distressing news that his brother had died in Copenhagen impelled Lauritz, not normally given to philosophical self-scrutiny, into examining his real goals in life. His ambition was undiminished, but most of all he wanted to be a good singer. "[At the Metropolitan] I was the new man, and I think that I was not always so excellent, but at any rate I was promising. Since there was nobody else on the market, they kept me," said Lauritz later. He had to admit he had never had a *fest* (seasonal, not single-production) contract as a tenor, by which a singer traditionally learns his craft through unceasing repetition of his roles. Kleinchen's measurement of success had more to do with financial security, but she reckoned with the fact that Lauritz's operatic reviews never reached the same heights of praise as did his concert reviews. Surely the normally abysmal circumstances under which opera rehearsals were (or, rather, *not*) held at the Metropolitan had something to do with it. In the eyes of the Metropolitan Opera, Lauritz was simply not schooled sufficiently to be considered a first-class Heldentenor. Under only one set of criteria could the Met prefer Laubenthal and Taucher to Melchior—they were experts in the style and routine of the major roles.

Artur Bodanzky spoke honestly to him: "Melchior, I know for sure that some day you will have the ability to become the world's greatest Wagner tenor, but you have come to the Met too early. You must work diligently with some opera house in Germany in order to gain routine and learn your roles perfectly." Telling the story in later years, Lauritz simply said, "That's why I went to Hamburg—to get rehearsals. You didn't get that at the Met."

The less-prestigious, although highly important Hamburg Opera, offered a one-year *fest* contract, which would provide the routine Melchior needed to forge his dramatic and vocal style. He was granted one year's leave of absence (1927–1928) from the Metropolitan. Gatti-Casazza generously offered to keep Lauritz's name on the roster during his absence. When asked about the future, however, he promised that they would discuss it . . . later.

CHAPTER 7

Learning Tristan

(1927–1930)

Lauritz and Kleinchen had long realized that if he was to prove himself as the quintessential Wagnerian tenor they both believed him to be, he must demonstrate his capacity to sing the great role of Tristan. They were not lulled into false security by his increasing success as a Heldentenor, his higher fees, or engagements at the great opera houses. They knew that Siegfried Wagner was anxiously awaiting Melchior's Tristan, and Gatti-Casazza's reservations surely had to do with the fact that Lauritz didn't yet know the role. Clearly he would need to learn it soon.

Other musical responsibilities, however, prevented Melchior from tackling Tristan immediately. First, his concentration was focused on his third season at Covent Garden. This 1927 London sojourn, which encompassed five performances during two weeks, came just after the first successful television transmission and just before Lindbergh landed in Paris. Melchior acquitted himself well and his appearance as Parsifal rendered the approving critics "astonished . . . at the quality of Melchior's performance."

Lauritz and Kleinchen were always happy to return to London. Hugh Walpole's friendship had transformed that city into a home for them. Here they had more social ties. Melchior was "enormously popular" with the British public, and not only in the opera house; he was a "frequent and welcome guest" at parties and receptions. In addition, Lauritz's London colleagues were artists whom he respected and whom both he and Kleinchen regarded as real friends. The great Russian basso, Feodor Chaliapin, was making his Covent Garden debut during this 1927 spring season, and the *Walküre* performance of May 6 featured at least four good friends—Lotte Lehmann, Frida Leider, Sigrid Onegin, Friedrich Schorr.

The Melchiors' best friends, however, were their constant companions Frida Leider and her husband, Rudolf Deman, who was concertmaster at the Berlin Staatsoper. (Often in later years Lauritz would sit back with his eyes closed remembering how wonderful a singer Frida Leider was—"an angel.") Leider, for her part, relished the reunion with the Melchiors each year: "Lauritz always created an atmosphere of jollity . . . . By upbringing and character, I was inclined to take life seriously. Lauritz's sanguine temperament, however, found all problems easy to solve."

Lauritz's habit of taking Frida and Rudi to the Danish Club on Hyde Park for "a light lunch of several courses" threatened her diet. His favorite "light lunch" was called "Figaro." It consisted of alternate layers of sausages, potatoes, and onions in a white sauce flavored with bouillon and Worcestershire sauce, accompanied by aquavit and beer. Lauritz enjoyed nothing so much as inviting colleagues and friends to supper after the performances. He favored a fashionable French restaurant named Boulestin's near Covent Garden. According to Frida, he couldn't be bothered to pronounce it correctly; he called it "Bulstein's." Leider was perhaps the first to describe in print the connection between Lauritz's eating and working habits. During the intervals of a performance he would be deliberating where to eat afterwards. "I usually got out of this," noted Leider, "as I needed sleep after a performance. But I understood very well that, for Lauritz, the thought of a good meal after he'd finished work incited him to his finest performances."

"Fritz" Schorr and Lauritz had hit it off from the very beginning of their acquaintance. Lauritz maintained that when Schorr "was one's friend, there were no reservations."

> Many times in the beginning of my career, when I was not always secure in the German text, he helped me right on stage. Also musically, especially when the problem was mezza voce, of which he was a master. For instance in Tristan in the delirium of the third act, where I sing *"wie selig her* [sic] *und milde,"* he worked with me until I mastered it as it should be sung.

Lauritz was moved by Fritz's ravishing vocal quality and exemplary singing, especially the "humor and love that would shine in his eyes" when he played Hans Sachs, and his "warmheartedness and passion" as Wotan. "He had in the texture of his voice a timbre that went straight to one's heart, and his fine character as a human being enriched his art. I would often hurry up taking my makeup off, so that I could go down in the wings and listen, and always a tear would run down my cheeks." Lauritz looked upon Schorr as a brother. Later at Bayreuth that summer, tenor and baritone actually recreated Wagner's "Gibichung Palace Scene." Each stabbed himself in the arm, cutting open a little vein. Then they mingled blood and wine and drank friendship and blood-brotherhood together in the spirit of the Nordic heroes they played.

In Bayreuth Lauritz was content. His friends were near, and his household snugly contained Kleinchen's parents, the Hackers, and Victor Beigel, "whom I still wanted to have with me, and whose unremitting interest in my progress was of inestimable usefulness and pleasure to me." Once again the tenor was doing new roles at Bayreuth. Sometimes it is difficult to assess the achievements of the young Melchior, unless one remembers that he honed his skills not in the usual "regional" circuit, nor in a tiny provincial theater, but before the educated, international Bayreuth audience. This summer his formidable responsibilities embraced both the young Siegfried (his first at Bayreuth) and the elder (his first anywhere).

Brünnhilde was played by Nanny Larsén-Todsen. Lauritz described the Swedish singer to his diary as one who cut an imposing figure on stage and a conservative old-style Bayreuth appearance offstage, but who turned in uneven performances. "Onstage she was so cleverly made up that she looked quite beautiful" was Frida Leider's backhanded compliment when she met the soprano in 1928.

Both Larsén-Todsen and Lauritz received a fine, if chauvinistic, review from the *Hamburger Nachtrichten* when they sang *Siegfried* together again the next summer:

> The stage was under the command of Lauritz Melchior. His Siegfried is perfection, doubtless because he has polished it at Hamburg. He began the first act still holding back, but he gave his reserves first during the rhythms of the "Forging Song." It was there he revealed the flashing brilliance and metal with which this tenor seems to identify itself.

When Melchior had successfully completed both Siegfried debuts under Franz von Hösslin's baton, he was told that Cosima had complimented him for the second time—a signal honor, said her son. Praising Melchior's performance, Brooklyn critic Patterson Greene astutely noted the difficulty of playing the young Siegfried:

> The role is a cruel one. It exacts about three hours of constant singing. It calls for pealing high notes, fiery declamation, light patter, and lyrical fervor. Melchior supplies all these. It is the best performance of a Wagnerian tenor role that I have seen. He has a beautiful voice and is an imaginative actor.

Bayreuth's close-knit family, in addition to congregating at Die Eule or Die Post after rehearsals and performances, organized picnics in the Franconian forests outside the town or visits to the eighteenth-century Eremitage with its beautiful elm groves, terraces, grottoes, and fountains. The year 1927 marked the beginning of another long-lived friendship for Melchior, this one with basso Alexander Kipnis, who had come to Bayreuth to sing Gurnemanz that summer. In a 1976 magazine interview, Kipnis was asked whom he would choose if given a chance to surround himself with the greatest singers of his lifetime: "Lauritz Melchior in the Wagner repertoire. . . . Melchior and I were very close friends. His voice was to my way of thinking, unique in this century—he had not only volume, but warmth as well. . . . Where . . . the voice alone matters, his is superb."

In a 1965 letter to German friends, Melchior recalled these early days in the German houses. "A better audience than the German one cannot be found anywhere. During my first steps as a young foreigner on the German stages I found friends for my entire life." Gotthelf Pistor and Fritz Wolff were two Bayreuth Heldentenors who remained Lauritz's "good and intimate" friends for life. Lauritz Melchior was never one to exclude other tenors from his circle of friends. If he was not friendly with a tenor colleague, it had nothing to do with his Fach.

Lauritz was anxious to begin work on routining his regular roles at Hamburg's Stadtteater, beginning with the opening night *Walküre* in August 1927. In addition he had learned three new roles for his Hamburg sojourn: Lohengrin, Radamès from *Aïda*, and Otello. The first one, performed on October 31, was Lohengrin. Melchior always held that there are two opinions on what type of voice is best for the role of Lohengrin. One is that it should be sung by the *jugendlicher Held*, a more lyric voice. The other view holds that it belongs to the *schwerer Held*, a voice that can manage tenderness in the right places but sing with heroic authority in the big moments. The "Bridal Chamber Scene," for example, clearly needs both weights of voice, lyric in the beginning and strong at the end. Melchior explained his feelings about the character thus: "Lohengrin becomes a human being the moment he comes to earth."

> That is why he has to *fight* with Telramund to preserve the right from wrong. But after Elsa has asked him the question, he ceases to be human, and has to go back to the Grail. Then, when Telramund attacks him, he is possessed of the spirit of God and his power is God-sent, so that he has no right to fight and needs only raise his sword as a cross.

Lohengrin was never to be one of Melchior's favorites (as was Siegfried), although he learned to command the role. An exception, perhaps, was one performance described by Hugh Vickers in *Even Greater Opera Disasters*, in which the prop man forgot to put Lohengrin's sword under the bed in the "Bridal Chamber Scene." As Telramund rushed in, Melchior reached under the bed for the sword that Lohengrin uses to defend himself. Finding nothing, Lauritz, ever resourceful, dispatched Telramund with a stagey left hook to the jaw.

Melchior sang the first of ten Hamburg *Aïdas* on January 30, 1928. As there was an international theater conference in Hamburg at the time, the Verdi opera was a gala performance for which the administration furbished the decor with real zebras and other animals brought over from Hagenbeck's Zoo. Lauritz was a bit concerned about competing with the animal population that crowded the stage, but he managed to come out on top, especially in his aria "Celeste Aïda," after which the performance was stopped by a full minute of applause (unheard of in Hamburg, said Kleinchen in her diary, since Caruso's Radamès some years earlier). "That role is one of my favorites," Melchior later wrote, "and it is somewhat of a sorrow to me that I have never had the opportunity to sing it in America."

As an adult Melchior's high spirits and unreserved friendliness were still equalled by his propensity for play. His inveterate passion for cards, absorbed during the musical evenings at home when members of his father's male quartet would play *l'hombre* until it was time to sing, colored his professional life as well. Other singers found it extremely difficult to maintain concentration during the endlessly long dinner intervals, but for Lauritz they could never be long enough. He played skat, a game he originally learned to please Bodanzky, with colleagues until the warning bell sounded. Then he would call the dresser and prepare hastily for the next act. According to Leider, however, he paid a price for his haste one night at Covent Garden. He had forgotten to wear Brünnhilde's ring for the second act of *Götterdämmerung*. In the recognition scene, when Brünnhilde opened her eyes and saw Siegfried, she noticed immediately that the ring was missing and whispered to Hagen: "Ring is missing." He passed the word to a chorus member who relayed it to the wings. A clever dresser slipped him the ring and Hagen deftly maneuvered it onto Melchior's finger by the time Brünnhilde sang "*Einen Ring sah' ich an deiner Hand*" ("A ring I saw on your hand"). Backstage between the acts, Kleinchen grumbled angrily in her Bavarian accent, "You and your silly old cards!" Lauritz just laughed and later went on to toss off the high C that he always produced to great effect in the scene with the Rhinemaidens, and everything was forgotten.

To some, stories like this indicated at worst a lack of seriousness, and at best a certain artlessness. In fairness, however, one must recognize that Melchior's sense of humor and lust for life allowed him to maintain a healthy equanimity of spirit offstage, which did not necessarily produce a lack of professionalism onstage. One is reminded of the great actress Judith Anderson, who did somewhat the same thing when playing in a Broadway run of Robinson Jeffers' *Medea*. The most arduous scene of this classic tragedy comes at the end, when Medea reenters the stage with the bloody bodies of her children in her arms, after twenty minutes offstage, during which she is supposedly making the decision and doing the deed. During rehearsals Dame Judith used the entire twenty minutes for her dramatic preparation, reliving the anguish of the decision and the killing. Later in the run it is said that she played cards with the stagehands until a few minutes before her entrance. Seen in this light, perhaps Melchior, too, well-routined in his roles, needed little time to prepare for plunging into character.

Similarly, Melchior's reverence for Bayreuth and its traditions did not check his sense of the ridiculous. He was vastly amused by the antics of the

Bayreuth tourists, later giving a sardonic description of the typical lady visitor to the festival:

Lady G. wants to go to Bayreuth because she is interested in good music and has heard that Wagner-Town has it. She travels, I believe, convinced that she comes to a fairyland where giants and dwarfs and elves are at home, the kind she has seen at Simpson's Department Store [a London emporium], who are so cute and old-Germany-like—Red Riding Hood and the seven dwarfs, Young Siegfried and the Evil Hagen, and the like. . . . And Siegfried, son of the Master and the Mistress, is the Loving God in this Paradise of elves and dwarfs. . . . Not so entirely wrong.

In sharp contrast to this reasonably polished writing style is an amusing letter, written to a sporting supply house in Maine upon arrival of the goods he ordered, that provides a sample of Melchior's own usual idiosyncratic syntax, strongly derived from the German language, although written in English:

I am very happy with the fishing trousers with zippers and the hunting trousers with zippers which I can wear. But I do not care for the fishing trousers without zippers and the hunting trousers without zippers which I cannot wear. I should like to exchange the fishing trousers without zippers for fishing trousers with zippers and hunting trousers with zippers. However, if you cannot send me those with zippers which I can wear, please do not send me those which I cannot wear because they are too small where I must sit down. I understand that I am entitled to a knife of fishing and an axe wood after I have spent $70 with you. I have now spent $78.77. Will you please send me the knife of fishing and the axe wood immediately?

Melchior's love for his enormous collection of decorations was sometimes viewed as an extension of his ingenuousness. Apparently, it was partially in response to an obvious admiration for military men and their derring-do. His last personal secretary, Marianne Tegner, reminds us, "Although [Lauritz] may have been a little naive about his decorations, [he] really and truly was proud of what they signified and of the fact that they were bestowed upon him because somebody thought he deserved them." The end of the Bayreuth season of 1927 was notable for the actual presentation of a decoration bestowed in 1924 by Lauritz's erstwhile benefactor, the former King Ferdinand. His son, King Boris of Bulgaria, presented Lauritz with the Cross of Civil Merit in December 1927. The extensive Melchior collection, thus begun, would increase to an amazing size during the next 25 years of his singing career. These decorations are most important for what they reveal about Melchior. He loved everything about his decorations: basking in the pomp of the ceremonies; putting the letters after his name; keeping count of the decorations and referring to them; and adorning his evening clothes with his ribbons and medals. When dressed in tails, he always wore around his neck in its full glory the last and most important Danish decoration, the Commander Cross of the Dannebrog, bestowed upon him by King Christian X. Lauritz wore miniatures of the most important decorations on his ample chest when clad in a dinner jacket. But no matter what other honors came his way, he cherished his Danish decorations above all.

In 1928, Zorobabel and Frederik to the Crowned Hope, a Danish Freemason lodge, elevated Melchior to Degree VII. (He had chosen in 1921 to go beyond the first three Craft Degrees to the Higher Degrees of the Knights Templar.) Melchior's predilection for the pomp and trappings of Masonry might also garner aspersions of lack of sophistication except for the fact that he took very seriously its philosophical tenets. He felt that he conducted his life according to the Masonic principles, and he claimed to have been "helped a great deal by the threefold Master Builder." In his correspondence he never failed to invoke the benevolence of "the great Architect" upon his friends: "May the great Architect keep you healthy and happy." He maintained membership in his original Danish lodge all his life, because "there is nothing more solemn . . . than Danish freemasonry. The men who are the leaders are the great men of the country, and one can learn a lot from that."

In a burst of self-assurance and fiscal courage born of Lauritz's operatic successes, the newly affluent Melchiors moved into their first German residence on February 1, 1928. Their nine-room apartment in the Curiohaus at Rothenbaum Chaussee 17 in Hamburg presented the first opportunity to indulge themselves in their new passion, auction-going and antique-buying. At one time the young couple had eight different chandeliers in the dining room! (Kleinchen also developed thereby the expertise—and an unabating appetite—to appraise the furniture and paintings of houses they visited.) When they found a choice objet d'art or piece of furniture, a lesser one was returned to be auctioned off. In this way the young couple was able to own antiques that they would otherwise have been unable to afford. "It's really extremely exciting to 'auction together' one's home like that. Every day, when you come back home, it looks different. . . . Every single piece in our home had its own history and was a kind of milestone on the way ahead," said Lauritz. Something more basic appealed to Kleinchen: "There is no cheaper way to live than auctioning," she wrote. That was undoubtedly because, in the Germany of 1928, the beautiful objects found in the auction houses were sold by those who were forced to live on the highly inflated German currency.

Like children in a candy store, the two Melchiors were greedy for the beautiful things that they found at auctions, as a story from Lauritz's diary illustrates. When her parents consented to give up their Mühldorf residence and live with them, Kleinchen insisted that Lauritz must buy a bed. Her parents could not sleep on the floor. With the best of intentions Lauritz went off to an auction where they had spied "a couple of wonderful beds. Unfortunately, the number that was auctioned before those beds was a collection of antique Chinese vases, among them two genuine 'pigeon's blood' vases, and I fell for them. They cost me six hundred marks and when the turn came for the beds, my wallet was empty."

Kleinchen scolded the antique-lover roundly; Lauritz responded passionately that they could live without an extra bed, but not without those particular vases. The good bed was given to the Hackers and the young couple made do with a mattress loaned them by Rudelheimer the (canny) auctioneer. For consolation, the beautiful vases were placed on the floor at the head of the mattress.

Yet, with all their professed love for beautiful antiques and objets d'art, the Melchiors evinced no interest in the Mies van der Rohe Pavilion, which was making history at the Barcelona Exhibition of 1929 when they were there. Apparently, their mania for studying and collecting art didn't extend to the modern era. Melchior's Irish-American daughter-in-law, Cleo Baldon, herself an environmental designer, explains their non-attendance another way. Using an Irish term of loving respect—"Himself"—to address and refer to her father-in-law, she states, "Another giant was in town and 'Himself' didn't pay any attention."

May 1928 once more found the Melchiors in England for the Covent Garden spring season. Bruno Walter was also there, conducting *Die Fledermaus* with singers that Melchior admired: Lehmann, Elisabeth Schumann, and Olczewska. The fine Russian basso, Feodor Chaliapin, was again singing his two great roles, Boris and Mefistofele. Kleinchen, who had seen him in his Metropolitan appearances as Don Quixote and Boris in 1926, called him "the greatest actor I have ever seen." After one of his own performances, Lauritz was in his dressing room preparing to leave when Chaliapin rushed into the room. Grabbing Lauritz in an appropriately bearish hug, Chaliapin shouted compliments and announced that he was going to give a party at the Savoy for his wonderful colleague. Lauritz found it difficult to take Chaliapin's extravagant words and behavior seriously, but the Russian was sincere. In a gesture that showed he could match his Danish friend not only in physical size, but in gargantuan appetite and zest for life, he gave a smashing formal dinner party in Lauritz's honor for twenty-four guests in a private salon at the Savoy. Nevertheless, Lauritz was struck by the fact that Chaliapin spent every minute of the party talking about himself. The only time the discussion even veered toward his guest of honor was when Chaliapin explained why he no longer sang in Lauritz's country: the Royal Opera didn't pay fees high enough to make it worth putting up with the inordinate criticism of the Danish critics.

The London performances as Siegmund, Tannhäuser (wherein Melchior "rose to unexpected heights"), and Siegfried (in which he was "vital from beginning to end," but "only awoke to an intelligent, sensitive style in the third act") were interrupted by a speedy and short trip back to Hamburg for his first *Otello* on May 31. This he managed with his much-vaunted panache and lack of nerves, although perhaps makeup and costume gave trouble: "I had made up my Otello as a complete negro [sic] and without a beard, which caused a critic to say that I looked like a chocolate figure. When I now look at the costume pictures from then, I must admit that he was right. My later Otello makeups, however, have been in Moorish style."

Melchior was delighted to find that Frida Leider would join him and Schorr at Bayreuth for the first time that summer of 1928. She was engaged to sing Kundry in *Parsifal* with Fritz Wolff under conductor Karl Muck (who had been at Bayreuth since 1901) and the three Brünnhildes with Gotthelf Pistor and Lauritz. Frida, who had worked with Muck often elsewhere, called him "very firm in judgment and very strict about tempi," but Lauritz found him dictatorial, "an unapproachable man." To prove his point, Lauritz related how the orchestra members tried to convey to Muck their dislike for his biting tongue and lack of humor by replacing his baton with a thick, gnarled stick, a real shillelagh. When he stepped up on the podium they all waited in silence to see his reaction. Muck said nothing, picked up the shillelagh, and competently conducted the entire opera with it, but as he never referred to the incident, the pranksters were denied their fun. For Lauritz and Frida, coping with his slow tempi did mean restudying breath distribution, dramatic timing, and the handling of words and phrases. Frida was challenged by this; Lauritz, simply annoyed.

Neither was Leider surprised by the internal politics of Bayreuth. As concertmaster in Bayreuth since 1914, her husband knew the Wagner family and the atmosphere of the festival. "There was, as always at Bayreuth, a feeling of trouble in the air," wrote Frida, but she was less oppressed by that than by the fiendishly heavy armor she had to wear as Brünnhilde. Lauritz, however, with his native cheerfulness, seems never even to have noticed trouble at all. In any case, he left all such problems to Kleinchen.

During the summer of 1928 three complete performances of *Der Ring des Nibelungen* were done in Bayreuth, one conducted by Siegfried Wagner. Melchior sang the same repertoire as in the previous season: the two Siegfrieds (this year with both Frida Leider and Nanny Larsén-Todsen). Frida was much disturbed by sharing the role with the Swedish singer, who was totally ensconced in Bayreuth as the ruling soprano. Consequently, when Siegfried

Wagner sent her a two-part cartoon in which a bench from one of the Bayreuth sets was occupied by Larsén-Todsen and Gunner Graarud together in one view and by Leider and Melchior in another view, Frida, taking it to imply that she and Melchior were considered the "second cast," refused to return (as it turned out, for the remainder of Melchior's tenure in Bayreuth).

At the end of the 1928 season, Siegfried Wagner engaged Melchior to sing the role of Tristan at Bayreuth during the next season of the festival (in 1930, since the festival was in abeyance in 1929), when he hoped to have plans for the new three-dimensional *Tristan* production completed. Now Lauritz had to be in earnest about learning the greatest Wagnerian tenor role. It could be put off no longer.

Developments in New York were not so favorable to Melchior's career as those in Europe. On March 29, 1928, Gatti-Casazza's assistant, Edward Ziegler, had sent a cable to Erich Simon, who now handled almost all the German and Scandinavian artists engaged by the Metropolitan, saying that the Met was looking for a "new man" for a three-month engagement since they were planning to reduce Kirchhoff's period during the season. This seems to suggest strongly that the Met was not altogether confident that Melchior was the answer to their Heldentenor problems. Responding to Ziegler's cable, Simon proposed, in addition to Melchior's friend Fritz Wolff, only a young tenor named Max Lorenz. From a letter written by Ziegler to Erich Simon on September 17 one sees rather clearly that Gatti agreed with the Melchiors about the importance of Tristan but was not yet very sanguine about Melchior's potential. Gatti offered a close-of-the-season contract for six performances at $650 plus an allowance for steamship fares. Ziegler stated that it was "difficult to offer him a long engagement because he has not yet got Tristan in his repertoire," nor the role of Jonny (from Krenek's opera *Jonny spielt auf!*). On October 9, Simon was informed by cable from the Met that it was "impossible [to] guarantee Melchior more than seven performances if [he] refuses *Freischütz*, *Meistersinger*, [and] *Rheingold*." Simon replied on October 11 that, since Melchior had never sung these operas and was earning 12,000 marks monthly in Hamburg, he would be forced, although regretfully, to refuse the contract unless given a guarantee of eight performances. (In point of fact, by constantly traveling between Hamburg and Berlin, Melchior was actually earning 28,000 marks monthly, singing four performances each week.)

Gatti capitulated on October 12, guaranteeing eight performances, and on October 17 Simon reported that the contract was signed. Doubtless Gatti's bitter complaint of November 1 to Otto Kahn, chairman of the Met board, was inspired by this battle of wills: "As to artists, the number of good ones is getting smaller and they are so in demand by all theaters of the universe that their fees increase automatically."

Lauritz was determined to be totally prepared for the challenge of Tristan and to give his best. As ever, the risk of failure did not throw him, if indeed it entered his mind. He spent untold hours working the role dramatically with Leopold Sachse in Hamburg (where he was at the same time preparing the role of John of Leyden in Meyerbeer's *Le Prophète* for his first of six performances on December 20). Melchior later confided to Danish broadcaster Arne Honoré his complete preoccupation with Tristan, even while asleep: "Suddenly one dreams . . . there are some words, some text that one cannot remember . . . out of bed to get hold of the score and look up that place to check whether it is correct, then back again to sleep as well as one can." In a 1965 letter, he recalled, "I studied my Tristan with Leopold Sachse, and he explained to me the meaning of Schopenhauer's philosophy. For a foreigner it was naturally very difficult to understand all that, but only when one understands something can one create a figure within oneself and give life to it."

Leopold Sachse, Hamburg's intendant and stage director, and conductor Egon Pollak were of greatest help, next to the work at Bayreuth, in the final forming of Melchior's dramatic and vocal persona as a Wagnerian artist. "There I really learned things the way they should be learned." Lauritz recollected that "Leopold took a personal interest in working out my roles dramatically with me. Also the chief conductor, Egon Polack [sic] helped me in every way with the musical work. What these two people have taught me together I can't thank them enough for." Being Melchior, he could not resist adding, "but I must say that it was a lot of work."

Sachse gave him some good advice: he suggested that Lauritz first perform *Tristan* outside Germany. In this way, should Lauritz's shaky German slip, a foreign audience would not be nearly as critical as a German one. Melchior could thus gain vital performance experience without the added pressure of linguistic perfection. (It is interesting to note that most Heldentenors worry about the vocal skills, the stamina, and the dramatic understanding required by this most demanding of all Wagnerian tenor roles, but in Melchior's case only his command of the German language caused concern.) An engagement was accepted with the Teatro del Liceo of Barcelona for Lauritz to sing both Tannhäuser and Tristan. There he would gain experience so that, when he sang Tristan in Bayreuth, he could be master of the role.

As he arrived in Barcelona in January 1929, Lauritz was afflicted with a cold so virulent that his range had shrunk to its original baritone parameters. As was to become his performing tradition, he went on nonetheless. A few of the highest of Tannhäuser's 3,908 notes were transposed down, and by the time the "Rome Narrative" came up, he was in brilliant form. His longtime friend Karl Laufkötter avers that Melchior always finished his performances brilliantly, even when handicapped by severe vocal indisposition at the outset of an opera. Normally the need to push his strength in order to get through *Tannhäuser* would render a tenor less able to command the

Tristan role a few days later, but Melchior possessed the fabled stamina that allowed him to surmount such vocal strain.

In Barcelona as always, the Melchiors presented a united front. Kleinchen nosed about the company, conversing with everyone and learning in the process a great deal about the local situation. She was horrified to discover that the company had no prompter who knew German, as Lauritz described:

> For that reason, Kleinchen offered to take over that task. She is, however, rather short. In order that we on stage could both see and hear her, they had to install in the prompter's cubicle a wooden box with a board across it, so that her nose could just stick up above the stage floor. Access to the prompter's box was not the most comfortable in the world, especially not for a female prompter, as one had to pass through a certain place for gentlemen. She had to announce her passage by loudly knocking and requesting [permission] in her female voice. . . . At one of the performances, we suddenly heard a terrible crash. It was the prompteress with score, the board, the box, the entire "throne" that had collapsed.

Leopold Sachse had been right: It took only one moment like this to break Lauritz's tenuous hold on his German words. The stupendous crash, coming during one of the quiet moments at the beginning of the act, frightened Lauritz so thoroughly that he forgot his German and translated his lines into Danish as he sang. Lacking a review of this first Tristan of February 1, 1929, we must fall back upon Walpole's journal, which remarked on Melchior's success, despite the Spanish audience who "talked and laughed all through the performance." The Teatro del Liceo invited Melchior back later in the year to sing the leading tenor roles in the *Ring*.

The Spanish Tristan proved to have been excellent practice and subsequent performances went better. Returning to the Metropolitan to sing the two Siegfrieds, and Siegmund as well as Tristan, Lauritz (now an old hand at the vagaries of the Metropolitan system) was not surprised to learn that there would be no "official" rehearsals for his *Tristan und Isolde*. Fortunately, it turned out that the March 6 Met performance on tour in Philadelphia served Melchior as an unofficial preparation for his New York Tristan debut, although a veteran Met coach told Danish record producer Hans Hansen that it took four prompters including himself—one in each corner of the stage—to get an accurate performance out of Melchior in Philadelphia. The cast included Gertrude Kappel as Isolde, Karin Branzell as Brangäne, and Friedrich Schorr as Kurvenal. Kappel had proven to be a most welcome addition to the Met. She was definitely preferred to Larsén-Todsen, especially in her best role, Isolde. A no-nonsense professional, she was happy to sing both Elisabeth and Venus, as well as Brünnhilde, Sieglinde, Fricka, and Kundry.

At a matinee on March 20, 1929 (his 39th birthday), Melchior revealed his new Tristan to New York. In the cast were Gertrude Kappel, Julia Claussen, and Clarence Whitehill. Melchior was somewhat disappointed by the reviews, which showed that the critics still looked upon him as merely a promising singer. Critic Samuel Chotzinoff, however, was pleased that Lauritz was a gentleman, finding "his very first gesture . . . revolutionary [for] he bowed to Isolde as, of course, any well brought-up knight would do on finding himself in the presence of a lady. Never to my knowledge had a Metropolitan Tristan shown that common courtesy to a Met Isolde."

Although one headline read, "A TRISTAN AT LAST," Kleinchen noted bitterly that her husband was still confined to matinee performances in New York. (Out of eight performances that season, five were matinees, one was a concert, and two were in Philadelphia.) Opera historian Irving Kolodin agrees that at this time Melchior was still considered to be "highly promising" but an "unformed performer whose lack of physical attraction put double burden on his singing," and tells us that Lauritz needed time for "a portrait to emerge from the rough sketch. He would, in the next few crowded years of worldwide performing, make steady progress not merely in audibility, but in credibility (especially when he took to playing the part with a beard)." When wearing his Tristan or Parsifal beard, Lauritz looked impressive and less childish; he also markedly resembled his father. Gatti-Casazza, for his part, tore up the old contract and signed a new three-year one, dated March 30, 1929 (significantly, only ten days after *Tristan*), to commence in February 1930 at a new fee of $800.

It was with *Tristan* that Lauritz began to grasp the physical as well as the vocal perils of the Heldentenor repertoire. The pitfalls of performing in armor were new to him. Playing opposite one soprano who was "trying to make up for lack of voice with what she considered acting ability" taught him to stay out of her way as she threw herself about the stage with dramatic fervor. When the moment approached for the duet, Lauritz was fearful lest her athleticisms would throw off his singing. At the first embrace he pulled her fiercely to him and whispered a threat to lay off the gymnastics. Instantly, she made a wild start backwards, almost breaking her tenor's arms. Lauritz clutched her once more, but she twisted and clawed so frantically that he was forced to release her. The same thing happened each time the stage directions called for an embrace. The scene ended in a rather undignified pursuit around the stage. The mortified Lauritz went to her dressing room to reprimand her. "What is the meaning of all this?" "Assassin! Brute! I'm going to sue you!" she cried. Eventually Lauritz discovered that a piece of metal had somehow been pried up in his armor in such a way that each time he tried to embrace her, she thought Melchior was attempting to stab her with his knife.

By April 1929 the Melchiors had arrived in London for the May season at Covent Garden, where the public was aflutter over the Norma and Gioconda sung by Rosa Ponselle in her first season there. Along with Siegmund and both Siegfrieds, he himself sang Tristan to rather grudging praise, although it was the high point of his year's efforts in that role. Speaking of the elder Siegfried, the *Musical Times* admitted that there was "no one better." Hugh Walpole, deeply moved, told the appreciative Lauritz, "With your performance as Tristan, all my help has been completely rewarded."

Only then, Lauritz later declared, was he informed that Inger had died in January, after almost a year's hospitalization in Copenhagen. Responding to sister Bodil's great concern for the welfare of the children, Lauritz and Kleinchen came up with the following plan: Gerda Henningsen, Inger's nurse, should put Ib, now eleven, and Birte, only eight years old, on the train to Hamburg. (Nurse Henningsen, a former friend of Lauritz's, had come into the family life when she assisted at Birte's birth. Lauritz had asked her to leave the hospital and move into the Melchior household, where she would take care of Inger and both children. There Tante Gerda, whom both children regarded as their second mother, remained even after the divorce.) They planned to be together in the Hamburg apartment at the end of May, when the new family would become acquainted. The children mainly remember this Hamburg trip as the time when Ib reassured his frightened sister that Kleinchen as a "stepmother" was not necessarily like the wicked one in *Cinderella*.

Kleinchen's first thought on becoming a stepparent (at the age of twenty-six) was of the education of her new charges. A fine education at a good school was of primary importance, it seemed to her. While she pored over a vast assortment of school brochures, her husband daydreamed about the resumption of his fatherly role. His children, however, remember less pleasant things about this time. To this day, his daughter Birte is most saddened by her father's not coming home for the funeral, and not wishing to pay for the stone marker for Inger's grave. "They were not married any longer, but she was our mother," Birte declared later. Lauritz's personal manuscript records no mention of Inger's death. Only in the Stambog is the date inscribed.

Clearly, at this point, the children could not have known their father very well. Says Birte, "It was only after . . . they tried to replant us in Germany . . . that we really got to know him a little better, if we ever really got to know him." In the years between the divorce and Inger's death, the meetings of the father with his children had been particularly stiff and formal. Whenever the Melchiors arrived in Copenhagen, Lauritz would call the house and announce the name of the restaurant at which they would meet. Inger cried when told that she must not accompany the children, who would be deposited there and told to wait. Soon their father would arrive accompanied by "someone else . . . a beautiful actress still in her childhood." It appeared to the children that "this woman who had already taken our father away now had the power to banish our mother." The children knew only that their father, as usual, was away most of the time and that their mother cried a great deal over it. These strange, ritualistic public meetings with their father and a stranger, who seemed to the unsophisticated children somehow too bright, too "on" all the time, had rather frightened them. It is no surprise that the new relationship was to prove a strain for all concerned, despite the fact that Lauritz allowed his children to address Kleinchen as "Mutti," rather than "Kleinchen," which might signal a lack of respect, or "Mor," which would usurp Inger's place.

Kleinchen's feelings were hurt, wrote Lauritz, when, upon their return to Hamburg, she discovered that the children considered her "the other woman." The children did not, they now say, regard their father with distrust, simply because they were too young and too uninformed to understand. "Kleinchen," says Birte, "was in a position to behave as a mother, but she was too young, and jealous, and envious of anything that might take something from her. I don't think we ever found the core of Kleinchen, my brother, and I." In addition, not only had the two children inherited both parents' love of pranks, but the apartment's valuable antiques and objets d'art were at real risk when they played their games in the house. Even making them sleep under lock and key in the chauffeur's tiny attic room did not assuage Kleinchen's worries about her possessions.

The decision made—to send the children away—must reflect Kleinchen's feelings, since she handled all such practical details. Clearly, their absence simplified life at home for her and for Lauritz, who knew that, by purchasing an expensive education for Ib and Birte, he had, in a sense, bought himself out of being a father and discharged his parental responsibilities. Birte was sent to live with Tante Gerda (whom she had missed dreadfully) while she attended a private school in Ordrup. Ib would be taken out of the public school that he had been attending and placed at Stenhus Boarding School to finish the first level of his education. The children appreciate the education they were given, realizing now that, had they traveled about with the Melchiors, their schooling would have been slapdash and faulty. They were pained at being separated from each other, however, because Ib was truly Birte's best friend.

Not only was Kleinchen in charge of the family problems, but financial arrangements of all kinds were now in her hands, and those who wished to discuss any business that had in any way to do with Melchior were compelled to do it with her. Kleinchen was the self-appointed architect of her husband's career. It was Kleinchen who had set up the engagement with the Teatro del Liceo in Barcelona. She communicated daily with Erich Simon about his dealings with the Metropolitan Opera. Trusting his wife completely, Lauritz didn't even try to keep track of the details of his business affairs. He did, however, notice his fees rising slowly but surely; Hamburg, Bayreuth, and Berlin were now paying him 800 DM for singing each of sixteen performances a month between Berlin and Hamburg (as well as seven or eight extra ones for indisposed colleagues). She continued to evaluate his possible competitors at the Metropolitan Opera as well. Next to each name she wrote an evaluation of each singer's talent, fees, frequency of performance, number of opera houses in which he sang, recording contracts, and royalties earned. The single most important name on her list—which included Laubenthal, Kirchhoff, and Martinelli—was now Beniamino Gigli, believed to be the highest paid singer in America. (Kleinchen was fairly near the mark: Metropolitan payroll accounts for the 1928–1929 season show that Martinelli was now earning $1,900 per performance, while Gigli was paid $2,000 for each of thirty-nine guaranteed performances.) It was a position that she coveted for Lauritz Melchior. She had heard Gigli sing at the Metropolitan in 1926 ("a terrible actor . . . a wonderful voice . . . plays up to the audience awfully . . . holds notes insanely long . . . toasts the audience from the stage, such nonsense"). In 1930 he sang *L'Elisir d'Amore* and was "excellent in that role because he looks so comical on stage and does not have to take the trouble to be so," she said tartly. She actually went to hear Gigli in a concert, returning persuaded that he was a wonderful singer, but unable to fathom why he was so universally lionized.

Kleinchen soon added to her list of Melchior competitors Ezio Pinza, the recently arrived young Italian bass who would upset tradition by singing the famous baritone role of Don Giovanni. After his name Kleinchen placed a question mark. Had she known that he was paid only $12,000 for a twenty-four week season during which he sang 63 performances, she might have erased his name. Melchior's eight performances at $800 were at least more lucrative than that. It is a testimonial to Kleinchen's persistence and persuasiveness that she came to possess such private information.

Melchior made a prestigious German debut as Tristan on June 18, 1929, at Berlin's Städtische Oper in Charlottenburg. In the cast were Leider, Onegin, Schorr, and Kipnis; the conductor was young Wilhelm Furtwängler, a favorite of Hitler's although not a Nazi, who had become the star of the German music world when he was named the director of the Berlin Philharmonic in 1922. The Melchiors then traveled to France for Lauritz's first engagement in Paris. During this June sojourn Lauritz proposed to Jacques Rouché, the very able director of the Opéra, the idea of a Parisian Wagner Festival. In a flash of inspiration Lauritz urged him to canvass the many German singers who spent every May in London. With them he could set up a Wagner season during June. Rouché fell in with Lauritz's plan, and the French had eight Wagner seasons in the years to come, commencing in June of 1930. Kleinchen's astonishment at this entirely uncharacteristic business insight on Lauritz's part was lessened when she heard of the unrestrained, utterly lavish parties being given by the French and by expatriate Americans. Her suspicions made sense: such experiences as singing with American soprano Grace Moore for the Baron Maurice Rothschild's sumptuous soirée had whetted Lauritz's social appetite, and he could have dreamt up the whole scheme to justify attending some of these legendary social affairs. Meanwhile Lauritz performed his two complete *Ring* cycles for Mme. Ganna Walska at her Théâtre Champs-Elysées, during which he was delighted to receive from the French Academy on July 6 a new decoration—l'Officier de l'Instruction Publique (with gold palms).

Most music historians agree that Melchior's international reputation was really launched with the New York *Tristan* of March 20, 1929. Certainly, his various Tristan debuts—Barcelona, Philadelphia, New York, London, Berlin—had served him well. Melchior now appeared an experienced Heldentenor, who could rank with the best in the world. New contracts came from opera houses all over Europe, and from the United States as well. He would sing Tristan (at fees nearly double what they were previously) in six countries with twenty-one different conductors, among whom, listed inside the cover of his first *Tristan* score, were Elmendorff, Furtwängler, Toscanini, Walter, Kleiber, von Schillings, Pollak, Blech, Bodanzky, Robert Heger, Werner Wolff, Johan Hye-Knudsen, and Georg Sebastian.

It was a scant year after his Barcelona Tristan that the Copenhagen Royal Opera invited Melchior to sing *Tristan und Isolde* there in January 1930. The strain of making his first appearance in Copenhagen in ten years was probably responsible for a nervousness more extreme, said Kleinchen, than she had ever witnessed in him. The reviews, however, "were a triumph." On January 9, King Christian X named Lauritz Melchior "Kammersanger," and the next day they were invited to lunch with the king and queen at Amalienborg Palace, in the company of the Todsens and the royal princes, Lauritz's friends. The title of Kammersanger meant a great deal to Lauritz because of his intense loyalty to Denmark, and because it proclaimed that he had followed in the footsteps of his teacher, Kammersanger Vilhelm Herold. He remembered his dream during his early studies with Herold: "To equal Vilhelm Herold would be the highest I could ever reach, would be to shoot beyond my goal in life." Now he had achieved the impossible. He had truly arrived. It was the apex of his career thus far.

CHAPTER 8

Tristanissimo

(1929–1931)

The glittering opening night performance of the 1929–1930 season of the Metropolitan Opera took place on October 28, the very night before the stock-market crash that would result in the Great Depression. Hearing the dreadful news in Berlin, Kleinchen had worried about the Metropolitan's ability to continue in its old style, but was reassured by her overseas information network that three million dollars in essential advance money had come in from Met subscribers. One month later her spirits were further raised by an announcement that the patrons of the Met would witness, during the following season, the first uncut performance of *Der Ring des Nibelungen* since 1899. Despite increased ticket prices, advance reservations were pouring in, and confidence ran high. In fact, the full impact of the crash was not to be felt by the Metropolitan until the next season. At the conclusion of the 1929–1930 season there would be, for the first time in twenty years, no profit—"a straw in the wind soon to become a gale."

Kleinchen fully appreciated the irony implicit in the Met's initial success and in the Melchiors' own growing celebrity during this period, because their success had virtually coincided with the stock-market crash. The fact was that, as the fortunes of the Metropolitan went steadily downhill, Lauritz was rising to the position of premier Heldentenor in the world.

Clearly Kleinchen was enjoying their new estate of comparative financial and professional security, for they leased an apartment found for them by the Schorrs at New York's Ansonia Hotel, where many of the Metropolitan artists lived during the season. Kleinchen was much annoyed because Lauritz was not behaving in a manner calculated to build his image as an international *primo tenore*. Not only did he make friends with the other singers, even fellow tenors, but he modestly took over thirty lessons with Gigli's teacher, Enrico Rosati. Of this he simply remarked later, "Since I was an admirer of Gigli, especially his mezza voce, I thought that [Rosati] was the right teacher. . . . He disappointed me somewhat but naturally my lessons with him did not hurt me." Kleinchen, on the other hand, was so impressed with what Rosati had to say and Lauritz's progress in "light singing" (which must have been her phrase for pianissimo singing) that she did not cavil at his "exorbitant" ten-dollar fee. Lauritz was working very hard: He practiced "technique" alone; he rehearsed *Fidelio* with a coach; he continued daily lessons with Rosati; and he even went to the opera several times a week. It is possible that Kleinchen assessed her husband's singing more objectively than believed, at least within the privacy of her diary. When on March 22, he sang his first Lohengrin at the Met, she found his voice at times "somewhat *klanglos* [without ring] and throaty," and his body "too fat . . . for Lohengrin." His March 28 Tristan still had "text mistakes," she wrote, but in *Tannhäuser* he sang "as beautifully as [she] had ever heard."

Profiting from his many Tristans since his first one at the Met the previous spring, Melchior was steadily improving his Tristan, as he showed in a fine portrayal on March 5, 1930, with Gertrude Kappel as Isolde, about which W. J. Henderson wrote:

> Lauritz Melchior looks more like a Tristan than some of those who have been seen here. He is a man of stalwart figure and bears himself well. His singing is what might be expected of the best type of Heldentenor. His voice is heavy but agreeable and he sang . . . with excellent art in the treatment of light and shade.

Henderson's opinion of Melchior's worth to the Met was clearly not that of Gatti-Casazza. Kleinchen noted grimly that Gatti marked Gigli's birthday on March 20 with a congratulatory telegram, but Melchior, whose birth date was the same, received nothing.

Taking heart, however, from the apparent fiscal health of the Met at the moment, Lauritz was emboldened to confront the general manager with his repertoire concerns. Referring to his new long-term contract, he said, he wanted Gatti to know that he would prefer not to concentrate exclusively on Wagner. Otello and Radamès were considered his best non-German roles. Without hesitation, Gatti flatly informed Lauritz that he would never be given either of the two roles. The Met already had a plethora of Italian tenors, and he had hired Melchior to be a Wagnerian tenor. Not only was *Otello* not in the repertory, but, were it to be revived, Gatti said conclusively, it would be given to Giovanni Martinelli, the dramatic tenor of the Met's Italian wing.

However, Gatti sweetened his refusal by diplomatically proposing an alternative: Walther in *Die Meistersinger*. "Not possible," Melchior said at once, listing these reasons, which he later confided to writer Harold Schonberg:

> I studied the role with Mme. Bahr-Mildenburg in Munich. We both agreed that it was not right for my voice. Too much of the part lies in the high register. The Heldentenor goes from low to high, then down-

hill, then up again. I can go high but I cannot sit there for a long time without coming down every now and then. I get tired from staying up high too long. In *Meistersinger* there are no real mountains and valleys, so a Heldentenor gets tired. When we walk on the same height all the time we lose strength. Even if I could manage the first part, I must then sing "Das Preislied" in a tired condition. I am a "schwerer Held," not a "jungendlicher Held." I am tired when I finish Stolzing, more tired than after Siegfried or Tristan. A singer must know his own voice.

The general manager was not convinced. The Met needed a Walther and Gatti wanted Melchior to do it. Melchior should rethink his attitude; Gatti offered a substantial increase in fee. He had emerged the loser in their first confrontation, over Loge and Max, but he intended to win out with Walther. In this ongoing battle, Lauritz was equally uncompromising. He never did agree to sing Walther, and Gatti never offered him Otello or Radamès.

More than one American critic has concluded from what resulted that Melchior was "too lazy" to learn roles outside his "narrow repertoire," but they were mistaken. Not only did he perform non-Wagnerian roles in countries other than the United States, but he longed to do them at the Metropolitan. San Francisco presented him in *Otello*, but neither Gatti nor Johnson, his successor, would do so.

Following the spring season at Covent Garden, where he performed *Götter-dämmerung*, *Parsifal*, *Siegfried*, and *Walküre* in the company of his friends Lehmann, Leider, and Schorr, Lauritz assisted at the inauguration of the Paris Wagner Festival, the idea for which he had proposed to Jacques Rouché the previous year. There he earned $1,000 for what the French called "the best Tristan who has ever been here." After extra performances in Berlin and Hamburg (with an eight-minute ovation—clocked by Kleinchen—after his aria "Celeste Aïda"), the Melchiors set off for Bayreuth, where they moved into their suite of rooms at 26 Ludwigstrasse.

The household accommodated the Melchiors, the Hackers, two servants, the two dogs, and, for the first time, the children, who had never heard their father perform in an opera before. Their principal reaction was one of amazement: The opera was so long that there were "eating intermissions" between the acts! (For years Ib and Birte thought that all operas were of this length.)

Ib Melchior, thirteen, was a guest at the Bayreuth high school for several weeks that summer. Ib and Birte both stalked deer with Lauritz and his hunting companion, ate chocolate generously supplied by Kleinchen, and sampled the champagne that stood open on the piano while Lauritz practiced. One visitor witnessed a revealing example of Lauritz's democratic ways, when the tenor gave a rehearsal pass to the municipal street cleaner. A few days later, the sweeper was working in front of the house when Lauritz got out of his car. As the worker complimented Lauritz on his singing to Brünnhilde at the end of the opera, Lauritz took him by the arm, pulling him and his broom into the house. Shortly after, Melchior's voice rang out in the Brünnhilde-Siegfried duet in honor of his guest, "the broom artist."

Uppermost in Lauritz's mind this summer of 1930 was his performance of *Tristan* under the baton of the formidable Arturo Toscanini, who had been invited to Bayreuth for the first time this summer. The Melchiors had been attending Toscanini's orchestra concerts since their first year in New York. Their reverence for the fiery Italian conductor was total, but they knew his personality only from gossip: When his temper erupted he hurled batons, threw scores, and furiously excoriated his musicians; but when his rage had spent itself, his tranquil face would reappear and all would be well once again. In reality Toscanini was in many ways different from what Lauritz had expected: "I can say that I had a good relationship with Maestro Toscanini, and since he is a good friend of beautiful ladies, it is understandable that Kleinchen was one of his favorites." Indeed, at the end of the summer when the Maestro said goodbye to Lauritz, the diminutive conductor even managed the difficult task of patting affectionately his tall Tristan's cheek.

Toscanini was an inspiration to the festival and to its artists. Lauritz later related details of Toscanini's artistry crucial to his own development:

> One day came Arturo Toscanini to Bayreuth. . . . He was so acclaimed that every child on the street of Bayreuth pronounced his name with awe. Arturo came, as all of us, as a Pilgrim. Richard Wagner was his pope. . . . [He] came full of respect and it is no invention that he cried tears when he stepped inside the Festspielhaus for the first time. We saw it, and we were all full of emotion. But all his respect did not hold him back from beginning the work. . . . He truly brought a new breath of air, although he did not wish a Revolution. . . . He took over the tradition, but lightly. He said to us: "You do it correctly, but it is more correct when you do so and so."

Nevertheless, the artists, the critics and the German audiences had spent an inordinate amount of time worrying about whether the Italian conductor would make Wagner indistinguishable from Puccini and Verdi. They were relieved to find that Toscanini had no intention of creating something new from the original score. "On the contrary," said Lauritz, "Wagner was for him the summit, as for us. . . ."

It was holy respect that had seized him, and he came as a Lohengrin.

[The other conductors] were not bad, but no Mucks and Toscaninis. . . . How did he direct? Very solemnly and dignified. I've read that he directed *Tristan* like *Bohème* or *Turandot*. That is the greatest nonsense! This is how the critics are, who have never lived it, but know everything.

"What Wagner meant is very clear. Just examine the score. You will find everything there," said Toscanini, who meant exactly what he said. At one rehearsal of the first act of *Tristan* he demanded, "Where is the cymbal crash?" He was assured that there was no cymbal crash and, as proof, was shown various editions (from which Cosima, however, had had it expunged). Unyielding, Toscanini waited while the original score was brought over from Wahnfried. His scholarship, long recognized as unimpeachable, proved itself again. There was the cymbal crash.

Considering his reputation for being arrogant and difficult, Toscanini generally behaved reasonably well, Lauritz found, to his intense relief, "Toscanini could be charming and kindness itself," but, "at other times, when something went against his grain, especially musical mistakes, he could be a devil. Everybody feared him and his will was autocratic. He did not yield an inch from the concept he had of a tempo and did not follow a singer who took a liberty." If a mistake was made during a rehearsal (and the Maestro could hear the tiniest mistake with the entire company at work), he would tap lightly on the stand with his baton. The offender would be expected to correct the error. When the error was made during a performance, one of the conductor's messengers would physically fetch the miscreant down to the Maestro's dressing room to receive a horrendous tongue-lashing.

Furthermore, Lauritz himself had seen what happened when Toscanini once took a monumental dislike to the tenor singing Tannhäuser. During one performance Toscanini repeatedly shrieked at the hapless fellow on stage, "*Cane!*" ("Dog!"), while continuing to conduct at a breakneck tempo. No one could hear the tenor as Toscanini "sang" along at the top of his voice, which was famous for its dreadfulness.

The *Tristan* cast happily witnessed one Toscanini explosion narrowly averted. During a pianissimo section Toscanini suddenly put down his baton, having been affronted by a loud, piercing noise that cut through the hall. He glared at the orchestra, and was about to erupt into Italian vituperation. The assembled instrumentalists and singers waited in nervous silence. The noise suddenly repeated. It had not been issued from the orchestra, but was merely the raucous horn of a passing automobile. Everyone laughed—except the Maestro.

Still the Bayreuth cast held its collective breath, assuming that sooner or later some cataclysm would befall one of them. This summer it was the unfortunate Anny Helm, playing Brangäne, upon whom the Italianate wrath descended. She was not fast enough in following Toscanini's directions. He shouted, "You sing like a rabbit! A rabbit!" For the entire two-hour rehearsal the malefactor was required to sing the same phrase, enduring with each repetition more calumny from the Maestro. In the end she fainted into Melchior's arms.

Lauritz had his own method of heading off Toscanini's wrath. He invoked a higher authority, namely, Richard Wagner.

When he [Toscanini] was very wild during rehearsals because it didn't go well, or because the horns didn't blow so sweetly as in New York, then I would point my forefinger upward, reminding him Who looked down on him and Who was listening. And then Arturo laughed and became quiet before the Genius who hovered over him. He pardoned himself and said, "Everyone is human."

Melchior was privileged to work on Tristan daily and privately with Toscanini. He insisted that the Italian conductor was paternal, kindly, generous, patient, and forgiving to those singers he respected. He always numbered the Maestro with conductors such as Leo Blech, Fritz Busch, and Fritz Reiner, who, together with the lesser known Egon Pollak and Max von Schillings, were his favorites because he believed they helped him to achieve a higher standard.

Toscanini's penchant for setting tempos and adhering rigidly to them is well-documented. Lauritz found security in the knowledge that there would be no deviations in rehearsal or in performance, no "personal" interpretations of Wagner's chosen tempo. Perhaps this affords us a clue as to his veneration of Toscanini as a conductor. With Toscanini on the podium, there was no "give and take" for Lauritz to accommodate. For him, it was simpler to spend rehearsal time working hard to learn the precise tempo, and then, on stage, to have the security of that familiar, and mercifully undeviating, tempo. Berta Geissmar, visiting Bayreuth as Furtwängler's secretary in 1931, also noted that Toscanini "rehearsed everything with the orchestra in minute and careful work to avoid . . . any risk at the time of performance. Nothing was left to chance."

The Maestro, nevertheless, must have been sorely tried by Melchior's legendary inability to follow the tempo in fast-moving passages of impassioned music. (After Siegfried Wagner's death a tasteless but pertinent joke made the rounds: Siegfried had finally given up, driven to his grave by the effort of trying to make Melchior stay in tempo.) Lauritz was certainly trying to be rhythmically responsible. In his *Tristan* score are a multitude of blue pencil marks, exhorting "*nicht eilen*!" ("don't rush!") and "*ruhig*!" ("calmly!"), together with beat numbers over every note. Daily, Lauritz and Toscanini studied tempos together. Toscanini, with his own score held in the familiar position recognized by all who had performed under the famous but near-sighted conductor—directly up against his nose—would set the tempo again and again until Melchior had it. While complimenting his tenor on a beautiful voice, Toscanini implored him to just *keep* the tempo, to just sing it *correctly*, Lauritz related. Apparently all those tempo difficulties could not dampen the Maestro's admiration for Lauritz, for it was in Bayreuth during this summer that Toscanini coined the term "Tristanissimo" to describe the Danish tenor. His sobriquet, "most Tristan of Tristans," is paralleled in suitability only by Conrad L. Osborne's description of the great Heldentenor: "a *Fach* unto himself."

One result of this hard work with Toscanini was that tempos Melchior learned from him were firmly set in his mind. No matter who his conductor was, he tended to sing at these very same tempos. Unlike his other Wagnerian roles, Lauritz learned his *Tristan* and *Tannhäuser* in large measure away from Bayreuth and the influence of Kittel, Siegfried Wagner, and Bahr-Mildenburg, but the finishing touches for these two roles came at the exacting hand of the Italian taskmaster. Melchior tended to be more musical when singing with Toscanini, even with repertoire other than *Tristan* and *Tannhäuser*.

Eventually a pronouncement joined the Melchior legend for which the musically fastidious conductor Fritz Busch may have been responsible (although Met conductor Fritz Stiedry later was credited with saying "once he learns a mistake he never forgets it"). At dinner one evening in Buenos Aires he said to conductor-pianist Ignace Strasfogel, "Melchior's obstinate tempos are the scourge of his conductors, but at least you can count on him to make the same mistake every time." Then he added, "But with all of that, give me Melchior anytime, because that intensity, and that voice, and everything about him is so electrifying." No one could accuse Lauritz of a total lack of musicality: he never committed, for example, the sin of dragging the tempo. Just keeping abreast of all the different cuts laboriously notated in his score— New York cuts, Philadelphia cuts, Buenos Aires cuts, London cuts, and Barcelona cuts—demanded great musical skill.

Melchior's appreciation of the larger Wagnerian principles was genuine. He understood well that the interpretation of Wagner's masterworks was a process of never-ending development, that a role like Tristan is ever beyond the performer's complete grasp: "It is like a well without a bottom. Every time you sing it you discover something new you hadn't discovered before. I feel I developed into the role gradually. I must have been lousy to start with." He was convinced that Tristan is the last role a Heldentenor should attempt because of the enormity of its challenge: "Acting, expressing feelings, musical and vocal technique—all these come together. They are all extreme, all on the same level, no letting down."

> [*Tristan*] is the greatest love story in the world because it sets forth the ideal of what love should be between man and woman. It is a drama of love, of love never dying. If there is anything after this world, these two people will certainly find it. In this world they must die together for they cannot die apart.

For that very reason Melchior always loved his Schattenstein portrait, which now hangs in Founders' Hall at the Metropolitan: "It shows in the eyes and the whole expression just what Tristan thinks in that moment."

Yet Melchior had always considered the role of Tristan more from a musical than a dramatic point of view, as he stated in 1936:

> No one will ever appear as the ideal physical Tristan for everyone. And since Wagner has made his music so expressive emotionally, I think it better to express the emotion of Tristan through the music and not through hampering and superfluous acting. For actual singing, there is nothing in all Wagner that is more emotionally uplifting and more deeply stirring than the love-duet in the second act of *Tristan und Isolde*. It is for the actual singing that I love this part of the opera best, and for the dramatic opportunities that I like the last act best.

The reviews of his Tristan provided a very enjoyable moment this summer; the same Nuremberg reviewer who had once predicted that the world would never hear from Melchior again wrote on the occasion of the first *Tristan*: "It is a great pity that Richard Wagner did not live to hear his noblest dreams fulfilled through Melchior." Another reviewer of *Tristan* appreciated the rare quality of the Melchior tenor: "In this artist is a perfect example of the (apparently dying out) breed of Heldentenor. . . . Not an instrument—a singing man."

For his second role this summer, *Siegfried*, the notice was more analytical, clearly written by an astute judge of musical and vocal matters:

> If this artist can add to his uniquely beautiful Heldentenor (with which he can tirelessly accomplish all registers) and his large, heroic presence, the aspiration toward a real perfection in singing and acting, then will he plainly *be* a Siegfried. But high artistic earnestness shows itself in iron diligence and is not his strong suit, and so he offered again only rough work.

Regrettably, this seems to indicate that Melchior was pleased with his Siegfried as it was.

Lauritz, whose enjoyment of Bayreuth was always heightened by the presence of his beloved colleagues, was unhappy with Frida Leider's absence that summer but was consoled to find Karin Branzell there singing Fricka in *Rheingold*. "The Swedish singer was an outstanding artist and I felt totally confident when working with her. . . . Unforgettable . . . were her Fricka and Ortrud and several Italian roles. . . . She was the best Brangäne I have ever seen." But his usual friendly relationship with his Heldentenor colleagues was not in evidence in the case of Gunnar Graarud. Lauritz was the target of a vituperative campaign by the wife of the Norwegian tenor. Graarud had sung Parsifal, Siegmund, and Siegfried in *Götterdämmerung* that summer, but had longed to do Tristan again, as he had in 1927 and 1928.

When the Bayreuth artistic administration decided to give that role to Melchior, Mrs. Graarud was furious. Kleinchen wrote: "The Graarud woman does everything to make things bad for us and makes no bones about it. She even told Lauritz to his face that she would spread all kinds of stories about him. Very nice. And she is keeping her word and is making Bayreuth hell for us."

It was Winifred Wagner who had delivered the paper and ink on which Hitler's *Mein Kampf* was written during his time in prison. Presumably it was the proceeds from his book that allowed Hitler to sport a suit, the famous trench coat, and highly polished, tall leather boots he now affected as he strode about Bayreuth with a dog whip in his hands. Privately Melchior brooded over the question of whether Hitler could be stopped at this point. Unemployment was now pandemic. Because so many citizens were seeking someone to lead Germany out of its postwar troubles, he worried that Hitler's National Socialist Party would win election to parliament in September. No German of real importance had taken Hitler seriously despite Nazi marches and violence, and no one bothered to stop him, thinking either that he could not succeed or that he could be used and controlled.

When Lauritz asked these questions of Minister Zahle at the Danish Embassy in Berlin, Zahle was not at all pessimistic. The thoughtless violence was not at Hitler's instigation. It was due to the unemployment, the lack of food, the fears about Germany's future. Lauritz should not worry. As a Danish citizen—more importantly, as a Singer to the Royal Court—he and his family would not be in danger. Now Melchior's honorary title of Kammersanger had a concrete value: physical safety.

Siegfried Wagner worried that the festival would be compromised by Hitler's presence, but did not know how to be stern with Winifred. Rumor had it that he was unable to control his wife's involvement in Nazi party affairs. To the company he appeared absentminded and unhappy, grieving for his mother, who had died on April 1 at the age of ninety-two. Barely four months after his mother's death, sixty-one-year-old Siegfried died, on August 4, 1930, sometime after collapsing on stage during a *Götterdämmerung* rehearsal. His wife was of the opinion that his death was probably due to the aggravation of his heart condition caused by the discord sowed by Karl Muck, who had worked unceasingly (and vainly) to prevent Toscanini from being invited to the festival.

Although Siegfried had been duty-bound to run the festival in Cosima's shadow during her lifetime, he had made the first real break with Cosima's tradition with his new innovative production of *Tannhäuser*, using three-dimensional sets. He designed the scenery in realistic style, insisted on a naturalness of movement that made the drama "seem to happen," and, perhaps most importantly, summoned Toscanini to Bayreuth. The first rehearsal of the new *Tannhäuser* that meant so much to him had taken place while Siegfried was hospitalized, and Toscanini wept throughout it. Birte Melchior, standing vigil with the crowd outside Wahnfried, had seen the curtain in Siegfried's room pulled down (signaling his death), and had run home with the news.

At the funeral Melchior joined his colleagues Fritz Wolff, Friedrich Schorr, and Rudolf Bockelmann as a pallbearer. A memorial concert was held in the Festspielhaus. Toscanini led the orchestra in "Siegfried's Funeral March" from *Götterdämmerung*. After Carl Braun's eulogy the orchestra, conducted by Karl Elmendorff, played an excerpt from one of Siegfried's own compositions, "Der Friedensengel." The concert concluded with Karl Muck conducting the Siegfried theme, which Richard Wagner had composed when his son was born. The largest of the floral offerings was from Adolf Hitler, a huge swastika covered with flowers and greenery.

In the weeks following Siegfried's death Melchior was scheduled to sing *Tristan* two more times. Lauritz did not doubt that the change he felt in the normally cheerful Bayreuth atmosphere was due in some part to Winifred, who sat at her husband's desk by 8:00 the morning after his death. "From the moment that Siegfried Wagner closed his eyes, the Bayreuther charm and friendly spirit among the artists was gone." The festival now reflected the emotional state of the country itself.

Upon his return to Berlin in the fall of 1930, Lauritz realized that things were not as before. A strange unrest, a vague tension, enveloped the German opera houses. Relations between colleagues, formerly friendly and open, now became a network of intrigues. The daily harassment of Jewish artists increased. Fritz Schorr, Lauritz's Jewish blood brother, was insulted and actually spat upon, whereupon he refused to renew his contracts with either Berlin house. In the future Melchior would always maintain that—like conductor Fritz Busch, whose entire (Gentile) family left Germany in protest at the treatment of Jewish artists—he had determined to stand on principle and do as Fritz Schorr had done. He fulfilled his standing contract with the Berlin houses, singing both Siegfrieds as well as an Otello—which Kittel, visiting, declared the greatest Otello he had ever heard. (In fact, he did, inexplicably, sing gratis performances of *Walküre* and *Tristan* with the Berlin Staatsoper in the fall of 1932, a gratis performance of *Tristan* in December 1933, and another performance of the opera in May 1934, for which he took a fee.) Although he could not bring himself to abandon Bayreuth, he included Hamburg, where he was truly beloved by the public, in his indictment, for in that opera house the attitude toward Jewish musicians was exactly the same. His last performance there was *Otello* on December 27, 1930.

Ill with bronchitis and down to 86 pounds, Kleinchen was sent by her doctor from Bayreuth to a Garmisch rest home for two weeks to gain weight. With her return, the Melchiors had moved from Hamburg to Berlin on September 1 (staying with the Wolffs until the new apartment was ready). The move was made partly to accommodate their new family and partly because the city was more centrally placed for Lauritz's work, even though he no longer intended to sing there. Kaiserallee 189 in the Wilmersdorf section of Berlin was big enough for all of them, even when the children came to join them during vacations. The Melchior family, when all together, now numbered six—Ib and Birte, Lauritz and Kleinchen, and her parents, the Hackers. Even when they finally moved in on November 15, even as they exclaimed over the view from the lovely, large balcony, Lauritz could not shake off his worry about living in Germany.

Pictures of their Berlin apartment reveal several large, airy rooms filled with oversized furniture and stuffed with antiques, which ranged from seventeen carved wooden panels that lined the dining room walls, to a collection of Meissen porcelain birds. The windows were dressed by glass-curtains inset with thickly reembroidered lace, over which hung heavy velvet or silk drapes falling to the parquet floors and onto the Oriental rugs. In the bedroom Kleinchen's dressing table, laden with crystal bottles, was at least eight feet long and draped with swags of silk. Carved flowers, fruits, and birds were featured on the enormous wooden bedstead. The place was unmistakably opulent. Even Kleinchen described it as "a palace."

By February the family was well settled in Berlin, and from their new home base the Melchiors traveled to Paris, where Lauritz appeared at the Opéra in both *Siegfried* and *Parsifal*. In May he returned to do his first *Otello*, his first non-Wagnerian opera in France (he singing in German and the rest of the cast in French) on the 28th. During the intermission he was presented with his second French decoration—Chevalier of the Légion d'honneur.

At this same performance a young French baritone sang the role of Iago. Martial Singher, in his own words, "had a name" the next morning, a fact due not only to his admirable performance, but also to an amusing circumstance. Melchior, singing the opera without orchestra rehearsal, joined with Singher and the others on May 27 for several hours of rehearsal with coaches, conductor Philippe Gaubert, and stage director Pierre Chéreau. With this sketchy blocking, "It is not surprising that at the performance the stage movements were not always very well coordinated," says Singher. Traditional staging dictates that, during their long scene together in Act II, Otello should shake Iago violently and force him to his knees. Singher remembers:

> Melchior was probably not used to a 155-pound Iago. He caught both my shoulders in his powerful hands and sent me flying across the stage.

I landed on the footlights, breaking a square of tinted glass and hurting my left arm which stayed numb the rest of the evening. But I got up with such an upsurge of energy that I rose almost to Lauritz's level of power and—so it was said—matched him in the final duet of the act.

During the eleven curtain calls, Lauritz publicly showed his chagrin over the incident by embracing Singher repeatedly.

At Covent Garden in the spring of 1931, Kleinchen learned to handle her business dealings with recording companies more effectively. At first she and Lauritz had naively accepted one-time fees for recordings, but she now understood the importance of guaranteed continuing royalties. Consequently, when they arrived in London for the 1931 Grand Opera Season in which Lauritz was scheduled to sing the *Ring* roles and Tristan, Kleinchen asked His Master's Voice (HMV), originally a British branch of the Victor Talking Machine Company, to send one of the directors for a chat during a rehearsal. She wanted to know why they had received no royalties to date on Lauritz's recordings from 1928 through 1930. During their discussion Kleinchen was enraged to find that Rudolf Laubenthal's recordings, distributed before Melchior's only because the German tenor had been on HMV's roster longer, meant that Melchior would receive no royalties. Infuriated at this state of affairs, Kleinchen physically attacked the British executive with his own umbrella. Somehow, despite, this display of temper (or perhaps because of it), she did eventually win his cooperation in the distribution of Lauritz's recordings.

Sales of Melchior's recordings were increasing, in any case. This may have been due to the recognition of Lauritz's fine singing and interpretation of both Siegmund and Siegfried, which, as one critic wrote, surpassed all his previous Covent Garden work by the "greater flexibility and subtlety of his character drawing, as well as by the perfect steadiness of his singing." Frida Leider, too, was singing very well, with "greatness . . . stamped on every note" of her Brünnhilde. Melchior's most treasured accolade, however, came from the formidable Ernest Newman, who, after complaining for years about Melchior's Wagnerian portrayals, finally complimented him on his Tristan:

> All our previous estimates of Lauritz Melchior will have to be revised. Hitherto he has been more remarkable as singer than as actor, and, as a tenor, more effective in *ff* than at any lower scale of vocal values. It is true that his softer tones still lack ideal beauty and body. But he manages now to lessen his disparity between them and his forte and fortissimo, and he handles them with such skill, and skates so dexterously over the thin spots on the ice, that for once we were spared the anguish

of hearing the quieter parts of the duet ruined in the usual manner of the German tenor. His more powerful tones are as brilliant as ever, but he now employs them with more poetic discretion than of old. As an actor he has improved beyond recognition. . . . His Tristan . . . was not only extremely dignified; it had a curious spiritual quality about it even in its moments of greatest frenzy.

Before leaving London, Melchior did four days of recording with the London Symphony under several conductors. The works performed under Sir John Barbirolli included the *Meistersinger* quintet (from the role Melchior had thought he would never sing) and yielded Barbirolli's most famous story about Melchior. At the recording session of May 16 Lauritz ruined one take after another. He could not manage to come in correctly, and the constant repetitions were making Elisabeth Schuman hoarse. Barbirolli was forced to come up with a creative solution to avoid a postponement of the session. The final take was done with Barbirolli's eyes riveted on Melchior. He held one hand over his mouth. Lauritz was bid to keep his mouth shut until Barbirolli removed his hand. By the time Barbirolli managed to get a reasonably correct reading everyone in the house knew the right notes. Despite all the trouble, Barbirolli often told how immensely fond of Melchior he was and that, in his opinion, this 78-rpm "classic" recording had turned out wonderfully. Melchior himself expressed his own opinion to American fan William Park that it was "amazing . . . if you think that it was sung by a heavy dramatic voice." Elisabeth Schumann may have become hoarse, but HMV's production man, Fred Gaisberg, rejoiced that "we had at last got a tenor who could sing and rehearse record after record without stress and without his voice going husky or becoming strained. . . . It takes a voice of iron to withstand that kind of strain."

In early June 1931, singing two Tristans and two elder Siegfrieds in the company of Leider, Olczewska, Janssen, and Andresen, with Blech as conductor, Melchior appeared in the second Paris Wagnerian Festival, which came off brilliantly. Then, before speeding off to sing Tristan on June 21 during the Vienna Opera's Festival Week, Lauritz and Kleinchen were summoned to attend a stupendous Paris party, this one hosted by Elsa Maxwell. Frida Leider, who called Elsa "America's most sharp-tongued society reporter," was not keen on going, but Lauritz was impressed by the fee of 12,500 francs (though it hardly compared with the 30,000 francs the Baroness Eugénie Rothschild had paid him for singing a few songs at one of her parties the previous May). Maxwell's specialty was organizing spectacular parties, for which she was paid by her wealthy clients. For her "*Louis Quatorze* Party," held in the Bois de Boulogne on June 13 in honor of the Baron Maurice Rothschild, she engaged Lauritz and Frida Leider to sing the love duet from *Tristan und Isolde*, a choice that Frida found "out of place amid the rococo surroundings." Still to some extent shockable (surprising in a couple accustomed to the infamous nightlife of Germany at the time), the Melchiors gaped at the parade of pet pigs, with bows around their necks, held on leashes by their fashionable lady owners. Other (more formal) entertainment was furnished by three internationally famous dance bands, a symphony orchestra, and an entire corps de ballet. The Melchiors' firm commitment to caviar and champagne was bolstered by kilos of Russian caviar and an actual fountain of Veuve Cliquot champagne.

In July 1931 the Melchiors arrived in Bayreuth, the last German opera company with which Melchior had retained a contract. Lauritz, missing Siegfried Wagner, felt the strain of the new Bayreuth. He contemplated the photo Siegfried had given him, dedicated to "Bayreuth's Latest Prize" and inscribed "my dear *tusind tak*" (the only Danish phrase Siegfried knew: "thousand thanks"), and remembered the warm tone of his voice when Siegfried called him by that nickname. Now everything was changed. Winifred was first lady of Bayreuth at last, but in name only, not in spirit. Lauritz had never faltered in his admiration, even veneration, of Cosima. That pale apparition in Wahnfried's gallery was for him the eternal embodiment of Wagner and his music. He had never brooked criticism of her methods or ideals, regarding such censure as uninformed. How could he turn his back on this place? Had it not been for Cosima and Siegfried Wagner, where would he be today? If they had not given him the most wonderful opportunity of the Wagnerian world, would he have made a career?

He was still very attached to the festival, but more than a little disappointed to find that Winifred had taken over completely. The festival was now her domain and she had chosen her own staff. Alexander Spring, a student of Seigfried's and formerly one of his stage assistants, was now stage director. Heinz Tietjen from Berlin's Staatsoper was engaged as general manager for the coming season, and was present this summer to check out his new responsibilities. The Melchiors fondly remembered Tietjen (a sometime critic) for his unstinting review of Lauritz's Canio at the time of his Berlin debut in *Pagliacci*, calling it "the best I have ever heard, including Caruso's." This welcome praise notwithstanding, Melchior found the gentleman to be a man without principles. Friedelind Wagner concurred, describing the little, dark man with thick spectacles as "one of the most sinister and astonishing of all the creatures who scrabbled to hold power in the early days of the Third Reich." Tietjen held a powerful position as artistic and business director of all the Prussian state theaters. Most felt that his business abilities outshone his artistic capability as a conductor, although he was an excellent musician and a fine stage director. Tietjen successfully outlived every change of government that might have unseated him, and, with his diplomatic cunning, was of great use to Winifred Wagner.

Another Bayreuth innovation was rather even more unsettling to Melchior. Adolf Hitler had actually moved into Siegfried Wagner's rooms in Wahnfried. His brown-shirts were evident everywhere. Hitler was not reticent concerning his own grandiose plans for Bayreuth: It was ridiculous to confine Wagner's operas to such a small stage; there ought to be room enough for ten thousand people. In Act II of *Tristan* the sky should be lit with a moon and innumerable stars. Wouldn't *Parsifal* be much more beautiful if the flower maidens were totally naked? In *Götterdämmerung* the three Norns should be placed on top of half a globe where they could sing about the end of the world. After the German Reich had bred a generation of racially pure young German women from which to cast a nude ballet, the "Venusberg Scene" in *Tannhäuser* would be marvelous!

A conductor much admired by Hitler was Wilhelm Furtwängler. With credentials such as his, it was natural that he should be invited to conduct at Bayreuth. He had enjoyed great success in a series of very important conducting posts from 1919 on, and by 1922, when he was 36, he was marked as one of the leading artists in his generation. Even so, he was not engaged at Bayreuth until Muck resigned in a huff because of the invitation to Toscanini. Gossip seethed about this tall, emaciated, now middle-aged man, made even more unattractive by his long, thin neck that supported an equally long, thin head. It was hard for Lauritz to understand how he captivated all those women who swooned when he conducted and threw themselves into his arms whenever they could get close enough. Part of his allure came from the incredible lifestyle he maintained. Winifred was obliged by Furtwängler's contract to provide a saddle horse, a stable, a stableboy, a car, and a chauffeur. He maintained a high profile by holding weekly press conferences, an innovation of his secretary, Berta Geissmar, whom he brought with him.

Melchior felt strongly that his practical needs as a singer were not being met by this conductor, and recognized that Furtwängler at that time was a better orchestra conductor than a conductor of opera. The simple reason, said Melchior, was that Furtwängler lost himself in his response to the music and often forgot what was going on onstage. (Frida Leider agreed.) This kind of behavior disturbs no one more than the singers, whose musical line is dependent upon span of breath. Moreover, it can destroy the integrity and flow of what is, after all, music-drama. One can see the influence of Toscanini (who despised the German conductor) in Melchior's thinking. Nothing could have been farther from Toscanini's ideal than the German mysticism espoused by Furtwängler. Furtwängler, said Melchior many times, would rather express his musical intentions than the composer's. Another camp held the exact opposite view: Toscanini, as an Italian, was only interested in the singers and pressed the orchestra parts far into the background. (Forgotten perhaps was Wagner's own admonition to the orchestra, "*Pian, pianissimo*— then all will be well.") Melchior genuinely preferred to be under the baton of the Italian conductor. "Have you heard my Ninth?" Furtwängler once asked the tenor. Melchior could not suppress his disrespectful answer, "No, I have only heard Beethoven's." Melchior was unhappy with Furtwängler's "creative solutions."

Toscanini too was unhappily wandering about the little town. He was not pleased by the Tannhäuser he was assigned (Hungarian tenor Sigismund Pilinszky), and declared his voice to be "weak and often guttural." He finally refused to conduct unless Melchior sang the title role. Clearly, Melchior's precision of detail, declamatory nobility, tonal clarity, clean and accurate attacks (unlike those of most German tenors), and unequalled vocal poise counterbalanced his weak sense of tempo. Lauritz was happy to oblige Toscanini by singing *Tannhäuser*, a first for him at Bayreuth.

Tristan und Isolde under Furtwängler's baton was Melchior's last performance that summer of 1931. For sentimental reasons, he and Kleinchen decided to go to the Festspielhaus in a horse and carriage that day. After the performance the enthusiastic Wagnerites did not leave Lauritz's side. A group of cheering young men unharnessed the horses and, followed by a devoted crowd, pulled the carriage, through the streets of Bayreuth to the Melchiors' home.

On August 4, the anniversary of Siegfried Wagner's death, a gala memorial concert that would include the artists and the festival orchestra and would be led by all the resident conductors was to take place. However, Heinz Tietjen had all too successfully exacerbated the existing animosity between Toscanini and Furtwängler. On the day of the memorial concert the two men had an explosive argument and Toscanini, also making an issue of Tietjen's official connection with the festival, absolutely refused to conduct. Following through, he later declined to return to Bayreuth, a stand that thoroughly irritated and embarrassed Adolf Hitler.

Disapproval of the racial distinctions at Bayreuth made many eminent singers drop out as well. They were equally displeased at the sight of Aryan colleagues furthering their own careers by making use of political connections. The atmosphere was downright unpleasant, and it became more so for Lauritz when Winifred Wagner hand-delivered an invitation to a personal conversation with Hitler that day. This invitation, however, was an order, which Lauritz refused emphatically. He told Winifred that he would never again sing in Bayreuth.

When writing his personal manuscript in 1946, Melchior regretted only his choice of words, ungentlemanly, he said, when addressing a lady:

> The widow . . . who tried to be a Cosima number two, but who had not the intelligence, personality, or the skills to support this inheritance, made the Bayreuther Festspiele impossible for me and many others, especially when later on, as if in love with the Führer Hitler, she Nazified and politicized them. If the Festspiel in Bayreuth never comes back again, she and she alone is responsible for this catastrophe. The importance of the Festspiele with regard to the training of the best Wagnerian voices in the world in the genuine Wagner style and tradition

Melchior as a child,
"Lalle Menkor."

Inger, Melchior's first wife, with her
children, Ib (left) and Birte.

Three generations: Jørgen Melchior, Lauritz, and Lauritz's baby son Ib.

Melchior at the age of twenty-one.

Melchior (right) at Marconi experimental station, Chelmsford,
Essex, with Marconi engineer Olaf Trost (left), 1920.

Melchior (right) and his mentor, Hugh Walpole, 1921.

Melchior and his second wife,
Kleinchen, at His Master's Voice
recording studios, London, 1929.

BARITONE ROLES

Melchior as Silvio in Leoncavallo's *Pagliacci* at his Royal Danish Opera debut, April 2, 1913.

As Baron Douphol in Verdi's *La Traviata* at the Royal Danish Opera.

As Morales in Bizet's *Carmen* at the Royal Danish Opera.

As Count di Luna in Verdi's *Il Trovatore* during the tour of Sweden in 1916. "You are a tenor with the lid on."

As Ottokar in von Weber's *Der Freischütz* at the Royal Danish Opera.

As Faninal in Strauss' *Der Rosenkavalier* at the Royal Danish Opera, at which the composer conducted.

TENOR ROLES

Melchior as Tannhäuser in Wagner's *Tannhäuser*, his first tenor role at the Royal Danish Opera, 1918.

(Right) As Canio in Mascagni's *Cavalleria Rusticana*, 1919.

As Siegmund in the Bayreuth
production of Wagner's *Die Walküre*,
1924.

As Parsifal in Wagner's *Parsifal*.

As Lohengrin in Wagner's *Lohengrin* at
the Hamburg Stadtteater, 1927.

As Siegfried in the Bayreuth production
of Wagner's *Götterdämmerung*, 1927.

As Otello in Verdi's *Otello* at Hamburg
Stadtteater, 1928.

As Radamès in Verdi's *Aïda* at Hamburg
Stadtteater, 1928.

Melchior in his first Bayreuth
performance of Tannhäuser in Wagner's
Tannhäuser, 1931.

Melchior's first Bayreuth Tannhäuser, 1931.

Melchior in his first Bayreuth
performance of Tristan in Wagner's
Tristan und Isolde, 1930.

As Florestan in Beethoven's *Fidelio* at
Teatro Colón, Buenos Aires, 1933.

Melchior and Bruno Walter.

Melchior and Kleinchen with Arturo Toscanini aboard the *Bremen*.

Melchior with Frida Leider and Wilhelm Furtwängler in Paris, 1933.

Melchior with Artur Bodanzky, Metropolitan conductor for the German wing.

Melchior in his Met dressing room, accoutered with his combination girdle/ breathing belt/suspenders for Tristan's chainmail leggings. When *Life* published this picture in 1944, one of his fans complained, "*Why* did you do it? Now when I look at you, instead of seeing the noble Tristan, what I see is a corset."

Lotte Lehmann and Lauritz Melchior. "We were the best Wälsepaar," said Lehmann.

Melchior with Kirsten Flagstad and Fritz Reiner.

Melchior and Kirsten Flagstad in London, 1936.

Melchior with Giulio Gatti-Casazza (left) and Fiorello La Guardia at the Metropolitan Opera after the 100th performance of Siegfried in Wagner's *Siegfried*.

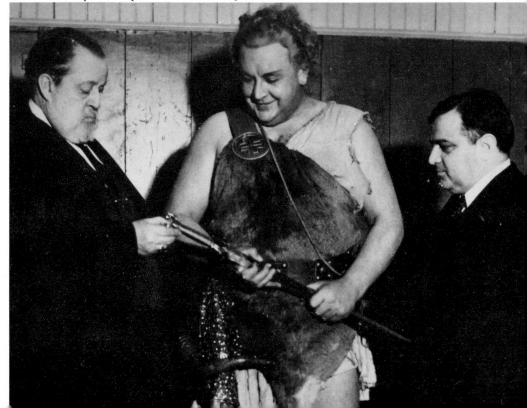

Melchior and Helen Traubel in Wagner's *Tristan und Isolde*.

Melchior and Helen Traubel at play.

under the right leadership without rush and in the Bayreuther atmosphere was immense to the artists and to the knowledge and style of Wagner, which they passed on to the big opera houses in the world. With the disappearance of these Festspiele this genuine style will suffer and gradually fade and succumb to the whims of the individual artists. . . . This year, for the first time, I did not stay in Bayreuth until the festival performances were finished.

Berta Geissmar, however, contradicts Melchior's description of his last summer in Bayreuth. She notes that Melchior was particularly unhelpful to Furtwängler during his Bayreuth debut season: "The first clash of the season was with Lauritz Melchior . . . who declared that he would leave immediately and never return; the management was apparently his source of irritation. He finally consented to fulfill his contract for the summer, but since then the world's greatest Wagnerian tenor has never set foot in Bayreuth."

The recollections of Rudolf Bockelmann (a distinguished baritone playing Tristan's faithful Kurvenal), cast yet another light on Melchior's decision to leave Bayreuth.

For a long time Nanny Larsén-Todsen had no longer been fresh-voiced. She pushed every tone from G up, stretching her arms high above her head. . . . The Danish giant, Lebrecht Hommel, with the stage name Lauritz Melchior, sang strongly and beautifully but horribly out of tune. This angered Furtwängler so greatly that he hinted to Winifred that he would never do *Tristan* again if this couple were entrusted with the drama. . . . Melchior's pitch and Larsén-Todsen's "shrill piping" made Furtwängler's efforts uneven. . . . Melchior and Larsén-Todsen attributed their failure to the "new fashion" of the Berliner. . . . But there was no replacement Tristan. . . . In order to save *Tristan* at all, they had to agree to all Melchior's special wishes. He was even granted the infamous "Metropolitan cut" in the second act love duet. . . . "Bockelmann," confided Furtwängler, "I must regenerate the orchestra from the bottom and will make my influence felt so that the soloists will be selected better. With Larsén-Todsen and Melchior I would have been as ashamed as a beginner in Lübeck."

It is said that Bockelmann's statements may not be totally reliable (certainly he was in error about Melchior's name), but Lauritz's later version of the events of the 1931 festival may also have been put forth in too noble a light. Surely he must have sorely missed the days when Cosima and Siegfried approved of him wholeheartedly.

Melchior always told a poetic little story of his departing from Wahnfried (it must, alas, come under suspicion since, according to Friedelind Wagner, the famous parrots died before she was born): As he left Wahnfried for the last time, he passed two parrots, the only two friends he had left in Bayreuth. With exquisite timing one of them burst into Brünnhilde's battle cry, "Ho-jo-to-ho! Ho-jo-to-ho!"

CHAPTER 9

The Wagnerian Ensemble at the Met

(1931–1935)

The Metropolitan Opera was not the only establishment to believe vainly that the stock market would recover in a few weeks or months from the crash of October 1929. Even before 1930 began, however, fortunes had been wiped out and thousands of workers had lost their jobs. By 1931, while workers from an estimated force of ten million unemployed Americans were staging hunger marches, Melchior's personal finances were in fine shape. The Metropolitan and other opera companies were forced to give him a raise in his new contracts—although still not as high a fee as the Italian-wing artists—because his success as Tristan had put him in a higher artistic echelon. The desperate conditions that prevailed in Germany made his foreign funds, derived from appearances outside Germany, even more valuable, with the result that the Melchiors could live lavishly in that country and have funds left over to invest. Kleinchen busied herself learning the ins and outs of the investment world. At the royal Marlborough House parties in Britain, while Lauritz stayed close to the bar and the buffet table, Kleinchen closeted herself in a secluded corner with gentlemen from the Bank of England, charming them out of their latest investment secrets.

An engagement at the Teatro Colón in Buenos Aires helped make up financially for all those performances lost in Germany. The Colón's offer of three performances of the entire tetralogy *Der Ring des Nibelungen*, plus two performances of *Tristan und Isolde* from August 20 through September 29, 1931, paid a hefty fee, $1,200 for each performance. In addition, their friend Frida Leider was going to sing Isolde, and they would travel comfortably for three weeks in what amounted to an all-expenses-paid sea voyage.

Frida and Rudi met the Melchiors in Genoa. The weather was terribly hot, the cabins claustrophobic in red plush and heavy velour, and Lauritz kept taking showers until the *Conte Verde* was at sea. Elated to find a full-fledged ceremony new to his experience—the ball celebrating the equator crossing—he bribed the chef to let him serve the buffet supper at the ball. Lauritz dressed as the head cook and Kleinchen as a charming kitchen boy. Lauritz was severely reprimanded for serving the caviar too generously. Otherwise, the trip was uneventful and restful.

This was fortunate, for after arrival all was strife and dissension. The enthusiasm of the Argentine public was running high because for the first time, the Colón's season would be under Otto Klemperer, a German conductor whom Señora Santas Elias, director of the opera, had engaged for the *Ring*. Use of the theater for extra rehearsals called by Klemperer forced the management to cancel six of the performances. The public's original elation over the unprecedented number of German opera performances turned to rage. The artists, on the other hand, were most disturbed by the cancellation of their lucrative performances. (Lauritz sang only eight out of the scheduled fourteen.) Despite the fact that all the leading singers had insisted upon a guaranteed fee for all the performances, whether or not they actually took place, payment for the canceled performances was not forthcoming.

While the Melchiors were trying once again to speak to the cashier about Lauritz's unpaid fees, the cashier made his usual attempt to slam the door in their faces and escape. "This was too much for Lauritz!" said Frida. "He banged his elegant silver-knobbed cane on the cashier's foot. The poor man, hopping up and down with pain, kept repeating, 'Mañana, mañana!'" The next day checks were promised for directly after the last performance of the single *Ring* cycle that survived uncanceled. Unfortunately, their ship, the *Giulio Cesare*, was scheduled to depart at 9:30 that night. Knowing that a government crisis had sent the stock exchange crashing, Kleinchen demanded cash. The company, she was told, paid only by check. With the help of a new friend, banker and wheat tycoon Señor Hirsch, she set herself to solve the problem. As Leider wrote:

> He telegraphed our checks through his New York bank so that they could be paid on time. . . . We were on stage, singing nervously, not knowing whether Kleinchen had succeeded in persuading the captain to delay the sailing for two hours. With the help of Rudi, we rushed to the ship half made up. Kleinchen had achieved the impossible and the anchor was being raised as we rushed breathlessly on board.

This saga reinforced Kleinchen's reputation for canny business sense and marked the end of the German regime at the Colón.

Clearly, for Melchior to return to Buenos Aires, still under the management of Señora Elias, would be madness, and Kleinchen decided that they would not go in 1932. By the summer of 1933, however, Elias had left, and Lauritz was pleased to sing his first Florestan in Beethoven's *Fidelio* at the Colón, having just learned the role that spring. Anny Konetzni and

Michael Bohnen were in the cast, and his friend Fritz Busch, whom he had met at Bayreuth, conducted.

In 1924 Melchior had witnessed the sadly truncated Bayreuth career of Fritz Busch. The conductor had been personally selected by Siegfried Wagner to conduct *Die Meistersinger* (not produced at Bayreuth since 1912), but his introduction to Bayreuth was an amusing case of mistaken identity. In June, as soon as he was settled in, Busch had headed toward the singing he heard coming from Rüdelsheim, a cozy little cottage occupied by the "grand and very charming" chorus master Hugo Rüdel, who used it for his rehearsals. Since it was a choral passage from *Meistersinger*, Busch decided to attend the rehearsal. Before he could introduce himself to Rüdel, who was expecting an extra second tenor, he brusquely took him to task for being late. "Go take your place over there," he commanded. Busch meekly did as he was told, and sang energetically with the others. Unsatisfied with the results, Rüdel pointed accusingly at the second tenors, singling them out for special blame. (Privately, Busch agreed with him.) "You must do better than this! How can I present a chorus like this to Herr Musikdirektor Busch when he arrives? Are you *looking* at the music? Let's hear the second tenors alone." When the break was called, Busch introduced himself. The embarrassed Rüdel took Busch to lunch at Die Post, and the two musicians became fast friends. Because Lauritz enjoyed Rüdel's fine little wine cellar, he often made up a third member of the party, as they drank wine and told stories.

As it turned out, Busch needed a friend. He had come to Bayreuth an outsider, a stranger to the other conductors. Karl Muck, in particular, had resented Busch's offers of help, interpreting them as interference by an upstart newcomer. The old guard of Bayreuth had stayed jealously aloof, and Busch's inability to keep his opinions to himself caused his first year at the festival to be his last, even though Siegfried did ask him to return. Busch himself admitted: "If again and again I made critical remarks or offered suggestions, they merely smiled." Since his hatred for Nazism was as intransigent as Toscanini's, Busch would not have remained long in any case.

Pleased as Lauritz was to be singing Florestan under Busch, the greatest excitement of the South American sojourn was, however, the thrilling return trip by airplane to Porto Alegre and Rio de Janeiro and then by dirigible, the great Graf Zeppelin, back to Europe, arriving on September 12. The airship floated up the coast of Brazil, then to Africa, the east coast of Spain, and across Switzerland to land in Friedrichschafen on Lake Constance. Rather than sitting by the windows admiring the beautiful scenery, however, the Melchiors could be found during much of the five-day trip in the cockpit with the captain, Ernst Lehmann (who played the accordian rather well), singing everything from operatic arias to street ballads. These sessions were most likely the noisiest part of the trip, for the dirigible itself flew so quietly that passengers could scarcely believe they were moving. Over South America the zeppelin's passing caused everyone to run outside to wave, but in Africa, as Melchior recalled, "not a single human being lifted his head to stare at us, much less to wave." Several times during the crossing Captain Lehmann took the zeppelin down low enough for Melchior—who had seven pairs of martinettas (an Argentine species of bird that he wanted to introduce into the game reserve of a hunting estate he had purchased) traveling below the zeppelin in a cargo ship—to have a conversation with the cargo ship's captain about the welfare of his birds, or to talk with the Karl Laufkötters, who were returning more economically by that ship.

In order to keep operating in the usual way during the 1930–1931 season, the Metropolitan had spent a third of its reserve fund. Worse, the subscriptions on which it depended so strongly declined by a disastrous ten percent. On October 28 of the 1931–1932 season Otto Kahn had retired from the chairmanship of the board of trustees, leaving the financially astute lawyer Paul Cravath to hold down the job. Gatti admitted to Cravath that in three years they had lost thirty percent of their subscribers, and the figures showed it was among the wealthiest class that subscriptions had shrunk the most. The general public, however, kept buying, and the Wagner patrons remained markedly steadfast, permitting Gatti to give Lauritz a new three-year contract with a raise. Interest in Wagner's music-dramas was so strong that lecture evenings for Wagnerites were popular, one of which Lauritz himself did at New York University in March 1932.

Gatti had written on November 3, 1931, to Otto Kahn, who was still included in the decision-making despite his retirement from the board. Apologizing for the "worst budget in forty years of being in the theatrical profession," Gatti, taking no fiscal chances, required those few artists (such as Lauritz) whose contracts were for more than one year to give the Met the right to abrogate the contract by the August preceding any season that the company was forced to cancel, now a very real possibility. On Christmas Day of 1931 the Metropolitan Opera had broadcast its first performance— *Hänsel und Gretel*—over NBC Radio. The management hoped the infusion of NBC's substantial yearly broadcast fee would revive the ailing budget.

Circumstances had left Melchior considerably better off than many other Met artists. As the Met was unable to find another Heldentenor for his parts, Lauritz was one of the few artists allowed a long-term contract; some singers were actually hired by the week. Also, Lauritz was singing rather more at the Met this year than before—his new contract guaranteed twenty performances at $1,000 (still less than Martinelli, whose fee for each of more than forty performances was $2,000). However, he had taken, like almost all the other Met artists—the exception being Gigli—a voluntary ten percent cut to help sustain the Met in its fight to keep going. At Covent Garden Friedrich Schorr had offered his own services gratis, and persuaded his colleagues to take cuts in salary. Paris soon followed suit with its own fee cuts.

By 1935 things would be so bad that a meeting of all the major artists of the Metropolitan would be called on January 21 to discuss the raising of a fund for the Met. Chairman Bodanzky opened the meeting—the first of its kind—by saying that a fund of one million dollars would guarantee the opera for the next three years and permit some improvements in the *Ring* scenery. Melchior, however, was against the goal of a paltry one million dollars. Why not try to get the government to support opera as was done in Europe, he inquired, where a tax on every radio, so much per week, went to support the opera and other cultural efforts? If the U.S. government charged everyone who had a radio only 25 cents a year, it could raise 28 million dollars. All present "objected and said that this country is too big and it is too hard to get the government interested." (Thirty-three years later, in fact, the Carnegie Commission on Broadcasting would recommend a tax on televisions for the same purpose.)

In September and October 1932, congratulations to Gatti-Casazza on the beginning of his twenty-fifth year as manager of the Metropolitan Opera Company poured in from all over the world. Plans for the gala celebration to be held on February 26 were in full swing when the Melchiors arrived in New York in January 1933. On February 14, the Associated Press, recognizing a genuine occasion when they saw one, sent a lengthy plea for a special interview, reminding Gatti that they had been observant of his unalterable rule of silence during all his years as general director. Although Gatti declined the interview, the questions posed in the letter suggest the concerns of many contemporary Americans regarding opera and the Depression: Did Gatti think "that it was likely, practically speaking, for there to be an increased interest in opera once the depression had passed?" the letter began. Might there be "a possibility for what is sometimes called 'democratic opera,' opera supported by the wider public?" Did Gatti think that "further Americanization" of the Metropolitan organization would be helpful? Which would be "more valuable, a new house, or tradition? Granted a season next winter, possibly shorter than this one," would Gatti attempt to produce more new works "in the hope of attracting new custom," or would he produce fewer "in the interests of economy?"

For Melchior, the one bright spot in all the gloom was the shower that the Met had installed for him! No longer would his dresser have to wash one part of the giant body at a time in the miniscule washbasin of the dressing room. Melchior knew full well why he had previously been without a shower. Plans to build a new opera house had superseded the necessary modernization of the fifty-year-old building, but the Depression that halted the planning was also to blame for the deterioration of the building. (Upon his arrival in

1950, Rudolf Bing, too, denigrated the dressing rooms as "a rabbit warren with worse plumbing than most rabbits are willing to tolerate.")

The stage facilities themselves had become downright perilous. Melchior had endured several accidents at the hands of the dilapidated sets and props, though managing to keep singing each time. Neither the props nor the scenery could be trusted: Brünnhilde's rock was a loose pile of boxes wrapped in canvas; the stage floor was so rotten that his leg once went right through it, requiring Kurvenal and the sailors to hold him up while he sang Tristan in that position; the dragon Fafner's breath, too realistically hot, scalded the singer when he approached for the fight. (This was a direct result of Melchior's bravery in approaching the dragon. The men who made up the front and back legs of Fafner declared that Melchior was the only tenor who did not spoil the scene by his cowardice.) One evening the bellows-rope of Mime's smithy broke as Melchior was in the middle of Siegfried's "Forging Song"— not too simple a task in itself. The tenor was able to divide his concentration, singing steadily along while he neatly spliced the rope together. "It was all stopgap refurbishing," admitted Met patroness Eleanor Belmont. "The productions were literally dropping to pieces."

The high point of the 1932–1933 season for Lauritz was the arrival of his favorite Isolde, Frida Leider. Back in 1931 Lauritz had suggested Frida Leider to the managing director as the very greatest Wagnerian soprano in the world. Gatti listened instead to his assistant manager, Edward Ziegler, a former critic, who insisted that Leider was not good enough for the Metropolitan. Melchior then sought out the one person with more influence than Ziegler, Artur Bodanzky, with whom he was now on good terms.

Originally Melchior and the conductor had clash after clash, usually over tempi. Their controversies had not been quiet and gentlemanly then.

> Since I was no less able in using abusive language, and since our dressing rooms were placed side by side with a small corridor between them, one can imagine the "flowers of speech" that flew from room to room. In the corridor stood Kleinchen to see to it that we really did not kill each other.

Now they had found agreement.

> When I became more knowledgeable, also musically, Arthur [sic] and I became very good friends, for he was, inside the coarse outer shell, a warmhearted human being, who went through fire and water for his orchestra musicians and artists on stage. To him the best was only just good enough.

Bodanzky's response to Lauritz's questions was surprising: Because Leider sang for Insull, the Met would not have her. (When the famous and successful businessman Samuel Insull took over the Chicago Opera from Mr. and Mrs. Harold McCormick, he turned the organization into a going concern, backed by his considerable personal resources.) Although this opera company was located way out in Chicago, the Met had considered Mr. Insull an upstart and his opera a competitor. Eventually the two companies had come to an agreement: they would not raid one another's roster. Mme. Leider had sung at the Chicago Opera for several seasons and would therefore not be invited to sing at the Metropolitan. Melchior was forced to back down, feeling the insecurity of his own present position. In 1931, he was seldom invited to sing on American radio, with American orchestras, or to record for American companies, whereas in Germany he had a fanatically admiring public and was constantly in demand for recordings, as well as for radio, operatic, and orchestral appearances.

One year later, when the hard times that hit Chicago Opera made Insull concede defeat at the hands of the Depression, Lauritz was able to persuade Bodanzky to engage the soprano for the 1932–1933 season. His dear Frida was not a member of the Met. For three years Melchior had been imagining what a magnificent occasion her Metropolitan debut as Isolde would be, and, on January 16, 1933, it happened exactly the way he had anticipated.

With Lauritz as Tristan and the newly-engaged contralto Maria Olczewska, Melchior's longtime colleague in Berlin and at Covent Garden, as Brangäne, it was a glorious performance. Said Olin Downes: "This performance . . . had, for once, the glamour, the authority, the finished dramatic art that it demands and so seldom receives." Henderson praised Leider's "power and conviction" and her "indescribable magic of genuineness" and called Olczewska "a Brangäne of first rank"; the principals, he wrote, displayed "admirable unity of purpose" and Melchior had sung "with depth of feeling and vocal finish." Bodanzky—clearly even he had felt the electricity— had conducted with "wonted fire and feeling." Gilman cited Leider's "deep and enlarging tenderness, richness of feeling, poetry of imagination." Cushing, while praising the performance as surpassing "any that memory can recall" since the postwar revival of *Tristan*, reminded his readers that, had honors been distributed solely on the basis of merit, "Mr. Melchior's share would probably have been the largest." Lauritz, surrounded with beloved friends who were superb artists, found it easy to sing from his heart. "At last a cast!" rejoiced Sanborn, joined by the 400 standees who broke into cheers at the end of Act I.

Lauritz had advised Frida to take an apartment in the Hotel Ansonia, where so many Met colleagues lived. Now Lauritz not only had his dear friend as a cherished colleague on stage, but also her husband Rudi Deman as a companion at the card table. Their inveterate card playing went on at the Ansonia as well as before, during, and after performances. Lauritz preferred to treat the Met as a sort of second home used for friendly gatherings for an evening of music, a kind of new 31 Nørregade.

Leider was surprised by the opulence of the Met: "Nothing in its monotonous facade prepares one for its splendid interior." Because Leider's debut was not the first performance of *Tristan* for the season, she would have to make do without an orchestra rehearsal. The prospect of having nothing more than piano rehearsals in the ladies' lounge increased the perturbation the soprano already felt because of Edward Ziegler's opposition. That her earlier notices invariably contained the word "incomparable" did nothing to soothe her jittery nerves. Lauritz did his best to help, accompanying her to the piano rehearsal and showing her the blocking on the huge Met stage.

Frida could not understand why no one asked her to sing on the radio in America. She found it difficult to believe that, as Kleinchen explained, opera singers were not regarded as popular enough to draw an audience. The conversation gave Lauritz an idea of how to take Frida's mind off her troubles. He called her on the telephone, disguising his voice in imitation of a radio contractor, and asked whether she would be willing to sing on a radio show that advertised a patent medicine for male potency. Her husband's strong physicality and handsome appearance would be featured while she sang in the background. Suddenly it dawned on her who was making this bizarre offer, and she hung up on the incorrigible Lauritz. Later he sought her forgiveness with an enormous bouquet of flowers.

Frida Leider was utterly astounded to see the shenanigans of the Met administration and artists at the "Save the Met" fund-raising Surprise Parties. Even though she had long known of Melchior's delight in playing the clown offstage, she was taken aback by the turn he and Lily Pons did as two curly-haired blonde acrobats—and in the opera house! Lauritz in yellow tights and body stocking (over his girdle), sequined shorts, and beribboned ballet shoes, stood center stage like a Colossus, while the diminutive Pons, in matching costume but sans girdle, climbed up on his back, paused on his shoulders, and finally walked out on his outstretched arm to a roar of applause. The side splitting conclusion to "Allez-Oop" had Lily holding Lauritz aloft by one foot, a feat achieved with some help from the technical staff.

Lauritz and Lily Pons were such a hit that they again teamed up in 1935 in the fourth annual Surprise Party, called "Oper-Tunities." Its most appreciated and applauded sketch featured an apache dance with tiny Pons in the role of the man, and black-clad, white-gartered, and gigantic Melchior as the buxom and brunette object of "his" wrath. (In an apache dance the girl was thrown about in acrobatic style by the man.) Both artists were often criticized for missing Met rehearsals, but the pair spent an entire month, three times a week, at a local dance studio learning fancy little steps and elegant twists for this one appearance. In 1936 the two singers repeated their apache dance for a dinner (billed as "Undignified Entertainment by Dignified Artists") given by Mrs. Vincent Astor. These two were not the only clowns on this occasion, for soprano Lucrezia Bori conducted a band in which violinist Jascha Heifetz played bagpipes and Melchior the drums.

During her second year at the Met, Frida Leider again enjoyed (while marveling at the kind of informality that a European house would never countenance) the "break from routine that was the famous Surprise Party," which continued efforts to raise money for the Met and always sold out the house. To be sure, the irreverent Melchior made the most of the opportunity. This year he combined forces with tenor Marek Windheim for a smashing satire of *Salome*, entitled "She Knew What She Wanted." In their version Herod sat in his court and telephoned John the Baptist to send Salome (played by Melchior) up from the cistern. Lauritz the Large cavorted through the dance of the seven veils. His gauzy costume with its low-cut top, rounded out to match his generous proportions with four strategically placed balloons fore and aft, was completed by big clown's feet with painted toenails. "What will you have, Sally old girl?" asked Herod. Salome whispered in his ear. A slave went into the well, and up came the heads of the New York music critics. In the middle of April, long after the Melchiors had left New York on the *Europa*, the fetching picture of Windheim and curly-wigged Melchior ("The Bewitching Jade from Judea") was still being reprinted in papers all over the country.

Melchior's lifelong addiction to hunting began as early on as his love of pranks and clowning. He was taught by the father of a friend, an ardent hunter, who gave Lauritz "the upbringing to be a good hunter with respect for a gun." When the Melchiors began to think of moving from Berlin to the country, Dr. Grohnwald, one of Lauritz's hunting friends, had suggested an estate in a little village called Chossewitz, located in Nieder Lausitz, a bit more than a hundred kilometers southeast of Berlin. Not uninfluenced by Hugh Walpole's criteria for a summer residence, they took one look at this peaceful, bucolic setting and fell in love with it. Without further consideration, they leased the smaller of the two villas along with hunting rights, and managed to return to Chossewitz by Christmas, when they were once again entranced by the gently hilly land extending to the calm, tree-lined lake. Lauritz settled in, making friendly overtures to his neighbors, cultivating the local hunters. This was the kind of life he had always envisaged for himself: Hiking for hours in the forest with his hunting dogs, Sturm and Tilla, stopping for a chat with the forest ranger, enjoying the quiet beauty of nature.

Nightly entertainment at Chossewitz in 1931 featured lengthy discussions about the future: How they were going to enjoy it when they could lease the main building as well, which was big enough to allow sumptuous and elegant hospitality. (Lauritz's criteria for hospitality were so exacting and so very important to him that, describing for his diary the 1926 visit to Sarah Cahier's castle, he noted only her "poor hospitality.") Long lists of intended guests—which featured Lauritz's sisters—were compiled. Kleinchen's parents would live at Chossewitz year-round, and the children would join them in the summertime.

With his Danish love for making a festival out of every possible occasion, Lauritz decided that the summer of 1932 should be a celebration of his new artistic status in France and Belgium. Accordingly, he invited a multitude of friends and as many family members to visit them at Chossewitz, where he was finally permitted to lease the larger main house. Scarcely a day passed that summer when the lodge did not hold a vast assemblage of guests, who joined in the hunting expeditions, the singing fests, the evening open-air card games. Hugh Walpole spent a week enjoying the pastoral joys of Chossewitz, which he described as being "miles from anywhere. It is very quiet and peaceful and just what I want. . . . It is all opera scandal and frogs in the pond and Wiener Schnitzel."

For Melchior, the romance of hunting lay in its many rituals and traditions, as well as the enjoyment of nature and comradeship it afforded the hunter. He never stopped trying to interest his son Ib in hunting. He touted the tradition of *Brüderschaft* (brotherhood): after the first deer of the day is killed, you take a leafy twig from a nearby tree and put it into your hatband; then you shake hands with your hunting companions. This summer Lauritz promised Ib his first buck. For Ib, however, the romance of Brüderschaft was not enough. "Hunting" from a comfortable *Hochsitz* (a platform hidden in the leafy branches of a tall tree) repelled him. "I cannot kill an animal. It isn't hunting; it's shooting. . . . Far [Father] was disgusted." Lauritz always maintained that he hunted only to thin out the herd, but Ib wasn't buying that theory. "Look at the trophies. Are those old and infirm animals?" he asked. In truth, it would be difficult to make a case for Lauritz's assertion. On one 1940 hunting trip, for example, he shot both a Kodiak bear and a bald eagle. Horrified conservationists actually made a visit to his California home to check out the circumstances of the kill, and Lauritz was forced to prove that he had shot the eagle in Canada, and before the law against shooting the bald eagle in the United States was enacted. As for the bear, Lauritz brought down the magnificent specimen, which weighed one thousand kilos, in the Alaskan wilderness. This trip resulted in a new lake added to the map of Alaska. When their flimsy old seaplane landed near the Bering Sea on a lake unknown to the guide, Lauritz promptly said, "We'll call it Melchior Lake." Alaska's governor blessed his choice, saying it would be a treat to have a lake that wasn't called Bear or Sand.

Not everyone viewed Melchior's hunting habits critically. One of his comrades who had hunted with him for forty years insisted that Lauritz was not only a very skilled but a humane hunter, eschewing, for example, the use of buckshot when shooting deer.

As his son didn't enjoy hunting, Lauritz took his daughter, who tells how even the guests had to help clear *Pürschwege* (paths where the hunters can walk without stones rolling noisily or twigs snapping with a cracking sound, both of which will frighten the animals away). Then a Hochsitz would be fashioned at the corner of the field where the deer came in the evening to rest and eat. When all preparations had been made, Birte would go with her father in Maxi the Ford, with its canvas top and four doors, driven by her friend, the chauffeur Walter Bock. She carried all the equipment except the gun, which Far trusted to no one but himself. Birte, an animal lover like Ib, had her own way of rebelling against the hunting. When it came time to shoot, she would do something to deflect Far's aim. Although she says (mitigating somewhat Ib's harsher criticism) that Far allowed himself to shoot a really good deer only once a year, she still called his collections of trophies "the horror cabinet."

Hunting was not the only sport at Chossewitz. The usual rash of practical jokes were also indulged in. Members of the family were customarily safe from the famous sense of mischief, but not the honored guests. One entire evening was spent with other guests nervously watching what they said or did in the presence of a celebrated soprano. Lauritz had secretly instructed the servants to tell his guests that she was a madwoman whose particular delusion was that she could sing.

With all the joy that Chossewitz gave the Melchiors, they had more important things on their minds in 1932. What would be the reaction of the world's great opera companies now that Lauritz Melchior no longer sang at the Bayreuth Festspielhaus or any other German houses? Where could a Heldentenor go when Germany was not an option? Would he be able to make a living elsewhere? Kleinchen brought her list of other Wagnerian singers at the Met up to date. Kirchhoff and Taucher were gone but Laubenthal still lingered. A new heroic tenor, Max Lorenz, Melchior's friend from the Grenzebach studio and from Bayreuth, had debuted on November 12 as Walther von Stolzing. A serious artist, an intelligent musician, he possessed a tone quality generally regarded in America as "hard and unyielding," although he was much admired in Europe, where he sang many Italian dramatic roles as well. Still, in the rapidly changing Metropolitan scene, the number of Lauritz's performances would increase each year until he was singing twenty-two times during the 1933–1934 season.

As for Paris, Lauritz was booked in each of Jacques Rouché's June Wagner Festivals, which would go on, against all odds, until the Nazis put an end to it. During these performances, the conductor was often Furtwängler, who was allowed by the Nazis to participate. (Lauritz always found it very hard work to sing with Furtwängler because—as Leider said—he fretted so about his own reputation that he insisted on rehearsing too much.) Melchior would also be booked for a yearly concert in Paris, as well as operas in the winter season. After his three 1934 performances of *Siegfried* with the

Paris Opéra, the French critic wrote, "Never did we hear a Siegfried more brilliant."

Antwerp and Brussels offered both opera and orchestral engagements. In 1934 Melchior sang Siegfried in Brussels. It was at Brussels' Théâtre Royal de la Monnaie that the Melchiors first met Kirsten Flagstad, although she made little impression on them at the time. Melchior had been, said Flagstad, "very helpful" and "as usual, in excellent humor." Lyons and Bordeaux offered opera engagements every year, Monte Carlo almost every year.

Copenhagen behaved as did the other major capitals. They invited Melchior to sing often, perhaps the most important appearances being two performances of *Siegfried* in January of 1932. It was his first chance to sing the opera with fellow Danes and the first time for singing Siegfried before his "fellow townsmen." Johan Hye-Knudsen (who did not much appreciate being addressed as "Mr. Toscanini") was the conductor on both occasions, but the casts differed. On January 1, at the "New Year Levee," Kammersanger Lauritz Melchior received one of his most prized decorations: King Christian X of Denmark made him a Knight of Dannebrog (or a Knight of the Danish Flag). After the ceremony he and Kleinchen were invited to lunch at the Amalienborg Palace. Teasingly he warned his wife about behaving herself this time. In 1930 when Lauritz had been named Kammersanger, Kleinchen had enjoyed the "good lunch with caviar," and had found the king, even taller than Lauritz, "so cheerful and so cordial." While answering a question posed by the monarch, however, she had, in her fractured Danish, made an inadvertent scatological remark. The king had laughed so hard that he almost fell off his chair.

Munich presented Melchior in concert and Vienna engaged him for five performances of five different Wagnerian operas during September 1934. After these performances, a critic from the *Neue Presse* remarked, "His international monopoly [of Heldentenor roles] becomes understandable."

Covent Garden remained loyal, engaging Melchior every season until the outbreak of World War II put an end to their German season. Awaiting Melchior in the spring of 1932 was a pleasant surprise, and Covent Garden's financial problems were the indirect cause. Since his first appearance there in 1924 the conducting chores had always been shared by Bruno Walter and Robert Heger. This year Bruno Walter was gone and in his place, as financial contributor as well as principal conductor, was Lauritz's old friend from Bayreuth Sir Thomas Beecham.

With Beecham's return to Covent Garden restoration of the opera season's prewar glitter was complete. Journalists reported on the long lines of limousines and taxis, the crowded vestibule and staircase, the gallery packed a full half hour before curtain, the crimson auditorium filled once again with elegant women and eminent men, the attendance of the king and queen at Lauritz's *Tannhäuser*, and the cheers from the gallery that met Sir Thomas when he appeared in the pit.

During their comradely gatherings in Bayreuth, Lauritz had found Bee-cham a charming social companion. Because he had behaved rudely to Hitler, Beecham had become persona non grata at Wahnfried, thereafter spending much of his time in the company he preferred, that of the singers and instrumentalists at the restaurant *Die Eule* (The Owl). This simple wood and plaster building, which still stands at 8 Kirchenstrasse, was the scene of many convivial gatherings that Beecham, like Siegfried Wagner, democrat-ically attended. Beecham the British conductor, however, proved vastly dif-ferent from the Beecham whose sense of humor had endeared him to the musicians at Bayreuth. Rudolf Bing would later describe Beecham as "an impossibly charming and impossibly difficult man." Yet, even when his famous temper was raging, Beecham would manage to elicit from the or-chestra a wonderful support for the singers he liked, one of whom was Lauritz, judging by a story Lauritz told often. During the supper interval for *Tristan und Isolde*, Sir Thomas would invite Melchior into his dressing room and treat him to fine French champagne. As they toasted and drank, the conductor admitted that Lauritz was virtually the only Wagner singer he could stomach. (Probably, Lauritz was also the only Wagnerian singer who could be given champagne during the interval and still be counted on to sing the next act in full command of his powers.)

Melchior was willing to limit himself to "pints of grapefruit juice" in his dressing room, where he was "scantily clad," surrounded by many friends keeping him company, and with Kleinchen busily autographing pictures with her husband's name, writing letters, or meeting with her London broker. The Covent Garden *Tristan* production Lauritz found too dry, however. The newly constructed ship in Act I of *Tristan* was placed in such a way that Tristan and Kurvenal were required to go on board before the curtain rose, and to sit there for an entire half-hour while Isolde and Brangäne sang. No longer could Melchior slip off stage, drink several more pints of grapefruit juice, and return just in time for his second scene, without the audience seeing him wade through the "ocean." The tenor lamented bitterly to Sir Tommy that he and Herbert Janssen had nothing to do back behind the mast. His suggestion was pure Melchior: "I think we deserve to have a drink served there." The answer was also pure—one might almost say vintage—Beecham: At the next performance there were two glasses and a bottle of excellent champagne waiting behind the mast.

Some years later Melchior overheard a young colleague telling about the best performance of *Tristan* that he had ever taken part in. It was at Covent Garden, where he found behind the mast—to his amazement and delight—an uncorked bottle of chilled champagne and two glasses. The di-rection inscribed in the stage manager's book, at the order of Sir Thomas, had become tradition!

Melchior's quest to sing Otello in the United States was given fresh impetus by an invitation to sing two concerts in Italy during November 1931, one a recital at the Conservatorio Santa Cecilia, and one at the Augusteo under the baton of Maestro Bernardino Molinari. Lauritz bragged a bit about the press response to his *Otello* arias: The Italian critics advised young singers to listen to this exemplar of "beautiful Italian language" and style.

Upon his return to the Metropolitan in February 1932, Melchior, observing Gatti-Casazza's good mood caused by the first broadcast from the Met stage, seized the opportunity to raise again the subject of singing Verdi. This time his arguments were more powerful: He knew all of *Otello* in Italian, and the Italian review from Rome had been unexceptionable. Covent Garden believed in him sufficiently to engage him to sing the role with *Italian* colleagues! Once more Gatti firmly repeated his original statement: the Met didn't need another Italian tenor, and they did need Melchior in the German wing. This time Melchior was prepared with the clinching argument: Martinelli had a desire to sing Tristan. "Let Martinelli have a go at *Tristan* and give me an *Otello*," said Lauritz. Alarmed and shocked, Gatti refused, revealing his true feelings about operatic repertoire: "I can't have Martinelli ruining his voice by singing Wagner!" (Indeed, he never did let Martinelli sing Tristan.)

Lauritz was doubly disappointed at not being given an *Otello*, because he had been working very hard at his Italian, necessary for him to do his Verdi roles in the international houses. A little man named Loria was his Italian teacher. Melchior had run across Gaetano Loria at Covent Garden, where the Italian taught French and Italian diction and interpretation. Previously Loria had taught "poetical declamation" to an impressive list of Italian opera stars—Caruso, Cavalieri, and Muratore—and later at the de Reszke Academy in Paris. Melchior's *Otello* score shows us that Signor Loria really knew his business. Inside the front cover is a lengthy document entitled "The role of Otello in Italian with character as described by Boito. Also with the English translation word by word; a reconstructed and free translation; hints on pronunciation; hints on phrasing, tone of voice and scenic action [extracted from Boito's and Victor Maurel's documentary sources] for the private and exclusive use of Mr. Lauritz Melchior."

Even with Loria's help and his own hard work, Lauritz's Italian was often criticized (though mostly by non-Italian critics), sometimes even called slovenly. It seems that his Italian had some of the faults evinced by many German singers who try the language (such as *appasso* for *abbasso*) whereas, as Conrad L. Osborne noted,

> Melchior's identification with the German language was complete. It is not that he merely pronounced it and enunciated it almost perfectly. He used every vowel to musical effect and employed the very consonants that choke many singers to lend a word forward thrust. . . . Though the Italian language gave him difficulty, the Italian style did not.

On the whole, critical opinion (particularly in later years when reissues of all Melchior's *Otello* excerpts were available) leans toward the belief that the 1943 Italian-language excerpts were not as fine as the German ones from 1930, when, as Osborne said,

> Melchior's unmatched tenor had all the juicy resonance and pliancy of his youthful prime. . . . He brings to these excerpts a musical and interpretive integrity beyond praise. . . . I would not hesitate to term his voicing of the monologue as the greatest ever recorded, every note of it sung, not ranted, very beautifully sung and with the most poignant inflection of the words. The effect of this bel canto treatment is infinitely more moving than the most carefully conceived parlando interpretation. If the whole of Melchior's Otello was ever up to this level, then it was certainly a genuinely great achievement.

His quest not deflected by Gatti's refusal, Melchior could scarcely wait to do his *Otello* at Covent Garden. In the spring of 1933 he sang the title role in an all-Italian cast with Rosetta Pampanini as Desdemona and Antonino Votto as the conductor. Melchior received great praise, of which he valued most that of Ernest Newman, the dean of British critics and a real Wagnerite. Ironically, Newman, who had never appreciated Melchior very much as a Wagnerian tenor until the *Tristan* of 1931, found that, as Otello, he was "holding his own beautifully among the Italians." While other critics called his work the best of the Italian season, some members of the audience received with great hostility his singing of the role in German.

Thanks to his work with Loria, by 1934 Melchior was prepared to sing the role in Italian for the first time. Beecham conducted Lauritz's three performances of *Otello* (as well as *Fidelio* with Lotte Lehmann and new productions of *Götterdämerung* and *Siegfried* with Frida Leider). Said the *Times*, "His voice has not that rich and effortless tone for which Verdi wrote, but his commanding qualities of voice and style make themselves felt and are completely admirable." Melchior found it very interesting

> to sing an Italian operatic role in the Italian language. . . . It was rather difficult for me, since I did not speak Italian. Even if I sang the role reasonably well, I think that there were many mistakes in the text. Also my way of singing was not common to Italian ears, and I imagine that I was not absolutely an Italian's idea of an Otello.

The British were again critical of his Italian when he again sang *Otello* with Maria Caniglia in 1939, complaining that "Melchior's Italian sounded not one whit better than it had in 1934."

San Francisco, however, welcomed his Otello in the fall of 1934 and responded with enthusiasm: "His Otello will go down in the history of the San Francisco Opera"; "he sang like a God." Lauritz felt sure that the excellent reception he was accorded as Otello in London and now in San

Francisco would sway Gatti-Casazza to cast his Heldentenor in something other than Wagner.

Gatti's refusal this time was due to two new factors: He had now made public his determination to resign after this season, his twenty-seventh with the Metropolitan. (The board of directors had known of his intention for two years, but persuaded him to remain while they sought his successor.) The Melchior/Otello problem could safely be relegated to the new administration. The second factor that stiffened Gatti's resolve, ironically, was the very popularity, newly won, of Wagnerian opera among the "ordinary" audiences. This Met season, the shortest in almost forty years, was historically noteworthy for another reason. The opera company was forced to depend utterly upon its general audience, and those standing in line at the box office were not there to buy tickets for Italian operas but for Wagnerian music-dramas.

At the start of the 1933–1934 Metropolitan season, Lauritz's happiness was complete. Frida Leider, his ideal Isolde, had returned; Lotte Lehmann, superb at those lighter roles that Leider no longer wished to sing, had arrived. Eventually all his very favorite singers would be at the Metropolitan, as critic Desmond Shawe-Taylor has pointed out:

> The singers whom Melchior called his friends had been singing together in London, Berlin and Bayreuth—eventually the Met—since 1924, creating with their ensemble a great period for Wagner. . . . Lehmann, Schumann, Leider, Olczewska, Janssen, Bockelmann, Schorr, and Kipnis, the list is staggering and went far to remove objections usually leveled against an "all-star cast."

On three continents, Melchior and his colleague-friends worked as "all-star" Wagnerian casts in well-nigh perfect artistic harmony.

Lehmann's New York debut as Sieglinde, with Melchior as her Siegmund, took place on January 11, 1934, when she was forty-six years old. Not only Lauritz fell in love with her; the critics, and the public, were enchanted with her: "The whole audience broke into cheering which lasted for ten minutes."

Lauritz and Lotte Lehmann had enjoyed singing together since their 1927 *Walküre* at Covent Garden, where they subsequently sang in *Tannhäuser*, *Fidelio*, and *Lohengrin*. Anyone who knew Melchior well would agree that Lotte Lehmann was his favorite soprano. Onstage, he found her irresistible. Lauritz was always outspoken about her; for example, years later he gave Leonard Eisner a curiously unsophisticated description of Lotte as "not just motherly as we now know her, once very active in men/women affairs." Another time, he pointed out (without a trace of disapproval) that Lehmann, whom he liked so much, had indulged in great flings in her youth. "She was quite a girl in her day, but has settled down now." Possibly his appreciation of his "adorable Sieglinde" was even enhanced by that side of her nature. During Lauritz's marriage to Kleinchen there was never a word of gossip about infidelity, but before—and even after—those years some innuendos were made, even in his old age. Certainly he never failed to pay serious and courtly attention to beautiful women.

Lehmann clearly returned his affection, for example, greeting him in her letters, *"Mein lieber* [my dear] *Siegmund,"* and closing equally often with *"Deine* [thy] *Sieglinde."* She also valued his professional counsel. When, in 1930, she was toying with the idea of learning Isolde, she pressed Lauritz for advice. Franz Schalk had insisted that she could do it, but only if she would be reasonable and restrain herself by husbanding her voice. But Lotte wanted to "enjoy it completely, to be able to act and sing that marvelous part without moderation or restraint." Lauritz, however, had aligned himself with Leo Slezak (who was horrified at the thought) and warned Lotte most strenuously against doing the role.

It is strange to contemplate the picture of this highly sophisticated woman, "the epitome of everything one means by Viennese aristocracy, charm and friendliness" (as Ivor Newton described her persona onstage and off), being attracted to the portly, fun-loving, slightly naive, unintellectual, hedonistic, game-playing, but supremely talented Heldentenor. A handsome and intelligent woman, she habitually eschewed the usual gossip of operatic circles, preferring to discuss painting, art, composers, acting, or music in general—subjects on which she spoke with considerable authority. She was a dedicated musician, something Melchior was never called, although he appreciated these superior facets of Lehmann's character. Her presence on stage stimulated his performance, and he recognized it. A 1935 New Year's Day *Tannhäuser* is an example of a performance in which the loving compatability between Melchior and Lehmann, clearly perceived, had the critics cheering:

> The electrifying spark which set off everything at white heat was the superb performance of Mme. Lotte Lehmann as Elisabeth. Responding to the contagion of her magnetic personality, the other principals gave of their best because they simply couldn't help it. Sparks flew at times with the fervor of Mr. Melchior's singing. . . . [He] sang with genuine tragic power.

Kleinchen was not entirely uncritical of Lehmann's work. Of the soprano's 1926 Manon Lescaut in Vienna, she wrote in her diary, "Lehmann does not fit . . . in the role. She lacks temperament and sensuality." According to Ignace Strasfogel, Lehmann was also somewhat censorious of Kleinchen: "[Lehmann] was a purist in certain matters. Her character was the opposite from Rabelaisian and not realistically inclined, and she knew that Kleinchen's was. They got along perfectly well, but Lehmann was altogether opposite in nature from Kleinchen." On the other hand, this perhaps explains the real friendship between Kleinchen and Frida Leider, whom Gaisberg called "harsh and intransigent in business."

Although Kleinchen was not as fond of Lehmann as of Leider, that did not mean she would miss an opportunity when it presented itself. One day press photographers came to the Met to take pictures of Lotte Lehmann. Kleinchen, on the alert, tried to keep her husband before the cameras, too, but was foiled by a young woman who cleverly rearranged the group, excluding Melchior from the picture. Kleinchen asked Lotte who she was. She was, said Lotte, Constance Hope, her personal publicity agent. Kleinchen was so astonished that she could barely speak, but it was from Lehmann, a newcomer to America, that she learned what "personal publicity" was. Constance Hope and her partner, Edith Behrens, had told Lehmann that opera singers had a difficult time of it in America. They were destined to be less than famous because very few Americans—only those in New York, Chicago, and San Francisco—attended the opera. In Europe, where the greatest opera singers were idolized by the entire population, it was different, of course. Yet Constance had assured Lotte that enough "publicity"—pictures and articles about a singer—could make an operatic artist famous, even here in America. Lehmann agreed, simply wanting to help the two nice girls who had just started their own business. Artists' representative Thea Dispeker, who knew her professionally, says that Constance Hope invented the idea of personal publicity.

Kleinchen immediately saw the possibilities, and she determined that Lauritz also must purchase this precious commodity, this "personal publicity." Fixing her eye on those lucrative American radio contracts, she had long since come to the conclusion that opera singers must be truly renowned before they would be invited to appear on radio. Although organizations such as the Metropolitan had employed a public relations manager, individual musicians had not thought to hire their own personal publicity representative.

As his new publicity team swung into action, Lauritz was immediately impressed by journalists' interest in what he had to say. Constance Hope must have sensed a great opportunity when, later in January, "someone" persuaded Melchior to go public with a manifesto he had delivered before the Wagner Society. The resulting squib—"Lauritz Melchior Asks Cuts in Wagner Operas—Leading Wagnerian Tenor of Metropolitan Advocates Wagner Society to Direct Work of Making the Great Music-Dramas Shorter and More Enjoyable for Average Opera-Goer"—touched off a critical barrage. Lawrence Gilman obviously believed the piece to be the product of a "spokesman," as he made clear in a lengthy February rebuttal to a debate that had been raging since January 23. He began by quoting Melchior's words from the offending release:

An American Wagner Society . . . could . . . secure great musicians to cut Wagner's works with skill and understanding so that they would make an average evening's entertainment and retain at the same time their grandeur and nobility. . . . Wagner is too long for the average operagoer. . . . The operas must be brought within the orbit of the average man who works all day and seeks two or three hours' entertainment in the evening. . . . I have no patience with those who shout, "Let us not touch a single note," and prefer to have the public ignore Wagner entirely.

Gilman then took Melchior to task for his failures: not stating that most Wagner scores were already liberally cut in most opera houses; not realizing that it is probably a mistake to offer Wagner's more formidable music-dramas to the average opera subscriber at all (abridged or not); not taking into account that Wagner intended his audiences to come to performances with a special mental attitude; and assuming that these works could be regarded as "diversions." Gilman suggested that the many magic potions Melchior had imbibed during his performances had befuddled his thinking. As "constructive criticism" (but, in fact, with devastating sarcasm), he offered his own plan for fitting *Tristan und Isolde* into the tempo of modern life: That formidably long opera could be cut to a total performing time of 27 minutes and used as a curtain-raiser for *Pagliacci*—but he and other Wagner-lovers would stay at home to peruse the score.

Lauritz (tutored by Bayreuth's best) defended himself by publicly pointing out that Richard Wagner had shared his point of view. Always worried about the audience being bored, Wagner had written three times (in 1861, 1864, and 1865) to Ludwig Schnorr von Carolsfeld about "the necessary shortening of *Tristan*." Cosima herself, according to Lauritz, was known to quote her husband's acceptance of the great difference between the conception of the artistic idea and its performance in the theater, as well as his belief that *Tristan* could possibly end with the second act, and the fact that he was contemplating cutting the entire third-act monologue!

Melchior's statements created a fresh surge of newspaper attention all over the United States. Several scholars came forward to support his position. A former student of de Reszke assured Melchior in print that one of Wagner's favorite conductors, Anton Seidl, and the great tenor had cut Wagner. W. J. Henderson, who treated Melchior's idea seriously, recalled an anecdote from the first Bayreuth Festival, when an eminent German critic complained of Wotan's lengthy monologue from Act II of *Walküre*, "If it is absolutely necessary that Brünnhilde should know all this, why doesn't Wotan buy her a libretto of *Das Rheingold* and let her read it between the acts?"

Loud protests came from Wagnerites across the country. The *Cleveland News* was disapproving. One might "as well knock another hunk off the Venus de Milo because she looks lopsided" it reported. "The great aim of getting tired businessmen in bed by midnight is a worthy one," was the snide rejoinder of the *Buffalo Times*. The foremost American Heldentenor, Paul Althouse, observed that to a non-Wagner-minded public, "even *cut* Wagner is apt to seem long and dreary," that education was the only answer to a public that "was not prepared to traverse the long stretches of musical scenery between the mountain peaks." Conductor Walter Damrosch considered it a mistake to offer Wagner to the average opera subscriber at all, and curtly stated that "the musical population of New York might be estimated at one percent." Fritz Reiner, Lotte Lehmann, and Sir Henry Wood (chiming in from England, where the brouhaha had penetrated) came out in favor of Melchior's plan, calling it "not nearly so revolutionary as it sounds."

Newspapermen seemed inspired by the subject to new flights of rhetoric, as in Gilman's felicitous phrase "[Melchior came west] to exhibit his zeal for Wagnerectomy." The war of words sputtered on into March, when the last half of the month was occupied with another publicity-generating idea. Melchior and others launched a competition for young tenors to determine the American heroic tenor of tomorrow. An all-star panel of judges—an array that included opera singers, two concert managers, three conductors, one composer (oddly enough, Arnold Schoenberg, then teaching in Boston)— provided their own aura of glamour. The contestants were so colorful that one might almost suspect them of being handpicked by Hope and Behrens. A theater doorman, an army officer, a civil engineer, a poultry-man, a garage man, and a bootblack, among 167 other entrants, inspired the press to total coverage. One reporter valiantly questioned why, if heroic tenors are so scarce, a public competition would be likely to find one. Perhaps that question was partly answered when the winner collected his Knabe grand piano and was never heard of again.

The economic facts of the 1933–1934 season at the Met had not escaped Gatti's attention. Observing that the Wagnerian operas, manned by superb casts, were being supported by the general audience upon whom the Met must now rely, he requested that Melchior and Leider return earlier the following year and stay longer. Melchior accepted at once, and happily, but Frida Leider had a problem—Adolf Hitler.

Hitler, who by June 1934 had assumed the office of president as well as chancellor, brought with him as his minister of cultural affairs, the notorious Hermann Göring. Göring immediately prohibited artists of the state opera from being given leaves of absence to perform in the United States. Since a longer period at the Metropolitan would conflict with Leider's Berlin Staatsoper contract, she was forced to choose between America and her native Germany. She said no to the Metropolitan and never returned. To Kleinchen she confided her fears that permission to sing in London and Paris would soon be withdrawn. There was nothing to do, wrote a saddened Frida to the Melchiors, but to stay in Berlin. Of her stay in New York there remained only eulogies, such as Pitt Sanborn's remarks about her *Walküre* Brünnhilde: "I suspect one would have to go back to Lilli Lehmann to find another soprano who has delivered the music with such perfection of phrasing and shading, so sure a sense of design, such subtlety and such nobility of expression, and so firm a control of her vocal resources."

True to his promise to Gatti, Melchior returned early to the Met in November 1934, considerably let down by the thought of being without Frida as his Isolde, but buoyed up by his many engagements outside the Metropolitan. St. Louis had presented him in two orchestral concerts before he went to San Francisco for one performance of *Otello* and two of *Tannhäuser*, making his debut there in the latter role on November 26. A concert tour—his first American tour since the 1926–1927 season—filled in the time before his prestigious Chicago debut as Tristan. Of this performance, one critic wrote that Melchior "is the great Tristan of this era, going to depths of tradition for the part and executing a monumental role with the freshest and most finished use of a virile and expressive voice."

Most importantly, the Melchiors' ambitions began to be realized with Lauritz's first American radio broadcast on January 27, 1935, when he sang three big Wagnerian arias on the "General Motors Hour." The next month he joined Rose Bampton in the radio studio to do *Samson et Dalila*, in English. (This was the only time he sang that role in America, and it must have been a refreshing respite from the same six Wagnerian parts in which he was repeatedly cast.)

Both Lauritz and Kleinchen were delighted by Melchior's new status and especially by the prospect of further radio work. In fact, the only disappointments he had sustained were the continued rejection of his pleas to sing *Otello* at the Met, and the postponement of the role of Florestan, which was even written into Melchior's 1934–1935 contract but never done.

Who is to say how much of Melchior's new and wider acceptance by impresarios in the United States was due to the efforts of Constance Hope? Clearly she had done her work well: She had accurately assessed what it would take to interest the wider American public in an opera singer and made Melchior well known across the country. Melchior's career was poised on the brink of a higher success than he or his advisers realized.

CHAPTER 10

The Golden Years

(1935–1939)

The mid to late 1930s were probably Lauritz Melchior's most important years as a Heldentenor. He had never been better as an artist, and much of his lasting legacy of recordings was done at this time. The decade not only saw Melchior in the best vocal form of his life, but it was a period during which the German wing at the Metropolitan Opera became preeminent. For the first time the American public began to go to hear Wagner with the same appetite they had once reserved for Verdi and Puccini. The everyday Wagnerian casts, which "now read like operatic mythology," were arguably some of the best in the world. Although Melchior may have been the finest Heldentenor, there were many other accomplished heroic tenors available. The steady stream of great Wagnerian sopranos and contraltos available to the Met was by any standards astonishing. The same can be said for the heroic baritones, basses, and Spieltenors. To assemble a legendary cast of impeccable artistry was not an incredible feat but simply a matter of matching schedules.

Another factor of great import was the rising influence of the Metropolitan radio broadcasts and the publicity they generated. Radio was creating a new audience for opera in the outlying regions of the United States, and publicity techniques were making celebrities out of operatic artists who had been virtually unknown previously unless they were fortunate enough to be recording or movie artists. The culmination of these trends is probably best seen in the performance of December 21, 1936, when the Metropolitan Opera opened with a German opera for the first time since 1901.

The spring of 1935 was blessed by the presence at the Met of a matched, and matchless, pair of Wagnerian titans: Lauritz Melchior and Kirsten Flagstad. In January the Melchiors learned that Gatti had engaged a Norwegian soprano to replace the absent Frida Leider. They had encountered this Kirsten Flagstad briefly in Brussels the previous year when Lauritz was rehearsing *Siegfried* as she had been performing Sieglinde with Lauritz's friend,

Gotthelf Pistor. The Melchiors knew as little of Flagstad as did the rest of the American public.

The Norwegian soprano was thirty-nine years old, and had sung a total of thirty-eight roles in operetta, oratorio, and opera over the preceding twenty-one years. When the Met engaged her she had been ready to abandon singing in favor of a second marriage, wanting to be together with her husband of only three years, Henry Johansen. Flagstad, it was said, had continued to sing only because it pleased her new husband.

The relative obscurity of her name and talents, even at this age, was attributable to an accident of fate. Back in 1929 Otto Kahn, who always listened purposefully to foreign singers during his travels abroad, had heard the young Flagstad singing *Tosca*. He then urged the Met to write and arrange for an audition, but the singer neglected to answer the Met's request for information and nothing came of this correspondence. Not until 1932 did word of her fine Wagnerian soprano filter its way to Bayreuth, where Tietjen and Winifred Wagner eventually auditioned her.

Flagstad described her Bayreuth audition for Lauritz after they became friends. Like him, she had been hired on the spot, and, under Karl Kittel, went through a strenuous period of indoctrination into the Bayreuth way of singing Ortlinde and the third Norn, two lesser roles. Returning to sing Sieglinde the following summer, she was heard by the agent Erich Simon, who must have reported his findings, as usual, to Bodanzky. Bodanzky bade her come to his summer home in St. Moritz, to audition before himself, Gatti, his wife, and Simon. The group thought that she sang with insight and intelligence, but, thanks to the heavily carpeted hotel room, with a small voice. Needing her to fill out the roster, which was depleted by Frida Leider's resignation and not quite covered by the six-week contract of newcomer Anny Konetzni, Gatti signed Kirsten Flagstad for one season to sing Isolde and the three Brünnhildes.

The Norwegian soprano made her Metropolitan debut on February 2, 1935, as Sieglinde. Paul Althouse was her Siegmund, with Friedrich Schorr, Emmanuel List, and Gertrude Kappel rounding out the cast. During a *Götterdämmerung* rehearsal (there was none scheduled for *Walküre*), Althouse missed his cue from sheer wonder at Flagstad's voice; Bodanzky, afraid to believe what he was hearing, put down his baton and rushed out to find Ziegler, to have him come listen. The press had paid only perfunctory advance attention. At her debut matinee, however, news of the astonishing events on stage swept through the building before the second act began, and the listening public was alerted to the extent of Flagstad's triumph by soprano Geraldine Farrar's intermission comments. It is doubtful that even Gatti himself recognized what a jewel he had found. Between acts of the debut *Walküre*, his ex-wife, soprano Frances Alda, called Gatti on his private line. "Who is that soprano?" she demanded "*Una certa Flagstad* [A certain Flagstad]," he answered with notable understatement. The reviews, however, were ecstatic—"an instantaneous and complete triumph."

Four days later Flagstad sang Isolde with Melchior and swept the audience and critics off their feet. Melchior, although a familiar face and voice, came in for his share of praise. "Certainly not since Jean de Reszke have we in New York known the vocal equal of this Tristan," said Sanborn. Downes admitted that because his article dealt "principally with a new singer, briefer mention is made here of Mr. Melchior's masterly treatment of his lines . . . the poignancy of the dialogue . . . the pathos and subtle vocal color," adding that Melchior's last act was "a triumph of great interpretation." As Kolodin concluded later, "the stimulating effect of Kirsten Flagstad's and Lehmann's presence were felt by Lauritz Melchior."

Flagstad appeared once more with Paul Althouse that spring—on February 15—and then sang the rest of the season only with Melchior. Lauritz finished that year as Flagstad's first Siegfried (in *Götterdämmerung*) and her first Metropolitan Tristan, Tannhäuser, Lohengrin, and Parsifal, but had to settle for being her second Siegmund in New York. They performed together sixteen times in the spring of 1935, making history every time.

On March 5 Melchior partnered Flagstad in her first American portrayal of Elsa—in Brooklyn, where the Met company often performed. She had been asked to do the role with four days' notice. Six years before she had sung Elsa in Norwegian, but she memorized the German text in a few days. It was all very well for Bodanzky to say, *"Die Kirsten kann alles* [Kirsten can do anything]," but Flagstad was also worried about having had, in usual Met style, no rehearsal. Lauritz, as always, was a staunch colleague. As she described it, "Melchior calmed me down and prompted me while I was on stage. 'Get up,' he whispered, 'Louder,' 'Come over here!.' 'Now go left!' He led me as in a dance."

Flagstad had totally captivated the entire Wagnerian public and the critics in a way unequalled at the Met in recent memory. Her colleagues, too, at once acknowledged the unique vocal presence that was Flagstad's. Strangely, however, the Melchiors did not instantly recognize the force she represented. Reviews of operas the two singers did together do not appear in Lauritz's enormous scrapbooks until a March 18 performance of *Lohengrin*. Presumably, it was only then that they began to perceive her importance as an artist. (Although he admired the amazingly big and beautiful voice and the assured technique of this woman whose great column of sound was seemingly inexhaustible, Lauritz tended to prefer the emotional depth of Frida Leider's performances, especially her Isolde.) As for the press, having exhausted their usual vocabularies of praise to describe the first few of Flagstad's performances, they were forced into encomiastic poetic and philosophical utterances with which to express their adoration of her talents. Lawrence Gilman, speaking of the 1935 Brooklyn *Lohengrin*, provides an example:

> That weary and jaded victim of a thousand deadening performances came suddenly to life . . . last evening. . . . This result was due in part to Mr. Melchior's Lohengrin which was sustained upon a rare level of

fervor and intensity . . . in part to the dramatic tension which Karin
Branzell . . . maintained throughout her great scenes in the second
act. . . . But it was the Elsa of Kirsten Flagstad . . . which raised last
night's performance to the plane of those occasional experiences which
give a new validity to the world of the imagination and the life of the
mind.

In the fall of 1935 Lauritz made his way to Chicago for a highly touted
concert with Kirsten Flagstad. Each of the two great stars was to do a solo
group, and together they would sing three big Wagnerian duets with Flagstad's accompanist, Edwin McArthur, at the piano. Despite a newspaper
campaign of huge proportions that had begun the previous summer, the
audience was inexplicably small. Critical success of the concert was absolute,
however: "What Mme. Flagstad and Mr. Melchior brought to Orchestra Hall
and to Wagner yesterday was sincerity and devotion, distinction of workmanship and the very peak of Wagner singing as it is to be found today."
Of personal concern to Lauritz was the strange behavior of Kirsten Flagstad.
Her manner seemed excessively reserved. Indeed, the Chicago concert was
not only their first together but would prove to be their last.

December of 1935, the start of Flagstad's second season at the Met,
marked the beginning of the avalanche of publicity that accompanied the
years of collaboration between the Norwegian soprano and the Danish tenor.
By today's standards of publicity for operatic personalities, with the possible
exception of Luciano Pavarotti, the scope of public interest in the Melchior-
Flagstad duo is staggering. Just in December Kirsten Flagstad appeared on
the cover of *Time*, and the glories of Chossewitz were celebrated in a complete
color spread by *House Beautiful*.

Despite all this attention, one facet of the two careers was overlooked
by the press—the timing. The timing of the productive years of each artist
is literally in the hands of fate. (It was, for example, too much to hope that
Birgit Nilsson's best years as Isolde should coincide with Lauritz Melchior's
best years as Tristan.) Yet the press did not comment on the happy coincidence of Flagstad's appearance at the Met with what were to be Melchior's
finest years. Possibly this was because there were many heroic tenors singing,
and no one was as yet excessively worried about the possibility of a lack of
partners for her.

Perhaps the biggest difference between the two artists and their respective Met careers was this: When Melchior first appeared in New York
he was an unformed and unfinished artist, having been a functioning Heldentenor for only two years. He polished his roles in full view of the Metropolitan audience, as he had first learned many of them before the Bayreuth
audience. Kirsten Flagstad, on the other hand, sang her first New York
appearance in full command of her powers. She had spent many years out
of the international limelight, working her way through a very broad collection of lighter roles, learning slowly to command some of the dramatic

soprano parts. Her magnificent debut inspired an explosion of admiration, whereas Melchior's debut had inspired only such words as "promising," and by the 1930s he was in many respects taken for granted as a familiar face and voice.

Some reviewers, however, kept a nice sense of perspective in the midst of the unbelievable, albeit well-earned, adulation surrounding Flagstad. On December 21 Lehmann and Melchior opened the broadcast season on NBC with *Lohengrin*. The *Times* found that Melchior sang "with a wealth of light and shade, splendor of tone, and significance of diction that were unforgettable."

This same December saw some caviling on the part of the critics with regard to the invincibility of Mme. Flagstad. Following the first *Tristan* of the 1935–1936 season on December 30, both Downes and Gilman complained that she was singing too many concerts, that her voice showed wear. The same reviewers acknowledged the contribution of Melchior in the operas they sang together. Said Downes:

> The Tristan of Mr. Melchior is one of the abiding glories of the Met stage. He sang his music with the loftiest feeling, the finest proportion. His stage demeanor is noble and his first act is as nearly the model of this role as seems likely to materialize in this day and age. His last act . . . is an achievement that surmounts every one of its immense difficulties and its interpretive responsibilities. It is great art, and the one possible preparation for Isolde's death.

Lauritz was, as always, an incorrigible teaser, and he did not recognize that his tomfoolery was an affront to Kirsten Flagstad's seriousness of artistic purpose. He began his habit of operatic teasing in Bayreuth of all places. There were several photographs taken of him there as he made an impish face, or sported a crazy accessory (like a derby hat) to dress up his Wagnerian wolfskins. His favorite musical moments for such pranks were those when Wagner calls for the soprano to stand in dignified immobility for long periods of time, preferably facing upstage while he was in the wings, but he had other methods as well. Once he horrified Frida Leider at Covent Garden. Coming on for her last scene as Brünnhilde, she slowly approached Siegfried's (Lauritz's) body: "I was absolutely shattered to see that it was not he, but a member of the chorus. I looked into the wings. There was Lauritz in a dinner jacket beaming at me. When he wanted to come on stage in evening dress to take the applause, I said a firm No."

Nonetheless Lauritz continued to believe innocently that these practical jokes pleased his leading ladies; perhaps he had been lulled into that misconception by Lotte Lehmann, who always thought him endearing and liked him too much to be judgmental. Kirsten Flagstad became extremely angry when faced with such unprofessional behavior, but in response, Lauritz teased her the more. Danish radio and recording producer Hans Hansen has his own theory about this:

> When Melchior was a motherless baby, everything he did was considered so wonderful by his family that he habitually, in later years, continued his childish kind of horseplay, even on stage during operatic performances. Some, like Flagstad, couldn't stomach this, but Lotte Lehmann loved it and loved Lauritz.

Lotte Lehmann may have regretted her inadvertent encouragement of his teasing habits on one occasion some years later at Melchior's California home. He had acceded to Lotte's request, inspired by modesty, to swim alone in the pool under cover of darkness. Once Lotte was enjoying the privacy of the pool, however, he turned on the underwater lights.

At this time Melchior found Flagstad shy and modest. Others judged her to be absolutely professional, pleasant, but stubborn and quick to take offense. The Melchiors admired the unfeigned amazement of her reaction to the outpouring of adulation from New Yorkers. Nevertheless, Lauritz and Kleinchen just couldn't keep up with her changing moods. They never knew what to expect, comradeship or indifference. Lauritz's own perennial good spirits were in some subtle way dampened by his inability to anticipate Flagstad's changes of humor.

Kleinchen had little time to brood over the recurring awkwardness of this relationship. Business was her first priority. Noting early in 1935 that the rarely performed *Fidelio* (which the Met had so often promised Lauritz he would sing in) was on the schedule for March of that year, she immediately assumed that it was being revived for Flagstad. Her well-developed business antennae dictated an investigation into the facts. Discovering that the tenor role of Florestan was to be sung by René Maison, new on the roster, she went immediately to the administration. There she was given an embarrassed but truthful answer: Flagstad had requested Maison. Kleinchen kept this unpleasant news from her husband as the 1935–1936 season proceeded.

In 1937 the ambiguous situation was resolved with a bitter quarrel that virtually called a halt to the friendship between Flagstad and the Melchiors. After a Metropolitan tour performance of *Lohengrin* in Rochester, New York, on April 18, 1937, a foursome composed of the Melchiors, Flagstad, and Edwin McArthur played bridge. The talk drifted to a discussion of certain current practices of the press with regard to the two prima donnas of the German wing, Lehmann and Flagstad.

Kirsten Flagstad had never needed nor hired a press representative. During the 1936–1937 season she began to see many gossipy items in the press asking the question, "Who is the prima donna at the Met?" Since each clipping sent by her service bore a marked resemblance to the others, she began to suspect that the items were planted. Similar comments in the corridors of the Met and in the trade papers annoyed her. As the bridge game continued, Flagstad began to make loud and tactless remarks about "phony promotion stunts," clearly implying that Constance Hope had something to do with these articles, and she vociferously expressed the wish that Lotte Lehmann's career could be built up without constant reference to Kirsten Flagstad as a rival for top of the prima donna list. Melchior was infuriated by the slight to Miss Hope and by Flagstad's insulting words about Lehmann. (Flagstad's diary entry for April 18, 1937, is cryptic, but includes three expressive exclamation marks: "April 18: bridge Melchiors and Edwin!!!").

The aftermath was an unbridgeable estrangement between the two artists. Idolized by a public that knew nothing of the hostility between them, the Wagnerian lovers kept up outward appearances of cooperation. Although mutual friends made repeated attempts to mend the relationship, it was never really repaired until long after their years of singing together. "She was a skilled singer, but not a warm-blooded woman," said Melchior, some years after her death.

Both artists' careers, however, were highly influenced by the results of the quarrel. The steadily increasing acrimony put an end to HMV's great plans to put entire Wagner operas, rather than excerpts, on the market. Offers from the important and lucrative music hours on radio had to be turned down by George Engels, agent for both singers, because Flagstad answered each query with a reiteration that she would neither make records with Melchior nor sing with him. Both the San Francisco and Chicago opera companies initially resisted her demands that Melchior not be cast with her; Chicago eventually capitulated. The Metropolitan temporarily placated the soprano by giving her *Fidelio* and *Der fliegende Holländer* for her own, knowing that Melchior could conveniently be eliminated from those operas without public outcry. Edward Ziegler was well aware that "sooner or later we have to face that situation," and pushed Johnson to hire another Heldentenor. If the Met had no tenor other than Melchior to sing Siegfried and Tristan, how then could they accommodate Flagstad's wish to sing with someone else? Taking Melchior's own advice to look in Scandinavia for new singers, Johnson did engage Carl Hartmann during the summer.

Hartmann, brought to the Met to be an alternate Siegfried and Tristan, made his debut in the role of Siegfried in December 1937. Found "personable, commanding in stature, virile and graceful in action, with a mobile and expressive countenance," he apparently possessed "imagination, a sense of humor, [and] a right instinct for the color and implications of a mood." The voice, however, was "not embarrassingly sensuous in quality," a phrase which must be saluted as a brilliant euphemism. Hartmann was a partial answer to Flagstad's aversion to Melchior. She sang *Tristan*, *Tannhäuser*, and *Walküre* with him, and another *Walküre* with Althouse.

When Kleinchen, who deplored the childish stubbornness of both, finally confessed to her husband the real facts behind Flagstad's behavior, Lauritz could not believe that Flagstad would allow their personal problems to interfere with career decisions. He asked her bluntly whether it was true that she did not want to sing with him. Equally outspoken, she said that she preferred to sing alone and be recognized alone, not everlastingly paired together with Lauritz Melchior. Lauritz responded sadly with a phrase he was henceforth to use often (even to Max Lorenz as late as 1967), "The opera is called *Tristan AND Isolde*, not *Tristan OR Isolde*, Kirsten."

Although it might appear that Flagstad was the more vindictive of the two, it does not necessarily follow that Melchior was the more generous, for he was actually in no position, despite his celebrity, to make similar demands. Flagstad, on the other hand, was beginning to take full advantage of her reputation. Early in 1938 she had empowered her management to begin discussions with the Met regarding her twenty-fifth anniversary as a singer, which was to be a performance of *Götterdämmerung* in December. Her sole condition was that the tenor on that evening not be Lauritz Melchior. The weapon she had selected against Melchior was effective—public and private humiliation. Surely everyone in New York, in the world, would question the absence of the foremost Heldentenor from the cast on the occasion of the world's most celebrated Wagnerian soprano's jubilee. (It worked. When, for example, Fred Gaisberg wrote of the great Wagnerian couple, he mentioned Melchior's absence from Flagstad's grand anniversary *Götterdämmerung*, mistakenly ascribing it, as did others, to a quarrel about "who deserved greater credit for the extraordinary success of their joint Wagnerian performances.")

As Lauritz grieved, Flagstad "gloated over the fact that she could . . . dictate the . . . cast for her twenty-fifth anniversary. She exulted in excluding Melchior from the cast," wrote her friend McArthur. Leaving aside the potent professional considerations, the punishment—being left out of the after-performance party—was exquisitely suited to Melchior's love of a grand celebration. Each person who worked for the company was included: ushers, telephone operators, stage doormen, cloakroom attendants, cleaning women, gofers, night watchmen, ticket takers, everyone but Lauritz Melchior.

Once Kleinchen had taken Kirsten Flagstad's true measure as an artist, she made her usual inquiries after the financial facts. Her sources were not as infallible as she might have believed, for they fixed Flagstad's cachet at $350 per performance, whereas in truth she was paid $550 per week for a guaranteed nine weeks, a figure that was to rise dramatically for the 1936–1937 season, a testament to her electrifying impact upon New York opera lovers.

An amusing feature of the 1935–1936 season was the banishment from the Metropolitan of the infamous "claque," those opera-lovers who make a business out of applauding efficiently for the artists who have paid them. (The claque's standard rates included a fee of $25 in exchange for two guaranteed curtain calls; succeeding bows were charged at a rate of $5.) When an attempt was made to outlaw the claque, it was discovered that feelings ran high on the subject. Some opera-lovers thought that the claque served a useful purpose; others abhorred the artificiality of purchased applause. Many felt that the American public didn't know how or when to clap, and needed an enlightened body of listeners to point out the great operatic moments. Removing the claque, in any case, would prove impossible, for keeping tickets out of the claquers' hands was hopeless, and educating the increasingly "popular" audience about opera etiquette was nearly as difficult.

When he first arrived at the Metropolitan, Lauritz told his son, he couldn't imagine why inferior singers were given so much applause by the audience, but that when the head of the claque arrived backstage to arrange a contract and collect from the new tenor, Lauritz finally understood. In the personal manuscript he wrote this about the claque in Vienna:

> The dreadful claque system I have always opposed, and I refused to pay for it here and later in other places where it was in use. I feel that if one sings so poorly that the audience boos you, a claque cannot help, and if one sings well, the audience will itself utter its satisfaction. Furthermore, there is very little opportunity for applause in the middle of the acts of Wagner's music-dramas, and an unmotivated applause will do more damage than good.

Kleinchen, as we have observed, never hesitated to keep unpleasant details from Lauritz while smoothing his path. His pious sentiment about not patronizing the claque was undermined by Kleinchen (who handled the money). She admitted in her diary that the Viennese "*chef de claque* got 100 Schillings, [because he] executed his job well."

As early as March 1933, Herbert Witherspoon—then the respected director of the Cincinnati Conservatory of Music and formerly a fine singer (he was a student of the great G. B. Lamperti)—had begun to marshall his forces to secure for himself the position that Gatti would be vacating in a year. He had enlisted in his campaign Percy Rector Stephens, president of the New York Singing Teachers Association, and John Erskine, president of Juilliard School, writing during this lively correspondence, "If we could win out on this thing I know we will have a new era and a chance to really develop American artists." His friends in turn had put pressure on Paul Cravath, president of the Met board.

On March 7, 1935, the Met's board of directors appointed Herbert Witherspoon the new managing director, to be assisted by Edward Johnson and Edward Ziegler. Gatti himself had recommended Johnson, a valuable

Metropolitan tenor, as his successor. Nevertheless the cabal formed two years previously won out, the Juilliard Foundation having bolstered its proposal of Witherspoon's name with a gift of $250,000 to be used for an extra spring season (which, as a compromise, Johnson would manage). In return for its help to the Metropolitan, the foundation extracted promises for a guarantee fund of $100,000, a vigorous campaign to increase subscriptions by ten percent, a supplementary season that would give opportunities to American singers, who were to be engaged for the regular season if they showed merit, a budget that showed a clear promise for breaking even, and three seats on the Met board set aside for members of the Juilliard Foundation board. Any failure to institute these reforms was to result in forfeiture of the promised funds.

Witherspoon began his duties before the singers left for the summer. He established Lauritz's fee for the new season at $1,000 (the former contract, dating from the Depression, had specified the strange sum of $1,080), while persuading Flagstad to accept a guarantee of 28 performances at $750 each. This was the last time that Flagstad received any fee below the very highest paid by the Met. In fact, Witherspoon, when he set a new top fee of $1,000, was taking the first step to show the board that he could mount superior productions while holding the budgetary line. Indeed, Witherspoon's handwritten ruminations on the budget noted that Melchior was now making more than twice any other tenor, $20,000 for the 1935–1936 season. (Martinelli was nearest with a yearly total of $7,500.) This circumstance did not please Witherspoon, as his notes make clear: "The great number of people employed in the opera during the past years is impossible for me to understand, and therefore I am certain that we can save money." At the same time, he was also contemplating cutting back from nine to five weekly performances with a top ticket price of $6.

Witherspoon was at the helm for a tragically brief time: on May 10, he died suddenly of a heart attack. Plans for the next season continued under the new administration, headed by Edward Johnson, who had inherited the permanent position. Johnson, a Canadian, was an elegant, courteous, cultivated, and sophisticated gentleman; after a sensationally successful career in Italy as Eduardo di Giovanni, he had returned to sing with distinction at the Metropolitan Opera. He had earned the respect of his fellow artists most of all for his unfailing ability to be "a good colleague" and, during his years as a primo tenore at the Met, helped to raise thousands of dollars with his before-the-curtain speeches. As the new general manager of the company he had great support from the board, the singers, the technical unions, the administration staff, the Guild members—even from the audiences. Responding to the news, Lauritz spoke well of him: "Both singers and public are fortunate that so fine an artist and so able an executive as Edward Johnson has taken on the duties of head of the Met."

By the spring of 1936 things were a bit different. Both Flagstad and Melchior were jockeying for the most advantageous contractual position.

Unlike his predecessor, Johnson had judged Flagstad's worth to the Met to be inestimable, and he wisely optioned her services for the next two years, acceding to the codicil that "If a higher fee is paid to any other artist, such a fee shall be substituted to apply on this contract." Melchior's new contract also contained such a proviso, undoubtedly with the impetus of Kleinchen's efficient information service. Once Lauritz was on top, she was not about to relinquish an iota of that advantage. The new Melchior contract included several other significant changes. For example, rehearsal time was reduced from two days to one day (now that he had perfected his roles, he began to appreciate the Met tradition of no rehearsals); the two Emergency Fund concerts were reduced to one only; and most important, the date on which he must be informed as to the exact dates of his engagement for the following season was changed from April 30 *back* to January 15. Flagstad had an identical arrangement. In the near future, this would prove to be of vital importance.

Edward Johnson inherited, along with his other duties, the Melchior/Otello contretemps. Critic B. H. Haggin of the *Brooklyn Eagle* noted a few continuing defects of the Metropolitan in March 1936: "And I have asked Mr. Johnson to be consistent. If he is willing to be a realist about *Carmen* with Miss Ponselle or *Rigoletto* with Mr. Tibbett, I want him not to be a perfectionist about *Otello* with Mr. Melchior." Presumably, these obscure references have to do with the fact that in each case the singer possessed some physical or vocal attribute that was not absolutely suited to the role mentioned. Evidently, however, the members of the music press wanted to hear Melchior sing Otello at the Met.

This active partisanship was an aftermath of the March 1935 Sunday evening concert, which took the form of a gala farewell to Gatti-Casazza. For the celebration Gatti had asked Martinelli and Pinza to sing a scene from *Lucia di Lammermoor* and requested that Flagstad and Schorr do the *Walküre* final scene. Now that Gatti was leaving, he felt free to ask (an elated) Lauritz to help celebrate this great evening by singing Act IV of *Otello* with Elisabeth Rethberg. Of Melchior's many versions of Gatti's words upon capitulating to the tenor's long-standing desire to sing the Verdi work at the Met, this is the one he seems to have relished: "I wanted you to sing this for a long time, but didn't dare because of the Italian wing."

A complete *Otello* had not been heard at the Met since Slezak did it twenty-two years before, and Lauritz was convinced that Otello might well be his very best role. When the critiques, published on March 20, his forty-fifth birthday, came in solidly for Melchior, his feelings were vindicated by their approval. Gilman said: "Mr. Melchior is a magnificent Otello. It is a pity that he has not sung the role before at the Met, for his performance last night brought down the house by its dignity, its passion, its restraint, its depth of feeling." Given such unqualified praise, who can fathom why the Met administration persistently denied Melchior the opportunity he so coveted—to sing roles other than those written by Wagner?

I never had the opportunity to sing [Otello] at the Metropolitan Opera, to my deep regret, since I find this role extremely interesting and am of the opinion that my interpretation of this character gradually became one of my best. Maybe I could have forced through a performance of the role at the Metropolitan, but to [put] pressure on a management has never appealed to me.

February 1935 was dominated by Lauritz's upcoming 100th performance of the young Siegfried. To mark the occasion Kenneth Lynch, scion of a 400-year-old family of metal craftsmen and the only American maker of medieval-style swords, fashioned a hand-wrought reproduction of an old Viking sword from the Metropolitan Museum of Art. Accompanying the Melchiors out to the Long Island workshop of Mr. Lynch were a crew from the Metrotone News and several members of the New York press, who decided that it would round out "the event" if Melchior were to sing the forging song from *Siegfried* for the cameras. To be sure of his pitch, Lauritz placed a phone call to Dorothée Manski's husband in New York. Four times Dr. Bransen gave the proper starting note on his piano over the open line while Melchior (as usual, thoroughly enjoying the occasion) obligingly sang four repeats of the "Forging Song" for the photographers.

On the afternoon of February 22, his 100th performance as Siegfried was followed by a backstage ceremony at which the Danish Consul-General, Georg Bech, formally presented Melchior with the new sword while Mayor Fiorello La Guardia, the Italian-American aficionado of Wagner, looked on. The hoopla did not obscure the singing:

His growth from season to season in this part has been so marked as to leave little basis for comparison between his Siegfried of today and that of ten years ago. Many another Heldentenor has counted his Siegfrieds in three figures, but it is not common experience to find the 100th performance better sung than the 20th. Bad vocal habits usually leave their mark before Siegfrieds have reached a normal maturity of their powers. The Danish tenor's voice was in its best estate. The tone was fresh, vital and pure.

There was always a polarization of views about Melchior's acting as Siegfried. The fashioning of the reed episode was "barely this side of clowning" to one critic but to another his "unaffected acting suggested the primal innocence of the forest child." Gilman once gently expressed his opinion that although Melchior as Siegfried might have "zest and humor and of poetry, a trace, . . . as a symbol of heroic youth, Mr. Melchior presents a considerable hurdle to the imaginations' vaulting eye." At the beginning of 1936 an "exuberant" *Siegfried* was well-received by some critics who seemed to enjoy "the robust good humor" of Melchior's collaboration with Marek Windheim as Mime. "[Melchior's] energetic deportment and the exuberance of his singing did much . . . to give the characterization of a working realism." Noel

Straus of the *Times* also approved of Melchior's Siegfried. Melchior's performance, he wrote in 1938, "was as fine as he can make it when at his best. It was a vocally eloquent and sensitively detailed portrayal, running the gamut of emotions from the heroic and impassioned to the boyishly tender or humorous with compelling ease and expressiveness."

During the Melchiors' absence from New York through the summer of 1935, the Metropolitan was cleaned, painted, and given new lighting. Grudgingly, a new, but useless, $200,000 "air-circulating system" (air-conditioning would have been too costly) had been installed at no expense to the boxholder-shareholders. Talk of a new 4,000-seat opera house was heard again. Ernst Lert, formerly a Met stage director under Gatti, maintained that Met productions still remained but "a variety show," despite having "the most experienced impresario, . . . lavishly paid conductor, . . . highly publicized star, . . . [or] bombastic scenic artist." Lert had routinely been given full responsibility—but no stage rehearsals—for the productions in his care, and his observations, echoing Witherspoon's concerns, presaged those of Rudolf Bing.

On December 18 Lauritz sang Siegmund as his first Met performance of the 1935–1936 season, an occasion made more glamorous by the debut of a new dramatic soprano, Marjorie Lawrence, as Brünnhilde. Jerome Bohm found her "comely to gaze upon, youthful, slender and tall," and her gestures "delivered with unerring dramatic instinct." Speaking of her voice, he was less enthusiastic. "The voice is large, powerful. . . . But its quality is not ingratiating." Another critic thought that Lawrence had "sung her way straight into the hearts of her New York audience," and Bagar contributed his opinion that "Mr. Melchior was at his best, which is very, very good." An Australian woman who had sung both mezzo-soprano and soprano roles, Lawrence had come to the Met by way of the Paris Opéra, where Lauritz had known her. He admired Lawrence as a wonderful actress—indeed thought her the best Ortrud—but frequently found himself wondering whether she had her voice under control in its now exclusively soprano Fach, because he had often noticed evidence of vocal fatigue by the end of the opera. (Doubtless his view was somewhat jaundiced, accustomed as he was to his own indefatigable power, and the incredible vocal stamina of Kirsten Flagstad.)

Exactly one year after Melchior's 100th Siegfried, in February, 1936, the Metropolitan was occupied with the preparations for his 100th performance of *Tristan*. By mistake the management went forward with plans to celebrate the occasion on February 14, although his 100th performance actually fell on the eighth. (Others might, but Lauritz would never miscount. At the beginning of each year, he would laboriously mark into his new daily diary, with a red pencil, all birthdays, debuts, and wedding anniversaries, and with a green pencil anniversaries of deaths in the family.) Before a press conference at the Ansonia Melchior enumerated some facts from his meticulously kept performance ledger: Although it was his 100th Tristan, it was only the thirty-fifth in New York. He had sung the role under twenty-two conductors (among them Toscanini, Blech, Bodanzky, Furtwängler, Kleiber, Schalk, Busch, Sébastian, Walter, Elmendorff, Pollak, and Beecham), in sixteen opera houses (including Berlin's two houses, Paris, Vienna, San Francisco, Copenhagen, Hamburg, Chicago, Barcelona, London, Bayreuth, New York, Buenos Aires, and Brussels), with thirty Isoldes, the most outstanding of whom were Leider, Flagstad, Kappel, and Larsén-Todsen.

As he told the reporters, Frida Leider had been his Isolde in one ill-starred *Tristan*. The two singers had just shared the love potion and stood transfixed for the breathless moments in which the essence of the tragedy is born. His suspenders chose precisely this moment to break. Pressing his legs together forcefully, Lauritz signaled Leider to come to him. From that point on, an unusually ardent Isolde made love to a stationary Tristan. (Of course, critics seized the opportunity to complain of his "wooden" acting.) Severely traumatized, Melchior subsequently designed the famous and elaborate corselette to hold up his armor.

On stage, after presentation of the Opera Guild's silver Tristan cup and an enormous, heart-shaped laurel wreath, Edward Johnson made a characteristically generous and graceful speech:

> I cannot say whether or not any previous heroic tenor ever succeeded in making a century mark in this tremendous and magnificent role, but I do know that this generation has been most fortunate in having had the occasion to hear a Tristan who possesses not only the vocal attainments and the *physique du rôle*, but also that quality of emotion and understanding which is absolutely necessary for a perfect rendition of this great lyric drama.

For all the attention that the Melchiors lavished on the exhausting events of the 100th Tristan, Lauritz had managed an appearance as guest artist for the Beethoven Association concert in Town Hall during the very same week, and demonstrated a command of the subtleties required of a recital singer. Melchior had now been singing a preponderance of stentorian Wagnerian roles for twelve years. Logic would dictate that his voice, influenced by the constant weighty delivery of the Heldentenor repertoire, would be finding it ever more difficult to manage the superfine shadings of songs. Yet, against all odds, his skills had not diminished. Taubman found him "able to adjust his style to the more intimate concert hall," and Kolodin expressed "regret that he is not heard more often in concert," citing his "subtlety of phrasing, variety of vocal color," and his "expressive and excellently controlled half-voice."

The week after these two events, the *New Yorker* issued this evaluation, which included an opinion about his non-Wagnerian talents:

> I [once] tried out what I imagined was a delightfully timely simile: "As friendless as a German operatic tenor at the Metropolitan Opera House."

German tenor was a generic term to cover singers of any nationality who happened to be working at Wagnerian roles and the simile retained its validity for about a year. Then Mr. Melchior of Denmark arrived to apply himself to German tenor roles and within another year the simile had become as dated as a play about a woman who smokes cigarettes. Last week was Melchior week even though there was no official pronunciamento, and Mr. Melchior not only sang Tristan for the 100th time in his career, but also helped out at the Beethoven Association, contributing two groups of songs. The ovations for Mr. Melchior, both as a Wagner tenor and as a *Liedersänger*, proved that if any vocalist about town is friendless it certainly isn't Mr. Melchior. In his own territory he's the greatest tenor of our time.

At the beginning of September 1936, in his fall appearance before the Metropolitan Opera Board of Directors, Edward Johnson demonstrated that he intended to take full advantage of the strong audience interest in the German wing, which was rapidly becoming the financial mainstay of the company. He announced that he had engaged several new Wagnerian singers and that the season would open with the public's favorite Wagner duo, Melchior and Flagstad, in *Die Walküre*—the first Metropolitan seasonal opening to present a German opera since 1901. It was believed that the larger Wagner audience was due in part to the rising number of German emigrés in New York. So strong was the trend that there were no longer any free tickets available to the staff for Wagner performances. (During the 1936–1937 season the Flagstad-Melchior duo was to garner for the company a gross of $150,000 in nine performances of *Tristan und Isolde*, a record for all the Broadway theaters. Doubtless it contributed to an end-of-the-year statement showing that the association was in the black for the first time since 1930, and by a gratifying fourteen percent.)

The cast Johnson presented on December 21, 1936, was splendid: Flagstad, Melchior, Rethberg, Kerstin Thorborg (in her debut), List, Schorr, and Bodanzky in the pit. Even before the premier, *Walküre* was a smash hit; hours before the box office opened, queues circled the block. After the performance, however, opinions about Melchior's vocal estate were as disparate as always. Downes said that while "it was distinguished by unusually fine proportions and carefully devised contrasts, more effective because of its fine simplicity and its merit of understatement . . . it was not Mr. Melchior's night, so far as his vocal condition was concerned." For another critic, "Melchior displayed his usual dramatic ineptitude, which probably would defy any stage director's care and foresight." Gilman thought that "Melchior sang with a lavish outpouring of his opulent voice . . . with a surge of passionate beauty." For Flagstad there was only praise.

The criticism of Melchior's dramatic ineptitude, and the predictable compliments to Flagstad's glorious simplicity and absence of excessive movement notwithstanding, the fact is that both Melchior and Flagstad, like others of the era, stood about semaphoring to each other. The amount of meaningful stage movement achieved by present-day Wagnerian principals is, by comparison, astonishing. Both Melchior and Flagstad had energy and strength to spare, and could have managed more, but stage directors, governed by lack of rehearsal time, asked only for the rigorously instilled, traditional Bayreuth attitudes.

When the dean of New York music critics, W. J. Henderson, gave Melchior perhaps the highest compliment possible, calling the tenor "a noble Tristan, the best the Met has known since Jean de Reszke," he used Act III of *Götterdämmerung* as an example, making it clear why de Reszke is constantly invoked in evaluations of Melchior to this day:

> The present writer has heard no delivery of the narrative of such absorbing character since that of Jean de Reszke. . . . [His] version was remarkable because of the astonishing ease and grace of its repetition of the bird music from *Siegfried*, a vocal tour de force in facile and flawless florid song. Mr. Melchior also sang this passage beautifully but his version won its hearers by exceptional variety and significance of elocutionary detail. It was dramatized with masterly insight and skill and communicated to the audience with an illusion of story-telling, certain to hold the listener breathless. . . . The last words . . . [were] profoundly moving, the utterance of a truly great Wagner singer.

The logistics of de Reszke's great career had impinged upon Melchior's life ever since his days with Victor Beigel. In Melchior's opinion he had heard altogether too much about de Reszke during the early part of his singing life. (Today's young Heldentenors undoubtedly have suffered in the same way from the constant invocations of Melchior's name.) Another Tristan had not been accepted worldwide since de Reszke's (last performed at the Metropolitan in 1901), and Melchior enjoyed the comparisons now that they were in his favor.

Among those Edward Johnson had engaged this season was Karl Laufkötter, a Spieltenor [*tenore buffo*], one of whose special roles was Mime. Although he and Lauritz had become friends after meeting in 1930 at the Berlin Staatsoper, and had fostered their friendship during appearances in South America, it was not until this fine performer joined the Metropolitan Opera Company that he and Melchior became inseparable. In the days before speedy air travel destroyed the leisurely companionship of trips between South America, the United States, and Europe, the Melchiors and the Laufkötters discovered how unusually compatible they were, not only as colleagues, but as a social foursome. The "new and excellent" Mime of Laufkötter, in which role he debuted on January 22, 1937, drew compliments. There was general surprise that this fiendish part could be sung, rather than shouted, snarled, barked, or whined. Melchior himself, although his "dependable routine stood him in good stead," was in less than his best vocal condition for this performance, due, many critics pointed out acidly, to a week of opera and recital appearances.

Having never performed Mime with his friend, Laufkötter was unprepared for two surprises. In Act I, while Mime is cooking up the poison with which he intends to kill Siegfried, the hero is forging his sword in another part of the stage. Suddenly Laufkötter was bewildered to find himself under attack with bits of coal being flung at him by this guileless-appearing youth. (Lauritz had always been unable to resist the impulse to play games with his Mimes. A 1927 photograph, shows gigantesque Lauritz sitting on a tiny knee of Walter Elschner, Bayreuth's Mime that summer, guzzling beer held by the smaller tenor. The caption, quoting one of Mime's lines, reads "From a tiny tot I brought you up.")

Laufkötter had a genuine success in his first role at the Met. Then, readying himself for the curtain calls, he was again surprised, this time to be picked up by the scruff of the neck and deposited before the curtain for a solo bow. Lauritz just walked off and left him there. The audience—and the press—was enchanted.

Melchior and Flagstad opened the next Metropolitan season, 1937–1938, with *Tristan und Isolde*, the second time in as many years that a Wagnerian music-drama had been presented on opening night. Oscar Thompson wrote the next day:

> Mr. Melchior's thrice-admirable Tristan has undergone no substantial change. Possibly no other Heldentenor of the day has elaborated so successfully the exhausting business of the final act, even aside from the vital and poignant singing that Mr. Melchior brings to the music of this scene. It is here that he is at his peak as Tristan and it is just here that most Tristans prove most lamentably that they are not the supermen Wagner expected them to be.

So great was the continuing demand for Wagner and the two great Wagnerian singers that Flagstad sang thirty-nine performances during the season although contracted for twenty-four. Melchior, contracted for twenty-seven, sang thirty-seven, and they sang together thirty-five times in a sixteen-week season. To appreciate this properly, one must project such figures against the number of Wagnerian music-dramas performed during the season these days. In 1981–1982, for example, there were nineteen Wagnerian performances during a thirty-week season. In the two seasons between 1987 and 1990, with the Metropolitan's new production of the *Ring* cycle, the incidence of Wagner performances increased somewhat to twenty-two Wagner music-dramas performed in the 1987–1988 thirty-week season and twenty-seven in the thirty-two-week 1988–1989 season.

By far the most exciting event of 1939 was the Wagnerian Festival put on at the World's Fair during May. Planning for the festival, begun in March 1937, had not been without its problems. Since it was unthinkable to mount such a series of Wagner performances without Kirsten Flagstad, Olin Downes of the executive music committee had approached her first. She consented to perform at her regular fee, which encouraged the other artists to fall in line. Yet only when Mayor La Guardia, who consistently supported the cause of opera, took a hand with the guarantee fund, did the Wagner Festival become a reality.

A schedule of nine performances was arranged around Flagstad's other commitments—a *Ring* cycle, *Parsifal*, and *Tristan und Isolde*—with Melchior, Branzell, List, and Schorr. The fair opened on April 30; on May 2 Melchior sang two songs for the opening of the Danish pavilion and marched in the first parade with the local chapter of the Royal Danish Guard Outside Denmark. That evening there was a gala performance of *Lohengrin* at the Met with the Danish crown prince and princess occupying the beautifully decorated honor box. As the opera house had been "dark" that night, Lauritz Melchior became an impresario himself, to gratify Crown Prince Frederik's wish to hear the tenor sing at the Met. He hired Rethberg, List, Thorborg, and Schorr to join him. (Lauritz's original idea, abandoned only after logistics proved it untenable, had been to have Crown Prince Frederik conduct the opera.) After the performance the Melchiors entertained 110 persons for supper at the Gripsholm Restaurant. Crown Prince Frederik, extremely musical and a Wagnerite, was the guest of honor. Lauritz was pleased that the Crown Prince, his friend since the prince's graduate student days, enjoyed himself so well that he stayed until 3:30 in the morning. Lauritz's love of dispensing good hospitality was genuine.

The domestic side of the Melchiors' life was full of activity. For a long time Kleinchen had been trying to persuade her parents to come to America. Her adored and handsome "Vati" was ready and willing, but Mutti was fearful of learning the language. She was determined not to add any burden to the complicated and busy life led by her two children (she was almost more Lauritz's mother than Kleinchen's by now), but was, in the end, persuaded by her very feelings of love. The Hackers arrived in December 1935.

Every winter Lauritz and Kleinchen had occupied an eight-room suite at the Hotel Ansonia on Broadway and 73rd Street, where they made a real effort to enjoy life to the fullest. There was but one imperfection to their apartment. Lauritz could not fit into the bathtub. Marjorie Lawrence, a fellow Ansonian, once saw him in the corridor wearing a bathrobe and carrying a cake of soap. He was on the way to the basement where a suitable bathtub—the swimming pool—was located. After a few such events, the manager capitulated and installed a made-to-measure, elephantine bathtub in the Melchior apartment.

Lauritz habitually arose at eleven. He would saunter into the trophy room to eat his breakfast, a reasonably ordinary morning meal except for ice-cold beer. This room had been turned into a "café" with a bar, black-topped, chrome-legged tables, red-leather banquettes, and numerous mounted hunting trophies, whose glass eyes stared at the rows of photos featuring his fellow artists. When Berta Geissmar was invited to have lunch with the Melchiors at the Ansonia, she reported that "they were all in their pajamas." Until he left the house Lauritz wore what he always referred to as his "Carmen" clothes, which he favored for Las Vegas gambling activities as well—voluminous black satin trousers and "an abundant silk shirt the color of ripe strawberries." He alternated this "at-home" costume with beach pajamas from a store for the full-figured woman.

Either set of garments made a relaxing change from his professional clothing—armor, helmet, and beard, or evening dress—especially for the games of pinochle that he and Karl Hacker played incessantly on the rosewood desk in one corner of the living room. This was Lauritz's own bailiwick in the suite. Beneath it lay a Canadian bearskin; on the wall behind the desk was mounted another of his trophies, a gigantic moose head. The hooves of a bison, made into two immense ashtrays, sat on the desk. Here, overseen by a huge drawing of Richard Wagner, Lauritz and Karl enjoyed themselves surrounded by the pleasant noises of a busy household.

Into this happy home Mutti set herself the task of bringing a "Danish-Bavarian Christmas." She knew that the way to Lauritz's heart was to recreate the cherished customs of his Danish youth. There must be a goose; the tree must have real candles; on Christmas Eve everyone must walk around the tree singing carols. The *pynt* (decorations) must be planned and executed by family members weeks in advance, featuring the favorite Danish motif, the heart, for the tree, mobiles, and table decorations, all to convey that the Danish Christmas is from the heart. As her contribution, Mutti employed an army of young men to transport a forest of evergreens into the apartment and finished off the "woods" with hand-painted, gilded stars on the ceiling. Real candles flickering on the many trees were so hazardous that a man (whose salary Kleinchen resented) stood watch with a sand bucket.

Christmas at the Ansonia always included friends, colleagues, and holiday "refugees," who were invited to join the family in their festive setting to sing Yuletide songs. Mutti's first Christmas in America was no exception. Lotte Lehmann, bursting with holiday spirits, appeared as a pillow-stuffed Santa sporting a long white beard and toting a large bag of gifts. Other guests usually included the Schorrs, the Bodanzkys, Karin Baranzell and her husband, and widower Edward Johnson. During all their years in America, including their years in California, the dinner was a Danish one. One of the traditional dishes was milk-boiled rice with an almond hidden somewhere within—whoever is served the almond gets a small prize. Like any good Danish paterfamilias, Lauritz was known to cheat in the serving so as to favor a particular person. Goose with apples and prunes, decorated with an American flag at one end and the Dannebrog at the other, prompting risqué jokes from Lauritz ("there's only one spot where we have *not* put a flag"),

was always the main course, followed most frequently by a dessert made
with apples, butter, jam, heavy cream, and shredded rye bread.

First place on the Melchior list of the accoutrements of "the good life"
were fine food and drink. Alma Strasfogel enjoys telling how festive the
Melchiors made each occasion:

> Their talent was a capacity for enjoyment. Some people are dull at 42,
> but not the Melchiors. They made living such fun. At supper after the
> opera in their hotel suite, it was part of the ritual for Lauritz to single
> out one of the ladies (I was very often the lucky one). Lauritz would
> ask the favored guest, who was seated at his right, "Now what will we
> drink? You decide." I would always pick champagne. How wonderful
> it was not to be jaded! As if champagne had not been discovered as yet.

Lauritz patterned himself after his father, who, as Melchior wrote, "enjoyed good food and good wines and tobacco and lovely and beautiful ladies
without ever exaggerating in one direction or the other. I never saw my father
even slightly intoxicated." Although his own habits were not abstemious,
one never saw Lauritz intoxicated either, not even during those much-publicized, extremely merry, night-long parties with his friends from the Association of Royal Danish Guards Outside Denmark.

About 1928, in fact, Lauritz had learned of the New York chapter of
former guards. Their ideal of comradeship among ex-guardsmen appealed
strongly to Lauritz, and he joined the association. After 1928 he took it upon
himself to form other chapters in Chicago, Argentina, California, and two
in Canada—making himself president of each of the chapters. Through Melchior's efforts the New York membership had increased into a sizable group
just right for a grand yearly celebration in the expansive Melchior style.

Every year the Melchiors mounted a gargantuan feast for the Guardsmen, usually at Christmas or on the king's birthday, even on Lauritz's own
birthday. A lengthy ritual evolved for these much-publicized affairs. At some
point Lauritz had come up with the splendid idea of a shooting match. He
donated a silver cup, onto which the name of the yearly winners were engraved; it could only be kept by the man who won the contest for three
consecutive years. The Ansonia boasted spacious corridors eight to ten feet
wide, just the right size for a shooting range. A target with a thick steel plate
on its back was set up at the end of the corridor. One Guardsman stood
sentinel at the elevator doors warning the passengers back with a white flag.
Now and then a bellhop, sent as ambassador by horrified guests trembling
in their rooms, would poke his head around a corner, only to retreat posthaste
at the next noisy volley. Before each apartment door stood one of the giant
Danes, making sure that no guest inadvertently come out into the line of
fire.

Charles O'Connell, never one to hold his tongue when it was more fun
to be indiscreet, was unconvinced about the charm of these occasions. He
termed the once-a-year fracas a "rout" to which Kleinchen invited "practically

everyone they had ever spoken to." (In fairness, those who were invited did feel privileged to be asked and still place the parties among their fondest memories. Artists' representative Thea Dispeker, for example, simply shakes her head in disbelief as she remembers the lavish hospitality dispensed by the Melchiors.) The revels lasted until the early morning hours. Berta Geissmar, who was in town on some business for Beecham, reported that her invitation asked whether she would "spend . . . the time from 7:00 P.M. to 7:00 A.M." After a lengthy breakfast the morning after, Lauritz and his closest pals would go into an inner room and play cards until noon. Thus Kleinchen had discovered (as do most hostesses) that it is easier to pay off all social obligations in one yearly (and cost-efficient) burst of energy. Simultaneously, she gave the publicity people a great story to write up (and front-page news it was, too).

Another organization to which Melchior gave his time and interest was AGMA, the American Guild of Musical Artists, chartered by the American Federation of Labor in 1937. Melchior was an original member, and not in name only. During the 1940 battle that AGMA fought to keep the American Federation of Musicians from gobbling it up, President Lawrence Tibbett, a Met colleague, described how hard Melchior had worked for the union: "Melchior stays right up to the last minute, then dashes home, eats a hefty meal, smokes a big black cigar, and beats it back to the Met to sing *Tristan*. A brute for punishment."

Two of the more distinguished visitors to Chossewitz the summer of 1935 were Henry Johansen and his wife, Kirsten Flagstad. The pictures show two happy and compatible couples enjoying the idyllic pleasures of an enchantingly beautiful country spot. Henry Johansen's appreciation of food, wine, and tobacco were on as high a level as that of the Melchiors. To Lauritz this was a passport to friendship. Kleinchen related to Flagstad's husband as an astute business person as well, and benefited from Johansen's financial acuity.

Melchior initially called Chossewitz a hunting lodge (soon, in his publicist's hands, it was transformed into a "robber baron's castle"). The loyal Dane had installed on the tower of the large villa a huge flagpole from which he hung the Danish flag, the Dannebrog. The descriptive details of Chossewitz that Lauritz gave to the press showed the priority of its attractions for him. It had 3,000 acres of huntable land; the estate included two enormous lakes and five streams; almost every room had a few of his trophies (some 300 pairs of antlers); and venison was served at least once a week, accompanied by Lauritz's favorite horseradish sauce.

Hunting wild boars was the favorite sport at Chossewitz (though Melchior insisted that the shooting of boars was more a necessity than a sport, for they were capable of killing an unarmed peasant or making a field of crops look like a battlefield). Melchior loved looking "like a savage during his vacation," and he strode through the village with rifle in hand, clad in muddy boots, dirty sweater, sloppy trousers, a strange hunting hat pulled over an unshaven face, and accompanied by his prize-winning hunting dog Jonny. When surprised by reporters while in such disarray, his ploy was ingenious. To their questions about where one could find Herr Kammersänger Melchior, he would give a wily answer, "Just go around the hill by that road and in about two kilometers you will find his house," directing them to the longest way. Meanwhile he would hurry home the back way and be properly dressed to greet them when they arrived. His attitude was aptly demonstrated by his yearly hunt meet at Chossewitz, where in the company of 150 other hunters he indulged in elaborate and unifying ritual, tests of skill, and the opportunity to play host: "I never let singing interfere with living."

During the summer of 1937 Nazism began to permeate the idyllic life at Chossewitz. The Nazis attempted to hold back money Lauritz had raised for the families of those who had died in the *Hindenburg* tragedy. Kleinchen mulled over the import of this turn of events. It did not augur well that Lauritz had not received any recording royalties from Germany since Hitler was named chancellor. While Kleinchen awaited answers to her inquiries to record companies Odeon and Polydor, a book called *Jews in German Art* was published, in which Melchior was listed. There was her answer; Lauritz's recordings were banned in Germany. Minister Zahle from the Danish Embassy forced the Germans to correct the error, but it was too late to avoid destruction of the waxes (from which record matrices were molded), dating from 1923.

When Melchior demanded monetary compensation for the destruction of his recordings, the ministry of cultural affairs refused. They were, however, prepared to be generous in other ways. First, they would give him a certificate proving him to be 100 percent Aryan; they would give him a fine medal, as well as a lifetime singing position with a munificent salary. They sweetened the proposition with the use of the former crown prince's hunting castle. As a special lure, Göring himself would come to Chossewitz to discuss hunting with Lauritz. Melchior, fuming, refused categorically "to see Mr. Göring at [Melchior's] home." Had the Reich not been behind the offer, he might have been tempted, especially by the decoration and the hunting rights. Minister Zahle tried to persuade him to accept the decoration by citing Charles Lindbergh, who had done so during the time when he and his wife lived in Europe.

Klaus Riisbro, Melchior's godson, reveals what happened next at Chossewitz: A few weeks passed. Early one morning there was a banging at the front door. "This is the Gestapo," barked a voice. "Open up!" Melchior stood at the top of the stairs holding the dogs on leashes as the maid, Lizzie, opened the door. She found two members of the secret police standing before it.

"Are you Lauritz Melchior?" one of them called up. "Yes" he replied. "Then you are under arrest. Come with us."

Melchior had sent five kroner to Copenhagen, although sending foreign currency out of Germany was prohibited. He admitted it, but sent Lizzie down with his Danish diplomatic passport, which removed him from their jurisdiction. As the men were leaving, he calculated the amount of time the men needed to reach the gate and then released his dogs, who dashed off in full pursuit of the fleeing Nazis.

Proof that this episode would not be forgotten by the Gestapo came when a "Melchior fan" asked Lizzie a number of pointed questions about foreign broadcasts and visitors. The questions frightened Lizzie, for she knew that Chossewitz was a way station for Jewish friends who were waiting to get safely out of the country.

At the time of Karl Hacker's death in January 1938, Kleinchen and Lauritz made a major decision, to buy Chossewitz after all these years of leasing it. Wanting a place of their own somewhere in the world, and believing that insurance against the Nazis would probably no longer be afforded just by their Danish passports, they decided it would be better to own the property. Accordingly they paid 100,000 marks for the two lodges, land, lakes, forests, and all. They, like the Danish government, did not believe that Hitler would bother to appropriate little Denmark into the Third Reich. The Melchiors now felt safe in their own domain, which they immediately began to modernize.

The stone hunting lodge had long been the place to store and use the rare antiques in which they took so much pride. Lauritz had cultivated a penchant for baroque art and pieces from the Biedermeyer period. Kleinchen, on the other hand, was a confirmed orientalist, and particularly loved porcelain of the Ming dynasty and old Japanese carved ivories. Both enjoyed their traveling as much for the antique-hunting as for the performing. On the white and gold Empire piano in the music room stood a gold candelabra bought in a shop on the Seine. On one wall of the bedroom was a brocaded velvet hanging from Denmark featuring the crest of that other Dane—the melancholy one. An inlaid grandfather clock, the work of a Dutch master, stood in the main entrance hall, and two torch-bearing angels of bronze flanked the library door. Priceless Flemish tapestries as large as rugs hung on the walls of the library, which was paneled with seventeen sculpted wooden panels from Trier Cathedral. An enormous Gobelin tapestry covered one entire wall of the dining room.

Evidence suggests that Kleinchen exercised a constant and firm control over her family's life by means of many a hidden agenda. Kleinchen asserted, for example, that Walter Bock, their chauffeur, had behaved traitorously, extorting from and informing against fellow Jews who were being helped by the Melchiors. She convinced Lauritz of Bock's perfidy.

Such actions by Bock are clearly inexplicable. He had been one of the top electrical engineers in Germany. As an intelligent man, an extremely wealthy man (in all probability wealthier than Far, says Ib) and a Jew, he had no difficulty realizing the true nature of the Nazi threat. By working as Melchior's chauffeur Bock was protected by the Dane's nationality and fame while he slowly and surreptitiously sent his money and his family out of Germany. They did survive. To this day Birte has great affection for Bock, and Ib says that he learned more about life from him than from anyone else (except perhaps Uncle Knud), as their father was always off somewhere. Bock was kind, patient, supportive—and present.

It is difficult to intuit what Kleinchen's hidden agenda might have been in this case. As a chauffeur and surrogate father to the children, Bock was useful to her. Lacking evidence, perhaps the conjecture must be that he had offended her in some way, for Kleinchen never forgave those who crossed her. Even after Bock had managed to join his family in England, Kleinchen campaigned relentlessly against him there.

There can be no doubt that Bock suffered from her actions and from Lauritz's tacit assent to her accusations, for years later, when Birte met Bock in a railroad station, he implored her, "Please, please tell your father that I did nothing wrong—so many lies have been told!"

Lauritz always referred to 1935 as the spring he "rescued Covent Garden from disaster." The Silver Jubilee Season of that year offered not only the usual Wagner, but featured a Rossini festival with Conchita Supervia starring in *La Cenerentola* and Lily Pons as Rosina in *Il Barbiere di Siviglia*. The season, Melchior's eleventh at the English house, was to open on April 29 with a glittering gala (*Lohengrin* with Lotte Lehmann and a new German tenor, Max Hirzel). The gala was but a small part of a three-month celebration of the twenty-fifth anniversary of King George V's reign. Both the king and the queen were to be present at Covent Garden, as well as the prime minister, and members of the government and the military. As Melchior was not scheduled to sing until the following evening, he and Kleinchen happily accepted the invitation to attend.

To many, the whole effect of Covent Garden Opera lies in the lingering smell (and leftover samples) of fresh vegetables and fruit. It was no different on April 29, when glamour and opening-night turmoil extended into the surrounding streets, which still held empty produce stands. Flashbulbs exploded on all sides as Melchior, in evening dress, sporting his beloved decorations, escorted Kleinchen, also dressed in "full gala," into the foyer of the opera house. Twenty minutes before curtain time, a distraught man emerged from the crowd and threw himself upon a startled Melchior, gasping out his message: Mr. Hirzel could not appear and there was no cover. This was a terrible disaster! Covent Garden could not cancel when the king and queen were in attendance. Would Melchior sing Lohengrin?

Although the *Lohengrin* was to be done uncut, and was a role Lauritz had never sung at Covent Garden, he accepted immediately, even designating, as was his custom, that the fee go to Mr. Hirzel. When a representative of the management stepped before the curtain to announce that Lauritz Melchior had consented to sing in place of ailing Mr. Hirzel, murmurs of pleasure were heard, over which the speaker tried to continue. A perfectly proper gentleman in the balcony would have none of these long explanations and called out, "That's all right. Let's have him!"

Backstage dressers stood waiting with Hirzel's costume, and Charles Moor, the doughty Scottish stage director, glowered nearby in his white uniform. Just looking at it, it was clear that Mr. Hirzel's tunic would not fit Melchior. No time to waste. Moor ordered the dressers to rip it up the back. Three men yanked valiantly, but the tunic would not close and the stockings would not reach Melchior's knees. Kleinchen surveyed him. He looked like Gulliver in Lilliputian clothing. The cut in the tunic was quickly bridged barely hidden by the long cloak. There was nothing for Melchior to do but remember to face the audience at all times (reserving the rest of his concentration, of course, for the vocalism of the role and for the music, with former cuts just opened by Beecham). Each time he left the stage, there were new tears to be repaired. Curved upholstery needles did the job so well that the costume eventually had to be cut off, and the Melchiors dined out for weeks on the story of these backstage machinations.

The Covent Garden stay during the spring of 1936 was marked by the absence of Hugh Walpole, who was once again in Hollywood plying his screenwriter's trade, and by the presence of Kirsten Flagstad, who debuted as Isolde. Melchior, her Tristan, recalled that the ticket queue was around the block twenty-four hours before curtain, and that she enjoyed even greater ovations in London than in New York. A critique written by "Beckmesser" of *The Gramophone* (possibly Walter Legge) set the tone: "She sat completely at ease in the middle of the stage . . . and poured out such a flood of tone as I have never heard from a woman's throat."

Before leaving for Europe, Melchior had given an interview for an American magazine in which he announced that plans were all but finished for a complete *Tristan* recording that summer with Flagstad, Melchior, and the Vienna Philharmonic under Bruno Walter. This did not come to pass, but during the 1936 and 1937 Covent Garden seasons recordings were made of live performances of *Tristan*, *Götterdämmerung*, and *Walküre*, and a few test sets were pressed. A fascinating saga of the fate of Kirsten Flagstad's set of these pressings is told by Knud Hegermann-Lindencrone, a Danish friend of both Flagstad and Melchior, which "relates to the sad fate of some of the rarest Wagnerian test pressings."

In May 1957, Hegermann-Lindencrone and Flagstad were relaxing over a bottle of her favorite Krug champagne in the bar of Vienna's Hotel Bristol, "after one of the final sessions of Decca's first great stereophonic enterprise, the recording of the third act of *Die Walküre* with Flagstad, Otto Edelmann, Marianne Schech, and the Vienna Philharmonic under Georg Solti." Their conversation moved as it always did to those legendary prewar Covent Garden tests in her collection. The Dane expressed again how eagerly he anticipated his coming June visit to her home, Kristianssand, when he would hear the performance of *Götterdämmerung* with Flagstad, Melchior, and Kerstin Thorborg, under Furtwängler. Then Flagstad dropped a bombshell. She remarked casually that she had thrown the recordings out because they took up too much space. Lindencrone thought she was joking. When she elaborated, telling him how she had asked Nielsen, her chauffeur, to destroy them, he tried to mask his utter horror at her deed lest it provoke a discussion that might disturb her before the remaining recording sessions.

Later, during a farewell dinner together, Flagstad made a semi-apology, saying, "you may be right. . . . I shouldn't have thrown them out. I will *not* say that I personally regret it." Seeing how distressed her friend was, she promised not to dispose of the other tests (*Tristan, Holländer*, etc.) as she had first planned.

At Kristianssand in June, Hegermann-Lindencrone, left to browse in the music room, found seven mint HMV test pressings from Covent Garden, the Waltraute scene up to Siegfried's entrance from the destroyed *Götterdämmerung*. Flagstad explained, as if it were a minor matter, that she had kept them "because Waltraute sings so splendidly," adding, as an afterthought, that "maybe I'm not too bad there myself." The Dane was allowed to take back to Copenhagen those seven tests together with the very primitive tapes of the fifty-four sides of *Walküre* Act III and her *Götterdämmerung* scenes, made locally before the tests were thrown into the fjord.

Later that summer of 1957, during her absence in Vienna, where she made a recording of the "Todesverkündigung" with Set Svanholm, Flagstad ordered, as a surprise for her friend, that a frogman be sent down to retrieve the test pressings from the sixteen-meter depths of Kristianssand Fjord where Nielsen had thrown them. "I don't care myself, but you looked so sad that day in Vienna," she told Hegermann-Lindencrone. "I hate to see my friends distressed." Hope for their good condition vanished, however, when it was discovered that Nielsen had broken each test in two before consigning it to the water.

Recording connoisseurs firmly believed during these years that these tests were the last of only two sets in private hands, Melchior's and Flagstad's, and that they were lost forever. Lauritz's set, kept at Chossewitz, was gone, used for target practice by Russian soldiers. The matrices were melted by EMI after the war because of their need for material for their normal production. Much later another set was located (allegedly from the Earl of Harewood) and transferred to LP.

Melchior celebrated another 100th anniversary on May 25, 1936, this time for Siegmund, which he had first sung at Covent Garden. He had sung the role at twenty opera houses under twenty-nine conductors, including Beecham, who conducted on this occasion. In an interview this month, he described the role:

> Siegmund, in my estimation, is a most human and likeable character. When he enters Hunding's hut, he is a depressed man, hunted and despised, without friends or weapons. Gradually, through the love of a woman . . . he acquires a new lease on life—and a sword to protect himself. When the promised weapon is discovered and withdrawn from the tree, he is truly a man reborn—ready to fight the whole universe to protect his honor and Sieglinde. I always thought it was easier for an artist on the stage to make the most of a part that is human.

The celebration was up to his exacting standards of what such an event should be. An enthusiastic audience cheered him and his colleagues, Flagstad and Rethberg. In commemoration of the date the princesses Marie Louise and Helene Victoria presented Melchior with an antique silver tray and diamond-studded gold cufflinks. "Beckmesser," however, found the performance amusing:

> Rethberg, Melchior, and List made such nonsense of Wagner's dramatic intentions that an audience composed of people understanding German would have laughed themselves hoarse. . . . Melchior bounded in so exuberantly that I believe he thought he had to sing Siegfried that night. Then hearing orchestra sounds that were obviously *Walküre*, he changed his mind and manner, and took on some of Siegmund's weariness. . . . For the love duet this Siegmund and Sieglinde clambered on to a pile of cushions like a couple of long-married and weary hikers seeking the softest piece of grass on which to rest their weary limbs before they settled down to their sandwiches.

In Paris, by contrast, Melchior continued to be well-received. His *Tristan* under Furtwängler at the sixth Paris Wagner Festival drew great acclaim from the press, who cited his unique ability to reduce that "gigantic voice to the most subtle and lyric pianissimo, always clear and limpid down to the faintest whisper."

For the 1936 festival, Melchior appeared in three performances, the success of which was overshadowed by disturbing news from Germany. It was more than probable that German artists would not be allowed to perform outside their country in the future. That would mean the end of the festival for 1937. All were grateful that this summer Göring had permitted Frida Leider to appear at both Paris and Covent Garden, where she shared all three Brünnhildes with Kirsten Flagstad. During both festivals all the singers were uneasy, their anxieties fed by recent events: Hitler had ordered troops into the Rhineland, and Italian troops and German bombers were openly aiding the Fascist forces of General Francisco Franco in Spain.

On a more personal level, the artists were not reassured by Lotte Lehmann's run-in with Göring during the 1935–1936 season. Although never a member of the Göring-controlled Berlin Staatsoper, she had appeared there each year as a guest. As she was giving a recital in Dresden, an SS trooper interrupted a song by walking down the aisle, holding up his hand, and loudly announcing that Göring had telephoned and ordered Mme. Lehmann to appear before him. The next day she duly presented herself at Göring's palace in Berlin. He gave Lehmann a choice: accept engagements in Germany only or never sing in that country again. She chose to leave Germany forever, influenced by a rising fear on behalf of her Jewish husband and her stepchildren. Frida Leider, too, had never made much of the fact that her husband was Jewish, but now her fears were mounting daily.

It was probably Goebbels, responsible for all music and art in Germany, who had interfered with an earlier recording project of HMV's. His Master's Voice had planned to record some *Walküre* excerpts in Berlin during June 1935 with Melchior, Lehmann, List, and Bruno Walter. When the three German artists were forbidden to record in Germany, the recording was done in Vienna. A newspaper review, written when this recording of *Walküre* Act I was reissued in 1956, gives us clues to Melchior's sound when he was at the peak of his powers:

> To be truthful, I had forgotten that Wagner singing of this quality had ever existed. The Melchior of 1935 is simply indescribable. The ease and power of his vocal emission and his ability to control and color his massive sound will be a revelation to those who heard him only in the movies he made at the end of his career.

At Covent Garden in 1937 Melchior, alternating with Max Lorenz (an "eminently cultivated . . . singer," but judged "lightweight" in the role of Siegfried) sang *Götterdämmerung*, *Siegfried*, and *Tristan* under Furtwängler and Beecham, with Leider and Flagstad sharing the Brünnhildes and Isoldes. Although Leider, now characterized as "past her vocal prime," was "still a noble and imposing Isolde," Lauritz was, on the other hand, "scarcely a Tristan for whose sake a woman would be likely to feel the world well lost." Not only were Melchior's reviews disheartening, but he also suffered an accident that was to haunt him (and other tenors) for some time. As he readied himself to cleave the anvil in Act I of *Siegfried*, the audience was enjoying the spectacle and the passages of heroic singing. Three seconds before Melchior was to hit it, the anvil fell apart, seriously gashing his leg. So common was the anvil's premature disintegration, that in years to come the younger members of the Covent Garden audience thought it a part of the opera's plot.

The Melchiors were now depressed by Frida Leider's troubles. Ill with worry about her husband Rudi's safety, Frida tried valiantly to enjoy the relief of being in London—a week without furtive schemes and dread for what tomorrow might bring, a week of normality with her friends. It was almost impossible. When Hitler began to persecute the Jews, Frida had expressed her fears to Heinz Tietjen. He had made several promises to lure her into coming back to Germany, promises that had forced her to cut her ties to the Metropolitan Opera. Now, one at a time, he was breaking every one of those promises, making life more difficult for Leider and her husband.

Cheerless as the 1937 season had been, the spirits of the Covent Garden artists were even lower in the spring of 1938, a state of affairs directly traceable to the recent German *Anschluss* with Austria. Herbert Janssen, who had earlier barely escaped arrest in Germany, was lucky again. Having concluded his engagement with the Vienna Opera the day before the *Anschluss*, he and his wife had left safely, and together. Kerstin Thorborg had refused to sing with Nazi houses from the very beginning, and in Austria she broke her contract within twenty-four hours of the arrival of the Germans. Yet London had profited much from the Nazis' banning of certain "non-Aryan productions." Artists, conductors, and the loan of the productions themselves made this Covent Garden season exceptionally brilliant.

Lotte Lehmann frightened the audience during the May 4 performance of *Rosenkavalier* when she threw up her hands in the middle of Act I and said, "I cannot go on." Management announced that Mme. Lehmann was suffering from a chill and another soprano came on. Many assumed that she had lost her voice. The truth was that May 4 was the night when Lotte Lehmann's four half-Jewish stepchildren were to slip through the Austrian border into Alsace-Lorraine. The Nazis had forbidden them to leave Austria, but a sleepy border guard failed to notice that their passports were stamped improperly. It was the uncertainty of the children's fate that forced her collapse during the opera. Lauritz and Kleinchen did their best to comfort her, but she did not relax until two days later, when she was united with her husband and the children in Paris.

Frida Leider's story did not have such a happy ending. She had not sung all winter because of a nervous breakdown. For years her Austrian citizenship had protected her and her husband, but now the *Anschluss* had rendered even that safeguard uncertain. In prior years the visit to England afforded Frida an opportunity to buy clothes, to eat well, to enjoy the small luxuries denied the common population of Germany, and to recuperate from illnesses brought on by the food shortages at home. This year, however, Frida and Rudi were limited to £9 a day for expenses, the rest being directly accountable to the Nazis. Kleinchen and Lauritz were shocked at Frida's loss of vitality; she appeared ill. They begged her to stay out of Germany, to save herself and Rudi, but Frida was incapable of listening. She was unable to bring herself to give up everything that she had struggled for her whole life, to leave her mother, to start over as a singer without a cent. "Now come the difficult years," she said knowingly.

As she wrote the Melchiors later, she hadn't known how very soon those days were to come. The Bayreuth Festival that summer was poisoned by the fear that hung over the Jewish artists. Although Tietjen had given Frida every assurance that she and Rudi would not be affected by the law against Jews, as the last day of June approached, the designated date by which all Jews must declare all their property—and lose it all, most probably—Tietjen did nothing. (Tietjen's handling of power was later described by Rudolf Bing: "Tietjen was my idol. . . . I admired boundlessly his mixture of charm, wit, and noncommittal diplomacy. I had no hope of imitating his level of high intrigue, supreme control through *attrition by indecision* mixed with charm. But I studied his performance.")

It was in this atmosphere of fear, distrust, and uncertainty that Frida arrived in Bayreuth in 1938. Understandably, she collapsed after the first performance. She returned to sing two Isoldes at the end of the festival. Her description of the town was particularly distressing to the Melchiors. All the principal streets were dotted with swastika flags, hiding the famous old houses. At the foot of the hill leading to the Festspielhaus were two red-draped columns topped by Nazi eagles. Hitler himself kept the artists and the Wagners awake for hours after performances with his bombastic ranting about The Nature of Art. The pollution of Bayreuth by Nazi values was complete.

In the fall of 1935 Melchior had begun a new pattern of performances that was to continue for several years, a pattern derived from the newly larger proportions of his yearly concert tour. With Lauritz singing a concert every two or three days, the Melchiors would work their way west for a ten-day San Francisco Opera engagement. (In San Francisco, Lauritz was paid a fine fee of $2,000—a fact so significant that Edward Ziegler mentioned it in his personal correspondence—for each of four Wagner performances in the company of Flagstad, Manski, Rethberg, Schorr, and Windheim.) His return to New York would then follow a similar concert-filled route. Frequently, as in 1936, when he and Flagstad were the big drawing cards in San Francisco for *Tristan*, *Götterdämmerung*, and several performances of *Walküre*, Melchior would also stop off in Chicago for some opera appearances before finishing up his concert tour.

For several years Melchior sang duo recitals with Lotte Lehmann as well. In opera they were a magnetic combination that never lost its appeal to the public and the critics. They were also an engaging couple in recital. In a January 1938 Carnegie Hall joint concert, the two artists inaugurated a series of joint appearances. Together they sang several Schumann duets, the end of the first act of *Walküre*, and the *Fidelio* duet as an encore. Lauritz offered songs by Strauss, Hageman, Trunk, and Scandinavian composers, while Lotte favored Beethoven, Handel, and the German lieder composers. Critics cited their work as "an effective team," and found in their joint efforts "warmth of feeling and integrated musicianship." Their management was pleased to find a partnership for Lauritz—Kirsten Flagstad having made herself unavailable—that would allow them to sell a tour of such duo-recitals for years to come. When the two were booked in other major cities, reviewers agreed that the recital displayed "showmanship, but not at the expense of the music or the mood."

Lotte was determined not to repeat the same concert repertoire ad nauseam as some singers did, but Lauritz did not share her enthusiasm. He was not at all disturbed at the prospect of singing the same song repertoire thirty to sixty times each season for years. In fact, he insisted that his accompanists be "assisting artists," and auditioned accordingly. The pianists periodically changed their program numbers out of boredom, but he did not.

Perhaps the most significant difference between Lotte and Lauritz was her interest in acquiring mastery of the art song. Melchior never developed as a lieder singer simply because he sang few serious recitals after the promising early years. Lehmann was entranced by the mysteries of Hugo Wolf and others and loved steeping herself in this literature, while Melchior did not.

Yet Melchior spoke often of "painting in detail" in songs and "adopting the larger canvas" in opera: "An opera is like an oil painting, laid on with a big brush; you have to go far away to see the whole picture. A song recital is like a series of aquarelles; you have to look at it from nearby."

He had absorbed an interesting outlook from the great lieder singer Gerhard Hüsch, who sang Wolfram to Melchior's Tannhäuser in the 1931 Bayreuth Festival. Hüsch was a firm believer in studying lieder before learning operatic roles. He felt that most opera singers, who often make the mistake of doing it in the reverse order, never quite succeed in being completely at home in song literature, feeling circumscribed by the smaller event. Melchior's concurrence with Hüsch's theory was not merely rhetorical: The role of Parsifal, he felt, needs a song recitalist's refinement in detail to point up the nuances of music and text more than it needs an opera singer's broad gesture and overt dramatic action. Melchior as Parsifal was dignified, unpretentious, and intense, while specifically revealing the emotional content with small changes in tone and declamation, as does a fine singer of art songs.

Without doubt Melchior's longer concert tours and higher fees were attributable in part to the work done by Constance Hope, who earned her fees by persuading a minimum of seventy-five papers to print each story she sent out. In addition, radio was acting as a publicity agent for the Metro-

politan Opera itself. It was Melchior's conviction—shared by the administration of the Met—that a grass-roots interest in opera was being stimulated
by the Met broadcasts. The tenor had long publicly maintained that the rest
of America could not be captivated by something that took place only in
New York. The future of opera in America was thus being doubly served
by the broadcasts from the opera house. Substantial fees from the network
supported the opera financially, and the radio broadcasts themselves awak-
ened listeners to a fascination with the operatic art.

An opera-loving New York resident of today would find it difficult to
imagine the domination of press and radio coverage enjoyed by the Metropolitan Opera of 1935. Every detail of the day-to-day operation of the opera
company was discussed at length, and painstaking perusals of the meta-
physical aspects of interpretation were regularly offered to the public. In our
time only rock stars command such coverage.

Kleinchen was a natural at the game of publicity. She soon became very
adept at exploiting, aggrandizing, and even inventing situations that the press
would devour. In March 1936, for example, as Melchior and Flagstad set
off to do *Tristan* in Rochester, Kleinchen was alerting the local paper that
she would be making her operatic debut. The Met administration, ever on
the watch for ways to limit expenses, asked Kleinchen to fill in for the page
girl, who has but one duty, to hand Isolde her crown and cloak. Sufficiently
small and slender to squeeze into the tight costume, Kleinchen executed the
maneuver right on cue. Ziegler praised her and gave her the standard super's
fee of one dollar. She promptly wrote out a placard saying "I AM ON STRIKE
FOR HIGHER WAGES," and picketed in front of the dressing rooms until promised a higher wage. The newspapers loved the story and printed pictures of
Kleinchen looking fetching in the page costume, carrying her placard. Hope
Associates and the Met publicity department cooperated in disseminating
the picture throughout the country.

Ever more creative steps were being taken by Hope. In an expensive
brochure titled "Hitch Your Program to a Star," Hope Associates attempted
to persuade businesses to use her roster of stars, including Heifetz, Lehmann,
Melchior, Pinza, Pons, Ormandy, and Reiner, "to add color and personal
interest to your publicity." In this highly effective and innovative procedure,
the artists were sometimes sold as a package to the sponsoring business. The
Melchiors and Fritz Reiner, for example, collaborated on an advertising
campaign for a total package of RCA recordings to fit different budgets. A
picture of the three of them received an impressively wide press distribution.
The Melchiors pasted into their 1935 scrapbook 145 reproductions of this
picture from as many papers.

Constance Hope's elegant brochure paid its way. Melchior signed a
contract with Lucky Strike cigarettes for the use of his name in advertising.
For this, plus two two-minute radio commercials, he received $7,000 and
free cigarettes for a year. It must have been Kleinchen who used the Lucky
Strikes, because Lauritz smoked only big, black, lethal cigars that smelled

like burning buggy whips. This did not prevent him from signing his name to such unworthy assertions as: "The hardest test I can give a cigarette is to try its effect on my throat after hours of intense rehearsal. . . . I favor Lucky Strike for the sake of my throat." Kleinchen's persuasive argument that her husband agree to promote cigarettes (he could say that "Lucky Strikes never harmed my voice" but omit the qualifier "because I never smoke them") typified not only her pragmatism but also her influence upon Lauritz. Of course, the Met was in no position to disapprove because their first sponsor of Saturday radio broadcasts was the American Tobacco Company, makers of Lucky Strikes.

Somehow it never seemed quite as undignified when Lauritz did these things as when Lotte Lehmann did them. In April 1938 on the Lucky Strike radio show Lotte told the announcer how she and Lauritz were going to do a tour on which they would both be smoking Lucky Strikes, which "never affected their throats." She seemed to understand the needs of the American public, as she wrote to Kleinchen:

> [Constance Hope] is fond of me but that does not prevent her from dragging me through the hells of publicity if she thinks it necessary. The great public wants to think of its favorites above all as just human beings. . . . A singer they want as uncomplicated and near to them as possible, not far removed and veiled in a cloud.

From the Melchiors, who not only did exactly as they were told but even invented some maneuvers, sprang forth a steady stream of quotable quips and picturesque photos that kept both of them in the public eye. Readers found Kleinchen modeling hats and clothes, giving household hints, telling American women "How to Be Tactful," and helping Lauritz cook— or diet. In March 1938 many newspapers carried an enormous layout of pictures and copy entitled "If Your Wife Puts You on a Diet It May Be a Sign of Love."

Wagner being irresistible as a source of humor, Melchior fans were kept amused with various pieces from the publicity mill, such as one piece variously called "Lover, Go Way from Me," and "Are Tenors Lousy Lovers?" A legitimate stage director had commented that an operatic tenor's conception of a love scene is just about as inspiring as the "vernal cavortings of an aardvark." Lauritz responded in print that this fellow never had to whisper sweet nothings to a robust female wrapped in twelve yards of stifling gauze and make each murmured endearment reach the last row of the gallery of a huge opera house while prompter yelled from his box and a seventy-five-piece orchestra played for dear life.

At the first dinner tendered Melchior after he and Kleinchen first arrived in the United States, the toastmaster said, "And Lauritz Melchior is a household name." Kleinchen, whose knowledge of English was very limited then, tugged at his sleeve and whispered urgently: "No, no, it's a *Danish* name."

By 1938 Lauritz really was becoming a household word. As evidence of how familiar the name "Melchior" had become, one need only consider the hefty price advertising people were willing to pay to borrow it. In addition, for the first time the Melchior face and name were now included in those big weekend newspaper articles about goings-on in the opera world. He had not yet arrived at the pinnacle of celebrity, for even now, when operas in which he played the *title* role were announced, the wording was almost invariably "Flagstad to Sing Isolde."

In Europe opera singers had always been celebrated in the popular press. A perfect example is provided by LaScala's visit to England during the 1950–1951 winter season. Every taxi driver and luggage porter in Milan knew all details of the London performances each day: who was singing in which opera, how the performance went, and how each singer was received. It would be difficult to imagine ordinary Americans sharing such a profound interest in someone other than an astronaut or a rock musician. America's popular culture has never been centered on opera singers. Lacking a tradition of popular interest in opera, America acquired it only when the institution of the Metropolitan Opera was celebrated on the air, and when its singers became popular celebrities. But what does it take to become a celebrated opera singer in the United States? Most casual listeners are certainly not interested in the singer's technical knowledge. His skills as a singer are taken for granted. His credentials are established by virtue of his employment in an opera house. Rather, the American public is insatiable about the personal details: the singer's slimming diet, the cost of his last safari, his favorite pasta sauce, whether he sleeps without pajamas. Lauritz and Kleinchen were willing to do the kinds of things demanded by the public, with the result that Lauritz was fast becoming one of the most well-known opera singers in the United States.

CHAPTER 11

Hitler Interferes

(1939–1941)

In the past, returning to their beloved Chossewitz after the year's work was done had always given the Melchiors great happiness. In the summer of 1939, however, going back to Germany only increased the apprehension they had been feeling ever since the 1938 German *Anschluss* with Austria. Like the rest of the world, they longed to believe in the few hopeful signs that war might, after all, be avoided. There was a pattern: Each week brought new rhetoric about peace—but also actions that belied the talk. When President Roosevelt opened the World's Fair in May, he had called it a symbol of peace, and the Melchiors grasped at that indication. Within a few days, however, they learned that the British were implementing nationwide conscription. Fear alternated with hope, and the Melchiors felt the strain.

Looking back at his time in Covent Garden during the spring, Lauritz could see how the entire season had been colored by the possibility of war. Inside the theater the beauty and majesty of *Otello* prevailed, but outside, the grim possibility that three million British children would have to be moved from the cities to the country inspired emergency planning sessions. Cancellation of the season was imminent when Sir Thomas Beecham and critic Ernest Newman took a hand: Beecham shamed the London public out of considering it, and Newman convinced the backers to continue their support. On the very last night of the season Lauritz sang *Tristan und Isolde* with the beautiful and temperamental French dramatic soprano, Germaine Lubin, who was a favorite of Hitler's at Bayreuth (and who was to influence Metropolitan Opera policy in 1941 when the war prevented her from honoring her contract in New York). The public didn't agree with Newman, who criticized Lubin for "attitudinizing," but they approved of Melchior. Much later, when it became apparent that this *Tristan* was Lauritz Melchior's last operatic appearance in London, those who were in that audience remembered with admiration how he emptied his voice as he lay dying in the third act, and how he played affectionately with Isolde's braid before whispering her name for the last time.

Summer vacation at Chossewitz began on June 17. Lauritz and Kleinchen attempted to keep to their normal jolly summer schedule of activities, but world events intruded daily, weakening their resolve to enjoy themselves. Precautions were taken. A danger signal was agreed upon; concealed compartments were constructed in the barn floor; and certain items were packed up and put into the embassy basement.

Tensions were growing, fed by the pressure of events. On August 23 the Germans and Russians joined in an alliance. On August 24 France mobilized, and the next day ordered Paris evacuated. Although Denmark officially proclaimed that there was "no reason to fear," the British sent reinforcements to the Mediterranean, called up the reservists, and ordered London windows blacked out. There was no way for the Melchiors to ignore the implications. On August 27 Kleinchen left Lauritz hunting at Chossewitz while she went to Berlin. She heard only bad news at the Danish embassy: Both London and Paris had stated their intention not to mediate further or retreat from their position as allies of Poland. Zahle, their contact in the Danish Embassy, gave her advice that galvanized her into action. As Lauritz described it:

> That evening I was just a short distance into the woods. I was watching an old stag with my binoculars when I heard the horn on my car blaring across the lake. It was the prearranged signal of danger at home. I rushed back and was told that Herluf [Minister] Zahle . . . had warned us to get out of Germany as fast as we could. We spent the entire night packing the most important things like music, costumes, etc.

By 4:40 A.M. the concealed compartments in the barn floor were full of silver, paintings, tapestries, and objets d'art, and the two cars were so loaded—twenty-nine pieces of luggage—that there was no room remaining for treasured things like the crystal chandeliers, the Meissen dinner service, the stamp collection, the wine cellar, the recordings, the weapon collection, the Otello and Radamès costumes, or their library. Kleinchen wept as they said their farewells; Lauritz caressed his horses and dogs for the last time. Before climbing into the car they photographed the lowering of the Dannebrog. When the film was developed, an ominous black cloud could be seen in the left corner. Lauritz later wrote under the photo in their album, "The dark clouds are approaching and the Danish flag is lowered on our wonderful hunting estate in Chossewitz."

They elected to stop briefly at the Danish Embassy when they arrived in Berlin at 6:10 A.M. Minister Zahle (who had previously told them repeatedly that they were perfectly safe as Danes in Germany) received them at his bedside. Even as he was advising them to go immediately to Denmark, the phone rang incessantly "with information of the coming world catastrophe." Hitler was going to keep his demands for Polish territory; the Poles were digging trenches. Time was very short, and the Melchiors had to move quickly. Keeping with them only their clothes, the scores, the Wagnerian costumes, and Kleinchen's jewelry, they moved the rest of their baggage to the basement of the embassy. There they had stored some big suitcases "just in case something should happen." This done, they fled to the railroad station in an attempt to catch the train that left at 8:00 for Warnemünde, which was just a ferry ride across Mecklenburg Bay from Denmark.

At Stettiner Station all was chaos. There was little chance of finding a porter. Lauritz placed Mutti and Kleinchen in a safe spot and forbade them to move. He was determined that they would board this train, which was clearly going to be one of the last allowed to leave. Knowing, however, that the baggage cars were already completely filled, he demanded to speak to the station master at once. His theory about the Nazi mentality was confirmed, as he later recalled: Behaving in a loud and overbearing manner with Nazi officials was the best way to produce results. Not only did the station master promptly appear, but he positively bowed and scraped. What a pleasure to meet the Kammersänger! It would be a great honor to find seats for the Kammersänger's party! He would have the luggage of those less important persons removed immediately! As the Melchiors left Germany, "a very happy chapter of our lives had come to an end."

Safe in Copenhagen, but unable to stop grieving over their loss, they absorbed like a blow each historic event as it happened in a rapid sequence of escalating tragedy: On September 1 the German army invaded Poland; on the third, England and France declared war against Germany; on September 17 Russia too invaded Poland; and by September 28, Russia and Germany had divided Poland between them.

Mutti, older and more philosophical because she had already experienced one war, had her priorities well in hand as she lectured her daughter. No family lives had been lost; America was safe; they were all healthy; they could make a fresh start if necessary. Kleinchen, so close to her mother, heeded Mutti's advice, as always. She would not think about Chossewitz; she would not even look at photos of it; instead, she would find reasons to be of good cheer. Lauritz had several engagements on the books: concerts in Danish towns, a recording of Danish songs for HMV, and—a real cause for rejoicing—he would finally do the role of Lohengrin at the Royal Opera House, for the first time since Vilhelm Herold had chosen it for him twenty-one years before.

Now the problem of his nineteen-year-old daughter had to be faced. Birte had been left with Gerda Henningsen in Copenhagen during the school years, visiting Chossewitz in the summertime. When she finished her schooling in 1937, she expressed a desire to go on with her studies in Switzerland, but was sent to a boarding school in Scotland to pursue a (virtually useless) domestic-science degree. The only foreign student, she was unhappy and made few friends, but did acquire her highly competent command of English and French to add to her knowledge of German. A combination of stress and unhappiness soon yielded a nervous breakdown, after which she was allowed to return to Denmark. When she informed her father that she wanted to become an actress, he responded with a warning about the uncertainties of the performing artist's life and advice to choose a practical education instead. Birte had listened and enrolled in a secretarial and business course.

Now Lauritz and Kleinchen had to make a decision regarding Birte's immediate future. In his personal manuscript Lauritz says that he and Kleinchen felt immobilized by the uncertainty of his future career in the United States. What if music by all Germanic composers should be banned from American concert halls and opera houses as it had been during World War II? Their only hope for the future, she felt, was the continuation of Wagnerian opera performances in America. (At no time was it even considered that Birte might live with Inger's relatives, for both children had long been forbidden to have contact with their mother's family—though they were never given a reason for this edict. Since the family of Uncle Knud, Inger's brother, was determined not to criticize Lauritz, they had—with the best of intentions—let the forlorn children assume that the Nathansen family had no interest in seeing them.) Finally it was decided that Birte would stay in Copenhagen, in the tenuous hope that neutral Denmark would remain safe, as it had in World War I.

How could Lauritz and Kleinchen have ignored the possibility that Birte was being left in danger? Would it not have been safer to bring a nineteen-year-old to America with them? Surely Melchior's career was blooming. He had never sung so much or for such enormous fees, nor had he ever been so well-known throughout the country. By what reasoning was it better to leave his young daughter alone in Denmark than to bring her with them to live in their roomy hotel apartment in New York? Most importantly, how could the Melchiors disregard the fact that Birte's mother was in part Jewish? For years they had been witnessing first hand the fate of their Jewish friends and colleagues at the hands of the Nazis. In no way could they plead ignorance. It has been said that Kleinchen would not tolerate the girl living with them. (Indeed, when Birte asked outright to come and visit the United States after the war—Inger's family was prepared to foot the bill—Kleinchen "wouldn't hear of it.") While this may or may not be the answer, no better one presents itself.

When asked directly whether she felt outraged over being left behind to face unknown dangers, Birte answers:

> This is a very delicate question. . . . Although my father and Kleinchen were fully aware of the dangers, they never even asked me whether I would like to go with them to the United States. They just left me, without work (I had been working for a Jewish firm), and without money. Yes, it is hard to understand that decision.

Until the occupation Birte did receive monthly from her father a small

amount of pocket-money through his Danish lawyer and friend, Poul Wiedemann. When the occupation came, Mr. Wiedemann asked whether he
should continue to pay Birte this pocket money out of his own account as
there was nothing left in Melchior's. Although Kleinchen's answer was,
"No," Wiedemann continued to give Birte money during the time that she
was without work.

Living in one small room and a tiny kitchen Birte (trained as an English
and German correspondent) tried to make a living, but, as she describes with
her deliberately emotionless British inflection, "it was very difficult because . . . I could use the German but not the English. I just got along. I
married a good friend of mine and had two children. I didn't love him, but
I married him." Later, Melchior's reaction was to complain that she had
"married poorly." When in 1944 a letter informing him of the birth of Birte's
son was smuggled to him, his response was typical, says Birte sadly. "My
father was always informed when my children were born. I *never* received
even a congratulation."

When the occupation started, Birte, desperate and convinced that she
had nothing to lose, defied her father and Kleinchen by seeking out her
mother's relatives, Uncle Knud Nathansen and his family. When the situation
with regard to the Danish Jews worsened, Uncle Knud expected to be investigated by the Germans and took steps to protect Birte also, by getting
them both an Aryan certificate. The unadorned truth—Birte's grandfather's
name had been changed from Mortensen to Nathansen and Birte had always
been a practicing Lutheran—made it appear that the family had, on some
bizarre whim, taken a Jewish name for the stage. Indeed, one night Knud
Nathansen was visited by the Nazis, but the documented fact that his name
had originally been Mortensen saved him. Who is to say what might have
happened to Birte without this paper? She was in the very worst position:
her being one-eighth Jewish resulted from descendancy on the mother's side,
which by Nazi logic was a death sentence.

It is not only extremely difficult to reconcile these facts with the Melchiors' decision to leave the young girl in Copenhagen, but the very process
of trying to come to an answer is troubling. Lauritz and Kleinchen took no
steps to assure Birte's safety, and brother Ib was already in America, appearing on Broadway. Only the Aryan certificate, obtained by Uncle Knud,
stood between Birte and danger. To be charitable, at the time it undoubtedly
seemed preposterous to the Melchiors that Birte's seemingly insignificant
Jewishness would endanger her, even as, in the beginning, millions of practicing Jews refused to believe that their fate would be so dire. It does not
explain Cousin Eva Andersen's story, however. During the occupation Eva's
former father-in-law, Clausen-Kaas, worried that he could not transfer money
to his daughter who lived in the United States. Through Sweden, Clausen-
Kaas contacted the Melchiors, proposing a deal: He would give money to
Birte if Melchior would do the same for Clausen-Kaas's daughter. His offer
was rejected.

Did Lauritz know everything that was going on? Or did Kleinchen keep some of these facts from him, as she had done on other occasions? There is no way to ascertain whether Melchior simply turned this affair over to Kleinchen, as he had so often with other matters. While no one fully knows Lauritz's rationale, it is probable that Ib's gentle assessment of his father as a man "lazy in human relationships" offers the best explanation. Kleinchen's complete management of the Melchiors' affairs required that Lauritz abdicate control. This he did in most things, for it was always easier to do as Kleinchen suggested, and he was a man who did not want to deal with the problems of daily life. He had no capacity to put himself out in family matters, or to be vigilantly protective as a parent must be. He was content to be the child.

October 4 saw Lauritz, Kleinchen, and Mutti board the *Kungsholm* in Göteborg for the voyage to New York. Though Birte was not taken along, Kleinchen had found passage for their Chossewitz maid and for the Laufkötters. Upon arrival in New York, Kleinchen was relieved to learn that the Met was not going to ban Wagner's music. Nonetheless, Birte was not sent for, confirming that it was not the insecurity of Lauritz's work that was uppermost in Kleinchen's reasoning. In reckoning the account one cannot escape the conclusion that Lauritz and Kleinchen—capable of going to great lengths of sacrifice and courage to save Jewish friends such as the Steinharters and Leo Taubman—had refused to aid Lauritz's own daughter.

"Don't ever mention Ib's name to Mr. Melchior, because he is such a terrible person that Mr. Melchior doesn't want to have anything to do with him," said Kleinchen to Ib's friend Tom, as she pulled him away from Lauritz at a big New York party in 1948. Tom reported to Ib what had happened when he, as an MGM executive, chanced to be introduced to Lauritz and Kleinchen at the Waldorf-Astoria. No sooner had Tom said that he knew Ib and thought him a fine fellow than Kleinchen took action. She had come up with a foolproof way to assure that no one would speak to Lauritz about his son.

Says Ib today, "I think that it was the first time I realized that this was the kind of thing Kleinchen did." (Reconstructing indications from before 1948, Ib recalled how Kleinchen, at the beginning of the war, had seized upon the very secrecy enforced upon him as a member of the OSS (he had volunteered after Pearl Harbor) to accuse him in front of Lauritz of keeping secrets from his father. There was also the stressful time at the end of the war when Ib, just demobilized, returned to America to find that his own son Leif, now three years old, might need kidney surgery. He applied to Lauritz for a loan, and the answer had been no; thereafter Kleinchen told Melchior intimates that Ib always wanted money, was "grabby," a thief, and a liar.)

Later in 1948 another incident heightened his suspicions. Ib, a freelance writer, had managed to sell a story to *Vogue* for the munificent sum of $1,000. At the time Lauritz rejoiced with him, but at the next meeting he accused Ib of lying, of trying to make himself look "a big man," because Kleinchen had found out that his fee was only $50. Showing his father the actual stub of the company check was useless. "This means nothing. Kleinchen told me."

The scope of Kleinchen's enmity began to escalate. No longer content to limit herself to family matters, she began to interfere in Ib's professional life. Still later in 1948 she learned of a project conceived by Ib and an independent movie producer, Marion Gering, to produce a film from Ib's script about Hans Christian Andersen and finance it with MGM funds still frozen in Denmark. The project had every chance for success until Kleinchen interfered. "Gering discovered that she had gone to MGM, saying that if they made any deals with me, my father would never work for MGM again," relates Ib. "Not wanting to become involved in a family squabble, they bowed out."

It was not until the early months of 1950 that Ib confirmed his suspicions: Kleinchen was systematically and methodically trying to discredit him in the eyes of his father. Previously, he had not heard stories of her machinations directly from anyone involved, but now CBS television personality Ed Sullivan, for whom he worked as an associate director, came to him and said, "Ib, your mother has just called and given me a very strange message." Kleinchen had declared that her husband would not appear on Sullivan's show so long as Ib was in his employ. Sullivan was totally amazed. Has this ever happened before? Why would even a stepmother do such a thing? Ib had no answer. Sullivan, incensed at this attempt to dictate to him, vowed to keep Ib on the show. Ib suggested a sensible alternative: he could be sent to work on another show until Lauritz's appearance was finished. That way Ed could honestly say to Kleinchen that her stepson was no longer working for him. And that is exactly what they did, with Kleinchen none the wiser. After this incident, Ib discovered that it was Kleinchen who, one year earlier, had spoiled his chances for an NBC job. Although Lauritz himself had introduced his son to General Sarnoff in the hope that a position might materialize, Kleinchen had written to Sarnoff, stating that her stepson would be unreliable as an employee.

Many have said that Lauritz withstood all tempests around him, standing with rocklike calmness in the center, untouched by the turmoil. Whether he knew the real facts of what Kleinchen was doing to his children or not, she managed her campaign without being challenged. Since Lauritz never answered the phone or the mail, it was simple to keep things from him. Indeed, her usual ploy to keep a caller at bay was to say that Lauritz was in the bath and couldn't come to the phone. His abdication of command made it all easy.

Ib accepts his father's neglect with an enviable philosophical composure:

One can break up the times that my father and I saw each other into four areas. First, the time until I was eleven years old, when I rarely saw Far, but he was my father, although somewhere else. Second, the time when I was at boarding school or the university, or acting with the English Company, or even during the war, when I saw my father and Kleinchen during vacations or leaves. Third, the time during which Kleinchen had convinced him that I was no good. It was a period of estrangement on their part, not mine, because I kept calling and writing but I could not get past her and through to him. This period lasted well beyond the end of World War II. Last was the time after Kleinchen died, when Far and I became very close. Then I was probably the closest person to him. . . . You could say that I had four different fathers.

Lauritz's friend and great admirer, Dr. Rudolf Steinharter, comments, "The children of prominent people very often have tragic lives." Yet Ib Melchior managed to triumph over the often difficult circumstances of his life. Not limited to a career as a television and motion picture director—more than three years directing "The Perry Como Show" and twelve feature films as writer and/or director—as an author he has produced ten successful books.

It was apparent to the music world that Flagstad and Melchior had reconciled their differences when the soprano was persuaded to record with Melchior in November 1939. (The Copenhagen newspaper, *Berlingske Tidende*, speculated that Henry Johansen had tired of the enmity between the two Scandinavians and put down a firm husbandly foot, a command that Flagstad obeyed.) The two singers, whom the public still regarded as the "golden couple," recorded the prologue duet from *Götterdämmerung* and the love duet from Act II of *Tristan und Isolde*. Charles O'Connell, in charge of the recording, described the session: Two minutes before recording time, Melchior had not appeared, and the staff's anxiety level was extremely high, for fear that it might give Flagstad "another opportunity to become obstinate." Just in time Melchior strode into the room smoking a big cigar, disheveled, dirty and tired—just back from a nightlong duck-hunting expedition. Lauritz cleared his throat a few times and got going. Most, including O'Connell, agree that he scarcely ever sang better. Clearly, Melchior was not overly disturbed by Flagstad's former stubborn dislike of singing with him. Were he so perturbed, he would most likely have prepared better, taken pains to be in good vocal shape for a "contest." Instead, he behaved exactly as usual and went hunting.

By this time Kirsten Flagstad's closest American friends were Edwin McArthur and his wife. McArthur served not only as her accompanist and preferred conductor, but also as a buffer between Flagstad and those who pursued her or solicited favors. In a February 1940 interview he was somewhat less than subtle about this relationship. "He leaned back and stuck a big cigar into his mouth," read the piece. "'Sure I've got a drag [influence]. I'm Mme. Kirsten Flagstad's accompanist.'" He told how he advised her about clothes, how he suggested that she not come on stage with a big black book of words. (Melchior and Traubel too resorted to a similar method to avoid reliance on their memory—large index cards or a book with the song texts in large block letters, Melchior's with red and blue transliterations from Danish to help his pronunciation. The cards were only slightly less visible than the black book, but would be equally unacceptable today.) McArthur said that he hoped some day to conduct at the Met, and added, with a sniff, that Leinsdorf, who was supposed to be twenty-seven, "has been twenty-seven for three years now."

In late November, just before Chicago Opera's opening night (where Martinelli was essaying his first Tristan with the hearty approval of Flagstad, his Isolde), Artur Bodanzky died suddenly after twenty-four years on the Met podium, leaving a vacuum in the German wing. Flagstad expressed her condolences by telegram and asked whether McArthur could be given an opportunity at the Met, a subject that she had never broached heretofore. Finally an evasive reply arrived from Johnson, whereupon Flagstad, amazingly enough, cabled Melchior for help. Perhaps because he wanted to stay on Kirsten's good side now that they had made up, Melchior went to bat for McArthur, a generous act by a man who had a high personal regard for McArthur but considered him far better as a pianist than as a "mediocre conductor." Johnson stonewalled for a while, and then chose the twenty-seven-year-old Erich Leinsdorf, who had conducted Wagner only four times during his two seasons at the Met.

Leinsdorf had been engaged by the Met in April 1937, partially because Hope Associates had repeatedly assured the economy-minded Met that Leinsdorf, in addition to being a conductor, was also an accompanist, chorusmaster, and musicologist. He was put to work assisting Bodanzky and made his debut in January 1938 conducting *Walküre* with Flagstad and Althouse. (Of this, Leinsdorf has written, "To me it was decidedly an advantage not to have Melchior in the cast at my debut, since he was unreliable and a nuisance to conductors with greater experience than I.")

Most insiders were astounded to see Johnson stand up to Flagstad's pressure. Money cannot have been the deciding factor, for Leinsdorf and McArthur would have made the same small amount—one could only describe it as a pittance—at the time. Flagstad was not trying to unseat young Leinsdorf, explained McArthur later; she just believed "that an American conductor of the same generation should have an equal opportunity."

Several jokes began to make the rounds, intimating that Leinsdorf would shortly be at the mercy of Flagstad whose ambitions for Edwin McArthur were well-known. Soon the press reported that a real fight was brewing between Flagstad and Melchior (both of whom were characterized as powerful, willful, and temperamental) on one side and Erich Leinsdorf (who was depicted as modest, talented, young, and defenseless) on the other. Melchior protested to the press that there never was a fight, just discussions between the stage and the pit, most of them regarding the tempos that had been set by Bodanzky. Flagstad, while preparing to leave for Toronto, gave her friends details that were duly recorded in the press: Flagstad had accused Leinsdorf of finishing the cup scene of a previous *Tristan* "a full minute" before she had completed her part. After two days of illness caused by the trauma, she brought this to his attention. Leinsdorf, she said, had responded, "I am doing it as Toscanini did." Flagstad protested: "When I am in full voice upstage I cannot hear the orchestra in the pit. I must see the cues from the conductor. Since Mr. Leinsdorf is inexperienced, he must watch his score. I see his arms moving, but I cannot tell where the music is. I need those cues."

Melchior (either momentarily untended by Constance Hope or encouraged by her because she had a vested interest in keeping both her clients on the front page) gave an interview in which he said that Leinsdorf was "too young" to take charge of the entire German repertoire and a "more experienced" conductor should be brought in. Leinsdorf, prudently without comment, sent away the reporters, who promptly went to the Met and asked to speak to Johnson.

Johnson, using brilliant tactics, managed to turn the situation to his (and the Met's) advantage. First he effectively disposed of the singers. "There are some 'old boats' in the company who have no competition for their roles and would be dictator." Next he rallied the protectors of the helpless young against the powerful oldsters: "There are old men who try to keep from the music scene much younger men who show genius . . . trying to gang up on a young man with a brilliant future." Within twenty-four hours, after a hastily convened board meeting, he had completed the job by announcing a campaign to make the Metropolitan into an independent, pay-as-you-go national opera company. One million dollars would be sought to buy back the opera house from the stockholder-boxholders.

Letters came in hot and heavy, a representative number supporting and criticizing each combatant. Those who felt that Flagstad was not the kind of temperamental singer who would say such derogatory things castigated Johnson for hurrying her retirement by his rudeness. Those who supported Leinsdorf criticized Flagstad for creating the whole imbroglio just to get a job for her protégé. Those who were sympathetic toward Melchior nagged that Leinsdorf had so little control over how loudly the orchestra played that Melchior and Schorr were seen by the audience with their mouths open and no sound coming out. Those against Melchior suggested not subtly that he lose weight before he criticized anyone for being too young. Impresario and personal manager Charles Wagner, an old hand at such machinations, made an informed guess in his letter: "While there's life, there's Constance Hope." In his P.S. he hinted that any man who could sing "under McArthur! What's *that*?!" should not complain about Leinsdorf.

Meanwhile behind the scenes powerful forces were at work to remedy the situation. Even Mayor La Guardia, whose command of public relations was legendary, joined the fray with a personal letter to Lauritz. His recommendation "*Sei nicht so dumm!*" ("Don't be so dumb!") was followed by a compendium of Melchior's virtues and a (correct) prediction that "the papers will eat this up. They will exaggerate what you say . . . and it will all result in injury to the Metropolitan." The mayor proposed a solution:

> Tonight take a bow with young Leinsdorf. Pat him on the back. . . . I know that you are generous and big enough to do it. Is it not better to have a young conductor in the pit and a seasoned, perfect Melchior on the stage? . . . You and Flagstad can make up any deficiency in the pit.

Despite letters from a group of standees who supported their tenor to the hilt, and a telegram saying "Old boats in good condition, and very seaworthy, A Good Friend," Melchior decided not to take on more trouble. On January 29, Melchior and Leinsdorf staged a potent public reconciliation scene in front of the curtain during *Die Walküre*. The audience on this evening featured a little group dedicated to booing the conductor, another small ensemble determined to hiss the tenor, and a large group prepared to see a fight. The brief booing and hissing were tame by Madison Square Garden standards, declared the *New Yorker*.

The entire thing was over in four days. The dispute left in its wake a beautifully timed, highly publicized (at no cost to the Met) million-dollar fund drive with which to purchase the opera house from the original stockholders and their heirs, to be headed by financial dynamo George Sloan (who was so ill-informed about the cast of characters that he referred publicly to the soprano as "Flagstaff"). By April of this year the guarantee fund had swelled to $833,342, and, at its successful conclusion in September of 1940, showed a final amount of $1,300,000, which had come equally from the campaign committee, Opera Guild members, and radio listeners.

Part of the credit for the favorable conclusion of this project must be laid to the Metropolitan's ability to present superb casts in the Wagnerian operas. In November, for example, the business leaders of New York had voted for Wagner over the traditional public favorite, *Carmen*. For two years Wagnerian music dramas starring Melchior and Flagstad had been overwhelmingly the choice of charitable organizations for their benefit evenings, which have long been recognized as an efficient financial barometer of the public's allegiance. There is no doubt that the splendid Wagnerian singing contributed handsomely to the Met's fund-raising. Speaking of one December performance of *Tristan*, critic-composer Virgil Thomson (never accused of effusive writing) almost gushed over the individual and ensemble work of Melchior, Flagstad, Kipnis, Branzell, and baritone Julius Huehn:

> It has never been the privilege of this reviewer to hear or to witness anywhere as sumptuous a performance . . . as that of yesterday's matinee. The cast was not only a list of faultless singers but a unit of

harmonious voices as well. . . . The resemblance among these [singers] in power and in style gave to the whole musical rendition a compositional quality of unity in variety as if the composer himself had asked for just those persons and those persons were a single family.

During the course of the fund-raising effort, the Met had bolstered its new high approval rating, and at the same time silenced those who criticized it for favoring foreign artists, by issuing figures on their artists' nationalities. On the roster as of October 7, 1939, were sixty-five Americans, seventeen Germans, fourteen Italians, four Swedes, three Hungarians, and no more than two singers each from fifteen other countries—plus one Dane—but, of course, only about ten of the Americans were doing leading roles.

On January 22, 1940, Lauritz Melchior joined the ranks of those privileged few whose pictures have graced the front cover of *Time*. Under his photograph as Siegfried blowing his hunting horn the caption read: "188 Siegfrieds; 163 Tristans; 138 Siegmunds; 104 Tannhäusers; 68 Lohengrins; 54 Parsifals." The article pronounced him "Prince of Heldentenors" and "the world's Number 1 Wagnerian tenor," and offered a description of him costumed as Siegfried: "his noble paunch encased in a deer skin, his stubby grey hair covered with a luxuriant blonde wig." Perceptively, the *Time* writers, after covering the popular trend toward Wagnerian operas (which they found traceable to Flagstad's 1935 appearance), recognized the contribution of the Met's other Wagnerians, declaring them "as fine a team of husky, seasoned . . . troupers as could be found in any opera house the world over," and "gargantuan jovial Tenor Melchior" to be the "sturdiest of all those sturdy troupers." *Time* did not neglect the frosty, "only limelight deep" relationship between Flagstad and Melchior, while taking care to note that the tenor's "triple-brass larynx" earned the same "top pay that Flagstad gets" for withstanding the wear and tear of Siegfried and Siegmund "without straining a capillary." Lauritz, the essay went on, "never forgets that he is a Dane." Most notable of the *Time* inclusions, however, must be the mention of his first wife and his children—a first of sorts—and its insistence upon the "parachute story," which was by no means a first.

This charming fairytale had played well, especially in America:

Lauritz Melchior, the young, talented Heldentenor, was relaxing in his garden in Munich, sitting beneath a large old tree studying a score. A whooshing noise above his head made him look up. Imagine his astonishment as he beheld, descending from the sky, a tiny, beautiful girl in helmet, goggles, riding breeches, and boots. She was suspended from a giant white parachute that had landed in his tree. Gallantly he climbed up to rescue the angelic creature from the clutches of the wicked garden tree. One of the great romances of the operatic world had begun!

Various versions of this romanticized fable of Kleinchen and Lauritz's initial meeting became a staple of Melchior's publicity after Constance Hope had taken over the reins. Completely untrue, it does, however, draw upon some facts from Kleinchen's life. As the 1926 shipboard interview in New York harbor affirms, "Maria Hacker, the 'German Mary Pickford,' . . . was prepared to give up her film career for a career in business in order to preserve her home life." Maria told how, shortly after her graduation from school, she joined a film company that was making a thriller patterned after "The Perils of Pauline," in which she (under her film name, Hannelore Meister) was called upon to do all the daredevil stunts, including those atop an airplane in flight. Some of the pictures in Kleinchen's own photo album show Hannelore scaling the side of a building with admirable insouciance.

It is apparent that all concerned had eventually realized how Lauritz's publicity could be enhanced by judicious stitching together of the various facts (after all, Kleinchen did do parachute stunts in the movies and Lauritz did have a garden in Munich), accented by a delicate embroidery of interesting details. Once locked into this fanciful verison, the couple stuck to it. By 1941 *Opera News* had published the story, and eight years later Kleinchen was still insisting in print that the story was true, "even though it sounds like a press agent's cooked-up story." To their close friends Kleinchen giggled about this brilliant concoction, and Lauritz laughed to Ib and the family about the gullibility of the public.

About the same time the gossip columns printed a bit of poetry composed by Lauritz. Tired of having his name mispronounced as "Melquire," he had often protested wittily, "They overestimate me; I am only one man." Finally he had this effort printed on cards (and disseminated to the press)

> There is a tenor big and jolly,
> Who's hardly ever melancholy;
> There's just one thing that can raise his ire:
> To have his name misspelled Mel-CHOIR;
> Such carelessness will bring a roar
> Of rage from Lauritz Melchi-OR.

In comparison with his fiftieth birthday, however, all other matters of 1940 were trivial to Lauritz. As the day approached telegrams and cables came not singly, but in batches from New York City, eleven states, Denmark, London, Oslo, Rome, and Germany. Mutti worked on the cakes, one for each of thirty-seven tables at the Copenhagen Restaurant, which Kleinchen had taken over for the party. Figures of Lauritz in all his roles were cut from postcards and pasted on little flagsticks to decorate the cakes. Presents, mostly fishing rods and guns, arrived constantly (and were hidden by Kleinchen) until the moment that they left for Philadelphia. Lauritz, who had begun to refuse singing dates on his birthday, nevertheless was booked to do *Parsifal* in Philadelphia the night before. Kleinchen carried a few presents and two bottles of champagne with them in case he "got fifty" on the train.

The birthday itself was a nonstop eating experience. The Danish Luncheon Club of New York tendered Lauritz a party at noon; he and Kleinchen gave a smallish dinner party for sixteen at the Rainbow Room that evening; then came the big party at the Copenhagen Restaurant for more than 500. The guest list was nothing if not democratic, from the diplomatic services through Met staffers, including several tenors (notably Crooks and Althouse). Lauritz passed a large portion of the evening kissing and being kissed by sopranos and contraltos of all sizes and shapes.

There is no evidence to prove that Constance Hope orchestrated this event, but the details certainly suggest that she and Kleinchen did not have Lauritz's typically Danish love of an anniversary exclusively in mind. As she had done with the Guard parties at the Ansonia, Kleinchen artfully wove business and pleasure together. Whether or not Lauritz so regarded it, it was a major publicity event, written, cast, and directed by Constance Hope and Kleinchen.

The press were obliged to use their usual word—"incredible"—for the food at a Melchior party. At 1:00 A.M. the cast of that evening's *Parsifal* production arrived. It was then that "a million dollars' worth of talent," led by Kirsten Flagstad, sang "Happy Birthday" followed by the Siegfried motif. This stellar moment led to Walter Slezak's reading of an epic poem (written by Constance Hope and Viva Liebling, wife of the critic Leonard Liebling) before the assembled multitude. A few verses of the poem, which show that Wagnerians had the wit to make fun of themselves, featured operatic heroines,

> Brünnhilde, the queen of the mounted police,
> Is all things to Lauritz excepting his niece.
> She's his sister, his aunt and his wife and his widow
> And it takes her three operas to express her libido.

his dresser, Angelo Casamassa,

> He protects all the clothes of this great Wagner hero
> For he knows that the chances to borrow are zero.

and tenors,

> With Althouse, his pal, Lauritz shares the same views,
> And when tenor loves tenor, my friends, that is news!

In the midst of the party, referring to the recent Leinsdorf contretemps, Melchior told the press, "I don't think the boat is so old that it will sink quite yet—unless it is torpedoed. . . . I guess I have a little noise left in me."

During the 1940 Met spring tour, the Nazis invaded the Scandinavian countries, and comments about the Scandinavians in the casts abounded. On April 12, 1940, the Met tour was in Dallas, where critic John Rosenfield wrote affectingly of Texas's delight that the heroic tenor had not been shot up in the last war or this. His piece revealed a total understanding of Melchior's command of Wagner's greatest principles and an unusual knowledge of the intricacies of operatic singing:

> Saved for us . . . is that pealing upper register, the heroic texture of the rest of the voice, that profound musicianship that realizes all subtle relationships of Wagner orchestra and voice. The dead hand of Bayreuth weighs heavily on some aspects of Melchior's art. (The costume described by Wagner ill becomes his gemütlich figure. The ecstatic spread-eagles, the stone bench cuddle . . . are saved from absurdity by the reservoir of Melchior dignity.) His faults at that are only those of an ineluctable Wagner tradition, and when a tenor can call the 15-bar "Wälse!" with incomparable clarity and firmness, suffuse his narrative with heartrending pathos and even elevate the . . . "Todesverkündigung" to the plane of epic tragedy, you must bow before opera-house greatness. Forgive him then if he is only a Wagner puppet. . . . Treasure him for the most meaningful Wagner proclamations today. Nor have his years and stentorian declamation destroyed his sense of cantilena. When the score changes unexpectedly into the Italianate arioso . . . Melchior lilts with it."

The tour company, however, was enveloped in despair because of the war news. Kleinchen and Lauritz could never endure for long such an atmosphere without taking matters into their own hands. Their determination to cheer people up usually took the form of a practical joke or a prank. The trip to New Orleans was no different. When a member of the company put forth an idea inspired by the depressing formality usually displayed by local welcoming committees, Kleinchen enthusiastically joined the plan for shaking up the New Orleans organizers a bit.

Between Dallas and New Orleans the makeup man was shanghaied and commanded to put whiskers and beards on every single tenor and conductor. From the luggage car they appropriated a suitcase full of false beards, side whiskers, wigs, and mustaches. Lauritz tried on several types of hirsute appendages until he was satisfied with a marked resemblance to von Hindenburg.

Kleinchen was busy capturing the ridiculous scene on the Melchior's movie camera as the gentlemen, in their hirsute glory—Crooks with black handlebars and strangely hued herbage on his chin, conductor Pelletier in matching gray beard and mustache, and Maestro Cimara looking, according to Leinsdorf, like "an early edition of Ho Chi Minh"—walked shaggily down the platform toward the committee. Sponsors and press stood in absolute silence, riveted to the platform, eyes round with shock. Once aware of the joke, the committee began to enjoy themselves, the press had a field day, and the company was once again ready to perform with zest—although they were not invited back for years.

Lauritz's January of 1941 was replete with large parties. The best was President Roosevelt's fifty-ninth birthday luncheon in the White House Blue Room on January 30. Kleinchen and Lauritz were invited, along with several movie stars, including Deanna Durbin, Maureen O'Hara, Red Skelton, and Glenn Ford. Mrs. Roosevelt, who sat between Lauritz and movie star Wallace Beery, succumbed to the Danish charm and pronounced the singer "a delightful companion" in her "My Day" column. The President invited Lauritz to return that evening to sing at the "cufflink dinner" which he gave each year for a group of old friends.

Lauritz acquiesced immediately, but didn't know what to do about an accompanist. The President offered to have anyone Lauritz wanted brought from New York, so Melchior called Otto Seyfert. The pianist, who had long suffered under Melchiorian pranks, listened calmly to Lauritz spin his long story full of details about how the motorized police would pick Otto up at home, how they would then transport him to the airport, where a military plane would be waiting to fly him to Washington, where he would then play for President Roosevelt in the White House. Seyfert laughed heartily, believing that for once he had forestalled a new joke of some sort. Kleinchen had to get on the phone and talk to Mrs. Seyfert before the pianist would believe either of them. By the time Seyfert arrived in Washington, the hotel manager had found them a piano—it was ancient, untuned, and almost unplayable, due to the thousands of drinks spilled inside. When the keys were pressed down, they would stay there until pried up again. Seyfert declared it impossible, even for a rehearsal.

As they waited in one of the White House reception rooms, the major-domo entered to ask them where their instrument was. Disconcerted, they stammered, "Well . . . we don't carry one wherever we go. . . . We naturally expected that there would be a grand piano at the White House." The performers were told that it would take too long to move the heavy and ornate mahogany piano from its usual place a few floors upstairs. On what had they rehearsed at the hotel? A rickety, barely playable upright. The gentleman left. After more waiting, the major-domo returned and asked Melchior and Seyfert to step into the hall. To their horror they saw two burly men carrying "our wonder of a piano from the hotel" up the main stairs of the White House.

> I remember clearly that both of them were wearing their hats, and as they entered the hall, our gentleman said in a thunderous voice, "Take your hats off, when you enter the White House!" And one of the workmen answered, "Sir, we are not paying a social call."

The two performers were ashamed to follow that hideous piano into the dining room where all the guests were congregated, Mrs. Roosevelt costumed as Whistler's mother in the famous painting ("I'm playing a joke on Frankie"). As the accompanist struggled with the ivoryless and/or nonfunctioning keys, Lauritz looked around. One gentleman was asleep. No one appeared to notice the strange effect of the piano, whose missing fourth leg was replaced by a small table contributed by "Whistler's mother." While Seyfert hammered energetically upon the stuck keys, Lauritz sang a few loud notes, virtually a cappella. The sleeping guest twitched and jerked with each high note, sent Lauritz "a very eloquent glance," and then went back to his nap. After their songs the two musicians had a glass of champagne with the president. Then the major-domo put a stop to that with a supercilious gesture. The piano was rolled out of the dining room and "we, like mourners at a funeral, shuffled silently after it."

By 1939 Flagstad expressed her intention to retire at the end of the 1939–1940 Met season. At the end of the season, however, she had informed a delighted Johnson that she was considering returning for the next season, although she had told him flat out, according to Melchior, that if McArthur were not allowed to conduct she would leave the tour. To this ultimatum he acceded, and McArthur conducted an April 1 Boston performance. (His debut was generally regarded as a success, although it was said that he had "mastered the rudiments but not the intricacies of conducting.") Thereafter, Flagstad planned to sing only part of the tour, and she was booked to sail back to Norway on April 22, 1940. The touring company of the Met left Boston on April 8 and headed for Cleveland. The Janssens, the Melchiors, and Kirsten Flagstad played cards aboard the train before turning in.

 With one glance at the next morning's headlines Lauritz learned that Germany had occupied Denmark secretly during the night in order to "protect the country against the British." Denmark had given little resistance, but Norway, also attacked on April 9, was now at war with the Nazis. Lauritz went immediately to Kirsten's compartment and told her the terrible news. Flagstad's first reaction was to fear that the Germans would not allow her to go home on April 22. She spent the remainder of the day trying by telephone and cable to get in touch with her family in Oslo. Eventually, she was forced by circumstances to remain in the United States.

 The performance of February 17, 1941, was a triply auspicious occasion. It marked the fifteenth anniversary of Melchior's Metropolitan debut, Flagstad's 100th Isolde, and McArthur's debut in the Met house. Very early that morning there came a knock at the door of Flagstad's suite at the Waldorf. She sat up in bed, startled. A voice called out sharply, "Your breakfast, Madame." But she had ordered none and called back to say so. The waiter persisted and she let him in. He entered with a beautifully decorated bed tray set with handsome crockery and silver. On the tray in large letters was engraved "To Isolde from her Tristan." It was a gift from Melchior. By her own admission, Flagstad wept. That evening Lauritz and McArthur, together with Ziegler, Johnson, and Earle Lewis of the business office, sent the soprano 100 roses with a touching poem.

McArthur's opportunity to conduct at the Met, not just on tour, was the result of a fierce battle of wills between Flagstad and the Met administration that had raged all fall. Flagstad was intransigent: The price of extending her contract to include more performances would be the engagement of McArthur in New York. On January 20, only one week before Flagstad was needed for *Siegfried* (because French dramatic soprano Germaine Lubin was prevented from honoring her contract), the Met had capitulated and given McArthur a contract for three performances. A summation of the general critical response to McArthur's debut came from Thompson: "If the results were not momentous, neither were they materially different from those of the *Tristan* performances in the last several seasons. The American conductor knew the score thoroughly and the orchestra played for him much as they played for Erich Leinsdorf."

All agreed that McArthur had a genuine talent for conducting and for opera. Indeed, he should have been commended for one amazing feat: in Act I his orchestra actually got *ahead* of Lauritz Melchior at the phrase "*zu König Markes Land.*" McArthur is probably the only conductor who could claim to have outrun the Dane.

As early as March, papers began to announce that Mme. Flagstad was intending to return to Norway at the completion of her scheduled performances in April. Although relations between Flagstad and Johnson had become strained by the battle over McArthur, artists' representative Marks Levine assured Edward Johnson by letter on March 25 that Flagstad had every intention of returning to New York after the summer trip, but that she realized "such plans are dependent upon world conditions. She does not care to learn *Oberon* but will submit a list of other roles."

It is curious that so much press was given to Melchior's lordly demeanor at the Met, while virtually no one mentioned the enormous change in Flagstad's attitude, as documented by McArthur. From a modest Norwegian singer, the adulation of America and the world had produced a diva. Every now and then, however, amid fulsome columns about Flagstad, one or another critic would take notice of Melchior's contribution: "With so much attention focused on the heroine, the singing of Tristan might be overlooked. Were anyone suddenly substituted for Melchior, it would at once become apparent how fine a Tristan he is."

About Melchior as Tristan in a Boston performance of April 2 a critic at the *Post* wrote, "this reviewer has been slow in realizing the tenor's true stature as a singing actor." His commendation of Melchior ("it is not easy to believe that a Tristan such as Mr. Melchior's walks any present-day stage") was accompanied by the heretical admission that "some of us have a sneaking desire to have another Isolde for a change."

At the last New York performance of Melchior and Flagstad together (as Tristan and Isolde), Melchior obtained permission from Edward Johnson to make a speech between the acts. During their curtain call Melchior stopped the applause and announced that Kirsten Flagstad was returning to Norway and her family after her two performances on tour. "Let's wish her a happy voyage and a happy return." Lauritz left the stage to the soprano amid repeated cheers of "Flagstad! Flagstad!"

After several curtain calls, and repeated cries of "Speech!" she responded: "My dear friends, I am very happy that I am going home, but I know that on the day I come back I will be even happier. Thank you—all of you."

In Cleveland after the *Walküre* performance of April 17, Lauritz Melchior and Kirsten Flagstad embraced. She cried on his shoulder as they said goodbye, never to meet again. Via Bermuda she flew to Lisbon, thence (after many delays) to Berlin and finally, after much waiting, to her family in Oslo.

CHAPTER 12

Another Legendary Partnership:
Melchior and Traubel

(1941–1946)

World War II, which made travel to the United States impossible for Kirsten Flagstad as well as other European artists, put American artists at the Metropolitan Opera on a new footing; in general, they were given better roles and sang more often. In the German wing, Kirsten Flagstad's prolonged absence opened up opportunities for other dramatic sopranos. Melchior, although blessed with a phalanx of Wagnerian sopranos, was holding the fort alone in the heavy Heldentenor Fach. Indeed, Melchior's lasting reputation would eventually rest primarily upon his recordings, precisely because the actions of Nazi Germany had prompted him to leave Bayreuth in 1931 (after taking part in only six festivals) and had caused him to abandon his singing career in Europe after 1939.

At this time, there was scarcely a day when one or both Melchiors were not in the papers for something or other, for Kleinchen had become an expert at the publicity business and was very proficient at sniffing out ways to exploit everything they did. Melchior was a deeply patriotic man whose allegiance to his two countries was utterly sincere, but he and Kleinchen simply became inured to the idea that whatever they did for charity or for the war effort could do double duty for publicity as well. In years to come, this attitude assumed the status of a principle: no publicity attached, no appearance. While effective in a business way, the behavior was to boomerang and to be seen as discreditable, if not downright tacky.

To balance the account it must be said that, even before financial stability allowed Melchior to absorb the loss of fees entailed in charity performances, he was more than willing to accept such engagements. As his fame grew, so grew the demands upon his time. In the early summer of 1932, as an example, he sang several benefits for Leo Blech and a gala performance of *Pagliacci*—

at which the Prince of Wales was present—for the Royal Danish Opera. According to Lauritz's meticulous records, the Dane did somewhere between two and thirteen benefits per year in the United States, a total of 179 from 1926 to 1960. Since his average fee was $2,000, this came to more than $500,000 worth of charity concert and opera appearances, not even counting those he did in Denmark, Canada, England, Spain, France, Germany, and Argentina.

Even before the Japanese bombed Pearl Harbor, Melchior had been haranguing his Washington acquaintances about the danger of Nazism. Although he and Kleinchen had decided that they would become American citizens, Lauritz felt that it would be disloyal to do so while the struggle continued. As a foreign national he could not fight, but he could help in his own way. For his soon-to-be-adoptive country he spoke and sang for the Red Cross, in theater canteens, at West Point and civil defense functions, in military camps, and for the U.S.O. Feeling honor-bound to do what he could to alleviate the suffering in Europe during the war, he made speeches, sang songs, and appeared for many Scandinavian organizations such as the Danish Seamen's Christmas Fund, the Danish Soldiers' Fund, and the Little Norway Fund. He gave help to groups such as The American Friends of Danish Freedom and Democracy, the National America-Denmark Association, Denmark War Relief, and the Friends of Denmark. He was not looking for reward when he organized several benefit concerts for "Help to Finland" during the winter war in that country, but he was proud to be given a decoration—the Cross of the Knight Commander of the Finnish White Rose—for his efforts.

His concern for the men of the armed forces was genuine. Long after the war when many had forgotten about the veterans, Melchior did not. On the Fourth of July, 1949, he made a day-long, fifteen-hour tour of veteran's institutions throughout the metropolitan area of New York under record conditions of wilting heat that would have daunted a younger man. "Melchior sang for us . . . on a holiday when everyone else went to the beach, and that was better than all the medicine in the world," said a veterans' newspaper.

Throughout the war Lauritz, member of the committee of prominent Danes in America, had been regularly briefed as to the actions taken by the Danish foreign service in exile, headed by Ambassador Henrik Kauffmann. Although his position as minister to Washington had been rescinded more than once by the German-controlled Danish Foreign Office, Kauffmann (and other Danish consular officers in the United States) stayed until the liberation of Denmark, and took actions "on behalf of His Majesty Christian X, King of Denmark," such as signing a diplomatic agreement with the United States that allowed the United States to occupy and defend Greenland. As Melchior reflected, "Thank God, here we had good Danish men who gathered around Kauffmann and Denmark's cause."

Just before the end of 1941 the Metropolitan summed up their achievements subsequent to closing the books on their million-dollar fund drive. The purchase of the opera house initiated many changes, physical, financial and artistic: installation of a new gold curtain and magnificently comfortable seats in the grand tier and balcony; hiring of new players for the orchestra and new conductors; institution of a program of public service, including low-priced tickets; addition of nineteen young American-born, American-trained singers, with a course of training for the younger artists; and a substantial reduction in the price of tickets for regular subscription performances. All in all, the board had every reason to feel proud of these accomplishments.

At the same time the papers were full of Henry Johansen's announcement that his wife was back in Norway to stay. Neither her management nor the Met had received direct word from Flagstad, and all feared that the Norwegian puppet government of the Nazis was behind the statement. Lauritz declared privately that personally he was convinced Kirsten knew nothing of and cared nothing for politics.

Duties were therefore being split on the dramatic soprano front. Melchior's partners included several fine Wagnerian singers, Helen Traubel, Astrid Varnay, and Rose Bampton, in addition to his beloved Lotte Lehmann. Marjorie Lawrence, who had contracted polio, was missing during 1941, while she gallantly worked to overcome the paralysis resulting from the disease. In 1942 Lawrence evoked the intense interest and sympathy of the entire United States as she came back to the Met one and one half years after suffering her paralysis. An audience of 3,800 persons crowded into the theater to witness the December "Welcome Back" gala concert, a tribute to the courageous spirit of this indomitable woman. Reclining on her throne she sang the "Venusberg" duet with Lauritz, as her part of the program, and was received with tumultuous applause. That 1942–1943 season she sang at the Met and on tour in Chicago, all four times as Venus, and all with Lauritz. Next season, her last, Lawrence sang Venus five times, and in her one performance as Isolde she was again received with great enthusiasm. "So strong was the lure of her personality and so apposite her gestures and facial play," said Jerome Bohm of her Isolde, that he hardly missed her ability to move around. Also it was noted that she was "the first in a long time to deliver [the love duet] with both high Cs" (a small gibe at Traubel and Flagstad, among others). Despite her total command of the role, Johnson hinted that some patrons were made uncomfortable by her presence on stage. After a few more performances in New York and on tour, she was never heard at the Met again.

Taking up some of the slack in the dramatic soprano ranks in the first season of Flagstad's absence was a young and inexperienced Norwegian soprano trained in America. Astrid Varnay, married to the Met's Wagner coach, Hermann Weigert, was singing her first season at the Met. Perhaps her seventeen performances during the 1941–1942 season (in contrast to the eight given Helen Traubel) had something to do with the fee schedule, for Traubel's cachet was almost three times that of Varnay. Certainly Varnay sang often because she learned roles speedily and accurately, something Traubel reputedly had difficulty doing.

In 1919 Lauritz had sung two performances of *Tannhäuser* in Oslo. On both those occasions the stage manager of that company, Astrid Varnay's father, had been very helpful and supportive to the young singer. Now, as Varnay's first Siegmund, Melchior was able to repay his kindness. Later he and Varnay would collaborate in *Tannhäuser, Lohengrin, Siegfried, Parsifal,* and *Tristan und Isolde.* Lauritz gave Astrid his greatest accolade, bringing her a deerskin for her Sieglinde costume after one of his hunting forays. Before and after her December 6 Metropolitan debut as Sieglinde, Melchior was openly Varnay's champion. He continued his vigorous attempts to further the young dramatic soprano's career at the Met and with the recording companies.

Although Lotte Lehmann was contracted to sing six performances in 1942, she sang only two. Her Sieglinde on February 15 (obviously a fine one, even for a woman who now wanted to avoid the role) elicited one of two diverting "sports" reviews for this month. Virgil Thomson wrote the horserace piece:

> Wagner continues to bring out the vocalism fans. Last night's *Walküre* was heard by a full house . . . with many standing and applause running high. Vocalism ran pretty high, too, with Lotte Lehmann leading the field, Helen Traubel and Lauritz Melchior placing. Julius Huehn, vocally limping from the start, was about to run in the third act in spite of his disabilities when your reviewer went off to write his piece.

The *Post* featured football: "MAISON TO CARRON TO MELCHIOR AS USUAL." The situation on February 1 described by the *Post* was but one of the several incidents this season that pointed up the Met's (unhealthy, some said) dependence upon Lauritz Melchior and his stamina: René Maison was indisposed; Arthur Carron's name appeared as a substitute; but, "as usual, it was the indestructible Lauritz Melchior who actually sang the performance." Later that month Melchior was supposed to have sung *Siegfried,* but begged off because of a rare indisposition. Johnson was forced to change the opera or go dark. People began to worry seriously about the fact that the Met was almost out of Heldentenors.

Helen Traubel, arguably Melchior's most distinguished soprano partner during the war years, certainly became the most celebrated, although not quite ever given parity with Flagstad, especially abroad where she never appeared in opera. Today, even the European music press calls her voice "one of the most beautiful ever heard," and believes that "it is time that Helen Traubel, also with us, is acknowledged as one of the really great ones."

Melchior enjoyed singing with Helen Traubel. When he spoke to *Time* about her in 1946, he admitted that her vocal technique and acting were not on a par with Flagstad's, but emphasized how he appreciated the special warm beauty of her voice:

> Flagstad's voice is like a shining diamond; Traubel's voice is like a beautiful ruby. In the last 20 years I've killed twenty-four Isoldes; Helen is the most agreeable. Flagstad was not so easy. She got a little swollen with success. Helen will always have both feet on the ground.

In the course of a historic two-week visit to Chicago in the spring of 1943, the Metropolitan presented *Tristan* with Traubel and Melchior, Leinsdorf on the podium. Traubel's great height and statuesque figure were viewed ecstatically by the audience, jokes about this twosome being unable to embrace due to their girth notwithstanding ("like a couple of two-ton trucks colliding in the middle of Broadway"). Apparently Traubel's command of Wagnerian acting traditions—"pulsating with life . . . she sang it incandescently"—had flourished with the years of experience since her 1937 Sieglinde in this city. (*Time* was to characterize her as "that rare breed of singer with the stature of a Valhalla deity, the projection of a diesel horn, and the stamina of a channel swimmer.") As for Lauritz, "Mr. Melchior's Tristan remains one of opera's irreplaceable treasures, a heroic conception, knightly in bearing and blessed with a matchless tenor." Together they made "a team to rival memories of Melchior and Flagstad."

Instantly compatible in their larger-than-life personalities, sharing a love of humor and cheer and a distaste for pretension, Traubel and Lauritz had been friends from the first time they met. When conductor Walter Damrosch had invited the Melchiors to dinner in the early spring of 1937, he had more than sociability in mind. During an appearance in St. Louis the conductor had become angry when told that a local soprano was to be his soloist, but after a few bars of the young woman's beautiful singing, his anger was transformed into admiration. At the dinner party his plan was to have this soprano perform for Lauritz, then ask him to recommend her to the Met— if he liked her singing. The next morning Melchior had gone to Ziegler and praised Damrosch's discovery, a thirty-four-year-old soprano named Helen Traubel. Her first engagement by the Met, also her first time on the operatic stage, had been for two performances of the world premiere of Damrosch's *Man without a Country* during the 1937 "popular" season. The critics had lauded her beauty ("a woman of noble and gracious beauty"), her voice ("of power and fine quality"), and her acting ("restraint and sincerity").

Their next meeting was on stage in a Chicago *Walküre* performance on December 3, 1937, when Helen Traubel was to sing her first Sieglinde. When the Melchiors arrived, Traubel had been in Chicago for three weeks, practicing the role but—indicating the curious kind of "staging" in use at that time—still ignorant as to where to walk and how to stand. It was the stuff of which singers' nightmares are made: You're on the stage with a once-in-a-lifetime opportunity, but you don't know the blocking. Traubel explained in a shaky voice that she had no idea where to go or what to do, but was calmed by Lauritz's promise to prompt her movements. During Act I Melchior constantly whispered instructions (as he had done for many another soprano), and Kleinchen stood sentinel in the wings to shove Helen back onstage every time she tried to hide in a corner. So did Helen Traubel make it through her first Wagnerian role.

Engaged as a Wagnerian soprano by the Met for the 1939–1940 season and gaining stature with each performance as Sieglinde and Elisabeth, by December 10, 1940, she garnered this prescient review at her Philadelphia *Walküre* debut: "Miss Traubel disclosed the really commanding quality of her voice, and in company with the formidable Flagstad, too." For her two seasons at the Met, Traubel had sung both her roles with Melchior, sharing them with Flagstad, Lehmann, and Lawrence. With Flagstad's absence, although scheduled for only four performances in 1941–1942, Traubel was pressed into service for eight, including both the Brünnhildes for the first time.

In February 1941, Toscanini engaged Traubel and Melchior to sing a Wagner program with the NBC Symphony in a broadcast from Carnegie Hall; this concert was later issued as a recording. Lauritz's veneration for the Italian conductor was still undiminished, judging by the way Melchior obeyed the slightest indication by Toscanini:

> Mr. Melchior sang strictly in time and the *"Wälse, Wälse!"* from *Walküre*, where he loves to hold on to these high tones for a time which is at least double the length of the notes in the score, were held for their exact values, and on observing a little wigwag of Mr. Toscanini's finger, he promptly renounced them.

On September 27, 1942, critic Jerome Bohm spent an entire column pointing out the inadequacies and deficiencies of the Met singers. Although he called Melchior "still the world's best heroic tenor," the only female singer he found to be distinguished was Helen Traubel, "a truly commanding figure in the world of operatic singing," citing her wide range, tremendous power, solidity of tone, and noble style of delivery. (A critic in Ann Arbor, Michigan had appreciated more than anything else the size of her voice: "Miss Traubel hoisted a couple of tones across Hill Auditorium that could have been used for girders.")

On December 4, 1942, Helen Traubel continued her series of debuts in the great Wagnerian roles with her first Isolde, opposite Melchior. The trustees of the Lillian Nordica Association presented Traubel, as the first American-born and entirely American-trained Isolde, with the jewels worn by Nordica, the first American Isolde. Traubel was also given thirty-three American Beauty roses, emblematic of the thirty-three years that had elapsed since the last appearance of an American Isolde. Lauritz sent her a magnum of champagne with one of his endeavors attached:

> There was a Tristan so alone,
> No girl, no love drink could atone;
> Today he sails again his ship,
> For Helen's aboard. Hooray! Hip! Hip!

She, in turn, giving evidence of her ebullient sense of humor, presented Lauritz with a picture of herself as Isolde: "To Lauritz, with my love, even if I had to wait in line for nineteen other Isoldes."

Traubel sang fourteen performances of Wagner (at a much higher fee) this season—Isolde, Elisabeth, and the Brünnhildes. She must have been gratified to see that her cachet was much increased, but, strangely, Jack Salter negotiated a deal whereby, in a separate agreement, she returned a substantial portion of it to the Met, and not for the purchase of war bonds as other singers were doing. Next year her fee was the same, but this refund was no longer part of the picture. Clearly, Traubel had finally proved her worth to the Met.

A performance on March 2, 1943, was distinguished by one debut and one farewell. Friedrich Schorr was making his operatic farewell, and Helen Traubel was singing her first *Götterdämmerung* Brünnhilde to Melchior's Siegfried. (One of Traubel's fondest remembrances of Lauritz was in this opera. She had been determined to show Brünnhilde's joy at seeing Siegfried. As she began her solo, she bent lovingly over his form in stage center. Lauritz muttered, absolutely true to form, "For God's sake, Helen, hurry it up! I'm hungry and I need a beer.")

Schorr had joined the Metropolitan two years before Melchior, eleven years before Flagstad, after ten years of singing in Austria, Czechoslovakia, and Germany. Sad to say, Schorr's final exit was marred by the general decrepitude of those ancient sets and props. Somehow Wotan's spear came apart without a blow from Siegfried's sword. As he left the stage of the Metropolitan Opera forever, said Kolodin, some heard him show his disgust by flinging the pieces of the sword upon the floor with violence. At a gathering on stage after the performance, Lauritz, representing Schorr's other colleagues, made an emotional goodbye speech to his blood brother, praising all the traits for which he loved the baritone.

Knowing that Lauritz not only loved his friend, but greatly admired his singing, it is easy to see similarities in their artistry, as Osborne points out: Schorr and Melchior had in common an even scale, superb skill at *piano* singing, and a true legato. Both were capable of great subtlety and unpretentious musicality, but most of all, they sang lyrically in a repertoire where this is seldom encountered. Each imaginatively revealed the compelling dramatic qualities of the music without sacrificing ease or lyricism. Schorr was commonly credited with being dramatic and insightful, but not so Melchior. Yet, as Osborne says, "there is nothing *wrong* with heroic, jubilant tone, with easy command and endurance, with every note honestly and fully sung, is there?"

An incident took place the following season, in the absence of Schorr, that amused Kleinchen because she took it as a delicious illustration of the fallibility of critics. At 6:00 one morning she was on the phone to Alma Strasfogel:

> I simply had to call and tell you the story! Julius Huehn was scheduled to sing Wotan in last night's *Walküre* performance. At the end of Act II Huehn told the stage manager that he could not go on. I put in a call to Herbert Janssen. "Come at once; there is a crisis," I said. During the time it took for Janssen to come to the Met, I went upstairs to make sure someone was there. Osie Hawkins, understudy for Wotan, was costumed and rehearsing like mad. Downstairs I found Herbert getting into his costume. Everyone was relieved because Osie was really a greenhorn at the role, although he looked wonderful. I was watching from the wings when the curtain went up. Herbert was on stage. Suddenly I saw Osie coming out from the other entrance! When I looked at the back of the stage, there I saw Huehn! He had not heard that other people were taking his place and thought he ought to chance it. There were three Wotans on stage and NOT ONE CRITIC NOTICED!"

Kleinchen dissolved in laughter. In their defense, it must be added that New York critics were required to leave before the last act of Wagnerian operas in order to meet their deadlines.

Behind the scenes Helen Traubel and Lauritz talked more about recipes and eating than music. They shared a unique ability to eat anything before singing, including peanuts and ice cream. But for fun on stage they would compete, holding notes as long as possible. Lauritz would always win, Traubel asserted. Without ever speaking of it, they would play a stately chess game on stage, one forcing the other into an unfavorable place upstage, one covering the other's face with a lover's embrace, jockeying for the best singing position under cover of theatrical moves while, in the prompter's box, Riedel would choke with laughter and have to disappear under the stage until he could function again.

Despite all the fun, Helen Traubel's serious assessment of Melchior's abilities is classic and undisputed: "A combination of temperament and tremendous physical qualities, coupled with a beautiful voice and stamina, equals the world's greatest Wagnerian tenor."

When, after fifteen years of collaboration, Melchior left RCA Victor to go with Columbia Records, Irving Kolodin, for one, was hard-pressed to understand his reasons. Yet he found it to Columbia's credit that it had (in April 1942) gone directly "to the heart of the much-pondered question 'Why Doesn't Melchior Sing Otello at the Met?' and produced their first record that is really newsworthy," with two Italian-language *Otello* excerpts, conducted by Erich Leinsdorf. Included in the set were two Wagnerian solos and two *Tristan* excerpts with Herbert Janssen, which were not, said Kolodin, as appealing as the *Otello*.

> There are . . . moments when Melchior produces some of the most remarkable sounds heard from any tenor since Caruso. And those who call the Danish temperament phlegmatic should hear the climax of ["*Dio mi potevi*"]. The quality of the death scene, if not as earshattering, is even more moving in its power and understanding.

Another recording, of songs, released by Columbia in the fall of 1942 elicited unanimity of opinion: Melchior's repertoire was unsuitable, unworthy, and not well sung, although he received very high marks for his English diction, as always. It was not the seven Scandinavian songs, nor the two Schubert, that offended, but the three songs in English. Whether the tenor himself or the recording directors chose the execrable array of light songs— Harding-Johnson's "There Shall be Music," Rogers' "The Star," and "Come You Merry" by Craxton—they would have been hard-pressed to select three songs less likely to survive in musical history and even harder to find someone less appropriate to sing them. Bohm felt that Melchior had offered here a large serving of his least condonable idiosyncrasies. "He hits notes on the nose as usual and brings his Tristan bluster to bear on the trifles in a way that dwarfs them even further," said another critic. Regrettably, these three songs are the same type of repertoire that he was to include in his programming when he started his campaign to introduce the mass audience of radio and the movies to more "serious music."

During a South American tour in 1943, August 21 and 31, and September 6 and 9, were devoted to recording sessions with Roberto Kinsky, Ferruccio Calusio, and Juan Emilio Martino conducting the Colón Opera House Orchestra. Under Kinsky and with the assistance of Herbert Janssen, seven sides gave a nearly complete account of *Tristan* Act III up to the death of Tristan. Of the six sides devoted to Italian arias (From *Tosca, Otello*, and *Pagliacci*), only the two from *Otello* were ever published.

Ever since Guglielmo Marconi came to his conclusions about the Melchior voice, there seemed to be unanimity about how well it recorded. Critic Robert Bagar, for example, noted that Melchior's "tones gather richness and color unto themselves via mechanical processing," and during the summer of 1935 electrical engineers from the Acoustical Society of America had reported in their journal that the voice of Lauritz Melchior was the most nearly ideal for recording.

Critic Irving Kolodin had an interesting way of capturing Melchior's vocal quality in words—"the purple-dark quality" of his lower register and the "tension of his upper notes." Others have designated these areas by the words "baritonal" and "forced." Their use of the word "forced" is a mystery to those who understand the vocal instrument. A succession of tenors (whose voices were never characterized as "forced") have appeared on the operatic scene, then soon found it necessary to sing half as often, unable to keep up the pace, or quickly disappeared, physically incapable of continuing to sing the heavy repertoire. How could a voice that was forced twenty to forty times a season, not counting an average season's sixty orchestral appearances or solo concerts (where Wagner was always sung), continue to sing exactly the same way in its sixtieth year of this cruel repertoire, and, furthermore, sing publicly at the age of seventy? A voice that has been truly forced, with intense muscular strain during so many performances (over a thousand performances, in fact: an unequaled record) will not function into old age, nor will the voice retain a range of dynamics. No one knows exactly when forcing is taking place except the singer, often not even his teacher. "Forced" is, however, a word that is easy to apply when the quality of the sound is in some way aesthetically objectionable.

It is quite possible that Melchior survived this repertoire precisely because of those high tones, much-criticized as "constricted" or "xylophonic." (This last adjective was applied in 1927 by Walter Legge after hearing a Covent Garden *Walküre* performance in which he said that "Melchior, apart from xylophonic high notes . . . was a good Siegmund.") These words imply a pinched and thin tone. It must be admitted that Melchior's vocal timbre was not a sensuous one, and that he did protect his high register by narrowing. This is not, however, an unusual technical ploy for any male voice, especially those who sing into their sixties, but is probably most important for a dramatic tenor whose repertoire calls upon him to sing heavily and with a dangerously baritonal color for a large part of each role. My opinion is that Melchior survived because at all times and at all costs he kept head voice (which Lilli Lehmann and other great teachers have called "the youth of the voice") mixed into his tone in that treacherous area just before the high notes, "the passaggio." Necessarily, this tactic produced high notes that were at times more brilliant than rich, even truly constricted on those few occasions when he miscalculated, but it was this that made them healthy and totally secure.

Melchior himself once explained this method to me in one short sentence: "I always begin each note in the small place and then expand." To a singer this concise phrase indicates that Melchior purposefully kept his vocal position very narrow, at least until after the attack had established the tone; then he allowed it to bloom. Melchior spoke to the *Brooklyn Eagle* at some length, and in uncharacteristic detail, about escaping from baritonedom and other vocal matters:

> The voice is like a skyscraper. It must be built on firm bedrock. Then you can always build upwards to new heights, but if you work first on superstructure and neglect the foundation, you can never build downward. . . . I do not believe there is any such thing as actual change of voice in a mature singer. What really happens is that, after one has sung

in public for a number of years, one's tone quality or . . . style of interpretation undergoes a change. There are only between three and four halftones between the baritone and tenor range after all. A dramatic tenor sings his notes differently, from a different vocal position. In the case of women, there are only three halftones between a contralto and a soprano, but a soprano must have a greater brilliance of tone than a contralto would ever need. . . . What we call vocal range is merely that vocal range which we use most often, either because it has become a habit with us or because we find it physically easiest. A good voice instructor will always try to help his pupils extend the range of their voices as far as possible so that when they have need for any one phase of their range, that phase will be ready for use. . . . The modern opera composer will express his feelings in music and will not stop to consider whether a baritone has a high C or whether a soprano lacks a low A. The good old days of bel canto are gone, it would seem. The dramatic singer is the pop singer of today.

In 1941 the Melchiors bought a magnificent property in Beverly Hills. The house, a minor contemporary masterpiece of what is called "streamlined moderne" with deco detail, was designed by Frederic Monhoff. Their distaste for living in hotels combined with the enjoyment of their first western trip taken in 1940, which was their first summer away from Chossewitz, had persuaded the couple to find a house they liked and buy it. Keeping her own counsel as they drove west, Kleinchen had reflected on her life in New York, whose changeable weather she loved. Others might be fatigued by New York's hustle and bustle, but she enjoyed it. She thrived on the constant telephoning—masterminding publicity, gratifying the requests of fans, keeping in contact with friends, fulfilling social obligations, maneuvering with the Met, making important decisions, supervising the management representatives, and in general keeping a wary eye on all the business transactions. She was stimulated by the activity; she was personally fulfilled by knowing that she did it well.

Lauritz and Mutti were not of the same mind. Their desire was to get out of the city, and the flora and fauna of California delighted both of them. Catching a glimpse of a new, sparsely-landscaped house on the top of a Beverly Hills "hill," they made an appointment to view it. Lauritz's great enthusiasm infected Kleinchen; she worked her magic on the owner; and 13671 Mulholland Drive was theirs before they left, for only $52,500.

The magnificent vistas from this property, which rose off the highway that runs between the San Fernando Valley and Beverly Hills, allowed one to see far out over the Pacific Ocean, all the way to Palos Verdes (although Lauritz insisted that it was Catalina) when conditions were right. Over there was the city of Los Angeles laid out in a panorama below them. In another direction the view encompassed the entire broad San Fernando Valley with the mountains beyond. The five-and-a-half acres boasted a guest house, tennis courts, and some newly planted lemon and orange trees that delighted Mutti. Lauritz was already making plans to fill the ample space around the hilltop property, which he considered its finest asset. They would plant hundreds of evergreen trees; they would build a swimming pool at the top; they would terrace the land below the house; they would hire an Italian mason to set off the pine woods and flowering trees with stone walls and meandering paths.

Five days later they moved into "The Viking." Lauritz had christened it for Holger Danske, the mythological Danish giant who slumbered until his country needed him. (Leonard Eisner remembers Lauritz going out into his California garden and blowing the Viking horn just for fun. "I really think he fancied himself a Viking. All he needed was a bearskin.")

By the spring of 1942, most of Lauritz's plans for the landscaping of his property had been completed, and Kleinchen was fast transforming the heroic house itself into an opulent and striking showplace. Actually, it does her a disservice to imply that opulence was her only objective; the comfort and pleasure of the house's inhabitants and guests were equal priorities. Indeed, ownership of this house would provide Kleinchen with a scope for another of her talents, described by Alma Strasfogel: "Kleinchen had all sorts of devices to adorn, to decorate life. She admitted that it was all part of a plan. In The Viking's swimming pool they had, for example, trays that floated so that no one would have to get out of the pool to eat or drink."

She set off the natural stone of The Viking's facade and parts of its interior by natural pigskin or seal upholstery and a zebra-skin rug in the inside dining room. All the furniture was as massive as the owner; couches seated eight and chairs two. The solarium/lanai alone had fourteen glass doors set in a curve around the swimming pool. Above the fifty-foot-long wall of the former porch a lifelike mural (serving as an "African veldt [grass country] habitat" for the lion and sheep trophy heads) had been painted by friend Karl Laufkötter, giving the impression that the animals were kneeling on the floor above the ceiling. From the outer dining area, surrounded with latticework, the diners were afforded a splendid view of the whole San Fernando Valley. So precious was the view that Kleinchen had glass installed on three circular sides of their bedroom, which made it seem to push into the trees, and had the fourth (fireplace) wall mirrored so that the vision would not be obscured.

Melchior had visited California's famous Bohemian Grove in 1940 as a guest of a fellow Dane, movie star Jean Hersholt. Obviously he had passed muster, for in April 1941 he received a welcome invitation to become a member himself. The Bohemian Club, a bastion of male camaraderie, owns its own building in San Francisco, but their "Grove" is located in the redwood forest on the Russian River north of the city. The Club is probably not any of the things it has been called—the touchstone of a military-industrial plot to take over the world; a collection of eccentric millionaires; even a quasi-Druidic cult that performs peculiar rituals during its annual campouts at the Grove—but there is no doubt that the members wield a lot of clout. The group that Ronald Reagan belongs to, for example, boasts George Bush, George Schultz, Caspar Weinberger, and Howard Baker. Former presidents Ford, Nixon, Eisenhower, Hoover, and Teddy Roosevelt also made the rolls. Bing Crosby, Walter Cronkite, and fellow opera singer Lawrence Tibbett came in, as did Lauritz, on a special membership for men professionally involved in the arts. After an initiation fee of $7,500, such professionals do not have to be put on a waiting list, which in 1986 numbered around 3,080 names.

The requirements of the Bohemians suited Lauritz Melchior perfectly! What better club for the Unmelancholy Dane than one that is "forever torn between a yearning for irresponsible fun and the style of genteel high society?" Aside from the philosophy and the companionship, the physical beauty of the Grove is breathtaking: gigantic redwoods surround the open spaces. No wonder Lauritz was thrilled to become a member, to live with his "Cuckoo's Nest" group among those glorious redwoods, where business talk is forbidden and the motto is "Weaving spiders, come not here." Our tenor might have invented it.

By 1950 Melchior would become a member of another colorful organization, the One-Shot Antelope Club. The Shoot took place at Lander, Wyoming, and Lauritz was a part of it for many years. He was a great favorite with the Indians, who immediately named him "great white hunter" and beaded a ceremonial belt for his world-class Brobdignagian waistline. The hunters, usually celebrites and crack shots as well, rode out in special four-men teams to comb the hills. If a hunter approached within 150 yards of an antelope, he was obliged to take his one shot. Lauritz was most famous among the members for having achieved the impossible: he once shot two antelopes with one bullet.

In his new home state of California Melchior speedily affiliated with no less than three Danish organizations in as many months. Unflaggingly sociable, he was always ready to entertain at The Viking and was unfailingly democratic, welcoming all Danes, from his butcher to the Copenhagen Boys' Choir. That the welcome mat was always out for Danes did not inhibit his countrymen from telling wild stories. A Danish mezzo-soprano told a tenor colleague a parcel of lies that defy reason: She tried to visit The Viking but, before being rudely turned away, noticed that in the garden there were statues of Melchior as Siegmund and Lohengrin. If one inserted a coin, they would sing an appropriate aria!

Melchior lost no time in inviting the California chapter of the Royal Danish Guard Society to their first shooting competition at The Viking on May 31, 1942, and donated a new silver cup, which was again, sadly, won by someone else. But at the Guard party of 1943 he accomplished his ambition and became at last the shooting king of the California chapter, a feat all the more impressive since it came after a prodigious intake of alcohol caused by the requisite toasts to the king and queen and Denmark and freedom, done with glass after glass of aquavit, each followed by a glass of beer.

Traveling west in June 1941, Lauritz and Kleinchen were shocked to hear on the car radio that Sir Hugh Walpole had died suddenly at Brackenburn, his country home. He had succumbed to a diabetic coma and coronary thrombosis, although some blame might have been assigned to the strains of war—noise, terror, and lack of sleep. In his letters to the Melchiors he always played down his many narrow escapes during bombing raids, although he admitted that the suicide of Virginia Woolf had depressed him greatly. Lauritz was saddened to be prevented by the war from attending Walpole's funeral, but he never failed to acknowledge that he owed his position as an international tenor to Hugh's belief in him. As for Walpole, his appreciation of Lauritz's character had been documented in a 1938 article, in which he described the people who "are worth their weight in rubies, . . . serenely balanced people who are not fools, who are not either too gaily optimistic nor too determinedly pessimistic, who love their fellow man without thinking him an angel, [and] who have a really strong and extensive sense of values." He named Lauritz Melchior one such person.

During the summer of 1942 the State Department asked Melchior to serve as a goodwill ambassador during a tour that included Mexico City, San José (Costa Rica), Balboa (Panamá), Santiago (Chile), Montivideo (Uruguay), and Lima (Peru), where he would sing at local orchestra concerts under the direction of his own conductor, Ignace Strasfogel. The two-month tour was to finish with ten operatic performances at the Colón in Buenos Aires. (As usual, Lauritz also sought out the local institute for the blind and offered to present a concert for them.

Five days before he arrived there, pictures of Lauritz were everywhere in Mexico City, which provides an example of the kind of reception that was usual wherever the tenor went. The concert was a tremendous success, and the audience only agreed to leave when the lights flared up and the stagehands closed the piano. In the dressing room crowds clamored for autographs and embraced the tenor, whom most South Americans believed to be "The Caruso of Wagnerian Opera."

Ignace Strasfogel gives us a good idea of the South American adventures. Once in Mexico, the touring party was given a small U.S. Air Force plane for their travels. This craft could only fly by day, so an extremely tight schedule was strictly followed. It was the same every day: an early morning departure; an airport reception by U.S. diplomats, the president of the local orchestra, and the press; then an afternoon orchestra rehearsal; an evening concert; a reception given by the U.S. Embassy; to bed; and up again early the next morning to do it all again.

The schedule went like clockwork in Mexico City. On the dot the next morning they flew off to San José, Costa Rica, where the schedule collapsed. Near the border of Guatemala a violent storm broke. The pilot, alarmed by the turbulence, decided to land at the closest airfield. At the hangar there awaited a hybrid vehicle, jerry-built of dented scraps from various automobiles. One of the two men sitting in it, an American, warned them with heavy irony that, although they had landed safely in this accursed place, they were not to assume that their troubles were over. He explained that the Palace Hotel was the only shelter offered by the town of Tapachula.

The three visitors clung together in fear as the driver started the conveyance (one could scarcely call it a car) by hot-wiring it like a car thief. A canvas roof and the absence of windshield and windows gave the passengers no shelter from the elements as they rode into "town." The American told them his story: During his two-week enforced sojourn in Tapachula, he had learned that the mañana culture held no brief for schedules. Here one did not ask, "At what time will the nine o'clock plane leave?" but, "Will the nine o'clock plane leave today?" As no one had an answer, he spent each day at the airport just in case. However, all the news was not bad. Happily, he had not experienced the latest earthquake, he said, pointing to the evidence that littered the streets.

The building that they stopped before was indescribable. At first the Melchiors and Strasfogel took it for a lean-to for animals, for the beaten-up chairs on the front porch of the Palace Hotel contained only pigs, hens, ducks, and goats. The American nodded bitterly at their looks of disbelief. Within the hotel, its door a large hole in the wall, sat a woman who spoke more animatedly to her chicken than to the three would-be guests. She laboriously "registered" them with a dull, stubby pencil on a filthy paper, then conducted the party to a room, also doorless, but containing three walls. The fourth wall revealed, through many holes in the curtain, a sidewalk directly outside the room, which contained an iron bed that had two sheets but no pillows or blankets.

Determined to be a good sport, Kleinchen suggested that they do some sightseeing. Any place would be better than that room. In the lobby they encountered a man who had a bit of pidgin English, which Kleinchen tried to match: What here to see? "Prison, fine show." Always prepared, Lauritz took out his honorary police captain badge from Passaic, New Jersey. It worked wonders. Outside across the plaza, they heard the prison gates open, followed by the sound of marching feet squishing in the wet streets. As the Americans went out onto the porch, a company of men stopped before the hotel and presented arms. The commander saluted his American counterpart, kissed Lauritz on both cheeks and Kleinchen on the hand. As dinner guests at the prison, they had a hilarious evening with extravagant speeches on both sides, each unintelligible to the others, but made palatable by the fast-flowing wine. The interpreter, however, was greatly disgusted. He had wanted them to see the "show," that other parade, composed of beautiful prostitutes who nightly visited the prisoners.

A cock crowing on their bedpost awoke them to the good news that the flight could be continued because the storm had passed. As they entered the "taxi," the prisoners assembled in the plaza, accompanied by impressive drum rolls. The commander again kissed Melchior on both cheeks with much ceremony, saying "Vaya con Dios." As Strasfogel says, "We loved Kleinchen. In a situation like this one, many people would have been easily upset. Not Kleinchen; she took it in her stride and turned it into a funny story." Strasfogel chuckles telling some of the adventures that followed Tapachula: In Bogotá the local manager presented Kleinchen with a bouquet of orchids with one hand, while, with the other, he considerately gave her a bag of flea powder. In one hotel where they had requested something to eat that came from a can so as to minimize the danger of illness, the manager removed the fish with his bare hands. In Lima, Peru, the travelers went to a restaurant where there was an arrangement of raw meats from which the diner could choose whatever he wanted. Kleinchen giggled to her husband about some favorite that she wanted. Having chosen, she took a long, slow, provocative walk back to the table followed by the waiter, who proudly bore her choice on a tray he held high. "It was the testicles of a steer or something like that. She had a Rabelaisian sense of humor," says Strasfogel.

Wherever Strasfogel and the Melchiors went, the Latin Americans were kindness itself and hospitable beyond belief. Therefore an invitation to return in the summer of 1943 for eighteen concerts and twelve operatic performances (including *Fidelio*) at the Colón was happily accepted. *Musical America* summed up this visit to the Colón, Melchior's last and Helen Traubel's first:

> Lauritz Melchior, great Wagnerian that he is, dominated by his style and expression in spite of a voice that had lost some of its freshness and darkened in timbre. Helen Traubel's . . . debut . . . shows the presence of a magnificent singer and a convincing actress who can compare with the greatest artists who have appeared [here].

On his previous trip to South America he had promised to return and sing Lohengrin at a gala performance in Santiago for Chile's National Festival on their Independence Day. A private audience with Chile's president was rewarding, but nothing could compete with a new decoration presented to him that evening, the Knight Commander Cross of El Merito. Pleased as he was with the panoply and pomp of his Chilean investiture, he (typically) enjoyed every bit as much a lesser honor that came to him a month later— being sworn in by Mayor La Guardia as an Honorary Auxiliary Fireman of the City of New York.

From Johnson in the fall of 1944 came a letter whose contents give a better sense of his methods regarding rehearsals as well as an example of how carefully the Met administration proceeded in dealings with Lauritz. Asking that Lauritz be in New York for rehearsals on November 24 and 25, Johnson explained that Leinsdorf, fortuitously released from the army just in time to replace Beecham (who was leaving for England), had extracted as part of his contract a promise of two stage rehearsals for the coming *Tristan* anniversary. Blandishing with a master hand, Johnson said: "This, dear Kleinchen, will make for a better *Tristan*, for better criticism, the maintenance of a higher artistic standard, and, we hope, sustain strong box office interest, things much to all our interests. Please be a darling and fix it in your usual clever way to see that Lauritz is here by then."

It seemed only yesterday that Melchior was celebrating his 100th performance as Tristan; yet the 200th had arrived by November 29, 1944. The real anniversary, which occurred at a Philadelphia performance, was a sentimental occasion. As Melchior recalled, "It was very nice that my faithful servant and friend, Kurvenal, was Herbert Janssen, who also sang with me at my first *Tristan*." Extensive press coverage of the New York performance, which took place on December 4, celebrated the fact that Melchior was the first singer ever to reach this mark.

For his regular visit to the San Francisco Opera, Melchior was joined in the fall of 1945 by Helen Traubel, who was to sing Isolde under William Steinberg as her operatic debut in that city. Her success was absolute, and the Act II duet by her and Melchior was called "the very essence of music."

Backstage a drama of a different sort was taking place. Kleinchen was preparing one of her practical jokes in an effort to keep up the spirits of the personnel, whose singing was oppressed by the persistently overcast weather. Lorenzo Alvary, a bass with the Metropolitan at that time, tells how she stole a sheet of stationery with the San Francisco Opera letterhead, on which she wrote, "Mr. Alvary: We note that you have broken the valuable mirror in your dressing room. The damage which amounts to $250 will be deducted from tonight's salary." This threatening letter she signed in a dashing but indecipherable hand and left propped against the broken mirror. When Alvary found the note that night, he was livid, rushing from one dressing room to another, protesting his innocence. When apoplexy seemed to threaten, Kleinchen confessed. After a good laugh, everyone in the company relaxed and sang well.

Alvary agrees that Melchior was a "superman," and tells a story that supports his contention. They sang together in a San Francisco Opera performance of *Walküre* in Los Angeles, after which the Melchiors hosted a party at The Viking. At four o'clock that morning, says Alvary, Lauritz once again sang "Winterstürme" with exactly the same strength and quality of voice as he had many hours earlier on stage.

The new Met season of 1945–1946 promised some postwar changes. The present crop of operatic stars, including Traubel, Munsel, Merrill, Tucker, Warren, and Varnay, were Americans, but once again European singers were anxious to sing at the Met. In the wings, readying for 1946–1947, was a "German tenor" from Sweden, Set Svanholm. Plans for the coming season were revealed by Edward Johnson at an October press conference. Torsten Ralf (new Heldentenor, and brother to Oskar Ralf, a 1927 Bayreuth colleague of Melchior's), Helen Traubel, and Fritz Busch as conductor, were to perform *Lohengrin* on opening night. In addition Ralf was going to do *Meistersinger*, *Tannhäuser*, and *Parsifal*. (Strangely, the fact that *Otello* would be revived with Ralf in the title role was rather played down.) A grudging compliment was bestowed upon the old and the new Heldentenor in the review of Ralf's November 26 debut as Lohengrin: "Considering what we have been enduring . . . when the performer of the evening was not Melchior, for these blessings we give thanks."

A clever and affectionate telegram came from manager Davidson, on Lauritz's fifty-fifth birthday, referring to the anniversaries Lauritz so prized:

PLEASE CONFIRM FOLLOWING ARRANGEMENTS COVERING NEXT 45 YEARS: 400 TRISTANS, 300 SIEGFRIEDS, 200 LOHENGRINS, 100 WALKÜRES, 50 MGM SPECIALS, AND 25 WORLD TOURS. THEN IN YOUR SPARE TIME WE PROPOSE RADIO ENGAGEMENTS AND POSSIBLY A FEW OPERETTAS. AM SURE YOU WILL AGREE THIS IS COMPLETELY REASONABLE SCHEDULE FOR THE BIG NOISE. PLEASE ACCEPT MY ADMIRATION, RESPECT, AND AFFECTION. JIM

Had Lauritz kept going at the same rate for another forty-five years, Davidson's figures would not have been all that far off the mark.

"By Lauritz Melchior is every other day some kind of anniversary," said a German colleague, referring to the Dane's twentieth year of association with the Metropolitan Opera on February 17, 1946. Preparations commenced in January. Lauritz was permitted to choose the repertoire, singers, and the conductor of the evening. For a while it was uncertain whether Lehmann, now retired, would consent to sing excerpts from Act I of *Die Walküre* with him, but, despite a bad cold, she did. Act II of *Tristan* with Astrid Varnay and Kerstin Thorborg was second on the program, and *Lohengrin* Act III— with Elsa sung by Irene Jessner, Astrid Varnay as Ortrud, and Nicola Moscona as King Henry—closed this festive program conducted by Fritz Busch. At the last of the curtain calls Lauritz made a graceful speech in which he pleaded for a helping hand for young American opera singers.

Melchior had been serious about not criticizing America while still a citizen of another country, as he had said in an interview with Otis Guernsey: "While I am a visitor here I must be polite. You don't tell your host what to do. But there are things I want to say and cannot say until I become an American citizen, one of the family. They are about indifference toward young people of musical talent."

Once he had informed King Christian of his intention to become an American citizen, he felt a bit more free to let go, as in the graceful little speech before the curtain this evening: "It seems to me that the future of opera depends on how much the cultural leaders of this country can do to bring it to the masses. . . . Opera can never be self-supporting. It needs financial assistance."

Backstage, Melchior and his colleagues were joined by Kleinchen, members of the administration, the board, and other artists for a brief ceremony. Mrs. Belmont presented the board's gift, a silver bowl, and Astrid Varnay gave him a gold plaque and a book of autographs from his fellow artists. Edward Johnson called Melchior "a national and international figure and a pillar of strength in the German wing." Lotte gave him a caricature she had drawn that showed Lauritz and her in wheel chairs, both frail and wrinkled, still in Siegmund and Sieglinde costumes, doing a 7,000th *Walküre* in 1976. But the most touching gift of all was a miniature replica of the Grail, a beautiful piece of workmanship designed and executed by the electrical department of the Metropolitan. Lit from within, the tiny chalice in the center stood on a pedestal formed by red-velvet-lined gilded wooden sides. A plaque read, "*'Enthüllet den Gral'* In honor of your twentieth anniversary as the outstanding interpreter of Wagnerian roles." Proceeds from the evening, a net of $5,113, were given to the Production Fund, Lauritz explaining:

> Most of all what we need at the Met is a new Met, but if we can't have that, what we need next is new scenery. I'm giving the money from this performance to help buy some new scenery. Since the money will run to several thousand dollars, it should provide a considerable number of buckets of paint.

After the performance, at the Swedish restaurant where Kleinchen and Lauritz drank aquavit and beer with their eighty-five guests, Melchior sighed deeply. "Now I can take a breath. Now I can start over again." At this date he had done 125 *Siegfried*s, 209 *Tristan*s, 171 *Walküre*s, 143 *Tannhäuser*s, 101

Götterdämmerungs and *Lohengrins*. *Newsweek* quipped, "The possibilities for new anniversaries are staggering!"

Lotte Lehmann, in a loving letter that thanked him for the gift he had sent her as appreciation for her participation, gives us another perspective:

> It is *I* who should thank *you*. Despite my illness, not to be with you on your honorary day, not to sing, *for the last time*, an act of Sieglinde (the role that I love above all others) with you, would have been unthinkable. You are right, we were the best Wälsepair [sic]. Do not be concerned over that word "were." You have preserved all. You are the same. You have the very same vocal technique that you had in younger years and you combine this young art with the wisdom of experience. You are very blessed, dear Lauritz. . . . Ever your true Lotte."

Lehmann, whose technical skills were, by her own admission, slipping, clearly saw her friend Lauritz as vocally invincible. In truth, 1946 had so far been a good year for him. On February 12, singing the elder Siegfried, Lauritz garnered a splendid critique: "To summon so much beauty of sound for the dying apostrophe to Brünnhilde after three and a quarter hours of singing is well worth noting." Back in April 1944, however, the reviews had been uniformly bad. The Met had visited Chicago and Milwaukee that month—for the first time in 34 years—and Lauritz was excoriated in three out of four reviews, one headline saying that *Parsifal* was "No Credit to Wagner or the Audience Here." Another article was headlined "Melchior Hits New Low in *Tannhäuser*," and a third stated, "[Melchior] sang very badly indeed."

Although Melchior's fabled stamina never lessened and his top range never failed, signs of a slight vocal deterioration were present in a February 7, 1945, concert given for the Town Hall Endowment Fund. The program was a fine one, in contrast to the ones that were to come after Melchior's movie career began in earnest: five Grieg songs, a group of other Scandinavian songs that included Sibelius, a long excerpt from *Otello*, two Schubert songs ("Der Doppelgänger" and "Der Atlas"), three by Wolf ("Gesegnet sei das Grün," "Schon streckt' ich aus im Bett," and "Ein Ständchen"), and two by Richard Strauss ("Heimliche Aufforderung," and "Cäcilie").

Reading the press comments, it is hard to remember the Lauritz Melchior of 1927, who drew from the demanding W. J. Henderson such magnificent reviews as a recitalist, or his success with song repertoire before the Beethoven Association just a few years before. Since the critics of the former era were nearly all gone, the event took on the character of a local concert debut. All agreed with *Musical America* that Melchior seemed "a fish out of water." Said the *Times*'s Noel Straus, "He had well-defined artistic intentions as an interpreter but possessed little of the vocal finesse needed to carry them out." Eighteen years before, Henderson had found it to be just the opposite. An even more serious matter was Melchior's present technical inability, chronicled by four major critics, to establish a middle ground between soft and loud, vocally a bad omen. "There was an excess of contrast between the tones he sang in full voice and those he sang in half voice. . . . The listener could almost feel him grip the more voluminous ones in his throat and then let go of the others that were virtually without support," said Thompson.

Functioning successfully for some thirty-five years in the heaviest repertoire known to the male voice had, as it must, taken a toll: on Melchior's flexible control of *pianissimo*. Yet, unlike most Heldentenors, his power, stamina, and range remained undiminished; he sang his roles exactly as written right up to the end of his operatic career. Oddly, full marks were always given to his female counterparts, when, with age, their top notes became less than secure and they began to take optional lower notes. Because the Wagnerian roles require such heavy singing in the middle register, critics found these results to be "expected" in the soprano voice.

Recitals, being by their nature vocally revealing and demanding great refinement, are judged according to a different standard than Wagnerian opera. Melchior could have avoided this more critical judgment by choosing less delicate material for his recital. Given the subtlety of the repertoire he programmed, however, there was no way to sidestep the need for superb technical control in the dynamic range of *pianissimo* to *mezzo forte*. Thus, he virtually put on display his one weakness, a lack of flexibility in head voice singing.

In his 1926 Metropolitan Opera debut Melchior had been praised for singing a beautiful head tone as Tannhäuser breathed the name "Elisabeth." Twenty years later that ability to sing a supported head tone had failed him. His technical work during the intervening years had been almost exclusively concentrated on "light singing," the most difficult thing for a big voice to manage. Eventually he had conquered it, but now, at the age of 55, it was no longer his. Such a vocal disability is a serious matter. For any other singer, in fact, it would have been a harbinger of bad tidings.

CHAPTER 13

From Opera Star to Movie Star

(1943–1946)

In the years since Constance Hope had first persuaded Lotte Lehmann and the Melchiors to try her (then rudimentary) "personal publicity" techniques, their effectiveness had been proven repeatedly. Beginning in 1943, these methods would bring Lauritz to genuine celebrity, not only as an opera singer, but as an idol of popular culture on radio and in the movies. He became what he and Kleinchen aspired for him to be: not merely a singer, but a famous singer.

Artist Andy Warhol, who was a master at the game of celebrity, said, "Publicity is like eating peanuts. Once you start, you can't stop." Kleinchen was addicted early on. An apt pupil, she quickly became as creative at publicity gamesmanship as was Hope herself. Lauritz, weighed down by a few faint scruples, tended to drag his feet at times, but was usually overruled by his wife. When publicity maneuvers were suggested that appeared questionable, both he and Lotte quickly learned to calm their doubts by parroting the principle that guided Hope's activities: "The public wants to believe that its favorites are just human beings, not remote and aloof artists." Every piece of publicity released by Hope Associates in some way bolstered this image of Lauritz as a "regular guy": He hunted, looking wonderfully unshaven and grungy in his hunting costume; he smoked cigarettes like an ordinary American; he helped with the dishes just like the man next door; he admitted that he ate too much and woefully described how Kleinchen nagged him about his diet.

One of the most appealing facets of Melchior's image as a normal fellow was his ability to see the funny side of being a Wagnerian lover. His quips were droll and frequently very witty:

The constant watching that the prima donna's hair is not caught in your armor while singing and acting as if in love is fatiguing. You could step away in a renunciation gesture and take the prima donna with you, her wig dangling from your breastplate like a scalp. I wish I could just wear a business suit and hold the soprano tightly. I would enjoy that.

Artists who enjoy working together are constantly checking each other's appearance. You think that Isolde is gently touching my forehead. Nope. She's fixing my wig. Because of the necessity to sing, the lovers cannot be curled up comfortably on the divan, each must leave the other room to sing; each must not cover the other from the audience's view; this makes the audience think that the lovers are restless rather than in love.

The love benches must constantly be checked for secure fastenings; otherwise the singers are left with their feet in the air as the bench tips over. I've been on benches so small that, as Siegfried, I had to step over Brünnhilde, sing for fifteen minutes, and *then* discover her. This is silly, even for Gary Cooper.

Too bad all operatic love is tragic. It is harder to be a tragic lover than a happy one. The tragic lover is usually dead. If he's not, then the loved one *is*. If *she's* dead, he is left alone on the stage clumping around in his armor. If *he's* dead, he is lying down smelling the floor. This is *not* passionate.

In the process of building Lauritz's celebrity the truth was first gently bent, then trampled: Friends never saw him play the piano, but fully half of his publicity pictures showed him at the piano. Copenhagen cronies recall that he had actually made use of every possible excuse on every possible occasion to be relieved of his duties when serving in the Guard; in his publicity, however, his love for a soldier's life was exaggerated and his passionate (and sincere) devotion to the Royal Danish Guard was exploited at every turn. Lauritz smoked only big black cigars, but in the ads he puffed on a Lucky Strike.

Clearly, Kleinchen and Lauritz had been lovers for three years before they were married, the ceremony a mere three days after his divorce from Inger. All publicity, however—even Kleinchen's obituary—pronounced the time between the two events to be anywhere from one to three years. To the very end of Melchior's life the myth about his meeting with Kleinchen (suspended from her parachute in the garden tree) was scrupulously maintained, and there is a great deal of skepticism about the Melchiors' assertion that Kleinchen had been a movie "star"; it is quite possible that the publicity upgraded her position from stunt girl to star.

It was not easy for an artist of the 1940s to tread successfully the line of demarcation between being too accessible (thereby losing his credentials as an artist) and being too remote (thereby losing his appeal to a mass audience), in part because there were no established rules at the time. Constance Hope was making them up as she went along. Today the opera singer's problem is much like that of the President of the United States, who in the 1980s has mastered the (now well-defined) skills required to win his election:

He must be seen to be qualified and serious about his job, but not so detached from the common man that he won't shake his hand and kiss his baby. (And if a presidential candidate ever admitted that he liked opera, his chances of becoming the common man's representative would plummet drastically.)

Lauritz's greatest celebrity was to come directly and indirectly because of Frank Sinatra. By 1943 Lauritz was an old hand at radio, but still known primarily as an opera singer. The Chamber Music Society of Lower Basin Street, a weekly radio comedy show, had used him several times because he was such a good sport, and a wonderful, larger-than-life character. For a November show the writer came up with a new wrinkle. He thought Lauritz was a nice guy, "But I couldn't spell his name; besides, I think opera is a waste of time. So in the script I suggested that if Mr. Melchior wanted to make $30,000 a week, he should become a crooner and change his name to Larry Melch." Melchior did not neglect his homework. He went to the Waldorf Astoria Hotel seven nights in a row to hear Frank Sinatra, and practiced the crooner's style for hours. When he eventually crooned for the radio public, his rendition of "That Ol' Black Magic" was a faithful duplication, even to the last unvocal but theatrical gasp.

At his Stage Door Canteen appearances for the U.S.O., Lauritz repeated this imitation of Sinatra. Word went round and the press picked it up, loving the picture of the massive Melchior trying to look like a half-starved boy clutching a microphone stand for support. Sinatra was called upon to return the compliment with an accurate imitation of Melchior singing *Tristan*. In response, he promptly scheduled a press conference, saying that he had hopes of singing a heavenly duet with Melchior some day. Constance Hope, seeing in the comparison of skinny Sinatra and mountainous Melchior a public relations match made in heaven, was beside herself with professional satisfaction.

A strange parallel was to exist between Sinatra and Melchior for the next six years. Each had come to his celebrity in large part because of a brilliant press agent. Gossip and society columnists wrote as much about one as the other. Serious music lovers were affronted by both men; the mass audience adored both singers. Both Lauritz and Sinatra were idolized by those strange creatures, the bobby-soxers, and both press representatives, George Evans and Constance Hope, exploited this idolatry in their publicity handouts. (It was Evans who had hired six girls to dress in bobby sox and drilled them to squeal and faint as Sinatra groaned. The whole mass-hysteria scene was his invention.) The constant press association of the two names was always good for a laugh: Sinatra, the skinny, underdog type, who needed the support of the mike stand to sing (Evans coached him in this maneuver, too) versus the well-fed strongman Melchior, who could blast down the nearest tree with his voice. Sinatra outraged high-brow music lovers by insisting that his singing style was in the best tradition of the *bel canto* Italian school as he sang with symphony orchestras; Melchior offended them by including pop tunes on his concerts. Elsa Maxwell gave as much space to

Melchior in her column as she did to Sinatra. President Roosevelt had them both to the White House, although he was heavily criticized for inviting the crooner. Not until 1949, when Sinatra was no longer at the top of the polls and Melchior was being castigated weekly for his transgressions, did the jokes die down.

Due to his new fame as a crooner, Melchior was asked to appear on the comedian Fred Allen's radio program on December 12, 1943. Part of the script ran:

ALLEN: For two solid seasons I played the Barber of Seville. Then the electric razor came in and BANG! the barber was through. But enough about me. What about you? You've been in opera many years, I know.

MELCHIOR: Yes, when I went into opera Madame Butterfly was only a caterpillar.

ALLEN: You must have known Boris before he was Goodenough.

MELCHIOR: (*petulantly*) Fred, I'm not here to tell jokes. I came to talk to you. I have a problem. I want to quit opera and go into radio.

ALLEN: You're kidding. What's wrong with opera?

MELCHIOR: Long hair and short dough. In radio they pay singers big money. Yesterday I read that some young boy on the radio is making $30,000 a week. $30,000 a week and what does he sing? (*croons a bit of a pop ballad in imitation of Sinatra*) Fred, make me another Sinatra!

ALLEN: But the Met audience is top hat and tails. You want to sing for sweat shirts and bobby sox?

MELCHIOR: (*angrily*) $30,000 for . . . (*croons a bit of the same song*) I'll drive that Sinatra off the Hit Parade!

ALLEN: But you're not the Sinatra type. You've got to be thin.

MELCHIOR: You think I'm too robust?

ALLEN: Robust? Why, your tonsils weigh more than Sinatra does. Why, when he's on the air, you can't tell whether Sinatra is singing into the microphone or the microphone is giving Sinatra a transfusion. Forget the whole thing! Sing me one of those adenoid rattlers of yours. (*Melchior sings the* Meistersinger *aria*) That's your racket. Stick to it. Think what it would be like otherwise: (*pretending to be an announcer*)

The makers of Pasternak's Pretzels present, "Life Can Be Melchior," the story of one man's struggle to be a failure. Little Larry Melchior was born in a motel in Ohio. The world knew that a great singer was born when the baby's first words were,

MELCHIOR: (*in a high-pitched baby voice*) Fiiiiiiiigaro, Fiiiiigaro, Fiiigaro, Figaro, Figaro!

ALLEN: At school his genius was immediately recognized. The teacher gave little Larry a pitch pipe, a metronome, and a picture of Rudi Vallee to inspire him. After graduation he forged ahead with his music; day after day, hour after hour, little Larry Melchior practiced.

MELCHIOR: (*in a slightly more mature voice*) Fiiiiiiigaro, Fiiiiigaro, Fiiigaro, Figaro, Figaro!

ALLEN: Four years at the Curtis Institute of Music, Melchior sang:

MELCHIOR: (*in a fuller voice*) Fiiiiigaro, Fiiiigaro, Fiiigaro, Figaro!

ALLEN: Eight years at the Juilliard School of Music Melchior carried on.

MELCHIOR: (*in a more operatic voice*) Fiiiiiigaro, Fiiiiigaro, Fiiigaro, Fiiigaro, Figaro!

ALLEN: And then came the crucial test: his audition for the Met. Melchior sang:

MELCHIOR: Fiiii, Fii, Fi . . . (*limping to a halt*)

ALLEN: He had forgotten the words. But this did not stop Lauritz Melchior. Ah no, back to ten years of . . .

MELCHIOR: Fiiiiigaro, Fiiiiigaro, Fiiigaro, Fiiigaro, Figaro, Figaro!

ALLEN: And now he was ready for his crowning achievement, starring on his own radio program, The Pasternak Pretzel Hour. Here is Lauritz Melchior bringing you the music he has spent a lifetime to achieve.

MELCHIOR: (*singing*) "Pasternak Pretzels are . . . FiiiiiiiiiiiiiiiiiiiiiiiiNE!!"

On the last word Melchior sang a full-throttle, exceedingly high blockbuster of a note, and the studio audience erupted into applause. That applause was only the beginning.

The combination of that wonderfully nasal voice of Allen's and the puncturing of the immense dignity that was assigned to a star of the Metropolitan Opera—plus Fred's ad-libbing on the air—made it a once-in-a-lifetime piece of inspired fun. Melchior was an extraordinary success as a foil for Fred. When *Variety* chose to repeat this program on its Weekly Hall of Fame, the tenor's fame was made, even in those tiny corners of the United States it had not yet reached. America, it seemed, immensely enjoyed the sport of mocking an opera star, and Lauritz didn't mind at all. After the Allen show there were streams of offers from producers of other top shows, carloads of letters from listeners, and invitations for guest appearances from such entertainment greats as Dinah Shore, Al Jolson, Bing Crosby, and Eddie Cantor.

In the 1940s most United States citizens still thought of opera as an elitist art form, incomprehensible to ordinary folk, patronized only by Europeans and extremely wealthy Americans. They pictured all opera singers as unapproachable and haughty, having an immense and lofty dignity that they managed to sustain despite the fact that they were fat and wore horns on their heads. The only well-known operatic tunes were "Ridi, Pagliaccio" from *Pagliacci* and Figaro's aria from *The Barber of Seville* (hence its inclusion in the Fred Allen script), which they had learned from radio and movies. Lauritz Melchior, whom most had heard—if at all—in concert, not in opera, provided a delightful surprise when he dared to clown on comedy shows. So astounding was this found that "We the People," a more serious radio show, dramatized the mere existence of a Melchior, and *Life*, the most important magazine of popular culture in the 1940s, covered his operatic anniversaries. What news! An opera singer could possess a sense of humor! A singer who had dedicated thirty-one years to performing opera of the most serious sort could have a comic talent!

But what about the opera fans and dedicated Wagnerites? They abhorred their Heldentenor's condescending to perform for the mass audience. They hated the indignity of opera spoofs on radio and in the movies. The operagoer of the 1940s, proud of his position in "high" culture, was far from democratic in his vision of opera and its singers: only a minority of the public was able to "appreciate" the exquisite (whereas the aficionados themselves knew—to the single note—how well the singer acquitted himself), and the mass audience could enjoy only the vulgar (they were content with radio and the movies). The knowledgeable opera fan could not conceive of a Wagner singer of Melchior's international status turning his back on his art. It was undignified and unforgivable. Although they had loved every moment of the skits he did at the Met Surprise Parties, they insisted that a Tristan should not be a comic as well. *Life*'s coverage of the 200th Tristan anniversary also provoked and offended the Wagnerites, but this was altogether understandable. It included a famous (but highly unappetizing) picture of the Heldentenor sitting majestically before the mirror in the dressing room once occupied by Enrico Caruso. Melchior was making up his face, wearing over a bare and bulky torso the heavy-duty corset that held up the chain-mail leggings of his Tristan costume. (It had also pushed the rolls of fat of his upper body into high relief.) Either Melchior was not as good at controlling the publicity photo event as he thought he was, or Kleinchen and Constance Hope had carelessly left him to his own inept devices. *Life* coverage certainly made him even more of a household word in Nebraska and Idaho, but it also spurred a furious letter from one fan, who was probably reacting typically: "*Why* did you do it? Now when I look at you, instead of seeing the noble Tristan, what I see is the corset!"

Aficionados, today as then, have no interest in an opera star who is unpretentious, uncharismatic, and resembles "the man next door." The singer should properly look and behave in such a fashion that the larger-than-life art form that is opera is maintained in their actions and appearance. Opera is not realistic, and its practitioners should properly be the instrument of transporting the audience away from the humdrum and into the realm of noble gods and adored goddesses. While Americans prefer to deify opera singers, Europeans are far more relaxed about the behavior and appearance of their opera stars; witness soprano Renata Tebaldi, who, when she came to sing at the Metropolitan, had to be taught by her American management how to dress as befits an opera star.

So timely was the issue in 1946 that an *Opera News* article was all but devoted to disputing criticisms of Melchior's "clown vs. singer" activities: "Tristan does not disintegrate because his interpreter runs riot in Duffy's Tavern!"

In truth, the publicity machine was voracious. Ultimately, the presence of a photographer to record an event became the only validation of its existence. Once the Pandora's box of personal public relations had been opened, no artist was free of its strong influence. The end (the mass audience's approval) was well worth the means (parodying one's art, stretching the truth, doing undignified comic turns on radio and in the movies—all to appear a "real human being"). High-principled Lotte Lehmann also succumbed to the siren call of publicity. When Melchior, teasing Lotte backstage, had presented her with a leftover bouquet of wilted flowers saying they were from her fans, she, true to her training, cried, "Get a photographer!" Even straightforward Kirsten Flagstad could not resist the insidious effect of publicity engineering; her quarrel with Melchior came about solely because of her concern with her press image. At Eisenhower's inauguration, when the new president descended from his box to thank Lauritz personally for singing, Kleinchen could not relax and enjoy the wonderful moment. As she indignantly complained later, "there was no photographer around to catch the picture!" Birthday parties, anniversaries, Guard functions, charity events, war bond rallies—all were eventually expected to do double duty, both as an occasion and as fodder for the publicist's efforts.

Grim as it may appear in retrospect, the Melchiors were not the least oppressed by these shenanigans. It was a game. They enjoyed matching wits with the press and giggled over winning each tiny victory. Lauritz relished being considered "good copy" and loved being a clown. The pleasure he derived from being funny was only increased when he was paid for doing it. He saw no lack of dignity in comedy, and certainly did not regard it as a prostitution of his art. Furthermore, he didn't mind in the least being portrayed as an "ordinary human being," for that is always how he regarded himself. Being a celebrity was a lot of fun, and he was thrilled to be in the presence of others of equal fame. Meeting his hero Eddie Rickenbacker at the Masonic ceremony where they both received medals was "a great honor," which made him "very proud and happy." True to one of his most endearing qualities, Melchior continued to enjoy thoroughly each new experience his fame brought him. Even after many years of fame, he never grew insensitive to the fun and festivity of being a celebrity.

Kleinchen's agenda was, as usual, somewhat different from her husband's. She knew to the penny the fruits of these non-operatic endeavors. She realized that although a career was built in the opera, opera was, in the end, a poorly paid stepping stone to the concert field, where the real money was to be made, the sum dependent only upon the price a singer's fame commanded. The situation has not changed appreciably in the 1980s. Concerts, solo or orchestral, are more lucrative because they can be scheduled seven nights a week if desired, whereas opera requires lengthy rehearsals and long stays in each city. What opera star who is not a media celebrity could fill as large a venue as Madison Square Garden, as Luciano Pavarotti has done? How would a discreet, albeit a real, success as an opera singer yield equal financial rewards? Kleinchen saw to it that, in consequence of the publicity blitz accompanying his radio and movie celebrity, Lauritz's concert fee rose to be twice his operatic fee.

In the years between 1943 and 1949 Allen and Melchior were often at it again. The jokes in the scripts almost always pitted Sinatra against Melchior to the greater gain of their respective publicity:

MELCHIOR: Last week I read that Frank Sinatra is giving up his radio program.

ALLEN: Lauritz, you mean that you . . .

MELCHIOR: Fred, you are looking at the new singing hoe handle.

ALLEN: Lauritz, don't tell me that you are giving up the opera?

MELCHIOR: I handed in my tights today.

ALLEN: Gad! not your tights!

MELCHIOR: The public has seen Melchior's knees for the last time.

ALLEN: What about your recitals? your concert tours?

MELCHIOR: Finished. I have blown my last kiss from the rostrum.

ALLEN: I don't get it. Why do you want to be another Sinatra?

MELCHIOR: It's the only way I can get something I've been striving for all my life—money.

The other running joke was the difference in mass of the two singers:

BOSS: Who is this, Allen, Mr. Pot Roast of 1947?

ALLEN: This is Lauritz Melchior, the Great Dane.

BOSS: I don't care if he is a cocker spaniel. I'm busy.

ALLEN: He would like to replace Sinatra.

BOSS: He could replace Sinatra and have enough body left over to replace 4 Chicks and a Chuck.

Their disparity in volume was also good for a laugh:

BOSS: Can he sing?

ALLEN: Can he sing!!! Let's go, Lauritz.

MELCHIOR: I'll sing "Without a Song."

ALLEN: He's doing it the haaaaaard way. (*another reference to Sinatra*)

MELCHIOR: (*sings*)

BOSS: Too loud!

ALLEN: Too *loud*?!! To sing like this takes years of training and breath control.

BOSS: Breath control? You mean you were breathing? Wait till Frankie learns that singers breathe. He'll die laughing.

MELCHIOR: I'll promise not to breathe.

ALLEN: Try him out as a hillbilly singer. It's just like the Met, but instead of singing in tights you sing in your underwear.

Melchior's first show with Fred Allen had prompted the summons to Hollywood. Joe Pasternak, producer of musicals for MGM, had heard that little spoof commercial, in which the product just happened to be called "Pasternak's Pretzels." Hearing his name, Pasternak listened, and the rest was history. He was smitten. He couldn't resist a *funny* opera singer. A few changes in the script of a new color film *Thrill of a Romance*, starring Esther Williams and Van Johnson, allowed it to accommodate an opera singer, Melchior the Dane. Said a jubilant Lauritz: "I wanted to vacation in California so I went there and bought a house. And there, after thirty-three years of professional life and twenty years at the Met, MGM discovered me." No one should have been surprised at the movie contract. It was inevitable that Melchior should be exploited as a clown, once the world out there had heard him on those radio comedy shows. He was genuinely funny.

Melchior finally submitted to a screen test, but only after signing the contract. (A salary of $4,000 per week brought joy to Kleinchen's heart, although, by Hollywood standards, it was probably not much.) Opera singer or no, Lauritz had to suffer the usual ignominies at the hands of the Hollywood philistines. After Lauritz's test was shown, one of the bigwigs commented sourly that a name like "Lawrence Something-or-other" would probably have to be changed for the movies. Neither Kleinchen nor Lauritz took umbrage at such treatment. It was all part of a whole new exciting world with new customs.

The first fallout from the screen test was recognition by the studio brass that the big fellow's operatic acting had to go. The job of scaling down operatic gestures intended to be seen in the last row of a 4,000-seat house was given to a speech coach, Lillian Burnes Sidney (also Sinatra's coach), who was to remake Lauritz into a movie performer. The necessity for underplaying on the screen meant that those studied gestures of Cosima's he had practiced so faithfully had to be unlearned. The singing, too, was different. He had thought that it would be just like making a record, where he sang and the engineer tended to the balance. But movie engineers bade him damp down the volume of his powerful voice. To do this with songs and popular ditties was not such a strain, but holding back on operatic arias required a lot of technical work. Yet to perform the eight songs in *Thrill of a Romance* was, on balance, less strenuous than one Wagnerian performance. Lauritz found the whole process of synchronizing his lips to the prerecorded songs a bit of a trial, but after thirty-three years of singing the same repertoire, this fresh territory waiting to be explored and mastered was a welcome change. It made him feel young again.

Movie work was not only easier but a lot more amusing than opera singing, said Lauritz. On a movie set one could do many things between shots: bring a secretary and dictate letters, sit around, read, or think, while the stand-in worked. And the comfortable dressing rooms sent him into paroxyms of delight. No airless, small, ugly rooms as at the Met. Imagine the pleasure of bathrooms right next door. No trekking up five flights to take a shower. No washing one foot at a time in the washbasin. And the scenery at MGM was far more stable than was, for example, the *Tristan* set, where he had crashed right through the old boards of the boat. Yes, the movies were really safe, restful work, and Lauritz "really preferred to die a natural death."

When the shooting of *Thrill of a Romance* had to be postponed from July 1 until the end of August 1944, there was time to take on another project, this one for the government. The Allied Forces, planning a landing somewhere in Nazi-occupied territory, were making contingency films in various languages. Once the site of the landing was ascertained, the army would use whichever one was suitable. Lauritz was asked to make a short film in Danish, requesting cooperation and giving information about the landing and the liberation. (Since the Allied landing took place in France, it was never used.)

Once the shooting of the feature film started, Lauritz's old, ingrained working schedule had to be discarded. No more singing in the evening, having a leisurely meal with friends, and then retiring in the wee hours of the morning. Instead, the horrors of early to bed (9:00) and early to rise (predawn) were topped by early to work. "6:30 in the morning! What a terrible time to go to work!" he told the press.

Of course, there were humiliating situations caused by the new movie star's ignorance of what "shooting" was all about. One particular scene had been allotted two days of shooting, but Lauritz had somehow escaped the watchful eye of his studio "keeper." For the second day of shooting he came on the set sporting a haircut. This precipitated much shouting and assigning of blame. All other activity came to a complete halt while two hairdressers fussed over his hair, brushing, combing, and even yanking at it. The director, the actors, and the crew of technicians stood by—expensively—and watched. Nothing made it look as it had on the first day. Bad boy Lauritz was banished, to be guarded by one of the hairdressers until his hair was the proper length once again.

Certainly he enjoyed the new life, new friends, and new work. "I want to make some fun for a while. I get a little tired of always being serious and walking around with a sword. I like a little vacation from Valhalla." The larger significance of his movie appearances, however, did not escape Lauritz. He himself had never found his position—as both a comedic radio star and a Wagnerian tenor—ambiguous. In addition, quite possibly he had been sustained by a broader purpose. In earnest about introducing "good" music to those whom he held captive in his radio appearances, the tenor had insisted upon singing one serious piece of music on every program. Now his old plan for radio was reactivated for the movies. He would seduce young moviegoers into liking arias. Radio had done well at bringing fine music to people, but the screen would spread its popularity even more rapidly:

> The chief trouble is that so much is said and written about good music that people are afraid they will not appreciate it. They must be introduced to it. . . . At all events, their ears are open and, if we are clever, we can catch them when they are young.

He subscribed to Beverly Sills's philosophy about poisoning the minds of the young at a very early age, expressed when she became general director of the New York City Opera Company.

The nature of Melchior publicity from Hope Associates changed radically in the summer of 1944. A whimsical picture of Melchior with Edgar Bergen and his two wooden dummies, Charley McCarthy and Mortimer Snerd, came first. Then a short piece appeared in entertainment columns across the country that immortalized the remarkable "Happy Birthday" quintet assembled in the MGM commissary for Louis B. Mayer in July: Lauritz Melchior in sports clothes, James Melton in a dress suit, Frank Sinatra still in his sailor costume, Kathryn Grayson in full makeup, and the redoubtable Jimmy Durante at the piano, causing a small problem, since he could only play in one key. Sinatra, fighting to be heard most of the way, finished after everyone else with a solo "boop-boop-a-doop." Next to inundate the country was a picture of Melchior, fellow guest for lunch at a social-register home in Montecito with the movie singer Jeannette MacDonald. The text under the photo claimed that Melchior was coaching her! (This may well be the only suggestion on record that Lauritz ever indulged in teaching voice.) Finally there came a movie-magazine picture—a first for the opera singer— of Sinatra standing next to Lauritz, listening while the tenor croons, "Boo, boo, boo, boo . . ." In the caption Melchior asks inscrutably, "How do you like my scrooning?"

As if to mitigate the undignified and movie-oriented tone of his publicity, Lauritz issued a statement in September 1944 saying that although Hollywood was showering him with dollars, he didn't intend to make more than one picture a year, because first and foremost in his work was his obligation to the Metropolitan Opera.

In March 1945, *Thrill of a Romance* was released. Movie stardom, Lauritz and Kleinchen discovered, was a completely different animal from opera stardom. "I had no idea that I would ever be an old girls' Sinatra," Lauritz gurgled merrily. But he was; his presence on the screen seemed to make some middle-aged hearts beat faster. Even more surprising, the teenage bobby-soxers who went to the Capitol Theater in New York to admire Van Johnson remained to burst into loud and spontaneous applause for Melchior's rendition of "Vesti la giubba," *five* times a day. (No wonder Lauritz believed that singing arias on the screen would extend the influence of opera.) Letters came by the score telling him that he was their introduction to "good music."

Hordes of autograph hunters now laid siege to him wherever he went. The result was that he was constantly late to appointments and was sometimes unsuitably testy. (Once, when too many autograph seekers approached at once, Lauritz growled and said, "I am starved. I might bite the next lady I shake hands with.") Kleinchen solved that problem by having an enormous number of already autographed photos made up. Now he could just hand them out as he passed. More passive evidence of his success at this new career were the numbers of children that were named after him, not to mention the gourmet dishes *à la Melchior*.

Lauritz and Kleinchen were keenly aware that a movie role gave him a chance to prove one all-important fact to the movie audience—that he was a real human being. In the movies made by Nino Martini, Lily Pons, and Gladys Swarthout there was only one plot to use with "grand opera" people, the one about how hard you had to work to become an opera star, but how anybody could do it. Being only half true, this plot soon wore thin. By Melchior's time other story lines were found, including funny ones, where he found his niche.

The judgment of most professionals held that it was the combination of that beautiful voice and his truly funny delivery that won Melchior his audience. *Thrill of a Romance* had a wonderful scene cribbed right out of *Don Giovanni*. Lauritz and Van Johnson go out to Esther Williams's house to serenade her and break down her resistance to Johnson. He stands on the lawn in clear sight, and pretends to be singing his serenade outside her window, but it is, of course, really the concealed Melchior who sings. Henry Travers and Beulah Bondi, the parents, get out of bed and stand at the window.

"Funny that he has an accent," remarks Bondi.

"Yes, and he can sing with his mouth shut," marvels her husband.

Lauritz's sunny personality was welcomed by all his new colleagues. He never tired of relating how nice the established movie people had been to him during his first difficult days. "They expected me to be complicated and think that I knew everything. I was worried a bit. I had to ask everyone how to do this and how to do that. I needed advice. They were all very good to me."

Most of the music critics, who wrote for the knowledgeable public, were clearly in the camp of the affronted Wagnerites. They, too, felt that Melchior's publicity and media appearances detracted from his artistic stature as a serious musician. (This attitude has not carried into the 1980s, when no one is offended to see Jean-Pierre Rampal playing his flute on the "Johnny Carson Show." On the other hand, a box at the opera is still a symbol of elitism to the mass audience, even though opera no longer has the cachet it once had, as can be seen by the radical change away from formality in the dress code of opera audiences.) Dissatisfaction with Melchior's vocal means, evinced by the music critics of the 1940s, was based, at least in part, on their perception that his voice was deteriorating because of his movie making and radio clowning.

An article in a 1946 issue of *The Musician* echoed other remarks being made around the country: Melchior was no fool to go into the movies because he knew himself to be passé and superannuated; Melchior got bookings because the public still had a certain veneration for a name and because there was no young singer to take his place; today's operagoers wanted to hear someone who could sing, and Melchior must know that his shouting no longer carried conviction over the footlights.

Chicago writer Henry Marx, however, did not join the attack. In 1946 he reminded his readers reasonably that "the Melchior situation [had] been acute for several seasons."

A prudent management would have begun to cast its eyes around for a successor long ago. While it was obvious to everyone that sometimes Melchior was performing under real difficulties, he is 55 years old, after all, little or nothing was done in that respect. Pointing to Mr. Melchior, who for good reasons is slowly retiring from the operatic stage, as a scapegoat is unfair. This deserving artist rounds out twenty years of devoted service with the Met this season.

The concerted press attention, which had begun with Melchior's transformation into a super-celebrity at the hands of Fred Allen, no longer referred to Melchior as being "of the Opera," but "of Hollywood, Radio, and the Opera" in descending order of importance. In 1944 Howard Taubman had fired an opening shot, heard across the nation, in what was to become a steady barrage of sniping disguised as news:

> Melchior has insisted on top pay, top billing, and top consideration. As long as he has had them, he has been as sweet as a soubrette, but when he thought that somebody was getting the better of him, he has turned difficult and stubborn. The tenor makes no secret of his disdain for those who would steal his throne. He cheerfully rates one aspirant as a "big donkey," another as the "stupidest man I ever met," a third as "an impossible singer, simply impossible."

The music press seemed to turn a jaundiced eye on all his endeavors. They even managed to cast as self-serving the benefit concerts that Melchior did when a tour engagement put him in Texas at the time of a disastrous explosion in Galveston. (Not so the Texas press, who appreciated the gesture, and the state government, who made Lauritz an honorary Texan. This was the beginning of his sporting a huge ten-gallon Stetson hat as his favorite headgear.)

The Metropolitan Opera had, until the departure of Gatti-Casazza, operated in a way totally removed from the lives of ordinary people. Once the shareholders wished to sell out their investment, and the company was forced to buy back the building, the support of the general public was crucial. Not only did the opera need contributions from the country at large for their fundraising effort, but it had to function within a budget predicated on selling tickets. It was the radio broadcasts that had made it possible to have an opera supported by a wider public.

When Melchior continued to do comedy on radio, eyebrows were raised and fingers wagged, but there was some support in high places—from pragmatic businessman George Sloan, president of the Metropolitan Board of Directors, who was clearly ahead of his time in an appreciation of the realities of selling tickets by means of publicity exposure. Not only did Sloan not chastise Lauritz, but he sent a letter expressing his regret that he had not heard the latest broadcast, wherein, he was sure, Melchior had made friends for the opera.

Sloan's approval was in sharp contrast to the attitude of most Met administrators, none of whom—until recently—recognized the value of this kind of publicity. So much was the issue on Rudolf Bing's mind that his first act, after Wagnerian soprano Birgit Nilsson's great success at the Met, was to ask her to sign a paper stating that she would not go out and sing "cheap music." Today, it is not enough for a singer to be expert at his or her art. Celebrity mandates media exposure. Not only do our prima donnas of the 1980s feel free to do commercial ads for such products as Japanese whiskey, but those opera singers who do *not* "crossover" into media turns are relegated to a semi-obscurity because of their lack of name recognition.

Understandably, it was and is difficult for those who love serious music and the opera itself to bear the constant use of the "opera singer" image as a source of comedy. Yet, beginning with Groucho Marx, "It isn't over till the fat lady sings" was an attitude endemic in American humor. Even now, when opera is broadcast on television and regional companies are flourishing, the mention of opera in commercial shows and advertisements usually features an unattractive person in a ridiculous costume performing a travesty of operatic music in a comically "loud, but ugly" voice, or a character being forced to attend the opera, where he is, of course, miserable. Playing to the stereotype bothered his fans, but never Melchior. In fact, when asked to compare opera and radio, he said that he found the latter more serious.

Shortly after the Germans unconditionally surrendered in May 1945, Melchior offered to go to Europe and sing for the troops. Because his status as a foreign national made for complications within the American army, he contacted the British, who, quick to accept his offer, had arrangements in place by August. The Melchiors left New York on September 16, flying over Labrador and Iceland to Stockholm and thence to Copenhagen. There for the first time in six years Lauritz saw his sister Bodil, seemingly in good health at sixty-eight, his daughter Birte, safe after all, with her husband and Lauritz's newest grandson, Hans Henrik. From the south where he was stationed with the CIC, Ib drove up to meet his father, his Jeep loaded with oranges, coffee, and other provisions for the family. Father and son drove in the Jeep from the airport to the Hotel d'Angleterre in the center of the city. Rather inappropriately, but characteristically, Lauritz waved to the multitudes like a victorious general riding triumphantly into a war-torn city. The picture was too much to be forgotten and several major cartoonists— the famous Jensenius among them—captured it for posterity.

With great sadness Lauritz learned that his sister Agge had died only six months before. During his years in the United States he had never ceased his activities in behalf of the blind and had maintained a real interest in his sister's work. As with the death of his brother many years before, Lauritz was forced to ponder what his life would have been without Agge. Had she not needed him to accompany her to the theater, where he learned to love opera as a young child, he might never have pursued the life he did.

The Melchiors took part in the Danes' celebration of their beloved King Christian's seventy-fifth birthday, in preparation for which the city was in an uproar of happiness. At a poignant reunion of the Melchiorianer Association Lauritz was treated to proud stories about the resistance fighters and their exploits, as well as tales of King Christian's bravery: he had refused to leave Denmark or to institute anti-Jewish laws; he had attended services in a synagogue in full regalia (saying, "we do not have a Jewish problem; we do not consider ourselves inferior to them"); he would not take down the Dannebrog from Amalienborg Palace (arriving to remove it by force, the Nazis had found it guarded by one officer of the Danish army in full uniform—the king).

During the intermission of the Royal Theater's gala birthday performance, at which he sang, Lauritz was called to the royal box. There, in the presence of the Danish royal family, the Swedish king and queen, and the Norwegian king and queen, King Christian presented Melchior with the Commander Cross of the Dannebrog, personally placing the cross around the singer's neck. It was a night Lauritz remembered all his life. (When they returned to the United States, they would—only half in jest—proclaim that they must be addressed as Sir Lauritz and Lady Melchior, now that Lauritz was a Commander, not a mere Knight of the Dannebrog.) Next morning he showed the film he had made for the Allied Forces and presented the king with a purse of 10,044 kroner (around $2,100) donated by the Guardists in America to the families of the Royal Guards that had fallen during the occupation. That evening the premiere of *Thrill of a Romance* was given at a huge movie theater, the proceeds also earmarked for the king's birthday fund. More importantly, it was then that Lauritz told the king that he and Kleinchen wanted to become American citizens. King Christian gave his blessing, saying, "Any boy who was born in Nørregade will be a Copenhagen lad all his life," a phrase that Melchior cherished forever. "In my left hand, which is close to my heart, there is my Dannebrog flag, and in the hand with which one struggles, the right hand, is my American flag, and holding those two flags, I try to fold my hands in friendship between Denmark and America," he explained.

Berlin was no longer recognizable to the Melchiors when they arrived there in the fall of 1945. It lay in ruins covering many square miles, here a hill of rubble as tall as a building, there an empty crater, pipes hanging from the girders of bombed buildings, not a tree or bush left in the entire city. Names and addresses were scrawled on the ruins for the benefit of searching family and friends. German civilians were rag-clad, living in dark makeshift dwellings within buildings that had not yet fallen down. Military debris littered the streets and filled the canals. Hundreds of thousands of bodies remained unburied, and the stench of corpses pervaded the air, already full of ash and dust. Kleinchen and Lauritz reeled at the total devastation and the eerie silence. "One's heart must bleed at the thought that a single man and his fanaticism could bring all this misery and destruction upon countries and peoples," wrote Lauritz.

Getting to Berlin after the first concert in Lübeck had been fraught with many obstacles. Permission for passage through the Russian zone was not obtainable, and driving was thus not possible. Finally, thanks to their two obligatory escort officers, one British and one American, the Melchiors were granted the use of a military plane.

When they asked to go out to the suburb Pausin, then in the Russian zone, where their friends the Grohnwalds had lived, the British aide-de-camp was sure that the necessary Russian permission would not be forthcoming. However, they had reckoned without "Kleinchen's charm" and Lauritz's "singing for the soldiers," which "softened the officer."

> When we arrived at the border . . . we found the road blocked with a gate, barbed wire, machine guns, even a tank. A Russian officer of non-commissioned rank asked for our papers, and my American officer, who knew some Russian, demanded to speak with the officer in command. When he appeared, it was a small, blond, boyish lieutenant, nineteen or twenty years old. In a mixture of Russian and German our aide-de-camp explained to him that I was a great singer from Moscow, who was on his way over to sing for the troops, but that we had no papers. He granted us two hours' time to return to his post.

Having cut through the red tape successfully, the Melchiors found the Grohnwalds in the most miserable conditions, with scanty furniture, almost without clothing, with no bed linen whatsoever, in a house without a single intact window. Happy to see their friends, the Grohnwalds called them "unexpected angels." After Hitler attacked Denmark, embassy personnel had transported as much Danish property as possible to the Grohnwald house, where they had sealed everything, including what belonged to the Melchiors, into a silo. The Polish, arriving first, respected the seal, but the Russians did not. After the trucks were loaded (they had taken everything but four stamp albums), Grohnwald had made the Russian officer sign a receipt. This, together with the trucks' license numbers, he gave to Lauritz. He had information about Chossewitz, and it was bad: Immediately after the Melchiors' departure, the SS informer who was wooing Lizzie had told the authorities about the property hidden in the barn, and it was confiscated. Himmler had wanted the house for himself, but he was overruled in favor of a Gestapo officers' club. Once the Russian soldiers had taken up quarters there, however, things were very different. Melchior would see for himself, if he could secure permission to visit.

Melchior made arrangements to sing for the Russians in return for being allowed to visit Chossewitz. A Danish officer with the Allied forces, Harry Rabinowitz, also a great Melchior admirer and a passionate collector of his records, obtained approval for the trip from the British authorities in Hamburg and served as chauffeur. Melchior dressed for the evening concert at two in the afternoon, all his colorful decorations dangling from the left side of his massive chest. The party arrived at the frontier of the Russian zone where a bulky Russian non-commissioned officer was on guard. Suspicious of foreigners, foreign permits, and foreign languages, she refused to let them pass. In Russian Rabinowitz told her that she was in the presence of the most famous tenor in the world, and that she was being rude to him in the bargain. Melchior, an impressive sight at any time, silently opened the left side of his overcoat where his medals gleamed in all their glory. Struck dumb, the Russian soldier came rigidly to attention and saluted. The car passed.

As they approached Chossewitz, the Melchiors saw on the lawn a huge hammer and sickle made out of what seemed to be colored stones. Upon closer inspection the gigantic mosaic, sadly, proved to be composed of their collection of Meissen china and porcelain birds, broken into small bits. Things were as Dr. Grohnwald had said. The barn was empty; the rest of the stamp collection (truly valuable) and some diaries, soaked with water and rotting in a pile of rubble, were all that was left. The recordings and the Covent Garden test pressings had been used for target practice. The caretakers, who were the same old couple who had worked there before the war, were so overjoyed to see the Melchiors that they wept, but the party left swiftly, for it was more painful to remain.

Approaching the Russian zone barrier some hours later, they were apprehensive, expecting to find a different soldier who would have to be convinced of their probity. The same one, however, was on duty, and long before the car reached her she had already snapped to attention. With her permission, the car passed swiftly, in top-brass style. There was just enough time to notice that the soldier had decked out her own impressive chest with an array of medals hardly less resplendent than those of the mysterious dignitary in the car.

Back in Berlin the Melchiors visited the building where they had lived and the Danish Embassy where they had stored possessions. Both sites were empty, the buildings having succumbed to bombs and fire. By night Lauritz sang concerts. By day they went about tracing friends and trying, unsuccessfully, to obtain restitution for their looted property. They were especially worried about Bayreuth colleagues who had not left Germany: Frida and Rudi, Gotthelf Pistor, Fritz Wolff, and their wives. With a lot of luck, they found the two Heldentenor friends. Fritz Wolff had lost his feet from frostbite and Pistor's daughters, who had been lost, were found when Lauritz asked for information about them during his broadcast concert. Kleinchen and Lauritz busied themselves providing the material aid so badly needed by the two families.

There was still no sign of Frida Leider. Finally it was learned that Rudi was still in Switzerland, where Frida had last seen him in 1943, when she was permitted to sing a concert there. She had not sung at the opera since 1941 and had lived in her Pausin home until 1944, subsisting on tea alone at times, painting, and awaiting "the end of the catastrophe" in desperate fear because the Russians used the suburb as a camouflage for their antiaircraft installations. Once her home and possessions had been confiscated by the Russians, she had gone to the British zone. After Germany's surrender, it took the Staatsoper only a few months to get organized again. In July 1945

Frida was summoned to the Admiralspalast, the opera's temporary home. Unable to sing anymore, she was given a position as artistic adviser and instructor. More importantly, opera lovers among the Russians were contributing welcome food to the opera personnel.

The Melchiors, knowing only that Frida had been with the Staatsoper when last they heard, headed for the Admiralspalast, which had just opened on September 8, hoping that the intendant would have her address. When his secretary regretted that he was in a meeting just then, they explained their errand. Smiling mysteriously, she invited them into the office. There they found Frida! Weeping from surprise and delight, the three embraced.

CHAPTER 14

The Hottest Dane Since Beowulf

(1946–1949)

The end of World War II coincided with Melchior's seriously advancing years and with his highly increased popular celebrity. It was the worst possible timing for his looming troubles. A euphoric America, having roundly beaten the Germans, had an appetite for everything new, from food to art. Out with the old and traditional; forget the furbelowed heritage; on with spare, stripped-down modernity. In the world of opera this took the form of intense dislike for the Met's outmoded sets and costumes, stock lighting, unfashionable Wagnerian acting, and uninspired direction. Out with the Met's antiquated Wagner productions, then; on with the new theatrical concepts. In the midst of these new trends, Lauritz Melchior appeared behind the times to some. The tone used by the serious music press even seemed to suggest that he was ranking Heldentenor only because he had no competition. Some critics began to suggest that the Met invite those European tenors who had not been able to visit America during the war.

Melchior was to some extent tarred with the same brush that attacked the out-of-date productions themselves. Other sins for which Melchior was being attacked were his alone. First, his acting was old-fashioned and uninspired. It cannot be denied that Melchior did cling willingly to the old Bayreuth traditions that he learned from Cosima and Siegfried. On the other hand, his acting was not markedly different from that of the other singers, who appeared in a "pattern of odd debuts and miscellaneous casting." Literally nothing in the German wing had changed since Gatti left. The threadbare sets, hard-worn costumes, and perfunctory stage direction provided the Wagnerian dramas by the Met were surely as old-fashioned as the acting being done by the singers. It is true that Melchior, who roundly detested the results when Wieland and Wolfgang Wagner were later given free rein to modernize Bayreuth productions by adapting the new theatrical techniques to Wagnerian opera, might have resisted innovative concepts had they been encouraged at the Met. Danish baritone Mogens Wedel met Melchior on the streets of Bayreuth during the 1950s, "disguised as a Tyrolese in short Lederhosen. . . . Melchior was polite, a little formal, and expressed a curious criticism of this new production of the *Ring*. Wieland Wagner's statuesque staging and special symbolism absolutely did not agree with Melchior's more naturalistic perception of the staging."

Another time Melchior and his son Ib attended the performance of a "modern" version of *Tannhäuser*. The production, as described by Ib, had "no costumes, no props, no sets, only large hangings of gauze on which constantly changing and shifting colors were projected. Instead of the 'Venusberg' ballet, a mobile picture screen was lowered on which was shown two people in intricate acts of love-making." In stony silence Lauritz glowered at the stage spectacle. During a soft passage, he turned to his son and, in his inimitable Wagnerian whisper that could be heard in the balcony's last row, muttered, "What kind of shit is this?" Still, after the act, a majority of the audience crowded around to shake the great singer's hand.

Secondly, it was pointed out, Melchior, behaving irresponsibly, would not rehearse. In fact, he did rehearse, but only when and where he chose. Charles O'Connell relates the story of a concert with the Choral Society of the University of Pennsylvania and the Philadelphia Orchestra. Melchior, the guest artist, turned up on time and rehearsed tirelessly and patiently in full voice with the amateur singers. Other artists of his rank, such as Lily Pons, also absented themselves from routine rehearsals, and without hearing about it in the press. It was a Met tradition for stars to let understudies take their rehearsals, and Edward Johnson, who could have put his foot down and changed things, did not.

Since there were virtually no new productions or renovated dramatic concepts in the Wagnerian wing of the Met during the 1930s and 1940s, rehearsals were limited to refreshing musical memories of the established artists and routining new singers in the old stagings. Clearly, many who charged that Melchior's musicianship was defective also believed that his problem stemmed from too little rehearsal time. His rhythmic memory was definitely weak, and his sense of tempo was always overridden by his dramatic involvement at moments of passion, but would more Met rehearsals have rendered Melchior's sense of rhythm flawless? It seems unlikely, considering that all the attention paid to this problem in his early career had not cured it. In fact, Fritz Busch and Fritz Stiedry were relieved to find that he always made the same mistakes in the same places. Furthermore, those mistakes were made in the very phrases that he had carefully marked in his scores ("nicht eilen!" [don't rush!], etc.), which he had rehearsed exhaustively during his years in the German houses.

Several critics also pointed out that Melchior was no longer singing as well as he should. "Tired out by his many non-operatic activities" was the reason most often advanced for this. Actually, the normal ravages of time were overtaking Melchior, as might be expected. Acquitting oneself well in the role of Siegfried at any age over 55 should have been a cause for rejoicing, but at this time, heritage and history were not uppermost in the minds of many music critics. Later, they would reassess what Melchior had been, but not now. Perhaps, had W. J. Henderson still been writing, things might have been different, but Melchior's outstanding place in the pantheon of Heldentenors was no longer considered by most writers, and the popular audience, who were, in any case, not objecting to anything about his singing, had no basis for comparison. The problem was exacerbated by Melchior's sinecure as "the best." The concept of "the best" must be tested constantly when a publicity machine has made the artist so visible. Each time he sings, the serious music public is assessing the technical skill he displays. Is he still "the best?" In Melchior's case, further pressure was exerted by the seriousness of his Wagnerian repertoire, the intense scrutiny of the Wagnerites, and the stamina required by the Heldentenor Fach.

Similarly, Melchior was criticized as being too fat and too old to be believable in his roles. Although many press pieces around this time concentrated on the ineptitude of his appearance as young Siegfried, a 1942 review had set matters nicely into balance: "As for his playing of the part— how would most of us look accoutered in a brief bearskin, romping on a big stage and trying to look half the age?" Once Set Svanholm began to sing at the Metropolitan, a great deal of space was devoted to comparisons between him and Melchior, which played up the gross differences in their *physique du rôle*. Too, another tenor, Giovanni Martinelli, who remained at the Metropolitan for thirty-two consecutive years, was permitted to grow old—and indeed portly—without being taken to task for showing it. On the contrary, he was accorded the usual courtesy given to an artist in his declining years. Even criticism of his singing was couched in the gentlest of platitudes such as "despite a few uneasy moments." Perhaps one of the most important criticisms was that Melchior was denigrating the whole operatic world when he clowned. A story from *Opera News* does double duty, proving that Melchior had attended at least one Met rehearsal, but that he played the clown during it: He passionately sang the "Rome Narrative," and then, when Wolfram tried to hold Tannhäuser back from going to Venus, Lauritz turned the baritone around and began to waltz with him. Radio shows and movies, however, knew only one way to deal with the kind of music that starred fat ladies and gentlemen, wearing horns and singing about German mythology in another language: They parodied it. Hence the radio scripts included a lot of buffoonery. Lotte Lehmann also did her share, without censure. In 1938 Martinelli appeared on the Eddie Cantor comedy hour and suffered no repercussions. He clearly enjoyed it: "I show them I can swing 'Dinah' and I yell 'Sock it, boys!' to the musicians. I laugh in tears when they swing 'M'apparì'." He did, however, ask, "You don't think it was wrong for me to make fun with them, do you?" To which the reporter answered, "Only musical prigs would think so." Lily Pons, Gladys Swarthout, Lawrence Tibbett, and Nino Martini appeared in movies, but, as leading men and women, their roles did no damage to their dignity as opera singers. Melchior, no leading-man type, had to be given character roles, usually with comic overtones, in a different type of plot. This kind of activity from one who was also the greatest Tristan, compounded by the profound lack of dignity in his publicity, was understandably viewed as embarrassing by the self-appointed protectors of Wagner, audience and critics alike.

From coast to coast, critics were in agreement that Melchior was singing cheap music, and had lame excuses for doing so. Melchior's concert programs now included what some considered contemporary romantic rubbish, operetta excerpts, and pop music. In all likelihood, these programs reflected an appreciation of how to reach a popular audience that Melchior had learned from his radio and movie experience. This audience was not interested in studying Wagner traditions. They went to see Melchior in concert mainly because he was a celebrity. It is doubtful whether many of them even knew that he was considered the world's best Heldentenor. Music critics were even more affronted by the constant pontificating on his methods for leading the mass audience to "good" music, the more so because he was singing what they regarded as trash. (Critic Harold Schonberg's opinion, for example, was that the tenor "had simply uttered the usual nonsense about 'bringing music to the people' that artists inevitably make when they soil themselves artistically.") Melchior was not just taking the easy way out, however. The music he sang was not as difficult as Tristan's, but the "Serenade" from Romberg's *The Student Prince*, which he sang very often, is a taxing piece; it sits so high that even lyric tenors have to work at it. In the 1980s we find mezzo-soprano Shirley Verrett exciting no comment when she included two (beautifully sung) pop songs—one of which was Melchior's old standby, "Without a Song"—in her PBS special, "The Life of a Diva."

Only Lauritz Melchior, who was still singing Wagner at fifty-six with his vocal skills virtually intact, singing all the notes as written, his voice untouched by having sung an unequalled, record number of heavy Wagnerian performances, was regularly singled out for heavy censure in the music press. Why?

One must wonder if he would have been criticized so thoroughly and so often had he not maintained so high a profile. Not only is it human nature to make a whipping boy out of the person who achieves celebrity, but the artist who keeps a low profile is looked upon as more deserving of respect. The pinnacle of fame Melchior occupied was regarded as suspect; in serious music this kind of celebrity was not supposed to come about. Yet the way to get an American identity is to attract attention, and Constance Hope had taught him how to do that. Martinelli once found it necessary to sue a chain of cafeterias for simply advertising that he had given them a recipe for artichokes. When he collected $20,000 for winning the suit, his lawyer explained, "It is essential to the career of a grand opera star that the grandeur surrounding such a career should at all times be scrupulously maintained." Melchior was simply not safeguarding his "grandeur" scrupulously, and serious people resented it.

There was a firm but unfair belief that Melchior's all-embracing celebrity was causing him to slight his operatic roles, "tending ever more to short Met visits and extended absences in Hollywood and on tour." No matter how it appeared, this was not true. It was Johnson himself and only he who decided how many performances Melchior was to do. All other commitments were routinely put off until the Met had made its decision.

Certainly in the 1980s we are hard put to understand such a furor over radio and movie appearances. Luciano Pavarotti, a popular celebrity, made a movie that was, all agree, a very bad one, as did Robert Merrill. No one held it against these gentlemen that their movie characters were decidedly bumpkinish, nor was it even discussed very much except in the popular press. Today we understand that they were simply playing a role. Many opera singers these days eagerly await a summons to the "Johnny Carson Show," where he or she will sing the most accessible piece of music from his or her repertoire. Marilyn Horne sings "Jeannie with the Light Brown Hair," sings it with great artistry, and makes no excuses for the fact that it is parlor music. The line of demarcation between serious music and popular music is no longer so strong as it was in Melchior's day. No one is affronted that Plácido Domingo records an album with John Denver, or that Kiri Te Kanawa sings a role in a recording of *West Side Story*, later appearing on television to say how much she enjoys this music. These are the very actions for which Melchior was disdained. Popular celebrity is now seen to encourage interest in opera performances, many of which are being given by grass-roots companies all over the country. Most of these local and regional companies were not in existence in the 1940s. In Melchior's time there were limited ways to introduce people outside metropolitan centers to music other than popular tunes: community concerts, radio, and movies. These were the avenues that Melchior used.

It can be argued that Melchior was ahead of his time in choosing material that would be enjoyable to the popular audience and yet a cut above what they usually heard. It is easy to program for the cognoscenti, and he proved that he could do it in his New York recitals. It is another thing to reach an audience untutored in the fine points of serious music. Certainly, hearing Vincent Youmans sung by Melchior provided an experience for this type of audience greatly different from hearing Frank Sinatra sing it. When Melchior sang a Wagnerian excerpt on radio or in the movies, he carefully chose something like the "Prize Song" from *Die Meistersinger*; a passage from Tristan's death scene would not do.

Even in the 1950s the most pervasive influence upon programming in cities outside of metropolitan centers was Columbia Concerts, which had a near monopoly on the concert business. Their absolute insistence upon the most familiar song and operatic literature in tour programs sung by their artists was based upon the sort of audience-preference ratings that lead television programming these days. Although most of these programs were, if anything, worse than Melchior's, they somehow escaped the contumely that was heaped upon his. Melchior's formula was most clearly seen in his constant tinkering with the choice of serious music programmed by the young singers in the "Lauritz Melchior Show" in the fifties. He was not satisfied until the song was of reasonably short length, had a beautiful melody, and projected a clearly identifiable, exciting dramatic theme (because the audience could not be counted on to understand the foreign words)—in short, a good, but accessible, piece of music.

Fed by the release of Melchior's second picture, *Two Sisters from Boston*, the disdain with which the serious music press and many fans regarded the Heldentenor's non-operatic escapades escalated. Its plot called for an opera performance starring Melchior as an egocentric singer—but Hollywood couldn't abide leisurely operatic conventions. "What Hollywood wanted was an overture, the curtain, and zowie, a tenor aria for Melchior," said a scornful but accurate *Time* piece. One of the musical pastiche artists employed by MGM borrowed from Mendelssohn's "Ruy Blas Overture" and the slow movement of the E Minor Violin Concerto, plus some Liszt preludes, Liszt's Hungarian Rhapsody no. 14, and "Liebestraum" to create an ersatz opera called *Marie Antoinette*. One of the barely literate verses for the "aria" sung by Melchior's character was: "Green is the hill and the valley/and gold is the grape on the vine;/Songs fill the air, of the harvest, Tra la la la la." RCA Victor released an album of the "opera" sung by Melchior and Metropolitan opera soprano Nadine Connor (who escaped criticism for her part in this exploit).

In this film Melchior made use of his early radio and recording experiences. From his description of the Marconi studio and the recording method, plus a few details from the recording session for his first Danish discs, the screenwriters derived an amusing bit for Melchior's rendition of the "Preislied." In the scene the recording director achieves louder and softer tones by yanking Lauritz toward the funnel and away from it; the fifteen accompanying musicians, clustered together like a bunch of grapes, keep marching forward and backward with him. Lauritz goes over to the couch and sits next to a little dog while the engineer rushes the cylinder into several baths to harden the wax, and then places it on a towel to dry. As the playback begins, the dog's ears perk up, and he goes over to the loudspeaker, contriving to look exactly like the trademark for "His Master's Voice."

Lauritz did not fare too badly in the actual movie critiques for his second film: "Melchior demonstrates considerable knack at being a villain as well as an opera star." Shooting of the new movie, *This Time for Keeps*, on Michigan's beautiful Mackinack Island in 1947 had the islanders agog. "Bicycle Built for Two" was to be sung by Lauritz and Jimmy Durante as a duet, which caused extensive problems for the engineering department. Because of his (slimmed-down for the movies) 250-pound bulk, Lauritz's seat on the tandem needed special springs, while wheel blocks had to be added to Durante's section of the bike to permit his short legs to synchronize with Melchior's. The publicity stills of the two men riding the bicycle were sensational. About one month later *Variety* reported that the tenor's fees for concerts had doubled since he started appearing in films. The film world would later honor him with an invitation to place his size-12 footprint—the largest one there—and a message ("Greetings and *Skål*") in front of Grauman's Chinese Theater next to those of the great movie stars.

Melchior had good reason to be proud of his movie work, for it had broadened public awareness of operatic music exactly as he had envisaged. In *Luxury Liner*, made during the summer of 1948, he sang "Winterstürme" from *Die Walküre* and a duet from *Aïda*. In *Two Sisters* he sang "Das Preislied." (Someone in the studio decided it was "a marvelous melody!") Observing that his performances were invariably sold out, most people agreed that Lauritz was not giving himself too much credit when he pointed to the new ticket buyers at the Metropolitan, as proof that he had made a difference. He explained his philosophy to *Opera News*:

> When you are introducing people to your art, it is as if you are at the top of the ladder and they are at the bottom. You have to step down to the rung just above them and catch their interest. Then you climb up again gradually, bringing them with you. . . . First they never go to an opera. Then they see an opera singer in a movie and find that . . . he is human. So the next time they go to his concert to see the animal in person. Finally they go to the opera.

Responding to a genuine controversial topic of the day—Is It a Good Thing for Opera Singers to Behave like Human Beings?—even Frank Sinatra was moved to defend his friend Melchior in a 1946 guest gossip column for Leonard Lyons: "There's nothing wrong in being hammy." From the admirers' side of this controversy came an invitation from the Metropolitan Opera Club for Lauritz to become an honorary member as "a token of your career as the greatest Wagnerian tenor in the world."

An interesting corroboration came from a fellow sufferer, the great Tito Gobbi, whose autobiography was published somewhat later.

> Oddly enough—unless a touch of envy accounts for it—my film work earned me small kudos among my operatic associates, who made a number of snide references to "the singing film star." [They] made more than one belittling comment about those who resorted to "film work for lack of something better."

Of all the pleasure Lauritz derived from being a celebrity, easily the most fun he ever had was his springtime of 1947 investiture as "fall guy" for the Circus Saints and Sinners Club. The "lucky" fall guy was the object of some two hours' worth of insults, lampoons, and libel at the hands of the club's members. Lauritz was borne into the luncheon on a chair fashioned like a swan, placed before a backdrop that represented the "Messapolitan" Opera House, and surrounded by a chorus of Vikings in Wagnerian opera garb. He spent the luncheon hunched over in his chair, his huge shoulders shaking and eyes welling with tears—unable to stop laughing. People had been telling him in not too polite language and in song that he was a jerk, that opera singers as a class were dimwitted poseurs and that Denmark should be ashamed of itself for ever exporting such a bulbous commodity. Lauritz's worst punishment was that he laughed too hard to eat more than a few bites.

Almost equally enjoyable was an appearance on Milton Berle's show in January 1949, in which Lauritz refused to turn the other cheek. During the rehearsal of some comedy scenes based upon *The Barber of Seville*, Berle made a sort of goat out of Lauritz, rubbing his ears the wrong way, prodding him in the stomach, and pushing up his nose. Lauritz took it all very well at the time, but when the show went on the air, he showed Berle that long years of operatic stage chicanery had taught him well. When Melchior crashed down his tin barber's basin from above his head squarely onto the great man's nose, it might have ended seriously. Berle suffered a bad cut, but the NBC management was appreciative that the nose was not broken. Meanwhile Berle had learned to curb humor at Melchior's expense.

Lauritz always felt, however, that he had the right to pull tricks on others. An unsuspecting Ignace Strasfogel was invited out to a seafood dinner one evening, for Lauritz had promised to teach his accompanist how to eat lobster. Strasfogel asked about the pieces of wood in the lobster's claws. Lauritz assured him that these wood pieces were the best part of the lobster, that one dipped these little delicacies in butter or sauce before savoring them. The pianist tried vainly to chew them. He finally gave up, saying, to the uproarious laughter of the Melchiors, that they tasted just like wood.

Kleinchen achieved a new level of fame of her own in 1948; she was named one of the best-dressed women of the United States, a title she was to keep for many years, together with occasional incursions into "best-tailored" and "best-hatted." Melchior once told this story about Kleinchen's famous hats to a New York columnist:

One afternoon Kleinchen had to go to a cocktail party and a funeral. For the party she bought a beautiful John Frederic hat trimmed with enormous lilies, reserving a severe black model for the funeral. After the party she switched hats and went to the funeral, where she placed her flowered hat on a table in the reception room. During the services she was horrified to see the coffin carried out with her lily hat on top!

She and Lauritz were no longer advertising Pabst Blue Ribbon Beer and Fanny Mae Candy, but had graduated to posh Romanoff Caviar. Sheila Graham featured Lauritz in her Hollywood column. This coverage was not all publicity fluff. Melchior was going to do a benefit concert for needy Navajo Indians (this was long before the Native American cause was "chic"). *Vogue* printed a wonderfully bizarre picture of Lauritz with Viking helmet, hunting horn, and pewter cup, wearing evening trousers with suspenders over ruffled shirt and tie. He was more than a household word; now regularly listed as a clue in newspaper crossword puzzles, he had become a fixture of American life.

Starting in 1946 Melchior took advantage of his new freedom, made possible by the presence of Torsten Ralf and Set Svanholm at the Met, and concertized across the country with a forty-piece orchestra conducted by Otto Seyfert. That season they traveled to sixty-six engagements in two private airplanes. Lauritz's joie de vivre was at a new high. He basked in the affection of his fans who waved him goodbye at the airport each morning. He enjoyed being flown by his very own chartered DC-3 Tiger planes piloted by two of General Clare Chennault's boys. He took pleasure in the salutations of his orchestra, "Morning, Boss!" He positively savored the ceremonial meetings of dignitaries and press upon arrival in each new city. So intense was the admiration of his audiences and so reluctant were they to leave the hall, even after several encores, that Melchior was forced to create a method of showing them that the concert was really finished: he walked on stage in his overcoat, waving his big Stetson hat. (By this time he had narrowed his choice of hats down to three: the ten-gallon Stetson for all formal wear, a baseball cap for Dodger games, and the disreputable Tyrolean hat he wore while hunting.) He reveled in the after-show party, for which his steak and a beer—National Premium in Baltimore, Rolling Rock in Ohio, and Champagne Velvet in Indiana— would be ordered ahead of time from the hostess of the evening by tour manager Walter Gould. Melchior even relished the fine sleep he managed in unfamiliar beds, and getting up for the next departure. The only thing he didn't like was his introduction, which would inevitably be "That great MGM star!" Melchior complained to Gould, "They dismiss my twenty-five years at the Metropolitan Opera and point to a few movie roles!"

Sometimes the troupe's welcome was of more than royal proportions: in Oakland the company aircraft was escorted by twenty-five navy planes. In San Francisco, the reviewers were skeptical:

> Of course it will be better when Melchior again sings complete Wagnerian roles with the San Francisco Opera Company, or when the symphony again signs him up as guest soloist. In comparison with such engagements his . . . concert . . . was pretty much a barnstorming event. Still the concert offered lively enjoyment. Melchior was surprisingly effective in the lyric "M'apparì."

The program included "Floods of Spring," by Rachmaninoff, Kurt Weill's "Lonely Night," and many songs and arias from his movies. It was roundly condemned by many.

In Washington, D.C., critic Paul Hume, a great admirer of Melchior's skills, delivered a devastatingly frank appraisal of the new concert program, while not omitting the usual epithet, "the Wagnerian tenor more lately noted for his antics in movies and on radio." Hume declared that the final group of songs was demeaning to an artist of Melchior's standing and past achievements, falling far below acceptable standards. He was the first to meet head-on in print Melchior's assertion that this type of program would win friends to serious music: "Be assured, American audiences are not won to Schubert and other great writers by being spoon-fed on Vincent Youmans."

Critic Claudia Cassidy in Chicago was less disturbed by the "usual terrible program." Hearing the fatigue in Melchior's voice at the opening of the concert, she suggested that even a bear hunter might spend a night resting between concerts. Nevertheless, she admitted that the longer he sang, the better he got and that his formidable powers of communication, in whatever repertoire, never failed.

> The man is really larger than lifesize. . . . He has the rare gift of communicating his personal stature and unquestioning conviction to anything he sings. And so, because he sang them, it was possible . . . to hear "Der Doppelgänger" and "Without a Song" on one program and not find them incompatible.

The true evaluation of Melchior's commercial and operatic activities at this time probably lies somewhere between Hume and Cassidy, both of whose positions are understandable. Here was a major artist of the century taking part in the "Hollywood Jackpot" show, and then singing on the highly respectable "Telephone Hour"; doing a commercial for Evinrude Motors, touting duck-shooting from a boat, then singing *Parsifal* at the Met; letting loose with "Open the Door, Richard" on Kay Kaiser's radio show, yet lecturing the Junior Stamp Club on the stamps issued by the Nazis for use in Poland. Not to wonder that people were so divided about what to make of his behavior.

Through no fault of his own, Melchior was again in the news in March 1947. Waiting in the Chicago airport, the pilot of their small plane delayed their takeoff for a Bloomington, Indiana, concert just long enough for hail to start falling. They waited an hour while the hailstorm became a blizzard, and then hired a limousine. "Take us to Bloomington. We must sing," said Lauritz. "Why not," said the driver, promptly skidding into a ditch—twice. Three hours later they were still slipping in and out of snowdrifts with regularity. Finally the exhausted driver spoke, "We're only a few miles out of town. Where do you want to go?" They suggested that they go straight to the university. "Can't. There ain't no university in Bloomington, Illinois."

After absorbing this shock, they acted. Wading through the snowdrifts, they managed to make their way into what could only be called a "joint." A phone call to the right Bloomington in the right state expressed their regrets to the capacity audience and their orchestra who were awaiting them. There being no rooms available, Lauritz was at the counter, staring vacantly into his coffee cup, when the keeper of the "joint" called him to the phone.

"It's my wife. I told her Lauritz Melchior was in my joint and she said that if I didn't lay off the hard stuff she'd come down and close me up. You gotta sing a coupla notes." So Lauritz lived up to the responsibilities of his celebrity by giving a short Wagnerian blast to convince the wife.

Set Svanholm, the new Swedish Heldentenor (also once a baritone), arrived at the Metropolitan in November 1946 while Melchior was on tour. He was to sing with Helen Traubel in *Siegfried*, with a new German conductor in the pit, Fritz Stiedry. The rejoicing was general over the appearance of another tenor who could sing this role. ("Since 1926 the role has become almost the exclusive property of Lauritz Melchior.") The Met would no longer be dependent upon Melchior! ("Lately Lauritz Melchior has found life more amusing and profitable as a movie star.") Svanholm was welcomed as much for his slim figure as for his voice and musicianship ("and besides [Melchior] has become more heavy in poundage and as a result less creditable as the radiant youth who grew up in the forest.") All agreed that Svanholm looked the perfect picture of a hero on stage, although he was under six feet tall and wore built-up sandals. He looked like Siegfried; he acted like Siegfried; he sang like Siegfried.

A slight drawback was the fact that Helen Traubel was built along far more heroic lines than Svanholm. Some were so ungentlemanly as to mention that this became a handicap when Svanholm was on the wrong side of the soprano, because he then disappeared behind the flowing robe designed by Adrian of Hollywood. A great advantage for the Met was that Svanholm was willing to cross between the heavy and the light heroic roles, singing Walther and Florestan as well as Tristan and Otello. With Torsten Ralf still around to sing Walther, Parsifal, Lohengrin, and Siegmund, the opera company was well protected.

Comparisons were inevitable, frequently invidious, and too often accompanied by sarcasm. It must have been infuriating to both Melchior and Svanholm. "The Met has at last found a satisfactory replacement for that Wagnerian veteran and up and coming screen star, Lauritz Melchior," wrote Douglas Watts of the *Daily News*. The *Sun* added, "If a certain celebrated Wagnerian tenor decides in the future to devote himself to films and the radio, it will no longer cause the agitation at the Met it might have a year ago. . . . [Svanholm's voice possesses] no remarkable aural beauty, but it is never even slightly unpleasant. A distinction not owned even by, let us say, Lauritz Melchior."

Irving Kolodin—who was responsible for some of the not-so-nice allusions to Melchior that purported to be reviews of Svanholm—devoted a whole column to answering angry mail from indignant fans of the touring Melchior. The critic said: "It should be a comfort to Lauritz Melchior . . . to know that his interests are being well cared for in his absence." One fan took exception to Kolodin's editorializing, demanding a public apology to Melchior, and others quibbled with Kolodin's assessment of Svanholm's abilities in comparison to Melchior's. In the end Kolodin had the last word. But while his statement provided a catalogue of what the music press hated about Melchior's celebrity, not even a die-hard Melchior fan could argue with it:

> I greatly doubt that the amiable Lauritz would care much for an apology, but if he will apologize to music lovers for being photographed in a hunting costume with a foot on a dead moose, for appearing on "Duffy's Tavern," for singing a vocal version of Liszt's "Liebestraum" in *Two Sisters from Boston*, and referring to himself . . . as "The Big Noise"— then I will apologize to the Melchior fans for having heard these things, and remembering them.

Melchior returned to the Metropolitan on January 22, 1947 as the young Siegfried. It was not the most advantageous of roles in which to be compared against the younger Svanholm, and the critics could not resist, having set the pattern while Melchior was away. Visually, Melchior was the loser, older and more corpulent than the young Siegfried should be, although he did indubitably have good legs (as his daughter said, "Most tenors have terrible legs, but Far's legs were beautiful"). As a musician, his tempo inaccuracies put him in second place, although his magnificent declamation and use of the language's rhythm should have been counted in his favor. As actors, the two tenors ended in a draw, Melchior being complimented for his energetic deportment, which gave the characterization a working realism and for the humor which he brought to the business of the reed pipe that must imitate the forest bird (which actually elicited audible chuckles from the audience). Regarding his vocalism, critics could not gainsay Melchior's considerable resources of power. In this area he might have been the winner but that his undeniable vigor and clarion tone were tagged with that "constantly forced" epithet, always with the implication that the movie activities had done the damage. The situation was as hard on Svanholm as on the veteran. Scarcely ever did a review mention Svanholm without rejoicing verbally over his being able to take Melchior's place ("nor has there been any necessity to shelve any Wagner operas during [Melchior's] absence").

Among the complaining reviews of the late 1940s was one from Los Angeles that involved extenuating circumstances.

> As Tristan, Melchior was hardly recognizable as the same tenor who sang such a memorable Siegmund. . . . He sounded like a tired baritone last night, and love potion or no, it's a wonder Isolde didn't send him packing back to Cornwall. . . . He had great difficulty sustaining long phrases in the love duet. . . . The tenor's portrayal of Tristan's delirium in the last act was a gripping interpretation and certainly his best work of the non-inspired evening.

For this, there was an embarrassing but amusing explanation that could not be made public. Fritz Busch was conducting a Met tour performance of *Tristan* with Traubel as Isolde. In Act II everyone noticed that the renowned clarion voice of Lauritz Melchior was weakening rapidly. The doomsayers surmised that the infamously cruel Heldentenor repertoire had finally caught up with Melchior, who had previously been immune to its hazards. Actually, Kleinchen had given him a laxative, which took effect midway through the act and made him chary of the strenuous breath support required for high notes. Act III opened with Melchior's voice miraculously restored.

When Melchior did sing well the critics tended to ascribe his glorious vocal estate, even his (temporarily) slimmer figure, to the new competition that Svanholm and Ralf provided him. Lauritz admired Ralf's great vocal and dramatic abilities and was friendly with him, but he was put off by the fact that Svanholm did not seem to follow the Wagner traditions. Furthermore, neither his voice nor his interpretations appealed to Melchior.

As for the relationship between Fritz Stiedry and Lauritz Melchior, it was difficult from the start. Without calling to make an appointment, the new German-wing conductor arrived at the door of the Ansonia apartment prepared to go over some tempi for *Siegfried*. Because no one was expecting him, Mutti mistook the short, thin man with glasses, carrying a big briefcase, for a salesman, and shut the door in his face.

Common lore has it that Melchior refused to rehearse this opera at all, and that he demanded that the conductor wait upon him at the Ansonia to set tempos. It is not true that he never rehearsed, and a conductor's appearance at a singer's apartment was, in itself, not unusual at the Met in those days, as Erich Leinsdorf has stated. Melchior thought that he was behaving in an exemplary fashion when he showed up for those rehearsals that involved new singers or new conductors. After all, he remembered his first days at the Met, when neither the leading singers nor the conductors attended rehearsals. (In former times stars often avoided rehearsals to spare their voices. Adelina Patti is said never to have gone to a rehearsal in her entire career.) Nor could it be held that the Ladies Lounge was an ideal rehearsal room. It was just as easy and far more pleasant for everyone to have the piano rehearsals in the Melchior apartment. If his schedule was particularly tight and the rehearsal had to do with the longest of the long operas (and he sang few of another kind), then his friend, Paul Althouse, would cover for him with the permission of the management.

By today's professional standards this behavior appears unbelievably high-handed. Certainly it annoyed the new conductor. When Stiedry demanded stage rehearsals with orchestra and full ensemble, Melchior was there, but he would refuse to sing full voice. What could he prove by doing so? He was adamantly against tiring his voice by rehearsing strenuous operas every week in full voice. Invariably, when asked to give singing advice to young Heldentenors, he told them not to rehearse full voice. "We do not sing for the conductor. We have to sing for the audience. They have paid

Melchior and Kleinchen (center) at Chossewitz with, left to right, sister Bodil, sister Agge, Karl Hacker, and Mutti.

Melchior with his daughter Birte at Chossewitz.

"The dark clouds are approaching and the Danish flag is lowered on our wonderful hunting estate in Chossewitz." August 27, 1939.

Melchior in his favorite disreputable hunting attire.

Melchior as Otello, with Elisabeth Rethberg as Desdemona, in Verdi's *Otello*, San Francisco Opera, 1934.

Melchior after his 100th Tristan, with Edward Johnson at the
Metropolitan Opera, 1936.

Melchior in his Met dressing room after his last opera performance on February 2,
1950, at the Metropolitan Opera.

"The Aladdin of song, assisted by forty black and forty white American slaves, presents to his former sultan [Frederik IX] an immense sum rounded up to 205 dollars by himself." (Cartoon by Hans Sørensen, *Svikmøllen*, 1948. Reproduced by permission of Lademanns Verlag.)

"Allez-Oop," with Lily Pons and Melchior at the "Save the Met" Surprise Party, 1934.

Melchior (she) and Lily Pons (he) as Apache dancers in "Oper-Tunities" at the Metropolitan Opera House, 1935.

Melchior with radio comedian Fred Allen.

Melchior with the stars of MGM's 1944 film, *Thrill of a Romance*, Van Johnson and Esther Williams.

Melchior with Frank Sinatra.

Melchior, comedian Danny Kaye, and singer Judy Garland
appear together on radio.

Melchior and Jimmy Durante, harmonizing on radio.

Melchior with movie star Jeanette MacDonald at his 25th wedding anniversary party, held at The Viking in 1950.

Melchior and comedian Ben Blue with Judy Garland on the last night of her legendary 1952 Palace Theater engagement, which the tenor's own show would follow.

Melchior in his favorite casual attire, Bavarian Lederhosen, rehearsing for a 1941 show at the Bohemian Grove in California. "Weaving spiders, come not here."

The Lauritz Melchior Show company sings "I'm going to Maxim's" in a Québec City, Canada, nightclub. (The author is shown at Melchior's left.)

Melchior with his co-star the elephant in the musical *Arabian Nights*, Jones Beach, 1955.

At the age of 70 Lauritz Melchior receives the applause of the studio audience at Radio House in Copenhagen before his last performance as Siegmund in Act I of *Die Walküre*, 1960. (Photo by Poul Petersen, Nordisk Pressefoto.)

Melchior with President Dwight D. Eisenhower, 1963. "Lauritz, nobody can sing our national anthem like you."

Melchior and his third wife, Mary Markham, 1964.

Melchior showing a picture taken with Pope Paul VI
at the Vatican, Rome, 1965.

The continuing Heldentenor crisis.
(Drawing by Ed Arno; © 1984 The New Yorker Magazine, Inc.)

"Is there anyone in the house who can sing Siegfried?"

Copenhagen's cathedral, Vor Frue Kirke, 1973 scene of the Lauritz Melchior memorial service according to the Masonic rite. Resting on the velvet cushion in front of a box containing Melchior's ashes are his decorations.

for it, and expect to hear a voice that is rested and ready to go," he wrote to one such young singer. Clearly, a Heldentenor ought to husband his resources prudently. It is even possible that Melchior's great stamina can be traced to his not wasting his resources on rehearsals: In 1979 an international team of otolaryngologists concluded on the basis of their research that operatic singing is by definition "forcing," because the type of vocal cord vibration used for this emission is so strenuous. When the audience of voice teachers queried the medical men as to what this meant to an opera singer, they answered, "Don't rehearse full voice any more than absolutely necessary."

Still, Melchior was often seen as a tempermental opera star throwing his weight around. Now and then a writer who understood vocal matters would define Melchior's greatness simply and without recourse to sarcasm.

> What Babe Ruth is to baseball, Lauritz Melchior is for opera and for the entire world of music. . . . It is one of the wonders of our time how the great Wagner singer at an age of fifty-seven has preserved the entire volume and flexibility of voice which he had as a young man. It was so much more remarkable last night, considering that Mr. Melchior has sung every night since March 15, and that he sang twice yesterday.

Rapport did not develop between Melchior and Stiedry during subsequent rehearsals. Lauritz's opinion of Stiedry's tempos as sleep-inducing would be suspect were it not for the fact that others also defined Stiedry's tempos as slow or even slower. Yet singer and conductor came to a compromise: Lauritz would follow Stiedry's (slow) tempos in certain passages if he could take other sections—as, for example, the fight with the dragon— faster. During the performance Lauritz thought that Stiedry did not live up to the agreement, excessively dragging the dragon-fight section. Therefore, he sang steadily ahead, making a real enemy of Maestro Stiedry. (However, even Rudolf Bing, his friend, admitted that Stiedry "was always taking offense at something or other.")

Those misbegotten, ancient *Ring* sets and props, always referred to as "man-eating" by Melchior, contrived to do him in again during the second Stiedry performance. It happened at the end of the first act of *Walküre* (whose sets were actually the most recently redone) right after he wrenched the magic sword from the tree trunk. He leaped from the table that the Met Siegmunds had to mount to reach the sword and caught his foot in the ragged cover, falling headlong, but he never dropped the note he was singing and even completed the few remaining measures. Kleinchen rushed backstage, passing Svanholm, who had also hurried there, ready to take over if necessary. During the intermission, which was extended eighteen minutes, the house physician put a splint on Melchior's big toe. He went on for the second act, singing as usual, but limping a bit. Later he admitted that, for the first time ever, he had forgotten to inspect the table personally, something singers learn to do, usually "the hard way," by having suffered a disaster on stage. His penance was a broken toe, and he hoped that his donation of $5,000 to the

Ring Fund would provide a new tablecloth. To the press flocking about to photograph the tenor gazing quizzically at the bandaged toe through a monocle, Lauritz declared dryly, "I really would prefer to die a natural death," a comment he liked well enough to repeat on radio several times.

Upon returning from Europe for the filming of his fourth movie, *Luxury Liner*, Lauritz read in a nationwide release that the Metropolitan had sustained a major deficit ($220,000) for the 1947–1948 season, despite increased attendance. In an August 5 letter the management "regretted to advise" that the 1948–1949 season plans were canceled due to lack of a basic contract agreement with the unions, for management could not meet union demands without irresponsibly increasing the existing deficit. The closing of the Metropolitan stunned disbelieving opera lovers and artists alike. Melchior issued an optimistic statement from Hollywood: He hoped that the cancellation would open the eyes of the American people to the need for government support; he promised to form his own company to do *Tristan* and *Lohengrin* on Broadway.

Actually, the previous three seasons had been conducted without a loss, but there had been only "token scenic construction," no new works, and very little attention to the substantial labor problems. As Kolodin later commented, an opera house could not go on like this. It would be like a library that never has a deficit, but never buys a new book. The 1948 deficit was caused primarily by the inefficient botch made of the new *Ring* production, wherein the sets were not only unsuitable and ugly, but, worse, could not be collapsed and taken on tour.

Headlines erupted all over the United States when Billy Rose, showman turned columnist, responded to the Metropolitan Opera cancellation by offering, in a public letter to George Sloan, to take over the management of the opera house for one year and personally guarantee the deficit. Showing his opinion of the productions at the Met, he didn't mince words. Because he believed that "a bit of streamlining would find favor with lovers of good music," he would "introduce modern lighting, staging, choreography, and certain other elements of present-day stagecraft." Those who had been following the annual turmoil over the presentation of a new season found his offer not so brash as it seemed. Billy Rose had proven himself as an impresario of colossal entertainment projects. No one expected the Met to accept his offer, but it spawned many raucous jokes: Might not the Rhine music become an accompaniment for Eleanor Holm's swimming act? Might this new streamlining not render Melchior's nightly struggle into his corset unnecessary?

All in all, the Met's problems did not inspire too much sympathy, especially among legitimate theater folk. Lauritz, for example, had heard the same noises from the management each and every summer since 1930. Johnson and his coterie were accused of crying wolf every year. "The only ones who cannot run [the Met] are those presently in power." *Variety* suggested that the art-minded financiers were tired of taking the rap and were voicing a familiar threat to pick up their marbles and go home, hoping for the opportunity to sell the well-located opera house and put up an income-producing office building. The Met's explanation that all that money representing the deficit went for wages and unions was roundly attacked. "A cleaning woman in my three-room apartment costs the same as a cleaning woman at the Met." "Broadway pays much more to its performers than the Met does." All the theatrical writers agreed that the ludicrous procedure of having to transport the sets in and out of the back door to make scene changes contributed greatly to the red ink.

After two weeks of front-page publicity, a letter arrived at The Viking from the Metropolitan, saying that there would be a season after all, but a shortened one. Lauritz sang only four performances in New York, due to the lateness of the contract settlement. Svanholm and Lorenz, with some assistance from Charles Kullmann as Parsifal, carried the rest of the season. Once again Melchior's being in especially fine fettle this month led some to conjecture that he was spurred on by the presence of other heroic tenors. Others simply noted: "Vocally Melchior was in good trim and about as we were hearing him many decades ago." "Melchior singing with greater ease and expression than he has exhibited in the past couple of seasons." "Melchior's Tristan from another artist would be a cause for headlines. From him it is a cause for gratitude that he endures and prospers." Once again, at the age of fifty-eight, Melchior's fine vocal technique and physical stamina had reasserted his claim to the title of "the world's greatest Heldentenor."

The Melchiors enjoyed fashioning the public's perception of themselves as celebrities, but they were not so expert as they appeared. To profit from publicity is to live by publicity. Vigilance must be constant, for the limelight shines indiscriminately. If not guided properly, publicity can boomerang.

Not the least of their failures in public relations was the image they projected in Denmark. As we have seen, when Melchior was not supervised carefully, he made blunders. In Denmark, however, a contributor to the frequent publicity debacles was the common Danish attitude toward those touched by fame. Danes generally follow something called "Jante's Law," named after the philosophy expressed by Aksel Sandemose: "You had better not believe that you are something special" and "Don't stick your head up above the crowds!"

Most Danes acknowledge that this national mind-set causes them to deny affection to their compatriots, however deservedly they achieve fame and however modestly they comport themselves. The Danish attitude toward Melchior was first illustrated in April 1939, at the time when he was attempting to arrange for Prince Frederik to conduct at the Metropolitan during the World's Fair. It manifested itself in an unflattering Danish newspaper cartoon of Lauritz in full evening dress adorned with all his medals, giving a news conference. The cartoon was accompanied by a poem of six increasingly satirical stanzas: at his *Lohengrin* performance Melchior would probably delegate the Court Chamberlain to sell tickets, an aide-de-camp to usher, and a lady-in-waiting to sell ice cream. With unmistakable irony, Lauritz was referred to as "Our world-famous Heldentenor," and was severely admonished: "Even Heldentenors can open their mouths too wide." The Danish press, for some reason, delighted in the fact that Melchior could not follow through on his plans to have Crown Prince Frederik conduct at the Met.

Melchior struck the Danes as offensively immodest and full of his own importance. He was not always diplomatic and at times was even overbearing. In his open, innocent way he would say, "I am not a complicated human being; I never put myself on a pedestal. Sometimes artists cannot take fame; they think that they are better than other human beings." This was an utterly sincere statement of what Lauritz felt, but the Danes, misinterpreting it as egotism, were even more offended. Yet Lauritz drew no lines from a social point of view. He beamed upon Danes, Danish-Americans, in fact all Scandinavians. One of the old Melchioriander, who did understand the real facts, felt it necessary to explain his comrade on a Danish radio show:

> Lauritz Melchior is judged wrong here in Denmark. . . . We have seen . . . examples where he comes over here and is misunderstood by the Danes because he is childish and behaves in the same way here as he does in America. . . . But that is something outward; inside, where you find the comradeship, charity, helpfulness, he is quite wonderful. I have letters from . . . former Royal Guard friends in America, many of whom do not hold prominent positions. All of them write, "You have no idea how much help we receive from Lauritz." . . . The very foundation that he builds all this work on is constantly his deep love of Denmark. . . . I think that Denmark cannot have a better ambassador than a man like him.

Often Melchior was done in by his love for speech-making. When Kleinchen was about, she controlled those events, but it was not easy. Holger Boland remembers a celebration set up for the Melchiors by operatic colleagues after a guest appearance at the Royal Opera.

> Cordial and naive, he stood up and said, deeply touched, "Dear singer friends, it is a special joy for me to be together with you. Now that I am standing here among you, I feel as if I am not at all superior to you." Kleinchen stepped on his toes, but it did not occur to him why. His childishly puzzled expression, however, quickly cleared up, and he continued his eloquent self-description.

Lauritz was hurt when he did not have the affection of his countrymen, when, as at his nephew Jørgen's wedding, the Danes were not nice to him ("envious of his success in the outside world," says Jørgen's wife Inga). Journalists in particular were unkind. One accurately but venomously described Melchior as living on his estate on Mulholland Drive "surrounded by German hunting dogs, African big-game trophies, Chinese elms, Swiss-French chefs, and cold running smorgasbord."

The next evidence of the Danish attitude toward Melchior came in 1948, which was a jubilee year—thirty-five years since his debut with the Royal Opera and twenty-five years since his Berlin debut with Leider and Blech. Having been made an American citizen in June 1947, the tenor was permitted to sing for the American occupation forces in various German cities. He also had a concert tour booked in England. First, however, he returned to Denmark for an anniversary concert. While there, Melchior advised King Frederik's equerry that he wished to present a contribution from the American chapters of the Royal Danish Guard Association Outside Denmark, intended as a donation for King Christian's sarcophagus. The audience was granted, and Melchior duly presented in person a purse of $208, which represented two dollars from each member, in obedience to the nationwide canvassing rules that no individual contribute more than 5 kroner.

Somehow the newspapers learned of the miniscule amount that this wealthy Danish-American had contributed. That it was done on behalf of the not-so-affluent Guards in America, and that a huge donation by Melchior himself would have put to shame that of his fellow Guards and violated the donation rules, were ignored. Melchior became a laughing stock across the country. Insulting and sarcastic songs were sung in the vaudeville shows. Malevolent articles were written in the unrelenting press. Cruel cartoons were printed depicting a gargantuan Lauritz kneeling before King Frederik and presenting an infinitesimal purse, while guards carried monstrously big treasure chests to the throne, or a grossly fat Lauritz dressed as Aladdin, kneeling before "his former Sultan" (Frederik IX) to present an "immense sum rounded out to $208" by Aladdin himself. Kleinchen fretted about all the bad publicity and the ignominy, regretting that Lauritz himself had presented the money. Lauritz, disheartened by the harsh attacks, was scarcely cheered by the actions of the king, who invited him to lunch and sent a kind letter of thanks to the former Guards. Stubbornly, Lauritz repeated to everyone who would listen that the men of the American Guard chapters wanted their gift presented personally and properly out of love and respect for the old king.

This was not the end. Melchior had been asked to wear a green Eisenhower jacket for his tour. Trying to look more military, he put a few of his decorations on the jacket. In the flurry of arrival a journalist asked about the decorations. Melchior, attempting to be as jocular in his remarks as his traveling companion, Victor Borge, changed the regular American phrase for decorations ("fruit salad") into a Danish expression for a chest full of medals, *Sildesalat* (he thus referred to his decorations as "my herring salad"). Lauritz could never manage a joke as well as Borge. Although the journalist laughed at the time, he later reported with big headlines about "the New American" who had insulted the Danish king and Denmark.

Andreas Damgaard, a staunch Danish fan, was a bystander at the Copenhagen airport. He overheard a visitor speak to one of the reporters who were covering Melchior's arrival: "Did you get any news?" "Yes, all too much," was the smiling, but pointed rejoinder. Damgaard also attended Melchior's concert, for which, although the hall was not sold out, the applause was long and enthusiastic. From one of the reviews we can see that the Danish press were as revolted by the type of program as the American critics had been, although they blamed "American taste" for the whole thing.

> A concert according to general standards it was not. If Melchior called it that, he would have had to take a beating for an outrageous choice of program. As it was, it became a show evening according to American taste. Good it is not, and one might have expected that Melchior gear his program more to European culture, but he did show us how they have fun musically, the masses of America, with arrangements, transcriptions, etc., in brief, all that we threw out here, and which, in the course of the next hundred years, they will also outgrow in America.

While not relishing the community sing of "Vive la compagnie" or the inclusion of Stravinsky's "Firebird" song transcription, the reviewers had appreciated the "personal silver trumpet ring" of the Melchior voice when he sang opera, "the domain . . . for which he will be remembered." One can see ample evidence of sarcasm in the opening description of Melchior's periodic trips to Denmark:

> He looks forward as a kind uncle, rich of fame, to return and let a little of his glory shine on his old country. It was shining last night . . . at the K.B. Hall, which was three-quarters filled at his concert. . . . On the whole people liked Lauritz Melchior—especially he himself. But that is the way he is.

Some days after the concert Damgaard asked respectfully and affectionately, "Do we hear you again soon, Kammersanger?"

"I don't know," said Melchior, who must have read the reviews. "It seems that you do not like me anymore."

The admirer was moved to comfort his idol. "That is those small newspapermen, Kammersanger. The public likes you."

"Yes, that is right. The public still likes me."

But, says Damgaard today, it was quite clear that the treatment of the newspapers had hurt him.

It is not difficult to understand how Danes would be put off by Melchior's heavy-handed (therefore seemingly patronizing) humor, especially when a journalist pointed it up, as in the following portion of a Danish interview of the same visit in which Melchior told how he would soon be going on a January safari. The reporter asked how the singer could take a vacation in the middle of the season. This was the printed version of Melchior's unwise answer: "Circumstances force me to. I must be careful not to make too much money. As it is now, I already pay eighty-four percent in taxes. If my income is increased further, I shall have to pay more, and then Kleinchen and I will have nothing to live on whatsoever." The reporter chose to headline his article in this way: "LAURITZ MELCHIOR CANNOT ALLOW HIMSELF TO MAKE TOO MUCH MONEY."

Each of these events devastated Melchior at the time, and, in fact, never ceased to be a source of deep sorrow. This was the dark side of his position as a "household word." As for the Danes, to this day most of them, sadly, remember only the parts of these incidents that reflect badly upon Melchior.

As an advance sixtieth birthday present, Kleinchen gave Lauritz a big cardboard box. Hidden within the crumpled tissue paper were plane tickets and reservations for a safari in Kenya and Tanganyika. Since childhood Lauritz had dreamt of going to camp in the African wilderness and seeing the African animals firsthand. The best part of the best birthday present of his life was the time off, six whole weeks in the spring of 1949. (Kleinchen did, however, talk him into doing a concert tour while there.)

Upon his safe return from Mount Kilimanjaro, Lauritz, down to 220 pounds, was a smash at his first concert in Johannesburg. Nothing dimmed the enthusiasm and gaiety of the full-house audience, who were not even affronted by the informality: When Lauritz did his usual conducting of a community sing at the end, they called it "coming down from Olympus."

While Lauritz was enjoying his first visit to Africa, a storm blew up around his head, fueled by the press's inclination for blaming his lack of seriousness whenever anything went wrong. Irving Kolodin raised questions in print: *Must* Melchior do a safari in Kenya during the last months of the season? Perhaps he just doesn't *want* to do *Parsifal* anymore. It has always been an ordeal for him to stand still without changing position for so long in that opera. This last remark was a reference to the controversy surrounding Melchior's habit of slipping surreptitiously offstage in the *Parsifal* "Grail Scene." Not only did he do so in apparent defiance of Wagner's express instructions that he professed to venerate, but he was ever so annoyed when the critics mentioned it disparagingly. Back in 1942 Melchior had written an open letter that he sent to all the major critics, explaining why he did leave the stage. It began, "Each year at this time with the regularity of the seasons, three major events take place in my life: my income tax returns, *Parsifal* at the Met, and the subsequent observations of the music critics concerning my departure from the stage during the first temple scene of the opera." He claimed that a frigid Arctic draft ("like a wind from hell") came in from the back when the scenery was changed (changes of sets often required the 40th Street doors to be open in the old house), and the cold put his health in jeopardy. Bodanzky himself had originally given permission for Melchior to leave fearing that the house would have to go dark if he were taken ill.

Lauritz's letter, of course, was no answer at all, or a lame one at best. It does not explain why the other tenors *did* remain on stage, nor why Johnson did not sanction a non-singing stand-in. In response to Melchior's open letter, one editor added this frivolous note: "Mr. Melchior does small justice to Met critics. Some of them sit in draughts through whole operas."

In any case, Melchior was innocent of Kolodin's other charges. Four days after his first piece, Kolodin reminded Melchior's manager that the tenor had never until this season failed to sing at least one *Parsifal*. Davidson countered flatly that even as they spoke there was nothing to keep Melchior from singing the role on Good Friday. He would be back in the country in time, and had no conflicting engagements. Davidson continued,

> We're getting a little tired of this talk of Melchior's availability. . . . The fact of the matter is he was not asked. . . . The post-safari dates were booked after the Met failed to show any interest in Melchior's plans for the time involved. . . . I do know that Melchior is disappointed not to be doing *Parsifal*.

Said Davidson, not only would Lauritz rather sing at the Met than do anything else, but he had, in the interests of the opera company, willingly sacrificed a whole month of concert bookings in order to conform to the Met's late start in the fall. Subsequently, the Met announced that Charles Kullmann would be singing the first *Parsifal* and the last two performances would be done by Set Svanholm (who would be brought all the way back from Europe for this purpose). The Met, having no lack of Heldentenors, felt free to dispense with Melchior's services except on a sporadic basis, although they did not see fit to make their policy public, thus giving the appearance that Melchior was opting for Hollywood and African safaris over the Met.

One must question why Melchior was made the culprit for legitimate money-saving strategies on the part of the management. Citing statistics for the 1946–1947 season, journalist Ross Parmenter showed clearly that Lauritz's movie making took the blame for a situation actually caused by a Metropolitan Opera policy. Even as far back as 1932, old, expensive, or independent stars were replaced with younger singers. By 1946, Melchior's performances at the Met were indeed fewer than in previous seasons, but he was not the only first-rank artist of whom this could be said. Every singer whose fee was exceedingly high suffered the same fate: his or her Met appearances were immediately reduced. The bulk of the season was being carried by little-known regulars and comprimarios, as always. Big-name singers *all* appeared less frequently. Thelma Votipka, George Cehanovsky, and Maxine Stellman sang thirty-odd performances each; Varnay, Peerce, and Ralf sang twelve. Svanholm sang ten and Melchior nine. Björling and Tagliavini sang only six performances; Milanov and Sayão, eight; Pons and

Albanese, seven; Melton, four. With these figures one can see that Melchior's attendance was neither better nor worse than others of this rank.

In the fall of 1945 there had been another furor of the same kind. Edward Johnson had made an unsuccessful attempt to slip an announcement ("no *Ring* this year") past Met audiences and press corps during his October 11 press conference. When both groups protested vehemently the projected absence of a *Ring* cycle with Melchior, Johnson countered: "The special *Ring* series has been dropped because Lauritz Melchior is our only proven Siegfried. So in the event that Mr. Melchior was unable to appear, the opera could not be given." He cited the unfortunate night of February 23, 1943, when the house had to go dark because, Melchior being ill, there had been no one to replace him. The company had no cover.

Judging by the amount of space devoted to this situation in his diary, Melchior himself was highly exercised over the injustice of being blamed for the *Ring* cancellation. The usual pattern of Melchior's contract negotiations gave Johnson alone the final decision about each conflict between the Met and other engagements. The tenor felt that Johnson, not wanting to disclose publicly the real reason for this—the dreadful dilapidation of those Wagnerian sets dating from 1913—had seized upon Melchior's indispensability as an excuse. Melchior's manager James Davidson, in a letter to Johnson, also took umbrage. From Johnson's remarks numberless fans had gathered that "the *Ring* cycle would be omitted for the first time in many years solely because Mr. Melchior had limited his Metropolitan engagements in favor of Hollywood picture commitments, thus failing in his artistic duty to the public." There must be some gross misunderstanding, added Davidson sternly, because

> at no time has Lauritz Melchior indicated that he would be unwilling to participate in the *Ring* cycle. On the contrary, Lauritz Melchior has repeatedly insisted that he would want nothing to interfere with his participation in the *Ring* until such time as you get a replacement for those roles. Lauritz Melchior is still available for the *Ring* performances during the usual period. In a future news release please clarify the fact that it was not Lauritz Melchior's unavailability that caused the Met to abandon the *Ring*.

In response, Johnson had simply stuck to his story, never stating publicly whether or not the Met had confidence in Melchior's loyalty to the company.

Other signs of the Met's increasing independence were probably evident to the press, who were not only knowledgeable about administration maneuvers but adept at picking up on implications. For example, Melchior's option for tour performances was not taken up in 1947. At the time, Lauritz sent an affectionate telegram to Edward Johnson:

WITH TEARS IN MY EYES I RECORD YOUR NOTICE REGARDING THE MET OPERA TOUR. IT LEAVES ME NOW

NOT ONLY WITH A BROKEN TOE, BUT ALSO WITH A BRO-
KEN HEART. SIGNED: LAURITZ MELCHIOR, A FORMER
PARTICIPATING ARTIST OF THE METROPOLITAN OPERA
TOUR.

And, indeed, he never again sang on the company tour.

Lauritz probably had no reason to feel events ominously closing in on him
in the spring of 1949, but the *Parsifal* contretemps and resultant publicity
should have warned him. In addition, the presence of bad reviews in increasing numbers during the past season is incontrovertible. These were not
petulant questions about why Melchior wasn't as thin as Svanholm or why
he spent so much time in Hollywood. They were addressing the fact of his
diminishing powers. Said Bagar in one such critique, "*Die Walküre* transports
nobody to the skies. Mr. Melchior coasted through his assignment, giving
his all only when he couldn't help it." (Bohm also noted the effects of age
when he wrote of a recording of two German lieder: "The Danish tenor's
voice sounds worn in both.") Whether or not the many poor reviews were
inspired by less good singing and acting, or colored by a prevailing attitude
of censure, it is clear that the artistic level of Melchior's performances had
begun to fluctuate widely.

From our vantage point we can see that Melchior had been poised at
the top of his fame and well-warranted artistic prestige for some time. There
are precious few years in a singer's career when he is not either on the way
up, or in the process of descent. The time when artistic mastery and physical
and vocal health combine felicitously with that most necessary ingredient—
luck—is short indeed. In 1948 the Metropolitan Opera was evidently beginning to phase Melchior out. Having found an acceptable replacement for him
in the heavy heroic roles, they no longer needed to fear dependence upon
him. Melchior was fiercely loved by some opera fans and just as ferociously
despised by others for his "selling out." The press was, for the most part,
critical. Nevertheless, this very controversy about his operatic and outside
activities had served their journalistic purposes well—quite simply, Melchior
filled a lot of space. But the publicity techniques that Kleinchen and Lauritz
had been at such pains to learn were about to backfire.

CHAPTER 15

A Dream Unrealized

(1949–1950)

Rudolf Bing, a pivotal character in the drama about to unfold, arrived in New York in the fall of 1949. In an uncharacteristically venturesome action, the Metropolitan board had boldly chosen to succeed Edward Johnson a man who was not just another singer, or conductor, or business manager (others being considered were Melchior himself, Lázló Halasz, Lawrence Tibbett, Richard Bonelli, and Frank St. Leger), but the artistic director of the Edinburgh Festival and general manager of the Glyndebourne Opera Company. Bing was not a complete stranger to the Met administration. Since 1935 his company had enjoyed the use of the Metropolitan's mailing list. In fact, the Met itself mailed out Glyndebourne prospectuses to their patrons, generously charging the British company only for the postage.

A combination of artistic background and broad theatrical experience together with excellent managerial and executive skills qualified Bing to tackle the Metropolitan's problems. Rudolf Bing was at this time forty-seven years old. He had once studied to be a singer, but giving it up, he took a position with a publishing house and concert agency in his native Vienna. In no time he was made director of the agency, where he widened its musical activities to include an opera department. From there he moved to a staff position at Darmstadt, and then in 1930 he joined the administration of the Städtische Oper of Charlottenburg in Berlin. With Hitler's rise to power, Bing was suddenly ordered to depart, by the S.A. itself. His first refuge was Vienna, the second, England. In 1934 he accepted John Christie's invitation (prompted by Fritz Busch's recommendation) to become part of the Glyndebourne Opera, where he soon rose to the position of general manager.

Watching Carl Ebert, "an extremely progressive director," in both Darmstadt and Glyndebourne, he said, "was to learn something about the theatrical possibilities of opera that many directors . . . (not to mention critics) have never even begun to understand." From that time on Bing committed himself to "dramatically valid operatic presentation." When he arrived in

New York, he had already determined that "stage direction was the key to the ways [his] management was to differ from previous managements of the Met," since, in his opinion, "staging of the first order [was something] the Met had never known."

In consequence of his European experience, Bing's reputation was that of a producer of a new kind of opera—one that depended for its effect on a skillful blend of teamwork, staging, and musical intelligence rather than sheer vocal power. At Glyndebourne, Bing had built a celebrated company, using the best singers, the best conductors and directors, and excellent stage management. He had also made a successful effort to cut out much of the snob appeal frequently associated with opera. Yet he was pragmatic and realistic— always in command of the organization's financial matters, proud of his achievement when he lowered the deficit and "even showed a profit at times."

Bing's first position as general manager had taught him many lessons, all of which were to be manifest in his leadership of the Met, one especially prophetic: In Darmstadt he came to the understanding of "why [he] had been so strongly drawn to a life in the theater. . . . Here was a microcosm complete in itself. Controlling such a world gave me the feeling of real power, without the evil that political power so often entails." His dealings and procedures in Glyndebourne were therefore based upon the practical wisdom he had acquired in Darmstadt: "An opera house must have one head. . . . A general manager must never give away any of his ultimate authority to a musical director." Bing learned, too, the convenience resulting from his singers "not running off to do guest appearances in . . . London or New York. . . . One had to worry about overworking them, but not about whether they would be [there] when they were needed." He had formed a policy for dealing with singers (which he seemed to change when he felt like it): "I think it is improper for a manager to appear to be on terms of personal friendship with any of the artists who work for him, since he cannot be personally friendly with all." Further, a profound dislike for "star" singers appears to have stemmed from a comparison he drew between the "star system" in operation during the 1930s and that which he encountered at the Metropolitan. In Charlottenburg singers "still had moral and artistic integrity. Their prime concern was the mastery of their craft, the preservation of their vocal ability, and— believe it or not—their duty to their public and to their theater."

Upon arrival in October, Bing, besieged by reporters, cultivated his official image as a mere observer and retained his reputation as a keen strategist with the press. To their questions about his opinion of the Metropolitan Opera, he responded that the Met was in good shape as regards vocal talent, but declined to be drawn out about the notoriously outdated scenery and costumes. "It would be rather tactless of me to be so critical now." He did not remain uncritical for long. (It is said that Johnson suffered much over Bing's relentless analyses of the Met's deficiencies.) The truth, which he wrote later, was that the Met was "much worse" than he had expected "in every way—physical conditions, artistic integrity, sense of professionalism, support from the board." He found them "all well below anything" he had encountered before."

Spurred by Bing's tactful silence, the rumor-mill went into operation: Plans for his new job—which he called "the biggest job of its kind in the world"—might involve a complete overhaul of the ancient building at 39th Street or construction of a new one. The plans might formulate a separation of the business and artistic management. More importantly, they might address the persistent question of rehearsal time, a matter that had driven at least two despairing conductors from the Met. Surely the Melchiors were hearing all this. Were they taking it in?

Edward Johnson's fifteen years, says Kolodin, could well have been titled "The Americanization of the Metropolitan." The forced pace of this process left in its wake many performances of less than professional quality. Too many singers were given one chance to show their mettle, but such an opportunity carried with it no rehearsal and no help except that of their colleagues. Music historian Martin Mayer has described the regime as "catch as catch can" and the assignment of roles as "resolute miscasting." Certainly it was a system that granted survival only to the fittest Americans. Those who "came through" artistically remained. The others were discarded.

Johnson, as a former singer, was sure that he understood the psychology of his artists. Allow them plenty of room, give them plenty of security, be a father to them—then they will do their best. Established artists like Melchior were permitted a great deal of freedom, and for pragmatic reasons. Unlike the younger, unproven singers, artists routined in their roles could be counted on to deliver without expensive rehearsals. The privilege that many established artists enjoyed—that of not attending routine rehearsals—was probably seen as an advantage by management, for it allowed the untried, younger singers their most prized boon, rehearsal time. As we have seen, Johnson had allowed Melchior many personal privileges, because of his great value to the company. In return the tenor rarely, if ever, canceled, sang an exigent repertoire gloriously, and in all other matters was totally reasonable and cooperative.

Rudolf Bing's style, on the other hand, was more that of an absolute monarch (it was certainly not that of a father). Living up to his personal code, he did not socialize with the singers and did not want to know them in any personal way. Bing's personal interpretation of the word "professionalism" was not yet a part of the Met work ethic. Observing Johnson's policies in place, he saw the result as "a competition among artists to see who can get away with the most," such competition being typical of "an ill-run house."

It is a fair guess that Rudolf Bing had arrived in America already planning to engage Kirsten Flagstad for his first season at the Met, if it were at all feasible. Although this could be logically painted as a self-serving move, since it would be a potent publicity lure for his first year at the Met, there is no doubt that it would also be viewed as simple and proper justice to an artist of Flagstad's calibre. Bing's credo offers a substantiation: "There is no financial decision that does not have bearing on artistic standards—and every decision involves human elements."

During November and December, in addition to his duties as an "observer" of his new bailiwick, he instituted a broad investigation of the Flagstad controversy: Had she or had she not been a Nazi sympathizer? He put together a file of evidence, compiled from her Paris agency, Oslo officials, the U.S. State Department, international Jewish organizations, her American management, the Norwegian Musicians Association, and the Norwegian Opera Association, all of which convinced him of the soprano's complete innocence. A four-page, exhaustive statement from Marks Levine, Flagstad's personal management representative, was a valuable addition to the ammunition that Bing and his assistants were storing up to offset the expected anti-Flagstad activities. Apparently he wished to be clear in his own mind about the charges and suspicions before moving to engage her.

Kirsten Flagstad had returned to the United States two years before. The very night that Lauritz's beloved King Christian died, April 20, 1947, Flagstad faced pickets outside and a capacity crowd inside Carnegie Hall at her first New York appearance in six years. The unmitigated success of this evening could not wipe out the horror of her experiences. Only a few days after the European war ended, Henry Johansen had been arrested as the couple walked in their garden at Kirstianssand. Without even being allowed to fetch his coat, Johansen was taken into custody and to prison. His wife never saw him again. He was charged with profiteering during the occupation and being a member of Vidkun Quisling's party.

Even before Flagstad's 1947 Carnegie Hall concert, Edward Johnson had maintained a very low profile: Until the question of Flagstad's reentry into the United States was solved, Johnson had "failed to see why the Met should even consider engaging her." Others had stood by her and spoken out for her, including Althouse, Martinelli, Farrar, and Damrosch. Kleinchen and Lauritz, however, had not even attempted to contact Kirsten while they were in Copenhagen in 1945.

Before leaving for Europe that September of 1945, Melchior had been asked his thoughts about Kirsten Flagstad. He did not seize the opportunity to uphold openly the integrity of his former colleague. Instead, his answer was a masterpiece of fence-sitting (it was this equivocation that so angered the friends and supporters of Flagstad—and still does): "I don't believe for a moment that *she* had any political thoughts. When she left America to go back to Norway, she didn't expect to stay there." Why then did she stay? he was asked.

It is, you might say, the European outlook on marriage. A woman belongs with her husband and in her home. If Kirsten Flagstad has done nothing else but be a faithful wife, I don't think she should be made to suffer. . . . But if she too has collaborated, that is an offense. If it has been done, it has to be punished.

At that, Melchior was not wrong in his assessment of Flagstad's view of marriage. In 1938 she had expressed it herself:

In order for a marriage to be happy, the husband must be the master. He must be the ruler. However—and this is important—he must be qualified to rule. If my husband says to me tomorrow, "You must stop singing in public," then I shall no longer sing in public. . . . Above all it is my duty to be something for my husband. That he is happy and content is to me more important than the ovations of my audiences. . . . Then you may say, "Your heart is not in your work." And my answer will be: Part of my heart is in my work . . . but my entire heart will be in this . . . to be happily married.

With the Norwegian singer's return to American in 1947 (and even before) the polemics were incredible, permeating all American society. In fact, the media space devoted to Kirsten Flagstad during the four years it took for her to return to her former status was almost as extensive as it had been during her first sojourn at the Metropolitan Opera. Sides were chosen: Erich Leinsdorf's words reflected a "we can get along perfectly well without her" attitude; Mrs. Belmont would have welcomed her; Walter Winchell called her a traitor. Elsa Maxwell, the society columnist, had mixed in from the beginning—with her usual stylish exaggerations, prevarications, and mis-representations: Flagstad had sung only in light operettas until Maxwell's friend Lauritz Melchior discovered and introduced her to the Met audience as Sieglinde, whereupon she won fortune and fame. (Out-and-out lies appear to have been Maxwell's stock in trade. In 1944 she had affixed herself to Lauritz's bandwagon of publicity by claiming that it was she who discovered him, she who had given him his "first chance" at that 1931 Paris soirée in the Bois de Boulogne, and she who had told Victor Beigel that Lauritz should be a tenor, not a baritone.) In 1945 she attacked Flagstad by writing of her horror that the soprano "like many others who backed the losing side is trying to get back to this country and to the Met where she gained her first niche in fame." The musical community was to hear more of this type of vitriol before Flagstad returned to the United States.

Not all attacks against Flagstad were public. At the many wartime Scandinavian benefit affairs, Melchior had been approached more than once by Norwegian Ambassador Morgenstierne, who pressed him to condemn Kirsten Flagstad publicly for her family's Nazi ties. (Even at the end of the war, Morgenstierne urged "strongly that if possible [Flagstad] be hindered from traveling to the U.S.A." Because of her many American admirers and "in her present state of mind . . . she will easily be able to confuse people's

concepts with regard to the difference between Norwegians and Quislings."
Morgenstierne's vanity was "virtually a disease." Flagstad had once refused
to allow him backstage during the intermission of a concert, and he never
forgave her the slight. This was the cause of his vindictiveness.

Lauritz refused to do as the ambassador asked. Nor did he speak out in
public in 1948. Privately, it was another matter. To Leonard Eisner he said,
"You know, Schubert, if push comes to shove, I think Flagstad is the greatest
in the world, but having been told about her politics, I would prefer to sing
with Traubel. Let someone else sing with Flagstad if she comes back to the
Met." (Melchior's hearsay information—however accurate—came, he told
Eisner, from Crown Princess Märta of Norway. Not until many years later
would he learn the truth about her innocence.)

Kirsten Flagstad herself, on the advice of close friends, kept a dignified
silence before her attackers. In print she said nothing about Lauritz and
Kleinchen either, but privately she admitted her grief at their lack of friendship. It must be said that, true to her nature, once things were going well
and she was once more a *prima donna assoluta*, Flagstad reverted to her strange
habit of replacing the friends who had stood by her in the terrible times with
new, more exciting, more exalted friends. Perhaps the Melchiors remembered
having been on the receiving end of such treatment from her. On the other
hand, knowing the veneration that the Melchiors had for a good press image,
it is possible that they had made a conscious decision (or were advised) early
on to stay well out of all the controversy.

The British were much quicker than the Americans to re-embrace their
idolized Isolde. In May 1948 Kirsten Flagstad came back for the first time
in ten years to Covent Garden, by that time restored to its prewar brilliance.
Her Tristan was August Seider. The *Musical Courier* gave its own explanation
for this casting in one pithy sentence, "The best tenors are in America:
Melchior, Ralf, Svanholm, and Lorenz." In 1949 Flagstad took part in two
complete *Ring* cycles at Covent Garden. Her partner, Set Svanholm, was
lauded as a "most personable young Wälsung" with "supreme musicianship
and intelligence." A November 1949 review from San Francisco touched
upon his dramatic skills as contrasted with Melchior's: "Svanholm, despite
a flawless rendering of Siegfried does not begin to compare to Melchior in
dramatic characterization. In this, as in other roles, his musicianship was
more apparent than his dramatic ability."

Later, it would become apparent that Bing had contemplated ridding
the Met of Melchior all along. However, he was civil at their one and only
meeting. When The Viking became their real home, Kleinchen and Lauritz
had begun staying at the Essex House hotel when in New York. On December 3 they were stopped on their way through the lobby by a gentleman
who introduced himself as Rudolf Bing. He paid Lauritz a compliment on
his Tristan of the previous evening. Pleased, Melchior thanked him during
their walk to the elevators. As Bing left the elevator, the Melchiors gave the

new general manager their congratulations. Melchior describes this as the only conversation he ever had with Bing.

The Bings attended the opening night *Der Rosenkavalier* on November 26, as did the Melchiors. Unmitigated horror was the new general manager's reaction to the sideshow of café-society figures. "I have never seen such antics in an opera house," he said. Contributing to the usual circus-like atmosphere was television coverage; two reporters described the lobby activities for the million people who were to see the Metropolitan Opera for the first time. Those opera singers who were not working that evening contented themselves with displaying their finery. (Gladys Swarthout, for one, set off her natural endowments by wearing a gown constructed with a décolletage so plunging as to be remarked upon by the press.)

Perhaps intending to point up the Melchior place in the operatic scheme of things, Kleinchen pulled out all the stops, wearing 375 carats worth of diamonds. These, still only part of her collection of precious stones, were dispersed in various places on her person. She wore five matching platinum sprays of wild roses encrusted with diamonds, two in her hair, two at the neckline of her white gown, and one at the waist. Her costume was completed by two wide bracelets at her wrists and around her neck two strands of huge diamonds sunk into platinum settings. Strawberry blonde hair set off the gleaming diamond tiara. Over this dazzling array Kleinchen wore one of her many furs, a full-length ermine coat. She looked, said Alma Strasfogel, "like a soignée Titania from *Midsummer Night's Dream*." She easily eclipsed the other ladies, with the possible exception of Gladys Swarthout. Normally irrepressible, Lauritz felt the dignity of the occasion and confined himself to one humorous remark during the television interviews in which the Melchiors, as first-nighters, were featured. "I am grateful to the movies. I have been discovered as a glamour boy before it is too late."

This occasion appears to be the first time that the Melchiors had attended opening night at the Met. Their infrequent attendance at musical events was not limited to the Metropolitan Opera (although during the first years of their marriage they had attended often). Seldom after the mid-1930s did the couple go to a concert as others do, for enjoyment. The consensus is that this was probably because Kleinchen was uninterested in any singing but Lauritz's, although the quality of operatic acting always elicited her attention and criticism.

For the same reason, Kleinchen never encouraged Lauritz to go deeply into his music, leaving to him everything but the German diction, where she was very helpful. Had there been a compelling financial reason to do so, she probably would have recognized it and acted accordingly. Thus as the years went on, there was no urgency for him to study his concert repertoire seriously or, indeed, to restudy any of his music, particularly as he was denied opportunities to sing repertoire other than Wagner. His remarks about Bayreuth indicate how strong was his belief that what he had learned from

Cosima and Siegfried was an extension of the will of Richard Wagner and not to be diluted by modern experimental sets and direction, which he neither understood nor liked. As for song literature, he did not seek to deepen his mastery. Consequently, the superlative lieder recitals of his early career were now a thing of the past, his rhythmic and tempo weaknesses completely ingrained, and his singing delivery hardened into a Wagnerian manner, no matter what the repertoire.

On September 16, before Bing landed in New York, a wire from Edward Johnson was delivered to The Viking:

> DEAR LAURITZ: OUR REPERTOIRE IMPASSE CANNOT BE SOLVED WITHOUT YOUR FRIENDLY COOPERA-TION STOP TRISTAN NEW YORK DECEMBER ONE AND PHILADELPHIA DECEMBER SIX IMPERATIVE LAT-TER UNACCEPTABLE LOCAL SUBSCRIPTION WITHOUT MELCHIOR STOP ... SERIOUS EMBARRASSMENT WILL ENSUE SHOULD IT BE NECESSARY TO REDUCE COM-MITMENTS ALREADY NEGOTIATED WITH OTHER ARTISTS ... DEPLORABLE CONSEQUENCE TO US SHOULD PHILADELPHIA TRISTAN BE CANCELLED STOP PLEASE RECONSIDER ... AND HELP MAKE MY LAST METROPOLITAN SEASON A HAPPY ONE   AF-FECTIONATE REGARDS   EDWARD JOHNSON

This "impasse" resulted from an apparent previous indication by Lauritz that he no longer wished to sing in Philadelphia. (Bing agreed: Going to Philadelphia on Tuesday nights was "a terrible burden.") Kleinchen did not, by her own description, say a word to Lauritz; she simply handed him the wire. This was his answer:

> DEAR EDDIE: AS SO OFTEN BEFORE I WILL AGAIN SHOW MY FAITHFULNESS TO THE METROPOLITAN BY SINGING DECEMBER FIRST AND SIXTH IN SPITE OF REMEMBERING LITTLE APPRECIATION I HAVE BEEN SHOWN BY THE MET AND SURELY WILL BE SHOWN IN THE FUTURE STOP AS COMRADE AND COLLEAGUE I WILL BE ONLY TOO GLAD TO MAKE YOUR LAST MET SEASON A HAPPY AND GLORIOUS ONE IF I CAN STOP GREETINGS   LAURITZ MELCHIOR

As Kleinchen wrote to Jim Davidson,

> Lauritz felt that he must do it, whereas I was very cold about the whole thing. For one time in my life I didn't make one suggestion or try to persuade him in the least way. Now, when you receive the contracts, please do not sign them until I have had a chance to look them over very carefully.

Perhaps Kleinchen's temper was short because she was trying so hard to persuade Lauritz to accept one of the offers for a Broadway show that were constantly coming his way. Pinza had enjoyed a great success in *South Pacific* after leaving the Met just the year before, she reminded her husband. But he would not budge from his conviction that singing the same music eight times a week would be insufferably boring. Besides, as he said often and tactlessly, "Signor Pinza is in the flat races and I am in the hurdles." Most importantly, he would never leave the Met before his twenty-fifth anniversary at that house, which would take place next year. After all, he was the only heroic tenor in history to survive twenty-five years of Wagnerian roles and continue to sing. Recognizing that this anniversary was of utmost consequence to Lauritz, Kleinchen had given up her campaign. Davidson could talk to the "new man" some time in November as usual, so that all details of the contract and the anniversary could be settled while they were still in New York.

Melchior and Bing may not have talked after their one meeting at the Essex House, but since Rudolf Bing took his study period seriously, he had sat in on rehearsals; he had held auditions; he had attended every performance at the Met, even repeats with different casts (and he probably had been told a lot of previous Met history). There is no evidence to show what Bing thought of Melchior's performances, but he surely read reviews containing such phrases as "with or without rehearsal," "slight hoarseness," and "slovenly musicianship." Yet, on balance, the reception given Melchior's four performances before Christmas was far more good than bad. The press noted "the familiar virtues" belonging to him and Helen Traubel,

> the sincerity of their characterizations and the ease with which they collaborate musically and dramatically. Others may sing Tristan with more vocal sensuousness, but Mr. Melchior's interpretation has a majesty and a sort of homely mastiff-like masculinity that are deeply convincing.

Kolodin declared that his Siegmund turned back the pages to his great days "with prodigal voice and an amount of youthful fervor astonishing in this phase of his career." Downes, too, insisted that his Siegmund had "an authority, a color, a sonority, and an effectiveness to reckon with." These were the performances that Bing attended.

Assuming that Rudolf Bing's definition of professionalism included good relations between singing colleagues, he should have approved the testimonial given Lauritz after the dramatic debut that enlivened the December 21 performance of *Die Walküre*. On four hours' notice soprano Regina Resnik sang her first performance of Sieglinde. When asked whether Lauritz, her Siegmund, had been helpful, she reinforced his excellent reputation for collegiality: "He was simply wonderful. He was as sweet and tender as could be.

We went over lots of details before the performance and he was a real friend on stage." In turn, Lauritz, after giving Miss Resnik a bear hug in full view of the crowd, said, "I am very proud of my colleague. She didn't make one mistake—and this with no rehearsal!"

Another story of Lauritz watching over his younger colleagues was told by mezzo-soprano Blanche Thebom. At Thebom's Philadelphia debut as Brangäne in December 1944, Lauritz had treated her "as a child, nodding when it was good."

> After the dress rehearsal of Act II, where I wore a heavy, clinging costume, Lauritz charged after me into the wings. Although he attempted to whisper, his "whisper" was so loud that it was enjoyed by all . . . [:] "Blanche, you have to wear a slip; I can see the line of your panties!"

Not only had Rudolf Bing observed everything at the opera house as he had been instructed by the board, but he had doubtless read all the daily papers. Headlines screamed "COURT RULES IT ISN'T NOISE IF MEL-CHIOR SAYS IT'S MUSIC!" and Lauritz looked just fine playing the washboard for the photographers from the *Herald-Tribune*. In the same month as the glamorous Metropolitan opening, Lauritz served as witness for the defense in the trial of the Korn Kobblers' Band. Accompanied by a few beauteous show girls, the Korn Kobblers were riding along Broadway in a hay wagon, celebrating their impending appearance at a restaurant in the vicinity. At 47th Street and Broadway they were handed a noise summons by a policeman who insisted that auto horns, washboards, and inverted spittoons were not orchestral instruments. Lauritz, brought along to court by the chief Korn Kobbler to help prove that it was music that they were making, spoke eloquently: "Sometimes it is difficult to determine what is noise and what is music; one generation's noise might be the next generation's music. Wagner's operas were at first described as unnecessary noise. The music of living composers is way ahead of the people." From the sublime to the ridiculous seemed to be the normal path of Lauritz's life. Could Rudolf Bing have missed this coverage? Most surely he heard Melchior's exuberant rendition of the Chevrolet radio commercial. The Wagnerian parody of "Seeeeeee the U! S! A! in a Che-vro-laaaaaaaay" was inescapable.

Melchior was also very visible in the New York papers on December 20, when Margaret Truman, daughter of President Harry Truman, would-be singer and protégée (but not student) of Helen Traubel, sang as guest soloist on a radio broadcast carried on the NBC network. Accompanied by the orchestra and chorus, she sang some Christmas carols and "O mio babbino caro." Critics praised her poise and personality but didn't think much of her singing. Carnegie Hall, however, was packed with an audience of socialites who wore very formal attire featuring a large number of rather bare backs and plunging necklines. Kleinchen, dressed more circumspectly, was so perturbed at her own lack of chic that she went home. Supporting by his presence a fellow member of James Davidson's roster of artists who was to become a good friend, Lauritz was very visible backstage, being photographed, kissing Margaret, saying, "She has the goods, but you can't expect her to be a Melba straight off." He even garnered a laugh, explaining to Margaret Truman, "My wife went home. She said she had too much on." All these details were faithfully recorded in the press. Rudolf Bing, impeccable autocrat, with his glossy British veneer layered over a Germanic hauteur, must have found such behavior irritatingly unprofessional.

Edward Johnson had spent many years as general manager during a time when Melchior was absolutely essential to the mounting of Wagnerian opera. Bing, however, may have viewed Melchior as expendable, for it was no secret that he did not care too much for Wagner. There were many reasons, Bing had said, among them the fact that the great voices needed to do Wagner no longer existed in sufficient numbers to support many such productions. A well-known conductor was said to agree with this cost-effective point of view, saying that "the damned things last five hours and they cost a fortune. When you consider all these things, it's easier to do Puccini."

Another contributing factor to Bing's attitude seems to have been Melchior's corpulence, which the cadaverously thin Bing always included in his written observances of the singer. Melchior's huge size was apparently personally distasteful to Bing (although he repeatedly handled any references to oversize sopranos with extreme tact). It began in 1939, when Bing saw Melchior in *Tannhäuser*, looking, he wrote, "like a moving couch covered in red plush," adding "although he sounded fine." Referring to Melchior in later years, he added to his evaluation, "the finest Heldentenor in the world," another mention of Melchior's size and age, "but distressingly fat and aging." Again he seemed preoccupied with weight when, reporting a later meeting with President Eisenhower in Washington, he quoted—apparently relishing the humor—the presidential question "How is that fat fellow?"*

Bing evidently felt that Melchior's failings, professional and physical, added up to make him dispensable, despite his incomparable voice. Knowing Bing's convictions about the proper place of singers in the operatic scheme of things, his objection to Melchior as "fat" perhaps equated with an objection to him as "powerful" or "controlling" as well. Certainly Lauritz's well-paid artistic life outside the Met made him suspect. In Bing's eyes Lauritz's age and weight, his narrow Wagner specialization, his outmoded acting, his

---

*Judging from the personal correspondence between Melchior and Eisenhower, it is difficult to believe this story. Autograph collectors say that anything written in Eisenhower's own hand is exceedingly rare. Yet in Lauritz's files, willed to his son Ib, there were official letters from Eisenhower typed by the White House secretary but containing hand-written postscripts signed "D" or "Ike"; there were post cards sent while the Eisenhowers traveled, completely hand-written and signed by "Ike," one headed "somewhere over the English Channel." The correspondence, which starts in 1943, spans many years, suggesting a real friendship.

undignified publicity, his lack of professionalism, and his position as a radio and movie star outweighed Melchior's position as the greatest Heldentenor of the twentieth century, his awe-inspiring voice, his vast European experience, his uniqueness in the repertoire, his long years of service to the Met, and even public opinion. Bing saw Melchior as a problem to be dealt with, but one he would deal with only when he was ready.

Constantly paired together by the press, Melchior and Traubel were uniquely qualified for the media attention they constantly received. Both were physical Titans whose larger-than-life bodies and personas typified "opera singer" to the average man; yet they were charming, amusing, and, most importantly, down-to-earth: Melchior hunted; Traubel played baseball—"real" people. In 1949 they were in two less highbrow projects together: the first, a new radio show, tentatively titled "Mr. and Mrs. Opera," which would star the two singers in a situation comedy with song; the second was a predigested, two-hour concert version of *Tristan und Isolde*, which would prove to be very successful.

The short *Tristan* had its tryout in June before 12,000 people in Philadelphia's Robin Hood Dell, Leonard Bernstein conducting. The reception was so "amazing" that by fall the dehydrated version of *Tristan* was booked to local orchestras and conductors by the enterprising Mr. Davidson in fourteen cities normally off the beaten path of operatic touring companies.

Melchior was, of course, on record as approving of shortening the Wagnerian music dramas. Bing's opinion of the venture is not known, but he did speak a lot about democratizing opera, presumably so that there might come a new opera audience out of the ranks of those who did not normally frequent opera houses. Ironically, Melchior, Traubel, and the truncated *Tristan* were doing exactly that. A huge number of people were being introduced to a Wagnerian opera in its most palatable form.

Almost every day during November and December, Melchior held press conferences about his coming concert tour of the shortened *Tristan*. Kleinchen, sitting nearby with Davidson, asked whether he had met with Bing. Each time Davidson repeated that, when he did manage to get the general manager on the phone, Bing simply would not discuss Melchior's next season. Davidson and Kleinchen were becoming increasingly anxious because they, and virtually everyone else, knew that Bing had already spoken with personal managers of other singers. In desperation Davidson resorted to the mails on December 20, asking in writing for an appointment to speak about his clients: Eleanor Steber, Leonard Warren, Melchior, and Traubel. There was no response. Melchior was scheduled for only two performances at the Met in January. *Tristan und Isolde* on January 2 was under the baton of Maestro Jonel Perlea, the Rumanian conductor who was equally at home in all three "wings" of the Met. One of his first three operas was *Tristan*, after which reviews spoke warmly about the new sweetness, richness, and clarity in the singing of both Traubel and Melchior, giving the credit for this subdued splendor to Perlea, who suggested tellingly that too many conductors were prone to mistake heroic for loud. Nonetheless, when the Melchiors, together with Traubel and her husband, left New York on January 8 for their *Tristan* tour, there had still been no answer from Bing.

Soon Bing's post as a mere observer weighed upon him. Rumors of his negotiations with Flagstad were circulating. He requested that he be allowed to speak to the press and explain his plans. Johnson objected strenuously but was overruled by the board, who were in this case prepared to support their new general manager and his methods. A press conference was announced for January 29, but before then, Helen Traubel proclaimed that she would not be singing at the Metropolitan in the coming season. Her feelings were wounded because Mr. Bing had been discussing contract issues with younger and less experienced artists but had not spoken to her management as yet.

At the press conference the general manager–elect announced that Kirsten Flagstad would sing again on the stage of the Metropolitan Opera. He had concluded from his private investigation that Flagstad was "obviously a non-political person, and that time for punishing her for her husband's misdeeds had ended." He stated, "This management will operate on artistic, not political or racist policies." When asked about Melchior, he was evasive, but emphasized that the roster was not yet complete. (Indeed, others also not on the list were Albanese, Pons, Steber, Peerce, Tagliavini, and Bampton.) He articulated his determination that the Met artists "put our interests first and not use the name as a label to improve their market value." A further slap at Melchior (and others) was his statement that he wanted his opera singers on tap at all times, not indulging themselves in concert, radio, or movie appearances for which they received three or four times as much as for a Metropolitan performance. A few less revolutionary statements closed the meeting: primary emphasis was to be given to the visual aspects of the stage, and the first priority was to be Quality. This inspired several headlines exploiting the alliterative possibilities of his name, such as "Bing Arrives with a Bang!"

The Melchiors first learned of these events via the newspapers in North Carolina where Lauritz was happily planning to hunt wild turkeys. It had not escaped the press that what the Met had acquired was not only a boss "uninhibited by either fear or humility" and capable of cracking the whip like a lion tamer, but a "really first-rate, high-class prima donna." Davidson called the Melchiors back to New York, citing rumors that Richard Tucker had already been signed.

It was at this moment that the Melchior forces failed to take the measure of the man.

Traubel stuck to her guns the next day, saying that she would wait to see what the Met had to offer. "No contract, no work is an awfully good policy." She and James Davidson thought that Bing should have settled things, if only on an informal basis, by November or December. Early in the fall, Johnson and Davidson had held meetings as usual regarding contracts for Melchior and Traubel. As it is noted in the Met files, Helen Traubel was to have a minimum of thirteen or fourteen performances at $1,000 for 1950–1951, and Melchior, at the same fee, a minimum of ten or twelve performances. To the Davidson contingent it must have seemed at that time as though business was proceeding as usual along comfortably familiar lines. However, that informal chat between Davidson and Edward Johnson now appeared to have been worthless. Bing insisted that he had written to the lady the previous week (indeed, there is a carbon of such a letter, dated January 27, in the Met files), and that this whole incident was unfortunate and ill-considered.

Communicating only through newspaper interviews seems foolish, but once again it happened. On January 30 Lauritz complained that Bing had not yet approached him about the 1950–1951 season. "It's a sentimental business. It's like loving a girl very much and having her leave you. It hurts." Then, lost in his role of the genuinely suffering *primo tenore*, he employed a childish tactic. One might almost believe that he tried a bluff, albeit unconsciously. His days at the Met might soon be over, he said. "I can only assume that if I don't miss the Swan Boat Thursday night, [that performance] will be goodbye to the Met public."

Bing's published answer contained no mention of a previous letter from Davidson asking for an appointment to discuss the Melchior contract, but said that contract talks usually start in February or March. This was patently untrue. Contract negotiations were conducted in a well-established pattern. Since the 1930s it had been regular practice for Melchior's management to reserve December, January, and February for the Met, with a few radio broadcasts and concerts in the vicinity. If the company desired Melchior's services for more performances, Johnson would let Davidson know in the fall, one year in advance so that no concerts (which were booked a year ahead) would be scheduled in that period. The middle of January was the very latest cutoff date for picking up an option. (Flagstad had the same arrangement, which the Met carelessly abrogated at least twice, the result being that Johnson had to give McArthur his chance to conduct both on tour and in the house.) In any case, Davidson would talk to Johnson before signing each concert contract, thus giving the Met preference whenever there was a conflict.

This information indicates that the real problem was caused by the mere existence of concert dates. They would be inconvenient for the opera administration. This is why Bing intended to prevent his artists from going off during the winter season, or trying to sandwich in concert dates between opera performances, a policy that would be very hard on the singers. Melchior himself may have been a wealthy man by now, but for the younger and less-publicized singers, whose Met fees were pitifully minimal, concerts provided the only real chance to make a living. On the other hand, as Bing knew only too well, without the all-important phrase "of the Metropolitan Opera" following their names, they were not as marketable.

By Monday noon, January 30, Melchior could no longer abide the endless waiting. After much discussion he decided to try a direct inquiry. Melchior's own draft was simple: two sentences, one asking for a conference and the second reminding Bing that they lived only two floors away from each other, in case it might be more convenient to meet at the Essex House. It was Davidson (according to Melchior) who suggested that they give a deadline; it might persuade Mr. Bing to respond.

James Davidson had started out as an accountant, then graduated to a career as a business manager for stars whose yearly income was high enough to need such help. When W. Colston Leigh broadened the scope of his lecture-booking agency to include a concert division, Davidson brought his financial clients under Leigh's umbrella and slipped into being a personal manager. Leigh's way of doing business, adopted by Davidson, was to guarantee a yearly income. In practical results, then, the artist, knowing none of the details of how this figure would be met, could have been paid different sums in different cities, or indeed missed out on an artistically important engagement solely because it did not pay enough—in management's opinion. Davidson knew and cared only about the final profit and loss statement. According to former management colleagues, he had an iron determination to keep matters firmly in his own hands, even to the detriment of his client's interests. (There is even some doubt whether Davidson had really been honest with the Melchiors during these events, for, when it was all over, Davidson told the press that he had said to Bing after the very first press conference, "If you're going to fire him, at least call him in and tell him you're going to fire him.") Most importantly, Davidson was totally (and contentedly) ignorant of artistic principles or personalities. This disability was about to influence Melchior's career irrevocably.

On the advice of Jim Davidson, then, an express telegram was sent off. Its text reflects well his ignorance about Bing's character and his artistic philosophy:

MR. LAURITZ MELCHIOR HAS REQUESTED THAT YOU ADVISE ME IMMEDIATELY OF YOUR PLANS CONCERNING HIM FOR NEXT SEASON. WOULD YOU THEREFORE KINDLY ADVISE ME NOT LATER THAN TWELVE NOON TOMORROW, TUESDAY, REGARDING FIRST, THE OVER-

ALL PERIOD OF AVAILABILITY DESIRED, SECOND, THE
ROLES INVOLVED, AND THIRD, THE NUMBER OF PER-
FORMANCES?

Davidson returned to his office and waited impatiently, as did the Melchiors in their suite. Nothing was heard from the Met that day, although
that afternoon the company did formally engage Helen Traubel. Bing maintained always that he received the Melchior telegram only forty minutes
before he was to leave for Philadelphia on Tuesday, but the telegram makes
it clear that it was *sent* early on Monday morning. On Tuesday Bing had his
assistant dispatch a special delivery letter (it arrived in late afternoon) that
acknowledged receipt of the telegram, stating "Mr. Bing regrets that due to
lack of time he is unable to give you an answer today."

Propelled by the unbelievable press attention, Bing held another conference on Wednesday, February 1. One of the first subjects he addressed
was that of Flagstad and her American counterpart, Helen Traubel. The
two sopranos were to share honors, each doing one *Ring* cycle and one Isolde.
Flagstad was to sing, in addition, Leonora in *Fidelio* and Traubel, the Marschallin in *Rosenkavalier*. Bing took public credit for evenhandedness, but it
was later revealed that the credit was due Flagstad, who had generously
insisted that the American soprano, having contributed so much during the
war years, be given equal status with her.

The unresolved issue of the press conference was whether Melchior
would be back. Bing refused to answer directly, denied that he had been
discourteous (only slow in coming to decisions), but added with his usual
brilliant command over the niceties and subtleties of the English language:
"I am not prepared to submit to an ultimatum, I don't care from whom,
specifically in forty minutes. . . . I will attempt to run this house—unmoved
by promises or threats—on the principle of quality only." (*Time*, however,
which kept good track of Bing's pronouncements for the next twenty-three
years, concluded that "Bing was notoriously unsympathetic to any ultimatum
but his own.") The Melchior team should not have failed to perceive this as
stonewalling. The question is why Lauritz did not just dig in and wait for
the negotiations to continue. Perhaps he had been too long a superstar, and
the public humiliation was simply too much to bear. Perhaps that was precisely what Bing was relying on.

Elaborating on his plans, Bing jolted more subscribers than singers.
Opening night would be taken out of subscription. This meant that the
regulars, who made a circus out of that evening with their pranks and exotic
clothing, would have to scramble—and pay dearly—to get in. The season
would be split into two subscriptions of ten weeks each, to give a break to
people with less income. Bing hinted again that the artists would be reined
in with longer contracts and more performances. Questioned as to his
thoughts on using black artists, Bing was caught uncharacteristically off
guard. "That's a new one. I would be glad to engage a Negro artist of suitable

voice for a suitable role. I am moved in running this opera house by artistic, not by racial considerations." He closed by saying that the goal was "an ensemble of stars, not comets."

Hope Associates released a statement on February 1, the eve of Melchior's last performance:

Mr. Melchior's present plans call for a heavy concert tour next season, and, as he has not yet been approached for the customary preliminary discussion by the Metropolitan management, his schedule does not include returning to the Metropolitan for what would have been his twenty-fifth anniversary season.

Melchior himself said, with some reasonableness:

I would have assumed that the natural courtesy of the management for the Metropolitan would dictate a call to any leading artist who had appeared regularly with the company for twenty-four years to determine his position with the company before information was released to the press.

The day of Melchior's *Lohengrin* performance, February 2, was a bitter one for Lauritz. While the press besieged his suite and the Met for answers, he sat quietly, brooding. How had this happened? In four days his entire life had changed for the worse. By late afternoon it was clear in his mind. He must make an effort to accept the facts. His aspirations for a twenty-fifth year at the Metropolitan were finished. He roused himself to draft a short farewell statement. That act gave birth to an optimistic thought: If he arrived at the Met earlier than usual, perhaps Bing or Johnson might come and speak with him. He would not give out his statement until the last minute. It was reported that the line at the box office was around the block, and hundreds of people were being turned away. Again Lauritz took heart. Perhaps Bing would realize what Melchior's name meant, if only to the house receipts. Perhaps he would relent.

Clearly, however, Rudolf Bing had no intention of conceding before he called Melchior's bluff that evening. It was a waiting game à la Tietjen (whose ability to rule by "attrition through indecision" Bing not only admired, but imitated), and Melchior had played directly into Bing's hands. Bing wrote, "I had not known, frankly, how to handle the Melchior problem, how to make him a responsible artist rather than a disturbing artistic influence in the house; his telegram now told me how." With the arrival of the Davidson telegram, Bing only had to sit back, do nothing, and wait for the ultimatum to run out.

Klaus Riisbro, Lauritz's godson and fellow Mason, gives a clue about the influence of secret Masonic principles on Melchior at that moment:

He therefore just turned the key and said, "This is my square. I am what I am and this would no longer be me." Being himself, Godfather would not play a calculated, cautious game, nor would he be dictated to. So he did not have a twenty-fifth anniversary. Godfather said, "Could he not have let me go my way until the anniversary was done, then ruled as he wanted?"

This suggests that even at this late date Melchior did not fathom why Bing was treating him in such a fashion; he simply accepted it.

When the swan boat entered the stage carrying Lauritz Melchior to his seventy-first *Lohengrin* performance on the night of February 2, 1950, having heard not a word from Rudolf Bing, he knew that he had lost the battle. Melchior appeared in the swan boat clad in silver armor. As his foot touched the stage, the audience erupted in a burst of applause. Although those within the opera house knew nothing of his decision, during the first act intermission he made his announcement to the assemblage of reporters.

> Not only as Lohengrin, but as Lauritz Melchior I have sung my swan song at the Metropolitan Opera tonight. For the opera lovers and my fellow artists I have the warmest affection; to the loyal audiences who have attended the more than 500 performances in which I have taken part, I express my deepest gratitude. I will not be back, and in departing I say, "Vive la compagnie!"

During the second intermission a reporter who found him asked, "Why?" Lauritz responded, "I don't believe I will feel happy working under the new setup. We artists have sentimentalities. So I swim off with the swan tonight." He kept up a brave front, but there were those who thought they saw tears in his eyes as the swan drew his boat off the Metropolitan stage.

The curtain went down at 11:48. The audience rose to give Lauritz Melchior fourteen curtain calls, one of the longest ovations in Met history. There was no speech. Union rules dictated the final closing of the curtain on the dot of midnight or payment of overtime. This put a stop to the applause. Backstage Melchior had trouble convincing his admirers—who stood two abreast in a line that stretched from his dressing room, through the long corridors of the house, all the way down to the stage exit—that he had just sung his last performance at the Met. "I never stay where I'm not wanted. This place has been my home for twenty-four years. I'm sorry to go but it can't be helped. You can't swallow everything."

Still in his Lohengrin costume, minus the helmet, he signed programs, autograph books, and librettos. "What will you miss most?" asked a young music conservatory student.

"My comrades and Angelo, my dresser."

"Supposing Mr. Johnson needs a Tristan in an emergency before the season is over?"

"I'll always be willing to help out as long as Mr. Johnson is here. You all know that I've been a trouper here for years."

Johnson remained silent. During the ovation he had taken one bow with Melchior and Traubel. Throwing circumspection to the winds, he had warmly embraced Melchior before the audience, but he would not speak. "No sir, you can't get a word out of me tonight!"

"Is it really goodbye?" asked a tearful young girl near the door.

"Yes, it is. It doesn't mean I won't sing anymore. I still have a little voice." Turning to someone else he explained, "It's hard to do *Lohengrin* for a goodbye because the words of Lohengrin's farewell are so well suited to a situation like this."

A cameraman asked Melchior to stand up in the center of the room and be photographed with an armful of girls. "That's not quite proper for the pure and saintly Lohengrin. You now, I made my debut as the bad boy Tannhäuser and I did my last performance as the good boy Lohengrin. I guess I made the grade."

Osie Hawkins, with a breaking voice, said, "You've done so much for me."

Irene Jessner said, "I won't say goodbye to you, Lauritz."

"No, I'm still playing pinochle with you tomorrow night." Lauritz got up and said energetically, "Any more business? Let's get it over with. I'm getting thirsty."

Kleinchen shooed them out, saying, "The poor man wants to dress."

The dressing room door closed.

In the 1950 daily appointment book Melchior wrote only: "It was my last performance at the Met. Went out to eat with Helen, Bill, Margaret." Asked for a statement the next morning, the Met management declared, "It was just another performance."

Echoing the headlines of the previous month, the papers now chorused, "Melchior Goes Out with a Bing!" Postmortems began all over the country the next morning. On Bing's side:

Bing has scarcely begun . . . but it is obvious tradition isn't going to bother him. There is no more tradition-encrusted institution in the world than the Metropolitan.

Bing reflects the European attitude of opera as a popular art [and where] . . . prices are scaled to the purses of large numbers of people.

Bing is not so much a new broom as a . . . tank model vacuum cleaner. It not only removes dirt from the carpet, but lifts the nap away from the rug as well. Undoubtedly this is going to be a very painful operation as far as the nap is concerned, but then it may be just what the Met rug needs.

On the Melchior side:

It would have been more forthright of Bing to have drawn the issue on principles.

The airy way he talks of refusing to make up his mind about Melchior in forty minutes smacks of arrogance, but almost worse than that, is smacks of ignorance. A heroic tenor is not lightly to be cast aside. . . . It's lunacy to fuss around. . . . It is no answer to try to balance two great sopranos like Flagstad and Traubel against the loss of Melchior. There are at least ten women capable of taking on Wagnerian soprano leads and doing well with them. There is only one singer in the world who can begin to approach Melchior's standards, and Set Svanholm needs seasons of experience to attain Melchior's authority.

At the very least, [Bing's] actions were lacking in grace.

Like all great celebrities, Melchior lived in a world that revolved around his career and its requirements. With no artistic peaks left to conquer, the principal activity of the Melchior team had been reduced to maintenance of the great singer's position at the pinnacle of fame. Melchior himself, so often referred to as "bigger than life," had expanded to fit his description. He basked in the public's incredible adulation, and lived according to professional mores and traditional ways of the past. He was still content to be doing those things which would have made Cosima proud. Instead of recognizing the new needs of the opera company, Melchior stood on his position as a loyal and longtime member of the company "family," who deserved, because of his many services and past loyalty, to be treated better. It was a reasonable point of view. The Met had kept—and still today does keep—other singers (some far less notable, some far less capable) on the roster, considerably giving them token performances until their twenty-five years have been completed. Reading Bing's two books, one sees the real compassion and respect with which he treated great, but aging, singers. Strangely, unless it resulted from Kleinchen's direction of his activities, Melchior was denied an equally considerate and respectful treatment. Sir Rudolf—he was knighted in 1971— normally unfailingly punctilious even when wielding a necessary scalpel, behaved in an uncharacteristically discourteous manner toward Melchior.

One fact was overlooked by everyone, including Lauritz and Kleinchen, but not by Danish discographer Hans Hansen: Lauritz had deluded himself all his life about the twenty-fifth Met anniversary. He conveniently passed over the year (1927–1928) that he spent away from the Metropolitan, singing in Hamburg and Berlin. His twenty-fifth anniversary would properly have come in the 1951–1952 season. Would the pain have been less, had he faced this?

The saga was not yet finished. On February 4 Bing topped his winning hand with a trump card. Paraphrasing neatly Melchior's reference to himself as a "leading artist," Bing said piously that he "disagreed with the distinction between Greater and Lesser Artists which Melchior had made." As for himself, he felt it "important to deal first with those of smaller reputations. Their livelihoods depended more directly on opera" and he wanted to "remove their doubts about paying the rent." With this stroke Bing had Lauritz neatly boxed into a corner and characterized as The Big Star who was selfishly pouting because he had not been reassured as to his position before the Lesser Singers were. Kleinchen responded for her husband, as this newsprint combat carried on:

> Mr. Melchior is definitely not interested in returning to the Met so long as Mr. Bing is the general manager. I hope that Mr. Bing, after he has been with the Met for twenty-four years—if he is there that long—will not receive the kind of treatment that Mr. Melchior has had.

Her husband, added Kleinchen, could never have made such a statement as that about "small singers." It was a feeble rejoinder at best.

In only eight days the austere Mr. Bing had won a major publicity skirmish, established his reputation as a tough adversary, and, with surgical precision and speed, deftly injected fear and caution into the minds of the "stars" of the Metropolitan Opera. Kleinchen was overmatched.

It was Lauritz Melchior's misfortune to be ending his operatic career just as the Metropolitan Opera was about to enter a new era. Fifteen years earlier, Herbert Witherspoon had scribbled with a pencil a list of his complaints and remedies for the ills of the Met. These notes, prophetically, almost exactly describe the changes Rudolf Bing made during his tenure:

* action of artists and chorus must be brought up to times . . . made more realistic and modern, new acting ideas, new principles of grouping chorus members, new life

* stage is old, obsolete piece of mechanism

* lighting equipment very old-fashioned . . . can be improved 100 percent

* all operas should be restudied . . . adjusted to new visualization influenced by movies

* repertoire should be changed, more French opera

* support of people at large must be obtained

* rigid but sensible economy . . . in every department; high prices for artists are gone for good

* all contracts should be on weekly basis, economy, giving radio privileges to opera company

* prices of seats should be based on new scaling of house

* opera school should be established in connection with opera, thus opportunity for American singers, save money for company

* discipline in attending rehearsals, overtime avoided
* foster alliances with labor, opera for people, not elite
* professional tour can be done, performances for school children

During his time as head of the Met, Edward Johnson had done little to effect such changes. Bing gives very good reasons for this when he describes the troubles he himself had with George Sloan, president of the board for both general managers: Sloan considered the Met part of his social life and expected the general manager to grace a constant round of parties with his presence; Sloan had no feeling of responsibility for those who worked at the Met; Sloan saw little reason why new productions had to be done or why money had to be spent on rehearsing; Sloan thought that opera should pay its own way. In the light of these observations, two conclusions can be reached: Johnson's hands were virtually tied until the board itself decided to permit changes; and Bing was the more determined antagonist.

At the time when Bing began his job at the Met, he found almost all productions done in the romantic realism style of the nineteenth-century scenic tradition—that is, mostly painted backdrop scenery. When he opened the 1950–1951 season with a production of *Don Carlo* (then virtually unknown to the New York audiences), directed by Margaret Webster, sets by Rolf Gerard, Bing "set a precedent for opera as a total theatrical experience"— just as he had planned—which "changed forever the art of designing for opera." In time, he made the Metropolitan Opera into a real theater, and it was never the same again. Sadly, unnoticed by the greatest Heldentenor of the twentieth century, the era of the all-powerful singer had passed, as had the era of the godlike conductor.

Production Values had arrived in the opera world, and with them, the reign of the director.

CHAPTER 16

Vacation from Valhalla

(1950–1959)

The press attention that followed Melchior's last Metropolitan performance had blanketed the United States, Canada, and even parts of Europe, but in sharp contrast to his daily public comments during the month of January, almost none of it was generated by the tenor. Typically, press and fans either excoriated Bing or insulted the other Heldentenors, or both.

Clearly, Melchior was still considered a major player in the world of singers. His audiences could hear that his voice was intact and his skills functional, and they were shocked at the cavalier treatment he had received. It was evident that the tenor's lack of ability had not been among the reasons for discontinuing Melchior's stay at the Met, and many critics took out their ire on Rudolf Bing. The *Houston Press*, on February 14, published this letter, which stated the case reasonably well.

> Dear Mr. Bing: A short time ago you relieved Lauritz Melchior of his duties at the Met, and in so doing, the music lovers of the entire nation— or Melchior-fans if you will—got the impression that a good friend had either been treated unfairly or had become old and weak in the service and had retired in order to vegetate. The answer to that riddle was given to 2,000 inhabitants last night when "the Great Dane" performed in our concert hall. They went home a little over two hours later, humming and whistling, finding that they had just heard the wonderful tenor of one of America's greatest singers. The music lovers were right. For Lauritz Melchior, a giant of a man with a giant gift, which he can share with others, had sung himself to a giant victory.

For some time after the event, Melchior fans continued to write letters to the Met, in which they made those who took their idol's place pay for the privilege. One such letter, which was addressed to Max Lorenz, offensively told him that his "effort to sing the part of Siegmund was the most excruciating agony I have suffered in many years of listening to opera, and especially after having listened to that *great artist*, Mr. Lauritz Melchior, sing the role."

The attention paid to Melchior did not lessen for the next ten years, as his personal mail shows. His sixty-ninth birthday in particular elicited much genuinely sentimental mail from admirers all over the world, such as a letter from an English gentleman, who wrote: "I have never forgotten you and never shall. It was you who first created my love for Wagner." A Texas school teacher wrote to thank Melchior "for the pleasure and joy" his "great voice" had given, for what he had done "to create an interest in good music among the young people," and for "the courageous, courteous and forthright manner" in which he had borne his success. Melchior's fame remained at a constant high level, even with the post office. An envelope arrived safely at his California home having come all the way from Copenhagen bearing only the skimpy address, "The Viking, U.S.A.":

FOR THE ROYAL CHAMBER SINGER, THE U.S. PRESIDENT OF THE ROYAL DANISH COURT'S LIFE GUARD, THE WORLD'S GREATEST TENOR, THE MALTESIAN KNIGHT, LAURITZ MELCHIOR, ESQUIRE

Melchior's supporters had rallied around him in every conceivable way. The Damon Runyon Fund was evidently not averse to affronting Mr. Bing. To help their admired Heldentenor realize his ambition of singing for twenty-five years at the Met, they offered to rent the Metropolitan Opera house for Melchior in 1951, to engage an orchestra, conductor and singers for a gala performance on the evening of his twenty-fifth anniversary at the house. He declined the offer.

Even on the lecture circuit Melchior was a big draw. Milton Cross's plummy speaking voice had given him a career as a rather anonymous staff announcer for NBC's Red and Blue Networks. When he took on the position of commentator for the Met radio broadcasts, the radio public transformed him into a celebrity. Thereafter, he wrote several books advising the radio audience how to listen and "appreciate" opera, and supplied plot summaries. He also became a sought-after lecturer around the country. So high was the public interest in the events of the final Melchior appearance at the Met that wherever Cross went after the February *Lohengrin*, he was asked to scrap his prepared speech and give the "lowdown" on the Melchior/Bing conflict.

In 1951 and 1952 two offers came from publishing firms, one for a book on Lauritz's big-game hunting adventures, and one for a biography to be written by Stephen Longstreet. Neither came to fruition, and the second is reported to have been stymied by Kleinchen's determination to suppress what she didn't want included.

Europe had not forgotten Melchior either. Following a May 1951 trip, which marked one million miles of air travel for the Melchiors, Lauritz sang a benefit radio concert in Berlin before an open-air audience of 30,000. Frida Leider told Mutti in a June letter of Lauritz's great success at this concert, saying with admiration how "all the people said unanimously that his voice was in magnificent condition, as ever it was. Yes, it is truly astounding what a magnificent condition Lauritz is in, bodily and vocally."

The media interest in Melchior did not seem to be waning. "As much of an American institution as baseball," declared a Nashville, Tennessee paper. As for the music press, in November 1950 Irving Kolodin had assessed matters at the Metropolitan Opera by reminding readers that December would bring "the season's first *Tristan*, but the Met's first Tristan will not be singing in it."

> That night finds Lauritz Melchior many miles away in Baltimore giving a concert. . . . Though Melchior is keeping his own counsel in this matter, there is no doubt that he as well as those close to him are still sorely exercised over the manner in which his Met career terminated last winter. . . . Those who know Melchior and his habits know that to round out twenty-five years singing leading Wagnerian roles at the Met was once one of his dearest ambitions. It is indeed a distinction worth cherishing, and no previous Heldentenor has even come close to such a record. Jean de Reszke, who is revered as the greatest Tristan in musical annals, sang those parts for a bare half dozen years before retiring, and there have been few tenors who have lasted as many as a dozen seasons in these roles.

Lauritz himself did not make a public statement about leaving the Met until January 1951, when—asked a question he presumably could not resist, "What, if anything, is currently wrong with opera, especially as conducted at the Metropolitan Opera House?"—he answered:

> Do you realize that opera in the Met will probably face a million dollar deficit at the end of the season? Appeals to radio audiences to send in their dollars and dimes, a humiliating recourse, will not save the situation. You cannot run an American opera company as a European opera company.

One might surmise that Melchior was simply seizing the opportunity to take a public blow at Rudolf Bing, except that he turned his criticism to a genuine concern of his, the hiring of foreign artists who took the place of Americans at the Met:

> There are many and costly museums of dead art in this city, but no proper building for live art. Here we have an ancient building, lacking air conditioning, filled with singers from abroad who are able to accept comparatively small pay because they can return to their own countries and get rich by transferring American gold into their own depreciated currency. Meanwhile young American singers of marked ability get little chance.

It appears that Melchior's public policy was to reveal a minimum of what he really felt, while not actually concealing his dislike for Bing and his methods. When asked by the press in 1953 whether he had any plans to sing again at the Metropolitan, the tenor gave this answer, "Bing has been signed to a new three-year contract, and by that time I will have a long white beard."

In 1959, soon after the great Rudolf Bing/Maria Callas controversy (which occupied the kind of space in the media that Melchior and Flagstad had filled in their time), perhaps spurred by the renewed public attention to Bing's treatment of his opera stars, Lauritz was finally ready to speak without equivocation. His answer to a reporter's question of whether he regretted leaving the Met revealed a bitterness even then unassuaged:

> I do not regret it in the sense that through the medium of television and pictures I have been able to expose millions to operatic music. I do regret leaving under the circumstances. I would like to have been able to celebrate my twenty-fifth anniversary, and I will be frank with you: it still hurts. But there is such a thing as pride, and I did what I had to do.

Most opera fans still remember, even today, the front-page stories elicited by the stormy quarrel between Rudolf Bing and Maria Callas. Callas, singing in Texas at the time, informed Mr. Bing that she could not manage her coming schedule at the Metropolitan, which called for her to sing a dramatic soprano role one night and a light soprano role a mere two days later. He, understandably, did not wish to change the schedule and held her to the legal contract. (Whether Bing knew it or not, the spectre he feared so much—concerts paying more than the Met—had raised its head in this squabble. Meneghini, Callas's husband, later revealed that they wanted Maria to be fired so that she could sing more money-making concerts.) Opposing points of view from these two glamorous combatants invariably made headlines. This occasion prompted the press to revive old grudges against Bing for his handling of the Melchior affair. Bing, "more a top sergeant than an artistic statesman," was castigated for breaking Lauritz Melchior and Helen Traubel "by petty derogation and insinuations that they had passed their usefulness." Others asked, "Who is Mr. Bing to dictate standards of behavior and chase Lauritz Melchior and Helen Traubel . . . and now Maria Callas?"

The reference to Helen Traubel concerned the launching of her nightclub career, at the Chez Paree in Chicago in September 1953. By October the papers were full of the details of her resignation from the Metropolitan. Bing had told her that she could not appear in nightclubs or hotel night spots, and handed her a token contract for three or four appearances at the Metropolitan. (The question of why Bing forbade his opera singers to appear in a nightclub while affirming his desire to remove the elitist image of opera remained unanswered.) Refusing to be bullied, Traubel took a public stand and tossed the contract back, incidentally gaining at the cost of three or four thousand dollars a million dollars' worth of publicity. (Kolodin commented wryly, "Bing is no scholar of American psychology." Still, Traubel's forays into "short-hair" music were not as successful or as lengthy as Melchior's. Somehow he seemed to be having more fun.) With the defection of Traubel, the leading singers of the German wing had now disappeared, as well as the Wagner matinee performance cycle.

American baritone Robert Merrill was, after Melchior, the next singer of whom Rudolf Bing made an example. Merrill went off to Hollywood in April 1951, violating his contractual obligations to the Met tour. Said Bing, "As of today [Merrill] is no longer a member of the Metropolitan Opera." The press made many comparisons with the Melchior case (which was probably what Bing desired) although Melchior had sinned only by omission. Bing made Merrill wait for absolution. When Merrill tried to effect a reconciliation in August at Bayreuth, Bing said, "He is still formerly of the Met. I usually mean what I say." In time Merrill humbled himself sufficiently and was restored to the fold, all privileges intact.

That Kleinchen was extremely apprehensive about the problems issuing from the Metropolitan disaster is apparent from a letter that Davidson wrote to her in February 1950 while the couple was in Texas fulfilling some of Lauritz's concert obligations. Davidson chided her a little about her impatience:

> Things are going along very nicely. Don't rush me. You may be sure that I am working constantly on radio, TV, and concerts. There is even some talk again about the Decca deal. I consider Lauritz's position as never better. It is not so much the business of grabbing things quickly; it is the business of taking only the best things.

Then Davidson referred to the "Firestone Hour," that most prestigious serious music program, on which Lauritz had appeared on February 6, the Monday following the excitement at the Met.

> I know very well the Firestone Show was a big success, and if you just let me work this business quietly I am quite sure Lauritz will be on Firestone next season. But all of these deals require time and patience.

A charming letter from California typifies the fine response to the highly successful broadcast: "Your performance . . . compelled me and all others . . . to accept you as the greatest heroic tenor alive today, and perhaps that has lived or will live. I know no greater." Kleinchen was not reassured, however, for she knew that when a major singer was not booked yearly on the "Firestone Hour," it was a bad sign. Already uneasy about the following year, she was taking it out on Davidson so as not to disturb Lauritz.

Was there really a need for worry about their financial condition? Davidson appeared unperturbed, unaffected by Kleinchen's pessimistic outlook. To him, interest in Melchior seemed to be unflagging. The short version of

Tristan was doing very well; it had drawn a crowd of 10,000 in St. Louis. In fact, for the 1950–1951 season he had been booked to sing thirty-six solo concerts, nine benefits, fourteen radio broadcasts, and many performances of the shortened *Tristan*.

But Kleinchen's instincts were to prove more accurate than Davidson's. The bonanza 1950–1951 season had all been booked in advance before the Met debacle, but for the coming 1951–1952 season very few concerts were on the books. Kleinchen did her part to swell the family coffers by doing ads for Wunda-Weve Carpets and Utica Sheets. She even, by sheer force of will, prevailed upon Lauritz to accept an invitation from an Allentown, Pennsylvania, department store owner named Hess, whose habit it was to invite Met artists—and pay them $5,000—to come to a party. Kleinchen thought it would be an easy and fun way to pick up such a fee. At the party no one asked Lauritz to sing and he was embarrassed to think he wasn't earning his money. Finally he asked timidly, "Does anyone mind if I sing?" Having sung only five songs, Lauritz wanted to return the check. Kleinchen forbade it. "It wouldn't be elegant," said Lauritz. Kleinchen retorted with finality, "You are not elegant. You are a singer."

As to artistic worries, Lauritz retained a dignified attitude toward his great disappointment, not speaking publicly about his feelings, admitting only that he didn't like the new administration, elaborating little even to his family: "Bing didn't want me there any longer, so I didn't sing again at the Met." Yet it was clear to all that his feelings were deeply hurt. It was the most profound sadness that life had dealt him. He would never recover fully from its effects. In the 1951–1952 season he had tried to reconstruct the semblance of a jubilee year even without the Metropolitan, but it had been uphill work. Only three events had given him pleasure.

At the January 28, 1951, silver jubilee of Melchior's American concert stage debut, President and Mrs. Truman joined in paying tribute to the tenor at his Constitution Hall concert. During the intermission the National Sesquicentennial Commission presented Melchior with a medal citing him as a "great artist and an outstanding American citizen."

Friends from the Met got together and designed a scroll titled "25th Anniversary, Metropolitan Opera, 1926–1951," which featured six original pencil drawings of Melchior as various Wagnerian heroes and one pose in evening dress, surrounded by the signatures of 182 Met associates, including Eleanor Belmont (Met patroness), Jussi Björling, Lucrezia Bori, Jerome Hines, Herbert Janssen, Robert Merrill, Jarmila Novotna, Fritz Reiner, Eleanor Steber, Richard Tucker, Bruno Walter, and Leonard Warren.

The Melchiors' silver wedding anniversary on May 26, 1950, was a matter of great joy and pride to Lauritz. He intended to celebrate it in New York, Copenhagen, and Los Angeles. With a group of their California friends and their wives they celebrated at The Viking: Nelson Eddy, Jean Hersholt, Victor Borge, Tom and Vally Knudsen, Walter Slezak, and Joe Pasternak, along with Jeanette MacDonald and Gene Raymond, plus many others less renowned. (One of their favorite Hollywood guests was Lassie, the collie movie star.) Lauritz bought a 56-carat emerald for his wife, but the real present was a yard-high red heart surrounded with white lace. In the center was a poem, composed by Lauritz. Originally in rhyming Danish, the English translation was much publicized:

Together for 25 years, we lived and fought;/God gave us happiness and calmed the waves, You paved my way; you created my name,/And sunshine we found in each other's arms, What can I give my darling today/Which she will really like? The warmth in my heart will never cool,/At daylight, or at night, when I sleep. If you were sad, I was to blame,/But you always forgave me. May sun more than rain be with us for long,/Until the time comes for the meadows of eternity.

Admittedly, since Lauritz left financial concerns entirely in Kleinchen's capable hands, she was more concerned about their "precarious" position than he. A 1957 robbery at The Viking did nothing to stem her fears. In fact, it left Kleinchen shaken by the trauma, in mental retreat, and feeling even more vulnerable to financial loss than before. In hindsight it is difficult to understand her money worries, when the total of the stolen items was known to be $250,000, a sum that now translates to several million, and fully insured.

Thanks to the enormous publicity surrounding the public appearances of the Melchiors, the beautiful jewels and furs owned by Kleinchen had been described in detail many times by the press. Everyone knew that the jewel collection, contributing to her personal aura of wealth and beauty, was grouped with those of Mrs. Alfred I. DuPont, Mrs. Robert Guggenheim, Jessie Woolworth, and the Duchess of Windsor. Kleinchen's nervousness about this proved justifiable one night in June. Lauritz was watching television when the doorbell rang. Kleinchen opened the door to find Willa the housekeeper standing on the doorstep. Immediately four men, faces hidden by nylon stockings pulled over their heads, stepped out of the shadows, and, brandishing .45-calibre automatics, pushed Willa aside. Kleinchen was told to keep her mouth shut. Nothing would happen to her. They just wanted the money and the jewelry. It was clear that they knew the household and exactly how many persons lived in it. Kleinchen had often stated her conviction that cooperation with thieves was the only sensible way to react to a robbery. Promising to give the robbers anything they wanted, she begged them not to hurt her mother, who was at the swimming pool in her wheelchair. The leader questioned Kleinchen: "Where are the jewels?" Lauritz was not entirely in agreement with Kleinchen's theory of passive cooperation, but he had not yet made up his mind what to do. He led them to the silver cabinet.

"Quit stalling. This isn't what we want. Where are the goodies?"

Kleinchen quickly capitulated. She took them to the library and opened the two safes. The criminals put thirty pieces of jewelry, including the

Anastasia diamonds, into a pair of socks. They stuffed the furs (leopard, nutria, seal, ermine, otter, and two sable coats worth $100,000) into shopping bags. One of the robbers said, "Let's go. I think we've got it all."

"This isn't all," said another. "how about the watch with the diamond bracelet? We know you've got an emerald ring worth $20,000. Where is it?" After they were given these pieces, the robbers stopped to pick up a box of 100 cigars. On the way back to the living room the leader tossed all of Lauritz's ties to his cohorts and told them to "tie 'em up." As they turned to deal with Lauritz, they froze with shock. As an expert at dying (227 hours of Act III Tristan-expiring alone), he put on a wonderful imitation of a heart attack. The sixty-seven-year-old huffed and puffed, rolled his eyes, sagged in his chair, and feigned death throes. When the robbers brought him a glass of water, he let himself fall onto the floor. There they tied him up and left him. The leader sent one man out to start the car and honk when it was ready. At the signal, he pushed the button that controlled the front gate. To Lauritz this meant the robbers *knew* how much time they had before the gate would close automatically. It took Lauritz less than a minute to untie himself after they fled. He spent no time untying the others, but rushed down the stairs to the hunting room, picked up his rifle, ran through the garage and fired some shots after them as they were turning the corner. Back into the house he ran, found the one phone whose wires they had not cut, called the police, and only then set the others free.

The robbery story filled newspapers from coast to coast. Lauritz was proven right in suspecting a former employee. The brains behind the $250,000 venture had been Melchior's 1947 butler. Once the jewels and the furs were recovered, every major magazine, including *Time*, *Life*, and *Look*, featured a picture of Lauritz and Kleinchen, knee-deep in recovered furs and jewels at the police station.

Although after the anniversary year Kleinchen tried to persuade Lauritz to spend more time enjoying the comforts of his home and the pleasures of California life, he would not face the realities of the situation and reiterated his intention to sing for another ten years. Casting about for a solution, Davidson came up with "variety shows," a new term for what was essentially vaudeville, now given between showings of a film. Chicago had made an offer for five half-hour shows a day. Melchior could choose the material, and he would begin on November 9, 1951, his act a companion to a Betty Grable movie.

Lauritz was as ignorant of this genre of show business as was Kleinchen, but he was captivated by the enormity of the challenge and persuaded by her calculation that Lauritz could reach 300,000 people in two weeks! Determined to begin with Siegmund's "Spring Song," he brushed aside the fact that Wagner would be a stranger to his audience. Eight strapping Scandi-navian singers, The Singing Vikings, would aid him in his latest crusade to bring good music to the masses.

To Wagner-lovers it was a disgrace that such a man should be reduced to performing in a vaudeville show, however it was disguised as a "star turn," and that "Winterstürme" should be sung in such a setting. They were shocked that Lauritz Melchior, the internationally revered Tristan, should be billed together with Sharkey the Seal, and even worse, that a most undignified picture of Melchior and that seal (the second attraction on the bill) should be reprinted nationwide. As might be expected, Melchior loved Sharkey almost as much as Sharkey loved him, and his evening clothes began to take on a distinct odor of fish. Nothing dimmed Lauritz's enthusiasm for the project. At sixty-one he was doing dress rehearsals at 7:00 A.M. and five shows a day with interviews, appointments, and veterans' hospital concerts all sandwiched in between shows.

There were, of course, larger ramifications to this appearance than the dismay it caused Wagnerites.

> On [Melchior's] first theater date, opera stars and theater men are watch-ing the experiment with bated breath. The path will be paved for other opera singers to reap the pot of gold waiting in the wings. Theater operators hit hard by TV will be pulling for Melchior to be a smash.

Everyone who was anyone in the business was watching. Statements that bore a surprising resemblance to sociological research, not untouched by business savvy, began to suggest that the legends of the Metropolitan Opera Company's stuffiness might have been only products of movie scripts. Grad-ually, it was noticed that ordinary folk relish the humbling of the mighty, and if the humbled mighty take it sportingly, they grow, paradoxically, to heroic stature. It appeared that opera stars could manage to be entertainers, too. *Variety*, as usual, saw beyond the obvious, and recognized the import of Melchior's choice of music:

> Melchior here in his vaudfilm debut has eschewed the usual trend of the longhair going comedic. He does straight singing with little devia-tion. That such a routine would excite bravos from an early morning audience is certainly a rarity in vaude, but that's exactly what greeted Melchior here. . . . Melchior at past 60 certainly can give pointers to many youngsters in this business during his five and six a day!

An enthusiastic Chicago critic caught the essence of the real Melchior as he waxed poetic:

> All the way down in the last row of the big auditorium I felt the old Melchior spell, the greatness of this man, the warmheartedness of this wonderful artist. He was himself on this new stage, was not conde-scending, and did not pretend his happiness. This is a man who loves life and wishes all the best for his fellow people.

With this pronouncement Lauritz felt himself vindicated and stopped apologizing for having performed in this branch of the entertainment industry. Strangely, however, Melchior continued to take the brunt of the criticism while many other serious singers escaped censure for their defections to show-biz's greener pastures. As we have seen, fellow Wagnerian Helen Traubel was pursuing a nightclub career. Pinza and Merrill would follow Melchior's trail-blazing footsteps in the gambling palaces of Las Vegas. Mimi Benzell, a most beautiful Queen of the Night at the Met, gave it up for Broadway musicals and very elegant nightclubs, as did mezzo-soprano Irra Pettina.

Stimulated by the Chicago engagement, Lauritz changed his mind about not singing on Broadway, although it was not to be a musical. Previously he had been adamantly against performing in musicals because he was convinced that it would be unbearably boring to sing the same music eight times a week. Not only did he capitulate in 1952, but, in defiance of his own logic, he accepted a contract that would make it necessary to sing the very same material for two shows every day.

Seven blocks up Broadway from the Metropolitan Opera, the Palace Theater had been host to Judy Garland that winter in a nineteen-week appearance that became a legend in show business. Lost in his Wagnerian and hunting world, Lauritz was completely unaware of the brilliant success Garland had enjoyed. The question soon came up concerning who should follow Judy Garland at the Palace. Great stars on both sides of the Atlantic— Gypsy Rose Lee, Jimmy Durante, Maurice Chevalier, and even Margaret Truman, it was said— had turned down the opportunity to do so, so great had been Garland's success. Jim Davidson mentioned none of this to Kleinchen when he tried to persuade her that Lauritz should be the next performer at the Palace. He merely told her that it would require only two shows a day for two weeks, and that other great Metropolitan singers had appeared there: Emma Calvé, the Ponselle sisters, Luisa Tetrazzini, to mention a few. Still Kleinchen hesitated. It was one thing to appear in Chicago, but in New York City itself! There would be much outrage from Wagner fans.

Lauritz recognized no risk. He accepted at once, genuinely inspired as usual by the prospect of reaching more people with his music, no matter that others thought his rationale merely a cover for self-serving financial interest. His thirty minutes would be a mini-concert, beginning again with Siegmund's aria, then "Die beiden Grenadiere" of Schumann, Grieg's "Jeg elsker dig," finishing with some show tunes. The story of Judy Garland's last performance at the Palace is folklore by now, but what few remember is that Melchior was in the audience that night. Garland had sung on and on. Finally, sitting on the stage apron in the famous clown costume with her legs hanging over the edge, she asked what more she could do. Lauritz stood up and started the audience singing "Auld Lang Syne." It was a glorious moment.

Similarly, one critic said about Melchior's Palace performances that the very sight of Melchior gave the audience its money's worth. But in his typical Melchior way he gave them generously of his rich voice and personality. . . . His voice was as fresh and powerful and beautiful sounding as always. . . . This wonderful strength and endurance . . . were still undiminished.

Nevertheless, Kleinchen's fears were realized when Irving Kolodin, juxta-posing Melchior and Flagstad in a cruel financial accounting, wrote:

> Final returns for the Lauritz Melchior engagement at the Palace Theater showed a skimpy $19,000 in business for his second week, $23,000 the first. By contrast, the first *Alceste* with Kirsten Flagstad at the Met brought in $26,265 for this single performance. To be sure, it was a benefit for the Metropolitan Production Fund at raised prices—but even so. . . .

When, in 1954, Melchior broke his vow never to do a musical comedy, there were extenuating circumstances. First of all, there was the fishing. Then there was the entrance on an elephant, and the harem of beautiful dancing girls. The part he was offered was the Sultan of Baghdad in Guy Lombardo's lavish production of *Arabian Nights* in the open-air Marine Thea-ter of Jones Beach on Long Island. Yes, the part was larger than life, and appealed to his sense of drama; yes, he would only have to sing four songs; but Kleinchen knew very well what had really tipped the scales to make Lauritz consent. When he realized that he could fish the lagoon during his offstage moments, he accepted at once. For her the $5,000 weekly salary was more important. To the various reporters who covered the opening Melchior offered several quips: "I'm a lucky man to get a new bride every night at my age," and, "It's a good summer job." The press, in return, noted that both Melchior and the elephant could be seen from the farthest seat in the house, and that the audience had complained that the Melchior voice when aided by microphones was far too loud for comfort.

On the night of the premiere, Lauritz rode the elephant, but after a slight accident on the second night, Kleinchen put an end to all that. Never-theless, Lauritz had long chats with the elephant, and soon they were as close as he and Sharkey the Seal had been. Like a pet dog, the elephant would follow him to and from the stage. Lauritz savored everything about the show: his colleagues, the $5,000 salary, the card games with the stage-hands, the beautiful "mermaids," even the storms. The cold, driving rains had an effect on all the voices except that of Melchior, who, by his continued good health, did his usual job of denying the cover singer a chance to appear. In this case, James McCracken, the understudy, collected his pay for two summers (it was done again in 1955) without going on a single time. As late as 1961, critic Herbert Kupferberg recalled Melchior's part in the production: "It wasn't much of a show. But in the midst of all the nonsense came one unforgettable moment when Melchior suddenly unleashed one of his well-remembered high notes, squarely on pitch and with all the gleam of his old days."

Lauritz's involvement in the *Arabian Nights* stemmed in part from his satisfaction with variety theater experiences. In addition to abandoning his interdiction against doing musical comedy, there had been another result of these appearances in Chicago and at the Palace in 1953. In the midst of Kleinchen's fretting about finances, television and radio offers continued unabated; advertising agencies still found Melchior's name attractive. Night-clubs, too, persisted in wooing the Great Dane, but the singer would not yield to their blandishments. Nightclubs meant singing while waiters wove their way through the audience delivering drinks. Never!

What he *would* like to do, he had decided, was a traditional tour for a live audience with a format inspired by his experiences singing with those young Vikings in his variety theater engagements. He would call it "The Lauritz Melchior Show," and it would have musical samples, "a music menu with opera as the main course and Hit Parade tunes for dessert," starring six young, attractive, and talented singers, and two pianists.

Lauritz's idea served two purposes: it created an opportunity to keep him singing, and it gave a larger purpose to his performing. In a sense, presenting these young singers to the world and helping them get started in their careers took the place of his former high calling and devotion to Wagner. Although it was evident to Kleinchen that Lauritz could not be happy without performing, she did not limit herself to cooperating with his dream. Making sure that it would be a money-making proposition as well kept her busy at the kind of business detail that fulfilled her. The first public announcement of the impending "Lauritz Melchior Show" went out in January 1952. By June their new manager, Martin Wagner of Hollywood (Jim Davidson had retired), succeeded in booking a four-month tour to start in January 1953. Kleinchen was going to act as company manager on the road, where, for the first time, Melchior did not take a set fee, but rather a fifty percent cut of the proceeds. Her first act was to strike a deal with the Chrysler Corporation for free cars in return for cooperation in their advertising.

Each detail of the actual implementation of this project gave Melchior pleasure. He happily devoted August and September to auditioning over 100 singers and pianists on both coasts. In October he made his final choice: Angelene Collins and I were to be the two sopranos; Val Valente and Alan Wemmer, tenors; Michael Roberts, baritone; and Edward Williams, bass. Angelene Collins recalls that Melchior did everything but check her teeth while he made sure that she was healthy enough to withstand the rigors of touring. George Roth and Ted Sadlowski were the pair of pianists he selected. (Roth's contribution to the program also included making the arrangements, one of which was a choral rendition of the musical introduction, which ended, "Presenting Lauritz Melchior!" in six-part harmony. Under the considerable stresses of touring for five long months, when devilish impulses occasionally run rampant, the group was known to rearrange these consonants so that the phrase ran, "Presenting Laurit Ssmellquire!")

Rehearsals began at The Viking before Christmas, Lauritz attired, somewhat to the amazement of us young singers, in gigantic Lederhosen and nothing else. Although not much was ever written about Melchior's predilection for nudity, there exist several highly amusing stories of his shedding clothing in semi-public places (such as between the stage and the dressing room). Best among them is this: Mutti, Kleinchen, and Leonard Eisner (who later remarked, "I think Melchior was a frustrated nudist") awaited Lauritz at the glass-topped table on the terrace of The Viking. He arrived for lunch, wearing not a stitch of clothing. As he sat, someone quietly murmured, "Bon appetit." Kleinchen, calmly averting her eyes, handed Lauritz an opened napkin, saying kindly, "At least cover it, Schatzi darling." Another time, when only the Laufkötters were present, Lauritz appeared wearing nothing but an open topcoat and a deftly placed bouquet. Kleinchen was always more fastidious than her husband about matters of exposure, but did find a humorous element in nudity. At one of the couple's California anniversaries, she and Lauritz entered ostensibly clad in evening dress. But when they turned around, their nether portions were bare.

Melchior especially enjoyed giving technical advice to the male singers, whom he had lying on the floor of The Viking living room with belts loosened and collars unbuttoned, in order to teach them the "difficult art of breathing" and to show Ed Williams, the bass, how to sing low notes. Curiously, Melchior never lost his childlike pride in his own bottom notes. Somehow, he seldom found it necessary to convince others of his capacity to sing high notes, but he never tired of showing off his ability to sing bass notes. Nor was he put off by having to lie on the floor to be able to gargle them on pitch. (Holger Boland, Danish opera singer and stage director, told how proud Melchior was, even in the 1960s, that he had once sung the bass role of Antonio: "I really think that I could still sing a bass role. Do you want to hear how I can manage the low D?" Melchior then pounded out the low D with a "trombone-like tone," adding with laughter, "And when we have partied after a *Pagliacci*, the following day I have a C . . . but then I cannot, damn it, sing Tannhäuser the following evening.")

No detail was too small to catch Kleinchen's eye. Ed Williams, being the tallest man in the company, was too close to Lauritz's height for Kleinchen, who told him to have the heels of his dress shoes redone with the thinnest lifts possible. "Lauritz is the star. He must be the tallest man on stage." The new lifts successfully rendered Williams one-quarter inch shorter than Lauritz and made Kleinchen content.

In order to lure Lauritz into performing in Las Vegas, Kleinchen took a calculated risk, suggesting that the young performers be given a chance to try out their roles one week before leaving on the tour proper. Lauritz surprised her by immediately championing the idea. But where could they do this?

"In Las Vegas," responded Kleinchen unhesitatingly. Forestalling any of Lauritz's objections, she quickly enumerated the advantages: there was a nightclub with a huge stage; there would be no food or beverage service during the performance; spending some time in Las Vegas could be a free vacation for them. What she didn't say was that Las Vegas was the most ruthless, cutthroat showplace in the world, that in that gambling town there had never been a show featuring serious singers, that the highest paid performers in the popular-music business would be his competition. Probably Lauritz would have elected to go on with it, even had his wife warned him. He was totally confident when it came to presenting his ideas to the public.

Lauritz intrepidly opened his show at the Congo Room of Hotel Sahara on January 6, 1953. When the review came out, he was honestly surprised to read in the *Daily Variety* that there had been "sombre predictions":

> Lauritz Melchior's amazing show at The Sahara hits dead center and must make pessimists eat their sombre predictions again. That Melchior chose one of the hardest places in the country for his premiere is either good judgment of his own show or contempt for death—or both. Despite the predictions, Melchior's name draws. Melchior himself and his entire company receive[d] loud and persistent applause from beginning to end. Such a form of appreciation is not found too often in this city of gambling, which is oversaturated with top names in showbiz.

As noted in trade papers, Melchior's success inspired "bosses along the Vegas Strip into hiring longhair," and changed the face of entertainment in that city. The "Lauritz Melchior Show" had made people recognize "the inferior products you usually settle for in the nightclubs." Lauritz, for one, was not the least surprised to find that his show had beat all audience records for any show presented in Las Vegas. "Melchior and his assemblage could tour indefinitely." So great was his success that the two performances a night (three on the weekend) were invariably sold out. The Sahara, rather amazed at the standing ovations ending each show, especially since the troupe offered such oddities as operatic arias and a view of the actual faces of the singers ("usually the faces of our nightery singers are stuck into the microphone. . . . The Melchior folk take a four-foot-away stance!"), asked the Melchiors to bring the show back any time that was convenient.

Kleinchen was generally delighted with the offers that were pouring in, but at a loss to explain the poor showing in the south. Soon she came to the conclusion that this state of affairs was directly traceable to my being the current winner of the Marian Anderson Award. Reasoning that southern impresarios assumed me to be a Black singer, she had a special photo taken of her husband and me. Disgracefully, she was proven right. After the picture was sent to southern bookers, all was well.

In her satisfaction with the way things were going, Kleinchen decided to dress up the show by allowing the two sopranos to wear her diamonds during the performance. My own share included a necklace of diamonds (so large that they resembled pebbles rather than precious stones) set in platinum, each setting connected to the next one by a tiny platinum hook that enabled the length to be altered; on my arm a platinum and diamond bracelet two inches wide, hinged to make the "leaves" float; on the neckline of my gown a platinum anemone-shaped brooch three inches in diameter and studded with diamonds. The three pieces totalled approximately 200 carats and must have been roughly 5,000 times more expensive than my gown. One night in the dressing room a beautiful, tall, scantily clad Sahara chorus girl looked disparagingly at the blinding brilliance with which I was accoutered.

"Don't you think all them rhinestones are a bit much, honey?"

"I beg your pardon," I said, affronted. "These are some of the Russian crown jewels."

"Tell me about it," she said dryly, turning her beautiful, bare back.

Who could fault her disbelief? Even Angelene and I couldn't imagine why we were loaned these valuable pieces. Our nervousness, already extreme, was heightened when Kleinchen failed to collect the jewels after the last show each evening. Protecting my own pieces was a difficult job in the spartan lodgings farther out of town to which company members were assigned. Our motel did have a safe, and that is where the royal jewels resided many nights, until the Melchiors' insurance man turned up and, thoroughly horrified at the circumstances, confiscated them. No longer were we allowed to spiff up our gowns with the genuine article, but the relief was enormous.

Melchior had a bit of trouble getting his *Pagliacci* segment—"Vesti la giubba" was the high point of the show—in shape. During the first rehearsal he spent a lot of time teaching the drummer from the dance band, pressed into service for the aria, how to do the few dramatic bars of percussion with which he wished the aria to begin. Finally, at a very early hour in the morning, he had it worked out his way. Unfortunately, at the opening that night a new drummer was substituted, a real jazz musician. Left alone in those few bars before Canio's entrance, he worked himself into an orgiastic frenzy of improvisatory riffs and explosions that were totally unrecognizable as Leoncavallo. Lauritz entered on cue in his clown costume, albeit clearly suffering from shock. Always a trouper, he gamely completed the aria, with an eye to disciplining the drummer before the second show.

The attractions of around-the-clock gambling were not lost on Lauritz. He arose at his usual late hour. After breakfast, he would immediately cruise the slot machines, clad in his Carmen clothes. Kleinchen had given him a gambling allowance of $20, which he promptly lost the first half hour of every day. When Mary Markham, the household secretary, arrived from Los Angeles, he persuaded her to loan him money from the household accounts. Apprised of the underhanded methods Lauritz was using to augment his gambling funds, Kleinchen shut off the supply without hesitation. Then, to his delight, Lauritz discovered that the hotel would advance monies against the hotel bill for gambling purposes. Taking advantage of this windfall, he continued to play, having discovered that the dollar slot machines were more fun and made more noise. (They also caused him to lose more money per hour than before.) Kleinchen was oblivious to this chicanery until it came time to check out of the hotel. The rest of us, privy to Melchior's losses, were uneasy as we assembled in the Sahara lobby, waiting for departure. Kleinchen approached the desk to check out. Suddenly there came a histrionic shriek: "Gott im Himmel! Vot you got here? Gold sheets? $7,000 for one week!!!" Sheepishly Lauritz hung his head, ten-gallon hat and all. By the time the "Lauritz Melchior Show" returned to the spa later that year, Lauritz no longer gambled at all.

It was in Bartlesville, Oklahoma, that Kleinchen's mania for saving money became embarrassingly apparent. The entire company had some rare free time after traveling and we decided to go to an afternoon movie. While waiting in the lobby for the next showing to commence, we were startled to see Kleinchen sweep in, followed by the great man himself. Kleinchen asked the ticket-taker to bring the manager out. Thereupon she announced portentously, "*I* am Mrs. Lauritz Melchior, and *this* is my husband."

The bewildered manager looked helplessly from little Kleinchen to giant Lauritz. "So?" he replied, clearly unenlightened by this announcement.

"Do you not wish to invite us to your theater?"

"Lady, if you mean do I want to let you in free, the answer is no. No one gets in here without a ticket."

Kleinchen exited in a huff, followed by a woebegone Lauritz. He had really wanted to see the movie, even if it did cost 40 cents.

Later in the tour Kleinchen tried to economize by purchasing an instrument for tuning a piano, intending to bypass the local piano tuner's fee. Unfortunately, she could not unravel the mysteries of its function, nor could the two pianists get the hang of it. In the end a real piano tuner was called when necessary, but Kleinchen never stopped grumbling about the unnecessary five-dollar expense.

When it came to holding trains and planes, however, she was a whiz. One day a record snowfall made it necessary for the company to take a train. As I came up the platform of the Oklahoma City station alongside the train that was clearly ready to depart, clad in my all-purpose, tent-like traveling coat, Kleinchen appeared out of the noisy clouds of steam. She pulled me aside. "Lauritz is still with the dentist. I have to delay the train. Go back to the station house and sit down. Keep your coat closed. You are pregnant and we are waiting for the doctor to give you permission to leave," she hissed, scarcely moving her mouth.

When Lauritz finally appeared at the station, Kleinchen hustled me on board and hovered around until the conductor had collected the tickets. With her prevarications about my "condition," she had charmed the engineer, the conductor, and the dispatcher into holding the train. That night, with a massive swelling on the side of his jaw, Melchior sang, aided by a swallow of whiskey handed him each time he passed Kleinchen's station in the wings. And how he sang! I, playing the Merry Widow, had always had some difficulty dancing with the Boss, whose waltzing style closely resembled a game of Snap the Whip. This night, on Tulsa's raked stage, with a partner who was by now definitely under more than medicinal influence, I held on to his enormous bulk more grimly than usual and worked harder at maintaining the smile on my face. The male members of the company had a pool going. Would this be the night when I would actually be cast into the pit during the waltz? As ever, Melchior's stamina triumphed. We finished the dance still clasped together.

Nothing could deter Melchior from taking part in the yearly celebration held by the Guards. Accordingly, the entire company detoured past New York for that occasion. The company members thoroughly enjoyed the entrance parade led by the commander-in-chief, Lauritz, to a cadence sounded by one violin and an accordion; the rousing cheers to King Frederik with each glass of aquavit; the wonderful food; Melchior's rendering of "Vesti la giubba" in which he confounded the efforts of the pianists who had mischievously put the aria back up into the original key without informing him. (His face changed from red to purple as he worked his way through the piece, but he triumphed.)

There were many examples of Melchior's famed waywardness with rhythm and pitch during the five months the company spent together, but none so amusing as an incident in Chattanooga, Tennessee, related by his accompanist, Roth. For some reason Melchior had fastened upon Ezio Pinza's *South Pacific* solo, "Some Enchanted Evening," as the piece for him. Unfortunately, he found both the rhythmic structure of the piece and the ascending minor thirds of the last coda difficult to negotiate. The accompanist patiently pounded out the tune and the rhythm on the piano for Melchior at odd moments before their arrival in Chattanooga, where it was to be sung with orchestra. As written, the famous first line, "Some enchanted evening," is echoed by the orchestra before the singer goes on to "You may see a stranger." Melchior, however, could never be bothered with waiting for the orchestral echo; he just forged ahead. Consequently, by the end of two lines, he was far ahead of the orchestra, and the distance was increasing with each succeeding line. Soon the situation was so ludicrous that the distraught conductor threw up his hands and the orchestra gradually stopped playing, leaving Melchior to tackle the coda on his own. Several times he tried to finish the ascending thirds that make up the last "Never let him go," but, not succeeding, somehow segued back to the beginning to have yet another go at "Some enchanted evening." The final ignominious ending was sung a cappella, and in the wrong key. A friend asked incredulously after the performance, "Who made that terrible arrangement?"

Next to musical foibles, the company suffered most from Melchior's black cigars. In a typically Melchiorian democratic gesture he had decreed that we would all take turns riding in the lead car with him and Kleinchen. What he never knew was that we drew lots to avoid this duty because of the debilitating effect of his cigar smoke in the enclosed car. Often the captive singer was also lectured on the salubrious effects of smoking cigars or breathing in secondhand fumes. We remained unpersuaded.

There were other major perils when riding with the Boss. One was the possibility of losing one's life. Seated in the right front seat, puffing on an enormous cigar that seemed never to diminish under our watchful eyes, he would direct the driver. Silently, he would shoot his hand and arm to the left, directly into the vision of the chauffeur, signalling a left turn. Another favorite gesture was the one used by John Wayne when calling "Wagons Ho!" In a gigantic left-hand movement akin to an overhand discus throw or a basketball "slam dunk," he indicated that the driver should proceed straight ahead. Even if the riders escaped a car crash resulting from these maneuvers, Melchior was inevitably wrong when choosing the direction in which to travel. The lead car was frequently lost, with the result that, upon arrival, those singers would have to choose between eating dinner, steaming wrinkles out of the evening wear, showering, or vocalizing. (Although Melchior never warmed up, the rest of the company, like most singers, found it expedient to do so.)

During the tour the Sahara phoned Kleinchen constantly, offering an outrageous fee, rumored to be $45,000 a week, if Melchior would come back at once. She persuaded Martin Wagner to postpone two weeks of the tour so that the company could again perform at the Sahara. The company members were still given the same fee per week as they had received on the road, even though Las Vegas demanded two shows an evening, three on Saturday. All complaints by the participants were fielded expertly by Kleinchen. She pitted performer against performer and stood her ground, winning each encounter hands down.

Clearly Melchior had drastically changed his opinion about me resembling Kirsten Flagstad (because of my excessive preoccupation with vocalizing), for, on our second trip to Las Vegas, he now announced that I was "just like Rosa Ponselle." Once again I was briefly thrilled until he went on to add, "all personality and very little voice." First, the great Ponselle scarcely seemed to fit this description, and secondly, it occurred to me that Melchior, notoriously suggestible, had been speaking to a Sahara busboy whose opinion I knew that to be.

Melchior was equally changeable in points of style. I was hired to sing Sieglinde to his Seigmund (a bit of casting for which I was understandably most grateful) in excerpts of *Walküre*. Before long, the realities of the American concert marketplace had suggested to him and Kleinchen another tack. I was instructed to prepare "Stormy Weather." As I limped my way through this classic in a fashion that could only be described as "square," Melchior (not too "round" himself) would stand in the wings and direct at me a Wagnerian whisper audible in the first twenty rows, "MORE SEX!!!"

The tour reviews were absolutely wonderful. The houses were full— that is, until the end of February when the audiences inexplicably began to shrink. The explanation was eventually discovered to be the pronounced innocence of the average American moviegoer. In April and May of the previous year Melchior had been shooting a movie for Paramount, *The Stars Are Singing*, in which he had a demanding role, that of a reformed alcoholic singer, opposite Anna Maria Alberghetti. As he had hoped, the movie proved that he was an excellent actor, perhaps too good. Thousands of his fans were convinced that he was the role he played: an unshaven drunkard who would have ruined his daughter's future. Although the movie contained flashbacks to his earlier days as a great opera singer and although, logically, these singing sequences must have been recorded during the shooting of the movie, the audiences stayed away from his concerts, believing he could no longer sing.

In the future Kleinchen never wavered from her conviction that this movie, by changing her husband's image in the minds of the movie public from an adorable, twinkly, good-natured, grandfatherly opera singer to a not-so-admirable character who scarcely sang at all, effectively ended his popularity and consequently his filmmaking days. When the image goes, said the popular Hollywood wisdom, so goes the career. "It is the greatest mistake I have ever made," she declared, forgetting the misadventure with Rudolf Bing. Kleinchen had moved mountains to have the movie released at exactly that time, believing that it would contribute to greater audiences during the tour. She had not known that so many people were innocent enough to identify the actor with his role.

Still, it was only the audience for his "classical" concerts that reacted this way, and nightclubs were clamoring for his appearances. They went so far as to offer to build stages to his dimensions and to suspend serving during his performances. Although Melchior, idiosyncratically, had refused to perform on stages built atop dance floors, or in a place where waiters served while he sang, Las Vegas had weakened his resolve, and eventually the monetary concerns became grave enough to force him to change his mind. In addition to the concerts, appearances at clubs in Reno, Dallas, Houston, Montreal, and Washington, D.C., would follow. Once the bad effects of *The Stars Are Singing* dissipated, the pattern of his performing life changed. A concert in a certain town would be followed by an invitation for a nightclub appearance the next year. Television shows swelled the family coffers until Melchior was making more money than any serious singer ever had in America.

After 126 performances, the first "Lauritz Melchior Show" tour (there was another the next year) ended at the Sans Souci nightclub in Quebec City, where the audience rose to its feet and applauded the singers. After the last show I went directly to the bridge spanning the river next to the Château Frontenac, where I joyfully rid myself of one of Kleinchen's "money-saver" tactics that had entailed extreme discomfort for me. For our "Merry Widow" segment, she had procured from the MGM costume department at a distress price a black dress formerly worn by Ann Miller, the great dancer. Unfortunately, Miller was narrower in the chest than I. Trying to breathe like a singer in the dress's narrow bodice was pure torture. At every performance I lost more fragments of the ostrich plumes that decorated the skirt. Soon the molting plumes had transformed the dress into a threadbare embarrassment. As the Boss and I waltzed in his usual athletic style, they floated about the stage. The entire company was hard-pressed to make our gestures appear dramatically motivated as we waved the feathers out of our mouths. I was determined to have a ceremonial disposal of this sartorial abomination after the last show. To the baffled police who, fearing the worst, interrupted me as I was shredding the dress and tossing the pieces over the side of the bridge, I explained that it was only the dress that I intended to do away with. Six singers cheered as they watched the wretched plumes and black tulle float away with the current.

CHAPTER 17

Melchior and the Heldentenor Crisis

(1960–1972)

When the brilliant Swedish soprano Birgit Nilsson appeared on the operatic scene, the entire international Wagnerian picture changed. After Melchior's last season at the Metropolitan Opera, for example, *Tristan und Isolde* had been performed only twelve times. A new production—the first in forty years—was mounted for Nilsson's 1959 debut at the Met. So brilliant was her success that it was carried on the front page of the *New York Times*. Along with the praise lavished upon Nilsson came the ubiquitous laments that she had no comparable tenor with whom to share her repertoire. Said Harold Schonberg, in an article that was a forerunner of many others,

> The world has not seen a true Heldentenor since Melchior was in his prime, and there are no signs of anyone coming along to replace him. . . . The trouble with a big voice like [Nilsson's] is that today there is not a man who can match it in the Wagner repertory. . . . Despite her appearance on the scene, there still may not be a Wagner renaissance, as there was when Flagstad electrified the operatic world a generation ago. Flagstad had her Melchior. For Nilsson's Isolde there is no Tristan, for her Brünnhilde no Siegfried.

Melchior's *amour propre* was given a lift by this lengthy article, and Birgit Nilsson's curiosity about Lauritz was heightened. They finally managed to meet through their mutual friends, the Strasfogels, although it was not to be until a few years after her debut.

Lauritz reflected on the meeting in a letter he sent to Birgit Nilsson on November 21, 1963:

> Also for me the first meeting with you, a famous Wagnerian soprano and a cousin from the other side of the Øresund, was an exciting experience. I felt on seeing you a little like young Siegfried awakening

291

Brünnhilde, and I was sorry that our musical roads came at different times. I am sure that we would have been a nice heroic couple on the stage. Your beautiful flowers will fade away and die, but when I want to look at future artists singing Wagner's works, I can always look at the picture of a great one who is carrying the music and the tradition on in the world until somebody else again carries on from where you left off. Once again my thanks, my admiration, and with the permission of your husband, my love.

A Wagner tenor who missed the boat, Lauritz Melchior

"They both had such a stentorian thrust of tone. How wonderful they would have sounded together," sigh the Strasfogels today. Said Nilsson herself in 1965: "Melchior, there's a real man of steel."

As distressed as Melchior was to have missed singing with Birgit Nilsson, he had not lost his distaste for what Rudolf Bing stood for. Just prior to his seventy-fifth birthday, in 1965, Melchior was interviewed (on the subject of the Metropolitan Opera and his own career there) by National Educational Television. When the release form arrived, Lauritz noted that the program was to be called "The Creative Person—Rudolf Bing." He wrote to NET asking for assurances that his name "would not be in any way whatsoever connected with that of Mr. Bing" since he had "no respect for or interest in what Mr. Bing is doing." Their response was revealing:

> It is essential that we draw a picture of the artists' world that did exist. . . . It is clear that the Met today is not a vital place, not an exciting world. It grows dull, and this is a tragedy. . . . Mme. Lehmann too made it clear that she wanted no part of lauding a man she does not like. . . . The voice of Lauritz Melchior will be used only to help illustrate the era before Bing arrived.

As on every one of his birthdays, affectionate messages poured in from all over the world, many in the form of poetry and, as always, at least one plea for Lauritz to begin his autobiography. One of the California celebrations of his seventy-fifth birthday featured a dinner at the Scandia Restaurant for 200 Danes, twenty former Guards among them, at which the Chancellor of the Knightly Order of Saint Brigitte presented Melchior with their decoration, the Grand Cross. For his eightieth birthday in 1970, there were many requests from British and American fans exhorting the singer, "*Do*, please start a book!" as well as testimonial dinners in New York, Los Angeles, and Copenhagen, and an invitation to the White House from President Nixon.

If it need be asked whether Melchior was esteemed as an important foreign-born citizen of the United States, the answer would be formulated in the August 1967 request from the National Park Service for five or six personal items for their new American Museum to be housed in the base of the Statue of Liberty. The exhibit was to depict the "vast and outstanding contributions of the foreign-born to our democratic way of life." About that same time, Syracuse University, Yale University, Boston University, and the University of Southern California had made repeated and strong suggestions to Melchior that his memorabilia would be welcome at their institutions. In the end, he left his effects to his son Ib, who, in turn, gave them to Dana College, a school founded by Danish pioneers in Blair, Nebraska, where he had sung his first concert in 1950 and to which he had later returned several times to sing with the college choir. The directorate of Dana founded the Lauritz Melchior Memorial Room because Ib Melchior felt that his father's memory would be best served in this manner. Boston University then generously contributed its own collection to that at Dana.

The legendary Melchior stamina, vocal and physical, was evident in his guest appearance at the 13th Annual Liederkranz Scholarship Award Concert at the age of seventy-three. The winners that year included tenor Daniel Marek, who remembers Melchior's baritonal, strong, clear, beautiful tone and the inspirational quality of his singing. The *Times* was in accord:

> But whatever loss of vocal power there is, and it is not as much as you might expect, his appearance brought a bygone age into focus for a few moments. . . . He gave the songs a familiar zest and the ringing exuberance that has been the keystone of his life and art.

Others spoke of Melchior as "brimming with life and erect as ever." The next month he managed "Winterstürme" and "Jeg elsker dig" of Grieg with Stokowski and the American Symphony Orchestra at Adelphi College with the same extraordinary results. All these activities he accomplished despite a grave problem with his left eye and increasing and irreversible deafness in both ears. Those backstage at Adelphi noticed how weakened by back stiffness and other problems he seemed, but the minute the lights hit him on stage, he became the old war horse, ebullient and indefatigable.

The details of the 1967 "Dodger safari" provide proof of Melchior's stamina at the age of seventy-seven, plus an eye-opening view of the expenses involved in such a venture, and evidence of the extremely luxurious conditions under which these safaris were conducted. The so-called "Dodger safari" was conceived by Walter O'Malley, manager of the Los Angeles Dodgers, and his son Peter, who, together with other friends, made up the hunting party. Planning for the trip scheduled for fall of 1967 began in the early months of that year. The fees for each participant covered some exotic items beyond the professional hunter, airfares, hotels, and beverages (this last, a large expense when Lauritz was involved); added to the initial package fee of $4,000 were crating and veterinary fees, fumigation, dipping, and insecticide expenses, dock charges, transportation of the trophies, and hunting licenses.

The Dodger safari went out from Nairobi on the morning of October 15. Complying with Melchior's usual hunting style, Mozambique provided every luxury that could be commanded. The main camp had a lounge/bar/eating "banda" (hut), a kitchen banda, several sleeping bandas with steel cots, bath houses with hot and cold running water, proper toilets, showers, and tub baths. The main camp also boasted a repair shop for the vehicles and equipment, a generator plant, two-way radio communication, a medical dispensary, a well-maintained air strip, and a trophy-handling area carefully positioned so that the odors would not waft into the camp. Even the sub-camps had an open-air eating hut, a kitchen, a laundry hut, and hot showers. Each location was chosen for its attractive physical details, an absence of insects, and the known presence of specific game. The hunters were flown into the main camp; Jeeps or Landrovers were used to set up permanent quarters at the sub-camps using a fifty-mile rotation system so that no hunting party would bump into another. Lauritz managed to bag, among other game, a prize trophy—a bushbuck, two-and-one-half inches bigger than the world-record specimen, and when he returned, burnt brown by the African sun, he looked, said the newspapers, "like a larger-than-life Ernest Hemingway."

When his wife Kleinchen died in February 1963, Lauritz Melchior was dealt the second devastating blow of his life. Although stricken with a heavy cold, Kleinchen had been busy with the preparations of the fiftieth anniversary of Lauritz's debut in opera. On February 23 Lauritz was to sing with the Norwegian Choir in Chicago as part of the celebration. The night before the Chicago flight, Kleinchen was still ill with a very bad cold that had plagued her the entire month of February. Not only would she not go to a doctor, but she insisted on attending the Danish party that evening. Cecily and Christian Castenskiold, close friends, noted how really virulent was Kleinchen's cold, but that a few drinks made her more her jolly self. Nevertheless, that evening she remarked to Mrs. Castenskiold, "I know I'll never make it to sixty." At home, she went to bed early, leaving Lauritz to watch television. The next morning, he decided to let her sleep a little longer and went to order breakfast. When he returned to awaken her, Kleinchen had died, her skin so pale and chalky that she had almost disappeared into the bedclothes.

Looking back later, Lauritz often reflected to his godson and others that Kleinchen had seemed wittier and more beautiful than ever during the Christmas holidays of 1962. Some who were present, however, saw that she had drunk too much, and no longer looked her old self but was actually rather bloated.

Twice, when the noise and revelry of a party were at their peak, Kleinchen had wondered aloud how many more Christmases they would have together. Although she always maintained humorously that she and Lauritz, traveling so often, would undoubtedly perish in a plane crash, many of those close to the Melchiors knew of the fortune teller who had predicted years before that Kleinchen would die when she was sixty. About this time she seemed to be settling her affairs, as if she really believed that she would not be around to deal with them. Lauritz also was entertaining thoughts of his own mortality this year. He had sounded uncharacteristically somber in a May interview:

Nature holds out at me several gifts, several magic senses which not only sharpen my awareness of God but have the power to dissipate my troubles. Nature's first gift is a sense of proportion. . . . I can look up at the heavens and realize what a little bit of a thing I am, a speck on a world that is itself a speck.

The medical reasons behind Kleinchen's death are murky. Whereas the autopsy certificate lists "acute hemorrhagic broncho-pneumonia," common gossip intimated that drink plus too many medications played a part. (The lethal effects of alcohol plus flu remedies were not known then.) During the years after Melchior left the Metropolitan Kleinchen still had duties such as managing "The Lauritz Melchior Show" to occupy her, but already then she was drinking more than she ever had before. In earlier years she had, by all reports, drunk only with dinner and afterwards, as evident in the story that nephew Jørgen Krause mischievously delighted in telling: At a dinner party given by the Melchiors in Copenhagen, Jørgen was the honored guest. The waiter, who knew him, asked, "Is that little lady your aunt?" Jørgen said she was. "I have served eight glasses of beer to that little lady. She has drunk them all and hasn't been to the toilet yet!"

Later, with too few publicity events to mastermind, with too few schedules to organize, leisure depressed her. The Laufkötters, visiting for card games, were disturbed by her frequent trips to the kitchen "for an apple," after which she would become steadily more intoxicated without drinking in front of anyone. This behavior had upset Lauritz terribly. In 1953 I recall her eating for most of her meals just one lone hamburger (without a bun) but drinking a great deal. As Birte said, "The last years were not nice when Far was not on top of the hill. That was too much for her." It is possible that her husband's retirement from an active singing life was more devastating to her than to him.

There is no denying that Kleinchen had been a living, breathing enigma to many. Her public image was an amalgam of her glittering accouterments and a charm so potent that it was awesome. Birte says, "When Kleinchen was near you she could persuade you to do anything she wanted. When she was gone away, you thought, 'Why did I do that?' She had a magic spell." Her approach to individuals and the public was well-planned, assured, and marvelously artful, eliciting both sympathy and admiration. No one could question her mastery of attractive feminine qualities—she was beautiful, always impeccably groomed, totally supportive of Melchior's career, in sum, a very good wife. She stopped well short of being a good mother, responding wittily to inquiries that she had no need of children because she had Lauritz. (Her friend Betty Smith reminded the family later that a Melchior estate existed precisely because Kleinchen had no children.)

Kleinchen had been a genuinely loving daughter herself, caring for her own mother with unfeigned affection until her death in 1960. Mutti, confined to her bed, died while the Melchiors were away. Kleinchen's conscience suffered for the remainder of her life because she had let her mother die alone while she accompanied Lauritz to Denmark for his gala birthday concert, but Mutti had always been conscious of her blessings. The close bond that united the three was expressed in Mutti's 1941 letter written to "the children" when she was sixty years old.

> Dearest Kleinchen and dearest Lauritz . . . I must above all thank you both that I am allowed to live with you. I must thank you for helping me over the terrible time with Karl. Lauritz, I know well what a lovable man Kleinchen lives with. I wish that it be forever so. Kleinchen, I thank you and am happy that you have always been such a wonderful child. . . . I wish only that we can stay always as we have been.

Kleinchen enslaved most masculine acquaintances and enraptured many women. She had all the magnetism, brilliance, and wit with which striking women of her era found it expedient to hide their shrewdness. "She was the very spirit of life itself," said one condolence letter from a male friend. Kleinchen's friend Rosa Ponselle said this in her March 8, 1963, letter:

> Kleinchen was such an extraordinary person. . . . I always thought of her as a sister. . . . She gave me advice the night before I got married. . . . We have shared girls' secrets. We have shared interest in your career, had discussion about investments, normal woman's gossip, and the kind of good sense I felt we both had about the important things in life. . . . I will never forget the night after my mother died. I went into the living room to turn off the lights. There was that adorable Kleinchen with a bottle of wine. She told us that she wanted to drink with us to the New Year because that was what Mother would have wanted us to do. She may have been called Kleinchen, but she stood awfully tall.

"She was your happy star, always filled with a love of life, gaiety, and dazzling temperament," wrote Frida Leider. One can only speculate whether Kleinchen ever told Lauritz how she had, in 1951, asked Frida for repayment of the money advanced to support Rudi Deman during his wartime exile in Switzerland. Frida's sorrowful reply at that time documented how she and Rudi tried unsuccessfully to sell their house, in which fifteen people lived by edict of the government, how they awaited the day when their stocks, now frozen, would be honored so that they could repay the Melchior's "so generous" help.

Lotte Lehmann wrote belatedly on April 26 to tell Lauritz that she had heard about the tragedy only when she read "that Columbia Records had wished to bring out a record with birthday greetings of your friends and fans, but that it had to be delayed due to Kleinchen's death."

So now I will say to you privately what singing with you has meant.

Not only as Siegmund—that has become almost a legend—but also your Tannhäuser, your Lohengrin, all these unforgettable roles that you created. It was a beautiful, golden time. That Kleinchen is no longer here to celebrate with you is something that you can only settle with yourself. But believe me, I feel her absence very deeply. One can simply not imagine Lauritz without his Kleinchen. I know this: you bear it with bravery. Life goes on. And Kleinchen would not wish that you sink into sadness. With heartfelt greetings I am your true friend. Lotte.

Kleinchen seemed to prefer the company of men, particularly well-informed men of business. But was she a genuine financial wizard as the legend would have it? Certainly, it was the pervasive opinion of her circle that she was a mastermind. Yet, after her death, many of the investments she had made proved to have been mistakes. In the 1950s she had told friends that she herself had one million dollars in stocks, but by 1963 she left an estate of roughly the same amount. Still, during only a single year soon after Kleinchen's death, Lauritz was able to spend $300,000 on his new wife, refurbishing the guest house, and general living expenses. In 1965 he could afford to settle his divorce for a very large sum and still live for eight more years in the style to which he had long been accustomed, including African safaris, the very best hotels, and cigars imported by the hundreds.

Would generous, congenial Lauritz Melchior have given away all his money without Kleinchen as his overseer? His sister Bodil thought so. Rumors abound that Lauritz's estate later suffered from the excessive trust he placed in friends acting as business advisers. Nephew Jørgen Krause and his wife Inga declared that Lauritz himself had no financial acumen whatsoever, nor did any member of the Melchior family. The Krauses believe that Lauritz would have had a lesser career without Kleinchen's guiding hand. Most of those who knew Kleinchen agree. (Hans Hansen, however, objects: "If it hadn't been Kleinchen, it would have been somebody else.") Kleinchen organized his singing like a business, and made it possible for him to remain charmingly "above" money matters. When money was the subject, he could simply and truthfully say in his most twinkly manner, "I do the singing and Kleinchen does everything else." There could be no dissension about her genius at publicity, which had two healthy results: The Melchiors not only dexterously exploited every opportunity to stay in the public eye, but they also managed, on the whole, to revel in it rather than to be oppressed by it.

Melchior surrendered his personal autonomy to Kleinchen and in return was given a gloriously pleasurable life. She kept everything disagreeable from him, watched his diet, drew up the contracts, planned their social life, invested their money, helped him into his costumes, attended to the details of his tours, assisted him on and off the stage, directed their many households, answered the mail, organized their extensive diversions and celebrations, and cared for both his operatic apparel and his personal wardrobe. Kleinchen cosseted Lauritz's genial, hedonistic nature in every particular. Unfortunately, her lack of comprehension of artistic principles may have helped to precipitate the biggest tragedy of Melchior's life, the premature discontinuation of his operatic career, and there is no doubt that she singlehandedly engineered the estrangements from his children.

Those whose admiration for Kleinchen is not unqualified attribute all her actions to a desire for power and control over her husband and his money. Her treatment of the stepchildren is an issue avoided by family members and by those who were close to the Melchiors. Some understandably wish to protect the memory of an illustrious and genuinely beloved man; others want to ensure that Kleinchen's less admirable qualities do not appear to overbalance her real virtues. Some fear accusations of carping or of paranoia. Nonetheless, from all the cautiously given clues, hearsay, innuendos, and facts, it appears undeniable that Kleinchen labored unceasingly to keep the Melchior children on the periphery of their father's life. (Birte provides some evidence for Kleinchen's lack of affection for her sisters-in-law as well: "She was jealous of everything that happened in Denmark. She was jealous of his sisters. When he came to Denmark, she always got insulted so that they had to go home.")

Kleinchen's unprovoked animus is hard to understand. She was, it is true, very young to be given the responsibility of stepmothering when Inger died in 1929. Possibly she felt threatened by the existence of two children from a former marriage and wanted Lauritz to herself. Jealousy in such a situation is not an unusual reaction. In addition, solidifying her position as the chief heir to the Melchior estate may have had a high priority for Kleinchen, whose natural acquisitiveness was at times described as that of a typical German Hausfrau. It was she, after all, who was tending to the business of building up that fortune, and, being so many years younger than her husband, she surely expected him to die before her. This conjecture was substantiated by Hilde Laufkötter, who believed that Kleinchen did her best to destroy Lauritz's relationship with his children so that she would inherit his full estate if he did predecease her.

Nothing had prepared Lauritz for the emptiness he felt, having lost his constant and beloved companion. The morning after Kleinchen's death he sat in his big reclining chair, staring out over the valley, just thinking, writing in his daily dairy: "When I wanted to wake my darling, I found that she had slept to the eternal life. . . . The three-times-great Architect will lead my life until I am called."

His godson Klaus Riisbro, who had been sponsored in America by Lauritz and had lived at The Viking for about ten days (until Kleinchen decreed that "a young man should be on his own"), heard of Kleinchen's death on a news broadcast. He immediately called his godfather. Told that

Melchior was mourning, Klaus sent a condolence telegram in lieu of speaking with him, as did Lauritz's real son, Ib, who interpreted his father's refusal to speak on the telephone as another rebuff.

The next day Melchior summoned Klaus to The Viking. The two men embraced. Melchior said haltingly. "Well, yesterday I cried. Today we have to live because life must go on. I want you to come to The Viking to live. This house is yours, you are my godson. I have my butler and his wife here and I'm going to hire a secretary. I just called New York and got the news. I have money, more than I thought."

"Congratulations, godfather."

"I want to tend to Kleinchen now. I want to do it in style, even though I do not believe in the Hollywood way." He insisted upon writing out a list of guests whom he wanted to invite to a dinner party after the funeral service. Both Hilde Laufkötter and Kleinchen's secretary Mary Markham tried to dissuade him, but he was adamant that this is what Kleinchen would have wanted.

Two days later the funeral took place, and in the Hollywood fashion after all. Limousines, movie stars, thirty-nine friends, a beautiful casket, an entire room full of flowers that filled the chapel from floor to ceiling. The Danish Consul General spoke; Amparo Iturbi played. Many conversations among the guests attested to their indignation at Mary Markham's bejeweled appearance as she bustled about telling everyone where to sit and what to do; as nearly as anyone could see, she wore "all of Kleinchen's jewels, everything but the tiara," says Cecily Castenskiold. After the service Melchior got up, went down to the front, opened the doors to the chapel and stood there, a magnificent figure. Condolences were tendered. The casket was closed.

The menu for one hundred guests at the Scandia Restaurant matched the one they had followed the last time Kleinchen had arranged a dinner here. Mary Markham again organized all seating and serving. Lauritz made a speech: Because Kleinchen had never liked people who wallowed in grief, he wanted them to remember her as she was in life, her usual joyous self. Lauritz spoke personally with each and every friend present, recalling something personal about Kleinchen's regard for that person.

"From that day on Lauritz Melchior was in charge of his own life," says his godson. "Within a year of Kleinchen's death he became The Old Viking."

Riisbro explained the analogy: The Old Viking, Holger Danske, of Kronborg Castle is a sculpture in which the figure just sits, his beard growing through the big round marble table. The myth says that Holger Danske rouses himself to fight only when enemies to Denmark are about. "Now Godfather sat like The Old Viking in his chair, not moving. When Kleinchen died, everyone asked, 'Who is going to look after the poor man now?' But he, like Holger Danske, threatened with enemies, roused himself and took his life into his own hands."

"Godfather had done everything as Kleinchen said, even to eating only what she let him eat," elaborated Riisbro. Strictly speaking, Lauritz sometimes won the daily games he and Kleinchen played over what he ate. A Philadelphia reporter noted that Kleinchen had her own way of discouraging Lauritz's prodigious caloric intake. When he in a loud and firm voice ordered cheese blintzes with strawberries and sour cream, he was using a standard tactic: Be definite so that the wife cannot easily contradict in public. Kleinchen showed herself a veteran in the battle over diet when she didn't come right out and say No, but just "suggested" flounder. As Lauritz eyed the rolls, she expertly countered with a piece of low-calorie brown bread, carried in her purse for such emergencies. Lauritz gave a sickly smile but won the last round when he ordered a beer. Kleinchen could not object because they were then negotiating a contract for Lauritz to endorse a certain beer.

Would we expect so strong a woman as Kleinchen just to fade away? Never, for she was in control to the very end—and beyond. Sometime after Lauritz's own death, Klaus Riisbro saw the ghost of Kleinchen and would never again go back up to The Viking. On her first visit to The Viking, after Kleinchen's death, Cleo Baldon (soon to become Ib's wife) was sitting alone in the trophy room while Ib and his father visited the wine cellar. She heard someone say, "Ja, hello." Turning sharply about, she saw no one. She had never met Kleinchen and did not know at the time that this was a habitual greeting of Kleinchen's. Later, at Klaus Riisbro's wedding, Cleo reentered the trophy room to check her gift of flower arrangements and caught a fleeting glimpse of a small, beautiful woman looking at the flowers. Everyone thinks from her description it must have been Kleinchen. Even Betty Smith told about having a long conversation with Kleinchen's portrait one night, precipitated by seeing Kleinchen's foot kick the gown right out of the picture.

Mary Markham alleviated Lauritz's loneliness by including him in her life. He liked being with her. She was lively, a businesswoman with projects of her own to occupy her time. Lauritz confided to his diary Mary's assertion that Kleinchen had intended her to take care of Lauritz:

> I thought I was too old for her, but she thought we should get married and wanted to be mine, hopefully for several years before the call to the big brigade up in the sky sounds for me. . . . Mary and I decided that we should get married because we are both so very lonely.

Those whom Kleinchen had told of her efforts to "train" Mary in how to dress, entertain, and behave, were not surprised to find that the blonde (her hair was now tinted Kleinchen's exact strawberry blonde shade), petite Mary reminded Lauritz of Kleinchen, or to note how closely Mary patterned herself after Kleinchen, even to the very color of nail polish she wore.

Mary was introduced to Lauritz's German and Danish friends and his

Copenhagen family during his 1963 trip to Europe. Acquaintances recognized Kleinchen's vicuña coat and her great emerald ring. Dressed so, Mary bore a striking likeness to her predecessor. Lauritz had been stricken with one of his periodic tidiness bouts—"now we shall put things in order"—which had previously yielded orderly arrangements of his guns (all in a row), hunting shoes (each pair classified by function), sweaters (each tagged with a note regarding size and warmth), and over fifty scrapbooks of clippings and pictures (arranged by dates). With the same thoroughness Lauritz cleaned out Kleinchen's medicine cabinet immediately after her death and rapidly gave away her clothes and accessories. Some were distributed to the family, but this did not mitigate their shock at seeing Kleinchen's great emerald on Mary Markham's hand.

Birte was told by everyone that Lauritz regarded Mary as a daughter. (But Klaus Riisbro says, "Godfather didn't think of any woman as a daughter. He loved women, loved to flirt, and flirted with them all. Did you ever see him be less than charming to a woman?") At the time Birte tried to be philosophical: "Well, if she is his daughter, then he doesn't need me. So be it." A tinge of bitterness would color her later words about the denouement: "After he found out that Mary Markham was not a daughter to him, he came back to me."

Lauritz hated the emptiness and the lack of activity at The Viking. Mary rescued him by taking him with her to visit her friends and by accompanying him on visits to his friends. Eventually Kleinchen's look-alike and Lauritz announced an engagement. "We were all such good friends that at one time they wanted to adopt me, but my mother was living and that made adoption difficult," burbled the bride-to-be, as she told the press of the wedding plans.

The reconciliation between Lauritz and Ib Melchior, which took place a mere five weeks after Kleinchen's death, had been effected in no small part by the insistence of Hilde Laufkötter, who knew the facts of the situation. "Look, Lauritz," she said, "you and Ib have got to get together." Several of Lauritz's California Guard cronies also urged him to see Ib. It is significant that none of these friends spoke up until after Kleinchen had died. Clearly, she had been open about her desire to keep father and son apart. The second time that Ib and Lauritz met after Kleinchen's death, at the beginning of May 1963, Ib, despite his good intentions, could not refrain from telling his father how Kleinchen had kept them apart. Tears ran down Lauritz's face but he remained silent, uttered no apologies, no recriminations, just said, "Let's not talk about it."

When, shortly after the reconciliation, Lauritz came to meet Cleo Baldon, his daughter-in-law-elect, he had presented himself at her door clad in a blinding white suit, endearingly clutching in one giant hand a bunch of flowers from the gardens at The Viking. He was on his best behavior and criticized her fledgling skill with Danish customs only minimally: When she did not return his *Skål* properly, he said, "You have a hell of a lot to learn." His roisterous singing of the "Drinking Song " as an accompaniment to the aquavit tempted Cleo to run to the windows and open them before the room exploded. Ib and Cleo were married at The Viking on January 18, 1964. For the wedding ceremony the father of the groom sang "Jeg elsker dig" and "Because," for which he rehearsed but didn't vocalize. During his last years his deafness prevented him from hearing the accompaniment. He would simply start to sing, and it was the accompanist's task to discover the key.

Lauritz asked that the new bride add to the Stambog all details of her ancestry. Cleo dutifully complied, tracing her family back to Alexander Chute of Taunton, Somersetshire, England, who died in 1268. Lauritz was somewhat put out because his ancestors could be traced only as far back as 1690. "Nevertheless," said he triumphantly, "don't forget that the Danish flag is the oldest flag in the world!"

At Lauritz's own wedding to Mary Markham the family was represented by Bodil from Denmark, Ib and Cleo, and Cleo's son Dirk. A little open car with an awning shuttled more than 500 celebrated guests from society and the movies to The Viking from their parking places down on Mulholland Drive. Cleo, an environmental designer by profession, created her own brand of magic, making an outdoor chapel of the tennis court. For the Danish Lutheran rites Lauritz wore a white swallowtail coat, its lapel lined with medals and the Commander Cross of Dannebrog around his neck. The bride wore a dolphin-green chiffon dress whose full skirt was covered with 10,000 handmade silk rose petals. Former members of the Royal Danish Guard stood at attention along the aisle leading to the altar. Jane Powell sang for the wedding, Wayne Newton for the reception, and Karl Laufkötter was the best man.

Immediate plans called for the couple to honeymoon briefly in Hawaii before Melchior and his friends Tom Knudsen and Walter O'Malley went off on their Alaskan polar-bear hunting trip. All details of this "safari" had been confirmed in January of 1964, and there was no way to cancel at this late date. Reporters dogged the footsteps of the bridal couple, and Lauritz's response to a question about the Beatles ("some dishes taste like caviar and some taste like soap") prompted an argument about Wayne Newton in their first joint interview.

"He was simply wonderful! He has personality, talent . . ." Mary paused.

". . . and a microphone voice," finished Lauritz. "*I* had to have my mike built inside here," he said, pointing to his chest.

The new bride countered, "Ah, but Wayne has personality. He doesn't need a powerful voice."

Mary's resemblance to Kleinchen proved to be predominantly physical. She left Lauritz alone at The Viking while she tended to her television commitments, rising as early as 5:00 and going to bed either too early or too late for companionship. "Still disharmony," confided Melchior to his diary. Friends, noting Melchior's increasing unhappiness, began to unburden themselves of facts they had tactfully refrained from mentioning previously: Mary had spoken indiscreetly the very day after Kleinchen's funeral, predicting her own future place as mistress of that household; Mary had not been circumspect in her choice of male visitors at The Viking during Lauritz's absence; Mary had sold the old furniture, replacing it with far less distinctive things before his return (painting the piano white and gold in the bargain), and charging her husband retail price rather than the customary "cost plus"; Mary and her friends had laughed publicly at Melchior's naivete in thinking that she had any intention of making a marriage and being a wife; Mary's lawyers had held up the wedding celebration at the last minute on her instructions, insisting, "Miss Markham must have these documents signed before the party begins." On the other hand, many asked how a man of seventy-four might believe that a thirty-eight-year-old woman could love him. Why not? was the answer. He was a famous man and accustomed to adulation since his youth. (More importantly, he believed that Kleinchen had wished them to be together.) A *Newsweek* reporter had spoken to Cleo before the wedding, saying, in effect, "This isn't true, is it?" Says Cleo sadly, "It was impossible to tell such things to an old bull elk who was in love."

On August 28, 1964, Mary and Lauritz had dinner at Ib and Cleo's house. Before dinner Mary took aside the other four guests and told them that Lauritz was impossible, that she had had enough of him. After a great show of drinking wine so that she could bear listening to Lauritz's opinions, Mary stood up, spilling her wine over Cleo's best tablecloth, and made an embarrassingly intemperate speech about how her husband was trying to tear down America (based on his comments that Denmark couldn't come up with as good a cherry tomato as America had, but that Danish veal was the best in the world). She stormed from the room and the house, announcing she could take no more. As Ib and Cleo drove Far home that night, Lauritz confessed that he was desperately unhappy. He felt "betrayed" and believed that there was no chance to work things out. "The only thing in my life now is having found my son again."

He could not understand Mary. After all, it was she "who, with her hairdresser friend Loretta, suggested that we get married and told me that she loved me. But now . . . she is completely cold." Ib and Cleo encouraged Melchior to travel, to go on safaris. He objected to the expense, but, remembering how surprised Far had been to learn the size of his fortune after Kleinchen's demise, the young Melchiors felt that his wife had imbued him with these fears about spending his money. They tried to convince him that he could use his money for his own pleasure. It was during the ride home that Far broached for the first time the idea of their living at The Viking: "I'll go to the guest house and give you the big house." At the end of his notes written that night, Ib wrote: "Of course we would never do that, but will do whatever we can to be a family to him."

Lauritz's loneliness had returned full force. In October Lauritz came alone to Ib and Cleo's Halloween party in Los Angeles. He wore his white satin Pagliacci clown suit, and sang "Vesti la giubba." More than once that evening, he replied to those who inquired about his marriage with these words, "There's no fool like an old fool." Cleo believes he felt a clown and this was his way of exorcizing that sensation.

During his marriage he had mentioned in his letters to granddaughter Helle how Mary was gone from the house most of the day, busy with her television work: "Morfar is very lonesome without his Kleinchen, and would like to hear from his little girl Helle for whom he wishes all good things." (Later, some of his loneliness would be palliated when, in 1965, beautiful blonde Helle came to live with him in California. In his usual fashion with family members, he would not show his affection overtly, but would be very strict with the seventeen-year-old girl. Although he felt that she "had had enough schooling in Denmark," he paid her college tuition, but he expected her to work in addition. On May 13, 1967, some time after the mother of movie actor George Hamilton introduced Helle to her other son David, the couple were married. Lauritz gave his granddaughter away, sang "Jeg elsker dig" in both Danish and English, and provided a smashing wedding dinner at The Viking, at which he and the brother of the groom vied for supremacy in charm, cigar-waving, and story-telling.)

Divorce was decided upon before the new year, but the decree was not granted until February 1965. The marriage of Melchior and Mary Markham had lasted a total of five months. Melchior's lawyers begged him not to give Mary all she asked for. As gallant as ever, perhaps even foolish, Melchior responded, "No, I was the old fool. Let me not be a bigger one now." In his sole gesture of retaliation, Melchior pasted over all pictures of Mary in the scrapbooks. Markham got what she asked, but she was forced to wait for Melchior's death to cash in the major part of her settlement.

Lauritz was urgent in his requests that Ib, Cleo, and her son Dirk come to The Viking, so in December 1964 they gave up their own home and moved up to Mulholland Drive to live with Far in the big house, whose master bedroom he ceded to the young couple. His seventy-fifth birthday and their presence provided a respite from the renewed loneliness of his life. Lauritz and Ib breakfasted and opened their mail together each morning, and when Ib returned from his morning's writing, they had an aquavit-replete lunch together. Their companionship was so close that Lauritz, although burdened by deafness most of the time, was nevertheless able to hear his son's voice, whether in English or Danish, at a conversational level. The young Melchiors were to stay for three years, until October 1967 (when Helle's continuing presence would help). When Lauritz was truly "Himself" again, his depression completely over, they would return to their own home, feeling good about getting Far on his feet.

As frequently happens with the elderly, the presence of a new person in the household acted as a tonic. Melchior told Cleo stories he had not repeated in years, and confided to her intimate thoughts that had remained unspoken previously. For example, he hated not having recognized the truth about his relationship with Mary Markham. Plaintively he explained, "All my women really loved me." An affectionate and genuinely admiring daughter-in-law, unfailingly attentive as a listener, Cleo was a superb audience for his funny anecdotes and one-liners: "Pop music is all right if you're holding a girl, but to listen to it, it's just noise." "Compared to modern music, Wagner's recitative sounds like the sweetest Italian cantilena." Cleo observed firsthand the amusing contradictions of Melchior the Hunter: He was immensely proud of his trophies; yet one of his sable antelope trophies set a world record, and he modestly took it for granted. At a dinner held at The Viking, Cleo told Far how wonderful the vension in cream sauce was. Without stopping his eating, Lauritz pointed to one of the many trophies above him on the wall, saying with mock callousness while mischievously enjoying Cleo's consternation, "Yes, you're eating that one up there." Yet he would plunge into the pool to rescue a bumblebee from drowning, and one of Cleo's cherished memories was Melchior in evening dress, answering a mockingbird in the Viking garden who had started a singing contest as Lauritz exited the car.

The younger Melchiors had, before their move, been concerned that living at The Viking be a positive experience for young Dirk, but Melchior enjoyed his step-grandson almost as much as his daughter-in-law. Dirk treated Lauritz with playful deference, and the two teased each other unmercifully. Sharing a love of baseball, the oldest and the youngest of the household attended Dodger games companionably. It was Dirk who inherited the ritualistic chore of bringing the cigar box to the dinner table, and, after Lauritz made the choice, cutting and lighting the cigar. (Lauritz was continuing a tradition he learned as a child. He had been given the honor of fetching his father's elaborate cigar case and taking part in the ceremonious lighting. When Jørgen preferred his long meerschaum pipe, Lauritz would run to get it. If he had been a particularly good boy, he was allowed to put the tobacco in, but it had to be done correctly as set forth in the old proverb, "First softly, with the virgin's hand, and then strongly, with the man's hand," quoted Jørgen.) He enjoyed tending bar for Lauritz's card-playing evenings with some of the most interesting men in town, among them the great Walter O'Malley, and it was Dirk who was finally given the responsibility for working the new Great Dane, "Fred." The dog had been well trained in obedience school, but with one-work commands: Sit; Back; Down. Lauritz stubbornly persisted in saying "Sit Down," thereby confusing Fred completely. Dirk adopted some of Lauritz's colorful vocabulary as well, such as his wonderfully descriptive phrase for lavish parties: "stink-fine affairs."

Ib and Cleo accompanied Lauritz on his 1965 European trip. In Denmark there were three parties belatedly commemorating his seventy-fifth birthday, one large and festive with family and friends, held at Josty's Restaurant. Another was a small private dinner given by his Danish fans, which the most fervent of these, Andreas Damgaard, describes thus: This small circle of Wagnerites eagerly awaited Melchior's arrival in a beautiful private home. Upon arrival of the great tenor a loudspeaker in the yard played the *Siegfried* horn-motif. Although Melchior had ordered his chauffeur to pick him up at midnight, he enjoyed the party so much that he stayed until 2:00 A.M. During dinner, table conversation included some Melchior remarks about *Tannhäuser* (it is very difficult because it shifts quickly between lyrical and dramatic sequences), and about Lotte Lehmann (when he was on stage with the great soprano he could hardly help falling in love with her). His reaction to hearing for the first time Maria Callas's rendition of Isolde's "Liebestod," which the Wagnerites played for him, was: "It is as I have always said, female Italian singers cannot sing Wagner." When they played Melchior's own recording of the finale of Act I of *Siegfried*, Melchior (no less honest about himself than he had been about Callas) said, "That last note was not quite in tune, was it?"

During this visit Lauritz took Birte to a restaurant, where they had an unusually frank conversation. (Says Birte today, "You know, I was not used to him being kind to me, but he suddenly was, and we had a sort of friendship. But I never really regarded him as a father. That is how it is when your father or mother is a celebrity. You just don't have a family.")

Far said unexpectedly, "I know you didn't like Kleinchen."

Startled, Birte nevertheless managed to hold her ground. "No, I didn't. She was a good wife for you, but I didn't like her. . . . Why did you keep us from seeing mother's relatives?" she found herself asking.

"Kleinchen knew that they were trying to do me harm, to hurt my career."

"How could those good-hearted, simple people manage to accomplish such a thing living here in Copenhagen? How could you believe that?"

He was silent before her logic.

After Copenhagen the Melchiors had an appointment in Naples. During a most solemn ceremony before the ornate, gilded and fretworked altar of a late seventeenth century Naples church, Lauritz Melchior and his son Ib received their knighthoods in the fourteenth-century Knights Templar order of Saint Brigitte. This rite completed the event that had started with the seventy-fifth-birthday presentation of the Grand Cross in California. The Grand Master, Prince Vincenzo Abbate de Castello Orleans, assisted by two archbishops, grand priors of the order, conducted the ceremony, and a former president of the Supreme Court of Italy was Melchior's knightly godfather. The pomp and circumstance of the occasion were unsettled only by an Italian working man clad in a threadbare brown suit, who passed right through the church (carrying a bundle that looked suspiciously like a fish wrapped in newspaper), paused to look about, and exited without a word.

While they were in southern Italy, the three Melchiors decided to visit Capri's Blue Grotto. Clad in his big brown overcoat and ten-gallon Stetson hat, Lauritz had to recline in the rowboat to pass through the low entrance to the grotto. Inspired by the quiet and the luminescent beauty of the place, he sang "Come Back to Sorrento" from his supine position in the boat more or less at the top of those famous lungs, his expressive arm gesture coming up from the boat bottom, At the end, after an odd pause, there came an explosion of applause from the other tourists, who, startled but appreciative, applauded while their Italian guides listened and watched open-mouthed.

Working their way back to Rome, they had stopped at a highly touted coastal restaurant whose owner had also been a famous opera singer. Everyone was very anxious that the two should meet. A group of bystanders were talking in Italian about "the great Melchior" and Lauritz was told in English about this famous Italian. They exchanged hellos; they embraced. As they departed Lauritz said to Ib, "Who the hell is this?" and in the corner Ib could see the Italian asking the same thing. Lauritz had never liked Italy very much for precisely this reason—not everyone recognized him.

Back in Rome Melchior was received in a private audience by Pope Paul VI. This occasion, too, was almost marred, because the taxi driver didn't know where to go. Far kept fuming, "People of prominence should not be late." The twenty-minute private conversation centered around the need for Christian unity and the role of music in religion. Lauritz wore all his medals in their large size, and over his tails, the cape of the St. Brigitte order. His vestments were almost as splendid as those of the pope. A wonderful photograph was taken of the great singer, his finger wagging toward Pope Paul's face, as Lauritz made a point.

One their way to Germany they moved so rapidly though Italy that Cleo was given only fifteen minutes to see Hadrian's Tomb. In Verona the stunning outdoor opera arena was accorded second status to eating. Lauritz opened the doors of four restaurants in a row, sniffed a bit, said, "No," and proceeded to the next. At the fifth door, he smiled and ushered Cleo and Ib inside. Viewing the skinned, gray carcasses of the *uccellini* (little birds) on display in the Italian fashion, however, he virtuously lectured that "in Italy, there are no birds; they shoot them and eat them." Cleo thought Far's concern somewhat suspect when she remembered his heartless comment after he watched her cooing over the beauty of a mother quail and her offspring as they trailed across The Viking terrace, "Yes, they taste very good."

The trip supplied yet another opportunity for Lauritz to flash his beloved (and useful) police badge. When the Melchiors were in Italy, Lauritz could scarcely wait to get to Munich so that he could don his more comfortable Lederhosen. As they drove on the Autodromo, he urged Ib, "Go fast!" Although genuinely worried about getting a ticket, Ib muttered sotto voce, "The hell with it." He sped along for a while, but then he noticed that they had attracted a police car. Soon it zoomed up beside them, signaling a stop.

"Don't worry," said Lauritz, as he sat up very straight in the front seat.

When the carabiniere walked up alongside, Lauritz withdrew from his wallet his Passaic, New Jersey, honorary police-chief badge. "American police," he intoned authoritatively.

Off they went, scot-free.

In 1970 another European trip was taken by father and son alone together. Before leaving California, Ib had made a vow to himself that this trip, in celebration of his father's eightieth birthday, would be thoroughly pleasant for Far. No disagreements over anything. Whatever Far wanted to do would be done, and exactly Far's way, even down to wrong directions and long shortcuts. What did it matter, after all, if two hours were lost on a fruitless search in the wrong direction? They would be together and in harmony. So Ib drove according to Lauritz's directions, with one exception. Because of a flooding Rhine River they were rerouted off the Autobahn to little roads that would have extended the trip to Mainz by ten hours. Crawling along in the heavy traffic, Ib spied a road sign on a dirt road. He suddenly recognized the terrain as territory in which he had operated during his cloak-and-dagger days as a member of the war-time Counter Intelligence Corps. When the unprepossessing route brought them to their destination in an hour, Lauritz showed new respect for his son. How he loved a successful shortcut!

This trip was clearly dedicated to leave-taking, says Ib. Those old friends and colleagues who were still alive, such as Frida Leider, Claire Wolff, and Max Lorenz, were visited one last time. Lorenz and Melchior had been friends since their days in the Berlin studio of Ernst Grenzebach. "Our friendship will always remain until some day we will sing our songs with a harp seated on a cloud," wrote Lauritz in a last letter to Lorenz, adding a closing thought that would do well as a singer's motto: "Stay well and keep your throat moist!

One of the truly memorable events of Melchior's professional life took place on March 31, 1960. One week after his seventieth birthday, an invited audience and the press attended a gala concert in Copenhagen's Danmarks Radio Concert Hall to hear the white-bearded, hearing-aid-equipped Melchior sing his last Siegmund with the radio symphony orchestra. This gala birthday concert featured Act I of *Die Walküre* with Dorothy Larsen, Mogens Wedel, and conductor Thomas Jensen, three fine Danish artists. Because he had conceived the idea for the concert, Knud Hegermann-Lindencrone was allowed to install his stereo equipment in "a little study just beside the concert hall." Here, with Kleinchen at his side, Hegermann-Lindencrone made a stereo recording, parallel to the broadcast mono version, that became the only stereo recording of Lauritz Melchior.

Hegermann-Lindencrone's idea for this gala performance was indirectly influenced by some interesting events back in 1952 and 1957. In October 1952, Kirsten Flagstad had given two concerts in Copenhagen, sponsored by *Berlingske Tidende*, the newspaper founded by one of Hegermann-Lindencrone's forebears. Afterward, two enthusiastic Wagnerites—Palle Alsfelt, program controller of Danmarks Radio, and Hegermann-Lindencrone, at that time co-owner of *Berlingske Tidende* and a member of the board—had a conversation. How sad it was, they remarked, that Melchior had not publicly given Flagstad a helping hand when she returned to the United States after the war. How marvelous it would be to have Flagstad and Melchior together again. What a pity it was that King Frederik IX, also a lover of Wagner's music, had never included anything by that composer in those private concerts that he conducted at the Royal Theater. An idea was conceived then and there to sponsor a radio concert of the *Walküre* Act I with Flagstad and Melchior, King Frederik on the podium, with royalties going to the Greenland Fund.

Before suggesting the Flagstad concerts to his paper in 1952, Hegermann-Lindencrone had for many years been assured of Flagstad's innocence by Arne Dørumsgaard, composer and cultural adviser to the Norwegian government, who knew the facts surrounding the earlier false accusations against her. This paved the way for Alsfelt, whose work had given him connections at court, to ask his friends in the royal entourage to investigate delicately King Frederik's feelings about such a concert. The answer was affirmative: It was very likely that the king would accept, not only because the Greenland Fund was close to his heart and Queen Ingrid's, but because he would relish conducting these special singers.

Next, Hegermann-Lindencrone wrote to both artists. Melchior's enthusiastic yes came by return post. In Norway a few days later, Flagstad invited Hegermann-Lindencrone to lunch. The postman rang and the mail was brought in to the table. Flagstad recognized Melchior's handwriting on one of the envelopes. "A letter from Lauritz! Excuse me, but I must read this at once." She read in silence and soon her guests saw a few tears start slowly down her cheeks. "We are friends again, just as we were so long ago." An unforgettable sight, says Hegermann-Lindencrone, "to see Kirsten smiling through tears of happiness."

Back in Copenhagen Alsfelt and Hegermann-Lindencrone, elated with their success, were beginning to put together the rest of an all-Scandinavian cast when the Biancolli Flagstad biography came out, bringing up again the accusations by Norwegian Ambassador to the United States Wilhelm Morgenstierne. It was given wide coverage in the newspapers and on the radio by the Ritzaus Bureau, which refused to publish Flagstad's protest. The two planners sorrowfully agreed that in a climate of such sensationalism, however falsely based, they could not ask the king to participate in the concert. Eventually Alsfelt and Hegermann-Lindencrone swallowed their regrets and recognized the good that had come out of their unrealized plans: at least the two great singers had become friends again.

The second half of the story leading up to the 1960 concert took place in 1957, when Hegermann-Lindencrone persuaded Vagn Kappel, then head of music for Danmarks Radio, to bring Flagstad to Copenhagen for a single radio broadcast of *Alceste*, which she sang with an all-Danish cast and in the Danish language, learned especially for that occasion. At a late supper after the 1957 concert, the Dane brought up the possibility of Flagstad doing a *Walküre* with Svanholm on the Danish radio. This plan also fell through ("too late for me," Flagstad had responded in 1960 when the subject was broached), but, when Hegermann-Lindencrone heard that Melchior was coming to celebrate his seventieth birthday in Copenhagen, he revived the original idea. He phoned Melchior in California, suggesting that he sing a gala performance as Siegmund to mark the occasion. With Melchior's seventieth-birthday radio concert in 1960, the 1952 plans were realized belatedly, albeit incompletely.

The Dane tells us how happy Lauritz was with the concert and how wonderfully he sang. "He was fantastic, and his 'Wälse! Wälse!' came out as in his most glorious days, but when Lauritz turned away from the mono microphone to face his public, the presence was not that good." (Interestingly, although Hegermann-Lindencrone himself resists the idea, many musicians concur that, even in those few moments when the voice showed its seventy years, the pitch was sharp, not flat.) During rehearsal, however, there had been some problems, described by Hans Hansen in his liner notes for the newest reissue of this recording:

> Thomas Jensen had apparently decided not to be impressed by Denmark's aging prodigal son, and at rehearsal a testy exchange developed between conductor and star, quite loud and increasingly excited due to the impaired hearing of both men. The discussion concerned mainly matters of rhythm, as it had for Melchior and a host of conductors for more than a generation. . . . Lauritz was applauded by the orchestra and responded with a little speech, expressing what it meant to him to be working in the country of his birth with this glorious orchestra.

There were over twenty curtain calls for the Great Dane that night. Lauritz could not resist appearing for the last calls wearing a top hat, only to take it off and wave it jovially in all directions like a boulevardier. Mme. Larsen, who, more than twenty years later, still had never heard an equal of "the warm timbre of [Melchior's] voice, its almost purely innocent sound, enormous strength and carrying power, combined with a striking effortlessness and the ability, rare for a Heldentenor, to sing a beautiful *pianissimo*," found also that "his boyish disposition was safe and sound." Mogens Wedel declared himself staggered by "the astonishing vitality and surplus of ringing, full sound, which simply had to seem almost against nature for a singer of his age." During the performance, recalls Wedel, at the famous "Wälse! Wälse!" "I was standing closest to Thomas Jensen and . . . he mumbled to me, 'God knows how long he is going to hang in there!' . . . Melchior stayed as long as he wanted to." He did, however, lose his concentration for a second, overcome—as was the audience—by the sound of the "Wälse!" ("as wonderful as in his youth"), and stopped for a fraction of a second at the beginning of the love duet. "Dorothy Larsen brought him back with such rapidity that only if you knew your first act very well would you notice it," says Hegermann-Lindencrone.

Mogens Wedel told about seventy-year-old Melchior's behavior at the supper party hosted by Danmarks Radio after the performance: "Melchior dived into an assortment of 'snaps' [drinking] songs. I kept pace as well as I could and the master remarked dryly, 'I am sure that you will make it, young man.' I was then forty-two years old."

The huge batch of congratulatory cables brought a surprise, a generous and poignant accolade from Kirsten Flagstad, who had heard the broadcast from Kristianssand, Norway. She had tried to telephone him after the concert, but the radio station receptionist didn't realize that everyone was at the supper party. Hegermann-Lindencrone, who had been "on pins and needles" during the party, expecting Flagstad's call at any moment, spoke to Kirsten by telephone the next day, and she repeated what she had said in the telegram. "Dear Lauritz: Thank you for tonight. Thank you for the old days. There is no one like you."

It was a source of great satisfaction to Knud Hegermann-Lindencrone, who had been working for so long behind the scenes, that he had helped bring about a reconciliation between these two artists who were bound together in every way by their adoring public. Lauritz's 1952 letter to Kirsten had asked her to forget the differences of opinion they had had, to remember their work together and what it had meant to both of them. Now, in 1960, Flagstad's telegram was not only congratulatory; it was a final step in their rapprochement.

When she died in 1962, Melchior taped a moving farewell for Hegermann-Lindencrone's Flagstad memoriam broadcasts and cabled masses of red roses to Oslo with a card, "From Tristan to Isolde." He was touched to read in a commemorative article that she had often listened to their *Lohengrin* and *Parsifal* duets. A close friend recalled that when Flagstad heard Melchior's voice, she always exclaimed, as if it were the first time she heard it, "What a singer!" Melchior returned the compliment in his commemorative piece for the British magazine *Opera:*

To be on the stage with Kirsten was always exciting because the one seemed to lift the other up to the highest in their art. I think that greater teamwork will never exist again. . . . Kristen's voice and technique were always perfect.

In a taped message on the occasion of a 1972 BBC tribute to Kirsten Flagstad, he added: "The fact that it was Norway and Denmark who carried German opera in the turmoil of the world was proof that art stands above politics."

On the day after the concert the Copenhagen critics said only nice things: The Danish tenor had sung the long and demanding music "with continuously increasing power and vocal strength," said *Dagens Nyheder*, and it did not cause him "the slightest physical trouble." *Information* found neither the fact that Melchior had "reached an amazing level artistically . . . despite his advanced age" nor "the great . . . firmness, volume, and brilliant ring" of his voice to be the essence of the occasion, but rather his interpretation, which "could still serve as an example to all dramatic tenors of the world." "One's memory went back to the time when Melchior . . . was quite simply *the* Wagner tenor, the supreme Heldentenor of Heldentenors," said *Berlingske Tidende. Politiken* noted that anyone who might have thought the concert would be "just a superficial show number . . . [or] a weak reflection of the former splendor and glory of the seventy-year-old Wagner world tenor" was certainly "taught something quite different."

Denmark had finally given Lauritz Melchior the uncensored, unreserved respect and affection he had longed for from his former countrymen. Is it possible that the Danes only now realized exactly how great a national treasure Melchior was? Surely it must have been an eye-opener not only to hear him sing Wagner at the age of seventy, but to hear him sing it as well or better than some much younger pretenders to the Wagnerian art. Even at this time, it was often said that after Melchior "there were no Heldentenors, only tenors in Helden roles." Perhaps this 1960 concert was so clear a measure of Melchior's true stature that it encouraged the Danes to forgive him for what they had perceived to be an inflated view of himself.

Denmark had not been alone in taking Melchior for granted when he was a young singer, and not alone in expecting the appearance of "another Melchior" right on cue. And they were not the only ones to view his stature differently in the new and harsh light shed by a definite void in the ranks of world-class Heldentenors. It was beginning to be apparent that "another Melchior" had not materialized, although Wieland Wagner, one of the composer's sons, who took his turn at the helm of the Bayreuth Festival after the war, didn't give up hope. When inquiring about the situation in Denmark, he always asked Danes "whether a new Melchior would soon be on his way."

In his travels throughout the world the tenor found himself paying closer attention to comments in music reviews. Although he had been criticized toward the end of his operatic career, often severely, he could not fail to notice that, since he left the Metropolitan Opera, the critics had begun to speak very kindly of him in retrospect. Seemingly, Melchior's uniqueness as a singer was being appreciated in increasing measure with each passing year after his retirement.

In 1960 recording companies paid tribute to Melchior and his colleagues. Angel came out with a new edition of his Wagnerian excerpts with Leider and Schorr, which was awarded the Grand Prix du Disque in France, and RCA issued a splendid record in honor of his fiftieth anniversary as a singer. Reviewing the RCA release, Conrad L. Osborne insisted that if Lauritz Melchior did not sing by the established rules, then the rules should be changed:

> No recording can . . . convey the stunning impact of that ceaseless vari-colored ring. . . . [People] assert that Melchior was not a conscientious or knowing interpreter, or that he merely unleashed a big voice and hoped to overpower his listeners. For refutation, listen to the way he caresses the opening phrases of the Bridal Chamber Scene in a mezza voce that changes color from phrase to phrase—even from word to word. Or select his immensely moving version of Otello's monologue and death, quite on a par with any interpreter you care to name. . . . Melchior's voice served him until his sixtieth year in a very active career. . . . He always adhered to a legato line. . . . His ideals are precisely those of the *bel canto* singer. . . . He never pressed down on the voice to give it weight, never barked or yelled. He always *sang*. This he shares in common with all the great Wagnerians of his era.

As early as 1963 Melchior had been asking himself why *he* should not be the one to help in the Heldentenor crisis. He ruminated on the help that he himself had received, from Mme. Cahier, from Hugh Walpole, from the Royal Danish Opera. He could still sing a good high C and a bass C. Surely it all boiled down to the technique. Most singers of the day seemed not to have time to learn a solid technique. By the time a singer is mature enough to become a Heldentenor, he frequently has a family and the consequent financial responsibilities. How can such a young man afford to stop earning and pursue new vocal studies, as he had?

As Lauritz pondered these problems, he realized that he needed advice and help from professionals. Accordingly, he wrote to many of his friends and colleagues to solicit their advice. In a letter to Max Lorenz, he explained,

> It looks sad with the new growth of Heldentenors, and therefore I have established a Heldentenor foundation in order to further the new growth of the "schweren Helden." There are still "jugendliche Helden," but you cannot find Siegfrieds, Tristans, and Tannhäusers, and therefore our dear Wagner operas will disappear from the opera stages. It is not called "Tristan OR Isolde," but "Tristan UND Isolde," and the poor

"hochdramatische" [dramatic soprano] ladies will all be without lovers. So I find that something must be done, and soon.

As a result of Melchior's letter-writing campaign, inspired and orchestrated by Betty Smith, an international fund to assist in the training of Heldentenors was in full swing by 1965.

Clearly money was required, funds sufficient to provide scholarships from the interest alone. Encouraged by his son's insistence that his fortune was his to dispose of, Lauritz drew up a new will in which twenty-five percent of his estate was earmarked for the Melchior Heldentenor Foundation, whose monies were to be administered by the Juilliard School. His rationale was spelled out in a two-page brochure:

Heldentenors are rare, usually developing with age, and most often created from a high baritone voice. This singer must stop singing for some time and concentrate on study. The Melchior Foundation will provide the financial assistance to make the training and support of the future Heldentenor possible. Applicants for grants can be nominated only by the director of an opera company, who will be expected to assist the singer's development in any way possible if he is selected. The director must engage the singer to perform Heldentenor roles for at least one season with his opera company. By the same token, the singer must have musical and dramatic experience already.

The original advisory council for the foundation included Karin Branzell, Herbert Janssen, Otto Edelmann, Alexander Kipnis, Lotte Lehmann, Karl Laufkötter, Birgit Nilsson, and George Szell (with a great deal of practical assistance from Betty Smith). Presumably, they too, like many others, were concerned that the incidence of Wagner performances had decreased so dramatically in the years since 1950. Lauritz had garnered some appalling figures: from the 1925–1926 through the 1949–1950 season there had been a yearly average of thirty-one Wagner performances at the Met; from 1950–1951 through 1963–1964, the number decreased to an average of seventeen per season; the 1964–1965 season promised only *Parsifal* and *Tannhäuser* for a total of ten performances.

He began to proselytize seriously. From small local arts clubs to the English Wagner Society, Melchior made speeches in behalf of his foundation. His standard response to the question about the status of Wagnerian opera in interviews now included a reference to the Heldentenor crisis:

Today there are only Isoldes and no Tristans. Birgit Nilsson is a widow before her time. No tenor can match her in voice and technique. We Wagner singers must look on our parts like a jockey who rides in a race. You cannot lead all the time, but must have the strength to lead in the end. A heroic tenor must be taught this control or he will ruin his voice in a short time.

He sent a fund-raising letter to his friends and acquaintances in Germany:

> Richard Wagner's operas are slowly disappearing from the operatic stages . . . because a certain voice type does not exist for the time being, the "schwerer Held." All other voice qualities can be found; only this voice, which develops later in life, disappears because the young singers who possess the material cannot . . . restudy. It takes a certain time, during which one must absolutely not sing in public, and during which one has to work only with the changing of some notes in the middle-high part of the voice. It is necessary that this voice reschooling take place; otherwise the young singer will ruin his voice in a short time.

Melchior devoted much of the rest of his life to this quest to discover and help those baritones with the potential to become Heldentenors. Given his knowledgeable use of the press and the professional help of Betty Smith, it was only a matter of time before serious attention was being paid to his crusade.

Of the journalistic reaction, probably the best piece was written in 1966 by Martin Bernheimer, Wagnerite and perceptive music critic for the *Los Angeles Times:*

> The world of Wagnerian tenors is in crisis. In the international community of singers there may be five or six performers who can even get through these roles, and then usually with the help of a sympathetic conductor, an editor's scissors, and some cleverly executed vocal cheating. . . . It is highly appropriate that [Melchior] should be the one to pick up the gauntlet. There have been compromise heroes since 1950. . . . There was Set Svanholm . . . an artist of tremendous intelligence, but not possessed of the world's most ringing tenor by any means. Then along came Wolfgang Windgassen, who still has a virtual monopoly on the repertoire, but often has to fake his way through. Hans Hopf has revealed good vocal potential but a rather unpredictable technique. . . . None [of the group of youngish tenors who have been successful in lyric Wagner roles] has thus far dared essay Tristan or Siegfried. And their caution would seem to be warranted.

Often the sadness engendered by retirement from an active singing career is mitigated by finding a protégé in whom the former artist can take a personal interest, or by beginning a new career as a teacher, in which capacity he passes on the knowledge gained during his performing life. The fact that Melchior did not teach might be traced to a marked distrust of voice teachers. Many times he declared that there were no good teachers, only intelligent pupils: "It is important to get the right help in voice training, but also to have the courage to seek elsewhere if it's wrong." He really believed that a successful singer was the product of an amalgam of the gift of proper material (he called it "a touch of God's little finger"), combined with do-it-yourself knowledge. Hilde Laufkötter, knowing Melchior very well, offered her opinion that it would have been impossible for him to teach in any case, because he could not explain technical matters. Since Melchior did not choose to teach, it is understandable that he was impelled to turn his interests in the direction of a foundation to facilitate the careers of future Heldentenors. Moreover, he was one of the few singers who had amassed a personal fortune large enough to make such a foundation possible.

During January 1968, when the first Lauritz Melchior Foundation competition was in its preliminary stages of auditioning, Melchior wrote to Birgit Nilsson, thanking her for her Christmas card and responding to her words about young tenor Jess Thomas:

> It was very interesting to learn that you feel that the new Jess Thomas has the possibility of being a good Tristan. I don't know much about him myself, but I hope for his own sake that he is not attacking those long operas without having enough knowledge of the technique of singing them. I would like to meet him and hear him one day. If he is really ready it will of course mean a lot in the way of keeping Wagner's operas in the repertoire and also giving you a partner to your liking. Of our auditions in New York, one singer has possibilities. He has been singing baritone before this, has fine low and high notes, and is of German descent so his German is good. . . . At present, we have only enough money for one potential heroic tenor, but there are more possibilities who, through the right guidance, could become tenors in the future.

Forty-four young men had been recommended by opera companies in Germany, Norway, and the United States, by teachers, singers, managements worldwide, and impresarios, one of whom was Wolfgang Wagner himself. The final auditions of February 1969, where nine men were heard, produced two splendid candidates for the Heldentenor Fach, John Russell, thirty-six, and William Cochran, twenty-five. One of Cochran's vital statistics illustrates the usual physical proportions of heroic tenors: this weight-lifter and former linebacker at Wesleyan University—now singing successfully in Germany—boasted a fifty-two-inch chest. (Two 1981 recipients of the Melchior awards, Timothy Jenkins and Gary Lakes, are also immediately recognizable as prototypical Heldentenors, tall and stocky.) After the auditions, Melchior marked the occasion in his usual way; he took all nine contestants and the judges (Birgit Nilsson, Karen Branzell, Otto Edelmann, Peter Mennin, Gideon Waldrop, Ignace Strasfogel, and Alexander Kipnis) for a smorgasbord accompanied, of course, by heroic quantities of aquavit and beer.

A letter written by Melchior to young Cochran in August 1969 offers advice from the veteran Heldentenor, in his own inimitable style, on when to essay certain roles, on singing full voice, and on acting with sincerity:

> Please take care that they do not put you on to parts you are not yet ready for! Even if Wolfgang is of my opinion, he may be forced to try

you in something where he has not got anybody else. . . . You are wise to postpone your *Siegfried* and *Götterdämmerung*. Before you do those, you should try *Tannhäuser*, and please wait . . . until you . . . make *Tristan*. . . . When you rehearse on the stage, don't always sing with full voice—only when it is necessary. Otherwise, transcribe your tones down so that you don't always tire your voice by singing the high notes. . . . And don't forget that 90 percent of what you are putting into your operatic roles are your personality and the coloring of the words plus the sentiment of them are the most important things to keep an audience awake. Never let Mr. Cochran stand next to the part he is performing but let him try to be, feel, and live that part. Then you will fulfill your obligations.

Melchior elaborated on this theme in his personal manuscript, where he cautioned the singer not to think he is

a machine because [he does] certain things exactly the same one evening after the other, for there is never a great artist in the world without personality. It will come through. But the young artist is clever only if he or she uses as much of the given help as possible and mixes that with his or her own feelings . . . and in this manner creates a character of heart and blood moving on the stage.

Melchior also lectured Cochran on the duty of artists' wives:

I wish that she will understand the great help she can be to you in your career by keeping away a lot of things which she can take care of and not bother you with them.

Some of the most interesting remarks Melchior made about singing and performing were contained in his correspondence with young singers, where we see clearly the ordering of his artistic priorities. With professionals he obviously felt it possible to be direct and technical, and imperative to be inspirational. He wrote earnestly to another young would-be Heldentenor whom he had consented to hear:

You seem to have a very powerful and good voice. In the Wagner operas it is not only the difficult solo parts which count most, because the difference lies in the length of the parts and the fact that these solo parts mostly in Wagner operas appear at the end of the opera. That means that you would have been singing for a couple of hours before you come to your climax. . . . In an artist's career it is not enough to possess a voice. With it goes looks, acting, and the coloring of your voice to suit the feelings in the words you sing. . . . Be humble in your approach to art. There is nothing worse than an artist who thinks that he is a prima donna because such behavior and thoughts will mostly be a disadvantage to you in your work and in your comradeship with your fellow artists. . . . a tenor of your kind who I feel is leaning toward Italian operas will have difficulties and gradually, by trying to get through the orchestra with his voice in the lower registers, will lose his high notes. This is what happened to . . . Mr. Vinay of Chile. He can now not sing any of the tenor parts anymore. . . . His voice has lost a lot of its shining beauty.

In 1966 the old plans for a new Metropolitan Opera House were finally about to be realized, and a celebration of the closing of the old house was being organized for the spring. On January 10 Eleanor Belmont wrote to Constance Hope, exploring the possibility of Melchior's attendance at this gala. Her letter read in part: "We desire to do him honor and this is the last opportunity in the old house to pay Lauritz Melchior a tribute that we have long yearned to deliver." Mrs. August Belmont, who Rudolf Bing called "a remarkable combination of charm, sense, and authority," had been a staunch friend to Lauritz and to the Met itself for many, many years. Not only was she a longtime board member, but she was the founder of the Metropolitan Opera Guild, which played a large part in the coming celebration.

On January 11 Constance Hope reported to Lauritz that she had raised the ticklish subject of the feelings between Bing and Melchior. Mrs. Belmont had assured her that they would inform Bing before corresponding with Melchior. When Mrs. Belmont wrote directly to Lauritz, asking him to be present for the final gala performance at the old Met on April 16, she further explained the plans. The Guild would list in a program insert those artists who helped to make the old house famous, but they wanted to honor in person as many as possible of those still living. Lauritz declined.

Eleanor Belmont was not one to take no for an answer. Using all the leverage she could muster, she tried to persuade Lauritz. Nor did she refrain from pointed reference to the debt he owed America. Lauritz's second letter of refusal (dated February 1) to Belmont explained well his point of view, not omitting a touch of bitterness:

When I am writing you, I write you first of all as a man of character and I think I can call myself a gentleman. I know exactly how much I owe the United States and the Metropolitan Opera in the way of my career and name. . . . The twenty-four years I had the privilege and happiness to perform in the German wing of the Met were the most wonderful years of my life. . . . Now most of my old friends have passed away and we are only some few left of the old guard. The most precious to me and my memories from that time is my dear Lotte, a friend and a woman artist unsurpassed in her womanly character and expression of that in her voice. Dear Mrs. Belmont, you can understand that it is not easy for me not to be present on the sixteenth. As I have told you before, a man who deprived me of continuing my art and work at the Metropolitan Opera, in which I am sure I can place myself as a faithful and dependable artist, in twenty-four years only cancelling three appearances out of 515 scheduled Wagner operas, is a person in whose company I will not and cannot be. . . . I do not want any unpleasant situation to arise. . . . I must say, although with a bleeding heart, that I am not going to be present.

By February 17, Eleanor Belmont wrote again. She finally accepted Lauritz's refusal to attend the final gala, but asked for permission to have his name listed with his colleagues together with a facsimile of the signatures of the most famous of them. To this he answered yes, and thus quietly did an operatic era end for the greatest Heldentenor of the twentieth century.

In his heart, Melchior did not really feel severed from the Met itself. At the Hollywood Bowl, he identified himself as "of the Metropolitan Opera," and clearly believed he was. Nor had the artists of the Met forgotten him. Schuyler Chapin later related how, while general manager of the Metropolitan, he had invited Melchior at the beginning of the 1972–1973 season, shortly before the tenor's death, to attend a performance of *Siegfried*. Melchior, deeply moved, replied that this was the first correspondence he had received from the Met administration in twenty-two years. (Covent Garden had cabled congratulations on his fiftieth anniversary, but the Met had remained silent—until Bing departed.) Although he could not come due to ill health, Melchior sent his regards to all hands. Chapin read the letter to the cast backstage at the end of the performance, whereupon "the company broke into thunderous applause."

Indeed, a real decline of Melchior's health began in the summer of 1972. There was the suspicion of a small stroke, thought at first to be a "fall." His declining physical powers and a stinginess learned from Kleinchen produced a determination not to spend money on his beloved house. The Viking property, appraised in 1964 for $350,000, was offered for $300,000 after his death, in part because it had become run-down and was in need of numerous repairs. Yet he had not lost his sense of humor. One evening in 1971 Ib and his father sat companionably before the television. A sober-faced newscaster came on to announce portentously, "The great Wagneran tenor, Lauritz Melchior, passed away today. He is remembered for his roles . . ." Lauritz picked up the telephone and called the television station. "Hello," he said, "this is a corpse speaking."

When Klaus Riisbro returned from Denmark in 1972, Melchior invited him to live at The Viking. "Young people make me feel young again." Lauritz had a fine time in his happy household with Marianne Tegner, his charming and efficient Danish personal secretary, a maid-cook, a chauffeur-butler, and his godson. "He led a super life, king-like," says Riisbro. He did nothing for himself. Whenever he wanted to go to town, they would help him. Whatever colors took his fancy, without regard to propriety, those were the ones in which he was dressed. Sometimes the result was outlandish. Mogens Wedel had been shocked at the giant-plaid jacket and white Stetson hat that Melchior wore to a performance at the conservative Bayreuth Festspielhaus. Guests to The Viking were surprised by the two gold-embroidered suits of yellow and green silk brocade that he had had made to order in Hong Kong during a 1971 trip. Cleo, recalling the brilliant costumes worn by Spanish bull-fighters, called each a "suit of lights." Lauritz wore them like comfortable pajamas.

Although Ib and Cleo no longer lived at The Viking, they often joined Far for dinner, or had him at their house for a good meal, or just kept him company as he watched television. Klaus's fiancée visited often. Lauritz said, "She can come and stay here, too. What the hell? If the bed is not big enough we'll get another. What a lovely way to wake up with a pretty little thing sitting and eating breakfast with me, while the sun shines and my crazy godson looks on."

But new symptoms arose: a shivering akin to that produced by malaria, an annoying itching on his back, an inability to taste his food. The tests were inconclusive. (Studying Melchior's medication list, a doctor's conclusions are now that he suffered from slight diabetes, a tendency toward congestive heart failure, some gout, and the medical-dermatological results of liver disease.) A male nurse was installed who tended Melchior day and night. He accompanied Lauritz to the parties he insisted on attending, although he could eat virtually nothing. Lovingly, Marianne had his suits altered surreptitiously, hoping vainly that Melchior would not notice that he had lost almost 50 pounds.

Marianne and Klaus fulfilled their function, keeping the house gay and alive. Christmas, spent with some old hunting friends, was a joyous occasion for Lauritz, and then New Year's Eve was made a special celebration by the younger people, who thought that it might be the last. There was champagne and wonderful food, but Lauritz, comfortably clad in his yellow "suit of lights," ate very little. Not surprisingly, he managed to drink to the new year.

Compared with any other eighty-two-year-old man, Melchior was extremely active—addressing the young singers of the San Francisco Opera Merola Program, conducting the orchestra twice (The Master of Ceremonies said, "Young Siegfried is still with us"), speaking before the national convention of the National Association of Teachers of Singing, singing the National Anthem at the Dodger season openers and other games, flying on the Dodger plane to the Bohemian Club in San Francisco for a centennial celebration, and attending the thirtieth anniversary of the Mid-America Guard chapter.

He took special care with the composition of his tribute to Frida Leider on the occasion of her eightieth birthday:

> I think there has never been a more sincere artist, and the greatness of her heart that you hear on the recordings is only a small percentage of what you heard when you saw and heard her on the stage. As she filled her parts absolutely, she also made her partners do their very best, and through that made the performances something very special. I wish that the great architect of the world will give her still many years of health, happiness, and sunshine before the day of sunset arrives, and I wish that I may be blessed with her friendship until then.

Frida Leider returned the compliment after Lauritz's death when she wrote for *Opera:*

> Our friendship during so many years was always of perfect happiness. . . . Even now his Tristan has not been equalled. To me he was always the perfect Tristan: My Tristan!

Not least, in November he invited himself to hunt in Denmark at the estate of Otte Svendsen, a prominent tenor and Kammersanger. Melchior had a good time, even though he couldn't hear very well and was too heavy to move as quickly as necessary, says Svendsen. They had amused themselves the night before by singing for each other. Then his host put Melchior in a huge double bed usually reserved for him and his wife. But, even at eighty-two, Lauritz wasn't about to alter his hunting customs to suit his age or physical infirmities. He insisted that they arise at sunrise. At three o'clock Svendsen barely touched him on the shoulder and Melchior awoke immediately. "What time is it? I'm ready to go! Give me my green socks." Helping him to dress, Svendsen noted that those green socks were as large as his own trousers, and the Melchior's trousers were more like a tent. Although, to his disappointment, Lauritz did not get a deer, he regaled his host with the story of his life while they hunted.

"Godfather loved sitting in the garden and talking about life. He was filled with human wisdom," says Klaus Riisbro. They would often sit up late together, and many times Klaus tried, unsuccessfully, to draw Lauritz out on the subject of singing. One evening he made another attempt, but Lauritz protested, "You cannot *talk* about singing. Put on a record." They listened to *Siegfried.* Melchior was very quiet, absorbed by the music. He ruminated aloud, "You must be *totally* the person described in the story. Kleinchen I owe a lot of this because she was the one who worked on my German and insisted that I spell it out." But Klaus, fortified by two margaritas, was not to be put off. Lauritz answered irritably, "All right, all right. This is a diaphragm," (pointing to his stomach), "and you do not do this," (making a raucous noise), "you sing like this," (making a good tone). "You put your tongue here," (touching the lower front teeth). "Get the idea?" he asked impatiently. "I am retired. I have no interest. My work is done. I could not get higher than that. My voice is gone; I cannot sing anymore." (Ib says, "He just couldn't hear himself. At our house he sang "Helan Går" [a drinking song] so that the rafters shook.")

They both lapsed into silence. Then Melchior continued: "Music is too damned complicated. I know so much about it, but I am so glad that I am retired. I don't have to work anymore. I can do exactly as I please. Everyone just says, 'Lauritz, sing a song,' but if anyone knew what it takes to learn the song and to act that song and to become that song. It's like pulling a load of hay up a hill alone. Lots of hours of aggravation. I want now to live, drink my aquavit and beer every day and have a good time. Be with young people. Go hunting and visiting old friends and all that."

CHAPTER 18

"Leb' wohl, mein Held"

(1973–1974)

Holding his granddaughter Helle's hand, Lauritz Melchior spoke his last words. "Have a good life," he said, wishing for her what he had always held dearest, then stopped breathing.

Ib and Cleo, Marianne Tegner, Klaus Riisbro, Helle Hamilton—all those close to him—had been to visit Lauritz at the hospital on Saturday. As they departed, he had said, "We'll see what happens tomorrow." On Sunday he received another round of visits from the family. For all but Helle, who came late in the day, it was to be a last farewell (a "Lebe wohl") to their hero. He died on March 18, 1973. "I believe he chose the moment and left me with the last of the many gifts he had given me in his life," says granddaughter Helle. By midnight, radio and television were broadcasting the news. In two days he would have been eighty-three years old. Already 104 birthday greetings had arrived at The Viking.

Melchior had been weakened by what were thought to be four different attacks of the Hong Kong flu. "I am so weak now, even when I wake up," was his only complaint, although food had begun to repel him, meat most of all. He would insist on going out, but had to hold his abdomen as he walked, saying, "It's nothing." His inability to swallow anything but carbohydrates was finally diagnosed, but incorrectly, as gall bladder dysfunction. January and February were not good months, but March was so much worse that a decision was made to operate. During the operation the surgeon found a primary cancer of the liver. When he awoke, Melchior, true to form, asked for beer despite his weakness. It is a testimony to his charm, even when ensconced in an intensive care unit, that the staff *gave* it to him. Ib and Cleo were present when Far suffered a cardiac arrest on March 11, soon after the operation. After the emergency medical team pulled him out of it, the first thing Melchior said, as he was coming to, was "My damned chest hurts!" As ever, his optimism was untouched, even by the decision to operate again as soon as he was stronger. During his six-day recuperation he insisted on giving instructions about the Royal Guards and planning the details for his coming birthday party, but he was never to leave the hospital. "He took it like a king," says his godson. "He lived his life right to the end."

There were two memorial services (four, if one counts the 1974 Dana College ceremonies for the opening of the Lauritz Melchior Memorial Room, and the ceremony that Riisbro and secretary Birte Appel conducted: They lit three symbolic Masonic candles at The Viking, believing that Lauritz would see them). In Los Angeles the City Council "stood in reverence;" a special banner over the Los Angeles *Times* headline read "Singer Lauritz Melchior Dies"; and the service was covered by all local papers, the *New York Times*, UPI, AP, and camera crews from all three major networks. There were full pages in *Newsweek* and *Time*, informational releases supplied by his publicity representative and friend, Betty Smith. All the articles cited in some way his "rare combination of artistry and humanity," as did Karl Laufkötter in his eulogy.

Condolence letters came from Richard Nixon, Frida Leider, Danish Ambassador Bartels, the Danish Consuls General, Walter Slezak, Walter O'Malley, the City of Los Angeles, among others. The immense display of flowers included a large bouquet from Lotte Lehmann. She apologized by letter for an illness that had kept her from attending the service: "I will have a private service in listening to the first act of *Walküre*." Ib Melchior designed the memorial program, and, as Melchior had requested, "Siegfried's Funeral March" from *Götterdämmerung* was played. For anyone else this music might have been pretentious; for Lauritz Melchior, as critic Martin Bernheimer said, "it was altogether fitting." Three years earlier Lauritz had told (with his usual tongue-in-cheek) of his fondness for the moment when he, as Siegfried, dies in *Götterdämmerung* and for that piece of music:

> I don't think he wrote anything so great as the "Funeral March." I hope that at my funeral I shall be carried out of the church with that music. You know, when you are singing you can't listen so well. But when you are dead, you can listen perfectly.

The journey of Lauritz Melchior's life finished where he had begun it— in Nørregade. A second, in all respects Masonic, memorial service was held at the square-towered, flat-roofed Cathedral of Copenhagen, Vor Frue Kirke, which had been Lauritz's neighborhood church when he was a boy. Masses of red roses mixed with white carnations and floral wreaths from the Danish Royal Family almost hid the well-known figure of Christ sculpted by Thorvaldsen that stood behind the altar. Birte's son (the only descendant of Lauritz to have served in his beloved Guard) was re-enrolled for one day so that he could be in uniform as he bore Melchior's decorations, resting on a velvet pillow, down the aisle to the font and its kneeling stone angel. Before him strode Ib Melchior, carrying his father's ashes. Royal Guardsmen lining the aisle in their dress uniforms and shakos mirrored the statues of the twelve Apostles that bordered the walls behind them, as the great singer's ashes were carried down the aisle to the organ strains of "Siegfried's Funeral March." Three hymns by B. S. Ingemann, one of Denmark's great hymn poets, were chosen, ones that Danish schoolchildren learned by heart in the early grades. The hymns were aptly chosen for the Melchior rites, for their spirit is one of simple religiousness. "At the end of the day the sun goes down and God himself spreads a blanket of stars over his earth so that all can close their eyes and rest safely, guarded by Him." "Dejlig er jorden" (known in America as "Fairest Lord Jesus") contains the kind of grand musical line coupled with a cheerful innocence of text that in a way symbolized Melchior's art.

There is no question that the loss of a twenty-fifth year at the Metropolitan Opera and the absence of affection from his Danish compatriots were the two great sadnesses of Melchior's life. Those who appreciate the awesome nature of Melchior's singing and the genuine humanity of the man find it tempting to rail at fate for the unfair treatment given him. For this legendary and unique artist to have been denied a fitting end to his operatic career (freely given to many other singers) because of the machinations of a petty administrator seems grossly unjust. For a man who was ever loyal to the country of his birth and unfailingly generous and loving toward his fellow Danes to have been denied the unreserved affection of his countrymen appears a genuine tragedy.

Still, the Metropolitan Opera Company issued a statement in response to queries: There would be no memorial service for Lauritz Melchior as there had been a disagreement between him and Rudolf Bing.

Having been repeatedly nudged by the trustees of the Melchior estate and the loyal Betty Smith, the Metropolitan administration finally yielded grudgingly and accepted the portrait of Melchior as Tristan, as well as the sword, horn, and ring used in *Götterdämmerung* and *Siegfried*. In March 1974 a small occasion was made of the presentation and hanging of the Schattenstein portrait, which was placed next to that of Kirsten Flagstad. Lotte Lehmann, regretting her inability to attend, showed with her pointed remarks that she understood the situation:

> I am very pleased that the Metropolitan Opera at last realizes that a painting of Lauritz should hang in the vestibule along with the others. . . . I am sending my best wishes for a ceremony which will be worthy of Lauritz.

In 1950 most of the musical community had accepted the erroneous story that Bing and Melchior had confronted one another over the rehearsal issue and that Melchior had refused to bend. Now, after his death, most suggested that a reasonable conversation between the two could have set the matter right without depriving the world of a still-functioning, peerless Heldentenor. (One obituary even recalled that Bing himself found the rehearsals "scarcely worth the time.") Sadly, the old canard about Melchior's "laziness" did surface in the obituary notices, asserting that Melchior had been "content" to stay within the narrow confines of a few roles. The truth—that Gatti-Casazza and Edward Johnson repeatedly denied his requests to perform non-Wagnerian roles—went unmentioned.

Ironically, although Denmark had found Lauritz Melchior more to its liking after the 1960 radio *Walküre*, it continued to pay him minimal attention at the end of his life. There was a newspaper strike at the time of his death; therefore immediate publicity was meager. Yet even when the strike was over, little was heard. Much was made of the fact that Melchior had gone into films and cabaret and amassed a fortune. *Information* said, "Now he has been taken into Valhalla where Wagner has awaited him for a long time. [Wagner] will find him quite a handful."

Ib had brought the urn containing his father's ashes from California for interment at the family's burial site. Some find it sad today that the old placard in Assistens Kirkegaard locating the graves of other renowned Copenhagen sons, such as Søren Kierkegaard and Hans Christian Andersen, has not been amended to include that of Lauritz Melchior. A well-known Danish actor has tellingly remarked, "We never forgave him that he did not adopt the obligatory mask of false modesty."

Those of us whose admiration for Lauritz Melchior as man and as artist never faltered (and those who have yet to know his singing) are indebted to Hans Hansen for the poetic assessment in his Danmarks Radio obituary of March 19:

> Nørregade, Denmark, God, the royal family, and the royal guards comprised the customary back-up group for . . . Melchior's many interviews. . . . Although his countrymen did not doubt Melchior's love for these entities, perhaps they had the feeling that . . . he exploited them in a purely elemental way. . . . There were conductors who said Melchior was lazy . . . and there were critics who found him unrhythmical and illusion-disturbing. . . . Perhaps even all [of this] is true. But the peculiar thing is that it matters so incredibly little. For he was the greatest tenor of his time—perhaps the greatest Wagner tenor who ever lived. God *had* touched him with his little finger.

As for the American press, it took up a felicitous phrase of the late Francis Robinson of the Metropolitan Opera Company, which suggested Melchior's awe-inspiring voice and persona: "Melchior was a natural phenomenon, something on the order of Niagara Falls." Without exception, the obituary notices carried on the journalistic trend that had begun after Melchior left the Metropolitan Opera, dividing the history of Heldentenors into two eras, Before and After Melchior. Criticisms of his "xylophonic" or "forced" high notes were nowhere to be found. Now those notes were recalled as brilliant, ample, and having ease. Critics noted that other, lesser tenors were forced to pace themselves carefully, "eyes popping as they sang all out"; that no other Wagner tenor in history had lasted so long, giving tirelessly of his awesome voice; that even other respectable Wagnerian tenors could not approach Melchior's glorious, clarion sound. The writers pardoned Melchior in retrospect for his huge, self-indulged body, which they had thought not credible as young Siegfried or Tristan. They now recalled that Ludwig Schnorr himself had looked "much like a watermelon," that Melchior the actor was doing exactly as Bayreuth had taught him to do, and that he worked his magic not only through vocal splendor, but through a touching humanity in his interpretations. Forgotten were all the old complaints. Now he was recognized as "a giant in every way: his appetite, his voice, his staying power, his repertory, his personality."

After Melchior's retirement, signs pointing to a continuing crisis in the international opera community were everywhere. Scarcely a year went by after 1960 without the publication of a major article that invoked the name of Melchior, while bemoaning the scarcity of singers who could manage the heavy Heldentenor Fach. Melchior's death in 1973 did nothing to interrupt the flow of such journalistic pieces (which were not limited to the United States), and their compliments to Melchior escalated as the years advanced.

In fact, Wolfgang Wagner, director of the Bayreuth Festival, responding to the cancellation of their *Tannhäuser* production for lack of someone good enough to fill the title role, seriously proposed in 1984 a "ten-year global moratorium on Wagner productions during which time the singers could mature and perfect their craft in order to live up to the requirements for this repertoire."

In 1990 the crisis continues unabated. Each heir-apparent who appears is proclaimed a "new Melchior," but only temporarily. Excellent candidates have raised hopes within the Wagnerian world, doing the lighter heroic roles for several years while preparing themselves for the challenge of Tannhäuser, Siegfried, and Tristan. Then, after singing the heavy roles for what seems to be a maximum of ten years, many have faded away or have dropped out, physically incapable of continuing as a *schwerer Held*, if indeed the experience has not rendered them incapable of singing at all.

Each time another Heldentenor was forced to abandon the heavy repertoire a conviction grew among the cognoscenti that there was not going to *be* another Melchior. Harold Schonberg was already certain in 1960 that "The Heldentenor species died with Melchior," and in 1968 the *New York Times* wondered anew "whether the century ever had a Heldentenor to match [Melchior's] kind of color, glorious tone, and effortless technique." Critic/conductor Robert Lawrence answered in 1971 that even then Melchior's Tristan and Tannhäuser still remained "unrivaled." In 1977 a French magazine listed Melchior "among the seven wonders of the world." In his *Record of Singing*, Michael Scott declared, "When Nature created Lauritz Melchior she broke the mold and having done so threw it away." In 1982 radio commentator George Jellinek stated without equivocation that "the more tenors [he heard] in Wagnerian repertoire the more [he was] convinced that Melchior [would] never be equalled, let alone surpassed."

All were in agreement about the discouragement that Melchior's recordings must engender in the new crop of Heldentenors. So pervasive was rhetoric of this sort that some critics were impelled to write articles that forcefully made the opposite case: Why Do All Heroic Tenors Have to be Compared to Melchior?!! When younger critic Peter G. Davis heard in 1985 the reissue of an ordinary Saturday Met broadcast from the 1940s, starring Melchior as Tannhäuser, he was stunned by Melchior's "magnificent performance," which seemed "to defy the laws of nature, and must surely be the despair of all tenors who have since attempted to sing Tannhäuser." Writer John Steane found in 1981 that no tenor had yet challenged Melchior's lifetime position as "the Wagnerian tenor supreme," and *Opus* magazine again made the point in 1987, saying that Melchior's records would in all probability "continue to impose a heavy burden on Melchior's successors, as they have for fifty years already."

To some degree, Melchior was taken for granted during his Metropolitan days, but now that we have had a taste of doing without a similar Heldentenor, we appreciate him. "Singers are not irreplaceable. Except one—Lauritz Melchior," wrote Lee Milazzo in the 1988 *American Record Guide*, adding, "When you hear [Melchior sing] the dying Tristan . . . you understand why the phonograph was invented." In fact, Melchior's reputation with contemporary music lovers rests solidly upon the many reissues of his recordings, which have made him, as German critic Clemens Höslinger wrote in 1970, "the ideal Wagner tenor of today's generation . . . the most important Wagner tenor of the total gramophone record history." When young Wagnerites hear Melchior's recordings for the first time, they are shocked because they have not heard anything comparable in their lifetime. In 1974, Dale Harris of the *New York Times* concurred, saying, "Nearly a quarter-century after his withdrawal from the opera stage Melchior's records serve to remind us that we have heard no tenor voice of comparable splendor since that time."

Is the Melchior story, then, simply the anomaly of a supremely glorious voice whose strength and quality resulted only from an accident of fate?

John Steane has concluded, to the contrary, that Melchior's recordings "bring out more and more clearly . . . [not only] the glory of his voice [but] . . . the sensitivity of his art. . . . What remains are voice and soul." Danish conductor John Frandsen also cited "that fabulous dramatic radiation . . . a kind of vocal illusion that allowed him to a rare degree to get his characters under his skin and give them vocal expression." While excluding a reliable sense of rhythm and tempo, Melchior's supreme gifts included a natural physical and vocal stamina, stemming in no small way from his rare physique. His voice, with its lusty Nordic timbre, was the ideal Heldentenor sound and the ideal Heldentenor size. It was a unique sound, and uniquely suitable for Wagner. To these natural advantages were added the inestimable benefits of good vocal training. Because of the voice's natural cutting edge, aided by a fine technique enabling him to hone that carrying power, it was not necessary for Melchior to force, nor to sing at the top level of his sound in order to cut through the huge Wagnerian orchestra. The audience was not stunned by an unremitting stream of sound from Melchior's throat precisely because he was able to vary dynamic levels constantly and still be heard. In short, Melchior set a standard for the heavy Heldentenor Fach that is valid in 1990 and has yet to be met.

That is not to say that several accidents of birth did not equip Melchior extraordinarily well for his career. Even his fun-loving attitude was an advantage in the long run. Equanimity of spirit made it easier for him to throw off the nervous strains of a singing life, as demonstrated in the 1935 Covent Garden crisis, which Lauritz surmounted with ease. In addition, he would probably not have been able to sustain this beneficial calmness and serenity without the inestimable advantage provided by Kleinchen's actions as overseer of all practical details. She even took over the responsibility of directing his career, handling all debilitating dealings with personal and operatic managements (often the true reason behind actions that elicit frequent use of the word "temperamental").

As for Melchior's acting, to which many writers took exception, it must be put in context with the history of operatic stage concepts. He was trained at Bayreuth, where Cosima Wagner had long resisted theatrical innovations, and where Siegfried had only started to make changes to accommodate the new concepts before his death. Melchior stayed at Bayreuth for only one more season, and was to remain ever frozen in the dramatic attitudes instilled by the two Wagners, thereafter "equating innovation with subversion." Nor was he helped by the staging practices of the Metropolitan Opera, which lagged far behind those of the European opera houses. Only with the appearance of Rudolf Bing were the innovative theatrical ideas that had been affirmed by Herbert Witherspoon fifteen years before finally put into execution at the New York house. Interestingly, with the Metropolitan's conservative 1989 *Ring* production, there may be a trend toward less "desperately novel" staging. There appears to be a suspicion abroad that "Wagner, at his best, is not about what we see on stage—that often defies belief—but what its dramatically incredible characters feel."

As much as it was despised, Melchior's insistence about resting his voice served in no small way to lengthen his career and sustain his vocal gifts. While the circumstances of World War II had made Melchior so important that he could make a rule about rehearsing too much or too often in full voice, today's young Heldentenors could never take such a stance. (Yet Lauritz was adamant in his advice to young singers: Whenever possible, do not sing full voice!) Today's smaller European houses sometimes demand full-voice singing at rehearsals for one opera back-to-back with performances of another. Another compelling reason for singing full voice at rehearsals these days is the new and cruel practice of having an audience for the dress rehearsal. In this situation a singer has no choice; not only is management displeased if he does not sing full voice, but the word gets around that he is either in vocal trouble or will not be well for the performance. His career concerns force a debilitating choice.

This is but one of the many influences that come to bear on the abilities of a young tenor whose physique and voice suggest that he is indeed destined to be a fine Heldentenor. There are several reasons why many of these young singers do not develop as expected: First, the avid desire of opera impresarios for new Heldentenors rages unabated. Promising young tenors suffer an enormous pressure to sing a wide variety of heroic tenor roles immediately. Only those well-advised or very strong can withstand it. (The career of Heldentenor Siegfried Jerusalem affords an example: within one year of his first performances as a singer, he was offered Parsifal and Lohengrin.) Second, a singer's daily life is now complicated by the ceaseless traveling required by today's singing career. The health of his body—which strongly influences the health of his vocal cords—is constantly undermined by the sheer physical fatigue caused by travel, not to mention the really dangerous vocal effects of all the hours spent in the airplane environment, which dehydrates the vocal cords. Third, in Melchior's day as a young singer, big cuts were made throughout *Lohengrin*, in Acts II and III of *Tristan*, and many places in *Siegfried*, including the "Forging Song." Today the trend is for conductors to open every cut, thereby making it even harder for singers to manage the heavy roles than it was for Melchior. Fourth—the list is completed by two factors that penalize the would-be Heldentenor: the big size of most opera houses and the conspicuous lack of interest in keeping the orchestra down for the benefit of the singer. (Ironically, at Bayreuth—the only place where a covered pit affords the singer an advantage—conductors have periodically requested its removal. Some have even been successful.)

Factors governing a Heldentenor's life and career may appear unimportant taken individually—the necessity for constant jet travel, uncovered pits, loud orchestras, ever higher orchestra pitches, deeper stages, larger auditoriums, uncut performances, lack of sound-reflecting backdrops, lighting from above that forces singers upstage, even the current cultivation of dramatic realism and the changed contemporary ideal of manly beauty—but in the aggregate they spell the difference between success and failure.

What then—forty years after Melchior's retirement from opera and seventeen years after his death—does the operatic world still await? A Heldentenor voice of steely power and clarion ring that can cut through the Wagnerian orchestra handily; a voice so strong that it never needs to operate at its limit, giving the sense of power in reserve; a voice, therefore, with the endurance to triumph at the end of the role; a voice, furthermore, not only so gifted as to strength and quality, but also so well-schooled in the idiomatic use of the German language that it reveals the poetry of the score, and so technically skilled that it can master the art of dynamic shading rather than capitulating to the adoption of a uniform fortissimo bellow. This is to say, a voice that is equal to Richard Wagner's own ideal.

Despite the vicissitudes of a Wagnerian career today, it seems clear that Lauritz Melchior would have surmounted even these problems as always, probably with power in reserve. What terrors could they hold for a man who splendidly survived 223 Tristans, 183 Siegmunds, 144 Tannhäusers, 128 Siegfrieds, 107 "elder" Siegfrieds, 106 Lohengrins, 81 Parsifals, and (at nearest reckoning) 2,100 concerts?

Leb' wohl, mein Held.

Notes

Whenever several quotes from the same source occur within one paragraph, only the first quote will be cited in the endnote, but the citation will give all the source page numbers in the order of their appearance in the text.

Abbreviations Used in Notes

APB	Associated Press Bulletin	NYE	*New York Enquirer*
AMO	Archives, Metropolitan Opera	NYHT	*New York Herald-Tribune*
BE	*Brooklyn Eagle*	NYJ	*New York Journal*
BET	*Boston Evening Transcript*	NYJA	*New York Journal-American*
BT	*Boston Transcript*	NYP	*New York Post*
CHN	*Chicago News*	NYS	*New York Sun*
CLN	*Cleveland News*	NYT	*New York Times*
CPD	*Cleveland Plain Dealer*	NYW	*New York World*
CTI	*Chicago Times*	NYWT	*New York World-Telegram*
CTR	*Chicago Tribune*	OPN	*Opera News*
DCM	Dana College Memorabilia	OP	*Opera*
DMN	*Dallas Morning News*	PASR	*Park Avenue Social Review*
ET	*Etude*	PB	*Philadelphia Bulletin*
HF	*High Fidelity*	PI	*Philadelphia Inquirer*
LAT	*Los Angeles Times*	PN	*Philadelphia News*
LMD	Lauritz Melchior diary	RG	*Radio Guide*
LMPM	LM personal manuscript	RL	*Radio Life*
LT	*London Times*	SFA	*San Francisco Argonaut*
MUM	*Musical America*	SFCB	*San Francisco Call-Bulletin*
MUC	*Musical Courier*	SFC	*San Francisco Chronicle*
MPM	*Motion Picture Magazine*	SFE	*San Francisco Examiner*
n.d.	no date on clipping	SFN	*San Francisco News*
n.p.	no paper or periodical on clipping	SR	*Stereo Review*
		ST	*Stage*
NOTP	*New Orleans Times-Picayune*	TI	*Time*
NWS	*Newsweek*	VA	*Variety*
NY	*New Yorker*	WP	*Washington Post*
NYA	*New York American*	WS	*Washington Star*
NYDN	*New York Daily News*		

Preface

p.xi *"The more tenors I hear"*: George Jellinek, SR, July 1982.
p.xi *"when nature created"*: Scott, p. 248.
p.xi *"[defied] the laws of nature"*: Peter G. Davis, *New York*, September 9, 1985.
p.xi *"Wagnerian tenor supreme"*: John Steane, liner notes for "Lauritz Melchior," Pearl, GEMM 228/229.

p.xii *"I never let singing interfere"*: *Parade*, August 7, 1949.

p.xiii *Berton Coffin has wisely*: Letter, Berton Coffin to Shirlee Emmons, July 29, 1984.

p.xiv *"How wonderful it must be"*: Interview, Cleo Baldon, Los Angeles, November 1987.

Chapter 1. Da Capo: "En København-Dreng" (1890–1905)

p.1 *"I was a Copenhagen lad"*: Interview, Hans Hansen, Copenhagen, August 1983.

p.1 Copenhagen background: Interview, Marianne Tegner, Copenhagen, August 1983.

p.2 *The Melchiors had been Lutheran ministers*: In Denmark there are two strains of the Melchior family: One emigrated from North Germany in the nineteenth century and is now prominent in politics, the garment industry, and the synagogue. The other strain descends directly from a seventeenth-century bellringer in the North Jutland coastal town of Grenaa and stops unbroken at Lauritz Melchior (letter, Hans Hansen to Shirlee Emmons, May 16, 1988).

p.2 *"bring music"*: J. Melchior, *Memories, Especially of Singing and Music*.

p.2 *"It caused immense sorrow"*: LMPM.

p.3 *a very big baby*: Bodil Melchior Termansen, Arne Honoré tape interview, "My Life's Adventure," Danmarks Radio, April 23, 1966.

p.3 *"She loved me and spoiled me"*: LMPM. Kristine Jensen's first cookbook sold 100,000 copies in Denmark, a country with only four million inhabitants. Miss Jensen's renown continues today: Singer Kim Borg has composed and performed a cantata entitled "Frøken Jensens Leverpostej" ("Miss Jensen's Liver Paste").

p.3 *"half a father"*: LMPM.

p.3 *"Lauritz could never spell"*: Interview, Hans Hansen, Copenhagen, August 1983.

p.4 *"getting into the hole"*: Letter, Knud Hegermann-Lindencrone to Shirlee Emmons, December 12, 1987, quoting Niels Peder Jørgensen of the Royal Danish Theater, who cites Karl Bjanhof's 1898 memoirs, which gives these details.

p.4 *"Down there, where the acoustics"*: Rose Heylbut, "A Little Touch of God's Finger," ET, n.d.

p.4 *"one of the most beautiful"*: Bodil Melchior Termansen, Arne Honoré tape interview, "My Life's Adventure," Danmarks Radio, April 23, 1966.

p.4 *Jorgen Melchior's musical genes*: J. Melchior, *Memories, Especially of Singing and Music*. Grandfather Hans Henrik Melchior had played the flute and piano, while Grandmother was "completely unmusical." Jørgen, given piano and violin lessons, was bored with the technical side and ceased studying—exactly as Lauritz would do—which he later regretted. Jørgen belonged to four different male quartets during Lauritz's youth.

p.4 *"probably played a great part"*: LMPM.

p.4 *"the best dancer in Copenhagen"*: LMPM.

p.4 *"he was a dandy"*: Bodil Melchior Termansen, Arne Honoré tape interview, "My Life's Adventure," Danmarks Radio, April 23, 1966.

p.5 *"medicine in [his] blood"*: LM interview, "The Fairy Tale of My Life," Danmarks Radio, produced by Hemming Hartmann-Petersen, December 20, 1970.

p.5 *"the idea of being able to help"*: LM, Arne Honoré tape interview, "My Life's Adventure," Danmarks Radio, April 23, 1966.

p.5   *"It was a little bit of a disappointment"*: Bodil Melchior Termansen, Arne Honoré tape interview, "My Life's Adventure," Danmarks Radio, April 23, 1966.

p.5   *"When the time came to choose"*: LM, Arne Honoré tape interview, "My Life's Adventure," Danmarks Radio, April 23, 1966.

Chapter 2. Training As a Baritone (1905–1916)

p.6   *"by 1908 it would be forced to close its doors"*: The old school had been torn down for sanitary reasons. The money spent on the new building caused cash-flow problems for Jørgen Melchior at the very time when the commune schools started in Denmark. The good teachers now to be found in commune schools, together with the taxes levied to support the schools, encouraged the "solid citizens," who had formerly been the bulwark of the Melchior Borger- og Realskole, to enroll their children in the public schools. 1908 saw the last recruiting for the school (LM, Arne Honoré tape interview, "My Life's Adventure," April 23, 1966).

p.6   *"Tante [Jensen] . . . loved to invite"*: LMPM.

p.6   *"choose a trade"*: LMPM.

p.6   *Helped by his father's musical connections*: Jørgen Melchior's connections with Copenhagen musical circles were many. He was a member of the highly prestigious Students' Choral Society, whose members were doctors, lawyers, teachers, composers, and performers. His election to the "small chorus of the S.C.S. afforded him the pleasures of sophisticated music-cum-social evenings in the company of such celebrities as J.P.E. Hartmann, one of Denmark's most celebrated composers of the romantic period, Peter Lange-Müller, a Danish Lieder composer, and even Edvard Grieg (with whom Jørgen studied some of Grieg's own male-quartet music).

p.6   *"At last, after all these trials"*: LMPM.

p.7   *"if she had not existed"*: LMPM.

p.7   *"At that time I had"*: LMPM. Poul Bang was the most celebrated voice teacher in Copenhagen at this time.

p.7   *"The basic thing of all singing"*: Rose Heylbut, "A Little Touch of God's Finger," ET, n.d.

p.8   *"your words and your emotions"*: LMPM.

p.8   *"He was the first one"*: LMPM.

p.8   *"My voice had developed"*: LMPM.

p.8   *"would absolutely have sung"*: Knud Hegermann-Lindencrone, quoting Gradman, *The Gramophone*, January 1939.

p.9   *"ransomed at the end of October"*: LMPM.

p.9   *"The only outstanding aspect"*: I. Melchior, p. 52.

p.9   *Previously, said his sister Bodil*: Bodil Melchior Termansen, Arne Honoré tape interview, "My Life's Adventure," Danmarks Radio, April 23, 1966.

p.9   *"at first glance"*: Birte Melchior, *Hendes Verden* #30, 1970.

p.9   *"her membership in that world"*: Inger's brother, sister, and sister-in-law were actors also.

p.9   *Inger's actor-father had lived*: Aalborg Stiftstidende, June 3, 1907.

p.10   *This flamboyant scandal*: Birte Melchior, *Hendes Verden* #30, 1970.

p.10   *"happy-go-lucky Lauritz"*: Mrs. Birgit Villaden, handwriting expert, having examined samples of Melchior's handwriting from the turn of the century and from the end of his life, has concluded from the substantial changes between the two that he did acquire a preoccupation with money later in life, possibly tutored by Kleinchen (personal communication, Birgit Villaden to Inga Hulgaard, December 1986).

p.10 Funeral story: Interview, Birte Melchior, August 1983; LM, Arne Honoré tape interview, "My Life's Adventure," Danmarks Radio, April 23, 1966.

p.10 *"promising"*: LMPM.

p.10 *"extraordinary aptitude"*: *Politiken*, May 4, 1920.

p.10 *"brilliant, for he had"*: Lilly Lamprecht, Arne Honoré tape interview, "My Life's Adventure," Danmarks Radio, April 23, 1966.

p.10 *"the most wonderful baritone"*: Bernhard Møller Petersen, tape interview, "The Fairy Tale of My Life," Danmarks Radio, December 27, 1970, produced by Hemming Hartmann-Petersen. Bernhard Petersen added, "When he came over to [my small apartment] and sang, we had to open the doors and windows; otherwise he would have blown us to the ground—already then he had such a big voice."

p.10 *"It was as if"*: Bodil Melchior Termansen, Arne Honoré tape interview, "My Life's Adventure," April 23, 1966.

p.11 *"Inger's dream of a cozy home"*: Birte Melchior, *Hendes Verden* #30, 1970.

Chapter 3. Metamorphosis: Baritone into Tenor (1916–1922)

p.12 *Gradman had engaged Sarah Cahier*: Mme. Charles Cahier, as she was known to Lauritz, was a very interesting character. Born Sarah Jane Layton-Walker in Memphis, Tennessee, she had won a reputation in concert and church singing as Mrs. Morris Black. She studied in Paris with Jean de Reszke and worked in Berlin with Mahler, who later engaged her as alto soloist in his "Das Lied von der Erde." In 1905 she married a Swedish gentleman and began to bill herself under his name, an idiosyncrasy that persisted throughout her singing career and her later teaching career at the State Academy of Vienna, at the Curtis Institute in Philadelphia, and privately in New York. Other than Melchior, one of her most celebrated students was Marian Anderson (NYT, April 16, 1951).

p.12 *"But you are not a baritone!"*: LM quoting Sarah Cahier, interview with Arne Honoré, "My Life's Adventure," Danmarks Radio, April 23, 1966.

p.12 *"could not understand"*: Birte Melchior, tape interview, "The Fairy Tale of My Life," Danmarks Radio, December 20, 1970, produced by Hemming Hartmann-Petersen.

p.13 *Herold had been Lauritz's idol*: Vilhelm Herold, like Melchior, had studied acting with Peter Jerndorff, reading Danish verse and prose with him for three years. After several auditions, the Royal Opera accepted him. He was particularly remembered for his poetic portrayals of Faust, Turiddu (*Cavalleria Rusticana*), and Lohengrin. Possessed of the same kind of stamina as his famous student, Herold sang 29 roles a total of 707 times at the Royal Theater. Like his successor, he was given the Order of Merit. At the time Melchior knew him, Herold was already a great teacher. Later he became a good stage director and a fine administrator of the Royal Opera (Vilhelm Herold Museum, Hasle, Bornholm, Denmark).

p. 13   *"He did for me the transition"*: LM, Arne Honoré tape interview, "My Life's Adventure," Danmarks Radio, April 23, 1966.

p. 13   *History does show us*: Pleasants, p. 159.

p. 13   *"low tenor"*: Jens Malte Fischer, quoting Julius Hey, *Opernwelt*, June 1986.

p. 13   *"Before the love potion"*: Wiesmann, et al, p. 84. It must be remembered that, in Gustav Mahler's period as Intendant, his ensemble had no specialists. All singers were expected to do a broad array of roles, spanning Fachs.

p. 14   *"only with a solid technical background"*: "Who's Who with Cobey Black," Maui, n.p., n.d.

p. 14   *"there is a big hole"*: LM, Arne Honoré tape interview, "My Life's Adventure," Danmarks Radio, April 23, 1966. A technical term for Melchior's term "grind down the voice" would be "to narrow the voice."

p. 14   *"Melchior believed"*: Interview, Leonard Eisner, New York, November 1984.

p. 14   *"The Heldentenor voice is one"* and *"If you start"*: Louis Biancolli, *New York World-Telegram and Sun*, March 5, 1944.

p. 14   *"exploded, and from experience"*: LMPM.

p. 14   *"I helped him a little"*: Holger Boland, quoting Herold, *Ascolta*, April 1983.

p. 14   *"You should not ask"*: Holger Boland, *Ascolta*, April 1983.

p. 15   *"Life does not give you"*: LM interview, "The Fairy Tale of My Life," Danmarks Radio, produced by Hemming Hartmann-Petersen, December 25, 1970.

p. 15   *"Speaking of emotional effects"*: *American Music Lover*, n.d., 1934.

p. 15   *"Tannhäuser is first of all"*: Knud Hegermann-Lindencrone, *The Gramophone*, January 1939. Vilhelm Herold's exact words were: "Tannhäuser is first of all a poetic dreamer, who does not care for this stupid world and its hypocritical conventions and who does exactly as he wants to do, without asking anybody's permission."

p. 15   *"His voice already seems to have"*: Gustav Hetsch, *Musik*, December 1, 1918.

p. 15   *how much more correct*: LMPM.

p. 15   *Strauss himself, in attendance as conductor*: LMPM; Nually, p. 30.

p. 16   *By any standards*: Another gentleman, the Danish ambassador to London, helped Melchior by arranging various parties at the embassy where the young singer could perform and have the opportunity to meet the right people. When this gentleman's grandson, Ulrik Ahlefeldt-Laurvig, visited California in 1962, Melchior insisted on repaying the hospitality shown him so long ago in London (Ulrik Ahlefeldt-Laurvig, tape interview, "The Fairy Tale of My Life," Danmarks Radio, December 27, 1970, produced by Hemming Hartmann-Petersen).

p. 16   *"second big luck"*: LMPM.

p. 16   *"I lived like a small prince"*: LMPM.

p. 16   *"Through the 1920s"*: Moore, *Furthermoore*, p. 39.

p. 17   *Some years later Kirsten Flagstad*: Biancolli, p. 30; Nually, p. 31.

p. 17   *Samson story*: Nually, p. 31.

p. 18   *"lacked the grand opera style"* and *"tower of strength"*: *Dagens Nyheder*, May 4, 1920.

p. 18   *"with great force and authority"*: *Berlingske Tidende*, May 4, 1920.

p. 18   *"strangely uneven"*: *Dagens Nyheder*, May 4, 1920.

p. 18   *Inger was fearful*: Birte Melchior, *Hendes Verden* #30, 1970.

p. 18   *"My father was"*: Interview, Birte Melchior, August 1983.

p. 18   *"He found the going hard"*: Gaisberg, p. 130.

p. 19   Description of the Chelmsford studio: NBC Press Book, 1938–1939.

p.19   *"I stepped up to the funnel"*: NBC Press Book, 1938–1939.

p.19   *Promenade Concert program*: Nually, p. 34.

p.19   *"his manly appearance"*: Wood, p. 312.

p.19   *Walpole, a Wagnerite, had heard Melchior at the Prom Concert*: Walpole had passed Queen's Hall on his way to a dinner party. Since he was early, he had decided to spend a few minutes listening to some music and bought a one-shilling standing room ticket. Just as he went in, Lauritz was singing one of his Wagner arias. Hugh enjoyed Lauritz's interpretation. Angered by the unfavorable review, he was moved to write Lauritz the note after sending off a letter to the critic. Writing to reviewers was one of Walpole's favorite diversions, second only to writing to authors. Melchior's concert was hardly Walpole's first opportunity to intervene with the press on behalf of a young artist. T.S. Eliot once remarked about Walpole's "capacity to admire generously the work of others" and his readiness "to help and testify to his belief in their future." When, at the time of his death, Walpole's wide acceptance in social and literary circles was denigrated in the official obituaries, a flurry of rebuttals came immediately from some of Britain's most admired writers, most of whom had been befriended by Walpole early on. Quick to divine new talent, he made extraordinarily few mistakes in his appraisals and gave solid financial help to countless young authors in addition to Melchior (Steele, p. 106, 110).

p.19   *"the joy of the evening"*: Hart-Davis, p. 197.

p.20   *"intimate friend"*: LMPM. Among the literary enthusiasts was Marjorie Scott, whose mother was president of the prestigious Pen Club. Marjorie was appalled at Lauritz's ignorance. As one of England's foremost authors and lecturers, Walpole was much in the public eye.

p.20   *Lauritz's friend presented him*: Walpole was a tall, rosy-faced man with thinning slicked-down blondish hair, a genial smile, and a face conspicuous for its strong, protruding chin. He wore horn-rimmed glasses with thick lenses. His excellent speaking voice and platform manner was combined with a pleasing demeanor with perhaps a hint of pomposity. Walpole clearly loved lecturing and could think well on his feet, two good reasons for his enormous success as a lecturer in England and America (Steele, pp. 19,22).

p.20   *his house near Regent Park*: Walpole had leased a house at 24 York Terrace upon returning in April 1920 from his very successful first American tour. Both ends of Regent Park fell within the vista afforded by the house, which sat on a corner lot (Hart-Davis, p. 192).

p.20   *"a great child"*: Hart-Davis, p. 197.

p.20   *"great deal of the child"*: Hart-Davis, pp. 74, 75.

p.20   *"six parts child and four parts living artists"*: Pathfinder, n.d., 1950.

p.20   *"He had the actual consciousness"*: Hart-Davis, p. 110.

p.20   "He loved every dog": Hart-Davis, frontispiece. This quote is taken from the writings of Jean Paul Richter, a German poet whose home was, coincidentally, very near Bayreuth.

p.20   *Among his friends*: Steele, p. 19.

p.20   *"Melchior is indeed"*: Hart-Davis, p. 202.

p.20   *Next came the literary circle*: Hart-Davis, p. 207.

p.20   *"The true quality of his voice"*: Hart-Davis, p. 205. Melchior's version of Walpole's statement was told in a radio interview in Denmark, "Here it is not going to work for you. If you are going to become somebody, you will have to get out in the big world. I have means so that I can help you" ("My Life's Adventure," interviewer, Arne Honoré, Danmark's Radio, April 30, 1966).

p.21 *Walpole's offer*: Nually, p. 41.

p.22 *Melchior had sung Chappell's popular songs*: One of the ways that Melchior had survived financially in London was to sing Chappell-published songs. "[Chappell] had to do with Queen's Hall, and if they liked you, when they had new songs to be presented, you were requested to sing these songs and act as an agent for them. Every time you could prove that one of those songs was printed in your program and had been performed in public, you were paid so and so much for it" (LM, Arne Honoré tape interview, "My Life's Adventure," Danmarks Radio, April 30, 1966).

p.22 Melchior suggests "Gluntarne": Nually, p. 42.

p.22 *Wigmore Hall was rented for April 6*: Walpole's diary disagrees, stating that the concert took place in March, which is a date LMPM assigns to a Liverpool concert. In this instance, Melchior's date, April 6, seems more logical, considering the short amount of time between the February 22 arrival and the concert.

p.22 *"a Croesus of his very own"*: LMPM.

p.22 *As Princess of Wales*: Wechsberg, p. 145.

p.23 *"They were two beautiful and fine"*: LMPM.

p.23 *"Does Your Highness recall"*: LMPM.

p.23 Inger's reactions to London: Nually, p. 44.

p.23 *a lieder and oratorio singer-turned-teacher*: Raymond von zur Mühlen had known Brahms, and Coenraad Bos had often accompanied for him. He first sang in England in 1901 at Bechstein Hall. On this occasion Busoni and Ysäye themselves were also on the program, accompanied by Hamilton Harty and Victor Beigel (Newton, p. 50).

p.23 *A bon vivant, Beigel*: Newton, p. 50.

p.23 *"there was no need to discover"*: Newton, p. 176.

p.24 Beigel audition story: LMPM; Nually, p. 44. Victor Beigel was invited to visit Bayreuth as a guest of Cosima Wagner every festival year. He was also the teacher of the fine black tenor, Roland Hayes.

p.24 *"a big Schnurrbart"* and *"He said to me"*: LM, Arne Honoré tape interview, "My Life's Adventure," Danmarks Radio, April 30, 1966.

p.24 *"in August when he died"*: Melchior often told of an incident involving Caruso. Lauritz was walking on a London street when he stopped to look in a window behind which was a poster advertising his own concert appearance. Suddenly he realized that the light was making a very sharp reflection on the windowpane. As he watched, the reflection showed Enrico Caruso coming up behind him on the sidewalk, then looking beyond him at the poster. Lauritz turned around. Caruso grunt, "Hmmff!" and left. The Melchior family, to whom the story was related more than once, believed the story, but others always questioned its credibility. Had Caruso really been in London at that time, or had Lauritz's own preoccupation with the world-famous Italian singer made him imagine the entire affair? Since Lauritz's first concert in London was in September 1920 and Caruso spent that spring and summer singing in Cuba, vacationing on Long Island, and on tour in Canada, the conclusion is that it was not possible in 1921. Even if Melchior had mistaken the year, Caruso was never in London when Melchior was there (Greenfeld, pp. 231–242). Nevertheless, Lauritz repeats the story at this point in the personal manuscript.

p.24   *"Victor Beigel costs"*: LMPM.

p.24   *"What he taught me"*: LM, Arne Honoré tape interview, "My Life's Adventure," Danmarks Radio, April 30, 1966.

p.25   *Walpole's influential connections*: His father was the Bishop of Edinburgh.

p.25   Copenhagen reception: Nually, p. 45.

p.25   *The Walpole-Beigel plan*: Hart-Davis, p. 218.

p.25   *"Beigel taught me a solid singing technique"*: LMPM.

p.26   *Beigel unexpectedly declared*: Beigel may have met Schalk on one of the conductor's two prewar visits to England, during the winter of 1907 and again in the autumn of 1911, when Schalk conducted the German seasons at Covent Garden. After conducting in Prague and Berlin, Franz Schalk had begun his directorship of the Vienna Staatsoper in 1918. At the time of Melchior's audition Schalk and Richard Strauss had been co-directors of the company since 1919 (Kralik, pp. 75, 79).

p.26   *Schalk recommended*: Anna Mildenburg's appearances at Bayreth had been arranged by Gustav Mahler, whose personal relationship with the singer before her marriage to Viennese playwright Hermann Bahr was apparently not at all a secret. Mahler had become her mentor when she was a novice singer at the Hamburg Opera. When he went to Vienna as director, he took his protégée with him. He introduced her to Cosima at Bayreuth, where she sang Kundry (the youngest ever) and Ortrud. Mahler chose her because she had the kind of voice he preferred, "bigger, harder, brittle . . . capable of a greater degree of expression." After 1919 she became a teacher at the Munich Academy and directed Wagner's works at the Munich Opera (Wiesmann, p. 83).

p.26   *"understood how to turn the spirit of the role"*: Wiesmann, p. 83.

p.26   *"the world to be at [his] feet"*: LMPM

p.26   *"vacation-time children"*: Birte Melchior, tape interview, "The Fairy Tale of My Life," Danmarks Radio, December 20, 1970, produced by Hemming Hartmann-Petersen.

p.27   *"Inger objected strongly"*: LMPM.

p.27   *Why could he not be content*: Interview, Birte Melchior, Copenhagen, August 1983.

p.27   *He intended to find*: Nually, p. 47.

p.27   *eighteen-year-old girl*: Maria Anna Hacker, it is generally agreed, was sixty when she died in 1963. That would put the date of her birth in 1903. (In the black pages of the old-fashioned photo album devoted to her childhood and early years in Germany all dates are covered with a tenacious white tape.) Born in Mühldorf, Bavaria, the daughter of Postmaster Karl Hacker, Maria Anna, named for her mother, was very pretty but still plump at the age of eighteen, and she did not really grow from mere prettyness to true beauty until around 1927. Shortly after graduation from school, she told the New York press, she joined a film company in which she was called upon to do all the daredevil stunts.

p.27   *he spent an enjoyable evening*: Interview, Cleo Baldon, Los Angeles, December 1983.

p.28   *"I think so"*: LMPM.

p.28   *he not only explained*: LMPM.

p.28   *her dreams of marriage*: LMPM.

p.28   *"intimate friend"*: LMD.

p.28   *"who had watched over me"*: LMPM.

p.28   *the catalyst for a telegram*: Hart-Davis, p. 231. Hugh Walpole stated his belief that the Berlin concert had precipitated Siegfried Wagner's telegram in a May 18, 1923, letter to his mother.

Chapter 4. A Bayreuth Beginning (1923–1924)

p.29   *Bayreuth's sumptuous Villa Wahnfried*: Wahnfried, much admired, became the model for other houses built by artists and those of artistic inclinations. The London *Daily Telegraph* had in 1876 disparaged it as a "house decorated with gaudy frescoes and mottoes, bearing a fantastic name." An elaborate sgraffito panel on the center wall above the entrance featured Siegfried Wagner as the "future"—and Cosima as "music"—in an allegory of drama and music united in the art of Richard Wagner. Three plaques placed on the face of the house by Wagner's order read, "Here where my delusions found peace, let this house be called by me 'Wahnfried' [Peace from Delusion]. (Hartford, pp. 39, 89; Skelton, *Wieland Wagner*, p. 27.)

p.29   *Yet Bahr-Mildenburg had told him*: Bahr-Mildenburg had admired Cosima from their first meeting. "I came to Bayreuth, stood one day in Wahnfried's twilight-filled hall, and then Cosima Wagner entered . . . [I stood] wordless and frightened without understanding what came over me or that life had spoken its most decisive word. Today I know that fate . . . had given my art a royal guidance on its way: Gustav Mahler and Cosima Wagner" (Bahr-Mildenburg, p. 50). Describing the effect of Cosima's presence upon her, Bahr-Mildenburg says, "One has the warm feeling that she advises one not only with her intellect, but also with her heart. . . . In front of her one is even ashamed of any trivial thought" (Bahr-Mildenburg, pp. 84, 85).

p.29   *"Soon you will stand"*: Bahr-Mildenburg, quoting Mahler, p. 27.

p.30   *When the old butler*: Nually, p. 49.

p.30   *Kittel, a Viennese who had come to Bayreuth*: Bayreuth Archives.

p.30   Bayreuth audition particulars: LMPM; Nually, pp. 49, 50.

p.30   *"Mother has complimented"*: LMPM.

p.30   *"motionless white apparition"*: LM tape interview, Danmarks Radio, December 25, 1970.

p.31   *"I stayed on in Bayreuth for a month"*: LMPM.

p.31   *"a very delightful and pleasant man"*: LMPM

p.31   *"What he taught me about my Wagner roles"*: LMPM. Later, Melchior added, "Kittel instructed me in the real old Wagner style, which is somewhat different from the modern one." (Arne Honoré tape interview, Danmarks Radio, April 30, 1966.)

p.31   *"In the works of Richard Wagner"*: Speech by LM, New York University, 1932, and New York Wagner Society, 1934. Melchior must have memorized Kittel's remarks verbatim, for they have been recorded elsewhere in almost exactly the same language.

p.31   *"the whole part through with me"*: LMPM.

p.31   *Often Siegfried would sit*: Nually, p. 51.

p.31   *"sign from 'Mama'"*: LM, Arne Honoré tape interview, "My Life's Adventure," Danmarks Radio, April 30, 1966.

p.31   *"Mother wants me to explain"*: LMPM; LM tape interview, Danmarks Radio, December 25, 1970.

p.32   *his duty to provide visual expression*: Skelton, *Wagner at Bayreuth*, p. 81. Melchior says in his personal manuscript only that Daniela also lectured him about Wagnerian tradition. Skelton has articulated her views, and I have combined them.

p.32   *"Frau Cosima stressed"*: Wessling, *Toscanini in Bayreuth*, p. 10.

p.32   *"chief remembrancer"*: Hartford quoting Shaw, p. 145.

p.32   *by means of leitmotifs*: Although Bayreuth bookstores offered the pilgrims of 1876 at least three enthusiastic volumes describing and listing the leitmotifs, and urged the serious listener to memorize a minimum of 23 in order to understand the Music of the Future, not all visitors to the festival embraced Wagner's compositional methods. Eduard Hanslick, the prickly Viennese music critic, dryly noted: "full enjoyment and reception are impossible when understanding and memory must be ever on the alert to catch the wary allusion" (Hartford, pp. 76, 77).

p.32   *"We are preserving"*: Marek, *Cosima Wagner*, p. 225.

p.32   *"superb* Tristan *conducted by"*: Skelton, *Richard and Cosima Wagner*, p.225.

p.33   *"what began as a general artistic principle"*: Skelton, *Wagner at Bayreuth*, p. 81.

p.33. *Conductor Felix Mottl noted*: Marek, *Cosima Wagner*, p. 216.

p.33   *"The Master [had] allowed everybody to express"*: Marek, quoting Lehmann, *Cosima Wagner*, p. 228.

p.33   *"not all could see beyond the drill"*: Skelton, quoting Bahr-Mildenburg, *Wagner at Bayreuth*, p. 83.

p.33   *Sadly, all the energy*: Hartford, 213.

p.33   *"was the last singer"*: LM, tape interview, "The Fairy Tale of My Life," Danmarks Radio, December 25, 1970, produced by Hemming Hartmann-Petersen.

p.33   *"came to him secondhand"* and *"I never spoke one word"*: LM tape interview by Arne Honoré, Danmarks Radio, April 30, 1966.

p.33   *Bayreuth artists really liked*: Siegfried Wagner was a charming and democratic companion. Said Lauritz, "It was an experience just for a young singer to be in an informal, friendly way with the big names of his art . . . [during] the jolly evenings in the restaurant Die Eule, where Siegfried always came" (LMPM).

p.33   *Winifred had been born in England*: F. Wagner, p. 4.

p.33   *"bewitchingly charming"*: Geissmar, p. 180. By 1923 Winifred had encountered Adolf Hitler at the Bechstein house in Munich. Because she felt deeply about the terrible conditions that prevailed in Germany after the war, Winifred was sympathetic to Hitler's nationalistic ideas and obsessed with his importance to the future of Germany. Siegfried shared the belief held by his mother and wife that the Germans were a master race, but his compassionate nature and deep interest in music did not allow space for a broad interest in politics. His daughter Friedelind said that her father's attitude toward Hitler, when he finally allowed him to visit Bayreuth, was that of a benevolent uncle. (F. Wagner, pp. 3, 8, 16, 17.)

p.33   *One afternoon in Siegfried's office* and *"Siegfried was not very Nazi"*: I. Melchior, p. 29; LM interview, "The Fairy Tale of My Life," Danmarks Radio, December 25, 1970, produced by Hemming Hartmann-Petersen. Melchior also stated in this interview, "I saw [Hitler] but I never said hello to him. I said to Siegfried that I did not want to meet Mr. Hitler."

p.34 *Their own versions of the Wagnerian music drama*: F. Wagner, p. 19.

p.34 *their wheelbarrow tours*: Skelton, *Wieland Wagner*, p. 36.

p.34 *"the congenial and natural society of children"*: O'Connell, p. 81. O'Connell tells a tender story about Melchior's disappearance from an adult gathering. When the host, previously alerted by an uproar from the children's quarters composed of manly laughter, childish squeals, feeble quacking, and indeterminate watery sounds, suddenly heard a total absence of sound, he went up to the third floor. The children had been given an assortment of barnyard animals, including a baby duck. In the bathroom he found the two boys gazing at the figure of Melchior, who held the "flaccid and dripping cadaver of a baby duck clutched to his massive bosom while he lamented, 'I didn't know he don't schwim. Nun he iss todt,' " (O'Connell, p. 82). Niece Eva Andersen still remembers Lauritz as the very best uncle a child could have, always in a good mood, always promoting fun and festivity (interview, Eva Andersen, Copenhagen, August 1986).

p.34 *"Your entire way of looking"*: Marek, quoting Wagner, *Front Seat at the Opera*, p. 212.

p.34 *"Don't think that your way of life"*: LM letter to William Arlock, March 26, 1965. Wagner's own remarks to his tenor Unger were practically identical to Melchior's words: "Don't think that normal behavior and stage acting are two separate things" (Skelton, *Wagner at Bayreuth*, p. 135).

p.34 *"I must constantly go"*: Ralf Stuckman, quoting Wagner's January 3, 1876, letter to Julius Hey, *"Mein lieber Schwan," NZ Forum*, June 1987.

p.34 *robust and sturdy body*: Both Siegfried Jerusalem and Timothy Jenkins, present-day Heldentenors, have said that they must work constantly at physical training in order to keep their bodies up to the demands of Wagnerian music. Melchior did not follow any physical regimen. Dr. Van Lawrence of Houston, Texas, one of the greatest otolaryngologists of the singers' world today, has discovered by an experiment of his own that vocal cords after an ordinary operatic performance are swollen and red, but recover by the morning if the singing has been well produced. He believes this to be a normal state for an opera singer's vocal cords, indicating that such performing requires the use of the limits of the human voice. Thus one must consider what is required of these cords during the performance of a Wagnerian opera, admittedly the most strenuous of all the repertoire (personal communication, Dr. Van Lawrence to Berton Coffin to Shirlee Emmons, 1985). Record producer John Culshaw reports conductor Georg Solti's opinion that "in the heat of composition, Wagner had not considered the question of singers' stamina," but that it came to the fore when he began to stage the works (Culshaw, p. 215).

p.35 *"that Wagner cannot be sung without shouting"* and *"you should sing Wagner"*: LM speech, New York University, 1932, and New York Wagner Society, 1934.

p.35 *"How can the spectator"*: Marek, quoting Wagner, *Front Seat at the Opera*, p. 203. Melchior's notes, taken at the 1969 Lauritz Melchior Foundation competition, reveal his own preoccupation with the contestants' size. Never did he fail to comment of the figure of the singer, clearly preferring tall, robust men for the Fach.

p.35 *coloring the voice*: Richard Wagner defined his concerns, "It is not any shortage of voices that worries me, but the bad manner in which these voices have been trained, resulting in a delivery which totally precludes all healthy speech" (Skelton, *Richard and Cosima Wagner*, p. 182). W. J. Henderson reminded his readers that Wagner believed the vowel sound as delivered to the consciousness of the listener in pure musical tone becomes an emotional power second to none. But because the poet has placed the words in a musical order with due recognition to their accentual power, it becomes the business of the singer to sing them exactly as they are written, to enunciate the consonants distinctly, but to preserve that fundamental emotional power of the pure vowel sound which is to be conveyed by the singer as musical tone only (Henderson, pp. 233–236).

p.35 *When Hugh Walpole arrived in Bayreuth*: Winifred Wagner broke the usual custom of keeping Wahnfried off-limits to the artists, and invited her countryman and Melchior to tea there. Hugh described Siegfried as "very much there, like a white, heavy, decaying bird," but he "took to Mrs. Wagner hugely," finding her "a simple, sweet woman, most plucky" (Hart-Davis, p. 235). Perhaps Winifred Wagner's hospitality was offered because Walpole was British. During World War II she begged the Nazis not to bomb England because there were so many friends and subscribers there (NYDN, July 15, 1982).

p.35 *Lauritz would study another year*: Hart-Davis, p. 232.

p.36 *several concerts in England*: The Scandinavian concert planned by Tillett and a private, command performance in Marlborough House for Queen Alexandra, the Queen Mother, were done in July 1923, followed by an August concert tour of England.

p.36 *under the baton of Leo Blech*: Conductor-composer Leo Blech (1871–1958) studied composition under Engelbert Humperdinck and pursued his conducting career in Aachen, Prague, and Berlin. In 1925 he served as artistic director of the Vienna Staatsoper. In 1926 he returned to Berlin, then on to Riga, and finally back to Berlin in 1949. One of his operas, *Versiegelt*, was produced at the Metropolitan Opera in 1911.

p.36 *The enormous expenditure*: Hart-Davis, p. 235.

p.36 *"Of all the conductors with whom I have worked"*: LM fund-raising letter, 1967.

p.36 *Yet, said Leider*: Leider, p. 93.

p.37 *"I left Berlin by train"*: LMPM.

p.37 *he found Siegfried and Winifred*: F. Wagner, p. 13.

p.37 *Opera intendants*: Nually, p. 74.

p.38 *"Achtung auf die kleinen Noten"*: Leider, p. 100; Skelton, *Wagner at Bayreuth*, p. 37.

p.38 *"Indifference, carelessness"*: Bahr-Mildenburg, p. 20, 15, 32.

p.38 *"but then, a nice sense of rhythm"*: Pleasants, p. 170.

p.38 *[Windgassen] had, and still has"*: Culshaw, p. 126.

p.38 *"a real maestro"*: LMPM.

p.39 *"exactly as he wanted them"*: Scott, p. 250.

p.39 *"the year 1924"*: LMPM. At his opera engagement in Nuremberg, Melchior sang the two roles Canio and Turiddu without rehearsal. This feat garnered him *two* laurel wreaths and much audience enthusiasm. Nevertheless, he was never asked back, and it rankled.

p.39 *Hugh had welcome news*: Hart-Davis, p. 242.

p.39 *"contributed to" and "really died"*: Interview, Eva Andersen, Copenhagen, August 1986.

p.40 *"competent, if not thrilling"*: Rosenthal, p. 425.

p.40 *"eight days ahead of time"*: LMPM.

p.40　*"[Walter] nearly had a stroke*: LMPM.

p.41　*The Covent Garden scouts*: Gaisberg, p. 131.

p.41　*Those singers who lived*: Interview, Emmy Hauser, New York, October 1983.

p.41　*"vocal manner always promised"*: Kolodin, p. 365. In London Ljungberg was lauded for her "pure and fresh singing" (Rosenthal, p. 425). In 1932, when she appeared in New York, here voice had lost some of its great beauty, and opinions of Göta Ljungberg were rather uniform. She was possessed of an "oboe sound where a trumpet quality was desired." W. J. Henderson complained that her *voix de velouté* did not cut through the Wagnerian orchestra (Kolodin, p. 365).

p.41　*"the most beautiful female voice"* and *"an actress of greatest intelligence"*: Rosenthal, quoting critic and Wagner scholar Ernest Newman, p. 426.

p.41　*Lauritz's new friend*: Leider, p. 69.

p.41　*"the performance went rather well,"* and *"In her nervousness"*: LMPM.

p.41　*some reviewers found*: Rosenthal, p. 426.

p.41　*"tremendous and dramatic voice"*: Rosenthal, p. 426.

p.42　*The famous English designer*: LMPM. Charles Ricketts again startled the London musical world when he ended the D'Oyly Carte Company's era of traditional Gilbert and Sullivan sets and costumes, creating a lovely but notorious re-dressing of their *Mikado* production in 1926.

p.42　*the conductor, Karl Alwin*: Karl Alwin was a conductor from the Vienna Staatsoper who shared the German season at Covent Gardent with Walter. Alwin was at this time married to soprano Elisabeth Schumann. The Alwins and the Melchiors were social as well as professional friends.

p.42　*"Very good publicity"*: Hart-Davis, p. 246.

p.42　*Lauritz and his British friends*: Leider, p. 70.

p.42　*"To this day"*: Leider, p. 79.

p.42　*"Siegmund is very depressed"*: Lilian Foerster, OPN, January 28, 1946.

p.42　*"it is not really suitable"*: Culshaw, p. 215.

p.43　*"You must have a good natural"*: Gerald Fitzgerald, OPN, March 28, 1970.

p.43　*"One must have the granite foundation"*: LM, "On Top of the Nose," MUM, April 1964.

p.43　*With some astonishment*: Mogens Wedel, *Ascolta*, April 1983.

p.43　*"with their naked voices alone"*: Ulrik Cold, *Ascolta*, April 1983. Not only Melchior admired the "shine" in a voice; in her master classes, Birgit Nilsson also refers to the "shine," which she demands from each and every singer on every note. Listening to those tones of which she approves, one hears that they are all possessed of the famous "ring," a frequency around 2,800 Hz. (Backus, pp. 255–56).

p.44　*"Good singing in Wagner"*: Conrad L. Osborne, "Voices from the Festspielhaus," OPN, August 1976.

p.44　*It is the concepts discussed*: Conrad L. Osborne, OPN, August 1976; OP, February 1, 1964; HF, October 1972; liner notes, Metropolitan Opera Historic Broadcast, January 4, 1941; *Records in Review*, 1961.

p.44　*"genuine passion"*: Conrad L. Osborne, HF, October 1972.

p.44　*"less dramatic"*: Conrad L. Osborne, OPN, August 1976.

p.44　*"I rarely think [about] technique"*: LMPM.

Chapter 5. From Bayreuth to the World (1924–1927)

p.45   Theater description: Hartford, pp. 31, 34, 35, 150; Skelton, *Wagner at Bayreuth*, pp. 33–35.

p.45   *The mechanism that whirled*: F. Wagner, p. 20. Rhinemaiden-mechanism description is by Friedelind Wagner. Melchior himself mentions in his personal manuscript only his sympathy for their plight—being nauseated.

p.46   *Kittle continued to drill Lauritz*: Skelton, *Wagner at Bayreuth*, p. 87.

p.46   *When the rehearsals were moved*: LM, tape interview, "My Life's Adventure," Arne Honoré, Danmarks Radio, April 30, 1966.

p.46   Discussion of eye positions: I. Melchior, p. 18; Skelton, *Wagner at Bayreuth*, p. 85.

p.46   *Cosima had also subdued*: Skelton, *Wagner at Bayreuth*, p. 87.

p.46   *unnecessary going and coming*: Marek, *Cosima Wagner*, p. 211.

p.46   *"A certain well-meaning realism"*: Skelton, quoting Cosima, *Wagner at Bayreuth*, p. 87.

p.46   *Yet even Maria Callas*: Rémy, p. 89.

p.46   *singers were not freed from the need*: Skelton admonishes us to keep in mind the source of Cosima's concern: Wagner himself in his day was "fighting . . . a tradition of histrionic attitudinizing and prescribed gesture that was rather . . . a comfortable substitute for acting than acting itself. . . . To preserve the drama intact required that singers be taught not to show consciousness of the audience." After Wagner's lifetime, "realism became the usual form of opera presentation." (So much so that audiences now have difficulty managing deliberate nonrealism, as used in the Brecht plays.) Cosima, when director of the festival, was determined to stay with the principles set up by her husband, regardless of the changes going on outside Bayreuth. She answered Adolphe Appia's written suggestions for new scenic designs by saying that since "the *Ring* was produced here in 1876 . . . there is nothing more to be discovered in the field of scenery and production." So great was the power of Bayreuth that Appia, "rejected by Bayreuth, was unable to translate his ideas on Wagner until 25 years later. [He did, however,] influence Siegfried Wagner in his three-dimensional productions of *Tristan* and *Tannhäuser*" (Skelton, *Wagner at Bayreuth*, pp. 84, 130, 131).

p.47   *"many singers had neither the aptitude"*: Skelton, quoting Bahr-Mildenburg, *Wagner at Bayreuth*, pp. 82, 83.

p.47   *"How necessary it is"*: LM speech to New York Wagner Society, 1934.

p.47   *"you can hear how the music paints"*: LMPM.

p.47   *"If Sieglinde thought"*: LMPM.

p.47   *"Normally such piano rehearsals"*: Mogens Wedel, *Ascolta*, June 1983.

p.48   *"He stops for a moment"*: LMPM.

p.48   *"the power of the voice"*: LMPM.

p.48   *"breathed in the old times"*: Wessling, *Toscanini in Bayreuth*, p. 9.

p.49   *"Second class?!"*: LMD; Nually, p. 67.

p.49   *having been delayed*: Hart-Davis, p. 252, 253, 255, 263.

p.49   *The imminence of Lauritz's debut*: Kleinchen, although innocent of operatic conventions, was amply experienced with mainstream acting values, and worried about the verisimilitude of a six-foot four, very robust man playing the sixteen-year-old Parsifal.

p.49   *"almost too much for the money"*: Hartford, quoting Mark Twain, p. 151. Along the same lines, the firm of Ricordi dispatched Puccini himself to Bayreuth during Cosima's regime to ascertain whether *Meistersinger* could be cut, and how much? She insisted not at all. During most of Melchior's career it was the custom elsewhere to make large cuts in the music-dramas, but never at Bayreuth (Hartford, p. 195).

p.50   *the building's interior*: Hartford, pp. 35, 151.

p.50   *It was so hot*: F. Wagner, p. 25.

p.50   *the lack of applause*: There was much confusion about Wagner's wishes regarding applause during *Parsifal*. In 1882 the audience applauded early on, and Wagner shouted, "Don't!" With respect for his wishes, the audience then remained totally silent at the end of the opera. Wagner later made it known that he wished for silence only *during* the performance. According to Earnest Newman, Wagner himself applauded at subsequent performances (Hartford, p. 201).

p.50   *"A tenor by the name of Lauritz Melchior"*: LMPM.

p.50   *"Perhaps reversed was the situation"*: Adolph Aber, *Berliner Tagblatt*, August 1, 1924.

p.50   *"My* Parsifal *was not at all recognizable"*: LMPM.

p.50   *"Never have I heard such singing"*: Hart-Davis, pp. 254, 255.

p.51   *"the greatest Parsifal"*: C. H. Heller, quoting Cosima Wagner, *Opernwelt*, Vol. 22, 1981; Scott, p. 249.

p.51   *"It is preferable to have them frail"*: Knud Hegermann-Lindencrone, quoting Cosima Wagner, *The Gramophone*, January 1939. Those voice teachers who successfully manage such baritone-to-tenor conversions have noticed that "thin" high notes signal the beginning of the switch to the higher Fach. Such notes, unacceptable in an operatic baritone, are typical of a Heldentenor early on.

p.51   *the longest he would ever have to learn*: A Melchior fan once took the trouble to count the notes in each of Melchior's roles and came up with a figure of 6,000 for Siegfried. Lauritz and Kleinchen would later sprinkle the word counts of the various roles—such as, Tristan: 4,140; Tannhäuser: 3,908; Parsifal: 1,606; Siegmund: 2,770; elder Siegfried: 2,832; Lohengrin: 2,662—into their conversations and interviews. Some accused Kleinchen of using the statistics to define Lauritz's fee structure.

p.51   *"A real . . . Siegfried cannot come"*: Alan Rich, NYHT, December 26, 1965.

p.51   *"[To be a Heldentenor you need]"*: Gerald Fitzgerald, OPN, March 28, 1970.

p.52   *"many tips"*: LM letter to Kleinchen, June 23, 1925.

p.52   *"The time of rehearsal"*: LMPM.

p.52   *"contempt for the human race"*: Daniel, quoting Olga Samaroff, p. 177. Back in 1892 Muck had been fired by Cosima after his first *Meistersinger* rehearsal, which he passed smoking one black cigar after another. What she heard did not please Cosima, and she got rid of him immediately. By 1901, however, he had returned to Bayreuth as conductor of *Parsifal*, a position he retained through Melchior's time (Marek, *Cosima Wagner*, p. 220).

p.52   *Fortunately, Michael Balling*: The German conductor Balling (1866–1925) had commenced his career as a string player in Bayreuth, becoming an assistant conductor in Bayreuth in 1896. Not only did he become one of the leading Wagnerian conductors of his day, but it was he who supervised the edition of Richard Wagner's collected works for Breitkopf und Härtel.

p.52 *"Parsifal was Lauritz Melchior"*: Adolf Weissman, *BZ am Mittag*, July 21, 1925.

p.52 *Adolf Hitler, after serving his year*: F. Wagner, p. 31.

p.52 *"Winnie" Wagner complained to Walpole*: Hart-Davis, p. 264.

p.52 *She asked "Wolf"*: Skelton, *Wagner at Bayreuth*, p. 20; F. Wagner, p. 37. An off-Broadway play, *The Music Keeper*, by Elliot Tiber and André Ernotte, about Winifred Wagner, tells that Hitler's intimates called him Wolf because he admired Walt Disney's Big Bad Wolf. Since the very first Laugh-O-Gram, "Little Red Riding Hood," was produced in 1922, Hitler could have seen it (Rex Reed, NYDN, July 19, 1982; Clive Barnes, NYP, July 22, 1982).

p.53 *From this vantage point Hitler listened*: Hart-Davis, p. 264.

p.53 *Melchior's son and daughter*: Interviews, Ib Melchior, Los Angeles, December 1983; Birte Melchior, Copenhagen, August 1983.

p.53 *Inger arrived in Berlin*: LMPM; Ib Melchior, interview, Los Angeles, November 1983; Nually, p. 69.

p.53 *The settlement was*: Interview, Eva Andersen, Copenhagen, August 1986.

p.53 *Birte remembers her mother crying*: Birte Melchior, *Hendes Verden*, #32, 1970.

p.54 Wedding details: Maria Hacker diary, 1925–1926.

p.54 Kleinchen tries hunting: Nually, p. 74.

p.54 *"he would not stop before"*: Interview, Karl Laufkötter, Ojai, California, November 1987.

p.55 *"He was the worst"*: n.p., n.d., DCM. Melchior's incessant card playing was often pointed out as evidence of his lack of seriousness as a singer. Caruso, too, was passionate about cards, and there was nearly always a poker game in his dressing room. "Caruso would finish the tenderest love song and rush backstage to ask, 'Who deals?' " (Marek, *Front Seat at the Opera*, p. 267).

p.55 *"My wonderful husband gave himself"*: Maria Hacker diary, 1925–1926.

p.56 *"I am . . . happy when a man adores me"*: Maria Hacker diary, 1925–1926.

p.56 *"Well, I've done my part"*: Hart-Davis, p. 266.

p.56 *"too inexperienced"*: LM daily diary, 1921.

p.56 *"I have heard in this time"*: Letter, Norbert Salter to Gatti, October 9, 1924, AMO.

p.56 *"I also have heard that the tenor"*: Letter, Gatti to Salter, October 14, 1924, AMO.

p.56 *Thereupon the Metropolitan transferred*: AMO.

p.56 Contract details: Payroll accounts book, AMO.

p.56 *Melchior was exceedingly disturbed*: Letter, Simon to Gatti, April 22, 1925, AMO.

p.56 *German wing conductor*: A typical Bodanzky performance was "fast, intense, and heavily cut": *New Grove Dictionary of Music and Musicians*, Vol. 2, p. 834.

p.57 "VERY MUCH SURPRISED": Cable, Gatti to Bodanzky, May 2, 1925, AMO.

p.57 "MELCHIOR READY": Cable, Bodanzky to Ziegler, May 5, 1925, AMO.

p.57 "SENTITO MELCHIOR": Cable, Bodanzky to Gatti, May 7, 1925, AMO.

p.57 *"Those who saw this performance"*: LMPM.

p.58 *"like a happy giant baby"*: Holger Boland, *Ascolta*, April 1983.

p.58 *"best so far"*: Maria Hacker diary, 1930.

p.58 *"very helpful"*: Maria Hacker diary, 1930.

p.58 *Siegfried is double*: Nually, p. 75.

p.59 *"It is the story of a youth and his development"*: LMPM.

p.59 *"The young Siegfried"*: Gerald Fitzgerald, OPN, March 28, 1970.

p.59 *"Unmatchable expectations"*: John Rockwell, NYT, February 7, 1988.

p.59 *"A Wagnerian L'il Abner"*: Herbert Kupferberg, *Playbill*, January 1988.

p.59   *at the piano with Mme. Bahr-Mildenburg*: Kammersängerin Bahr-Mildenburg died in 1947, having survived the war years in great privation, subsisting in a Viennese cellar (Jay Lissfelt, *Pittsburgh Sun-Telegraph*, February 23, 1947).

p.59   Details of first Siegfried performance: Nually, pp. 75, 76.

p.60   *occasionally slipped into his own language*: Lauritz had his own linguistic affinities, which he described thus: "German for singing; Danish for secrets; English for company" (*Boston Advertiser*, March 1, 1936).

p.60   *"Lauritz's first Siegfried!"*: Maria Hacker diary, 1925–1926.

p.60   *"very enthusiastic"*: Marie Hacker diary, 1925–1926.

p.60   *"I was not a sensation there"*: LMPM.

p.60   *"a dirty theater"*: Maria Hacker diary, 1925–1926. It is at this point in *his* personal manuscript that Lauritz describes the contretemps between Walpole and Kleinchen thus: Hugh had been sulking for some time since the wedding. It was his *idée fixe* that Kleinchen wanted to put an end to his friendship with Lauritz. Worse still, Hugh felt dispensable. Kleinchen, however, surprised him, and with her famous charm she swiftly changed Walpole's attitude, was pronounced worthy, and was allowed to enter the circle of his most intimate friends. Kleinchen, for her part, wrote at great length in her own diary about how compatible the threesome was, and how dear Hugh was to her. "We are so happy together, Hugh, Lauritz, and I."

p.60   Melchior and Beigel prepare for the United States: Nually, p. 77.

p.61   *"crazy happy"*: Maria Hacker diary, 1925–1926.

p.61   *"Our first view of New York"*: Maria Hacker diary, 1925–1926.

p.61   *"the nice good humor"*: Maria Hacker diary, 1925–1926.

p.61   *"A genius with languages"*: Interview, Birte Melchior, Copenhagen, August 1983.

p.61   *"so stupid as the other German artist-wives"*: Maria Hacker diary, 1925–1926.

Chapter 6. The Metropolitan Debut (1926–1927)

p.63   *"show up at the opera house"*: LMPM.

p.63   *"granted an audience with Gatti-Casazza"*: LMPM.

p.63   *"Our conversation took place"*: LMPM.

p.64   *rehearsal practice at the Metropolitan*: The impressive statistics of Bayreuth rehearsals, as once recorded by Karl Kittel, are in sharp contrast with Metropolitan practice. In 1927, from June 15 to the end of the Bayreuth Festival, there were:

    439 musical coachings with soloists
    76 piano rehearsals with groups
    23 orchestra rehearsals
    47 position and acting rehearsals on stage
    79 acting rehearsals in the rehearsal room
    15 children's chorus and chorus rehearsals
    159 coachings of soloists in style and presentation
    26 rehearsals of Parsifal bells and Rheingold anvils
    23 scenic and lighting rehearsals
    24 stage rehearsals with orchestra
    16 rehearsals of stage music (Skelton, *Wagner at Bayreuth*, p. 122.)

p.64   *Even in Germany, Frida Leider*: Skelton, *Wagner at Bayreuth*, p. 125.

p.64   *every hour of rehearsal saved*: Gatti had arranged matters so that there was no "need" to rehearse. Critic W. J. Henderson once responded in print to a member of the musical public who had castigated him for not holding the Met to a higher standard of performance, saying that years of experience had taught him the uselessness of such a course, for the Metropolitan was not touched by newspaper criticism and would do absolutely nothing when taken to task (W. J. Henderson, NYS, November 28, 1924).

p.64 *Conductor Artur Bodanzky's contract*: Payroll accounts book, AMO.

p.64 *In 1883 Cady had made his building*: Kolodin, pp. 50, 51.

p.65 *"a tall, lean . . . gentleman"*: LMPM. Melchior was in error when he stated that Bodanzky never conducted anything but Wagner. Bodanzky also conducted operas by Mozart, Krenek, Strauss, Korngold, Rimsky-Korsakov, and Meyerbeer at the Met. He was Caruso's conductor for his last Met performance, *La Juive* (Halévy). Outside the Met he conducted Purcell, Pizzetti, and Zemlinsky, and in New York alone he premiered *Das Lied von der Erde* of Mahler, *Le Roi David* of Honegger, and Janácek's Glagolitic Mass (Geissmar, p. 161).

p.65 *"was a great artist"*: LMPM.

p.65 *"one of the greatest singer-actors"*: LMPM.

p.65 *"gorgeous-looking and -singing Elisabeth"*: LMPM.

p.66 *"Many are the stories of fights"*: LMPM.

p.66 *"Mr. Gigli is not nice to me"*: Maria Hacker diary, 1925–1926.

p.66 *Jeritza was box-office queen*: Payroll accounts book, AMO.

p.66 *"she was not good either"*: Maria Hacker diary, 1925–1926.

p.66 *"I threw out my chest"*: LMPM.

p.67 *"To parallel at all"*: Tuggle, quoting Pitt Sanborn, p. 194.

p.67 *"shook like ash-tree leaves"*: Maria Hacker diary, 1925–1926.

p.67 *who were in America at the time*: Daniel, *Stokowski*, p. 247.

p.67 *"He had the audience at once"*: Maria Hacker diary, 1925–1926.

p.67 *"like a student with a good voice"*: Maria Hacker diary, 1925–1926. Indeed, Miss Talley's stardom was not long-lived. During the 1926–1927 season she received $500 per week, but sang 36 performances. During the 1928–1929 season her guarantee was reduced to four weeks at $350 per week. By the next season she was gone, though she turned up on NBC radio during the 30s.

p.67 *"the thrill of authentic discovery"*: Edward Cushing, BE, August 30, 1925.

p.67 *"gasped his way from note to note"*: Hartford, quoting Shaw, p. 167.

p.67 *"a great Wagnerian tenor"*: Edward Cushing, BE, August 30, 1925.

p.68 *"no denying that the music"*: Olin Downes, NYT, February 18, 1926.

p.68 *"warmth and fervor"*: W. J. Henderson, NYS, February 18, 1926.

p.68 *"an improved variety"*: Lawrence Gilman, NYHT, February 18, 1926. Irving Kolodin took advantage of hindsight to assess Melchior's debut in his Met history: "Melchior was unquestionably the most important artist to debut during the 1925–1926 season or for several previous ones. He had no rehearsal, no meeting, no conversation with Bodanzky. . . . awkward and ungainly . . . he was and remained. Although some of the outbursts in Act 1 taxed his range, the beautiful head tone on 'Elisabeth' was a sensation" (Kolodin, p. 331).

p.68 *"recitative passages in strict values"*: R. Wagner, p. 175.

p.68 *"That is your business"*: Hartford quoting Lilli Lehmann, who quoted Wagner, p. 49.

p.68 *"entire justice"*: Edward Cushing, BE, February 18, 1926.

p.69 *"it is always so here"*: Maria Hacker diary, 1925–1926.

p.69 *"It is difficult to start off so excited"*: Gerald Fitzgerald, OPN, March 28, 1970.

p.69   *"sang the fiercely demanding role"*: M. Owen Lee, OPN, January 30, 1982.

p.69   *"literally worthless"*: W. J. Henderson, NYS, February 21, 1926.

p.69   *"an insolence"*: Maria Hacker diary, 1925–1926.

p.70   *Brünnhilde was sung*: Nanny Larsén-Todsen's debut had been postponed because, according to the Met paybook, "horse at rehearsal of *Götterdämmerung* stepped upon her." W. J. Henderson declared rather nastily that her heavy tremolo "was likely to restore life to the long dead theory that operas can be given without good singing." Worse, Otto Kahn, chairman of the Metropolitan board, obviously was not an admirer, for Gatti wrote him with the "good news" when he replaced her with Gertrude Kappel for the 1928–1929 season (Tuggle, p. 196; Kolodin, p. 326).

p.70   *"mountain top"*: Tuggle, p. 194.

p.70   *"Mr. Lauritz Melchior, who is singing"*: Program insert, AMO.

p.70   *stricken with a swollen polyp*: Alden Whitman, NYT, March 20, 1973.

p.70   *"the* Parsifal *sets and the chorus"*: Maria Hacker diary, 1925–1926.

p.70   *"[He] seems devoted"*: W. J. Henderson, NYS, April 4, 1926.

p.70   *"an interesting opera"*: Gerald Fitzgerald, OPN, March 28, 1970.

p.71   *"Parsifal is the embodiment"*: Lilian Foerster, OPN, January 28, 1946.

p.71   *"were anxious, for we knew"*: Maria Hacker diary, 1925–1926.

p.71   *"It would be cataloguing"*: W. J. Henderson, NYS, April 1, 1926. Lauritz himself was not completely satisfied with his vocalism that evening, and thus found some amusement in Henderson's change of tune. But, as Edward Albee once wrote, "I count it rare to get a good review for the right reason" (*Playbill*, December 1964).

p.71   *"better reviews one cannot wish for"*: Maria Hacker diary, 1925–1926.

p.72   *arrived in London*: During this stay in England, Walpole invited them to the country for a visit, during which this amusing incident took place. Kleinchen revealed her typically earthy German sense of humor by recounting it at every opportunity. It seems that Hugh's huge collection of books began to overrun the Piccadilly apartment, the main building of Brackenburn, and the three rooms he had constructed across the lawn, and had to be housed even in the lavatories. Making a friendly visit to the loo where Hugh had placed some of his valuable first editions, Kleinchen found no toilet paper. Happening upon a page with almost no printer's ink on it, she decided that Hugh must have had some books made up especially for this purpose and tore it out. Unfortunately for Walpole, it was an extremely rare first edition. (As told to Marianne Tegner by LM.)

p.72   *"not helpful"*: LMPM. Ezio Pinza, on the other hand, likened Walter to Toscanini in his ability "to raise the singers and orchestra musicians to the greatest heights. . . . But there was this difference: whereas [Toscanini] achieved his goal through a will of iron, [Walter] made us partners in his search for the right interpretation of the work" (Magidoff, p. 151).

p.72   *"Melchior! My left hand"*: Tuggle, p. 196.

p.72   *When Maria Jeritza and Lauritz Melchior*: LMPM.

p.72   *"improved as an artist"*: Rosenthal, p. 446.

p.72   *"I have no objection"*: Rosenthal, quoting Ernest Newman, p. 446.

p.73   *Szigeti was the shy and retiring violinist*: Parade, August 7, 1949.

p.73   *"The singer imparted a fine manly strength"*: W. J. Henderson, NYS, April 16, 1927.

p.73   *"It has the stamp of authoritative"*: NYT, April 16, 1927.

p.73   *"unfortunate that . . . the most musical voice"*: BE, February 19, 1927.

p.73   *"his bounce upon the table"*: NYW, February 19, 1927.

p.74   *"manly and beautiful"*: MUM ad, March 1, 1927, quoting NYT.

p.74   *"of unusual beauty"*: MUM ad, March 1, 1927, quoting NYA.

p.74   *"convincing and emotionally contagious"*: MUM ad, March 1, 1927, quoting NYT.

p.74   *"musicianly judgment"*: MUM ad, March 1, 1927, quoting NYA.

p.74   *"his voice rang out rich and free"*: MUM ad, March 1, 1927, quoting Pitt Sanborn.

p.74   *"a great evening of song"*: MUC ad, January 13, 1927, quoting *St. Louis Globe Democrat.*

p.74   *"grandly gifted man"*: MUC ad, January 13, 1927, quoting *St. Louis Globe Democrat.*

p.74   *"veritable god of song"*: MUC ad, January 13, 1927, quoting *St. Louis Times.*

p.74   *"success came too fast"*: William King, NYS, January 8, 1928.

p.74   *"It was really a big handicap"*: Gerald Fitzgerald, OPN, March 28, 1970.

p.74   *"If only he knew"*: Maria Hacker diary, 1925–1926.

p.74   *"lightening my middle range"*: NBC Press Book, 1934–1935. Mme. Cahier, a Berlin friend of Wagner scholar Gunther Kossodo's mother, told Mrs. Kossodo that Melchior never paid her for the lessons she gave him. These lessons must have been the sessions held (after Victor Beigel's departure) in preparation for the New York debut concert and this work the two did in Sweden. Lauritz noted in his diary that it was "because of her impossible husband [that] this visit was not a success" (LMD). Kleinchen went further: "Charles Cahier looks like a swindler . . . a horrible man" (Maria Hacker diary, 1925–1926).

p.75   *"Do you remember, Lauritz"*: Interview, Ib Melchior, Los Angeles, December 1983.

p.75   *highest paid Metropolitan artists*: Nually, p. 87.

p.75   *The Met payroll accounts show*: Payroll accounts book, AMO.

p.75   *He had participated*: Seltsam, pp. 435–449.

p.75   Taucher, Laubenthal, Kirchhoff, Schorr salary figures: Payroll accounts book, AMO.

p.75   *"a piquant combination"*: O'Connell, pp. 87, 88.

p.76   *"an iron-clad lady"*: Interview, Leonard Eisner, New York, November 1984.

p.76   *"I was devoted to her"*: Interview, Alma Strasfogel, New York, April 1985.

p.76   *during their visits to Buckingham Palace*: Interview, Alma Strasfogel, New York, April 1985.

p.76   *"In every family"*: Interview, Leonard Eisner, New York, November 1984.

p.76   *In March 1927 the distressing news*: Melchior described his brother "Mils" in this way, "My brother, who was a scenic designer, was rather well-known in Denmark. He was the president of the Designers Association" (Arne Honoré tape interview, "My Life's Adventure," Danmarks Radio, April 30, 1966).

p.76   *"[At the Metropolitan] I was the new man"*: LM, Arne Honoré tape interview, "My Life's Adventure," Danmarks Radio, April 30, 1966.

p.77   *"Melchior, I know for sure"*: LMPM.

p.77   *"That's why I went"*: Gerald Fitzgerald, OPN, March 28, 1970.

Chapter 7. Learning Tristan (1927–1930)

p.78   *"astonished . . . at the quality"*: Rosenthal, p. 449.

p.78   *"enormously popular"*: Leider, p. 77.

p.78   *the* Walküre *performance of May 6*: Waspish critic Walter Legge, upon hearing this performance, remarked, "Melchior, apart from xylophonic high notes and doubtful intonation . . . was a good Siegmund" (Schwarzkopf, p. 19). Legge's cruel term, "xylophonic," became a favorite with other critics in later years.

p.78   *"an angel"*: Interview, Ib Melchior, Los Angeles, December 1983.

p.79   *"Lauritz always created"*: Leider, p. 78.

p.79   *"a light lunch of several courses"*: Leider, p. 77.

p.79   *His favorite "light lunch"*: Letter, Marianne Tegner to Shirlee Emmons, June 7, 1988.

p.79   *he called it Bulstein's*: Leider, p. 86.

p.79   *"I usually got out of this"*: Leider, p. 77.

p.79   *"was one's friend"*: LMPM.

p.79   *Many times in the beginning*: LMPM. In this quote we have an example of how Melchior's musical memory worked. The line should read, *"wie sie selig hehr und milde."*

p.79   *"humor and love"*: LMPM.

p.79   *"whom I still wanted to have with me"*: LMPM.

p.80   *"Onstage she was so cleverly made up"*: Leider, p. 99.

p.80   *"The stage was under the command"*: *Hamburger Nachtrichten*, July 28, 1928.

p.80   *under Franz von Hösslin's*: Conductor-composer von Hösslin debuted in Danzig in 1907, conducted in Lübeck, Mannheim, and the Berlin Volksoper before coming to Bayreuth to conduct the *Ring* in 1927. He also conducted Melchior in the *Ring* of 1929 at the Wagner Festival in Paris.

p.80   *"The role is a cruel one"*: Patterson Greene, BE, August 12, 1927.

p.80   *"Lauritz Melchior in the Wagner repertoire"*: James Drake, Joseph Tempesta, HF, March 1976.

p.80   *"A better audience than the German one"*: LM fund-raising letter, 1965.

p.81   *"good and intimate"*: LM fund-raising letter, 1965.

p.81   *Melchior always held*: Gerald Fitzgerald, OPN, March 28, 1970.

p.81   *"Lohengrin becomes a human being"*: Lilian Foerster, OPN, January 28, 1946.

p.81   *An exception, perhaps*: Vickers, *Even Greater Opera Disasters*, p. 52.

p.82   *"That role is one of my favorites"*: LMPM.

p.82   *He had forgotten to wear Brünnhilde's ring*: Leider, p. 121.

p.82   *in her Bavarian accent*: Perhaps it was the influence of Kleinchen's Bavarian German that led *Stage* magazine to comment: "Melchior's German in singing is the formal, classical enunciation of the Bayreuth tradition; in speech it is full of Bavarian colloquialisms, slurrings, and nonsense" (ST, February 1936).

p.83   *"Lady G. wants to go to Bayreuth"*: Wessling, *Toscanini in Bayreuth*, pp. 60, 61.

p.83   *"I am very happy"*: Letter, LM to L. L. Bean Co., March 1966.

p.83   *"Although [Lauritz] may have been"*: Letter, Marianne Tegner to Shirlee Emmons, June 7, 1988.

p.83   *The extensive Melchior collection*: Melchior cherished titles of slightly less grandeur as well, such as his singularly apt position as a Compagnon de Rabelais. By the end of his life Melchior's collection included: the three Saxonian medals, the Bulgarian Cross of Merit, four Danish medals (Ingenio et Arti, the Cross of the Order of the Men of Dannebrog, the Commander Cross of Dannebrog, and the Christian X Freedom Medal), the Finnish Commander Cross of the White Rose, the Chilean Commander Cross of Merit, the German Grand Cross of Merit, the American Institute for Fine Arts Medal. In addition he was an officer of the French Academy (with gold palms), and held the title

Chevalier of the Légion d'honneur. Directly above the doorbell outside the Ansonia hotel suite in years to come would be posed Melchior's calling card with his most prized titles listed: "Lauritz Melchior, Kgl. Kammersanger, K af D., DM., I et A., p.p." (Royal Singer to the Court, Commander of the Dannebrog, Man of the Dannebrog, Talent and Arts, etc.) Melchior should be given credit for good taste (and loyalty)—he only put the Danish titles on his card even when, eventually, he had nine others he could have listed. The all-inclusive "p.p." (etc.) stood for them (Letter, Marianne Tegner to Shirlee Emmons, June 7, 1988; *Saturday Evening Post*, February 27, 1945).

p.84 *"helped a great deal"*: LM tape interview, Danmarks Radio, "The Fairy Tale of My Life," December 27, 1970, produced by Hemming Hartmann-Petersen.

p.84 *"the Great Architect"*: Interview, Marianne Tegner, Copenhagen, August 1983; Los Angeles, November 1987.

p.84 *"there is nothing more solemn"*: LM tape interview, Danmarks Radio, "The Fairy Tale of My Life," December 27, 1970, produced by Hemming Hartmann-Petersen. Melchior's remarks went on: "One learns . . . not [to] let success and flattery go to one's head, [to] keep the feet on the ground. . . . Many . . . artists think that because they are put on a pedestal, they are better than other people. . . . we are not. We just try with the tools that we get as Freemasons to repair ourselves, to make ourselves worthy to be called a human being, to help out when needed, especially with people who . . . have difficulties accepting charity. . . . I have never known a Freemason and I never will. It is something as unattainable as becoming an angel."

p.84 *"It's really extremely exciting"*: LMPM.

p.84 *"There is no cheaper way"*: Maria Hacker diary, 1925–1926.

p.85 *"a couple of wonderful beds"*: LMPM.

p.85 *"Another giant was in town"*: Interview, Cleo Baldon, Los Angeles, November 1987.

p.85 *"the greatest actor I have ever seen"*: Maria Hacker diary, 1925–1926.

p.85 Chaliapin story: LMPM; interview, Ib Melchior, Los Angeles, December 1983.

p.86 *"rose to unexpected heights"*: Rosenthal, pp. 454, 455.

p.86 *"only awoke to an intelligent"*: John Steane quoting *Musical Times*, liner notes, "Lauritz Melchior," Pearl GEMM 228–229.

p.86 *"I had made up my Otello"*: LMPM.

p.86 *"very firm in judgment"*: Leider, p. 76.

p.86 *"an unapproachable man"*: LMPM.

p.86 Muck story: I. Melchior, p. 49.

p.86 *coping with his slow tempi*: Muck's tempi were generally on the slow side. Records kept by Bayreuth orchestra members show that his *Parsifal* Act 1 lasted for 116 minutes, whereas Mottl's took 106 and Levi's, 107. Toscanini broke the record for slowest: 122 minutes. Lauritz, to be expected, hated Toscanini's "too slow tempo" for this opera. Young Wolfgang Wagner described Richard Strauss's version (the fastest, with a 95-minute Act 1) in this way: "Strauss's *Parsifal* is wonderful. It's like a waltz all the way through. You actually stay awake. Pierre Boulez was eventually to beat Strauss's tempo and finish the opera 80 minutes earlier than Toscanini had. (Bayreuth Archives; Schwarzkopf, p. 24; F. Wagner, p. 102.)

p.86 *Neither was Leider surprised*: But she was very impressed by the covered pit which ensured that no well-trained voice would fail to carry over the orchestra (Jens Malte Fischer, "Sprachgesang oder Belcanto," *Opernwelt*, June 1986).

p.86 *"There was, as always at Bayreuth"*: Leider, p. 97.

p.86 *Consequently, when Siegfried Wagner*: Leider, p. 110.

p.87 *"new man"*: Cable, Edward Ziegler to Erich Simon, March 29, 1928, AMO.

p.87 *Simon proposed*: Cable, Erich Simon to Edward Ziegler, April 10, 1928, AMO.

p.87 *Gatti agreed*: Letter, Edward Ziegler to Erich Simon, September 17, 1928, AMO.

p.87 *"difficult to offer"*: Letter, Edward Ziegler to Erich Simon, September 17, 1928, AMO.

p.87 "IMPOSSIBLE [TO] GUARANTEE": Cable, Met to Erich Simon, October 9, 1928, AMO.

p.87 *Simon replied*: Letter, Erich Simon to Met, October 11, 1928, AMO.

p.87 *Melchior was actually earning*: LMPM.

p.87 *"As to artists"*: Letter, Gatti to Otto Kahn, November 1, 1928, AMO.

p.88 *"Suddenly one dreams"*: Arne Honoré interview with LM, "My Life's Adventure," Danmarks Radio, April 30, 1966.

p.88 *"I studied my Tristan with Leopold Sachse"*: LM fund-raising letter, 1965.

p.88 *"There I really learned things"*: LM, Arne Honoré tape interview, "My Life's Adventure," Danmarks Radio, April 30, 1966.

p.88 *"Leopold took a personal interest"*: LMPM.

p.88 *His longtime friend, Karl Laufkötter*: Interview, Karl Laufkötter, Ojai, California, November 1987. In a lengthy and busy career, the times when Lauritz Melchior canceled can be counted on two hands or, in the case of the Metropolitan Opera, on only one hand.

p.89 *"For that reason, Kleinchen offered"*: LMPM. In this performance Lilli Hafgren Weil (whom Melchior knew from Bayreuth) sang Isolde; old friends Herbert Janssen and Ivar Andresen were also in the cast. The conductor was Max von Schillings, of whom Melchior said, "Exactly like Blech, he was interested in my development into a first class Wagnerian tenor" (LMPM).

p.89 *"talked and laughed all through"*: Hart-Davis, p. 303.

p.89 *A veteran Met coach*: Interview, Hans Hansen, Copenhagen, August 1983. Hans Hansen, author of the Lauritz Melchior discography, has been Senior Opera Producer and Commentator for Danmarks Radio, Copenhagen, since 1964. He also produced the recently issued and universally praised Lauritz Melchior anthology on LP records and compact discs.

p.89 *Kappel had proven to be*: Gertrude Kappel's singing was called "genuinely beautiful . . . and sometimes ravishing" by critic W. J. Henderson. At the time of her 1928 debut, Olin Downes called her a "highly gifted artist" (Kolodin, p. 345; Downes, NYT, January 17, 1928).

p.90 *"his very first gesture"*: Samuel Chotzinoff, NYW, March 21, 1929.

p.90 "A TRISTAN AT LAST": Samuel Chotzinoff, NYW, March 21, 1929.

p.90 *"highly promising"*: Kolodin, p. 348. Yet Robert Lawrence, conductor and author, says: "Until Lauritz Melchior's first New York Tristan, one was used to hearing the role attempted rather than sung. The Isolde and the music had to carry the occasion" (Lawrence, p. 12).

p.90 *markedly resembled his father*: Interview, Inga Krause, Copenhagen, August 1983.

p.90 *"trying to make up"*: *Junior League Magazine*, May 12, 1938.

p.91 *"no one better"*: John Steane quoting *Musical Times*, liner notes "Lauritz Melchior," Pearl GEMM 228–229.

p.91   *"With your performance as Tristan"*: Hart-Davis, p. 306.

p.91   *a former friend of Lauritz's*: A family member has said that Miss Henningsen was the source of much pain as well as solace for Inger because "Lauritz could not stay away from other women." Birte Melchior was convinced that Gerda Henningsen was in love with her father (interview, Eva Andersen, Copenhagen, August 1986; letter, Birte Melchior to Shirlee Emmons, December 29, 1986).

p.91   *The children mainly remember*: Birte Melchior, *Hendes Verden* #48, 1970.

p.91   *A fine education*: Nually, p. 101.

p.91   *"They were not married any longer"*: Interview, Birte Melchior, Copenhagen, August 1983.

p.91   *"It was only after"*: Birte Melchior, tape interview, "The Fairy Tale of My Life," Danmarks Radio, December 20, 1970, produced by Hemming Hartmann-Petersen.

p.91   *"someone else"*: Birte Melchior, *Hendes Verden* #48, 1970.

p.91   *"this woman who had already"*: Interview, Ib Melchior, Los Angeles, December 1983.

p.92   *It is no surprise that*: Birte Melchior, *Hendes Verden* #48, 1970.

p.92   *"Kleinchen was in a position"*: Interview, Birte Melchior, Copenhagen, August 1983.

p.92   *The children appreciate*: Interview, Ib Melchior, Los Angeles, December 1983.

p.93   *an evaluation of each singer's talent*: Rudolf Laubenthal had been criticized in the press for an inadequate vocal technique, an insecurity of pitch, and an insufficient range for the roles he sang, a formidable list. Kirchhoff, no youngster, had made his debut in Berlin in 1906 and would be gone from the Met by 1931. When Taucher, married to Met soprano Johanna Gadski, had made "difficulties" (Gatti's word) over the Met's refusal to re-engage his wife, Kleinchen was able to dismiss him from her calculations. She found Laubenthal "terrible" as Siegfried and Kirchhoff "atrocious" as Siegmund (AMO; Maria Hacker diary, 1930).

p.93   Martinelli and Gigli fees: Payroll account books, AMO.

p.93   *"a terrible actor"*: Maria Hacker diary, 1929–1930.

p.93   *"excellent in that role"*: Maria Hacker diary, 1929–1930.

p.93   *he was paid only $12,000*: Payroll accounts book, AMO.

p.94   *American soprano Grace Moore*: Grace Moore made both her Paris Opéra-Comique debut and her Metropolitan Opera debut in 1928 and went on to star in several films before here tragic death in an airplane crash in 1947.

p.94   *"were a triumph"*: Maria Hacker diary, 1930–1931.

p.94   *The title of Kammersanger*: Salmonsen's Konversations Leksikon.

p.94   *"To equal Vilhelm Herold"*: LM tape interview, "The Fairy Tale of My Life," December 25, 1970, Danmarks Radio, produced by Hemming Hartmann-Petersen.

Chapter 8. Tristanissimo (1929–1931)

p.95   *"a straw in the wind"*: Kolodin, p. 361.

p.95   *"Since I was an admirer of Gigli"*: LMPM.

p.96   *"light singing"*: Maria Hacker diary, 1930.

p.96   *he rehearsed* Fidelio: Although Melchior's diary mentions nothing about preparations for another German role that he never did at the Met, Florestan in Beethoven's *Fidelio*, Kleinchen documents in her diary nine rehearsals on the role that Melchior had with Maestro Riedel and a coach named Rührseitz during this spring, with even, inexplicably, some stage rehearsal time. He was to sing it at the Colón in Buenos Aires in 1932 for the first time, and it was written into his 1934–1935 Met contract, although never done. Again in the summer of 1943, Edward Johnson promised him some *Fidelio* performances, but did not follow through (AMO).

p.96   *"somewhat* klanglos": Maria Hacker diary, 1930.

p.96   *"Lauritz Melchior looks more like a Tristan"*: W. J. Henderson, NYS, March 6, 1930.

p.96   *Gatti marked Gigli's birthday*: AMO.

p.96   LM's confrontation with Gatti: Nually, p. 104.

p.96   *"Not possible"*: Schonberg, *The Glorious Ones*, p. 391.

p.96   *"I studied the role"*: Schonberg, *The Glorious Ones*, p. 391.

p.97   *"too lazy"*: Schonberg, *Facing the Music*, p. 316.

p.97   *"the best Tristan who has ever been here"*: Maria Hacker diary, 1930.

p.97   *"eating intermissions"*: Interview, Ib Melchior, December 1983.

p.98   *"the broom artist"*: Dr. Ottmar Friedman, "Bayreuther Pennälerjahre" (III), *Nordbayerischer Kurier*, Monatsbeilage, July 1987.

p.98   *"I can say that I had a good relationship"*: LMPM. After this summer Melchior took to addressing all conductors as "Mr. Toscanini," rather than "Maestro" (when he thought he would get away with it).

p.98   *"One day came Arturo Toscanini"*: Wessling, *Toscanini in Bayreuth*, p. 11.

p.98   *"Wagner was for him"*: Wessling, *Toscanini in Bayreuth*, p. 12.

p.99   *"What Wagner meant is very clear"*: LMPM.

p.99   *"Where is the cymbal crash?"*: Marek, quoting Toscanini, *Cosima Wagner*, p. 216.

p.99   *"Toscanini could be charming"*: LMPM.

p.99   *During one performance Toscanini repeatedly shrieked*: I. Melchior, p. 225.

p.99   *The* Tristan *cast happily witnessed*: I. Melchior, p. 225.

p.99   *"You sing like a rabbit"*: Wessling, *Toscanini in Bayreuth*, pp. 66, 68.

p.100 *"When he [Toscanini] was very wild"*: Wessling, *Toscanini in Bayreuth*, p. 63.

p.100 *He always numbered*: Nually, p. 105.

p.100 *"rehearsed everything with the orchestra"*: Geissmar, p. 250. Those Wagnerites who call the Italian an "aria-conductor" do not mean to say his conducting contains inordinate "Italianate" rubatos, as we might infer. Rather, as Wagner scholar and lecturer Gunther Kossodo points out, they mean that Toscanini's choice of tempo was dictated by his concept of incorporating all of Wagner's instructions *without* deviating from the chosen tempo. Thus Toscanini's *Parsifal* is the longest on record (122 minutes), although he is known as a "fast" conductor. To choose another example, Wilhelm Furtwängler, supposedly a "slow" conductor, ended up with a shorter all-over time for the same opera by using the rubatos that he believed were implicit (although not marked) in the score.

p.100 *After Siegfried Wagner's death*: Interview, Lawrence Chelsi, New York, September 1983.

p.100 *Toscanini, with his own score*: Nually, p. 106.

p.101 *"a Fach unto himself"*: Conrad L. Osborne, HF, October 1972.

p.101 *Melchior tended to be more musical*: When in the 1940s Melchior and Helen Traubel sang a Wagner program with Toscanini and the NBC Symphony, critics remarked how well the Italian conductor made "bad-boy" Melchior behave with his tempos and rhythms (NYT, February 23, 1941).

p.101 *"once he learns a mistake"*: William Livingstone, SR, June 1974.

p.101 *"Melchior's obstinate tempos"*: Interview, Ignace Strasfogel, April 1985.

p.101 *"It is like a well without a bottom"*: Gerald Fitzgerald, OPN, March 28, 1970.

p.101 *"Acting, expressing feelings"*: Lilian Foerster, OPN, January 28, 1946.

p.101 *"[Tristan] is the greatest love story"*: Lilian Foerster, OPN, January 28, 1946.

p.101 *"It shows in the eyes"*: Gerald Fitzgerald, OPN, March 28, 1970.

p.102 *"No one will ever appear"*: American Music Lover, May 1936.

p.102 *"It is a great pity"*: I. Melchior, p. 234. Hugh Walpole had counted on being present at the Bayreuth Tristan debut, but was prevented from coming by a protracted and convoluted battle he was fighting behind the literary scenes over Somerset Maugham's *Cakes and Ale*, in which Walpole was savagely caricatured as a literary and social snob. In public Walpole put on a good face, but the Melchiors were privy to the "heartbreak [which] was left for more private moments" (Steele, p. 126; Hart-Davis, p. 316).

p.102 *"In this artist is a perfect example"*: Bernhard Diebold, *Frankfurter Zeitung*, July 25, 1930.

p.102 *"If this artist can add"*: Joseph Stolzing, *Völkischer Beobachter*, August 7, 1930.

p.102 *"The Swedish singer was an outstanding artist"*: LMPM.

p.103 *"The Graarud woman does everything"*: Maria Hacker diary, 1930.

p.103 *It was Winifred Wagner*: F. Wagner, p. 17.

p.103 *Presumably it was the proceeds*: F. Wagner, p. 7. Hitler was clearly unaccustomed to the concerns of sartorial splendor, for, as Friedelind Wagner related, he had allowed his evening suit to be constructed with one lapel shorter than the other (p. 100).

p.103 *LM asks Zahle about Hitler*: Nually, p. 108.

p.103 *His wife was of the opinion*: F. Wagner, p. 7.

p.103 *Although Siegfried had been duty-bound*: Skelton, *Wagner at Bayreuth*, p. 131. Poor Siegfried had suffered as much for his innovations, which had been labeled by some critics "a betrayal of his father's trust," as from his staunch defense of tradition, which was seen as "being tied to his mother's apron strings." Nonetheless, this new production of *Tannhäuser*, especially under Toscanini, was considered to be the most brilliant of Siegfried Wagner's conceptions. He had been planning it since 1925, but was unable to manage the expense until a group of friends made up a fund as a sixtieth birthday present (Skelton, *Wieland Wagner*, p. 37; F. Wagner, p. 57).

p.104 *Birte Melchior, standing vigil*: Birte Melchior, *Hendes Verden* #49, 1970.

p.104 *"From the moment that Siegfried Wagner closed his eyes"*: LMPM. From Friedelind Wagner we learned that her father was hardly cold in his coffin, let alone buried, when the mayor and the city fathers called on Winifred to ask her to turn Villa Wahnfried over to the town of Bayreuth as a museum. Although they had even found another house for her and her family, Siegfried's widow refused the offer (F. Wagner, p. 54).

p.104 *He fulfilled his standing contract*: Maria Hacker diary, 1930.

p.104 *(In fact, he did, inexplicably*: LM performance ledger.

p.105 *Pictures of their Berlin apartment*: DCM.

p.105 *"a palace"*: Maria Hacker diary, 1930.

p.105 *"had a name"*: Letter, Martial Singer to Shirlee Emmons, April 6, 1986.

Melchior and Singher remained friends, singing together in *Parsifal, Tannhäuser, Lohengrin,* and *Fidelio* in Europe and both Americas.

p.105 *"It is not surprising"*: Letter, Martial Singher to Shirlee Emmons, April 6, 1986.

p.105 *"Melchior was probably"*: Letter, Martial Singher to Shirlee Emmons, April 6, 1986.

p.106 *Kleinchen physically attacked*: LMPM.

p.106 *"greater flexibility and subtlety"*: Rosenthal, p. 472.

p.106 *"greatness stamped on every note"*: Rosenthal, p. 473.

p.106 *"All our previous estimates"*: John Steane, quoting Earnest Newman (*Sunday Times*), liner notes "Lauritz Melchior," Pearl GEMM 228–229. To evaluate Newman's statement, it helps to remember that his express opinion was that, "In a hundred respects the odds are against first-rate acting in opera" (Newman, *From the World of Music*, p. 49).

p.107 *At the recording session of May 16*: Barbirolli, p. 70.

p.107 *Despite all the trouble, Barbirolli always told*: Interview, Hans Hansen, Copenhagen, August 1983.

p.107 *"amazing . . . if you think that it was sung"*: Letter, LM to William Park, November 20, 1960.

p.107 *"we had at last got a tenor"*: Gaisberg, p. 132.

p.107 *"America's most sharp-tongued society reporter"*: Leider, p. 136.

p.107 *"Louis Quatorze" party*: Nually, pp. 102, 103.

p.107 *"out of place"*: Leider, p. 136. Kleinchen's diary, while documenting each memorable meal eaten by the couple in every titled household and their enjoyment of that conspicuous consumption, did not, however, mention in any way the disparity between the Melchiors' relative wealth and the financial depression that was raging outside their charmed life.

p.108 *"Bayreuth's Latest Prize"* and *"my dear* tusind tak"*: LMPM.

p.108 *"the best I have ever heard"*: LMPM.

p.108 *"one of the most sinister"*: F. Wagner, p. 63.

p.108 *Most felt that his business abilities*: F. Wagner, p. 92.

p.109 *Adolf Hitler had actually moved into*: F. Wagner, p. 139.

p.109 *It was ridiculous*: F. Wagner, pp. 143, 144.

p.109 *Gossip seethed about this tall*: F. Wagner, p. 153.

p.109 *(Frida Leider agreed.)*: Leider, p. 136.

p.109 *"Pian, pianissimo—then all will be well"*: Skelton, *Richard and Cosima Wagner*, p. 223.

p.109 *"Have you heard my Ninth?"*: LMPM.

p.110 *"weak and often guttural"*: Bernhard Diebold, *Frankfurter Zeitung*, July 25, 1930. It was probably Pilinszky at whom Toscanini had yelled the epithet *"Cane!"*

p.110 *He finally refused to conduct*: LMPM.

p.110 *Carriage-ride story*: Nually, p. 111.

p.110 *However, Heinz Tietjen had done*: F. Wagner, pp. 63, 64.

p.110 *They were equally displeased*: Skelton, *Wagner at Bayreuth*, p. 145.

p.110 *This invitation, however, was an order*: Said Lauritz later regarding this, "Hitler absolutely wanted me to sing in Germany, but I refused to be introduced to him" (tape interview, "The Fairy Tale of My Life," Danmarks Radio, December 25, 1970, produced by Hemming Hartmann-Petersen).

p.110 *"The widow . . . who tried to be"*: LMPM.

p.111 *"The first clash of the season"*: Geissmar, p. 50.

p.111 *"For a long time Nanny Larsén-Todsen"*: Wessling, *Furtwängler*, pp. 226–229.

p.111 *"with the stage name Lauritz Melchior"*: It is a mystery why the idea that Melchior had changed his name is so prevalent. (Bockelmann obviously believed the tale.) Several of the tenor's obituary notices contained the note that the name Melchior was a stage name. To this day *The Music Index* precedes each entry concerning Melchior with the words, "real name, Lebrecht Hommel." If the family Stambog (where his name was inscribed as Lauritz Lebrecht Hommel Melchior on the day of his birth) is not to be believed, Holger Boland (*Ascolta*, April 1983) tells of running across Lauritz Melchior's 1915 *Figaro* score in the Royal Danish Opera Library, his name abbreviated inside the cover in his own handwriting, "L.L.H. Melchior."

p.111 *"He was even granted"*: Wolf Rosenberg, author of *Krise der Gesangskunst* [Crisis in Vocal Art], warns that this is a "kind of absurd statement [that] should only be quoted when one has researched" and adds that there was "an anti-Melchior clique, which had already tried to 'defame' the tenor as 'non-Aryan' " (Ralf Stuckmann, quoting Rosenberg, "Mein lieber Schwan," *NZ Forum*, June 1987).

p.111 *according to Friedelind Wagner, the famous parrots*: F. Wagner, p. 15.

Chapter 9. The Wagnerian Ensemble at the Met (1931–1935)

p.112 *Kleinchen busied herself*: Interview, Alma Strasfogel, New York, April 1985.

p.112 Details of voyage to South America: Leider, pp. 137, 138. From the first grade on, Melchior was inspired to buffoonery by almost any situation, but those skills seemed to flourish during ocean voyages. Another trip, a departure for England on the *Europa*, precipitated a splendid prank. Feeling the need for a little levity, he and Kleinchen turned night into day for their own amusement. The ship was so crowded that it was not as comfortable as it might have been. Accordingly, they bribed one of the cooks and a steward to help them in their whimsical gambol. The Melchiors, and a group of fellow passengers who were amused by the idea, took over the lounge just about the time other passengers were turning in for the night. At midnight they had lunch, after which they played cards and cavorted as they desired until it was time to dress for dinner at 5:00 A.M. When the other passengers were rising, the Melchior group, in evening dress, was congregating for a nightcap at the ship's rail and bidding each other a goodnight. It was one of their more enjoyable larks ("The Big Noise," *Saturday Evening Post*, February 27, 1945).

p.113 *"This was too much for Lauritz"*: Leider, p. 140.

p.113 *"He telegraphed our checks"*: Leider, p. 141.

p.113 *By the summer of 1933*: Caamaño, p. 88.

p.114 *the sadly truncated Bayreuth career*: LMPM. Lauritz enjoyed the company of Hugo Rüdel, chorus master for the Berlin State Opera as well as Bayreuth, very much. The wine cellar of Rüdelsheim, his cottage near the Festspielhaus (which survives today as a restaurant), was but one of its attractions for Lauritz. Rüdel was also an excellent raconteur. Lauritz recalled one story in his personal manuscript: It was about a little, fat tenor with a glorious voice whom Rüdel wanted to work for him in the chorus of the Berlin State Opera. . . . But the opera company where this tenor was under contract would not let him out of it. Rüdel came up with a solution. During a performance of *Lohengrin*, at the place in the opera where the chorus is on stage, the trumpets blare and the

Herald calls out, "Who will champion Elsa?" just before the dramatic arrival of Lohengrin, the little, fat tenor stepped out from the ranks of the chorus, slapped his mighty stomach and shouted: "I will!" He was ejected from the stage immediately and also from the opera company. And Rüdel received him in Berlin with open arms.

p.114 *"If again and again"*: Marek, quoting Busch, *Cosima Wagner*, p. 271.

p.114 Details of Graf Zeppelin trip: Phone interview, Karl Laufkötter, December 1983; LMPM.

p.114 *"not a single human being"*: LMPM.

p.115 *Gatti admitted to Cravath*: Kolodin, p. 362. So oppressive were the Met's financial worries that they even prompted a letter to Julius Mattfeld, music librarian for CBS, asking whether the network would care to purchase the Met's orchestral arrangements of highly unoperatic tunes, like "Deep River," left over from the Opera Ball (AMO).

p.115 *"worst budget in forty years"*: Letter, Gatti to Otto Kahn, November 3, 1931, AMO.

p.115 *better off than many other Met artists*: Payroll accounts book, AMO.

p.115 Martinelli's fees: Payroll accounts book, AMO.

p.115 *At Covent Garden Friedrich Schorr*: Rosenthal, p. 487.

p.116 *a meeting of all the major artists*: January 21, 1935 meeting notes, AMO. Bodanzky eventually spoke his mind publicly, saying that the artists had saved the Met while the backers and bankers had quit. Even at that time, the major contribution to the financial health of the Met remained those "voluntary" ten percent cuts, still in place, taken by the artists. Gatti's much publicized voluntary salary reduction still left him with $47,000 a year—surely not a pittance in those days—while artists like Grace Moore and Gladys Swarthout, making around $75 a week (and only during the season), reduced their pitiful fees by ten percent.

p.116 *congratulations to Gatti-Casazza*: AMO.

p.116 Interview questions: Letter, Associated Press to Gatti, February 14, 1933, AMO.

p.116 *Melchior knew full well*: Nually, p. 119.

p.117 *"a rabbit warren"*: Bing, p. 137.

p.117 *The men who made up*: NY, January 23, 1937.

p.117 *"It was all stopgap refurbishing"*: Belmont, p. 272. Socialite Mrs. August Belmont was a longtime board member and founder of the Metropolitan Opera Guild, one who contributed much to social causes as well as artistic pursuits.

p.117 *"Since I was no less able in using abusive language"*: LMPM.

p.117 *"When I became more knowledgeable"*: LMPM.

p.118 *whereas in Germany he had*: Nually, p. 123.

p.118 *"This performance"*: Olin Downes, NYT, January 17, 1933.

p.118 *"power and conviction"*: W. J. Henderson, NYS, January 17, 1933.

p.118 *"deep and enlarging tenderness"*: Lawrence Gilman, NYHT, January 17, 1933.

p.118 *"any that memory"* and *"Mr. Melchior's share*: Edward Cushing, BE, January 17, 1933.

p.118 *"At last a cast!"*: Pitt Sanborn, NYWT, January 17, 1933.

p.118 *Lauritz had advised Frida to take*: Leider, p. 148.

p.118 *Lauritz preferred to treat the Met*: Melchior prized the comradeship of his colleagues, saying in 1970, "In my time we had much more comradeship on stage than they have now. It was a pleasure to go to work on stage. Now it is not fun; there is not the same atmosphere, the same spirit, the same atmosphere of comradeship. When we had finished the performance, we all went to a restaurant and had some beer and got a little to eat. Now . . . they sing, then they part and go home. We also got together in our various homes or hotels . . . we had a wonderful time together" (LM tape interview, "The Fairy Tale of My Life," Danmarks Radio, December 25, 1970, produced by Hemming Hartmann-Petersen).

p.119 *"Nothing in its monotonous facade"*: Leider, p. 152. Marjorie Lawrence, too, spoke in her memoirs of her distaste for the outside of the Metropolitan Opera building, but how "dazzled" she was by its interior (*Interrupted Melody*, p. 130).

p.119 *how to take Frida's mind off*: LMPM.

p.119 Frida Leider/LM story: Nually, p. 121.

p.119 *Lauritz in yellow tights*: Leider, p. 162.

p.119 *Its most appreciated and applauded sketch*: NYT, April 1, 1935.

p.119 *the pair spent an entire month*: NBC Press Book, 1934–1935.

p.119 *"break from routine that was the famous"*: Leider, p. 162.

p.120 *This year he combined forces*: NYT, March 12, 1934. Tenor Marek Windheim debuted at the Metropolitan during the 1929–1930 season. In addition to his most important roles, which were David in *Meistersinger* and the poet in *Rondine*, he did the lighter Wagnerian tenor parts.

p.120 *"the upbringing to be a good hunter"*: LMPM.

p.120 *"poor hospitality"*: LMPM.

p.121 *"miles from anywhere"*: Hart-Davis, p. 331.

p.121 *He touted the tradition of* Brüderschaft: Interview, Birte Melchior, Copenhagen, August 1983.

p.121 A *Hochsitz*, protected from the weather and equipped with cushions, gun-rests, and telescopic sights, is built in an area where the animals come to feed and drink. All the hunter has to do is sit and wait, in comfort. The outcome is never in doubt.

p.121 *"I cannot kill an animal"* and *"Look at the trophies"*: Interview, Ib Melchior, Los Angeles, December 1983.

p.121 *horrified conservationists*: Interview, Marianne Tegner, Copenhagen, August 1983.

p.121 *"We'll call it Melchior Lake"*: Phone interview, Karl Laufkötter, December 1983.

p.121 *Lauritz was not only a very skilled*: Kaj Olsen, tape interview, "The Fairy Tale of My Life," Danmarks Radio, December 27, 1970, produced by Hemming Hartmann-Petersen.

p.121 Chossewitz hunting details: Interview, Birte Melchior, Copenhagen, August 1983. Birte hated the custom of allowing one of the dogs to drink the deer's blood after the head was cut off, but she liked to eat the venison cooked with cream. The family and guests ate all the game that was shot. Only once did Far shoot something no one wanted to eat. On a year when there were very few ducks on the Chossewitz lake, Far, after much waiting, finally shot something. He commanded his dog Tilla to fetch it. Tilla hesitated, but Far, angry, made her go. As the procession of hunters, baying dogs, and children returned home, the ladies all laughed to see Birte at the head, carrying the lone shoot of the day, a black crow.

p.122 *"the horror cabinet"*: Interview, Birte Melchior, Copenhagen, August 1983.

p.122 Mad soprano at Chossewitz story: NBC Press Book, 1938–1939.

p.122 *"hard and unyielding"*: Kolodin, p. 364. Gatti had given Max Lorenz fifteen performances at a fee of $600. His roles this season included Erik, Lohengrin, Siegmund, and Siegfried (payroll accounts book, AMO).

p.122 *he fretted so much about his own reputation*: Leider, p. 136.

p.123 *"Never did we hear a Siegfried more brilliant"*: *Du Jour*, Paris, November 3, 1934.

p.123 *It was at Brussels' Théâtre Royal de la Monnaie*: Salès, p. 233.

p.123 *"very helpful"*: Biancolli, p. 60. Flagstad recalled the year as 1933 in Biancolli's book, but she did not sing Sieglinde in Brussels until 1934, and Melchior appeared there as Siegfried—which she recalled him singing—only in 1934. In his Flagstad biography, Gunnarson corrected the date to 1934.

p.123 In Lyons Kleinchen indulged in another prank, described by Frida Leider: "On the same day Lyons was expecting movie director Ernst Lubitsch and film star Lillian Harvey. A large crowd had been outside the hotel since early morning. The Melchiors and I were watching the crowd when Kleinchen had the crazy idea of appearing on the balcony with a bouquet in her arms. With her graceful figure, beautiful blonde hair, she easily passed for a film star at a distance. The crowd gave her a great reception and dispersed delighted" (Leider, p. 157).

p.123 *"Mr. Toscanini"*: Interview, Hans Hansen, Copenhagen, August 1983.

p.123 *"good lunch with caviar"*: Maria Hacker diary, 1930.

p.123 *"His international monopoly"*: *Neue Presse*, Vienna, September n.d., 1934.

p.123 *Covent Garden's financial problems*: Rosenthal, p. 477.

p.123 *Beecham's return to Covent Garden*: A direct and amusing comparison of Beecham's and Toscanini's conducting was given by Nevill Cardus, a friend of the Italian conductor: "Beecham directs as a connoisseur who serves up the one and only wine to our and his own amusement; Toscanini was the wine merchant" (Wessling, *Toscanini at Bayreuth*, p. 77).

p.124 *"an impossibly charming"*: Bing, p. 72.

p.124 *"pints of grapefruit juice"*: Geissmar, p. 234.

p.124 *"I think we deserve to have a drink"*: Geissmar, p. 234.

p.124 *Some years later*: Nually, p. 117.

p.125 *"beautiful Italian language"*: LMPM. Melchior elaborated further in a Danish radio interview. The critics had said, "Italian singers, come and hear how to sing in Italian." He also made an interesting statement about singing in another language: "One has to learn to feel so much in that other language that 'threadlessly' one can pass on the feelings to the listeners. Therefore one has to master another language well, because it is the color of the word that is important. One can say 'I love you' in many different ways, but there is only one way that can move the heart. . . . That is the way it is with words. When I listen to my records, there is something important: one understands everything that I sing, every word, and that is most important" (Danmarks Radio, December 25, 1970).

p.125 *Once more Gatti firmly repeated*: LMPM.

p.125 *"I can't have Martinelli ruining"*: LMPM.

p.125 *Loria biography*: AMO.

p.125 *"Melchior's identification"*: Conrad L. Osborne, *Records in Review*, 1961.

p.126 *"Melchior's unmatched tenor had all"*: Conrad L. Osborne, HF, December 5, 1963.

p.126 *"holding his own beautifully"*: Nually, p. 127.

p.126 *the best of the Italian season*: Rosenthal, p. 483.

p.126 *"His voice has not that rich"*: Rosenthal quoting *The Times*, p. 493. There was another legacy from his performances with the Italian cast. Melchior, despite his love for food, developed a strong aversion to garlic and forbade the use of it in his food, even to the end of his life. His abhorrence of that substance he blamed on one of his Italian Desdemonas, who had imbued the fur of his Otello costume with an irradicable scent of garlic.

p.126 *"to sing an Italian operatic role"*: LMPM.

p.126 *"Melchior's Italian sounded"*: Rosenthal, p. 549. The Italian tenor Lauri-Volpi assets in his book *Voci Parallele* (p. 129) that Toscanini himself had encouraged Melchior to study the role of Otello and went to Covent Garden to hear him do it, but "that voice, which to the Magician had appeared magnificent in German repertoire, revealed itself to [Toscanini] with all the fissures and defects which were so well masked by the declamation and the orchestral Wagnerian sonority." (This statement is, to my knowledge, without corroboration from other sources.)

p.126 *"His Otello will go down in the history"*: Ada Hanafin, SFE, December 9, 1934.

p.126 *"he sang like a God"*: SFCB, November 27, 1934.

p.127 *"The singers whom Melchior considered"*: Shawe-Taylor, p. 59.

p.127 *"The whole audience broke into cheering"*: NYP, January 12, 1934.

p.127 *"not just motherly"*: Interview, Leonard Eisner, New York, November 1984.

p.128 *"She was quite a girl in her day"*: Interview, Leonard Eisner, November 1984.

p.128 *"Mein lieber Siegmund"*: Melchior correspondence, DCM.

p.128 *"enjoy it completely"*: Lehmann, p. 178.

p.128 *"the epitome of everything"*: Newton, p. 178. Ivor Newton, British pianist and accompanist to Kirsten Flagstad and other notable singers, author of a book of memoirs entitled *At the Piano—Ivor Newton*.

p.128 *"The electrifying spark"*: Jerome Bohm, NYHT, January 2, 1935.

p.128 *"Lehmann does not fit"*: Maria Hacker diary, 1925–1926.

p.128 *"[Lehmann] was a purist"*: Interview, Ignace Strasfogel, New York, April 1985.

p.129 *"harsh and intransigent in business"*: Gaisberg, p. 129.

p.129 Kleinchen/Lehmann publicity story: Nually, pp. 123, 124.

p.130 *"An American Wagner Society"*: Lawrence Gilman, quoting LM, NYHT, February 11, 1934.

p.130 *Richard Wagner had shared*: Julian Seaman, n.p., April 9, 1934.

p.130 *A former student of de Reszke*: Letter, William Thorner of New York, written January 26, 1934, to the *New York Times* editor, published NYT, February 11, 1934. Anton Seidl (1850–1898), one of the great Wagner conductors of his day, assisted Wagner in the preparation of the score and the first performance of the *Ring* in Bayreuth. His early experience at cutting Wagner was gained on an 1882 European tour as conductor of the "Nibelungen" opera troupe. *Grove's Dictionary of Music* describes the music drama as being "sadly mutilated" by this company.

p.130 *"If it is absolutely necessary"*: W. J. Henderson, NYS, n.d., 1934.

p.130 *"as well knock another hunk"*: CLN, January 23, 1934.

p.130 *"The great aim of getting tired businessmen"*: *Buffalo Times*, January 25, 1934.

p.131 *"even cut Wagner is apt"*: Paul Althouse, *Nutley* (New Jersey) *Sun*, March 9, 1934. Althouse, a student of Percy Rector Stephens, made his Met debut in 1913. With the company until 1921, he left and gradually made the change to Wagnerian tenor, singing in Berlin, Stuttgart, Stockholm, Chicago, and Salzburg, before returning to the Met as a member of the German wing as the first American Tristan. Retired from the Met in 1941 to teach singing, he produced many distinguished singers, among them Eleanor Steber and Richard Tucker.

p.131 *"the musical population of New York"*: Columbus (Ohio) *State Journal*, February 1, 1934.

p.131 *"not nearly so revolutionary"*: NYT, February 7, 1934.

p.131 *"[Melchior came west] to exhibit"*: Lawrence Gilman, NYHT, February 11, 1934.

p.131 *An all-star panel of judges*: NYT, April 1, 1934.

p.131 *One reporter valiantly*: BT, March 23, 1934.

p.131 *he requested the Melchior and Leider*: Memo, Gatti to Ziegler, March 30, 1934, AMO.

p.131 *There was nothing to do*: Nually, p. 126.

p.132 *"I suspect one would have to go"*: Pitt Sanborn, NYWT, February 23, 1934. Leider's ensuing absence from the Metropolitan Opera is still attributed by many to Melchior's callousness. It was a common belief at the time that he had cavalierly cast aside his old friend in favor of the new Norwegian soprano, Kirsten Flagstad, because their partnership had caught the public fancy. Leider's letters would appear to refute this theory. Furthermore, Flagstad was auditioned only after the Met knew that Leider would not return.

p.132 *"is the great Tristan of this era"*: Eugene Stinson, CHN, December 17, 1934.

p.132 *to do* Samson et Dalila: Some sources state that Melchior performed Samson in *Samson et Dalila* a total of three times. According to his own performance ledger, however, he performed it once on stage at the Royal Danish Opera and once on radio.

Chapter 10. The Golden Years (1935–1939)

p.133 *"now read like operatic mythology"*: Donal Henalhan, NYT, April 2, 1989.

p.134 Kirsten Flagstad bio: Kolodin, p. 381; Mayer, p. 195.

p.134 *Back in 1929 Otto Kahn*: Mayer, p. 130.

p.134 *Not until 1932*: The great Wagnerian soprano Ellen Gulbranson was one of those who heard one of Flagstad's first four Isolde performances in Oslo during June of 1932. Gulbranson insisted that her young colleague should be singing abroad, and wrote to Winifred Wagner suggesting an audition for her compatriot. Tietjen then invited Flagstad to audition for Bayreuth on the further recommendation of Alexander Kipnis, who had sung with her in the otherwise all-Norwegian cast of *Tristan* in August 1932 (Rein, pp. 94–96).

p.134 Flagstad Bayreuth audition particulars: Vogt, pp. 97–101.

p.134 St. Moritz audition particulars: Ewen, pp. 71, 72.

p.134 *newcomer Anny Konetzni*: Konetzni, wrote Kolodin, sang "powerfully, but with frayed tones" at the Metropolitan (Kolodin, p. 380).

p.134 *rushed out to find Ziegler*: Noble, p. 150.

p.134 "Una certa Flagstad": Biancolli, p. 243.

p.134 *"an instantaneous and complete triumph"*: Leonard Liebling, NYA, February 3, 1935.

p.135 *"Certainly not since Jean de Reszke"*: Pitt Sanborn, NYWT, February 7, 1935.

p.135 *"principally with a new singer"*: Olin Downes, NYT, February 7, 1935.

p.135 *"the stimulating effect of Kirsten Flagstad's"*: Kolodin, p. 383.

p.135 Flagstad/Melchior/Althouse performance numbers: Payroll accounts book, AMO.

p.135 "Die Kirsten kann alles" and *"Melchior calmed me down"*: Gunnarson, p. 80.

p.135 *"That weary and jaded victim"*: Lawrence Gilman, NYHT, March 19, 1935.

p.136 *"What Mme. Flagstad and Mr. Melchior brought"*: CHN, October 21, 1935.

p.137 *"with a wealth of light and shade"*: NYT, December 22, 1935.

p.137 *"The Tristan of Mr. Melchior"*: Olin Downes, December 31, 1935.

p.137 *an incorrigible teaser*: As a school boy, Lauritz entertained his fellow students with his mischievous pranks and practical jokes but got himself in trouble with his father, the principal. As the Melchior School was known for its modern educational techniques—such as no indiscriminate use of the stick—Jørgen Melchior alone had the privilege of administering physical punishment to a student. Summoned by the teacher, he would arrive with a length of hollow bamboo known by the Danish term "Spanish cane." So customary an event was the spanking of little Lalle that, in honor of a school anniversary, his brother Henrik Emil drew a cartoon of one of Lauritz's encounters with the infamous Spanish cane.

p.137 *"I was absolutely shattered to see"*: Leider, p. 120.

p.138 *"When Melchior was a motherless baby"*: Interview, Hans Hansen, Copenhagen, August 1983.

p.138 Lehmann swimming at The Viking story: Interview, Leonard Eisner, New York, November 1984.

p.138 *Others judged her to be*: Mordden, p. 190.

p.138 Description of Melchior/Flagstad quarrel: McArthur, pp. 47, 48.

p.138 *"Who is the prima donna"*: Such publicity tactics inspired a letter to the *Times* editor from John Hastings, Highland Park, Connecticut, January 19, 1937 (printed NYT, January 24, 1937). Hastings' words give some idea of the rhetoric being used in the battle of the prima donnas. The "epidemic of idolatry" for Mme. Flagstad was "preposterous and entirely out of proportion to her artistic and histrionic, as exclusive of her vocal, endowment." Illustrating the "excessive preciosity indulged in by the critics," Hastings quoted a phrase describing Flagstad's singing of the "Liebestod": "the whole intolerable pathos of the moment is in her singing of the little grace note before the B flat." The naturalness and simplicity for which Flagstad was constantly eulogized were "useless as a basis of appraisal" when compared with Lehmann's inspirational and instinctive acting and her voice that conveyed "undreamt-of revelations in the music she sings."

p.139 *"April 18: bridge Melchiors and Edwin!!!"*: Gunnarson, pp. 101, 102. Melchior's own version of this quarrel appears exclusively in Nually, p. 34. (His personal manuscript omits all reference to the quarrel, and he, to the author's knowledge, never discussed it with outsiders who are willing to go on record.) In Nually, the date is given as March 18, 1936, rather than 1937. Gunnarson (pp. 101, 102), using Flagstad's diary, corroborates the 1937 date used by McArthur. In Melchior's story, Constance Hope's publicity efforts do not play a part: After several champagne toasts to Kleinchen's fine performance as the page in the Rochester *Tristan*, the Melchiors sat down to play cards with Kirsten. Then she brought up the subject of Lotte Lehmann and, to the surprise of the others, began to excoriate her soprano colleague's singing, her vocal quality, her recent Town Hall concert, and more. Melchior's loyalty to friends and colleagues is well-documented, as is his admiration for Lehmann's singing. He responded as might be expected, speaking bluntly to Kirsten about the lack of heart and tenderness in her singing, and, worse, her woeful lack of femininity—all compared unfavorably to Lehmann. Even Kleinchen was silent in the face of his fury. The damage was done.

p.139 *"She was a skilled singer"*: LM tape interview, "The Fairy Tale of My Life," December 25, 1970, produced by Hemming Hartmann-Petersen.

p.139 *"sooner or later we have to face"*: Memo, Ziegler to Johnson, May 21, 1937, AMO.

p.139 *Taking Melchior's own advice*: Memo, Ziegler to Johnson, May 21, 1937, AMO.

p.139 *"personable, commanding"*: NYT, December 13, 1937.

p.140 *"The opera is called* Tristan *AND* Isolde": Letter, LM to Max Lorenz, February 6, 1967.

p.140 *Early in 1938*: McArthur, p. 46.

p.140 *"who deserved greater credit"*: Gaisberg, p. 135.

p.140 *"gloated over the fact"*: McArthur, p. 86.

p.140 *she was paid $550 per week*: Payroll accounts book, AMO. For purposes of comparison, Lehmann was paid $700 per performance and Leider $750, while the Italian stars were still in the ascendancy: Claudia Muzio at $1,000 and Rosa Ponselle at $1,500 (all before the voluntary cuts of the 1934–1935 season). (Payroll accounts book, AMO.)

p.141 *The claque's standard rates*: NYT, December 19, 1935; AMO. The most expensive part of maintaining one's claque was getting the members of the claque into the opera house. This is why leading singers insisted on an allotment of complimentary standing-room tickets, which they then gave to the leader of the claque, who sometimes had as many as fifty henchmen. Johnson's ban took the form of cutting off the artists' free admission tickets. Caruso, of all people, was said to rely heavily upon the claque, to the tune of several hundred dollars a month (NYT, December 19, 1935).

p.141 *he couldn't imagine why inferior singers*: Interview, Ib Melchior, Los Angeles, November 1987.

p.141 *"The dreadful claque system I have always opposed"*: LMPM.

p.141 "chef de claque *got 100 Schillings*": Maria Hacker diary, 1930.

p.141 *"If we could win out"*: Draft of letter to Stevens, no date, handwritten by Witherspoon, AMO.

p.142 *the foundation extracted promises*: Musical Leader, March 16, 1935.

p.142 Details of Witherspoon's fees and contracts: Payroll accounts book, AMO.

p.142 *"The great number of people employed"*: Handwritten notes, no date, AMO. Witherspoon's budget made room for an "Italian soprano at $7,000" [for the season], an "Italian mezzo at $5,600," a "coloratura at $4,000," and a "basso at $4,200." According to his notes, he was prepared to "let go" a shocking list of artists (including Ponselle, Martinelli, De Luca, Pons, Moore), who for some reason he felt were not giving enough value for the money. Many of the artists whom Witherspoon was considering were indeed engaged at a future date—Marjorie Lawrence, Josephine Antoine, Gina Cigna, René Maison, Salvatore Baccaloni. On his list of conductors were Reiner, Szell, Walter, but he was also on the lookout for a young conductor "whom we can build into popular favor." Presumably this position was filled by Erich Leinsdorf. As to the number of weeks in a season: from 1883 to 1889 the Metropolitan season was sixteen weeks long. In 1907 it was extended to a twenty-week season, and from 1923 to 1932 it remained at twenty-four weeks, when the economy-minded administration again returned to sixteen weeks. By 1981 it had been extended to a thirty-week duration (AMO).

p.142 Johnson biography: NY, December 14, 1935.

p.142 *"Both singers and public are fortunate"*: MUC, January 4, 1936.

p.143 Flagstad and Melchior contractual details: Payroll accounts book, AMO.

p.143 *"And I have asked Mr. Johnson"*: B. H. Haggin, BE, March 22, 1936.

p.143 *"I wanted you to sing this for a long time"*: LM's notes of interview with Judd Bernard, California press agent, DCM.

p.143 *"Mr. Melchior is a magnificent Otello"*: Lawrence Gilman, NYHT, March 20, 1935.

p.144 *"I never had the opportunity"*: LMPM.

p.144 *Accompanying the Melchiors out to the Long Island*: NYT, February 23, 1935.

p.144 *"His growth from season"*: NYT, February 23, 1935.

p.144 *"barely this side of clowning"*: NYT, January 21, 1933.

p.144 *"unaffected acting suggested"*: NYT, April 10, 1931.

p.144 *"zest and humor, and of poetry"*: NYHT, March 7, 1931.

p.144 *"exuberant"*: Lawrence Gilman, NYHT, January 4, 1936.

p.144 *"the robust good humor"*: Henriette Weber, NYJ, January 4, 1936.

p.144 *"[Melchior's] energetic deportment"*: Robert Bagar, NYWT, January 4, 1936.

p.145 *"was as fine as he can make it"*: Noel Straus, NYT, February 25, 1938.

p.145 Metropolitan Opera refurbishing details: AMO.

p.145 *"a variety show"*: Ernst Lert, *Chord and Discord*, December 1935.

p.145 *"comely to gaze upon"*: Jerome Bohm, NYHT, December 19, 1935.

p.145 *"sung her way straight into the hearts"*: Henriette Weber, NYJ, December 19, 1935.

p.145 *"Mr. Melchior was at his best"*: Robert Bagar, NYWT, December 19, 1935.

p.145 *He admired Lawrence as a wonderful actress*: Nually, pp. 156, 157.

p.145 Details of 100th Tristan anniversary and story of suspenders breaking: Morris Goldberg, NYE, July 11, 1955. Longtime friend and professional colleague Karl Laufkötter asserts that Melchior wore the girdle for several reasons: to look thinner; to hold up the mail trousers; for a breathing aid (letter, Karl Laufkötter to Shirlee Emmons, March 9, 1984).

p.146 *"I cannot say whether or not"*: Copy of Johnson speech, AMO.

p.146 *"able to adjust his style"*: Howard Taubman, NYT, February 11, 1936.

p.146 *"regret that he is not"*: Irving Kolodin, NYS, February 11, 1936.

p.146 *"I [once] tried out what I imagined"*: Robert A. Simon, NY, February 22, 1936.

p.147 Edward Johnson report to the board: Copy of speech, AMO.

p.147 *So strong was the trend*: Noble, p. 155.

p.147 Financial details of 1936–1937 season: AMO.

p.147 *"it was distinguished by"*: Olin Downes, NYT, December 22, 1936.

p.147 *"Melchior displayed his usual"*: B. H. Haggin, BE, December 21, 1936.

p.147 *"Melchior sang with a lavish"*: Lawrence Gilman, NYHT, December 24, 1936.

p.148 *"a noble Tristan"*: W. J. Henderson, NYS, December 22, 1936.

p.148 *"The present writer has heard"*: W. J. Henderson, NYS, December 25, 1936.

p.148 *Another Tristan had not been accepted*: Of de Reszke's last Tristan, critic Henry E. Krehbiel wrote, "little short of a miracle: every word, every pose, every action brimming over with youthful energy, vigor, and enthusiasm" (Pleasants, quoting Krehbiel, p. 259). There is, however, general agreement that de Reszke's subsequent vocal limitations were brought on by the strain of performing Siegfried and Tristan. Also, de Reszke's most strenuous seasons had found him singing every two and one half days not only Siegfried but Rodrigue in *Le Cid*, Vasco da Gama in *L'Africaine*, or Werther (Pleasants, p. 261), whereas Melchior's most strenuous seasons found him singing on the average slightly more than once every three days, but all within the heaviest Wagnerian repertoire. Frequently he sang Siegfried and Tristan, or even three roles, with only one day's rest between them. Such combinations as Siegfried, day off, Tristan; or Siegfried, travel day, Siegmund, day off, Lohengrin, two days off, Tristan, day off, Siegfried; or Parsifal and Tristan back to back—these were commonplace for Melchior in the 1930s. In these feats of stamina he was evenly matched by Kirsten Flagstad.

p.148 *"new and excellent"*: Olin Downes, NYT, January 23, 1937.

p.148 *There was general surprise*: Lawrence Gilman, NYHT, January 31, 1937.

p.148 *"dependable routine"*: Winthrop Sargeant, NYA, January 23, 1937.

p.149 Mime/Siegfried horseplay: Interview, Karl Laufkötter, Ojai, California, November 1987.

p.149 *"Mr. Melchior's thrice-admirable"*: Oscar Thompson, NYS, November 30, 1937.

p.149 *So great was the continuing demand*: Payroll accounts book, AMO.

p.150 *She consented to*: Letter, Marks Levine to Johnson, May 9, 1938, AMO.

p.150 *Yet only when Mayor LaGuardia*: Letter, Fiorello LaGuardia to committee, May 6, 1938, AMO.

p.150 *After the performance*: Interview, Karl Laufkötter, Ojai, California, November 1987. Lauritz had asked the crown prince, his friend from the time of the prince's graduate days, whom he wished to include in the party. There was no question. Surfeited with talking to diplomatic personnel, Prince Frederik opted for artists.

p.150 *Marjorie Lawrence, a fellow Ansonian*: Marjorie Lawrence, *Interrupted Melody*, New York: Appleton-Century-Crofts, 1949, p. 133.

p.151 Description of bar-café: S. J. Woolf, NYT, February 17, 1946.

p.151 *"they were all in their pajamas"*: Geissmar, p. 161.

p.151 *"Carmen clothes"*: Alden Whitman, NYT, March 20, 1973.

p.151 *"an abundant silk shirt"*: NYP, December, n.d., 1945.

p.151 Mutti decorating for Christmas story: Nually, p. 137.

p.151 *"there's only one spot"*: Interview, Klaus Riisbro, Copenhagen, August 1983.

p.152 *"Their talent was a capacity"*: Interview, Alma Strasfogel, New York, April 1985.

p.152 *"enjoyed good food"*: LMPM.

p.152 Guard shooting parties: "The Big Noise," *Saturday Evening Post*, February 27, 1945; George Tucker, "Man about Manhattan," syndicated column, n.p., February 3, 1941.

p.152 *"rout"*: O'Connell, p. 85.

p.153 Artists' representative: Interview, Thea Dispeker, New York, February 1986.

p.153 *"spend . . . the time from"*: Geissmar, p. 161.

p.153 *"Melchior stays right up"*: NYHT, August 14, 1940.

p.153 *"robber baron's castle"* and Chossewitz description: NBC Press Book, 1938–1939; home movies, LM's photograph albums.

p.153 *"like a savage"*: Birte Melchior, *Hendes Verden* #49, 1970. Once asked how many dogs he had at Chossewitz, Melchior responded with his customary wit and jollity: "Five, and *I* am the Great Dane."

p.154 *"I never let singing interfere"*: *Parade*, August 7, 1949. The Melchiors held a yearly hunt meet at Chossewitz. One hundred and fifty strong, the group rose with the 8:00 reveille sounded by the gamekeeper and ate fried eggs, coffee, and mountains of rolls. The panoply that Lauritz so loved began at 8:00 with the traditional greeting to guests sounded on four hunting horns. Melchior formally welcomed his guests and told them the program for the day. After the call to the hunt was blown, the "Pürschwagens," garlanded with leaves and branches, left for the deep woods—hunters, beaters, dogs, and supplies all crowded on the wagons' long benches. The hunting horns announced each event all day, first the call to begin shooting. Villagers, together with young boys from the Hitler Youth, hired as beaters, noisily drove the animals toward the hunters. The fur-coat-clad women set lunch out by a tremendous bonfire in a cleared spot. At dark, the entire kill of the day was gathered in front of the house while a special call was blown for each kind of animal. On the last night, the festivities peaked with a ball in the village inn—The Pitcher with the Green Handle—which every resident of the village, healthy or infirm, infant or eighty-year-old, attended.

p.154 Lauritz in *Jews in Art*: Nually, p. 141; TI, June 27, 1938.

p.154 *"to see Mr. Göring"*: LM tape interview, "The Fairy Tale of My Life," Danmarks Radio, December 25, 1970, produced by Hemming Hartmann-Petersen. Göring was reasonably well-known to Lauritz, for he often hunted in the state forest contiguous to the Chossewitz property. Ib Melchior remembers one such hunt: Göring took up a position in a field about one hundred feet from the edge of the forest and sat on his three-legged folding seat, waiting for the game to be driven toward him. Far and I were nearby at some trees. Suddenly, while the noise-making drivers were still far off, a hugh boar broke unexpectedly and made straight for Göring. There was not even time to get his gun up before the boar bowled him over and took off. Göring went flying, legs in the air. I began to laugh, and was silenced by the murderous glares of the Göring entourage, who came running to the rescue." Coincidentally, one of the Chossewitz cars (other than "Maxi" the Ford and "The Professor," a 12-cylinder Packard) was called "Hermann," for it had once belonged to Göring. The Melchior household, especially Walter Bock, the chauffeur, enjoyed the "Heil" salutes given "Hermann" when it was driven in Berlin (B. Melchior, *Hendes Verden* #49, 1970).

p.154 Nazis at Chossewitz story: Interview, Klaus Riisbro, Copenhagen, August 1983.

p.155 *Calculating the exact moment*: Interview, Cleo Baldon, Los Angeles, November 1987.

p.155 *seventeen sculpted wooden panels from Trier Cathedral*: In July 1952, the Melchiors presented New York's Metropolitan Museum of Art with most of these panels, among the few items recovered after the war, and later the last three to the Los Angeles museum. Carved by a master craftsman and twenty-one assistants, they had been made in Mainz between 1723 and 1726 for a Carthusian monastery there. Eight years after the monastery was secularized, the choir stalls were sold. Acquired for the Cathedral of Trier in the middle of the nineteenth century, the stalls had been removed and stored when the cathedral was later restored to its original Gothic condition. A private collector of Berlin, into whose hands they had come, sold them to the Melchiors some fifty years later. The museum curator described them as the finest examples of German baroque woodwork in this country (*Musical America*, August 1952; NYT, July 10, 1952).

p.156 *in all probability wealthier than Far*: Letter, Ib Melchior to Shirlee Emmons, September 18, 1986.

p.156 *"Please, please tell your father"*: Letter, Birte Melchior to Shirlee Emmons, December 29, 1986.

p.156 *"rescued Covent Garden from disaster"*: Nually, pp. 130, 131; letter, LM to Johnson, June 3, 1935, AMO.

p.156 *glamour and opening night turmoil*: Geissmar, p. 241.

p.157 *"That's all right"*: Rosenthal, p. 497.

p.157 *Lohengrin* performance details: LMPM On May 6, thanks to the royal princesses Helena Victoria and Marie Louise, granddaughters of Queen Victoria, the Melchiors, Frida and Rudi were able to watch the elaborate public ceremonies commemorating King George V's silver jubilee from the balcony of St. James Palace in Pall Mall. All four commoners were thrilled when the princesses and the queen waved to them from their carriages (LMPM; Leider, p. 167). The royal princesses had been great Wagner enthusiasts since the time when they first were taken to rehearsals by Cosima at Bayreuth. At Covent Garden they eschewed the royal box when attending Wagner operas, preferring the better acoustics of the stalls. Their kindness toward the artists who came to London was legendary (Geissmar, p. 240).

p.157 *"She sat completely at ease"*: John Stean, quoting "Beckmesser," *The Gramophone*, June 1936.

p.157 *he announced that plans were all but finished*: American Music Lover, May 1936.

p.157 *a Danish friend*: Knud Hegermann-Lindencrone, friend and admirer of both Flagstad and Melchior, fell in love with Wagner as a young man in Paris, attending the gala performances of the Wagner Festivals at the Opéra, where he was introduced to Melchior by his niece, Yvonne Sorne, daughter of Henrik Emil Melchior, and a singer (mezzo-soprano) herself. After returning to Denmark, Hegermann-Lindencrone began monthly broadcasts featuring famous singers in 1938 (the first about Lauritz Melchior), continuing through the 1960s. His tape collection of live theater and music repertoire—the first of its kind in Europe—began at the newspaper *Berlingske Tidende* in 1949, which was the 200th anniversary of both the newspaper and the Royal Theater. This priceless and unusual collection, "containing such gems as Benjamin Britten conducting his own *Rape of Lucretia* and *Albert Herring* in 1949, and the first European stereo recording from 1958, is still going strong after forty years" (Letter, Hegermann-Lindencrone to Shirlee Emmons, May 17, 1989).

p.157 *"relates to the sad fate of some"*: Letters, Knud Hegermann-Lindencrone to Shirlee Emmons: February 7, 1987; April 4, 1987; July 5, 1987; July 12, 1987; August 9, 1987; December 7, 1987; November 2, 1988; June 6, 1988.

p.158 *she had thrown the recordings out*: Many people believed that Flagstad ordered the Covent Garden tests destroyed because she didn't like them, but Hegermann-Lindencrone has confirmed that it was rather "in bitterness and sadness that they never came . . . little knowing that EMI (stated to [him] in a letter from Walter Legge) was planning a complete *Götterdämmerung* in Vienna with Furtwängler. Instead she had accepted Decca's offer" (Letter, Hegermann-Lindencrone to Shirlee Emmons, May 17, 1989).

p.158 *a frogman be sent down to retrieve the test pressings*: Says Hegermann-Lindencrone of the rescue attempts, "The records, each in two pieces with a clear break, were in those huge light-brown parcels in which HMV always packed their things. Several were saved, as the grooves were intact except for the break. I put them together, transferred them to a 15″ tape. Then, with the clicks cut out, they sounded perfect in every way. Unfortunately they were not all like that, only a minor part." In January 1989 representatives of the Flagstad Hamar Museum came to Hegermann-Lindencrone and took the tests. They, together with other rare recordings, will be published to commemorate her one hundredth anniversary. The originals of the 1937 tests are transferred to cassettes and can be heard at the Hamar Museum (Letter, Hegermann-Lindencrone to Shirlee Emmons, May 17, 1989).

p.159 *"Siegmund in my estimation"*: *American Music Lover*, May 1936.

p.159 *"Rethberg, Melchior, and List"*: "Beckmesser" (possibly Walter Legge), *The Gramophone*, June 1936.

p.159 *"gigantic voice to the most subtle"*: *Paris Excelsior*, NBC Press Book, 1934–1935.

p.160 *Lotte Lehmann's run-in with Göring*: F. Wagner, p. 134.

p.160 *"To be truthful"*: FXK, *Catholic Standard and Times*, January 11, 1956.

p.160 *"eminently cultivated . . . singer"* and *"lightweight"*: Rosenthal, p. 527.

p.160 *"past her vocal prime"*: Rosenthal, p. 528.

p.160 Anvil story: Mordden, p. 187.

p.161 *Ill with worry*: F. Wagner, p. 180.

p.161 *When Hitler began to persecute the Jews*: Leider, p. 160.

p.161 *Herbert Janssen, who had earlier*: F. Wagner, p. 184.

p.161 *Kerstin Thorborg had refused*: F. Wagner, p. 194.

p.161 *Yet London had profited much*: Rosenthal, p. 529.

p.161 *"I cannot go on"*: *Philadelphia Record*, November 5, 1938. Like the rest of the audience, Fred Gaisberg also assumed that she had lost her voice, and his opinion probably represented that of the knowledgeable musicians of that time. "It was a sad finale to the hundreds of Marschallins she had played and our hearts went out to her in sympathy" (Gaisberg, p. 135).

p.161 *Frida Leider's story*: F. Wagner, p. 193.

p.162 *"Now come the difficult years"*: F. Wagner, p. 195.

p.162 *"Tietjen was my idol"*: [emphasis added by author to "attrition by indecision"]: Bing, p. 31.

p.162 *It was in this atmosphere*: F. Wagner, p. 195.

p.162 *(In San Francisco, Lauritz was paid*: Letter, Ziegler to John Erskine, August 6, 1935, AMO.

p.163 *"an effective team"*: NBC Press Book, 1938–1939.

p.163 *"showmanship, but not at the expense"*: BT, October 31, 1938.

p.163 *"assisting artists"*: Interview, Leonard Eisner, New York, November 1984.

p.163 *"An opera is like an oil painting"*: Lilian Foerster, OPN, January 28, 1946.

p.163 *Hüsch was a firm believer*: Moore, *Furthermoore*, p. 112.

p.164 Kleinchen as page girl story: Noble, p. 116; NYS, April 1, 1936.

p.165 Lucky Strike story: Interview, Klaus Riisbro, Copenhagen, August 1983; commercial ads, DCM.

p.165 *"[Constance Hope] is fond of me"*: Letter, Lotte Lehmann to Kleinchen Melchior, April 23, 1939.

p.165 *"If Your Wife Puts You on a Diet"*: Ida Jean Kain, n.p., n.d.

p.165 *"Lover, Go Way from Me"* and *"Are Tenors Lousy Lovers"*: ST, January 1939; PASR, November 1938.

p.165 Melchior as household name story: Interviews, Ib Melchior, Marianne Tegner, Los Angeles, November 1987.

Chapter 11. Hitler Interferes (1939–1941)

p.167 *Beecham shamed* and *Newman convinced*: Rosenthal, p. 544.

p.167 *"attitudinizing"*: Rosenthal, p. 546.

p.167 *how he emptied his voice*: Rosenthal, p. 546.

p.168 *"no reason to fear"*: NYT, August 25, 1939.

p.168 *"That evening I was just a short distance"*: LMPM.

p.168 *"with information of the coming world catastrophe"*: LMPM.

p.169 *"just in case something should happen"*: LMPM.

p.169 Stettiner Station story: LMPM.

p.169 *"a very happy chapter of our lives"*: LMPM.

p.169 Mutti's lecture to Kleinchen: Nually, p. 147.

p.169 *she was unhappy*: Letter, Birte Melchior to. Shirlee Emmons, December 29, 1986.

p.170 *he and Kleinchen felt immobilized*: LMPM.

p.170 *Their only hope*: Nually, p. 147.

p.170 *both children had long been forbidden*: Interviews, Ib and Birte Melchior, December and August 1983.

p.170 *"wouldn't hear of it"*: Letter, Birte Melchior to Shirlee Emmons, December 29, 1986.

p.170 *"This is a very delicate question"*: Letter, Birte Melchior to Shirlee Emmons, December 29, 1986.

p.170 Wiedemann story: Interview, Eva Andersen, Copenhagen, August 1986.

p.171 *"it was very difficult because"*: Interview, Birte Melchior, Copenhagen, August 1983.

p.171 *"married poorly"*: Interview, Leonard Eisner, New York, November 1984.

p.171 *"My father was always informed"*: Letter, Birte Melchior to Shirlee Emmons, December 29, 1986.

p.171 *When the occupation started*: Letter, Birte Melchior to Shirlee Emmons, December 29, 1986. The suicide and attempted killing of his second wife by Ludvig Nathansen (Inger's father) had prompted exhaustive newspaper reports in June 1907. In this *cause célèbre* all facets of Nathansen's life were thoroughly investigated and reported: Ludvig's mother, Inger's paternal grandmother, had married a Mr. Mortensen who, after the birth of the children, disappeared to America, whereupon the mother reappropriated her maiden name of Nathansen in order to be eligible for help from the Danish Jews. She and her children became members of the Jewish congregation. Her son Ludvig later married Thora Schmidt, Inger's mother, his first wife (*Aalborg Stiftstidende*, June 2, 1907).

p.171 *Indeed, one night Knud Nathansen*: Interview, Eva Andersen, Copenhagen, August 1986. Cousin Eva, despite a bad heart like her Aunt Inger, had joined the resistance, acting as secretary to the leader of the underground. After he had been imprisoned by the Nazis for something minor, she too was arrested, but never gave him away even when the Nazis tortured her by putting out lighted cigarettes on her breasts. Those scars she still bears. (Interviews, Eva Andersen, Copenhagen, August 1986; Cleo Baldon, Los Angeles, November 1987.)

p.171 Clausen-Kaas story: Interview, Eva Andersen, Copenhagen, August 1986; letter, Birte Melchior to Shirlee Emmons, December 29, 1986.

p.172 *"lazy in human relationships"*: Interview, Ib Melchior, Los Angeles, December 1983.

p.172 *Kleinchen had found passage*: Interview, Karl Laufkötter, Ojai, California, November 1987.

p.172 *"Don't ever mention Ib's name to Mr. Melchior"*: Interview, Ib Melchior, Los Angeles, December 1983.

p.172 *"I think that it was"*: Interview, Ib Melchior, Los Angeles, December 1983. Ib's army life began when he volunteered his services to the U.S. Armed Forces, writing to the War Department: "How can I help? I speak six languages and know Europe well." After delay for investigation, he was called to the Capitol and summoned to an ensign's office where he was told to sign a paper that said, "I hereby volunteer for hazardous duty, no questions asked." In the buff, carrying only his yellow toothbrush and a new identity, Mel G8, he was sworn in with others to the cloak-and-dagger department, the OSS, although later he was inducted into the MIS (Military Intelligence Service). Both the U.S. Army and the King of Denmark decorated Ib Melchior after the war ended.

p.172 Leif Melchior kidney operation story: Interview, Ib Melchior, Los Angeles, December 1983; letter, Ib Melchior to Shirlee Emmons, June 28, 1989.

p.172 *"grabby"*: Interview, Ib Melchior, Los Angeles, December 1983.

p.173 *Vogue* magazine incident: Letter, Ib Melchior to Shirlee Emmons, January 9, 1987.

p.173 Marion Gering/MGM incident: Letter, Ib Melchior to Shirlee Emmons, December 10, 1986.

p.173 Ed Sullivan incident: Interview, Ib Melchior, Los Angeles, December 1983. Ib Melchior had begun a theatrical career directly out of the university as a member of the English Players, a touring English language repertory company. He ended up in New York before the war and pursued an acting (specializing in foreign accents) and stage-managing career before and after the war, writing on the side. Nowadays he is a most successful and prolific writer of intricate spy stories.

p.173 General Sarnoff incident: Letter, Ib Melchior to Shirlee Emmons, June 28, 1989.

p.173 *Many have said*: Phone interview, Marianne Tegner, March 1989.

p.173 *"One can break up the times"*: Interview, Ib Melchior, Los Angeles, November 1987.

p.174 *"The children of prominent people"*: Interview, Dr. Rudolf Steinharter, New York, April 1985. It appears that Melchior was selectively generous, as one can see from the efforts he made on behalf of Rudolf Steinharter. In 1933, after young Rudolf had spend three years waiting in Switzerland for a certain required affidavit from a Cincinnati relative that would facilitate his emigration to America, it became apparent that the Cincinnatians feared the exposure of their income required on the form. Dr. Stefan Steinharter, Rudi's father, and doctor to both Melchior and Leider, asked help from Lauritz. He traveled to the home of the recalcitrant relatives, took the man of the family by the collar and said, "You give that boy his affidavit. I'll take care of everything else." The Melchiors deposited money in Switzerland as a guarantee that young Rudolf would not become a ward of the state, and he was allowed into America. Says the younger Dr. Steinharter today, "I'll never forget because he saved my life. He was a mensch."

p.174 *The Copenhagen newspaper,* Berlingske Tidende, *speculated*: Gunnarson, p. 124.

p.174 Details of November recording session: O'Connell, pp. 83, 84.

p.175 *"He leaned back and stuck"*: Henry Beckett, NYP, February 27, 1940.

p.175 *"has been twenty-seven for three years now"*: Rochester, NY, n.p., February 26, 1940.

p.175 *Flagstad expressed her condolences*: Gunnarson, p. 128. Martin Mayer quotes the telegram (Mayer, p. 198). Torstein Gunnarson, one familiar with Flagstad's way of speaking, says that this telegram, cast in a style clearly not that of the soprano, is "a striking example of the influence which McArthur had on Flagstad." He intimates that this "unwise telegram" had much to do with Edward Johnson's postwar antipathy toward the Norwegian soprano (Gunnarson, p. 129).

p.175 Flagstad/Johnson dealings: McArthur, pp. 106–110.

p.175 *"mediocre conductor"*: LMPM.

p.175 *Hope Associates had repeatedly assured*: Letters, Hope to Johnson, October 15 and November 25, 1936; memo, Ziegler to Hope, April 6, 1937, AMO.

p.175 *"To me it was decidedly an advantage"*: Leinsdorf, p. 67. "Unreliable" is a word generally adopted in the music profession to refer to those musicians who do not discharge their artistic responsibilities, perhaps by cancelling at the last moment or cracking high notes. Since this is patently not true of Melchior, Leinsdorf must have been referring to his rhythmic problems.

p.175 *Leinsdorf and McArthur would have made*: Payroll accounts book, AMO.

p.175 *"that an American conductor"*: McArthur, p. 105.

p.176 *Melchior protested to the press:* Nually, p. 150.

p.176 *"a full minute"*: UP Bulletin, January 25, 1940. Nowhere in the biographies based upon Flagstad's diaries are these newspaper accounts corroborated.

p.176 *"too young"*: NYHT, January 25, 1940. By February 4 Olin Downes, in an attempt to explain the incident, had conjectured to the *Times's* readers that perhaps Leinsdorf "did not reckon with the practical situation as an older and more experienced conductor would have done." The critics were on the *qui vive*, however. Later in the season in his review of *Tannhäuser* (Lincoln Center Research Library, 1940 NYHT clipping, no exact date), Jerome Bohm made reference to difficulties undergone by Flagstad, that flawless musician: "Mr. Leinsdorf's decision to give his singers no cues led during a few infelicitous moments to the soprano's apparent beating of time with her arms and shoulders." The *Boston Transcript* (February 20, 1940) added its opinion: "Critics and audience alike have felt Leinsdorf to be a talented conductor, but there has been equally general feeling that his tempi are generally too fast. Yesterday it was clear that the singers were hampered and that Wagner's vocal line had lost much of its freshness and beauty." Nonetheless, by 1941 good relations between Leinsdorf and the superb leading Wagnerian singers of the day were completely restored.

p.176 *"There are some 'old boats' "*: NYHT, January 26, 1940.

p.176 *a campaign to make the Metropolitan*: Dayton Journal, February 4, 1940.

p.176 *"While there's life, there's Constance Hope"* and *"under McArthur!"*: Letter, Charles Wagner to Johnson, January 25, 1940, AMO. Impresario of his own opera company in which Beverly Sills, among others, gained operatic experience, and a personal agent to such singers as Jussi Björling, Charles Wagner knew all the players and the game very, very well.

p.177 "Sei nicht so dumm!": Letter, LaGuardia to Melchior, January 25, 1940, AMO.

p.177 *"Old boats in good condition"*: January 26, 1940 telegram, LM correspondence.

p.177 *On January 29*: SFCB, February 4, 1940.

p.177 *The brief booing and hissing*: NY, February 3, 1940.

p.177 *"Flagstaff"*: Lincoln Center Library clipping, n.p., February 2, 1940.

p.177 *the guarantee fund had swelled*: TI, April 22, 1940.

p.177 *For two years Wagnerian music dramas*: Payroll accounts book, AMO.

p.177 *"It has never been the privilege"*: Virgil Thomson, NYHT, December 13, 1940.

p.178 *On the roster were*: October 7, 1939 memo, AMO.

p.178 *"188 Siegfrieds"*: TI, January 22, 1940.

p.179 *"Maria Hacker, the 'German Mary Pickford' "*: NYW, October 28, 1926.

p.179 *By 1941* Opera News *had published*: OPN, January 13, 1941.

p.179 *"even though it sounds like a press agent's"*: American Family, February, 1949.

p.179 *"They overestimate me"*: Personal communication, LM to Shirlee Emmons, February 1952.

p.179 *"There is a tenor big and jolly"*: NYHT, April 14, 1940.

p.179 Fiftieth birthday party details: NYHT, March 21, 1940; Dixie Tighe, NYP, March 21, 1940.

p.180 *Walter Slezak's reading*: Walter Slezak, actor son of the great Leo Slezak, persuaded Melchior to be godfather to his child.

p.180 *"I don't think the boat"*: NYHT, March 21, 1940. Melchior did not neglect to remind the press that de Reszke was over fifty when he sang his first Walther von Stolzing in German at the Met, that Albert Niemann had made his Met debut in 1886 at the age of fifty-five, that Martinelli sang his first Tristan after fifty, whereas he, Melchior, at the age of fifty had already done 167 Tristans, 144 Siegmunds, 115 young Siegfrieds, and 106 Tannhäusers. As for Lohengrins and elder Siegfrieds, who was counting? (NYHT, March 21, 1940.)

p.181 *During the 1940 Met spring tour*: The logistics of the former Metropolitan Opera tours are interesting for those unaware of their enormous scope. The spring tour of 1938 took up 22 70-foot baggage cars. The 20 opera productions required 500 70-foot backdrops and tabs, 4,000 set pieces, 3,500 pieces of lumber. The Electric Department requisitioned 150 large boxes in which they packed music stands, lamps, batteries. Props amounted to 110 boxes and crates containing 2,000 pieces. The Wardrobe Department used 125 baskets for costumes, 10 trunks for shoes—in all, 5,000 complete costumes. The orchestra required 68 trunks of instruments and music, and the artists carried 100 pieces of luggage. Altogether the personnel numbered 360 persons—50 artists, 20 accompanying relatives, 94 chorus members, 91 orchestra musicians, 21 stage hands, 36 dancers, 30 staff, and 8 business staff. All this was necessary simply to transport the opera to three cities (AMO).

p.181 *"Saved for us . . . is that pealing upper register"*: John Rosenfield, DMN, April 17, 1940.

p.181 New Orleans prank story: NOTP, April 19, 1940.

p.181 *"an early edition of Ho Chi Minh"*: Leinsdorf, p. 107.

p.182 *"a delightful companion"*: Eleanor Roosevelt, syndicated column "My Day," January 31, 1940.

p.182 President Roosevelt's birthday story: LMPM; interview, Ib Melchior, Los Angeles, November 1983.

p.182 *"I remember clearly"*: LMPM.

p.183 *"mastered the rudiments"*: SFN, April 3, 1940, quoting *Boston Transcript* review.

p.183 Boston to Cleveland train journey and Flagstad's plans: Gunnarson, p. 132.

p.183 *It marked the fifteenth anniversary*: NYHT, February 18, 1940.

p.183 *Very early that morning*: NYHT, March 27, 1955.

p.184 *That evening Lauritz and McArthur*: McArthur, p. 135.

p.184 *McArthur's opportunity to conduct*: McArthur, p. 134.

p.184 *"If the results were not momentous"*: Oscar Thompson, NYS, February 18, 1941.

p.184 *"such plans are dependent"*: Letter, Marks Levine to Johnson, March 25, 1941, AMO.

p.184 *the enormous change in Flagstad's attitude*: McArthur, p. 89.

p.184 *"With so much attention focused"*: Miles Kastendieck, BE, February 10, 1941.

p.184 *"this reviewer has been slow"*: *Boston Post*, April 3, 1941.

p.185 *"Let's wish her"*: NYT, April 13, 1941.

p.185 *"My dear friends"*: NYJA, April 13, 1941.

Chapter 12. Another Legendary Partnership: Melchior and Traubel (1941–1946)

p.186 Charity concert figures: LM performance ledger.

p.187 *appeared for many Scandinavian organizations*: In 1944 Melchior arranged a concert at the Metropolitan Opera House to benefit Danish refugees. Many Scandi-navian-Americans who sang in the 300-voice chorus that evening are still very proud of their part in that event.

p.187 *"Melchior sang for us"*: *The Bronx Cheer*, July 7, 1949.

p.187 Kauffmann/U.S. State Department details: Private report, Kauffmann to LM.

p.187 *"Thank God, here we had good Danish men"*: LMPM.

p.188 *the Metropolitan summed up*: Memo, Ziegler to Johnson, September 15, 1941, AMO.

p.188 *Henry Johansen's announcement*: NYT, June 19, June 21, 1941.

p.188 *Lauritz declared privately*: Interview, Leonard Eisner, New York, November 1984. Most agreed with LM. Tor Myklebost, press attaché at the Norwegian Embassy at that time, said that her "attitude to the world crisis was extremely neutral" (Gunnarson, p. 136).

p.188 *Duties therefore were being split*: Payroll accounts book, AMO. American soprano Rose Bampton studied at Curtis Institute before making her mezzo-soprano debut at the Metropolitan Opera as Laura in *La Gioconda* in 1932. She spent eighteen years at the Metropolitan, again debuting there, this time as a soprano, in 1937, also singing leading roles with the Covent Garden, Dresden, Buenos Aires, San Francisco, and Chicago Opera companies.

p.188 *In 1942 Lawrence evoked the intense interest*: Kolodin, p. 441.

p.188 Details of Lawrence gala concert: Irving Kolodin, NYS, December 28, 1942; Jerome Bohm, NYHT, December 28, 1942.

p.188 *"So strong was the lure"*: Jerome Bohm, NYHT, December 28, 1942.

p.188 *"the first in a long time"*: Jerome Bohm, NYHT, April 15, 1944.

p.188 *Despite her total command of the role*: Kolodin, p. 441. Many complained at this discrimination. It was especially unfair as Lawrence's command of the role was absolute, while Flagstad and Traubel often substituted lower notes for those in the extremely high range.

p.189 *Perhaps her seventeen performances*: Payroll accounts book, AMO. In addition, because of her slow learning speed, it was said, Traubel always tried to keep her roles as short as possible, resisting opening any cuts, an attitude which Melchior upheld in later years, but in his case probably out of laziness.

p.189 *Astrid Varnay's father*: Nually, p. 157.

p.189 *Melchior was openly* and *He continued his vigorous attempts*: O'Connell, p. 85.

p.189 *Lotte Lehmann was contracted*: Payroll account book, AMO.

p.189 *(even for a woman who now*: Mme. Lehmann did not relish the roles of Elisabeth and Sieglinde any longer, as one can see from the Constance Hope letter of March 17, 1942, to the Met. "This is to confirm that Lehmann will do *Rosenkavalier* and *Tannhäuser* (if she may 'punctier' [to touch lightly, not sustain] the high B) and she will do the Sieglinde if you find it necessary to schedule her" (AMO).

p.189 *"Wagner continues to bring out"*: Virgil Thomson, NYHT, February 17, 1943.

p.189 *"MAISON TO CARRON TO MELCHIOR AS USUAL"*: John Briggs, NYP, February 2, 1943.

p.189 *"as usual it was the indestructible"*: John Briggs, NYP, February 2, 1943.

p.189 *"one of the most"*: Jens Malte Fischer, *Opernwelt*, June 1986.

p.190 *"Flagstad's voice is like"*: TI, November 11, 1946.

p.190 *"like a couple of two-ton trucks"*: Traubel, p. 125.

p.190 *"pulsating with life . . . she sang it"*: Claudia Cassidy, CTR, April 1, 1943.

p.190 *"that rare breed of singer"*: TI, February 28, 1969.

p.190 *"Mr. Melchior's Tristan"*: Claudia Cassidy, CTR, April 1, 1943.

p.190 *"a team to rival"*: Claudia Cassidy, CTR, April 1, 1943.

p.190 Traubel/Damrosch meeting: NYT, April 9, 1937.

p.190 Damrosch's dinner party details: LMPM; Nually, p. 155.

p.190 *"a woman of nobel"*: NYT, May 13, 1937.

p.190 Traubel's Sieglinde debut in Chicago story: LMPM; Nually, p. 156.

p.191 *"Miss Traubel disclosed"*: PI, December 11, 1940.

p.191 *With Flagstad's absence*: Payroll accounts book, AMO.

p.191 *"Mr. Melchior sang strictly in time"*: NYT, February 23, 1941.

p.191 *"still the world's best heroic tenor"*: Jerome Bohm, NYHT, September 27, 1942.

p.191 *"Miss Traubel hoisted"*: TI, November 11, 1946.

p.191 *The trustees of the Lillian Nordica Association*: Mary Braggiotti, NYP, June 2, 1943.

p.192 *"There was a Tristan so alone"*: Mary Braggiotti, NYP, June 2, 1943.

p.192 *"To Lauritz with my love"*: TI, February 21, 1943.

p.192 Traubel financial details: Payroll accounts book, AMO.

p.192 *"For God's sake, Helen, hurry"*: Traubel, p. 176. Although his name does not appear on the program, Lothar Wallerstein is credited with the staging of this February 12, 1942, *Götterdämmerung* performance, which placed the body of Siegfried in the center of the stage so that Brünnhilde could sing the "Immolation Scene" from that vantage point.

p.192 Schorr bio details: NYT, February 20, 1943.

p.192 *Sad to say, Schorr's final exit*: Kolodin, p. 437.

p.192 *At a gathering on stage*: PM, March 3, 1943.

p.192 *Schorr and Melchior had in common*: Conrad L. Osborne, OPN, August 1976.

p.192 *"there is nothing wrong"*: Conrad L. Osborne, OPN, August 1976.

p.193 *"I simply had to call and tell you"*: Interview, Alma Strasfogel, New York, April 1985.

p.193 *Behind the scenes*: Traubel, p. 123.

p.193 *But for fun on stage*: Traubel, p. 108.

p.193 *Without ever speaking of it*: Traubel, p. 124.

p.193 *"A combination of temperament"*: Traubel, p. 123.

p.193 *"to the heart of the much-pondered question"*: Irving Kolodin, NYS, August 21, 1942.

p.194 *"There are . . . moments"*: Irving Kolodin, NYS, August 21, 1942.

p.194 *Melchior had offered here*: Jerome Bohm, NYHT, November 22, 1942.

p.194 *"He hits notes on the nose"*: *Listen*, January 1943.

p.194 *"tones gather richness"*: Robert Bagar, NYWT, July 1, 1949.

p.194 Acoustical Society report: NYT, September 8, 1935.

p.194 *"the purple-dark quality"*: Irving Kolodin, NYS, August 21, 1942.

p.194 *"forced"*: NYT, January 23, 1942.

p.195 *"Melchior, apart from xylophonic"*: Schwarzkopf, quoting Legge, p. 19.

p.195 *"the youth of the voice"*: Coffin, quoting Lehmann, *Overtones of Bel Canto*, Metuchen, New Jersey: Scarecrow Press, p. 74.

p.195 *"I always begin"*: Personal communication, LM to Shirlee Emmons, 1953.

p.195 *"The voice is like a skyscraper"*: BE, February 21, 1937.

p.196 *She thrived on*: SFC, October 31, 1937.

p.197 *Lauritz was already making plans*: Interviews, Ib Melchior, Marianne Tegner, Cleo Baldon, Los Angeles, December 1983.

p.197 *"I really think he fancied himself"*: Interview, Leonard Eisner, New York, November 1984.

p.197 *"Kleinchen had all sorts of devices"*: Interview, Alma Strasfogel, New York, April 1985.

p.197 Description of The Viking: *House Beautiful*, April 1, 1942; Interview, Cleo Baldon, Los Angeles, November 1988.

p.197 Bohemian Grove details: *Northwest Airlines Magazine*, February 1986; Interviews, Ib Melchior, Marianne Tegner, Los Angeles, November 1987; Interview, Elisabeth Mosher, Graz, Austria, July 1985.

p.198 *"great white hunter"* and other One-Shot Antelope Club details: NYT, April 19, 1963 and NYHT, September 21, 1951; Interview, Marianne Tegner, December 1983; Letter, Marianne Tegner to Shirlee Emmons, July 21, 1989.

p.198 *A Danish mezzo-soprano told a tenor*: Interview, Otte Svendsen, Copenhagen, August 1983. Ib Melchior says in rebuttal: "If a Dane was ever turned away from The Viking, it was not by my father."

p.199 *Sir Hugh Walpole*: 1937, Melchior's thirteenth season with Covent Garden, was a Coronation Season. At the end of 1936 Edward VIII abdicated (in order to marry Wallis Simpson) in favor of his brother, then George VI, who was crowned on May 12, 1937, the best press reports of the occasion being Walpole's. In April he had received a letter from No. 10 Downing Street asking on behalf of the new king and queen whether he would like to have a knighthood. "Accepted at once!" wrote Walpole, and he was made Sir Hugh in June.

p.199 *"are worth their weight in rubies"*: Hugh Walpole, "If I Were Twenty-One Today," n.p., n.d., probably 1938, DCM. Walpole had been totally serious about friendship. At the end of each year he compiled a list of the First Fifteen and the Second Thirty of his friends. Not until 1929 was Lauritz demoted to second place in the First Fifteen. Assessing their long friendship, Sir Hugh declared: "In my entire life, I have had only three true friends. One of them was David" (Hart-Davis, p. 404).

p.199 Central and South American tour: LM performance ledger.

p.199 Mexico City details: Alma Lubin, *Cincinnati Inquirer*, September 20, 1942.

p.199 *"The Caruso of Wagnerian Opera"*: El Pueblo, Buenos Aires, NBC Press Book, 1934–1935.

p.199 Tapachula story and South American tour stories: Interview, Ignace Strasfogel, New York, April 1985.

p.200 *Always prepared, Lauritz took out*: Nually, p. 168.

p.201 *"We loved Kleinchen"*: Interview, Ignace Strasfogel, New York, April 1985.

p.201 Bag of flea powder story: Nually, p. 169.

p.201 *"It was the testicles of a steer"*: Interview, Ignace Strasfogel, New York, April 1985.

p.201 *"Lauritz Melchior, great Wagnerian"*: MUM, August 1943.

p.201 *Pleased as he was*: NYHT, January 15, 1944.

p.202 *"This, dear Kleinchen"*: Letter, Johnson to Kleinchen, September 10, 1944.

p.202 *"It was very nice"*: LMPM.

p.202 *"the very essence of music"*: SFCB, October 6, 1945.

p.202 Alvary/Kleinchen story: Phone interview, Lorenzo Alvary, New York, May 1985.

p.202 *"superman"*: Phone interview, Lorenzo Alvary, New York, May 1985.

p.203 Details of 1945–1946 Met season: Payroll accounts book, AMO.

p.203 *"Considering what we have been enduring"*: Noel Straus, NYT, November 26, 1945.

p.203 "PLEASE CONFIRM FOLLOWING ARRANGEMENTS": Davidson to Melchior, March 20, 1945.

p.203 *"By Lauritz Melchior is every other day"*: Irving Kolodin, NYS, January 25, 1946.

p.203 Description of 20th anniversary program: S. J. Woolf, NYT, February 17, 1946.

p.204 *"While I am a visitor here"*: Otis L. Guernsey, Jr., NYHT, April 7, 1946.

p.204 *"It seems to me that the future of opera"*: Irving Kolodin, NYS, January 25, 1946.

p.204 *Mrs. Belmont presented*: Memo, George Sloan to board, February 16, 1946, AMO.

p.204 *"a national and international figure"*: Howard Taubman, NYT, February 18, 1946.

p.204 *Lotte gave him a caricature*: Nually, p. 180. Another Lehmann painting of Melchior is now housed at Dana College. At the lower corner of the portrait of her dear friend costumed as Tannhäuser she inscribed *"Meinem herrlichen* [to my magnificent] *Tannhäuser. Lotte."*

p.204 "Enthüllet den Gral": DCM. The miniature Grail is part of the collection of Melchior memorabilia at Dana College.

p.204 *"Most of all what we need at the Met"*: Irving Kolodin, NYS, January 25, 1946.

p.204 *"Now I can take a breath"*: TI, February 18, 1946.

p.204 *At this date he had done*: Howard Taubman, NYT, February 18, 1946.

p.205 *"The possibilities for new anniversaries"*: NWS, February 18, 1946.

p.205 *"It is I who should thank you"*: Letter, Lotte Lehmann to LM, February 20, 1946.

p.205 *"To summon so much beauty"*: NYS, February 12, 1946.

p.205 *"No Credit to Wagner"*: Carleton Smith, CHN, April 26, 1944.

p.205 *"Melchior Hits New Low"*: Remy Gassmann, CTI, April 26, 1944.

p.205 *"[Melchior] sang very badly indeed"*: Richard S. Davis, *Milwaukee Journal*, April 28, 1944.

p.205 *"a fish out of water"*: "P," MUM, March 10, 1945.

p.205 *"He had well-defined artistic intentions"*: Noel Straus, NYT, February 8, 1945.

p.206 *"There was an excess of contrast"*: Oscar Thompson, NYS, February 8, 1945.

p.206 *"expected"*: Mordden, p. 189.

p.206 *"light singing"*: Maria Hacker diary, 1925–1926; LMPM.

Chapter 13. From Opera Star to Movie Star (1943–1946)

p.207 *"Publicity is like eating peanuts"*: Andy Warhol, Museum of Modern Art Catalog," Andrew Warhol, A Retrospective," February, 1989; "Today Show," NBC, February 3, 1989.

p.207 *"The public wants to believe"*: Letter, Lehmann to Kleinchen Melchior, April 23, 1939.

p.207 *"The constant watching that the prima donna's hair"*: Lauritz Melchior, "Lover, Go 'Way From Me," ST, January 1939.

p.208 *Copenhagen cronies recall*: Interview, Hans Hansen, Copenhagen, August 1983.

p.208 *and there is a great deal of scepticism*: Letter, Ib Melchior to Shirlee Emmons, March 12, 1987.

p.209 *"But I couldn't spell"*: Jay Somers, n.p., December 22, 1943.

p.209 *He went to the Waldorf-Astoria*: Kelley, p. 91; LMPM.

p.209 *When eventually he crooned*: NYP, November 15, 1943.

p.209 *Word went round*: NOTP, November, n.d., 1943.

p.209 *In response, he promptly*: PN, December 18, 1943.

p.209 *(It was Evans who had hired*: Kelley, p. 113.

p.210 *Not until 1949*: Kelley, p. 155.

p.210 Fred Allen script: "Fred Allen Show" tape, December 12, 1943.

p.212 Life's *coverage of the 200th Tristan*: *Life*, December 25, 1944.

p.212 *"Why did you do it?"*: Fan letter to LM, January 5, 1944. This brings up the old question regarding a singer's use of such a girdle or belt. Melchior wore the corset "partly to look thin, partly to hold up the chain mail trousers, and partly to help his breathing," said Karl Laufkötter (letter to Emmons, March 9, 1984). Sbriglia, teacher of Jean de Reszke (whose influence upon Melchior's teacher Victor Beigel has been noted), is known to have invented a "breathing belt." No picture of it has been located, but Sbriglia's thoughts on breathing are documented in a 1942 *Etude* article (Byers, p. 337–338): "a. . . chest held high without tension by developed abdominal and lower back muscles and a straight spine . . . will give the uplift for perfect breathing." Berton Coffin, renowned voice teacher, scientist, and historian, confirmed (letter, Coffin to Emmons, July 7, 1984), "The belt was to assist . . . in holding up the chest. . . . An 1895 book, *On Breathing in Singing*, states that it was *not something to be pushed against* as has been the practice of some singers."

p.213 *"Tristan does not disintegrate"*: Lilian Foerster, OPN, January 28, 1946.

p.213 *"Get a photographer!"*: Personal communication, LM to Shirlee Emmons, 1953.

p.213 *"there was no photographer around"*: Personal communication, Kleinchen Melchior to Shirlee Emmons, 1953.

p.213 *"a great honor"*: NYT, May 4, 1944.

p.214 Fred Allen script: "Fred Allen Show" tape, February 2, 1947. 4 Chicks and a Chuck were a pop vocal quintet.

p.215 *"I wanted to vacation in California"*: Otis L. Guernsey, Jr., NYHT, April 7, 1946.

p.216 *"Lawrence something-or-other"*: MUM, July 1944.

p.216 *The first fallout from the screen test*: J. Carmody, WS, February 21, 1945.

p.216 *speech coach, Lillian Burnes Sidney*: Kelley, p. 150.

p.216 *The singing, too, was different*: J. Carmody, WS, February 21, 1945.

p.216 *Yet, to perform the eight songs*: Cue, April 7, 1945.

p.216 *Movie work was not only easier*: J. Carmody, WS, February 21, 1945.

p.216 *And the comfortable* and *And the scenery*: Cue, April 7, 1945.

p.216 *"really preferred to die a natural death"*: Cue, April 7, 1945; NYT, February 4, 1947.

p.217 *"6:30 in the morning"*: J. Carmody, WS, February 21, 1945.

p.217 Haircut story: Interviews, Ib Melchior, Marianne Tegner, Los Angeles, November 1987.

p.217 *"I want to make some fun"*: Louis Biancolli, NYS, March 5, 1944.

p.217 *"The chief trouble is that"*: S. J. Woolf, NYT, February 17, 1946.

p.217 *Then a short piece appeared*: MPM, n.d.

p.218 *In the caption Melchior asks*: MPM, July 1944.

p.218 *although Hollywood was showering*: n.p., September 6, 1944.

p.218 *"I had no idea that I would ever be"*: Eileen Creelman, RL, February 11, 1945.

p.218 *the teenage bobby-soxers*: Otis L. Guernsey, Jr., NYHT, April 25, 1945.

p.218 *"I am starved"*: Interview, Ib Melchior, Los Angeles, December 1983.

p.218 *In the movies made by Nino Martini*: J. Carmody, WS, February 21, 1945.

p.219 *"They expected me to be complicated"*: RL, February 11, 1945.

p.219 *Melchior was no fool*: The Musician, November 1945. In conjunction with these venomous scribblings, it is arresting to note that either already in the movies or negotiating for a contract at this time were pianist Artur Rubinstein (scarcely superannuated even when eighty-three), cellist Gregor Piatagorsky (whom the film industry considered a colorful personality "of the Melchior/Iturbi type" [*Variety*, February 2, 1946]), conductor William Kapell, and even Igor Stravinsky, who allowed one of his pieces to be revamped for more popular taste. (Stravinsky was approached by a go-getting record producer who reminded the composer of what Tin Pan Alley grave-robbers had done to Tschaikovsky and Chopin. In any case the practical Stravinsky did not have much choice. He allowed the Rondo from "Firebird" to become a foxtrot because it was not under copyright in the U.S.A.) Lou Singer arranged it and wrote words to what was called "Summer Moon." Copies went out to "the Guys with the Big Pipes," Melchior and Nelson Eddy, said *Movie News* [n.d., 1945]). Melchior programmed the piece often.

p.219 *"The Melchior situation"*: Henry Marx, Music News, n.d., probably 1945.

p.220 *"Melchior has insisted on top pay"*: Howard Taubman, NYT, April 20, 1944.

p.220 *Not so the Texas press*: APB, April 18, 1944.

p.220 Sloan letter: Nually, p. 171.

p.220 *"cheap music"*: Personal communication, Birgit Nilsson to Shirlee Emmons, New York, November 1988.

p.221 Description of Copenhagen airport reunion: Interviews, Ib Melchior, Los Angeles, November 1987; Birte Melchior, Copenhagen, August 1983.

p.221 *With great sadness*: In 1970 Melchior described Agge thus: "I had a blind sister who was a concert singer and a teacher, the only blind teacher at the Institute for the Blind. She had a gorgeous voice, trained by [Valdemar] Lincke" (LM tape interview, "The Fairy Tale of My Life," Danmarks Radio, December 20, 1970, produced by Hemming Hartmann-Petersen).

p.222 Stories about King Christian: Ib Melchior, *Bien*, February 17, 1977.

p.222 *presented the king with a purse*: Kleinchen was increasingly unhappy about the amount of time and money her husband spent on Guard business. Not only did he turn down engagements in order to tend to his presidential duties, but he started a magazine called *Vagtparaden* [*Changing of the Guard*]. As editor and adman, he embarrassed Kleinchen by approaching their friends and even strangers to canvass for ads, and angered her by the amount of time he spent writing the magazine. She eventually withdrew her support completely from Guard activities (Interview, Marianne Tegner, Los Angeles, November 1987).

p.222 *the premiere of* Thrill of a Romance: Inga Hulgaard, who was in Denmark at the time, relates, "When *Thrill of a Romance* came to Denmark after the war, it was a sensation. One of the first color movies, if not the first, and many people's first chance to see LM perform. America was a fairyland to us in those days."

p.222 *he and Kleinchen wanted to become American citizens*: In 1966 Melchior earnestly explained to the Danish public on radio: "The reason why I took up American citizenship was not because I didn't want to be a Danish citizen, but because I felt that, when in a country one has enjoyed all the benefits that I have enjoyed in America then one cannot, when the time is up say, 'Thank you. Now I have had enough of you. I have skimmed the cream. Now I will take along the cream and you can do what you want!' No, you have to take the good with the evil. When you are educated in a country, or when you have worked in a country, you must belong to that country. I would never have become an American citizen if my country had not been freed. I did not take out my American citizenship as long as Denmark was occupied by the Germans. No one can . . . say that I picked up my hat and walked out because Denmark had been occupied. I waited til the war was over and we were free again. . . I asked His Majesty whether he thought it would be right of me to take out American citizenship. He approved of it completely but said, 'If you ever feel like having your head rest in Danish soil, then I know that you will always be received with the honor and gratitude that we owe you as a good ambassador out in the world' " (LM, Arne Honoré tape interview, "My Life's Adventure," Danmarks Radio, April 30, 1966).

p.222 *"Any boy who was born in Nørregade"*: LMPM.

p.222 *"In my left hand"*: LM tape interview, "The Fairy Tale of My Life," Danmarks Radio, December 27, 1970, produced by Hemming Hartmann-Petersen.

p.222 *Berlin was no longer recognizable*: Leider, p. 178; LMPM.

p.222 *"One's heart must bleed"*: LMPM.

p.223 *"Kleinchen's charm"*: LMPM.

p.223 *"When we arrived at the border"*: LMPM.

p.223 *"unexpected angels"*: LMPM.

p.223 Trip to Chossewitz: Virgil Thomson, NYHT, October 12, 1945; letters, Knud Hegermann-Lindencrone, February 2, 1987, February 7, 1987, April 9, 1987, August 9, 1987.

p.224 Description of Chossewitz: Interview, Klaus Riisbro, Copenhagen, August 1983.

p.224 Finding Pistor and Wolff: LMPM.

p.224 Details of Leider's life during war: Leider, pp. 172, 176, 178, 181, 198.

p.224 *"end of the catastrophe"*: Leider, p. 180.

p.225 Finding Frida Leider story: LMPM.

Chapter 14. The Hottest Dance Since Beowulf (1946–1949)

p.226 *"pattern of odd debuts and miscellaneous casting"*: Kolodin, p. 451.

p.227 *"disguised as a Tyrolese in short Lederhosen"*: Mogens Wedel, *Ascolta*, June 1983.

p.227 *"no costumes, no props, no sets"*: Interview, Ib Melchior, Los Angeles, November 1987.

p.227 *"What kind of shit is this?"*: Interview, Ib Melchior, Los Angeles, November 1987.

p.227 *concert with the Choral Society*: O'Connell, p. 85.

p.227 *Other artists of his rank*: Mayer, p. 213.

p.227 *his failing was in one area only*: Lotte Lehmann admitted to a faulty sense of rhythm but was never charged with it. Said Lehmann in her book, "Rhythm was my weak point. . . . Again and again I heard the voice of my singing teacher saying, 'Wrong, be more careful. You've no idea of rhythm' " (p. 39). Wolfgang Windgassen's running ahead of the beat was considered a charming imperfection (Culshaw, p. 126), and Max Lorenz "in his drive for expression" discarded note values on occasion, with minimal censure from critics (Jens Malte Fischer, *Opernwelt*, June 1986).

p.228 *"As for his playing of the part"*: NYHT, February 7, 1942.

p.228 *"despite a few uneasy moments"*: Lincoln Center Research Library clipping, n.p., March 13, 1943.

p.228 *A story from* Opera News: Lilian Foerster, OPN, January 28, 1946.

p.228 *"I show them I can swing 'Dinah' "*: William G. King, "Music and Musicians," n.p., 1938.

p.229 *"had simply uttered the usual nonsense"*: Schonberg, *The Glorious Ones*, p. 388.

p.229 *Shirley Verrett exciting no comment*: "Creative Edge," PBS, February 12, 1989.

p.229 *"It is essential to the career of a grand opera star"*: NYT, December 5, 1941.

p.230 *"tending ever more to short Met visits"*: Kolodin, p. 465.

p.231 *"What Hollywood wanted"*: TI, June 24, 1946.

p.231 *"Melchior demonstrates considerable knack"*: NYHT, June 7, 1946.

p.232 *About one month later* Variety *reported*: VA, June 26, 1946.

p.232 *"marvelous melody"*: LMPM.

p.232 *"When you are introducing people"*: Lilian Foerster, OPN, January 28, 1946.

p.232 *"There's nothing wrong in being hammy"*: Frank Sinatra, NYP, August 21, 1946.

p.232 *"a token of your career"*: Letter, Metropolitan Opera Club to LM, September 10, 1946.

p.232 *"Oddly enough—unless a touch of envy"*: Gobbi, p. 64.

p.232 Details of Circus Saints and Sinners lunch: *Look*, March 4, 1947. The club, begun by a group of circus press agents, was at this time an aggregation of 850 New Yorkers. The proceeds from each of their lunches, once earmarked for down-and-out circus performers, were handed over to some worthy cause, now far removed from the circus.

p.233 Milton Berle Show story: Lawrence Perry, *North American News Alliance*, January 10, 1949.

p.233 *An unsuspecting Ignace Strasfogel*: Interview, Ignace Strasfogel, New York, April 1985; Tex McCrary, Jinx Falkenburg, NYHT, September 15, 1949.

p.233 *"One afternoon Kleinchen had to go"*: Tex McCrary, Jinx Falkenburg, NYHT, September 15, 1949.

p.233 *This coverage was not all*: Sheila Graham, *Hollywood Citizen News*, January 1, 1948.

p.233 Vogue *printed a wonderfully bizarre picture*: *Vogue*, February 12, 1948.

p.234 *"They dismiss my twenty-five years"*: Interview, Walter Gould, New York, May 1985.

p.234 *in Oakland the company aircraft*: *Alameda* (California) *Times Star*, November 8, 1946.

p.234 *"Of course it will be better"*: SFE, December 3, 1946.

p.235 *"the Wagnerian tenor more lately noted"*: Paul Hume, WP, February 25, 1947. Melchior had risen from a sick bed, where he was confined with ptomaine poisoning, to go to Constitution Hall to deliver his concert.

p.235 *"Be assured, American audiences"*: Paul Hume, WP, February 25, 1947.

p.235 *"usual terrible program"* and *"The man is really larger"*: Claudia Cassidy, CTR, March 10, 1947.

p.235 *"Open the door, Richard"*: a repetitious nonsense song of the genre of "Mairzy Doats 'n Dozey Doates" (Mares Eat Oats and Does Eat Oats) that, nonetheless, achieved a notoriety of wondrous proportions. A major newspaper found it appropriate to make this insignificant bit of fluff the subject of an editorial. The ultimate incongruity was achieved by having a Wagnerian tenor intone it.

p.235 *lecturing the Junior Stamp Club*: Ib Melchior, a stamp collector himself, had pursued during his army service in Europe the complete set of presentation booklets prepared at the direction of Adolf Hitler especially for the infamous Dr. Hans Frank, the Nazi governor-general of Poland who was eventually condemned by the War Crimes Tribunal. These booklets contained examples of all the stamps used by the Nazis in Poland during their occupation, forming the basis of the Melchior "Hitler Collection," about which Lauritz was lecturing here (NYHT, February 2, 1947).

p.235 Bloomington, Illinois, story: APB, March 25, 1947.

p.236 *"Since 1926 the role"*: NWS, November 25, 1946.

p.236 *"Lately Lauritz Melchior"*: NWS, November 25, 1946.

p.236 *"and besides [Melchior]"*: NWS, November 25, 1946.

p.236 *He looked like Siegfried*: NWS, November 25, 1946.

p.236 *Some were so ungentlemanly*: NWS, November 25, 1946.

p.236 *"The Met has at last found"*: Douglas Watts, NYDN, November 16, 1946.

p.236 *"If a certain celebrated Wagnerian tenor"*: NYS, November 16, 1946.

p.236 *"It should be a comfort"*: Irving Kolodin, NYS, November 30, 1946.

p.237 *"I greatly doubt"*: Irving Kolodin, NYS, November 30, 1946.

p.237 *"Most tenors have terrible legs"*: Interview, Birte Melchior, Copenhagen, August 1983.

p.237 *"constantly forced"*: NYT, January 23, 1947.

p.237 *"nor has there been"*: NYT, January 23, 1947.

p.237 *"As Tristan, Melchior was hardly"*: *Hollywood Citizen News*, April 20, 1948.

p.238 *For this, there was*: Interview, Ib Melchior, Los Angeles, December 1983.

p.238 *When Melchior did sing well*: Kolodin, p. 465.

p.238 LM on Ralf and Svanholm: Nually, pp. 180, 181.

p.238 *As for the relationship*: LMPM; Nually, pp. 181, 182. Fritz Stiedry (1883–1968), a Viennese conductor, succeeded Bruno Walter at the Berlin Staatsoper in

1924; after 1923 he spent some time in Dresden, Prague, and Nuremberg, before following Weingartner into the Vienna Volksoper in 1924, and then back to the Städtische Oper in Berlin from 1928 to 1933. Another casualty of the Nazi years, he stayed in Russia until he came to New York in 1937; he conducted at the Metropolitan Opera from 1946 to 1958.

p.238 *a conductor's appearance at a singer's apartment*: Leinsdorf, p. 64.

p.238 *"We do not sing for the conductor"*: Letter, LM to William Arlock, March 26, 1965.

p.239 *"Don't rehearse full voice"*: National Association of Teachers of Singing national convention, Denver, Colorado, July 1981. One need only compare the singing of Siegfried or Tristan with the singing of Nemorino (the light *L'Elisir d'Amore* tenor) to see how much more this concept would apply in the case of a Heldentenor.

p.239 *"What Babe Ruth is to baseball"*: *Philadelphia Evening Bulletin*, April 8, 1947.

p.239 *"was always taking offense at something or other"*: Bing, p. 42.

p.239 Description of *Walküre* accident: NYT, February 4, 1947.

p.240 *"I really would prefer to die a natural death"*: NYT, February 4, 1947.

p.240 *"regretted to advise"*: Letter, Johnson to LM, August 5, 1948, AMO. The cancellation brought an immediate protest from Local 802, which resented being presented as the chief culprit. The union said that it had already dropped wage demands in an effort to reach a settlement, and had insisted only upon pensions and unemployment benefits. Indeed, it was later to be revealed, by author Martin Mayer among others, that the Met had been showing a profit during Johnson's early years after all (NYT, August 5, 1948; Mayer, p. 213).

p.240 *Melchior issued an optimistic statement*: LAT, August 12, 1948.

p.240 *"token scenic construction"*: Kolodin, p. 461.

p.240 *"a bit of streamlining would find favor"*: Billy Rose letter, NYHT, August 7, 1948.

p.240 *"The only ones who cannot"*: John Chapman, NYDN, August 22, 1948.

p.240 Variety *suggested*: John Chapman quoting *Variety*, NYDN, August 22, 1948.

p.241 *"A cleaning woman"*: John Chapman, NYDN, August 22, 1948.

p.241 Details of fall season 1948: Seltsam, First Supplement, pp. 11–20.

p.241 *"Vocally Melchior was in good trim"*: DMN, November 25, 1948.

p.241 *"Melchior singing with greater ease"*: Douglas Watts, NYDN, December 12, 1948.

p.241 *"Melchior's Tristan from another artist"*: Irving Kolodin, NYS, December 13, 1948.

p.241 *"You had better not believe"*: Interviews, Andreas Damgaard, Otte Svendsen, Copenhagen, August 1983; Inga Hulgaard, New York, November 1984.

p.242 *"Our world-famous Heldentenor"*: *Berlingske Tidende*, n.d., 1939.

p.242 *"I am not a complicated human being"*: Arne Honoré tape interview with LM, "My Life's Adventure," Danmarks Radio, April 23, 1966.

p.242 *"Lauritz Melchior is judged wrong here in Denmark"*: Arne Honoré interview, with Melchiorianer Aage Buchardt, "My Life's Adventure," Danmarks Radio, April 30, 1966.

p.242 *"Cordial and naive, he stood up"*: Holger Boland, *Ascolta*, April 1983.

p.242 *"envious of his success in the outside world"*: Interview, Inga and Jørgen Krause, Copenhagen, August 1983.

p.243 *"surrounded by German hunting dogs"*: Interview, Ib Melchior, Los Angeles, December 1983.

p.243 Presentation of the $208 purse story: Interviews, Marianne Tegner, Andreas Damgaard, Otte Svendsen, Hans Hansen, Copenhagen, August 1983.

p.243 *"his former Sultan"*: Captions of cartoon from LM photo collection, probably by Hans Bendix, published by Gyldendal.

p.243 *Sildesalat* story: Interviews, Andreas Damgaard, Knud Hegermann-Lindencrone, Hans Hansen, Copenhagen, August 1983; personal communication, Mogens Benthin, October 15, 1988. Birte Melchior adds to the story her personal knowledge of how "angry and hurt" he was because he was exposed to public contempt (Birte Melchior, tape interview, "The Fairy Tale of My Life," Danmarks Radio, December 25, 1970, produced by Hemming Hartmann-Petersen).

p.244 *"Did you get any news?"*: Interview, Andreas Damgaard, Copenhagen, August 1983; letter, Damgaard to Shirlee Emmons, December 9, 1987.

p.244 *"A concert according to general standards"*: N. Sch., *Nationaltidende*, May 21, 1948.

p.244 *"personal silver trumpet"*: N. Sch., *Nationaltidende*, May 21, 1948.

p.244 *"the domain . . . for which"*: N. Sch., *Nationaltidende*, May 21, 1948.

p.244 *"He looks forward as a kind uncle"*: K.F., *Berlingske Tidende*, May 21, 1948.

p.244 *"Do we hear you again soon, Kammersanger?"*: Interview, Andreas Damgaard, Copenhagen, August 1983; letter, Damgaard to Shirlee Emmons, December 9, 1987.

p.244 *"Circumstances force me to"*: F. Haagen, Nationaltidende, May 18, 1948.

p.245 "LAURITZ MELCHIOR CANNOT ALLOW HIMSELF": F. Haagen, *Nationaltidende*, May 18, 1948.

p.245 *"coming down from Olympus"*: NYT, February 20, 1949.

p.245 *Irving Kolodin raised questions in print*: Irving Kolodin, NYS, March 12, 1949.

p.245 *"Each year at this time"*: Letter, LM to critics, March 22, 1942. Remaining on stage during the "Grail Scene" was a point of great contention and importance to the Wagnerites. A September 21, 1943, letter of protest written to the Met by a member of the New York Singing Teachers' Association points out that knowledgeable people had laughed at Melchior's published letter in which he attempted to justify his actions. This singing teacher had found out from a friend of Maestro Bodanzky's that "it was allowed the first time due to an attack of gout, not a draft." Others, who wrote to the Metropolitan expressing their disgust with Melchior's radio clowning, invariably referred to the "Grail Scene," deploring the Met's having allowed Melchior to get away with it for so many years (AMO).

p.246 *"Mr. Melchior does small justice"*: NYT, March 27, 1942.

p.246 *He reminded Melchior's manager*: Irving Kolodin, NYS, March 16, 1949.

p.246 *"We're getting a little tired"*: Irving Kolodin, quoting Davidson, NYS, March 16, 1949.

p.246 *sacrificed a whole month*: In July 1946 Davidson and Johnson had already come to an agreement on sixteen performances at $880, with a caveat: Should anyone else at the Metropolitan receive a higher fee, then Melchior's would be raised to that figure. Clearly the Metropolitan had done again what it always did. When the ten percent voluntary decrease was no longer needed, the fees were still kept at that level for as long as no one complained. Now that the war was over, the ten percent deduction for war bonds purchased out of salary somehow had become a permanent part of the fee schedule (AMO).

p.246 *Citing statistics for the 1946–1947 season*: Ross Parmenter, NYT, March 9, 1947.

p.247 *("no* Ring *this year*: NYHT, October 12, 1945.

p.247 *"the* Ring *cycle would be omitted"*: Davidson to Johnson, October 17, 1945. Melchior was proven right in his suspicions when, two years later, Johnson admitted in a memo to the board that the *Ring* had been withdrawn for the last two seasons because of the "worn condition of the sets." During the intervening two years Eleanor Belmont and Lucretia Bori had undertaken, on behalf of the Guild, to raise a special fund for new sets, and, with the help of Melchior's $5,000, did so (memo, Johnson to board, March 27, 1947, AMO).

p.247 *"at no time has Lauritz Melchior"*: Letter, Davidson to Johnson, October 17, 1945.

p.247 "WITH TEARS IN MY EYES": Telegram, LM to Johnson, February 17, 1947.

p.248 "Die Walküre *transports nobody"*: Robert Bagar, NYWT, February 14, 1948.

p.248 *"The Danish tenor's voice sounds worn"*: Jerome Bohm, NYHT, n.d., probably 1948.

Chapter 15. A Dream Unrealized (1949–1950)

p.249 *(others being considered were*: Kolodin, p. 483.

p.249 *use of the Metropolitan's mailing list*: AMO.

p.249 Rudolf Bing background: Herbert Kupferberg, NYHT, June 4, 1949; Bing, pp. 15, 18–20, 30, 53, 56.

p.249 *"an extremely progressive director"*: Bing, p. 37.

p.249 *"was to learn something about the theatrical"*: Bing, p. 86.

p.249 *"dramatically valid operatic presentation"*: Bing, p. 139.

p.250 *"stage direction was the key"*: Bing, p. 146.

p.250 *"staging of the first order"*: Bing, p. 146.

p.250 *"even showed a profit at times"*: Bing, p. 78.

p.250 *"why [he] had been so strongly drawn"*: Bing, p. 37.

p.250 *"An opera house must have one head"*: Bing, p. 39.

p.250 *"not running off to do guest appearances"*: Bing, p. 35.

p.250 *"I think it is improper"*: Bing, p. 123.

p.250 *"still had moral and artistic integrity"*: Bing, p. 42.

p.250 Description of first press conference: Kolodin, pp. 483, 484.

p.250 *"It would be rather tactless of me"*: NYT, November 10, 1949.

p.250 *"much worse"*: Bing, p. 130.

p.251 *"the biggest job of its kind"*: Herbert Kupferberg, NYHT, June 5, 1949.

p.251 *"The Americanization of the Met"*: Kolodin, p. 495.

p.251 *"catch as catch can"* and *"resolute miscasting"*: Mayer, p. 213. Mayer also tells us that Melchior was only one of those stars with this privilege. Young soprano Pierrette Alarie was overjoyed to understudy Lily Pons, because she never came to rehearsals.

p.251 *"a competition among artists"* and *"an ill-run house"*: Bing, p. 138.

p.252 *"There is no financial decision"*: Bing, p. 37.

p.252 Details of Bing investigation of Flagstad: AMO.

p.252 *Henry Johansen had been arrested*: Biancolli, p. 184. By November 1945, it was clear that Johansen's arch enemy, who had sought the position of prosecuting attorney in this case, was determined to take all of Johansen's wealth and property, and all of his wife's, too. During the long battle to prove to the Norwegian court that the allegations were not true, not only did Flagstad feel forsaken by many old friends and colleagues, but she was close to financial destitution, said McArthur. The death of her husband in June 1946 had changed nothing. Although there were offers of singing engagements, she was not able to accept them until her passport was returned with the complete clearing of her name in October 1946 (McArthur, p. 16).

p.252 *"failed to see why the Met"*: NYT, October 15, 1947.

p.252 *Others had stood by her*: Mayer, p. 227.

p.252 *Kleinchen and Lauritz, however*: McArthur, p. 171.

p.252 *it was this equivocation*: Interview, Knud Hegermann-Lindencrone, Copenhagen, August 1983; letters, February 2, 1987, April 9, 1987. Hegermann-Lindencrone phoned LM after the Nually book came out in 1969, saying that Melchior should have spoken out in the book, setting things right between the two singers, and protecting Flagstad's good name. Melchior protested that "he never knew" the true facts of Flagstad's suffering.

p.252 *"I don't believe for a moment"*: Seymour Peck, PM, September 14, 1945.

p.252 *"It is, you might say"*: Seymour Peck, PM, September 14, 1945.

p.253 *"In order for a marriage to be happy"*: Kirsten Flagstad, *Smith's Weekly*, July 2, 1938.

p.253 *Sides were chosen*: Mayer, p. 228. Popular belief had it that Mme. Flagstad had traveled back to Norway on a German passport; that she had sung for Hitler and for the Germans in Norway; that she engaged in "wartime activities"; and that she had gone home to her "Quisling husband." As Levine documented, the truth was that she had traveled on her Norwegian passport, visas arranged by her management and influential American friends, sung nowhere but neutral Sweden and Switzerland, gone neither to concerts nor parties in Norway, and returned to a husband whom she loved and whom she believed to be a loyal Norwegian. Levine also made a point of the fact that Norway's king had never rescinded his country's highest decoration, bestowed on Flagstad in 1940. Furthermore, says historian Richard Petrow, "when facts are separated from fiction," Quisling's party was a "negligible factor in the German conquest of . . . Norway" (Petrow, p. 6).

p.253 Elsa Maxwell prevarications: Elsa Maxwell, Hearst Syndicate column, November 10, 1945.

p.253 *"first chance"*: Elsa Maxwell, Hearst Syndicate column, February 6, 1944.

p.253 *"like many others"*: Elsa Maxwell, Hearst Syndicate column, November 10, 1945.

p.253 *"strongly that if possible"*: Gunnarson, p. 167.

p.254 *"virtually a disease"*: Gunnarson, p. 167.

p.254 *"You know, Schubert"*: Interview, Leonard Eisner, New York, November 1984.

p.254 *privately she admitted*: McArthur, pp. 238, 239, 302.

p.254 *"The best tenors are in America"*: MUC, May 1, 1948.

p.254 *"most personable young Wälsung"*: NYT, June 10, 1949.

p.254 *"Svanholm, despite a flawless rendering"*: SFA, November, n.d., 1949.

p.254 Meeting with Bing at the Essex House: Nually, p. 196.

p.255 *"I have never seen such antics"*: Bing, p. 133.

p.255 Description of opening night: NYP, November 27, 1949.

p.255 Description of Kleinchen's jewels: *Pathfinder*, February 25, 1950.

p.255 *"like a soignée Titania"*: Interview, Alma Strasfogel, New York, April 1985.

p.255 *"I am grateful to the movies"*: NYT, December 5, 1949.

p.255 *His remarks about Bayreuth*: Wessling, *Toscanini in Bayreuth*, p. 10.

p.256 "DEAR LAURITZ: OUR REPERTOIRE IMPASSE": Johnson to LM, September 16, 1949.

p.256 "DEAR EDDIE: AS SO OFTEN BEFORE": Telegram, LM to Johnson, September 16, 1949.

p.256 *"Lauritz felt that he must do it"*: Kleinchen Melchior to James Davidson, September 16, 1949. It seems clear that, though Kleinchen was in charge when she wanted to be, Lauritz sometimes put his foot down, and that both Lauritz and Kleinchen were now feeling ill-used by the Metropolitan.

p.257 *But he would not budge*: Lawrence Perry, *North American Newspaper Alliance*, November 30, 1949.

p.257 *"Signor Pinza is in the flat races"*: Tex McCrary, Jinx Falkenburg, NYHT, September 15, 1949.

p.257 *"new man"*: Nually, p. 196.

p.257 *"with or without rehearsal"*: Irving Kolodin, NYS, December 13, 1949.

p.257 *"slight hoarseness"*: NY, December 19, 1949.

p.257 *"slovenly musicianship"*: Jerome Bohm, NYHT, December 14, 1949.

p.257 *"the familiar virtues"*: NY, December 19, 1949.

p.257 *"the sincerity of their characterizations"*: NY, December 19, 1949.

p.257 *"with prodigal voice"*: Irving Kolodin, NYS, December 13, 1949.

p.257 *"an authority"*: Olin Downes, NYT, December 13, 1949.

p.257 *"He was simply wonderful"*: Louis Biancolli, NYWT, December 22, 1949.

p.258 *"as a child, nodding when it was"* and *"After the dress rehearsal"*: Blanche Thebom statement for LM Memorial Room Opening at Dana College, October 11, 1974. Lauritz not only looked out for his younger colleagues, but was also a pushover for despairing singers, of whatever age. One evening he and Kleinchen were approached by an old gentleman who asked if this was truly the famous Lauritz Melchior. After the introductions the stranger asked to sit down. Lauritz, never able to be unkind, and ignoring the baleful looks from his wife, agreed. The singer began a eulogy of his vocal skills, while Lauritz continued to eat his much-delayed dinner. "Listen!" said the man. He began to hum. The hum became half voice. Soon he was singing an aria (badly) at the top of his voice. The concert lasted a full half-hour while the victim bore his torture by counting the pictures on the wall—ten times (Alma Lubin, *Record Review*, April 1940).

p.258 "COURT RULES IT ISN'T NOISE": NYHT, November 5, 1949.

p.258 *"Sometimes it is difficult"*: NYHT, November 5, 1949.

p.259 *"She has the goods"*: NYHT, December 21, 1949. The chorus on this occasion was prepared by Robert Shaw and numbered in its ranks soprano Shirlee Emmons.

p.259 *"My wife went home"*: NYHT, December 21, 1949.

p.259 *There were many reasons*: Howard Taubman, NYT Magazine, March 5, 1950.

p.259 *"the damned things"*: Howard Taubman, NYT Magazine, March 5, 1950.

p.259 *"like a moving couch"*: Bing, p. 9.

p.259 *"the finest Heldentenor in the world"*: Bing, p. 155.

p.259 *"How is that fat fellow?"*: Bing, p. 254. Lauritz told an interviewer that Eisenhower always said, "Lauritz, no one can sing our national anthem like you" (LM, tape interview, Danmarks Radio, December 25, 1970).

p.260 *"Mr. and Mrs. Opera"*: RL, May 31, 1949; NYT, June 14, 1949.

p.260 *increasingly anxious*: Nually, p. 196.

p.260 *Davidson resorted to the mails*: Nually, p. 196.

p.260 Melchior and Traubel under Perlea: Kolodin, p. 489.

p.261 *Soon Bing's post as a mere observer*: Kolodin, p. 484.

p.261 *"obviously a non-political person"*: Bing, p. 151.

p.261 *"This management will operate"*: NYT, January 30, 1950.

p.261 *"put our interests first"*: NYT, January 30, 1950.

p.261 *"Bing Arrives with a Bang!"*: Inez Robb, International News Service, February 6, 1950.

p.261 *"uninhibited by either"*: Inez Robb, International News Service, February 6, 1950.

p.262 *"No contract, no work"*: NYT, January 30, 1950.

p.262 Contract details: Payroll accounts book, AMO.

p.262 *"It's a sentimental business"*: NYT, January 30, 1950.

p.262 *"I can only assume"*: NYT, January 30, 1950.

p.262 Contract details: Payroll accounts book, AMO.

p.263 Sending the telegram: Nually, p. 198.

p.263 Davidson bio and W. Colston Leigh business details: Interview, Thea Dispeker, New York, October 1985; Walter Gould, New York, May 1985. Both Ms. Dispeker and Mr. Gould were former management colleagues of Davidson.

p.263 *"If you're going to fire him"*: NYHT, February 3, 1950.

p.263 "MR. LAURITZ MELCHIOR HAS REQUESTED": Nually, p. 198.

p.264 *Bing maintained always*: Bing, p. 155.

p.264 *"Mr. Bing regrets that"*: Judith Crist, NYHT, February 1, 1950.

p.264 Second Bing press conference details: Louis Biancolli, February 2, 1950.

p.264 *Bing took credit for evenhandedness*: McArthur, p. 251.

p.264 *"I am not prepared to submit"*: NYT, February 2, 1950.

p.264 *"Bing was notoriously unsympathetic"*: TI, March 23, 1973.

p.264 *"That's a new one"*: NYT, February 2, 1950. One wonders if he ever saw the continuing file labeled "Colored," to which every general manager of the Met had contributed. With regularity, the names of Paul Robeson, Marian Anderson, Dorothy Maynor, Camilla Williams, Muriel Rahn, Carol Brice, Roland Hayes were suggested as worthy of engagement at the Metropolitan. The tenor of the management's answering letter never changed: "These artists are concert artists and have not had the proper training for opera." On November 30, 1947, *Washington Post* critic Paul Hume took Johnson to task for his patently contrived excuse that these black artists lacked operatic experience. In rebuttal Hume cited Astrid Varnay as the most recent of those who made their Metropolitan debuts with no previous stage experience whatsoever. To his credit, Mr. Bing changed all this very swiftly.

p.265 *"an ensemble of stars"*: NYT, February 2, 1950.

p.265 *"Mr. Melchior's present plans"*: NYHT, February 1, 1950.

p.265 *"I would have assumed"*: NYHT, February 1, 1950.

p.265 Details of Melchior's activities on February 2: Nually, p. 198. Melchior's last live broadcast from the Met was his previous *Lohengrin* performance of January 7, now on the market in a Danacord release of 1983. Stiedry, Traubel, Janssen, and Varnay were his colleagues.

p.265 *"attrition through indecision"*: Bing, p. 31.

p.265 *"I had not known, frankly"*: Bing, p. 155.

p.265 *"He therefore just turned the key"*: Interview, Klaus Riisbro, Copenhagen, August

1983. The symbols of Masonry are a square ("this is where I stand") and a compass ("our mercifulness") together with a G ("God, the great architect of the world") in the center.

p.266 *"Not only as Lohengrin"*: John O'Reilly, NYHT, February 3, 1950.

p.266 *"I don't believe I will feel happy"*: John O'Reilly, NYHT, February 3, 1950.

p.266 *thought they saw tears*: NYE, July 11, 1955.

p.266 *"I never stay where I'm not wanted"*: Louis Biancolli, *New York World Telegram and Sun*, February 3, 1950.

p.266 Dialogue and details backstage after the performance: Louis Biancolli, *New York World Telegram and Sun*, February 3, 1950.

p.267 *"It was my last performance"*: LM daily diary, February 2, 1950. Judging from other, previous entries, the names "Helen, Bill, Margaret" refer to Helen Traubel and her husband, and to Margaret Truman.

p.267 *"It was just another performance"*: NYHT, February 3, 1950.

p.267 *"Bing has scarcely begun"*: Hartford Times, February 4, 1950.

p.267 *"Bing reflects the European attitude"*: *Providence Journal*, February 4, 1950.

p.267 *"Bing is not so much a new broom"*: Inez Robb, International News Service, February 6, 1950.

p.267 *"It would have been more forthright"*: Kolodin, p. 485.

p.268 *"The airy way he talks of refusing"*: Bayonne (New Jersey) *Times*, February 4, 1950.

p.268 *"At the very least, [Bing's] actions"*: SFA, February 4, 1950. Bing "just *looked* like a gentlemen," says artists' representative Thea Dispeker (interview, October 1985).

p.269 *"disagreed with the distinction"*: NYT, February 4, 1950.

p.269 *Mr. Melchior is definitely not interested*: NYT, February 4, 1950.

p.269 *"small singers"*: NYT, February 4, 1950.

p.269 Witherspoon list: Witherspoon correspondence file, AMO.

p.270 Bing's description of George Sloan: Bing, p. 131, 132.

p.270 *"set a precedent for opera"*: Ming Cho Lee, "Designing Opera," *Contemporary Stage Design, U.S.A.*, International Theater Institute of the U.S., Inc., 1974.

Chapter 16. Vacation from Valhalla (1950–1959)

p.271 *"Dear Mr. Bing"*: Houston Press, February 4, 1950.

p.271 *"effort to sing the part of Siegmund"*: Fan letter of March 19, 1950, AMO.

p.272 *"I have never forgotten you"*: Fan letter to LM, Melchior birthday scrapbook, DCM.

p.272 *"for the pleasure and joy"*: Fan letter to LM, Melchior birthday scrapbook, DCM.

p.272 *"FOR THE ROYAL CHAMBER SINGER"*: DCM.

p.272 *"The Damon Runyon Fund was evidently not averse"*: Nually, p. 200.

p.272 *wherever Cross went*: Constance Hope letter to LM, March 14, 1950.

p.272 *a book on Lauritz's big-game hunting adventures*: VA, February 7, 1951.

p.272 *one for a biography*: NYHT, July 23, 1953.

p.273 *"all the people said unanimously"*: Frida Leider letter to Mutti Hacker, June 26, 1951.

p.273 *"As much of an American institution"*: Nashville Banner, January 9, 1951.

p.273 *"the season's first Tristan"* and *"That night finds Lauritz Melchior"*: Texarkana

Gazette, February 3, 1951, quoting Irving Kolodin, *Saturday Review of Literature*, November 1950.

p.273 *"What, if anything"* and *"Do you realize that opera"*: Lawrence Perry, *Buffalo Evening News*, January 15, 1951.

p.273 *"There are many"*: Lawrence Perry, *Buffalo Evening News*, January 15, 1951.

p.274 *"Bing has been signed"*: Irving Kolodin, NYS, October 11, 1953.

p.274 *"I do not regret it"*: *Pittsburgh Press*, December 4, 1959.

p.274 *"more a top sergeant"*: *Carolina Israelite*, November/December 1958.

p.274 *"Who is Mr. Bing"*: John Rosenfield, DMN, November 8, 1958.

p.274 *"Bing is no scholar"*: Irving Kolodin, NYS, October 11, 1953.

p.275 *"As of today"*: NYT, April 8, 1951.

p.275 *"He is still formerly of the Met"*: NYT, April 8, 1951.

p.275 *"Things are going along"*: Letter, Davidson to Kleinchen, February 18, 1950.

p.275 *"I know very well"*: Letter, Davidson to Kleinchen, February 18, 1950.

p.275 *"Your performance"*: Fan letter, Redwood City, California, February 6, 1950.

p.276 Hess story: Nually, p. 204; clipping, n.d., n.p., DCM.

p.276 *"Bing didn't want me there"*: Interview, Ib Melchior, Los Angeles, November 1987.

p.276 *"great artist and outstanding American citizen"*: WP, January 28, 1951.

p.276 *"25th Anniversary"*: Scroll, DCM.

p.276 *With a group of their California friends*: Guest list, LM correspondence files; photo album.

p.277 *One of their favorite Hollywood guests*: Interview, Leonard Eisner, November 1984.

p.277 *"Together for 25 years"*: Nick Kenny, *New York Mirror*, September 24, 1950.

p.277 Robbery story: TI, July 1, 1957. In interviews these jewels were referred to by the Melchiors as both the "Russian crown jewels" and the "Danish crown jewels." Although Melchior's publicity spun a more romantic tale, the probability as supplied by Professor Tage Kaarsted, Danish historiographer of the Orders of Chivalry, is that they had been the property of the Grand Duchess Anastasia Mikhailovna of Meklenburg-Schwerin, mother of Princess Alexandrine, the wife Crown Prince Christian of Denmark, later Christian X. Following Anastasia's death it was revealed that, in the aftermath of World War I, she had pawned her jewels. Although it is not verifiable, doubtless Melchior purchased them on the open market. (He did hunt in Meklenburg many times.) Lauritz maintained that after Kleinchen's death he sold them in Denmark that they might remain in Danish hands. The royal family declines to substantiate this, but a printed notice of such a sale by a Danish jewelry firm is contained in Melchior's papers.

p.278 *knee-deep in recovered furs*: The number of furs Kleinchen possessed, in every recognizable species and in every conceivable length, was astonishing. Her cachet was enhanced when the publicity pointed out that the full-length leopard coat (and the panther coat and the gazelle coat) was made from the skins of animals her famous husband had shot on safari.

p.278 Details of Davidson and "variety" shows: Nually, p. 203. To outsiders, Melchior's spirits seems high. Graduates of the University of Florida, for example, remember vividly how he joined a fraternity group for their panty raid and accompanying serenade after his concert on campus. The rest of the singers finished the serenade by yelling, "Go Get'em Gators!" Melchior joined in with his own version, making more noise than all of them, "Goo Gattem Goters!"

p.279 *"On [Melchior's] first theater date"*: Irv Kupcinet, *Chicago Sun-Times*, November 8, 1951.

p.279 *ordinary folk relish the humbling*: Ed Sullivan, NYDN, November 2, 1951.

p.279 *"Melchior here in his vaudfilm debut"*: VA, November 14, 1951.

p.279 *"All the way down in the last row"*: CTR, November 12, 1951.

p.280 Details of Jim Davidson persuading LM to play the Palace: Nually, pp. 204, 205.

p.280 The story of Judy Garland's last performance: Letter to the Editor, NYT, April 22, 1973.

p.281 *"the very sight of Melchior"*: Nually, p. 205.

p.281 *"Final returns for the Lauritz Melchior"*: Irving Kolodin, NYS, March 19, 1952.

p.281 *"I'm a lucky man"*: Morris Goldberg, NYE, July 11, 1955.

p.281 *"It's a good summer job"*: Morris Goldberg, NYE, July 11, 1955.

p.281 *"It wasn't much of a show"*: Herberg Kupferberg, NYHT, March 5, 1961.

p.282 *Nightclubs meant singing*: Nually, p. 206.

p.282 *"a music menu"*: "Lauritz Melchior Show" flyer.

p.282 *Angelene Collins recalls*: Interview, Angelene Collins Rasmussen, Long Island, December 1985.

p.283 *"I think Melchior was a frustrated nudist"*: Interview, Leonard Eisner, New York, November 1984.

p.283 *"At least cover it, Schatzi"*: Interview, Leonard Eisner, New York, November 1984.

p.283 Two nudist stories: Interview, Karl Laufkötter, Ojai, California, November 1987.

p.283 *"I really think that I could"*: Holger Boland, *Ascolta*, April 1983.

p.283 Kleinchen persuading LM to sing in Las Vegas story: Nually, p. 208.

p.284 *Lauritz Melchior's amazing show*: VA, January 13, 1953.

p.284 *"bosses along the Vegas strip"*: VA, October 14, 1953.

p.284 *"the inferior products"*: Bill Roberts, *Houston Press*, November 12, 1953.

p.284 *"Melchior and his assemblage"*: VA, October 14, 1953.

p.284 *"usually the faces"*: Bill Roberts, *Houston Press*, November 12, 1953.

p.285 *in his clown costume*: The two sopranos amused their colleagues by trying on the pants of Melchior's *Pagliacci* clown suit. Their figures, in the way of operatic sopranos, were not those of high-fashion models; even so, one soprano fit easily into each leg, with plenty of room to spare.

p.287 "Some Enchanted Evening" story: Personal communication, George Roth to Shirlee Emmons.

p.289 *In the future Kleinchen never wavered*: Interview, Leonard Eisner, New York, November 1984.

p.289 *"It is the greatest mistake"*: Nually, p. 209.

p.289 Details of nightclub offers: Nually, pp. 209, 210.

Chapter 17. Melchior and the Heldentenor Crisis (1960–1972)

p.291 *"The world has not seen"*: Harold Schonberg, NYT, January 10, 1960.

p.291 *Also for me the first meeting*: Letter, LM to Birgit Nilsson, November 21, 1963.

p.292 *"They both had such"*: Interview, Ignace and Alma Strasfogel, New York, April 1985.

p.292 *"Melchior, there's a real man of steel"*: NYDN, January 31, 1965.

p.292 *"would not be in anyway"*: Letter, LM to Jerome C. Karpf, NET, March 31, 1965.

p.292 *"It is essential that we draw"*: Letter, Jerome C. Karpf, NET, to LM, April 2, 1965.

p.292 *"vast and outstanding contributions"*: Letter, National Park Service to LM, August 17, 1967.

p.293 *But whatever loss of vocal power*: Howard Klein, NYT, April 29, 1963. *The New York Herald Tribune* (April 29, 1963) averred that Melchior was "brimming with life."

p.293 *Those backstage at Adelphi*: Interview, Angelene Collins Rasmussen, December 1985. When LM sang at Dana College for the last time in 1968, he is reported to have sung out of tune due to the deafness, and to have lost his place in the music because his glasses were inside his choir robe. Not even this affliction put a damper on his sense of humor, however. In a 1970 *Opera News* interview, he quipped, "Could you speak a little louder? All the Wagner I've heard has made me a little deaf."

p.293 Dodger safari details: LM hunting scrapbook, DCM.

p.294 *Since childhood Lauritz had dreamed*: Birte Melchior told a story related by her father about his safari that points up his stamina even at the age of seventy-one: they had come to a place where there was a river, in the middle of which was a small island where oil drilling was being done. Wanting to see the rig for himself, Melchior did not hesitate to use the only method of transportation. He jumped into the big basket and let the crane hoist it and him up and over to the island (Birte Melchior, tape interview, "The Fairy Tale of My Life," Danmarks Radio, December 25, 1970, produced by Hemming Hartmann-Petersen).

p.294 *"like a larger-than-life"*: Norman Nadel, *Scripps-Howard News*, December 9, 1967.

p.294 *"I know I'll never make it to sixty"*: Telephone interview, Cecily Castenskiold, April 1988.

p.294 *her skin so pale and chalky*: Interview, Cleo Baldon (quoting LM), Los Angeles, November 1987.

p.294 *Kleinchen had seem wittier*: Interview, Klaus Riisbro, Copenhagen, August 1983.

p.294 *Some who were present*: Telephone interview, Cecily Castenskiold, April 1988.

p.294 *Although she always maintained*: Interview, Marianne Tegner (quoting LM), Copenhagen, August 1983.

p.295 *"Nature holds out at me"*: Lauritz Melchior, *Guidepost*, May 1960.

p.295 *"Is that little lady your aunt"*: Interview, Jørgen Krause, Copenhagen, August 1983.

p.295 *"for an apple"*: Interview, Cleo Baldon (quoting Hilde Laufkötter), Los Angeles, November 1987.

p.295 *"The last years were not nice"*: Interview, Birte Melchior, Copenhagen, August 1983.

p.295 *"When Kleinchen was near you"*: Interview, Birte Melchior, Copenhagen, August 1983.

p.295 *Her friend Betty Smith*: Interview, Ib Melchior, Los Angeles, December 1983.

p.296 *"Dearest Kleinchen"*: Letter, Mutti Hacker to Kleinchen and LM, May 12, 1941.

p.296 *"She was the very spirit"*: Letter, George Weigl to LM, March 5, 1963.

p.296 *"Kleinchen was such an extraordinary"*: Letter, Rosa Ponselle to LM, March 8, 1963.

p.296 *"She was your happy star"*: Letter, Frida Leider to LM, February 25, 1963.

p.296 *Frida's sorrowful reply*: Letter, Leider to Kleinchen, March 30, 1951.

p.296 *"that Columbia Records had wished"*: Letter, Lotte Lehmann to LM, April 26, 1963.

p.297 *His sister Bodil thought so*: Interview, Marianne Tegner, Copenhagen, August 1983.

p.297 Nephew Jørgen Krause: Interview, Inga and Jørgen Krause, Copenhagen, August 1983.

p.297 *"If it hadn't been Kleinchen"*: Interview, Hans Hansen, Copenhagen, August 1983.

p.297 *"I do the singing"*: Interview, Leonard Eisner, New York, November 1984.

p.297 *Melchior surrendered his personal autonomy*: Singers have a difficult time finding a suitable mate, says conductor Ignace Strasfogel, well acquainted with the problem. "Every artist has to find a balance between his professional life and his personal life. Male singers can manage more easily than female. Women tend to marry later and there is always the suspicion that the suitors are backstage Johnnys who will live off the woman's earnings. Men can manage more easily."

p.298 *the biggest tragedy of Melchior's life*: The press blamed Lauritz for the inept response to Bing's strategy, but Metropolitan Opera colleagues felt that Lauritz said what Kleinchen told him to say. In William Zakariasen's *Opera News* (March 19, 1973) obituary, he describes Melchior's departure being "at the instigation of his petite, go-getting wife, Kleinchen." The musical community also entertained a silly rumor at the time: Kleinchen had prevented Lauritz from calling Bing to straighten out the problem because she was against a rapprochement, viewing his relationship with Kirsten Flagstad as too friendly. The facts as related in Melchior's diary would appear to discount such a theory, and close friends ridicule the idea: Lauritz was totally faithful to Kleinchen.

p.298 *"She was jealous of everything"*: Interview, Birte Melchior, Copenhagen, August 1983.

p.298 *Kleinchen did her best*: Interview, Ib Melchior, Los Angeles, December 1983.

p.298 *"When I wanted to wake my darling"*: LM daily diary, February 23, 1960.

p.298 *"a young man should be on his own"*: Interview, Klaus Riisbro, Copenhagen, August 1983.

p.299 *"Well, yesterday I cried"*: Interview, Klaus Riisbro, Copenhagen, August 1983.

p.299 *Two days later the funeral took place*: Significantly, the dates for the Melchior marriage vis à vis his divorce from Inger were altered in the funeral notice to say that Inger and Lauritz had divorced in 1924 and Lauritz had married Kleinchen in 1927, whereas in reality divorce and remarriage took place within three days of each other.

p.299 *"all of Kleinchen's jewels"*: Telephone interview, Cecily Castenskiold, April 1988.

p.299 Description of funeral service: Interviews, Klaus Riisbro, August 1983, and Cecily Castenskiold, April 1988.

p.299 *"From that day on"*: Interview, Klaus Riisbro, Copenhagen, August 1983.

p.299 *"Now Godfather sat"*: Interview, Klaus Riisbro, Copenhagen, August 1983. Dear to the Danish national pride, the name Holger Danske was adopted by one of the resistance groups during the occupation, eventually numbering some 400 members (Petrow, p. 186).

p.299 *"Godfather had done everything"*: Interview, Klaus Riisbro, Copenhagen, August 1983.

p.300 Kleinchen keeping LM on a diet story: PB, July 13, 1951.

p.300 *Klaus Riisbro saw the ghost*: Interview, Klaus Riisbro, Copenhagen, August 1983.

p.300 *"Ja, hello"*: Interview, Cleo Baldon, Los Angeles, November 1987.

p.300 *Even Betty Smith*: Interview, Ib Melchior, Los Angeles, December 1983. Lauritz found the painting "excellent," an opinion not shared by everyone. He believed that their dislike stemmed from the fact that a still painting could never capture Kleinchen's joie de vivre and liveliness.

p.300 *"I thought I was too old for her"*: LM daily diary, December 19, 1963.

p.300 *Those whom Kleinchen had told*: Interview, Angelene Collins Rasmussen, Long Island, December 1985.

p.301 *during his 1963 trip to Europe*: During this trip Melchior made an appearance at Tivoli, at which he sang three songs. Presumably it was at this time, when he had Kleinchen's body interred at Assistens Cemetery, that he made his gravest error in German spelling. On the granite tombstone of Maria Melchior is chiseled "KLEINSCHEN."

p.301 *"now we shall put things"*: Interview, Cleo Baldon, Los Angeles, November 1987.

p.301 *their shock at seeing*: Letter, Birte Melchior to Shirlee Emmons, July 15, 1987.

p.301 *"Godfather didn't think of any woman"*: Interview, Klaus Riisbro, Copenhagen, August 1983.

p.301 *"Well, if she is his daughter"*: Interview, Birte Melchior, Copenhagen, August 1983.

p.301 *"After he found out"*: Interview, Birte Melchior, Copenhagen, August 1983.

p.301 *"We were all such good friends"*: NYT, March 31, 1964.

p.301 *"Look, Lauritz," she said*: Interview, Ib Melchior (quoting Hilde Laufkötter), Los Angeles, December 1983.

p.301 *"Let's not talk about it"*: Interview, Ib Melchior, Los Angeles, November 1987.

p.302 *"You have a hell of a lot to learn"*: Interview, Cleo Baldon, Los Angeles, November 1987. (To "Skåle" properly, one must pick up the glass and look directly into the eyes of the person being toasted.)

p.302 *"Nevertheless," said he*: Interview, Cleo Baldon, Los Angeles, November 1987.

p.302 *500 celebrated guests*: Among the wedding guests were Cornell Wilde, Risë Stevens, Lloyd Bridges, Agnes Moorehead, Rory Calhoun, Cesar Romero, Dan Duryea, Buster Keaton, Vic Damone, Bobby Darin, Eartha Kitt, and Richard Chamberlain.

p.302 Hawaiian Islands interview: Maui dateline, n.p., n.d., LM scrapbooks, DCM.

p.303 *"Still disharmony"*: LM daily diary, July 17, 1964.

p.303 *Mary had spoken indiscreetly*: Interview, Ib Melchior, quoting Hilde Laufkötter, Los Angeles, December 1983.

p.303 *Mary had not been circumspect*: Interview, Ib Melchior, quoting Hilde Laufkötter, Los Angeles, December 1983.

p.303 *Mary had sold the furniture*: Interview, Cleo Baldon, Los Angeles, December 1983.

p.303 *Mary's friends had laughed publicly*: Interview, Ib Melchior, Los Angeles, November 1987.

p.303 *"Miss Markham must have these documents"*: Interview, Cleo Baldon, December 1983. Melchior financed Ms. Markham's production company, ownership of which, by terms of the settlement, she retained even after the divorce.

p.303 *"This isn't true, is it?"*: Interview, Cleo Baldon, Los Angeles, November 1987.

p.303 *"It was impossible to tell"*: Interview, Cleo Baldon, Los Angeles, November 1987.

p.303 *Mary and Lauritz had dinner*: After returning from taking his father home, Ib Melchior wrote complete notes documenting the contretemps at the dinner table and the conversations in the car, from which the narrative is derived.

p.303 *"The only thing in my life now"*: Notes taken by Ib Melchior on August 28, 1964.

p.303 *"who, with her hairdresser friend"*: LM daily diary, August 30, 1964.

p.303 *"I'll go to the guest house"*: Notes taken by Ib Melchior on August 28, 1964.

p.304 *"There's no fool like an old fool"*: Interview, Cleo Baldon, Los Angeles, November 1987.

p.304 *"Morfar is very lonesome"*: Letter, LM to Helle Melchior, September 1964.

p.304 *"had had enough schooling in Denmark"*: Letter, Helle Hamilton to Shirlee Emmons, July 28, 1987.

p.304 *"No, I was the old fool"*: Interview, Cleo Baldon, Los Angeles, November 1987.

p.305 *"All my women really loved me"*: Interview, Cleo Baldon, Los Angeles, November 1987.

p.305 *"Pop music is all right"*: Interview, Cleo Baldon, Los Angeles, November 1987.

p.305 *"Compared to modern music"*: Interview, Cleo Baldon, Los Angeles, November 1987.

p.305 *"Yes, you're eating that one"*: Interview, Cleo Baldon, Los Angeles, November 1987.

p.305 Details of Dirk/LM relationship: Interview, Cleo Baldon, Los Angeles, November 1987; letter, Cleo Baldon to Shirlee Emmons, October 21, 1988.

p.305 *"First softly with the virgin's hand"*: Interview, Jørgen Krause, Copenhagen, August 1983.

p.306 *"It is as I have always said"*: Letter, Andreas Damgaard to Shirlee Emmons, December 9, 1987.

p.306 Birte/LM luncheon story: Interview, Birte Melchior, Copenhagen, August 1983.

p.306 Saint Brigitte ceremony details: Interview, Cleo Baldon, Los Angeles, November 1987.

p.307 Capri Blue Grotto story: Interview, Ib Melchior, Los Angeles, November 1987.

p.307 *"Who the hell is this?"*: Interview, Ib Melchior, Cleo Baldon, Los Angeles, December 1983.

p.307 *"People of prominence should not"*: Interview, Cleo Baldon, Los Angeles, November 1987.

p.307 *"in Italy there are no birds"*: Interview, Cleo Baldon, Los Angeles, November 1987.

p.307 Speeding in Italy story: Interview, Ib Melchior, Los Angeles, November 1987.

p.308 *"Our friendship will always remain"*: Letter, LM to Max Lorenz, August 21, 1970.

p.309 *"a little study just beside"*: Letter, Knud Hegermann-Lindencrone to Shirlee Emmons, March 2, 1988.

p.309 *the only stereo recording of Lauritz Melchior*: Letters, Knud Hegermann-Lindencrone to Shirlee Emmons, April 9, 1987. Since the recording put out by Edward J. Smith, the record entrepreneur (for many years the only available record of this occasion), was taken from the radio broadcast, it was a monophonic disk. A hallmark of Smith's idealistic lifelong work was the gift of fifty copies of each recording to the international official collections, as was done with the 1960 *Walküre* Act 1.

p.309 *Hegermann-Lindencrone's idea for this gala performance*: Letters, Knud Hegermann-Lindencrone to Shirlee Emmons, April 9, 1987; August 9, 1987; March 2, 1988; February 28, 1989.

p.309 *"A letter from Lauritz!"*: Letter, Knud Hegermann-Lindencrone to Shirlee Emmons, March 2, 1988.

p.309 *"to see Kirsten smiling"*: Letter, Knud Hegermann-Lindencrone to Shirlee Emmons, March 2, 1988.

p.309 *accusations by Norwegian Ambassador*: Letters, Knud Hegermann-Lindencrone to Shirlee Emmons, February 2, 1987; March 8, 1987; April 9, 1987. Not until many years later, when Morgenstierne had died, could the Norwegian government officially present its regrets by naming Flagstad head of the newborn Norwegian Opera.

p.310 *"too late for me"*: Letter, Knud Hegermann-Lindencrone to Shirlee Emmons, November 11, 1988.

p.310 *"He was fantastic"*: Letters, Knud Hegermann-Lindencrone to Shirlee Emmons, April 9, 1987; November 2, 1988.

p.310 *Thomas Jensen had apparently*: Hans Hansen, liner notes, *Melchior Anthology*, Volume 3, Danacord DACO 119–120.

p.310 *"the warm timbre"*: Dorothy Larsen, *Ascolta*, June 1983.

p.311 *"the astonishing vitality"*: Mogens Wedel, *Ascolta*, June 1983.

p.311 *"as wonderful as in his youth"*: Letters, Knud Hegermann-Lindencrone to Shirlee Emmons, June 6, 1988; November 2, 1988.

p.311 *"Dorothy Larsen brought him back"*: Letters, Knud Hegermann-Lindencrone to Shirlee Emmons, June 6, 1988; November 2, 1988.

p.311 *Melchior dived into*: Mogens Wedel, *Ascolta*, June 1983. Revealing his opinion about "snaps," LM said in 1970: "Unfortunately, all my male friends have passed away. Probably they have not drunk enough 'snaps.' If they had, they would probably still be around. It is the 'aqua vitae,' the water of life" (tape interview, "The Fairy Tale of My Life," Danmarks Radio, December 25, 1970, produced by Hemming Hartmann-Petersen).

p.311 *"on pins and needles"*: Letters, Knud Hegermann-Lindencrone to Shirlee Emmons, October 20, 1988; November 2, 1988.

p.311 *"Dear Lauritz: Thank you"*: LM interview, "The Fairy Tale of My Life," Danmarks Radio, December 25, 1970, produced by Hemming Hartmann-Petersen.

p.311 *"What a singer"*: Interviews, Knud Hegermann-Lindencrone, Copenhagen, August 1983; Ib Melchior, Los Angeles, December 1983.

p.311 *"To be on the stage with Kirsten"*: Lauritz Melchior, OP, February 21, 1963.

p.312 *"The fact that it was Norway"*: LM taped interview, BBC, 1972.

p.312 *"with continuously increasing power"* and *"the slightest physical trouble"*: *Dagens Nyheder*, April 1, 1960.

p.312 *"reached an amazing level"*: *Information*, April 1, 1960.

p.312 *"One's memory went back"*: *Berlingske Tidende*, April 1, 1960.

p.312 *"just a superficial show number"*: *Politiken*, April 1, 1960.

p.312 *"there were no Heldentenors"*: Hansgeorg Lenz, *Information*, March 22, 1973.

p.312 *"whether a new Melchior"*: Hansgeorg Lenz, *Information*, March 22, 1973.

p.313 *"No recording can . . . convey"*: Conrad L. Osborne, *Records in Review*, 1961.

p.313 *As early as 1963*: Nually, pp. 221, 222.

p.313 *"It looks sad with the new growth"*: Letter, LM to Max Lorenz, February 6, 1967.

p.314 *"Heldentenors are rare"*: Lauritz Melchior Foundation brochure.

p.314 *"Today there are only"*: Norman Nadel, *Scripps-Howard News*, December 9, 1967.

p.315 *"Richard Wagner's operas"*: Fund-raising letter, 1966.

p.315 *"The world of Wagnerian tenors"*: Martin Bernheimer, LAT, March 10, 1966. With the phrase "sympathetic conductor," Mr. Bernheimer was referring to a then-new ploy of conductors like von Karajan. By holding the orchestra way down, he made it possible for a light Heldentenor to manage the repertoire formerly reserved for genuine heavy heroic-tenor voices.

p.315 *"It is important to get the right help"*: Rose Heylbut, ET, n.d., 1931.

p.316 *it would have been impossible*: Interview, Cleo Baldon, quoting, Hilde Laufkötter, November 1988.

p.316 *"It was very interesting to learn"*: Letter, LM to Birgit Nilsson, January 13, 1968.

p.316 *"Please take care"*: Letter, LM to William Cochran, August 13, 1969.

p.317 *"a machine because [he does]"*: LMPM.

p.317 *"I wish that she will understand"*: Letter, LM to William Cochran, August 13, 1969.

p.317 *You seem to have a very powerful*: Letter, LM to William Arlock, March 26, 1965.

p.318 *"this is what happened to . . . Mr. Vinay of Chile"*: Melchior's use of the word "shine" as a description of vocal quality echoes that of Wagner himself, who wrote to Liszt during his preparations for the first performance of *Lohengrin*: "The singer above all must have one quality: shine in the appearance and in the voice" (Jens Malte Fischer, "Sprachgesang oder Belcanto," *Opernwelt*, June 1986). Angelene Collins Rasmussen who sang on both tours of "The Lauritz Melchior Show" recalls another LM/Ramon Vinay story: Melchior came out of the room where he was listening to the afternoon broadcast of *Tristan und Isolde*, starring the Chilean tenor, and said, shaking his head sadly, "A child could have done better" (Interview, December 1985).

p.318 *"We desire to do him honor"*: Constance Hope (quoting Belmont) to LM, January 11, 1966.

p.318 *"a remarkable combination"*: Bing, p. 133.

p.318 *asking him to be present*: Letter, Eleanor Belmont to LM, January 16, 1966.

p.318 *Lauritz declined*: Letter, LM to Eleanor Belmont, January 23, 1966.

p.318 *she tried to persuade Lauritz*: Letter, Eleanor Belmont to LM, January 27, 1966.

p.318 *"When I am writing to you"*: Letter, LM to Eleanor Belmont, February 1, 1966.

p.319 *asked for permission*: Letter, Eleanor Belmont to LM, February 17, 1966.

p.319 *"of the Metropolitan Opera"*: Interview, Cleo Baldon, Los Angeles, November 1987.

p.319 *"the company broke into"*: Schuyler Chapin, NY, May 5, 1973.

p.319 *"The great Wagnerian tenor"*: Interview, Ib Melchior, Los Angeles, December 1983.

p.319 *"Young people make me feel young again"*: Interview, Klaus Riisbro, Copenhagen, August 1983.

p.320 *"He led a super life"*: Interview, Klaus Riisbro, Copenhagen, August 1983.

p.320 *Mogens Wedel had been shocked*: Mogen Wedel, *Ascolta*, June 1983.

p.320 *"suit of lights"*: Interview, Cleo Baldon, Los Angeles, November 1987.

p.320 *"She can come and stay here, too"*: Interview, Klaus Riisbro, Copenhagen, August 1983.

p.320 Details of LM illness: Phone interview, Marianne Tegner, August 1986.

p.320 *"Young Siegfried is still with us"*: Phone interview, Marianne Tegner, August 1986.

p.321 *"I think there has never been"*: Draft of statement for Leider's eightieth-birthday tribute.

p.321 *"Our friendship during so many years"*: Frida Leider, OP, May 1973.

p.321 *"What time is it?"*: Interview, Otte Svendsen, Copenhagen, August 1983.

p.321 *"Godfather loved sitting"*: Interview, Klaus Riisbro, Copenhagen, August 1983.

p.321 *"You cannot talk about singing"*: Interview, Klaus Riisbro, Copenhagen, August 1983.

p.321 LM lecture about singing: Interview, Klaus Riisbro, Copenhagen, August 1983.

p.322 *"He just couldn't hear himself"*: Interview, Ib Melchior, Los Angeles, November 1987.

p.322 *"Music is too damned complicated"*: Interview, Klaus Riisbro, Copenhagen, August 1983.

Chapter 18. "Leb' wohl, mein Held" (1973–1974)

p.323 *"Leb' wohl, mein Held [Farewell, my hero]"*: The chapter title is inspired by a phrase used by Martin Bernheimer (LAT, March 25, 1973) as the last line of his superbly moving obituary notice for Melchior, "Leb' wohl, O Held" [Farewell, o hero"].

p.323 *"Have a good life"*: Letter, Helle Hamilton to Emmons, July 27, 1987.

p.323 *"We'll see what happens tomorrow"*: Letter, Ib Melchior to Shirlee Emmons, March 12, 1987.

p.323 *"I believe he chose the moment"*: Letter, Helle Hamilton to Shirlee Emmons, July 27, 1987.

p.323 *Melchior had been weakened*: Letter, Marianne Tegner to Shirlee Emmons, June 7, 1988.

p.323 *"I am so weak now"*: Interview, Klaus Riisbro, Copenhagen, August 1983.

p.323 *"It's nothing"*: Letter, Marianne Tegner to Shirlee Emmons, June 7, 1988.

p.323 Details of medical problems: Letter, Marianne Tegner to Shirlee Emmons, June 7, 1988.

p.323 *When he awoke, Melchior*: Phone interview, Marianne Tegner, August 1987.

p.323 *It is a testimony to his charm*: Phone interview, Marianne Tegner, August 1987.

p.323 *"My damned chest hurts"*: Interview, Ib Melchior, Los Angeles, November 1987.

p.324 *"He took it like a king"*: Interview, Klaus Riisbro, Copenhagen, August 1983.

p.324 Riisbro/Appel ceremony: Interview, Klaus Riisbro, Copenhagen, August 1983.

p.324 *"stood in reverence"*: Letter, Los Angeles City Council to Ib Melchior, March 22, 1973.

p.324 *"Singer Lauritz Melchior Dies"*: LAT, March 19, 1973.

p.324 *"rare combination of artistry"*: LAT, March 19, 1973.

p.324 *"I will have a private service"*: Letter, Lotte Lehmann to Ib Melchior, March 20, 1973.

p.324 *"it was fitting"*: Martin Bernheimer, LAT, March 25, 1973.

p.324 *"I don't think he wrote anything so great"*: Gerald Fitzgerald, OPN, March 28, 1970.

p.324 *Masonic, memorial service*: Interview, Birte Melchior, Copenhagen, August 1983; NYT, April 6, 1973.

p.324 *Vor Frue Kirke*: Vor Frue Kirke, the Church of Our Lady, has an awesome history. It is believed that, late in the twelfth century, Bishop Absalon, founder of Copenhagen, built a small chapel on this site, whose ruins can be seen in the basement today. Ravaged by fire in 1728 and badly damaged by Admiral Lord Nelson's bombardment of Copenhagen in 1807, it was restored and, in 1924, named the Cathedral of Copenhagen. (Interview, Marianne Tegner, Copenhagen, August 1983.)

p.325 *There would be no memorial service*: NYT, March 19, 1973.

p.325 *Having been repeatedly nudged*: Melchior estate trustee correspondence.

p.325 *"I am very pleased"*: Letter, Lotte Lehmann to Metropolitan Opera, December 4, 1973.

p.326 *"scarcely worth the time"*: Paul Hume, WP, March 20, 1973.

p.326 *Sadly, the old canard*: Harold Schonberg, NYT, March 25, 1973.

p.326 *"Now he has been taken into Valhalla"*: Hansgeorg Lenz, *Information*, March 22, 1973.

p.326 *"We never forgave him"*: Hans Hansen, quoting anonymous Danish actor, Danmarks Radio, March 19, 1973.

p.326 *"Nørregade, Denmark, God"*: Hans Hansen, eulogy, Danmarks Radio, March 19, 1973.

p.327 *"Melchior was a natural phenomenon"*: Alden Whitman, quoting Francis Robinson, NYT, March 20, 1973.

p.327 *Before and After Melchior*: Conrad L. Osborne, OPN, August 1976.

p.327 *"eyes popping as they sang all out"*: Harold Schonberg, NYT, March 25, 1973.

p.327 *"much like a watermelon"*: Harold Schonberg, NYT, March 25, 1973.

p.327 *"a giant in every way"*: John Ardoin, DMN, March 25, 1973.

p.327 *"ten-year global moratorium"*: Barrymore Laurence Scherer, OPN, March 3, 1984.

p.328 *"The Heldentenor species"*: Reprint of 1960 article, Harold Schonberg, *Facing the Music*, p. 279.

p.328 *"whether the century ever had"*: NYT, n.d., 1968.

p.328 *"unrivaled"*: Lawrence, p. 59.

p.328 *"among the seven wonders of the world"*: André Tubeuf, *L'avant Scène, Opéra*, January/February, 1977.

p.328 *"When Nature created"*: Scott, p. 248.

p.328 *"the more tenors"*: George Jellinek, SR, July 1982.

p.328 *Why Do All Heroic Tenors*: John Rockwell, "The Heroes," OPN, March 23, 1974.

p.328 *"magnificent performance"*: Peter G. Davis, *New York*, September 9, 1985.

p.328 *"the Wagnerian tenor supreme"*: John Steane, liner notes, "Lauritz Melchior," Pearl GEMM 228/229.

p.328 *"continue to impose"*: Opus, February 1987.

p.328 *"Singers are not irreplaceable"*: Lee Milazzo, *American Record Guide*, March/April 1988.

p.328 *"the ideal Wagner tenor"*: Clemens Höslinger, *Fono Forum*, December 1970.

p.328 *"Nearly a quarter-century"*: Dale Harris, "Without Melchior," NYT, February 24, 1974.

p.329 *"bring out more and more"*: John Steane, liner notes, "Lauritz Melchior," Pearl GEMM 228/229.

p.329 *"that fabulous dramatic radiation"*: John Frandsen, tape interview, "The Fairy Tale of My Life," Danmarks Radio, December 20, 1970, produced by Hemming Hartmann-Petersen.

p.329 *"equating innovation with subversion"*: John Rockwell, "Wagner's 'Ring': Stage-craft as Ideology," NYT, March 26, 1989.

p.329 *"desperately novel"*: Donal Henahan, "The 'Ring' Bypasses the Brain," NYT, April 2, 1989.

p.330 *"Wagner, at his best"*: Donal Henahan, "The 'Ring' Bypasses the Brain," NYT, April 2, 1989. Melchior was, however, committed to one Bayreuth practice that predated an important modern concept, that of ensemble acting. No one ever accused Melchior of a lack of cooperation or of grandstanding on stage.

p.330 *The career of Heldentenor*: Deborah Seabury, "Alles Stimmt," OPN, January 16, 1988.

p.330 *loud orchestras*: Sir Georg Solti conducted his 1983 *Ring* at Bayreuth without the pit cover (Ralf Stuckman, "Mein liebe Schwan," *NZ Forum*, June 1987).

p.330 *uncut performances*: Many German and international houses sanctioned cuts in the Wagner scores during Melchior's performing days (e.g., Tannhäuser sang only two verses of the "Preislied" before entering the valley). Tenor Tichat-schak, a favorite of Wagner's, asked the composer for cuts in that opera. Conductor Felix Weingartner justified his many Wagnerian cuts at the Vienna Hof-Oper by saying that if he did not cut, "the singers would be ruins" (Ralf Stuckman, "Mein lieber Schwan," *NZ Forum*, June 1987).

p.331 *Despite the vicissitudes*: Barrymore Laurence Scherer, OPN, March 3, 1984.

Sources

The family of Lauritz Melchior has graciously given me official access to their papers, as well as their uncritical cooperation and generous help with my work, for which I am sincerely grateful. To be associated with Melchior's immediate family—Ib, Birte, and Cleo—has been a privilege.

Some quotes whose citations are incomplete appear in the text. They come from those clippings entered into the scrapbooks at the end of Melchior's life when he was less than careful about cutting off dates or credits, and from the Lincoln Center Library for the Performing Arts clipping files, where age has often crumpled the yellowed newsprint. I have tried to reconcile dates from the anecdotal sources, but sometimes it has been impossible.

Lauritz Melchior prided himself upon his ability as a raconteur. He told and retold the major stories of his life, relishing most the humorous ones. Whenever possible, I have preferred to use the versions as told to family and friends by Melchior in person, rather than those that appear in interviews, articles, and books.

The chief sources for this book are:

1. The diary that Melchior kept, dating from 1896 (retrospectively), through 1945.

Clearly, at the time when he began the diary, probably around 1920, he went back and filled in dates from his childhood and youth. These entries vary from one line to half a page. They have proven to be reasonably reliable. Whenever the dates conflict with those given by Hart-Davis, quoting Walpole, I have given precedence to Walpole.

2. Melchior wrote the personal manuscript, covering 1907 to 1950, in later years; it consequently has slips of memory. I have noted these discrepancies as they arise in the text. In most of the extracts I have retained the idiosyncratic syntax used by Melchior. Only when the sense might be impaired have I changed his grammar or punctuation for clarity.

3. Over fifty scrapbooks, each 18″ × 24″ × 3″, maintained by Melchior and his second wife, containing special interest material and all publicity items dating between 1918 and 1973. On October 11, 1975, Dana College in Blair, Nebraska, the only college in the U.S. with a Danish orientation, and a college with which Melchior had close ties, dedicated a museum to him on the campus: The Lauritz Melchior Memorial Room. Ib Melchior honored his father's memory by donating most of the memorabilia he had inherited. These include the scrapbooks, photographs, hunting trophies, an oil painting, costumes, artifacts, and mementos, as well as the record collection. This museum is open to the public.

4. A book in which Melchior kept a record of all his performances and fees. Opera entries include casts and conductors.

5. The family history book, the Stambog, now maintained by Ib Melchior.

6. Two handwritten diaries of Kleinchen Melchior, for the years 1925–1926 and 1930–1931.

7. Several special scrapbooks relating to hunting, the Royal Danish Guard

Association Outside Denmark, the family, the fiftieth and eightieth birthday parties, all of which are a part of the Dana College collection.

8. Home movies, some eighty photo albums, correspondence, daily appointment books, and copies of the MGM movies.

9. Two cassette tapes recorded by Melchior in 1961, containing memories of his childhood, which are part of the Dana College collection.

10. A 286-page document titled "Memories, Especially of Singing and Music," written by Melchior's father in the year of his death, 1925.

11. Copies of Melchior's speeches and interviews, including those in Denmark.

12. Cassette copies of the Fred Allen shows.

13. An unpublished manuscript compiled and edited by Ib J. Melchior, "The Golden Years of Bayreuth."

14. Two series of 1970 articles in five parts published by a Danish magazine, *Hendes Verden* [*Her World*], written by Birte Melchior: "Mother Was the Best in the Whole World," #30,31,32, and "Good and Bad Aspects of Being Children of Artists," #48,49.

15. Clippings from the Lincoln Center Research Library. In some cases, the newspaper or magazine credits and dates have been lost. These have been documented in the endnotes with the abbreviations n.d. (no date) and n.p. (no paper or periodical).

16. Materials, and memories, presented either in writing or by personal interview from relations and friends whose names are given below, are gratefully acknowledged: Lorenzo Alvary, Eva Andersen, Mogens Benthin, Christian and Cecily Castenskiold, Andreas Damgaard, Leonard Eisner, Walter Gould, Helle Melchior Hamilton, Hans Hansen, Robert Herring, Knud Hegermann-Lindencrone, George Jellinek, Jørgen and Inge Krause, Hilde and Karl Laufkötter, Birte Melchior, Ib and Cleo Melchior, William Park, Angelene Collins Rasmussen, Mark Rehnstrom, Klaus Riisbro, Martial Singher, Dr. Rudolf Steinharter, Ignace and Alma Strasfogel, Otte Svendsen, Marianne Tegner, William Zakariasen.

17. Reminiscences, biographies, history books, and magazine articles mentioned in the bibliography and in the source notes.

18. The book *Lauritz Melchior*, written by Betty Smith, which was published only in Danish under her pseudonym, Jana Nually, and (according to Ib Melchior and Marianne Tegner) contained material related to Ms. Smith by Melchior.

19. Recordings owned by me, recordings given me by Andreas Damgaard and Hans Hansen, recordings from the library of Robert Herring, recordings from Lincoln Center Library for the Performing Arts Rodgers and Hammerstein collection, and from the Dana College Lauritz Melchior Memorial Room.

20. Materials from the Metropolitan Opera Archives: reviews, programs, correspondence, and payroll accounts.

21. Tapes of recorded interviews on Danmarks Radio: (1) "My Life's Adventure," April 23 and 30, 1966, interviewer, Arne Honoré; (2) "The Fairy Tale of My Life," December 20, 25, and 27, 1970, produced by Hemming Hartmann-Petersen.

Bibliography

Arnold, Elliott. *A Night of Watching*, New York: Charles Scribner's Sons, 1967.

Backus, John. *The Acoustical Foundations of Music*. New York: W.W. Norton and Company, Inc., 1977.

Bahr-Mildenburg, Anna. *Erinnerungen*. Vienna: Wiener Literarische Anhalt, 1921.

Beecham, Thomas. *A Mingled Chime*. New York: G.P. Putnam's Sons, 1943.

Belmont, Eleanor. *The Fabric of Memory*. New York: Farrar, Straus and Cudahy, 1957.

Biancolli, Louis. *The Flagstad Manuscript*. New York: G.P. Putnam's Sons, 1952.

Bing, Sir Rudolf. *5,000 Nights at the Opera*. Garden City, N.Y.: Doubleday, 1962.

Busch, Fritz. *Pages from a Musician's Life*. Trans. Marjorie Strachey. London: The Hogarth Press, 1953.

Caamano, Roberto. *The History of the Colón Theater 1908–1968*. Buenos Aires: Ed. Cinetea, 1969.

Cairns, David. *Responses*. New York: Alfred A. Knopf, 1973.

Culshaw, John. *Ring Resounding*. New York: Viking Press, 1967.

Davis, Ronald L. *Opera in Chicago*. New York: Appleton-Century, 1965.

Drake, James. *Richard Tucker: a biography*. New York: E.P. Dutton, Inc., 1984.

Eaton, Quaintance. *Opera Caravan*. New York: Farrar, Straus, and Cudahy, 1957.

Ewen, David. *Men and Women Who Make Music*. New York: Thomas Y. Crowell Co., 1939.

Finck, Henry T. *My Adventures in the Golden Age of Music*. New York: Funk and Wagnalls Co., 1926.

Gaisberg, F. W. *The Music Goes Round*. New York: Macmillan, 1942.

Geissmar, Berta. *Two Worlds of Music*. New York: Da Capo Press, 1975.

Gilman, Lawrence. *Wagner's Operas*. New York/Toronto: Farrar & Rinehart, Inc., 1937.

Gobbi, Tito, and Ida Cook. *My Life*. London: MacDonald and Jane's, 1979.

Gunnarson, Torstein. *Sannheten om Kirsten Flagstad*. Oslo: Universítetsbibliotekets Hustrykkeri, 1985.

Hanslick, Eduard. *Vienna's Golden Years of Music, Musical Criticisms, 1850–1900*. Trans. and Ed. Henry Pleasants. New York: Simon and Schuster, 1950.

Hart-Davis, Rupert. *Hugh Walpole, A Biography*. New York: Macmillan, 1952.

Hartford, Robert. *Bayreuth, The Early Years*. London: Victor Gollancz, Ltd., 1980.

Henderson, W. J. *The Art of Singing*. New York: The Dial Press, 1938.

Herman, Walter. *Max Lorenz*. Vienna: Oesterreichischer Bundesverlag, 1981.

Hetherington, John. *Melba*. New York: Farrar, Straus and Giroux, Inc., 1968.

Hey, Julius. *Richard Wagner als Vortragsmeister*. Leipzig: 1911.

Hines, Jerome. *Great Singers on Great Singing*. Garden City, N.Y.: Doubleday and Co., 1982.

Kelley, Kitty. *His Way*. New York: Bantam Books, 1986.

Kennedy, Michael. *Barbirolli, Conductor Laureate*. London: MacGibbon and Kee, Ltd., 1971.

Klein, Hermann. *The Golden Age of Opera*. New York: Da Capo Press, 1980.

——— . *30 Years of Musical Life in London*. London: Heinemann, 1903.

Kolodin, Irving. *The Metropolitan Opera: 1883–1966*. New York: Alfred A. Knopf, 1966.

Kralik, Heinrich. *The Vienna Opera*. Trans. Richard Rickett. Vienna: Verlag Brüder Rosenbaum, 1963.

Kutsch, K. J. and Leo Riemans *A Concise Biographical Dictionary of Singers*. Trans., Harry Earl Jones. Philadelphia: Chilton Book Co., 1969.

Lawrence, Robert. *A Rage for Opera*. New York: Dodd, Mead and Co., 1971.

Lehmann, Lilli. *Mein Weg*. Leipzig: 1920.

Lehmann, Lotte. *Midway in My Song*. Freeport, N.Y.: Books for Libraries Press, 1938.

Leider, Frida. *Playing My Part*. New York: Meredith Press, 1966.

Leinsdorf, Erich. *Cadenza*. Boston: Houghton-Mifflin Co., 1976.

MacHaffie, Ingeborg S. and Margaret A. Nielsen. *Of Danish Ways*. Minneapolis: Dillon Press, 1976.

Magidoff, Robert, with Ezio Pinza. *Ezio Pinza, an Autobiography*. New York: Rinehart, 1958.

Marek, George. *Cosima Wagner*. New York: Harper and Row, 1981.

———— . *A Front Seat at the Opera*. Freeport, N.Y.: Books for Libraries Press, 1948.

Mayer, Martin. *The Met—100 Years of Grand Opera*. New York: Simon and Schuster, 1983.

McArthur, Edwin. *Flagstad—A Personal Memoir*. New York: Alfred A. Knopf, 1965.

Mead, W. R., and Wendy Hall. *Scandinavia*. New York: Walker and Co., 1972.

Melchior, Ib. *The Golden Days of Bayreuth*, unpublished manuscript.

Melchior, Jørgen. *Memories, Especially of Singing and Music*. Unpublished manuscript.

Moore, Gerald. *Farewell Recital*. New York: Taplinger Publishing Co., 1978.

———— . *Furthermore*. London: Hamish Hamilton, 1983.

Mordden, Ethan. *Opera Anecdotes*. London: Oxford University Press, 1985.

Newman, Ernest. *Wagner as Man and Artist*. London: J. M. Dent and Sons, Ltd., 1914.

———— . *From the World of Music*. London: John Calder, 1956.

Newton, Ivor. *At the Piano—Ivor Newton*. London: Hamish Hamilton, 1966.

Noble, Helen. *Life with the Met*. New York: G.P. Putnam's Sons, 1954.

Nually, Jana. *Lauritz Melchior*. Copenhagen: Steen Hasselbalchs, 1969.

O'Connell, Charles. *The Other Side of the Record*. New York: Alfred A. Knopf, 1947.

Petrow, Richard. *Bitter Years*. New York: William Morrow and Co., 1974.

Pleasants, Henry. *The Great Singers*. New York: Simon and Schuster, 1966.

Rein, Aslaug. *Kirsten Flagstad*. Oslo: Ersnt G. Mortensens Forlag, 1967.

Rémy, Pierre-Jean. *Maria Callas—A Tribute*. New York: St. Martin's Press, 1978.

Robinson, Frances. *Celebration: The Metropolitan Opera*. New York: Doubleday, 1979.

Rosenthal, Harold D. *Two Centuries of Opera at Covent Garden*. London: Putnam and Co., Ltd., 1958.

Rushmore, Robert. *The Singing Voice*. New York: Dodd, Mead and Co., 1971.

Salés, Jules. *Théâtre Royal de la Monnaie*. Nivelles, Belgium: Editions Havaux, 1971.

Schepelern, Gerhard. *Wagners Operaer i Danmark*. Copenhagen: Amadeus Forlag, APS, 1988.

Schonberg, Harold C. *Facing the Music*. New York: Summit Books, 1981.

———— . *The Glorious Ones*. New York: Times Books, 1985.

Schwarzkopf, Elisabeth. *On and Off the Record*. New York: Charles Scribner's Sons, 1982.

Scott, Michael. *The Record of Singing, Volume II.* London: Duckworth, 1979.

Seltsam, William H. *Metropolitan Opera Annals.* New York: The H.W. Wilson Co., 1947.

Shawe-Taylor, Desmond. *Covent Garden.* New York: Chanticleer Press, Inc., 1948.

Sheean, Vincent. *First and Last Love.* New York: Random House, 1956.

Skelton, Geoffrey. *Richard and Cosima Wagner.* Boston: Houghton Mifflin Co., 1982.

———. *Wagner at Bayreuth.* New York: George Braziller, 1965.

———. *Wieland Wagner:* The Positive Skeptic. New York: St. Martin's Press, 1971.

Steele, Elizabeth. *Hugh Walpole.* New York: Twayne Publishers, Inc., 1972.

Taubman, H. Howard. *Opera Front and Back.* New York: Charles Scribner's Sons, 1938.

Traubel, Helen. *St. Louis Woman.* Coll. with Richard G. Hubler. New York: Duell, Sloan, and Pearce, 1959.

Tuggle, Robert. *The Golden Age of Opera.* New York: Holt, Rinehart and Winston, 1983.

Vennard, William. *Singing, the Mechanism and the Technic.* New York: Carl Fischer, Inc., 1967.

Vickers, Hugh. *Great Opera Disasters.* New York: St. Martin's Press, 1979.

———. *Even Greater Opera Disasters.* New York: St. Martin's Press, 1982.

Vogt, Howard. *Kirsten Flagstad.* London: Martin Secker and Warburg, Ltd. 1987.

Weingartner, Felix. *Buffets and Rewards, a Musician's Remembrance.* Trans. Marguerite Wolff, London: Hutchinson and Co., Ltd., 1937.

Wagner, Friedelind, with Page Cooper. *Heritage of Fire.* New York/London: Harper and Bros., 1945.

Wagner, Richard. *Richard Wagner's Prose Works,* Volume 3. Trans. William Ashton Ellis. London: K. Paul, Trench, Trübner and Co., 1892–1899.

Wagner, Siegfried. *Erinnerungen.* Stuttgart: 1923.

Wechsberg, Joseph: *Red Plush and Black Velvet.* Boston: Little, Brown and Co., 1961.

Wessling, Berndt. W. *Furtwängler.* Stuttgart: Deutsche Verlags Austalt, 1985.

———. *Lotte Lehmann . . . mehr als eine Sängerin.* Salzburg: Residenz Verlag, 1969.

———. *Toscanini in Bayreuth.* Munich: Verlag Kurt Deach Dition, 1976.

Wiesmann, Sigrid, ed. *Gustav Mahler in Vienna.* New York: Rizzoli, 1976.

Wood, Sir Henry J. *My Life of Music.* London: Strand, 1938.

Grove's International Dictionary of Music and Musicians, Stanley Sadie, ed. London: Macmillan Publishing Co., 1981.

Den Blåbog, 1983.

Salmonsens Conversations Leksikon, 1928.

Sohlmans Musiklexicon, 1977.

Metropolitan Opera Archives, New York. Robert Tuggle; Kenneth Schlesinger.

Richard-Wagner Museum, Bayreuth, Germany. Günther Fischer.

Hamar Kommune Kulturkontoret (Kirsten Flagstad Museum), Hamar, Norway. Erik Østby.

Vilhelm Herold Museum, Hasle, Bornholm, Denmark.

Lauritz Melchior's Roles

DANISH ROLES

Baron (Merlesac's [sic] *Kongen har sagt det* [The King Said It])
Forsanger (Hofmannthal's *Det gamle Spil om enhver* [Everyman])
Majordomus (Enna's *Komedianter* [Comedians])
Per (Heiberg's *En Søndag, paa Amager* [A Sunday on Amager])
Sammensvoren (Heise's *Drot og Marsk* [King and Marshall])
Sverkel [tenor] (Hartmann's *Liden Kirsten* [Little Kirsten])

AS A BASS

Antonio (Mozart's *Le Nozze di Figaro*)
Baker (Wagner's *Die Meistersinger*)

AS A BARITONE

Brander (Gounod's *Faust*)
di Luna (Verdi's *Il Trovatore*)
Douphol (Verdi's *La Traviata*)
Faninal (Strauss' *Der Rosenkavalier*)
Germont (Verdi's *La Traviata*)
Grahlsridder, "Knight of the Grail" (Wagner's *Parsifal*)
Heinrich der Schreiber (Wagner's *Tannhäuser*)
Moorish Doctor (Tchaikovsky's *Iolanthe*)
Morales (Bizet's *Carmen*)
Ottokar (Weber's *Der Freischütz*)
Silvio (Leoncavallo's *Pagliacci*)

AS A TENOR

Canio (Leoncavallo's *Pagliacci*) total: 21 performances
    Berlin Staatsoper, 1928, 1929, 1930
    Copenhagen, 1919, 1921, 1932, 1936
    Hamburg, 1927, 1928, 1929
    Nuremberg, 1924
    Stettin, 1925
Florestan (Beethoven's *Fidelio*) total: 8 staged performances, 1 concert performance
    Buenos Aires, 1933, 1943
    London, 1934
    New York Philharmonic, 1 concert performance, 1935
    San Francisco, 1939
John of Leyden (Meyerbeer's *Le Prophète*), total: 11 performances
    Hamburg, 1928, 1929
    Berlin Staatsoper, 1930
Lohengrin (Wagner's *Lohengrin*), total: 106 performances
    Antwerp, 1932

Baltimore, 1937
Boston, 1935, 1938, 1940–1942
Bremen, 1928
Brooklyn, 1935
Buenos Aires, 1942
Chicago Opera, 1936, 1941
Cleveland, 1937, 1939, 1942
Hamburg, 1927, 1928, 1929
Kiel, 1928
London, 1935, 1938
Los Angeles, 1937
Lyons, 1932, 1933
Paris Opéra, 1932, 1934
Philadelphia, 1937, 1945
Rochester, 1937
Metropolitan Opera, New York, 1930, 1933–1947, 1950
New Orleans, 1939
Santiago di Chile, 1943
San Francisco, 1937
Vienna, 1934

Otello (Verdi's *Otello*), total: 31 performances
Berlin Staatsoper, 1929, 1930
Bremerhaven, 1928
Hamburg, 1928, 1929, 1930
London, 1933, 1934, 1939
Paris Opéra, 1931
Radio Berlin, concert performance, 1931
San Francisco, 1934

Parsifal (Wagner's *Parsifal*), total: 81 performances
Bayreuth, 1924, 1925
Berlin Staatsoper, 1930
Berlin Städtische Oper, 1924, 1925
Boston, 1938
Breslau, 1925
Buenos Aires, 1933, 1942
Chemintz, 1925
Chicago, 1944
London, 1927, 1930
Metropolitan Opera, New York, 1926, 1931—1948
Paris Opéra, 1931
Philadelphia, 1929, 1930, 1940, 1943, 1944, 1948

Radamès (Verdi's *Aïda*), total: 25 performances
Berlin Staatsoper, 1928, 1930
Bremen, 1928, 1930
Hamburg, 1928, 1929, 1930
Hanover, 1929
Kiel, 1928

Samson (Saint-Saëns's *Samson et Dalila*), total: 2 performances, one staged and one on radio in the U.S. in 1936.
Copenhagen, 1 performance, 1920

Siegfried (Wagner's *Götterdämmerung*), total: 107 performances
  Barcelona, 1929
  Bayreuth, 1927, 1928
  Berlin Staatsoper, 1929, 1930, 1931
  Boston, 1934, 1937, 1940
  Buenos Aires, 1931
  Hague, 1931
  Hamburg, 1928
  London, 1929–1939
  Metropolitan Opera, New York, 1929–1946, 1948, 1949
  Paris Opéra, 1931, 1933
  Paris Champs Elysées Opera, 1929
  Philadelphia, 1939, 1942, 1945, 1948
  San Francisco, 1935, 1936
  Vienna, 1934
Siegfried (Wagner's *Siegfried*), total: 128 performances
  Antwerp, 1930
  Barcelona, 1929
  Berlin Staatsoper, 1925, 1929–1931
  Berlin Städtische Oper, 1931
  Bordeaux, 1932
  Bremerhaven, 1927
  Brussels, 1934
  Buenos Aires, 1931
  Copenhagen, 1932, 1934, 1936
  Hamburg, 1927, 1928, 1930
  Hartford, 1940
  London, 1926, 1928–1939,
  Lübeck, 1927
  Lyons, 1932, 1933
  Magdeburg, 1925
  Metropolitan Opera, New York, 1926, 1929, 1931–1945, 1947, 1948
  Paris Champs Elysées Opera, 1929
  Paris Opéra, 1930–1932, 1934
  Philadelphia, 1932, 1938, 1939
  St. Louis, 1939
  San Francisco, 1935
  Vienna, 1934
Siegmund (Wagner's *Die Walküre*), total: 183 performances
  Baltimore, 1939
  Barcelona, 1939
  Bayreuth, 1924, 1925, 1941
  Berlin Staatsoper, 1924–1926, 1928–1932
  Berlin Städtische Oper, 1925, 1926
  Bordeaux, 1933
  Boston, 1935, 1938–1940, 1942
  Braunschweig, 1925
  Breslau, 1925
  Brooklyn, 1932, 1936
  Buenos Aires, 1931

Chicago Opera, 1936, 1937, 1940
Cleveland, 1939, 1941
Copenhagen, 1930, 1939
Dallas, 1940
Hamburg, 1927, 1928, 1930
London, 1924, 1926–1932, 1935, 1936, 1938, 1939
Los Angeles, 1939, 1948
Lyons, 1933
Magdeburg, 1924
Metropolitan Opera, New York, 1927, 1929, 1931–1949
Paris, Champs Elysées Opera, 1929
Paris Opéra, 1930–1933, 1935
Philadelphia, 1926, 1937, 1939, 1940, 1943, 1946
Rochester, 1940
St. Louis, 1939
San Francisco, 1935, 1936, 1939, 1945
Vienna, 1925
Tannhäuser, Dresden version (Wagner's *Tannhäuser*), total: 40 performances
Copenhagen, 1918, 1921
Berlin Städtische Oper, 1925, 1926
Bremen, 1928
Bremerhaven, 1928
Buenos Aires, 1942
Hamburg, 1924, 1927–1930
Leipzig, 1928
Oslo, 1919
Vienna Staatsoper, 1925
Tannhäuser, Paris version (Wagner's *Tannhäuser*), total: 104 performances
Atlanta, 1940
Baltimore, 1939
Barcelona, 1929
Bayreuth, 1931
Berlin Staatsoper, 1929, 1930
Boston, 1934, 1936, 1939, 1941
Brooklyn, 1935
Chicago, 1944
Chicago Opera, 1937, 1943
Cleveland, 1938, 1940, 1944
Dallas, 1939
Hanover, 1929
Hartford, 1938
London, 1928
Los Angeles, 1941
Lyons, 1932
Metropolitan Opera, New York, 1926, 1930, 1932, 1933, 1935–1946, 1948
Milwaukee, 1944
New Orleans, 1940
Paris Opéra, 1931, 1933, 1936
Philadelphia, 1932, 1941
Portland, 1941

Rochester, 1935
San Francisco, 1934, 1941
Seattle, 1941
Vienna, 1934
Tristan (Wagner's *Tristan und Isolde*), total: 223 performances
Antwerp, 1931
Baltimore, 1933, 1936, 1945
Barcelona, 1929
Bayreuth, 1930, 1931
Berlin Staatsoper, 1929, 1932, 1933, 1934
Berlin Städtische Oper, 1929, 1930
Boston, 1936–1941
Brooklyn, 1934
Brussels, 1933
Buenos Aires, 1931, 1933, 1943
Chicago, 1943, 1944
Chicago Opera, 1934, 1937, 1940
Cleveland, 1937, 1938, 1940, 1941, 1945
Copenhagen, 1930, 1933
Hartford, 1936
London, 1929, 1931–1933, 1935–1937, 1939
Los Angeles, 1937, 1939, 1945, 1948
Lyons, 1933
Metropolitan Opera, New York, 1929–1950
Paris Opéra, 1930–1936
Rochester, 1936
San Francisco, 1936, 1937, 1939
Vienna, 1931, 1934
Turiddu (Mascagni's *Cavalleria Rusticana*), total: 5 performances
Hamburg, 1927
Nuremberg, 1924
Stettin, 1925

Discography by Hans Hansen

The Melchior discography was first compiled almost twenty-five years ago and made public in 1965 by informal arrangement with the Danish Nationaldiskotek of the National Museum. A revised edition was issued in 1972, after which the activity was curtailed. The present and third edition, a comprehensive updating, is much enlarged, due primarily to the very great number of 78-reissues on LP, publication of off-the-air recordings of the last thirty years, and numerous reissues of complete Wagner operas featuring Melchior in "live performance." Particular effort has been made to facilitate two-way reference and identification.

For almost thirty years, until his retirement in March 1989, Hans Hansen was Program Secretary for Opera Presentation and Production with Danmarks Radio. His expertise on the career and recorded legacy of Lauritz Melchior has been widely recognized. Hans Hansen was responsible for the recent complete LP and CD anthology of Melchior's European recordings (1913–1939) issued on Danacord.

The discography is organized in four sections:

I. 1–301 78 rpm.

The three groups to the left of each title are, respectively: (a) chronological discography number, (b) most common coupling, and (c) matrix numbers. The vertical line to the right of titles divides "0" numbers (referring to the separate LP listing, Section II) and the various 78 rpm catalog numbers.

II. 01–080 LP transfers of 78 rpm records.

Numbers following each entry refer back to the chronological discography numbers in Section I.

III. x1–x52 Wagner in "live performance."

Live commercial and noncommercial recordings of Lauritz Melchior in the seven Wagner roles for which he is famous.

IV. Miscellaneous special issues, recitals, etc.

PREFIXES					
78 rpm records		3000	MGM, DK	17000	Victor, USA
03000	Odeon, DK?	5000	Odeon, AUS?	17000D	Columbia,
080000	Nordisk	6000	MGM, GB		USA
	Polyphon, DK	7000	Victor, USA	18000	Victor, USA
2-280000	HMV, DK	8000	Victor, USA	30000	MGM, USA
3-82000	Nordisk	9000	MGM	40000	Decca, USA
	Polyphon, DK	9700	Victor, USA	50000	Brunswick,
10-1000	Victor, USA	9800	Victor, USA		USA
11-8000	Victor, USA	10000	Brunswick,	60000	Polydor, D
100	MGM, USA		USA	70000	Polydor, D
1000	Odeon, AUS?	11000	Victor, USA	70000D	Columbia,
1800	Victor, USA	15000	Victor, USA		USA
1900	Victor, USA	15648	Columbia,	80000	Nordisk
2000	Victor, USA		CDN		Polyphon, DK
		16000	Victor, USA	260000	Columbia, RA

284200	HMV, DK	DM	Victor, USA	LOX	Columbia,
284300	Nordisk	E10000	Parlophone,		AUS
	Polyphon, DK		GB	M	Victor, USA
A14000	Odeon, DK	E18000	Brunswick	M550	Columbia,
A73000	Brunswick	EC	HMV, AUS		USA
AM	Victor, USA	ED	HMV, AUS	MGM	MGM, USA
AU	Decca, USA	EJ	Electrola, D	MM550	Columbia,
AW	HMV, I	ES	HMV, A		USA
B9000	HMV, GB	GQX	Columbia, I	ND	Victor, Japan
B20000	Polydor, D	JAS	Victor, Japan	P	Parlophone, D
D0000	HMV, GB	K	MGM	W	HMV, F
D25000	Parlophone	19000	Deutsche	X200	Columbia,
DA	HMV, GB		Gramophon, D		USA
DB	HMV, GB	61000	CBS, USA	X7000	HMV, DK

Section I. 78 rpm

The Baritone Records
ODEON Copenhagen, January-February 1913

1	Kpo 252	Verdi, *La Traviata*, Act 2: "Di Provenza il mar" (Danish).	01	011	055		A 144293
2	Kpo 253	Kjerulf, "Mit Hierte og min Lyre."	01	011	055		A 144261
3	Kpo 254	Heise, "Ørnen løfter med stœrke Slag."	01	011	055		A 144262
4	Kpo 255	—, "Om Strømmen mod dig bruser."	01	011	055		A 144294
5	Kpo 256	Nessler, *Der Trompeter von Säckingen*: "Behüt dich Gott" (Danish).	01	011	055		A 144295

Copenhagen, March 1913

6(7)	Kpo 410	Friedman, "Meet Me Tonight in Dreamland" (Danish).	01	055			03067 A 144329
7(6)	Kpo 411	Bechgaard, *Sømandsliv*: "Farvel."	01	055			03068 A 144356
8(9)	Kpo 413	Gade, *Elverskud*: "Olufs Serenade."	01	055			A 144374
9(8)	Kpo 414	Verdi, *Il Trovatore*, Act 2: "Il balen" (Danish).	01	053	054 055		A 144375

GRAMOPHONE COMPANY (HMV) Copenhagen, August 5, 1913

10	5030ab	Bechgaard, *Sømandsliv*: "Ved Land" (w. piano).	01	015	2-282437
11(12)	5037ab	Heise, *Bertran de Born*: "Herre Konge,	01		284227

		bliv her" (w. Astrid Neumann).				
12(11)	5038ab	Hartmann, *Liden Kirsten*, Act 2: "Tavlebordsduet" (w. Astrid Neumann).	01	015		284228
13(14)	5039ab	Heise, *Bertran de Born:* "Fager er den blide Vaar."	01	056		2-282160
14(13)	5040ab	—, "Ørnen løfter med stœrke Slag."	01	056		2-282161

Nos 1-9 and 11-14 have anonymous orchestral accompaniment.

Copenhagen, March 26, 1915

15(19)	17631L	Hassler, "Befal du dine Veje" (w.organ and bells).	01	055		2-282615
16(18)	17632L	Berggreen, "Velkommen igen, Guds Engle smaa" (w. harmonium).	01	055		2-282743

Copenhagen, March 29, 1915

17(20)	17660L	Weyse, "Den signede Dag" (w. brass).	01	011	055	2-282745
18(16)	17661L	Anon., "Lover den Herre den mœgtige Konge" (w. brass).	01	055		2-282742
19(15)	17662L	Berggreen, "Tœnk naar engang den Taage" (w.brass).	01	055		2-282616
20(17)	17663L	Anon., "Lovet vœre du Herre Christ" (w. brass)	01	011	055	2-282744
21(22)	17664L	Weyse, "Altid frejdig naar du gaar" (w. brass)	01	011	055	2-282808
22(21)	17665L	Mortensen, "Nattens dœmrende Taager" (w. orch.).	01	011	055	2-282809

The Early Tenor Records
NORDISK POLYPHON
Copenhagen, 1920–1921

23(24)	742½ar	Wennerberg, *Gluntarne* (w. Holger Hansen): "Slottsklockan."	01	054	056	84316
24(23)	743ar	—,—,—: Avskedet på Flottsund."	01	056		84317
25(26)	744ar	—,—,—: "Glunten på föreläsning."	01	056		84318
26(25)	745ar	—,—,—: "Upsala är bäst."	01	056		84319

27(33)	746ar	—,—,—: "Nattmarschen."	01	056			84320
28(29)	766ar	Lange-Müller, *Letizia*: "Firenze."	01	056			3-82075
29(28)	767ar	Allen, "Solen ler saa godt og mildt."	01	056			3-82076
30(41)	768ar	Andersen,S., "Nu brister i alle de Kløfter."	01	056			3-82077
31(40)	769ar	—, "Der flyver saa mange Fugle"	01	015 024 056			3-82078
32(39)	771ar	Kjellerup, "Elskede min fra den unge Vaar."	01	056			3-82079
33(27)	772ar	Wennerberg, *Gluntarne* (w. Holger Hansen): "Dagen därpå."	01	056			84307
34(38)	776ar	Heise, *Twelfth Night*: "Dengang jeg var kun saa stor som saa."	01 056	011 057	124		3-82080
35(36)	313as	Wennerberg, *Gluntarne* (w. Holger Hansen): "Magisterns misslyckade serenad."	01	056			084032
36(35)	314as	—,—,—: "En solnedgång i Eklundshofskogen."	01	054			084031
37(42)	842ar	Andersen, S., "Kongeaas Bølger."	01	056			3-82081
38(34)	844ar	Rygaard, "Flaget."	01	056			3-82082
39(32)	845ar	—, "Danmark."	01	056			3-82083
40(31)	856ar	Bonnén, "Da Freden drog over Lande."	01	015 056			3-82084
41(30)	857ar	Howalt, "Kristiansborg."	01	056			3-82085
42(37)	859ar	Wagner, *Die Walküre*, Act 1: "Winterstürme" (Danish).	01	011 056			3-82086
43(44)	860ar	Puccini, *Tosca*, Act 3: "E lucevan" (Danish).	01	011 056			3-82087
43A	860½ar	—,—,—,—, (unpublished)	01				3-82088
44(43)	861ar	—,—, Act 1: "Recondita armonia" (Danish).	01	011 056			3-82089
45(46)	318as	Wagner, *Lohengrin*, Act 3: "In fernem Land" (Danish).	01 015	011 056			082102
46(45)	319as	Hartmann, *Liden Kirsten*, Act 2:	01 015	011 056			082103

		"Sverkel's Romance."				
47(51)	862ar	Widéen, "Tinrande				284326
		frage stjärna."				
48(49)	863ar	Körling, "Det				284327
		skymmer."				
49(48)	864ar	Henriques, *Canta-*				284328
		Sangene: "Dagen er				
		omme."				
50(52)	865ar	Lange-Müller,				284329
		"Kornmodsglansen."				
51(47)	866ar	Kjerulf,				284330
		"Solvirkning."				
52(50)	867ar	Hellmuth, "Jenny i				284333
		Rugen."				

23–36 have piano accompaniment, 37–46 orchestra, while 47–52 are unaccompanied, performed by "Skandinavisk Kvartet," its members being Lauritz Melchior, Holger Hansen, Olaf Peelmann, and Holger Madsen.

THE RED POLYDORS

Germany 1923 (November–December ?); Leo Blech and anonymous orchestra

The 7000– and 72000–series numbers given are the double-sided and most common order numbers. Some of the Red Polydors were also issued single-sided under other numbers, although the catalogue or B-numbers are consistent.

53(54)	2779ar	Sjöberg, "Tonerna."				unpubl.
54(53)	2780ar	Strauss, R.,				unpubl.
		"Cäcilie."				
55	2790ar	Weingartner,	02	018		70599
		"Liebesfeier."				B2110
56(57)	1481as	Wagner, *Siegfried*,	02	011	012	72857
		Act 1: "Nothung!	014	036		B22176
		Nothung! . . .was				
		musstest."				
57(56)	1482as	—,—,—,:	02	011	012	72857
		"Schmiede, mein	014	036		B22177
		Hammer."				
58(59)	1483as	—, *Tannhäuser*,	02	012	014	72863
		Act 3: "Inbrunst im	037	041		B22180
		Herzen.				
59(58)	1484as	—,—,—: "Nach	02	012	014	72863
		Rom gelangt' ich.	037	041		B22181
60(61)	1485 ½as	—, *Die Walküre*, Act	02	012	014	72934
		1: "Du bist der	035	054		B25033
		Lenz" (w. Leider).				
61(60)	1486as	—,—,—: "Wie dir	02	012	014	72934
		die Stirn" (w.	035	054		B25034
		Leider).				
62(63)	1488as	—,—,—: "Fried-	02	012	014	72867
		mund darf ich nicht	035			B22182
		heissen."				
63(62)	1489as	—,—,—: "Siegmund	02	012	014	72867
		heiss'ich."	035	054		B22183
64(68)	1490½as	—,—,—: "Ein	02	012	014	72869

		Schwert verhiess mir der Vater."	015	038		B22184
65(66)	1491as	—, Rienzi, Act 5: "Allmächt'ger Vater."	02	012	014	72870 B22185
66(65)	1500as	—, Die Meistersinger von Nürnberg, Act 3: "Morgenlich leuchtend."	02 014	011 039	012	72870 B22186
67(70)	1501½as	Verdi, Aïda, Act 4: "Gia i sacerdoti" (w. Arndt-Ober) (German).	02 016	011 034	014 039	72936 B25035
68(64)	1502as	Wagner, Wesendonk-Lieder: "Schmerzen."	02 015	012	014	72869 B22187
69	1503as	—,—: "Träume."	02 015	012	014	72884 B22188
70(67)	1504as	Verdi, Aïda, Act 4: "Di lei non più" (w. Arndt-Ober) (German).	02 016	011	014	72936 B25036

THE PARLOPHONE RECORDS

Berlin, December 3, 1924 (71–72), January 5, 1925 (73–76), January 6 (77–78), January 28 (79–80); Paul Breisach and anonymous orchestra

71(72)	7742-2	Wagner, Die Walküre, Act 1: "Winterstürme."	02	051	054	1011 E10352	P1903
72(71)	7743-2	—, Parsifal, Act 3: "Nur eine Waffe taugt."	02 024	014	018	1011 E10352	P1903
73(74)	7821	—,—, Act 2: "Amfortas! die Wunde!	02 032	014 033	018	1010 E10298	P1902
74(73)	7822	—,—,—: "Es starrt der Blick."	02 032	014 033	018	1010 E10298	P1902
75(76)	7824	—, Tannhäuser, Act 2: "O Fürstin" (w. Bettendorf).	02	014	016	E10332	P1927
76(75)	7825	—,—,—: "Doch welch ein seltsam" (w. Bettendorf).	02	014	016	E10332	P1927
77(80)		Grieg, "Eros" (German).					
78(79)	7827-2	Trunk, a)"Mir träumte von einem Königskind," b)"Als	02	018(b)			P1928

		ob ein Toter im Grabe."			
79(78)	7900	—, a)"In einer Heimat," b)"Erster Strahl."	02 018(b)		P1928
80(77)		Grieg, a)"En svane,"b)"Jeg elsker dig" (German).			

Berlin, September 16, 1925; Frieder Weissmann and anonymous orchestra

81(82)	8307-2	Wagner, *Siegfried*, Act 2: "Dass der mein Vater nicht ist."	02	014	018	E10442	P2088
82(81)	8308	—,—,—: "Du holdes Vöglein."	02	014	018	E10442	P2088

Berlin, September 29, 1926; Frieder Weissmann and anonymous orchestra

83(84)	2-8880	Wagner, *Lohengrin*, Act 3: "Das süsse Lied verhallt" (w. Bettendorf).	02 017	011 031	013	5115 E10515	D25384 P9027
84(83)	2-8881	—,—,—: "Wie hehr erkenn' ich (w. Bettendorf).	02 031	011	017	5115 E10515	D25384 P9027
85(86)	2-8882	—,—,—: "Atmest du nicht" (w. Bettendorf).	02 031	011	017	5116 E10527	D25385 P9085
86(85)	2-8883	—,—,—: "Höchstes Vertrau'n" (w. Bettendorf).	02 031	011	017	5116 E10527	D25385 P9085
87	2-8884	—,—,—: "Hörtest du nichts?" (w. Bettendorf).	02 031	011	017	5117 E10540	D25386

THE ELECTRIC POLYDORS

Germany, 1926; with anonymous orchestra

88(90)	147bm	Sjöberg, "Tonerna" (German)	02	015	016	66440 B22306
89(91)	148bm	Meyerbeer, *L'africaine*, Act 4: "O paradis!" (German).	02 017	011	015	66439 B22303
90(88)	149bm	Strauss, R., "Cäcilie."	02	015	018	66440 B22305
91(89)	150bm	Wagner, *Tannhäuser*, Act 3: "Als ich erwachte."	02 016	012 018	015 037	66439 B 22304

THE BRUNSWICK RECORDS

Chicago (?), 1926; with anonymous orchestra

92(93)	E18845	Klenau, "To My Bride"	02	018			10245	E18845
93(92)	E18846	Hagemann, "Do Not Go, My Love" (w. Fredric Fradkin, violin).	02	018			10245	E18846
94(95)		Wagner, *Die Walküre*, Act 1: "Winterstürme."	03 018	014	015		50085	A73057
95(94)		—, Die Meistersinger von Nürnberg, Act 3: "Morgenlich leuchtend."	03	015			50085	A73057

THE HMV RECORDS

Berlin, June 19, 1928; Leo Blech and Berlin State Opera

96(97)	CLR 4275-II	Wagner, *Die Walküre*, Act 1: "Ein Schwert verhiess mir."	03	018		EJ300	ES456
97(96)	CLR 4276-III	—,—,—: "Siegmund heiss'ich" (w. Guszalewicz).	03	018		EJ300	ES456
97A(97B)	CLR 4277-II	—, *Tannhäuser*, Act 3: "Inbrunst in Herzen."		018			ES454
97B(97A)	CLR 4284-I	—,—,—, "Als ich erwachte."		018			ES454

Berlin, June 20, 1928; Leo Blech and Berlin State Opera

98(99)	CLR 4031-III	Wagner, *Lohengrin*, Act 3: "Höchstes Vertrau'n."	03	013 018	014 019	D1505	EJ302 ES455
99(98)	CLR 4032-IV	—,—,—: "O Elsa! Nur ein Jahr."	03	013	017	D1505	EJ302 ES455

London, May 6, 1929; Albert Coates and London Symphony

100(101)	Cc16620–IIa	Wagner, *Tristan und Isolde*, Act 2: "O sink' hernieder" (w. Leider).	03 019 044	09 022 045	013 027	7274 AW288 D1724	EJ483 ES606 W1149
101(100)	Cc16621–Ia	—,—,—: "Soll ich lauschen?" (w. Leider).	03 019 027	09 022 044	013 046	7274 AW288 D1724	EJ483 ES606 W1149

London, May 16, 1929; Albert Coates and London Symphony

102(103)	CR2197-III	Wagner, *Siegfried*, Act 1: "Fühltest du nie" (w. Reiss).	04	019		9805 D1690	EJ449
103(102)	CR2198-IIb	—,—,—: "Nothung! Nothung!. . . . was musstest (w. Reiss).	04 019	010 020	013 050	9805 D1690	DB1858 EJ449

London, May 17, 1929; Albert Coates and London Symphony

104(105)	CR2199-IIIa	Wagner, *Siegfried*, Act 1: "Nothung! Nothung! nun schmolz" (w. Reiss).	04	010	013	9806 D1691	EJ450
105(104)	CR2200-II	—,—,—: "Er schafft sich ein scharfes Schwert" (w. Reiss).	04	010	013	9806 D1691	EJ450
106(107)	CR2401-II	—,—, Act 2: "Dass der mein Vater nicht ist!"	04	010	019	9807 D1692	EJ451
107(106)	CR2402-IIa	—,—,—: "Du holdes Vöglein."	04	010	019	9807 D 1692	EJ451
108(109)	CR2403-I	—,—,—: "Gönntest du mir wohl . . ." (w. Grühn).	04	010	020	9808 D1693	EJ452

London, May 22, 1929; Albert Coates and London Symphony

109(108)	CR2404-IIb	Wagner, *Siegfried*, Act 2 "Da lieg'auch du."	04 020	010	019	9808 D1693	EJ452
110(111)	CR2405-III	—,—, Act 3: "Kenntest du mich?" (w. Bockelmann).	04 019	010 026	013 032	9811 D1694	EJ453
111(110)	CR2406-II	—,—,—: "Zieh' hin! Ich kann dich nicht halten" (w. Bockelmann).	04	013	026	9811 D1694	EJ453
112(113)	CR2407-I,-II	—, *Tannhäuser*, Act 3: "Inbrunst im Herzen."	03 019	013 058a	016	9707 D1675	EJ433 ES454
113(112)	CR2408-I	—,—,—: "Da sah ich ihn."	03 019	013 058a	016	9707 D1675	EJ433 ES454

Berlin, June 15, 1929; Leo Blech and Berlin State Opera

114(115)	CLR 5458-IIa	Wagner, *Götterdämmerung*,	03 019	013 030	017 032	D1700 EJ471	ES619

		Act 1: "Hast du Gunther, ein Weib?" (w. Schorr).					
115(114)	CLR 5459-Ia	—,—,—: "Was nahmst du am Eide?" (w. Schorr, Topas, Watzke).	03 030	017 032	019	D1700 EJ471	ES619
116(117)	CLR 5460-II	—, *Die Walküre*, Act 1: "Ein Schwert verhiess mir."	03	013 019	017 020	D2022	EJ475
117(116)	CLR 5461-I	—,—,—: "Siegmund heiss' ich."	03 020	017	019	D2022	EJ475

Berlin, September 13, 1929; Albert Coates and Berlin State Opera

118(119)	CLR 5612-I	Wagner, *Tristan und Isolde*, Act 2: "Isolde! Tristan! Geliebter!" (w. Leider).	03 019	09 022	013 027	7273 AW287 D1723	EJ482 ES605 W1148
119(118)	CLR 5613-I	—,—,—: "Doch es rächte sich" (w. Leider).	03 019	09 022	013 027	7273 AW287 D1723	EJ482 ES605 W1148

London, May 12, 1930; Robert Heger and London Symphony

120(121)	CR2498-III	Wagner, *Siegfried*, Act 3: "Selige Öde auf sonniger Höh'."	04	010		9812 D1836	EJ485 ES680
121(120)	CR2499-I	—,—,—: "Das ist kein Mann!"	04	010		9812 D1836	EJ485 ES680
122(123)	CR2500-I	—,—,—: "Wie end' ich die Furcht?"	04	010	020	9813 D1837	EJ486 ES681
123(122)	CR2501-II	—, *Tristan und Isolde*, Act 2: "Wohin nun Tristan scheidet."	03	09	017	11136 D1837	EJ486 ES681

London, May 13, 1930; Robert Heger and London Symphony

124(125)	CR2502-II	Wagner, *Götterdämmerung*, Act 3: "So singe, Held" (w. Helgers).	03 043	013	021	7659 D1838	EJ487 ES682
125(124)	CR2503-II	—,—,—: "In Leid zu den Wipfeln" (w. Helgers).	03 043	013	021	7659 D1838	EJ487 ES682

126(127)	CR2504-II	—,—,—: "Brünnhilde! Heilige Braut!"	03 013 019 021 040 043	D1839	EJ488 ES683
127(126)	CR2505-I	—, Tristan und Isolde, Act 3: "Wie sie selig."	03 09 013 019 022 032	11136 D1839	EJ488 ES683

London, May 17, 1930; John Barbirolli and New Symphony Orchestra

128(129)	CR2509-I	Verdi, Otello, Act 3: "Dio! mi potevi!" (German).	03 011 013 014 016 052 058	D2037	EJ574 ES676
129(128)	CR2510-III	—,—, Act 4: "Niun mi tema" (German).	03 011 013 014 016 052	D2037	EJ574 ES676

London, May 29, 1930; John Barbirolli and London Symphony

130(131)	Cc19608-Ia	Leoncavallo, I pagliacci: "Vesti la giubba" (German).	03 011 013 014 016	EJ582	ES694
131(130)	Cc19609-Ia	Wagner, Tannhäuser, Act 1: "Dir töne Lob!"	03 014 016 025	7656 D2057	EJ583 ES695
132(133)	Cc19610-IIa	—, Rienzi, Act 5: "Allmächt'ger Vater."	03 013 016 019	7656 D2057	EJ583 ES695
133(132)	Cc19612-Ia	Meyerbeer, L'africaine, Act 4: "O paradis!" (German).	03 013 014 016	EJ582	ES694

London, May 9, 1931; Robert Heger and London Symphony

134	2B530-I	Wagner, Die Meistersinger von Nürnberg, Act 3: "Abendlich glühend (w. Schorr).	03 019 023	7681 D2000	EJ700
135	2B531-II	—, Siegfried, Act 1: "Hoiho! Hau' ein" (w. Tessmer).	04 010	7691	DB1578
136(137)	2B532-IIa	—,—,—: "Das ist nun der Liebe" (w. Tessmer).	04 010 020	7692	DB1579
137(136)	2B533-IIa	—,—,—: "Jammernd verlangen Junge" (w. Tessmer).	04 010 020	7692	DB1579
138	2B534-Ia	—,—,—: "Soll ich der Kunde glauben?" (w. Tessmer).	04 010	7693	DB1580

London, May 16, 1931; John Barbirolli and London Symphony

139	2B543-IIIa	Wagner, *Die Meistersinger von Nürnberg*, Act 3: "Selig wie die Sonne" (w. Schumann, Schorr, Parr, and Williams).	03	09	019	7682	EJ693
			023	047	049	AW289 D2002	ES761
140(144)	OB 544-II	—, *Die Walküre*, Act 1: "Winterstürme."	03	020	042		DA1227
141(103)	2B545-I	—, *Die Meistersinger von Nürnberg*, Act 3: "Morgenlich leuchtend."	03	017	050		DB1858

London, May 21, 1931; Robert Heger and London Symphony

| 142(143) | 2B556-II | Wagner, *Siegfried*, Act 2: "Wohin schleichst du" (w. Habich and Tessmer). | 04 | 010 | | 7696 | DB1583 |
| 143(142) | 2B557-Ia | —,—,—: "Haha! da hätte mein Lied" (w. Habich). | 04 | 010 | | 7696 | DB1583 |

London, May 23, 1931; Lawrance Collingwood and London Symphony

| 144(140) | OB564-II | Wagner, *Die Meistersinger von Nürnberg*, Act 1: "Am stillen Herd." | 03 | 019 | | | DA1227 |

London, May 29, 1932; Robert Heger and London Symphony

145(146)	2B2896-II	Wagner *Siegfried*, Act 3: "Heil dir, Sonne!" (w. Easton).	04	010	019	7762	DB1710
146(145)	2B2897-Ib	—,—,—: "O Siegfried! Siegfried!" (w. Easton).	04	010	019	7762	DB1710
147(148)	2B2898-II	—,—,—: "Wie Wunder tönt, was wonnig du singst" (w. Easton).	04	010	019	7763	DB1711
148(147)	2B2899-IIb	—,—,—: "O Weib, jetzt lösche den Brand" (w. Easton).	04	010	019	7763	DB1711

149	2B2901-Ib	—,—,—: "Dich lieb' ich" (w. Easton).	04	010	019	7764	DB1712
150	2B2902-Ib	—,—,—: "Ob jetzt ich dein?" (w. Easton).	04	010	019	7765	DB1713

Originally HMV issued 4 *Siegfried* albums:
Set I: D 1530-5 (no Melchior).
Set II: D 1690-4 (10 sides Melchior) = EJ 449-53.
Set III: DB 1578-83(6 sides Melchior) = 7691-6 (M 161 "Siegfried", Set 2).
Set IV: DB 1710-3 (6 sides Melchior) = 7262-5 (M 167 "Siegfried", Set 3), (AM 167:7766-9), (DM 167: 16590-3).
plus: D 1836-7 (3 sides Melchior) = EJ 485-6.
By drawing 4 sides (D 1533-4: Erda-Wotan Scene) from set I, and including all of sets II, III, IV plus 3 sides of D 1836-7, HMV later issued a 38-side (final side contains leitmotives) collated *Siegfried* set with Melchior as Siegfried throughout, and containing about two-thirds of the vocal score (DB 7252-70, automatic sequence only).

Bruno Walter and the Vienna Philharmonic

Vienna, June 20, 1935

(In addition to the excerpts indicated, the following 14 sides, nos. 151–164, are all included on 04 06 07 and 08.)

151(152)	2VH94-I	Wagner, *Die Walküre*, Act 1: "Wess' Herd dies auch sei."		DB2636
152(151)	2VH95-II	—,—,—: "Ein Fremder Mann?" (w. Lehmann).		DB2636
153(154)	2VH96-II	—,—,—: "Kühlende Labung gab mir der Quell" (w. Lehmann).		DB2637
154(153)	2VH97-I	—,—,—: "Einen Unseligen" (w. Lehmann).		DB2637
155(157)	2VH99-II	—,—,—: "Trägst du Sorge" (w. Lehmann und List)	020	DB2638
156(158)	2VH100-I	—,—,—: "Wunder und wilde Mähre" (w. Lehmann and List).	020	DB2639

Vienna, June 21, 1935

157(155)	2VH98-IIIa	Wagner, *Die Walküre*, Act 1: "Müd am	020	DB2638

		Herd" (w. Lehmann and List).					
158(156)	2VH101-I	—,—,—: "Die so leidig" (w. Lehmann and List).					DB2639
159	2VH103-II	—,—,—: "Mit Waffen wehrt sich" (w. List).					DB2640
160	2VH104-IIa	—,—,—: "Was gleisst dort hell" (w. Lehmann).					DB2641
161(162)	2VH106-Ia	—,—,—: "Dich selige Frau" (w. Lehmann).			013		DB2642
162(161)	2VH107-I	—,—,—: "Du bist der Lenz" (w. Lehmann).	058b		013		DB2642
163(164)	2VH108-I	—,—,—: "Wie dir die Stirn" (w. Lehmann).			013		DB2643

Vienna, June 22, 1935

164(163)	2VH109-I	Wagner, *Die Walküre*, Act 1: "Siegmund heiss'ich" (w. Lehmann).	013	048	DB2643

Complete Act 1 *Die Walküre*

78: HMV auto DB 8039-46; Victor M 298 8932-9, AM 298 8940-7, DM 298 16933-40; Italian Columbia GQX 10889-96.

165	2VH110-11	Wagner, *Die Walküre*, Act 2: "Raste nun hier" (w. Lehmann).	04 029	06	07	09	DB3724
166(167)	2VH111-I	—,—,—: "Hinweg! Hinweg!" (w. Lehmann).	04 029	06 028	07	09	DB3725
167(166)	2VH112-I	—,—,—: "Horch! O horch!" (w. Lehmann).	04 029	06 028	07	09	DB3725
168(169)	2VH113-IIa	—,—,—: "Zauberfest bezähmt ein Schlaf" (w. Lehmann).	04 029	06	07	09	DB3728
169(168)	2VH114-II	—,—,—: "Wehwalt! Wehwalt!" (w. Lehmann, List, Flesch, Jerger).	04 029	06	07	09	DB3728

THE VICTOR RECORDS

U.S., April 27, 1937; Ignace Strasfogel, piano

170(173) BS07871-1	Strauss, R., "Heimliche Aufforderung."	059	1853	DA1626
171(172) BS07873-2	a)Hildach, "Der Lenz"; b)Trunk, "Erster Strahl."		1882	
172(171) BS07874-2	a)Sjöberg, "Tonerna"; b)Grieg, "Jeg elsker dig."	059	1882	
172A BS07875	La Forge, "Into the Light."	059	unpubl.	
172B BS07876	Hagemann, "Do Not Go, My Love."		unpubl.	
173(170) BS07877-1	Strauss, R., a)"Zueignung"; b)"Cäcilie."	059	1853	DA1626
174(177) BS07878-1	a)Jordan, "Hører du?" b)Grieg, "En Svane."	059	2007	DA1648

U.S.A., April 11, 1938

175(176) BS07872-3	Strauss, R., "Traum durch die Dämmerung."	059	1980	
176(175) BS022422-1	Lembcke, "Majsang."		1980	
177(174) BS022425-1	Jordan, "Drick."	059	2007	DA1648
177A BS022421-1	Wolf, a) "Schon streckt ich aus im Bett"; b) "Ein Ständchen Euch zu bringen."	059	unpubl.	
177B BS022426-1	Brahms, "Auf dem Kirchhofe."	059	unpubl.	
177C BS022424-1	Trunk, a) "Mir träumte von einem Königskind"; b) "Stilles Lied II."	059	unpubl.	

Philadelphia, April 17, 1938; Eugene Ormandy and the Philadelphia Orchestra

178(180) 022322	Wagner, *Siegfried*, Act 1: "Nothung! Nothung!"	059 065	060	2035	DA1664
179(183) 022323-2/1	—, *Lohengrin*, Act 3: "Mein lieber Schwan!"	059	070	15213 DB3664	M516

180(178)	022324	—, *Die Walküre*, Act 1: "Winterstürme."	060	066 058c	2035	DA1664
181(182)	022325-1	—, *Parsifal*, Act 2: "Amfortas, die Wunde."	059	064 060(It.)	15212 DB3781	M516
182(181)	022326-1	—,—,—: "So rief die Gottesklage."	059	064 060(It.)	15212 DB3781	M516
183(179)	022327	—,—, Act 3: "Nur eine Waffe taugt."	059	060	15213 DB3664	M516

THE HMV RECORDS (continued)

Berlin, September 19, 1938; Bruno Seidler-Winkler and Berlin State Opera

184(185)	2RA 3256-II	Wagner, *Die Walküre*, Act 2: "Siegmund! sieh auf mich" (w.Fuchs).	04 07	06 09	DB3726
185(184)	2RA 3257-III	—,—,—: "In Walhalls Saal" (w.Fuchs).	04 07	06 09	DB3726
186(187)	2RA 3258-II	—,—,—: "Du sah'st der Walküre sehrenden Blick" (w. Fuchs).	04 07	06 09	DB3727
187(186)	2RA3259-III	—,—,—: "So jung und schön" (w. Fuchs).	04 07	06 09	DB3727

Nos 165–169 and 184–187 represent sides 12–20 in the complete HMV-Victor Act 2 *Die Walküre*. HMV DB 3719-28, auto DB 8737-46; Victor M 582 15506-15, DM 582 16058-67. LP: Nos 184–187 issued separately as HMV DB 4606-7.

THE VICTOR RECORDS (continued)

U.S., January 30, 1939; Bruno Reibold and Victor Orchestra

188(191)	BS031860-1	Schumann, "Er und sie" (w. Lehmann).	063	071	1906 DA1716 M560
189(190)	BS031861-2	—, a) "So wahr die Sonne"; b) "Unter'm Fenster" (w. Lehmann).	063	071	1907 DA 1717 M560
190(189)	BS031862-1	—, "Familien-Gemälde" (w. Lehmann).	063	071	1907 DA1717 M560
191(188)	BS031863-1	—, "Ich denke dein" (w. Lehmann).	063	071	1906 DA1716 M560

U.S., April 30, 1939; Eugene Ormandy and the Philadelphia Orchestra

192(193)	CS035834-2	Wagner, *Lohengrin*,	059	060		11-8676	DB3936	M749
(214)		Act 3: "In fernem	068			11-8683	DM979	M979
		Land."				17726	ED232	
192A	CS035836	—, *Wesendonk-Lieder*:	059	060				
		"Schmerzen."						
193(192)	CS035837	—,—: "Träume."	059	060			DB3936	
194(195)	CS035838-1	—, *Die Meistersinger*	059	060		17728	(DB3951)	M749
		von Nürnberg, Act 3:						
		"Morgenlich						
		leuchtend."						
195(194)	CS035839-2	—,—, Act 1: "Am	059	060		17728	(DB3951)	M749
		stillen Herd."						

THE HMV RECORDS (continued)

Copenhagen, September 15, 1939; Chorus and Herman D. Koppel, piano

196(197)	OCS1521-1	Rung, "Hvor Nilen	05		2191	M851
		vander."			DA5211	

Herman D. Koppel, piano

197(196)	OCS1522-1	Lange-Müller, "I	05		2191	M851
		Würzburg ringe."			DA5211	

Johan Hye-Knudsen and Orchestra of the Royal Opera House, Copenhagen

198(199)	OCS1523-1	Rygaard, "Flaget."	05		2192	M851
					DA5212	
199(198)	OCS1524-1	Rygaard,	05		2192	M851
		"Danmark."			DA5212	
200(201)	OCS1525-1	Hornemann,	05		2193	M851
		"Kongernes Konge."			DA5213	
201(200)	OCS1526-1	Kröyer, "Der er et	05		2193	M851
		yndigt Land."			DA5213	

Johan Hye-Knudsen and Studentersangforeningen's chorus on the occasion of the glee club's 100th anniversary

202(203)	2CS1527-1	Hartmann, "Flyv,	05		18078	DB5233
		Fugl, Flyv."				
203(202)	2CS1528-1	Lange-Müller, *Der*	05		18078	DB5223
		var engang:				
		"Serenade."				

THE VICTOR RECORDS (continued)

San Francisco, November 11, 1939; Edwin McArthur and San Francisco Opera Orchestra

204(205)	CS042231-4	Wagner, *Tristan und Isolde*, Act 2: "O sink' hernieder" (w. Flagstad).	059	062	063a	11-8674 15838 16238	DB6016 ED60 ND394	M644 M671 M979
205(204)	CS042232-1	—,—,—: "Wonnehehrstes Weben" (w. Flagstad).	059	062	063a	11-8674 15838 16238	DB6016 ED60 ND394	M644 M671 M979
206(207)	CS042233-1	—,—,—: "Doch der Tag" (w. Flagstad).	059 067	062	063a	11-8675 15839 16239	DB6017 ED61 ND395	M644 M671 M979
207(206)	CS042234-1	—,—,—: "Soll der Tag" (w. Flagstad).	059	062	063a	11-8675 15839 16239	DB6017 ED61 ND394	M644 M671 M979

AM 644: 15843-6; DM 644: 15960-3; DM 671: 18477-8; DM 979: 11-8679-82; JAS 98: ND 394-5.

San Francisco, November 12, 1939; Edwin McArthur and San Francisco Opera Orchestra

208(209)	PCS042244-	Wagner, *Götterdämmerung*, Prologue: "Lass'ich Liebste" (w. Flagstad).	063	17729 (DB5885)	ED418 M749
209(208)	PCS42245-	—,—,—: "Zu neuen Taten" (w. Flagstad).	063	17729 (DB5885)	ED418 M749

U.S., November 22, 1940; Edwin McArthur and the RCA Victor Symphony Orchestra

210(213)	CS057525-1	Wagner, *Siegfried*, Act 1: "Ho-ho! Schmiede, mein Hammer."	059 060	11-8678 11-8680 17725 17777 17782 DM755	DM979 ED359 M749 M755 M979
211(212)	CS057526-1	—, *Tannhäuser*, Act 3: "Inbrunst im Herzen."	059 060	11-8677 11-8682 17727	DM979 M749 M979
212(211)	CS057527-1	—,—,—: "Da sah ich ihn."	059 060	11-8677 11-8681 17727	DM979 M749 M979
213(210)	CS057528-1	—, *Der fliegende Holländer*, Act 1: "Mit Gewitter und Sturm" (w. chorus).	060	11-8678 11-8679 17725	DM979 ED359 M749 M979
214(192)	CS057529-2	—, *Tannhäuser*, Act 1: "Dir töne Lob!"	059 060	11-8676 11-8683 17726	DM979 ED232 M749 M979
214A	CS057529-1A	—,—,—; "Dir töne Lob!"	069	unpubl.	

U.S., November 23, 1940; Edwin McArthur and the RCA Victor Symphony Orchestra

215(216)	CS057530-2A	Wagner, *Lohengrin*, Act 3: "Das süsse Lied verhallt" (w. Flagstad).	063a	061 062	11-8159 11-8161	DM897 M897
216(215)	CS057531-1	—,—,—: "Da wollte ich" (w. Flagstad).	063a 058c	061 062	11-8159 11-8162	DM897 M897
217(218)	CS057532-1	—,—,—: "Wär'das Geheimnis" (w. Flagstad).	063a 058c	061 062	11-8160 11-8162	DM897 M897
218(217)	CS057533-2A	—,—,—: "Hilf Gott, was muss ich hören" (w. Flagstad).	063a	061 062	11-8160 11-8161	DM897 M897

U.S., November 23, 1940; Edwin McArthur and the RCA Victor Symphony Orchestra

219(220)	CS057534-1A	Wagner, *Parsifal*, Act 2: "Dies Alles hab'ich nun geträumt" (w. Flagstad).	063a	061 063	17774 17778	17782 AM755	DM755 M755
220(219)	CS057535-2	—,—,—: "Nur Weinen war sie" (w. Flagstad).	063a	061 063	17774 17779	17783 AM755	DM755 M755
221(222)	CS057536-3	—,—,—: "Die Mutter, die Mutter konnt'" (w. Flagstad).	063a	061 063	17775 17780	17784 AM755	DM755 M755

U.S., November 24, 1940; Edwin McArthur and the RCA Victor Symphony Orchestra

222(221)	CS057537-1	Wagner, *Parsifal*, Act 2: "Es starrt der Blick" (w. Flagstad).	063a 058c	061 063	17775 17781	17785 AM755	DM755 M755
223	CS057539-1	—,—,—: "Den ich ersehnt" (w. Flagstad).	063a	061 063	17776 17779	17784 AM755	DM755 M755
224	CS057540-1	—,—,—: ". . . sein Fluch—ha! (w. Flagstad and Dilworth).	063a	061 063	17777 17780	17783 AM755	DM755 M755

U.S., May 16, 1941; Ignace Strasfogel, piano

| 225(226) | BS065619-1 | Heise, "Skovensomhed." | 05 | 2189 | M851 |
| 226(225) | BS065620-2 | a) Henriques, "Vaaren er kommett"; b) Heise, *Twelfth Night*: | 05 | 2189 | M851 |

227(229)	BS065621-1	"Dengang jeg var kun saa stor som saa." a) Henneberg, "Flyg mina tanker"; b) Körling, "Hvita rosor."		2190	M851
228(230)	BS065622-1	a) Hannikainen, "Stille mit Hjerte"; b) Grieg, "Til Norge."		2188	M851
229(227)	BS065623-2	Sibelius, "Svarta rosor."	059	2190	M851
230(228)	BS065624-1	Grieg, "Eros."	059	2188	M851

THE COLUMBIA RECORDS

New York, April 10, 1942; Erich Leinsdorf and the Columbia Orchestra

231A	XC032698	Wagner, *Lohengrin*, Act 1: "Nun sei bedankt" (w. Janssen).	073	unpubl.
231B	???	—,—,—: "Mein Held! mein Retter!" (w. Varnay).	073	unpubl.

New York, April 10, 1942; Ignace Strasfogel, piano

231(232)	CO32699-2	Lange-Müller, *Renaissance*: "Serenade" (w. chorus).	073	17361D-4 X233
232(231)	CO32700-1	—, a) "Skin ud, du klare Solskin"; b) "Kornmodsglansen."	073	17361D-3 X233
233(234)	CO32701	Schubert, "Leise flehen meine Lieder" (Ständchen).	073	17509D
234(233)	CO32702	Schubert, "Dem Unendlichen."	073	17509D
235(236)	CO32703-1	Andersen, S., a) "Der flyver saa mange Fugle"; b) "Nu brister i alle de Kløfter."	073	17360-2 X233
236(235)	CO32704-1	Heise, a) "Husker du i Høst" (Lille Karen); b) "Vildt flyver Høg."	073	17360-1 X233
237(238)	CO32705-1	Branson, "There Shall Be Music."		17353D
238(237)	CO32706-1	a) Rogers, "The Star"; b) Craxton, "Come You, Merry."		17353D

New York, April 14, 1942; Erich Leinsdorf and the Columbia Opera Orchestra

239(240)	XCO32711	Wagner, *Rienzi*, Act 5: "Allmächt'ger Vater."	073	073a	15648 71388D	264747 LOX571
240(239)	XCO32712	—, *Tristan und Isolde*, 072 Act 2: "O König, das kann ich dir."			15648 71388D	264747 LOX571

New York, April 15, 1942; Erich Leinsdorf and the Columbia Opera Orchestra

241	XCO32713-1	Wagner, *Tristan* *und Isolde*, Act 3: "Die alte Weise" (w. Janssen).	072		71595D 71601D	M550 MM550
242(245)	XCO32714-1	—,—,—: "Nun bist du daheim" (w. Janssen).	072		71596D 71602D	M550 MM550
243(244)	XCO32715	Verdi, *Otello*, Act 3: "Dio! mi potevi."	073	074	71389D	264748
244(243)	XCO32716	—,—, Act 4: "Niun mi tema."	073	074	71389D	264748

Buenos Aires, August 31, 1943; Juan Emilio Martino and the Colon Opera House Orchestra

244A	C13085	Verdi, *Otello*, Act 2: "Ora e per sempre."	011	073	unpubl.
244B	C13086	—,—, Act 1: "Si pel ciel" (w. Janssen).	011	073	unpubl.
244C	C13090	Leoncavallo, *Pagliacci*, "No, pagliaccio non son."			unpubl.
244D	C13091	—,—: "Vesti la giubba."			unpubl.
244E	C13092	Puccini, *Tosca*, Act 3: "E lucevan le stelle".			Arg. Col.
244F	C13093	—,—, Act 1: "Recondita armonia."			Arg. Col.

(On August 16 and 21 apparently unsuccessful takes of "Che gelida manina," "O paradis," "No, pagliaccio non son," and "E lucevan le stelle" had been made, Ferrucio Calusio conducting.)

Buenos Aires, September 6, 1943; Roberto Kinsky and the Colon Opera House Orchestra

245(242)	C13103-1	Wagner, *Tristan* *und Isolde*, Act 3: "Wie schwand mir seine Ahnung?" (w. Janssen).	072		71596D 71603D	M550 MM550

246(247)	C13104-1	—,—,—: "Isolde kommt."	072	71597D 71604D	M550 MM550
247(246)	C13105-1	—,—,—: "Noch ist kein Schiff" (w. Janssen).	072	71597D 71604D	M550 MM550
248(249)	C13106-1	—,—,—: "Wie vom Herz zum Hirn" (w. Janssen).	072	71598D 71603D	M550 MM550
249(248)	C13107	—,—,—: "O Wonne! Nein!" (w. Janssen).	072	71598D 71602D	M550 MM550

Buenos Aires, September 9, 1943; Roberto Kinsky and the Colon Opera House Orchestra

| 250(251) | C13108-8 | Wagner, *Tristan und Isolde*, Act 3: "Und Kurwenal, wie, du säh'st sie nicht?" (w. Janssen). | 072 | 71599D 71601D | M550 MM550 |
| 251(250) | C13116-1 | —,—,—: "O diese Sonne!" (w. anonymous soprano). | 072 | 71599D 71600D | M550 MM550 |

THE VICTOR RECORDS (continued)

Hollywood, December 27, 1944; film arrangements from *Thrill of a Romance* with orchestra

252(255)	D4RB-496-3	Schubert, "Leise flehen meine Lieder" ("Ständchen") (English).	076	10-1148	M990
253(254)	D4RB-497-4	Grieg, "Jeg elsker dig" (Danish and English).	076	10-1147 B9446	M990
254(253)	D4RB-498-4	Hubay, "Lonely Night."	076	10-1147	M990

Hollywood, December 30, 1944; film arrangements from *Thrill of a Romance* with orchestra

255(252)	D4RB-523-4	Anon., "Vive l'amour" (English) (w. chorus).	076	10-1148	M990
256(257)	D4RB-524-4	Fain, "Please Don't Say No" (w. chorus).	076	10-1149 B9446	EC137 M990
257(256)	D4RB-525-3a	Herbert, "I Want What I Want."	076	10-1149 EC 137	M990

U.S., September 6, 1945; orchestra conducted by Charles Previn ("operatic sequences" based on the Liszt Liebestraum, the Mendelssohn Violin Concerto, and other themes from the motion picture *Two Sisters from Boston*)

258(259)	D5RB-1121- 1M	*Marie Antoinette*, I (w. Nadine Connor and chorus).	076	10-1222 10-1226 DM1056	M1056 X7328
259(258)	D5RB-1122- 1Hi&1CM	*Marie Antoinette*, II (w. Nadine Connor and chorus).	076	10-1222 10-1226 DM1056	M1056 X7328
260(261)	D5RB-1123- 1M	*My Country*, I (w. chorus).	076	10-1221 10-1224	DM1056 M1056
261(260)	D5RB-1124- 1M	*My Country*, II (w. chorus).	076	10-1221 10-1225	DM1056 M1056

Hollywood (Lotus Club), January 29, 1946; orchestra conducted by Fausto Cleva

261A	D6RC-5042-2	Leoncavallo, *Pagliacci*, "Vesti la giubba."	059	unpubl.
261B	D6RC-5043-2	—,—, "No! Pagliaccio non son."	059	unpubl.

Hollywood (Lotus Club), January 30, 1946; orchestra conducted by Jay Blackton

262(264)	D6RB-1633- 1M	Robinson, "The House I Live In" (w. chorus).	076	10-1223 10-1225 10-1227	DM1056 M1056 X7329
263(262)	D6RB-1634	d'Hardelot, "Because."	076	10-1227	
264(262)	D6RB-1635- IP	Romberg, *Student Prince*: "Serenade" (w. chorus).	076	10-1223 10-1224	DM1056 M1056 X7329
264A	D6RB-1636	del Riego, "Homing."		unpubl.	

THE M-G-M RECORDS

Culver City, California; M-G-M Studio Orchestra conducted by Georgie Stoll (265–288) and Giacomo Spadoni (290–293). 269 and 294 include chorus. 289 is accompanied by Georgie Stoll, piano, Lou Raderman, violin, and Albert Sendry, organ. 277 and 294 are from the motion picture *Luxury Liner*.

October 12, 1946

265	46-S-3001	Hildach, "Der Lenz" (English).	077	
266(267)	46-S-3002	Youmans, "Without a Song."		112 30005
267(266)	46-S-3003	Geehl, "For You Alone."		112 30005

December 31, 1946

268(271)	46-S-3000	Lehár, *Das Land des Lächelns*: "Dein ist mein ganzes Herz" (English).	077	3003 30014

269(270)	46-S-3021	Andersen, F., "I det Frie."			30006
270(269)	46-S-3022	Bizet, "Agnus Dei."			30006
271(268)	46-S-3023	Porter, "Easy to Love."		3003	30014

June 16, 1947

272(273)	47-S-3118	Gruber, "Stille Nacht" (English).	078		30036
273(272)	47-S-3119	Adam, "Cantique de Noël" (English).	078		30036
274(275)	47-S-3120	Nevin, "The Rosary."	078	6015	30053
275(274)	47-S-3121	Bach-Gounod, "Ave Maria."	078	6015	30053

June 23, 1947

276(279)	47-S-3122	Heuberger, "The Kiss in Your Eyes."	077	K30471B	30030
277(294)	47-S-3123	Rotter, "Spring Came Back to Vienna."		MGM8872	30136
278	47-S-3124	Anon., "Why Is It All a Dream."		unpubl.	
279(276)	47-S-3125	Strauss, J., "Kaiserwalzer" (English).	077	K30471A	30030

December 16, 1947

280(283)	47-S-3339	de Curtis, "Torna a Surriento."		MGM26	30113
281(282)	47-S-3340	Kern, "The Song Is You."		MGM26	30112
282(281)	47-S-3341	Stravinsky, "Summer Moon."		MGM26	30112
283(280)	47-S-3342	Leoncavallo, "Mattinata."		MGM26	30113
284	47-S-3343	Adams, "The Holy City."		unpubl.	

December 18, 1947

285	47-S-3346	Anon., "The Last Chord."		unpubl.	
286(289)	47-S-3347	Schubert, "Who Is Sylvia?"		MGM26	30115
287(288)	47-S-3348	de Koven, *Robin Hood*: "O Promise Me."		MGM26	30114
288(287)	47-S-3349	Bond, "I Love You Truly."		MGM26	30114

| 289(286) | 47-S-3350 | Anon., "All mein Gedanken" ("Minnelied") (English). | | | MGM26 | 30115 |

December 26, 1947

290(291)	47-S-3381	Puccini, *Tosca*, Act 1: "Recondita armonia."	075	077	9133 K30469B	30308
291(290)	47-S-3382	—,—, Act 3: "E lucevan le stelle."	075	077	9133 K30469A	30308
292(293)	47-S-3383	Leoncavallo, *I pagliacci*: "Vesti la giubba."		077	9063 K30470A	30264
293(292)	47-S-3384	—,—: "No, pagliaccio non son!"		077	9063 K30470B	30264
294(277)	47-S-3385	Anon., "Helan går" (Swedish drinking song) (Swedish and English).				30136

THE DECCA RECORDS

New York, April 27, 1950

295	76229	Romberg, *Student Prince*: "Golden Days" (w. Lee Sweetland).	079	AU771	40166
296(299)	76230	—,—: "Drinking Song."	079	AU771	40167
297	76235	—,—: "Finale."	079	AU771	40165

New York, April 28, 1950

| 298 | 76232 | Romberg, *Student Prince*: "Deep in My Heart" (w. Jane Wilson). | 079 | AU771 | 40168 |

New York, April 29, 1950

| 299(296) | 76233 | Romberg, *Student Prince*: "Serenade." | 079 | AU771 | 40167 |

LP-issues: 10 inch US Decca 7008, GB Decca 8626.
          12 inch US Decca 8362, GB Decca AH8.
The 12-inch versions are one-sided (backed with a non-Melchior *Vagabond King*).

U.S., June 13, 1954

300(301)	MG3723	Lombardo-Loeb, *Arabian Nights*: "Hail to the Sultan."	080
301(300)	MG3724	—,—: a) "A Long Ago Love"; b) "Marry the One You Love."	080

Section II. LP Transfers of 78 RPM Records

01 *Lauritz Melchior: The First Recordings, Baritone 1913–15, Early Tenor 1920–21— Melchior Anthology Vol. 1.*—Danacord DACO 115-6 (2) (1983). DACOCD 311–312 (1987).
1–46

02 *Lauritz Melchior: Red Polydors and Blue Parlophones 1923–1926—Melchior Anthology Vol. 2.* Danacord DACO 117-8 (2) (1984). DACOCD 313–314 (1987).
55–76, 78–79, 81–93

03 *Lauritz Melchior: Electrola and His Master's Voice 1928–1931—Melchior Anthology Vol. 3.* Danacord DACO 119–20 (2) (1985). DACOCD 315–316 (1987).
94–101, 112–119, 123–124, 139–141, 144

04 *Lauritz Melchior: The Legendary Interpretations 1927–1938, Siegmund—Siegfried— Melchior Anthology Vol. 4.* Danacord DACO 171–6 (6) (1986) (includes additional stereo Act 1 *Walküre* from 70th birthday concert—see x33).
102–111, 120–122, 135–138, 142–143, 145–169, 184–187
(For the complete Danacord Compact Disc Melchior Anthology, the Vienna-Berlin *Die Walküre* Acts 1 and 2 are issued as DACOCD 317–318, the *Siegfried* scenes and the 70th Birthday concert as DACOCD 319–320–321 [1987].)

05 *Melchior and Flagstad in Copenhagen.* Danacord DACO 168 (1986). DACOCD 325 (1987).
196–203, 225–226

06 *Die Walküre Acts 1 and 2*—Unvergänglich-Unvergessen Folge 128. Electrola WCLP 734–6 E80686-8 (3) (1962).
151–169, 184–187

07 *The Art of Bruno Walter—Die Walküre Acts 1 and 2.* Angel EAC 57039-52 (Japan) (*Walküre* on discs 12-4) (14) (1984).
151–169, 184–187

08 *Die Walküre Act 1.* RCA Victor LVT 1003 (Vault Treasures) (1956) and LCT 1033; EMI COLH 133 (Great Recordings of the Century) (1963); FALP 50013; Electrola Dacapo 049-03023 (1976); 45RPM RCA WCT 58.
151–164

09 *Les Introuvables du Chant Wagnerien.* HMV 2902123 (12) (1985).
100–101, 118–119, 123, 127, 139, 165–169, 184–187

010 *Siegfried Scenes*—Unvergänglich—Unvergessen Folge 181. Electrola WCLP 803-4 E80744-5 (2) (1963).
103–110, 120–122, 135–138, 142–143, 145–150

011 *Lauritz Melchior 50th Anniversary 1911–1961.* American Stereophonic Corporation ASCO Records LP 121 (2) (1961) (includes an *Esultate* [May 1960] and *Ujuraks*

Udfart from Børresens opera *Kaddara* (1941).
1–5, 17, 20–22, 34, 42–46, 56–57, 66–67, 70, 83–87, 89, 128–130, 244A, 244B

012 *Berlin Damals (III) Lauritz Melchior singt Richard Wagner.* Heliodor 2548 749 (1971).
56–66, 68–69, 91

013 *Das Lauritz Melchior Album—Der Wagner-Tenor des Jahrhunderts.* Electrola Dacapo
1C-147-01259/60 (2) (1971).
83, 98–101, 103–105, 110–114, 116, 118–119, 124–130, 132–133, 161–164

014 *Lauritz Melchior.* Pearl GEMM 228-9(2) (1981) (includes *Walküre* "Raste nun hier"
to end of Act 2 with Lehmann, Flagstad, conductor: Reiner, San Francisco
1936).
56–70, 72–76, 81–82, 94, 98, 128–131, 133

015 *Lauritz Melchior.* Rococo 5318 (1970).
10, 12, 31, 40, 45–46, 64, 68–69, 88–91, 94–95

016 *Lauritz Melchior I: Lebendige Vergangenheit.* Preiser LV 11.
67, 70, 75–76, 88, 91, 112–113, 128–133

017 *Lauritz Melchior II: Lebendige Vergangenheit.* Preiser LV 124.
83–87, 89, 99, 114–117, 123, 141

018 *Lauritz Melchior III: Lebendige Vergangenheit.* Preiser LV 226.
55, 72–74, 78b, 79b, 81–82, 90–94, 96–97, 97A, 97B, 98

019 *Wagner on Record 1926–42* HMV HLM 7281-7/HMV RLS 7711 (7) (1983)
98, 100–103, 106–107, 109–110, 112–119, 123, 126–127, 132, 134, 139, 144–150

020 *Top Classics 9048.*
103, 108–109, 116–117, 122, 136–137, 140, 155–157

021 *Great Recordings of the Century* (Les Gravures Illustres). EMI COLH 105 (1959).
Scenes from *Walküre* and *Götterdämmerung* with Leider and Schorr.
124–126

022 *Great Recordings of the Century* (Les Gravures Illustres). EMI COLH 132 (1963);
FALP 50025. Scenes and arias with Leider.
100–101, 118–119, 123, 127

023 *Great Recordings of the Century* (Les Gravures Illustres). EMI COLH 137 (1963);
FALP 50023. Schorr, scenes from *Meistersinger.*
134, 139

024 *The Record of Singing Vol. 2* (1914–1925). HMV HLM 7181-93/HMV RLS 743
(13) (1983).
31, 34, 72

025 *The Record of Singing Vol. 3* (1926–1939). HMV EX 290169-3 (13) (1985).
131

026 *Rudolf Bockelmann: Lebendige Vergangenheit.* Preiser LV 9.
110–111

027 *Frida Leider: Lebendige Vergangenheit.* Preiser LV 30.
100–101, 118–119

028 *Das Lotte Lehmann Album.* Electrola Dacapo 1C147-29 116/117 (2) (1971).
Die Goldene Stimme—Lotte Lehmann. Electrola E73396.
166–167

029 *Bruno Walter Conducts Wagner.* Turnabout THS 65163 (1980).
165–169

030 *Friedrich Schorr.* HMV HQM 1243 (1971).
114–115

031 *A Tribute to Dr. Frieder Weissmann.* Ritornello R1001-02 (2) (1983).
83–87

032 *Sänger auf den Grünen Hügel.* HMV 181-30 669-78 (10) (1978).
73–74, 110, 114–115, 127

033 *100 Jahre Parsifal.* Electrola Dacapo 1C 137-78 174-5 (2) (1983).
73–74

034 *Die Alten Linden Oper.* DGG 19180 (1959).
67

035 *Grosse Sänger der Bayreuth 1900–1930.* DGG 2721 109 (2563 618-9) (2) (1976).
60–63

036 *Grosse Sänger der Bayreuth 1930–1944.* DGG 2721 110 (2563 620-1) (2) (1976).
56–57

037 *100 Years of Bayreuth.* DGG 2721 115 (2) (1976).
58–59, 91

038 *Die Hamburgische Staatsoper—*DGG 2721 176 (2) (1979).
64

039 *Berlin damals—Berliner Oper I.* DGG 2700 708 (2548 738-9).
60, 66–67

040 100 Jahre Bayreuther Festspiele—22 weltberühmte Wagner-Interpreten Electrola
Dacapo 1C 049-30 679.
126

041 DGG 2563 630.
58–59

042 *Stätte der Tradition—Festspielhaus Bayreuth II.* Electrola E73388.
140

043 *Götterdämmerung—Querschnitt.* Electrola WCLP 712 E80655 (1962).
124–126

044 *Die Goldene Stimme: Frida Leider.* Electrola WCLP 799 E83386 (1963).
100–101

045 *Great Voices of the Century.* Seraphim 60113 (1970).
100

046 *The HMV Treasury: The Grand Tradition.* HLM 7026.
101

047 *Glorious John: Sir John Barbirolli.* HMV ALP 2641-2 (2) (1970).
139

048 *A Treasury of Immortal Performances—Collector's Issue.* RCA LCT 1001; 45RPM
WCT 2.
164

049 *A Treasury of Immortal Performances—Collector's Issue.* RCA Victor LCT 1003
45RPM WCT 4.
139

050 45RPM HMV 7P 350.
103, 141

051 *Top Artist Platters.* TAP 322.
71

052 *Potpourri No. 2: Golden Age of Opera.* EJS 142 (1958).
128–129

053 *Potpourri No. 14: Golden Age of Opera.* EJS 223 (1961).
9

054 *Lauritz Melchior 75th Birthday: Golden Age of Opera.* EJS 322 (1965).
9, 23, 36, 60–61, 63, 71

055 *Lauritz Melchior Memorial Album 3*. Unique Opera Records UORC 160 (1973).
1–9, 15–18, 19–22

056 *Lauritz Melchior Memorial Album 4*. Unique Opera Records UORC 165 (1973).
13, 14, 23–35, 37–46

057 *Danske Klassikere: 100 Years of Recorded Sound 1877–1977*. IFPI K (2) (1977) (plus 1937 live Foster: "Se det summer af Sol").
34

058 *Les Introuvables du Chant Verdien*. HMV 2910753 (8) (1987).
128

058a *Great Tenors of the World: The HMV Treasury*. HLM 7004.
112–113

058b *75 Jahre EMI: Die Stimmes seines Herrn—47 berühmte Solisten, Orchester und Dirigenten*. Electrola 1C 147-30 636 (2).
162

058c *Wagner: Ses Grands Interprètes*. RCA 630752 ARTISTIQUE.
180, 216, 217, 222 (not complete)

058d *Lauritz Melchior Chanté Siegfried*. Pathé Marconi 2C 051–43389.
103–107, 109–111, 114–115, 134–136

059 *Lauritz Melchior, Heldentenor of the Century*. RCA CRM3-0308 (3) (1973) (includes Toscanini February 22, 1941, *Walküre* and *Götterdämmerung* duet scenes with Traubel, the first reduced to start at "Winterstürme," the second omitting Rhine Journey with spliced-in concert ending).
170, 172, 172A, 173–175, 177, 177A, 177B, 177C, 178–179, 181–183, 192 192A, 193–195, 204–207, 210–212, 214, 229, 230, 261A, 261B

060 *Lauritz Melchior/Wagner: Immortal Performances*. Victrola VIC-1500 (1970); 731067 Victor GB; "Il mio Wagner" VL47217 Italy (plus 181-182).
178, 180, 183, 192–195, 210–214

061 *A Treasury of Immortal Performances—Collector's Issue*. RCA Victor LCT 1105; HMV ALP 1276; 45RPM WCT 1105.
215–218, 219–224

062 *A Treasury of Immortal Performances*. RCA Victor LM 2618; RB 6517 GB; HR 208 Germany.
204–207, 215–218

063 *A Treasury of Immortal Performances*. RCA Victor LM 2763; RB 6604 GB; HR 219 Germany.
188–191, 208–209, 219–224

063a *Kirsten Flagstad and Lauritz Melchior, The Incomparable Wagnerian Duo*. RCA Victor VIC-1681.
204–207, 215–218, 219–224

064 *Immortal Performances, Unforgettable Voices*. Victrola VIC-1455 (1969).
181–182

065 RCA Victor LM 2631 (1964); RB 6515 GB; HR 212 Germany.
178

066 *50 Years of Great Operatic Singing*. RCA Victor LM 2372-C (1963); HMV CLSP 503; RB 16198 GB.
180

067 RCA Victor LM 6171.
206

068 RCA Victor LM 20132.
192

069 *MET: 100 Years, 100 Singers.* RCA Victor CRM8-5177 8LPs (1984).
214A

070 *Five Treasured Recordings*—Ormandy/Phil. RCA Victor SP-33-555 (1969).
179

071 *Schumann: Lotte Lehmann*—*Lauritz Melchior.* Electrola 430661
188–191

072 *Legendary Performances.* Columbia Odyssey 32 16 0145.
240–242, 245–251

073 *Legendary Performances: Heldentenor of the Century*—*Lauritz Melchior.* Columbia Odyssey Y31740 (1972). Germany: Die historische Reihe.
231A, 231B, 231–236, 239, 243, 244, 244A, 244B

073a *Legendaryt Performances: Fabulous Forties at the Met.* Columbia Odyssey 32160304.
239

074 *Musical Gems.* Philips 45RPM SBF 288.
243, 244

075 *Lauritz Melchior Memorial.* Unique Opera Records UORC 158 (1973).
290, 291

076 *The Lighter Side of Lauritz Melchior.* RCA Camden CAL-424 (1958).
252–264

077 *Lauritz Melchior Recital.* M-G-M E109
265, 268, 276, 279, 290–293

078 *Lauritz Melchior.* M-G-M 45RPM: X1056 (US); EP-577 (GB).
272–275

079 *Lauritz Melchior in The Student Prince.* Decca 10 inch 7008 (US), 8626 (GB); 12 inch 8362 (US), AH8 (GB).
295 (only on 12 inch), 296–299

080 *Lauritz Melchior in Arabian Nights.* Decca DL 9013 (1954).
300, 301

081 *Lauritz Melchior Chante Wagner.* Pathé-Marconi 322 2.C 051-43389.
103–105, 106–107, 108–109, 110–111, 114–115, 124–126

Section III. Wagner in "Live Performance"

A significant portion of the recordings listed in this section were issued by the late Edward J. Smith, onetime music critic for the *Brooklyn Eagle*, whose labels included The Golden Age of Opera (EJS), Das Goldene Ära Richard Wagners (GAW), Unique Opera Records Corporation (UORC), A.N.N.A. Record Company (ANNA), American Stereophonic Corporation (ASCO), Top Artist Platters (TAP), and Harvest. Also interrelated are these labels: Bruno Walter Society, Educational Media, Discocorp (all with the prefix RR), and I Grandi Interpreti (IGI).

Tannhäuser

x1 January 18, 1936, Metropolitan, w. Flagstad, Halstead, Fleischer; Tibbett, List: Bodanzky.   EJS 109 (3)

x2 January 4, 1941, Metropolitan, w. Flagstad, Thorborg, Stellmann; Janssen, List: Leinsdorf.   GAW 300 (3)

x3 December 19, 1942, Metropolitan, w. Traubel, Thorborg, Stellman; Janssen, Kipnis: Szell.   Raritas OPR 400 (3)
Melodram 306 (3)

x4 February 5, 1944, Metropolitan, w. Varnay,   UORC 168 (3)
Lawrence; Stellman; Huehn, Kipnis: Breisach.

x5 Excerpts, Acts 2 and 3. January 12, 1935,   EJS 504D (1 side)
Metropolitan, w. Müller; Bonelli: Bodanzky.

x6 Excerpts, December 19, 1942, Metropolitan, w.   EJS 544
Traubel; Janssen, Kipnis: Szell. Act 2: Beginning to
Entrance of Guests; "Dir, Göttin der Liebe" to end of
act; Act 3: "Allmächt'ge Jungfrau!" to end of act.

x7 Excerpts, February 5, 1944, Metropolitan, w.   UORC 158
Lawrence; Huehn: Breisach. Act 3: "Inbrunst in
Herzen" to end of act.

Lohengrin

x8 January 27, 1940, Metropolitan, w. Rethberg,   EJS 135 (3)
Thorborg; Huehn, List: Leinsdorf.

x9 January 2, 1943, Metropolitan, w. Varnay, Thorborg;   UORC 170 (3)
Sved, Cordon: Leinsdorf.   Melodram ?

x10 January 25, 1947, Metropolitan, w. Traubel, Harshaw;   Cetra LO 24 (4)
Janssen, Ernster: Busch.

x11 January 7, 1950, Metropolitan, w. Traubel, Varnay;   Danacord 111-3
Janssen, Ernster: Stiedry. (LM's next-to-last   DCOCD 322-324
Metropolitan performance)   DS-VOA 1493-1506

x12 Excerpts, March 24, 1934, Metropolitan, w. Rethberg,   EJS 504 (3 sides)
Olszewska; Schützendorf, Hofmann: Bodanzky.

x13 Act 2, February 19, 1938, Metropolitan, w. Flagstad,   UORC 194
Branzell; Huehn, Hofmann: Abravanel.

x14 Excerpts, January 7, 1950, Metropolitan, w. Traubel,   UORC 158
Varnay; Stiedry. Act 3: "In fernem Land" to end.

x15 Excerpts, August 26, 1948, Hollywood Bowl, w.   VOCE 94
Traubel: Ormandy. Act 3: "Das süsse Lied verhallt";
"In fernem Land."

Tristan und Isolde

x16 March 9, 1935, Metropolitan, w. Flagstad, Branzell;   GAW 301 (3)
Schorr, Hofmann: Bodanzky.

x17 May–June 1936, Covent Garden, w. Flagstad, Kalter;   EJS 465 (4)
Janssen, List: Reiner.   Educ. Media RR-471

x18 January 2, 1937, Metropolitan, w. Flagstad, Thorborg;   EJS 157 (3)
Huehn, Hofmann: Bodanzky.

x19 June 18 and 22, 1937, Covent Garden, w. Flagstad,   ANNA 1050 (3)
Klose (Acts 1 and 2), Branzell (Act 3); Janssen (Acts 1   DISCOCORP RR-
and 2), Schoeffler (Act 3), Nilsson: Beecham.   223
(DISCOCORP includes both second acts on 4 records;   Melodram CD 37029
ANNA 1051 contains alternate second act, and UORC
302 alternate first act.)

x20 March 23, 1940, Metropolitan, w. Flagstad, Thorborg;   UORC 182 (3)
Huehn, List: Leinsdorf.

x21 February 8, 1941, Metropolitan, w. Flagstad,   MET 3
Thorborg; Huehn, Kipnis: Leinsdorf.   Melodram 301 (4)

x22 Excerpts, March 3 and 11, 1933, w. Leider,   EJS 499 (2)
Olszewska; Schorr (11), Schützendorf (3), Hofmann:
Bodanzky.

x23 Excerpts, January 6, 1934, w. Kappel, Doe; Schorr,   EJS 502
Hofmann: Bodanzky.

x24 Excerpt, June 18, 1937, Covent Garden, w. Flagstad,   EJS 258
Klose; Janssen: Beecham. Act 1: "Liess ich das Steuer."

x25 Excerpts, February 6, 1943, Metropolitan, w. Traubel,   EJS 556 (2)
Thorborg; Huehn, Kipnis: Leinsdorf. Act 1: "Wer
wagt mir zu höhnen" to end of scene 3, and from
"Begehrt, Herrin" to end of act. Act 2: "Isolde! Tristan!
Geliebter!" to end of act. Act 3: "Bist du nun todt" to
end.

x26 Excerpt, August 26, 1948, Hollywood Bowl, w.   VOCE 94
Traubel: Ormandy. Act 2: "O sink hernieder."

x27 Excerpt, February 8, 1941, Metropolitan, w. Kipnis: ACANTA 40 23 502
Leinsdorf. Act 2: "Tatest du's wirklich?"   (Wagner sein Werk–
     19 LP)

x28 Excerpt, March 23, 1940, Metropolitan, w. Flagstad: UORC 159
Leinsdorf. Act 2: "Isolde! Tristan! Geliebter!"

Die Walküre
(see also 04, 06, 07, and 08)

x29 February 17, 1940, Metropolitan, w. Lawrence,   UORC 186 (4)
Flagstad, Branzell; Huehn, List: Leinsdorf.

x30 March 30, 1940, Metropolitan (Boston), w. Lehmann,   EJS 178 (4)
Lawrence, Thorborg; Schorr, List: Leinsdorf.

x31 March 30, 1946, Metropolitan, w. Varnay, Traubel,   Dept. of State
Thorborg; Berglund, List: Breisach.   QND6MM 9317-32

x32 Act 2, November 13, 1936, San Francisco, w.   EJS 234
Lehmann, Flagstad; Meisle; Schorr, List: Reiner.   RR 426
(Excerpt: "Raste nun hier" to end on 014.)

x33 Act 1, March 31, 1960, Copenhagen, w. Dorothy   EJS 410
Larsen; Mogens Wedel: Thomas Jensen and the   (see also 04)
Danish Radio Symphony Orchestra. LM 70th Birthday
Concert.

x34 Excerpts, December 6, 1941, Metropolitan, w.   EJS 543
Varnay, Traubel; Schorr: Leinsdorf. Act 1: "Ein Schwert
verhiess mir" to end of act. Act 2: Beginning to end
of Brünnhilde's Battlecry. "Todesverkündigungs-scene."
Act 3: "Im festen Schlaf" to end.

x35 Excerpt, December 6, 1941, Metropolitan, w. Varnay;   EJS 451
Kipnis: Leinsdorf. Act 1: "Heilig ist mein Herd" to
end of scene 2.

x36 Excerpt, February 27, 1943, Metropolitan, w.   UORC 158
Leinsdorf. Act 1: "Ein Schwert verhiess mir" to
entrance of Sieglinde.

x37 Excerpt, February 22, 1941, NBC Broadcast, w.   LM 2452 HR 200
Traubel; Toscanini. Act 1, scene 3 (the many versions   RB 16274 VIC 1316

include stereo and half-speed metal mastering; see also   RCA AT 400
059 and x50).   RCA CD RD85751

Siegfried
(see also 04 and 010)

x38 January 30, 1937, Metropolitan, w. Flagstad,   EJS 173 (4)
Thorborg, Andreva; Laufkoetter, Habich, Schorr, List: IGI 373
Bodanzky.

x39 Excerpt, January 30, 1937, Metropolitan, w. Flagstad: UORC 159
Bodanzky. Act 3: "Heil dir Sonne!" to end.

x40 Excerpt, January 30, 1937, Metropolitan, w.   UORC 158
Laufkoetter: Bodanzky. Act 1: "Nothung! Nothung!
Neidliches Schwert!" to end of act.

x41 Excerpt, January 30, 1937, Metropolitan, w. Schorr: BASF HB 22 863
Bodanzky. Act 3: "Den Weg, den es zeigte."   RCA RL 30439
(100 Jahre Bayreuth 4LP; Legendäre Zeit der Berliner
Opera 2LP).

x42 Excerpt, Act 3: "Im Schlafe liegt eine Frau" (to)   EJS 238
". . . sei mein!" Composite of Melchior's HMV
Siegfried set and Flagstad's HMV BLP 1035.

Die Götterdämmerung

x43 January 11, 1936, Metropolitan, w. Lawrence, Manski,   EJS 489 (4)
Meisle; Schorr, Hofmann, Habich: Bodanzky.

x44 Excerpts, May 12, 1939, Metropolitan, w. Flagstad: EJS 167 (2)
Bodanzky. Prologue: "Zu neuen Taten."
May 1936, Covent Garden, w. Leider, Thorborg,
Nezadal; Janssen, List: Beecham. Act 1:
"Altgewohntes Geräusch. . . . jagst du mich hin!" Act 2:
"Gegrüsst sei, teurer Held!" to end of act.

x45 Excerpts, May 1936, Covent Garden, w. Leider,   UORC 234 (2)
Thorborg, Nezadal; Janssen, Weber/List: Beecham.
Act 1: "Siegfried—mein!" (just before "Hagens Wacht")
to "Stärker als Stahl" (just before end). Act 2: "Hoiho!
Hagen!" (Siegfried's Entrance) to end of act.

x46 Excerpt, same performance as x45, Act 2: "Brünnhild',
die heerste Frau" to Siegfried's exit.
(Berlin—Die Staatsoper unter den Linden 1919–1945)   ACANTA MA
(8 LP)   22177
(Furtwängler (!) dirigiert Opern von Richard Wagner)   ACANTA 40 23 520
(5 LP).

x47 Excerpts, June 1, 1937, Covent Garden, w. Flagstad,   EJS 431 (2)
Nezadal, Thorborg; Janssen, Weber: Furtwängler.   RR 429 (2)
Prologue: "Zu neuen Taten." Act 1: "Altgewohntes
Geräusch" to end of act. Act 2: "Heil! Heil!
Willkommen!" to end of act. Act 3: "Schweigt eures
Jammers" to end.

x48 Excerpt, June 7, 1938, Covent Garden, w. Leider,
Stosch; Janssen, Schirp: Furtwängler.

"Heil! Heil! Willkommen!" to end of act.	EJS 342
"Helle Wehr!" to Siegfried's exit.	UORC 159
"Heil! Heil! Willkommen!" to Siegfried's exit (100 Jahre Bayreuth) (4 LP).	BASF 22 863-0
"Heil! Heil! Willkommen!" to Siegfried's exit (Richard Wagner—sein Werk in dokumentarischen Aufnahmen) (19 LP).	ACANTA 40 23 502

x49 Excerpt, September 30, 1934, Vienna State Opera, w. Konetzni; Manowarda: Weingartner. Act 2: "Schweig' ich die Klage" ("Helle Wehr!").   Belvedere TELETHEATER 120841

x50 Excerpt, February 22, 1941, NBC Broadcast, w. Traubel; Toscanini. Prologue: Daybreak, "Zu neuen Taten," Siegfried's Rhine Journey (the many versions include stereo and half-speed metal mastering; see also 059 and x37).   LM 2452 HR 200 RB 16274 VIC1316 RCA AT 400

Parsifal

x51 April 15, 1938, Metropolitan, w. Flagstad; Schorr, Cordon, List: Bodanzky (Acts 1 and 3), Leinsdorf (Act 2).   EJS 484 (4)

x52 Excerpt, September 28, 1939, Danmarks Radio, Danish Radio Symphony Orchestra: Nicolai Malko. Act 2: "Amfortas! die Wunde!" (Grosse Sänger der Bayreuther Festspiele 1900–1930; Great Singers in Copenhagen—Danacord).   DG 2721 109 DACO 131-133

Section IV. Miscellaneous Special Issues, Recitals, etc.

Foster, "Majvise" ("Se det summer af Sol") (see also 057)	Polyphon S50704-A
Rygaard, "Flaget" (May 17, 1937, Christian X Silver Jubilee, Radio City broadcast)	Polyphon S50705-A
Verdi, *Otello*, Act 1: "Esultate" (May 1960)	ASCO 121 (see 011)
Børresen, *Kaddara*: "Ujuraks Udfart" (1941)	ASCO 121 (see 011)

Lauritz Melchior 75th Birthday: Golden Age of Opera Pacius, "Suomis sång," w. Flagstad, Branzell, and Tibbett (Finnish Relief Rally 1939)   EJS 322 (see 054)

Schubert, "Der Atlas"; Schubert, "Der Doppelgänger"; Strauss, "Heimliche Aufforderung"; Strauss, "Zueignung"; de Curtis, "Torna a Surriento"; Malotte, "Lord's Prayer"; Styne, "I Believe"; Verdi, *Aida*, Act 1: "Celeste Aida" (German); Meyerbeer, *Le prophète*: "Roi du ciel" (German); Grieg, "Jeg elsker dig" (Adelphi College, conductor: Leopold Stokowski) (Der Atlas, Aida and Grieg recorded 1963, balance April 1961)

Potpourri No. 12: Golden Age of Opera   EJS 213
Flotow, *Martha*, Act 3: "Ach, so fromm" (Italian) (1945 soundtrack)

Verdi, *Rigoletto*, Act 4: "La donna è mobile" (1945 sound-track)

Potpourri No. 13: Golden Age of Opera   EJS 215
Verdi, *Aida*, Act 3: "Aida! . . . Tu non m'ami . . . va!"
w. Marina Koshetz (1947 *Luxury Liner* soundtrack)

Tenor Recital: Golden Age of Opera   EJS 288
Lange-Müller, *Der var engang*: "Midsommervise"; Ry-
gaard, "Flaget"; Grieg, "Jeg elsker dig," w. Band of the
Tivoli Boys Guard (June 1963)

Lauritz Melchior Memorial. Unique Opera Records   UORC 158 (see 075)
Wagner, *Die Meistersinger*, Act 3: "Morgenlich leuch-
tend," conductor: José Iturbi. 1937 broadcast. (also EJS
425) §§§ *Vive la compagnie* radio show December 6, 1966.

American Personalities Parade—Department of State conduc-   DS 1071
tor: Frank Black (1949?) Bach-Gounod, "Ave Maria";
d'Hardelot, "Because"; Jordan, "Drick"; Sjöberg, "To-
nerna"; Rotter, "Spring Came Back to Vienna."

Horneman, "Højt fra Træets grønne Top"; §§§ "Dejlig
er Jorden" (Old Silesian hymn); Gruber, "Stille Nacht"
(Danish) (strung together with Melchior's Yuletide sentiments for use in Danish radio Christmas program,
recorded at Universal Recorders, 6757 Hollywood Bou-
levard)

Prokofiev, *Peter and the Wolf,* January 14, 1951, Lauritz   SONIC B7671-2
Melchior (narrator), Austin (Texas) Symphony, Ezra
Rachlin (conductor). (Melchior did the Prokofiev narration on several occasions, including an unpublished
recording with the Chicago Symphony and Fritz Reiner.)

Index

Acoustical Society of America, 194
Albanese, Licia, 247, 261
Alberghetti, Anna Maria, 289
Alda, Frances, 134
Alexandra, Queen Mother, Princess of Wales, 22–23
Alexandrine, Queen, 222
Allen Fred (The Fred Allen Show), 210–212, 214–215, 220.
   See also Melchior, Lauritz: radio work
Alsfelt, Palle, 309–310
Althouse, Paul, 131, 134–135, 139, 175, 180, 238, 252
Alvary, Lorenzo, 202
Alwin, Karl, 42
Amalienborg Palace, 25, 94, 123, 222
American Museum at Statue of Liberty, 292
American Federation of Labor, 153
American Federation of Musicians, 153
American Guild of Musical Artists, 153
Andersen, Eva (née Nathansen), 39, 53, 171
Andersen, Hans Christian, 173, 326
Anderson, Judith, 82
Andresen, Ivar, 74, 107
Ansonia, Hotel, 95, 118, 145, 150–153, 170, 180, 238
Anti-Semitism, 104, 105, 110, 161
   King Christian X, 222
   Wagner, Cosima, Siegfried, and Winifred, 33
Appel, Birte, 324
Appia, Adolphe, 46
Arabian Nights, 281–282
Assistens Kirkegaard, 10, 326
Astor, Mrs. Vincent, 119

Bahr, Hermann, 198
Bahr-Mildenburg, Anna, 26, 28–29, 31, 33, 36, 38–39, 47, 51, 59, 96, 101
Baldon, Cleo, 85, 300–305, 307, 320, 323
Baldon, Dirk, 302, 304–305
Balling, Michael, 52
Bampton, Rose, 132, 188, 261
Bang, Poul, 7, 9
Barbirolli, Sir John, 107
Bayreuth Festival, 8, 16, 26, 37, 40–41, 45–54, 64, 67–68, 74, 79, 80, 81, 82–83, 86–88, 92, 97, 103, 109, 114, 122, 127, 130, 127, 146, 149, 162, 163, 167, 203, 224, 226–227, 275, 320, 329–330. See also Bayreuth style
   Cosima as administrator, 32–33

Leider and Melchior at Bayreuth, 86–87
   Melchior audition, 28–31
   Melchior debut, 49–50
   Melchior decides not to return, 110–111, 186
   Melchior humorously on Bayreuth, 83
   Melchior on his debut, 50
   Melchior training, 31–35, 46, 88, 130
   Siegfried as administrator, 30
   Siegfried's innovations, 103–104
   Toscanini and Melchior, 98–102
   Wieland as administrator, 312
   Winifred as administrator, 108
   Wolfgang as administrator, 327
Bayreuth style, 29, 31–33, 46–47, 82, 96, 110, 134, 148, 181, 190, 226, 229, 238, 255–256, 327, 329. See also Bayreuth Festival: Melchior training
Bech, Georg, 144
Beecham, Sir Thomas, 40, 123–124, 126, 146, 153, 157, 159, 160, 167, 202
Beery, Wallace, 182
Beethoven Association, The, 146, 205
Behrens, Edith, 129, 131
Beigel, Victor, 23–28, 51, 58, 60–61, 66, 71, 74, 79, 148, 253
Bel Canto Choir, 6
Belmont, Eleanor (Mrs. August), 117, 204, 253, 276, 318–319
Bennett, Arnold, 20
Benzell, Mimi, 280
Bergen, Edgar, 217
Bergonzi, Carlo, 13
Berle, Milton, 233
Berlin Staatsoper, 60, 78, 104, 108, 127, 146, 148, 160, 224–225, 268
   Melchior debut, 51
Berlin Städtische Oper, 10, 53, 56–58, 104, 127, 146, 249–250, 268
   Melchior debut, 51
   Melchior's first German Tristan, 93
Bernstein, Leonard, 260
Bing, Rudolf, 69, 117, 124, 145, 162, 220, 239, 252, 255, 257, 258, 259, 272, 274, 292, 318, 319, 329
   becomes new manager of Metropolitan, 249–251
   forces Melchior from Metropolitan, 254–257, 259–271, 273–276, 289, 325, 326
Björling, Jussi, 246, 276
Black, Mrs. Morris. See Cahier, Mme. Charles
Blech, Leo, 36, 38, 72, 94, 100, 107, 146, 186, 243

Bock, Walter, 122, 155–156
Bockelmann, Rudolf, 104, 111, 127
Bodanzky, Artur, 56–57, 64–67, 69, 74,
       77, 82, 94, 116–118, 134, 135, 146–
       147, 151, 175, 176, 246
Bohemian Club, The, 197–198, 320
Bohemian Grove, The, 197–198
Bohnen, Michael, 65, 114
Boito, Arrigo, 125
Boland, Holger, 14, 58, 283
Bondi, Beulah, 219
Bonelli, Richard, 75, 249
Boosey, William, 17
Bordeaux Opera, 123
Borge, Victor, 243, 276
Bori, Lucrezia, 119, 276
Boris, King of Bulgaria, 83
Brackenburn, 199
Branzell, Karin, 65, 89, 102, 136, 150,
       151, 177, 314, 316
Braun, Carl, 104
Brunswick Gramophone Co., 56, 72
Brussels Opera (Théâtre Royal de la
       Monnaie), 123, 133, 146
Buckingham Palace, 76
Bülow, Daniela von, 32, 34
Bülow, Hans von, 30, 32
Busch, Fritz, 100–101, 104, 114, 145,
       203–204, 238, 249
Bush, George, 198

Cady, Josiah Cleaveland, 64
Cahier, Mme. Charles (née Sarah Jane
       Layton-Walker), 12, 16, 67, 71, 72,
       74, 120, 313
Callas, Maria, 46, 274, 306
Calusio, Ferruccio, 194
Calvé, Emma, 280
Caniglia, Maria, 126
Cantor, Eddie, 211
    Eddie Cantor Comedy Hour, 228–229.
       See also Melchior, Lauritz: radio work
Carnegie Commission on Broadcasting,
       116
Carnegie Hall, 163, 191, 252, 258
Carolsfeld, Ludwig Schnorr von, 130, 327
Carron, Arthur, 189
Caruso, Enrico, 24, 43, 74–75, 82, 108,
       125, 194, 212
Casamassa, Angelo, 180, 266
Castello Orleans, Prince Vincenzo Abbate
       de, 306
Castenskiold, Christian and Cecily, 294,
       299
Cavalieri, Anna, 125
CBS (Columbia Broadcasting System), 75
Cehanovsky, George, 246
Chaliapin, Feodor, 65, 75, 78, 85
Chamber Music Society of Lower Basin

St., The, 209. See also Melchior,
       Lauritz: radio work
Chapin, Schuyler, 319
Chaplin, Charlie, 20
Chappell and Company, 17, 22
Chéreau, Pierre, 105
Chevalier, Maurice, 280
Chicago Opera, 56, 118, 132, 139, 146,
       162, 175, 190–191
Chossewitz, 115, 120–122, 136, 153–155,
       167–169, 172, 196
    take over by Russians, 167–169, 172,
       196
Christian X, King of Denmark, 21, 25, 83,
       94, 123, 152, 187, 204, 221–222,
       243, 252
Christie, John, 249
Cimara, Pietro, 181
Circus Saints and Sinners Club, 232–233
Claussen, Julia, 90
Coburg-Gotha, Duke of Saxe, 49
Cochran, William, 316–317
Cold, Ulrik, 43
Collins, Angelene (Mrs. Lawrence
       Rasmussen), 282, 285
Colón, Teatro (Buenos Aires), 101, 112–
       114, 145, 199, 201
Columbia Concerts, 230
Columbia Records, 193–194, 296
Connor, Nadine, 231
Constitution Hall, 276
Cornelius, Peter, 25
Cotogni, Antonio, 58
Covent Garden, 22–23, 60, 74, 78–79, 82,
       91, 94, 97, 101, 107, 115, 118, 125,
       127, 131, 137, 146, 158, 160, 161,
       195, 224, 250, 254, 319, 329
    Beecham returns, 123
    George V's Silver Jubilee, 156–157
    Melchior and Beecham, 124
    Melchior and Chaliapin, 85–86
    Melchior and Jeritza, 72–73
    Melchior's debut, 36, 39–42
    Melchior's last performance, 167
    Melchior's Otello, 126
    Newman on Melchior's Tristan, 106–
       107
Cravath, Paul, 115, 141
Cronkite, Walter, 198
Crooks, Richard, 180–181
Crosby, Bing, 198, 211
Cross, Milton, 272

Dagmar, Empress Maria Feodorovna, 23
Damgaard, Andreas, 244, 306
Damrosch, Walter, 131, 190, 252
Damon Runyon Fund, 272
Dana College, 293, 324
Danish Luncheon Club of New York, 180

Danish Royal Guard, 9, 10, 13, 207, 208, 292, 324, 325, 326
  Melchior's induction, 8
Danish Royal Guards Outside Denmark, 150, 152, 180, 198–199, 213, 222, 242, 243, 287, 301, 302, 320, 324
Danish Royal Opera, 3–4, 12–13, 17–18, 21, 22, 25, 43, 85, 94, 123, 146, 169, 187, 222, 242, 243, 313
  debut as baritone, 10
  debut as Heldentenor, 14–15
  Melchior enters royal Opera school, 8–9, 70
  resignation, 22
Darmstadt Opera, 249, 250
Davidson, James, 203, 246, 247, 256, 257, 259, 260, 261, 262, 264, 265, 268, 275, 276, 278, 280
  becomes Melchior's personal manager, 263
Decca Records, 158, 275
Decorations. See Melchior, Lauritz: medals and awards
Deman, Rudolph, 78–79, 86, 112–113, 118–119, 161–162, 224, 296. See also Leider, Frida
Denver, John, 230
Dessay, Paul, 57
Dispeker, Thea, 129, 153
Domingo, Plácido, 13, 230
Dørumsgaard, Arne, 309
Duffy's Tavern, 213, 237
Dupont, Mrs. Alfred I., 277
Durante, Jimmy, 217, 231, 280
Durbin, Deanna, 182

Ebert, Carl, 249
Eddy, Nelson, 276
Edelmann, Otto, 158, 314, 316
Edinburgh Festival, 249
Ed Sullivan Show, The, 173
Edward, Prince of Wales, 187
Eisenhower, Dwight D., 198, 213, 259, 259fn
Eisner, Leonard, 14, 76, 127, 197, 254, 283
Eliot, T. S., 20
Elmendorff, Karl, 94, 104, 146
Elschner, Walter, 149
EMI Records, 158
Emmons, Shirlee, 35fn, 282, 284–290, 295
Engels, George, 139
English Wagner Society, 14
Erskine, John, 141
Essex House, 254, 257, 263
Eule, Die, 52, 80, 124
Evans, George, 209

Farrar, Geraldine, 134, 252
Ferdinand, King of Bulgaria, 48–49
Films. See Luxury Liner; The Stars are Singing; This Time for Keeps; Thrill of a Romance; Two Sisters from Boston
Firestone Hour, The, 275
Fischer-Dieskau, Dietrich, 23
Flagstad, Kirsten, 17, 35, 43, 135–138, 140, 142–143, 145–150, 153, 157–160, 162–164, 166, 175–178, 180, 186, 188–192, 268, 274, 281, 288, 291, 325
  debut at Metropolitan, 133–134, 137
  death, 311–312
  estrangement from Melchior, 138–140, 213, 253–254
  first meeting with Melchior, 123
  first reconciliation with Melchior, 174
  leaving Metropolitan, 183–185
  political accusations, 188, 252–254, 309–310
  return to Metropolitan, 261–262, 264
  second reconciliation with Melchior, 309–311
Ford, Gerald, 198
Ford, Glenn, 182
Franco, General Francisco, 160
Frederik IX, King of Denmark, 243, 287, 309–310, 324
  as Crown Prince Frederik, 150, 154, 241–242
Frey, Freitag, 58
Furtwängler, Wilhelm, 93–94, 100, 109–111, 122, 146, 158–160

Gaisberg, Fred, 18, 107
Galsworthy, John, 20
Garland, Judy, 280
Gatti-Casazza, Giulio, 61, 63, 74, 77–78, 87, 90, 96, 115, 131–132, 145, 220, 226
  Flagstad engaged, 133–134
  Leider engaged, 117–118
  Melchior engaged, 56–57
  refuses non-Wagner roles to Melchior, 96–97, 125–127, 326
  rehearsal policy, 64
  retires, 141–143
  twenty-fifth anniversary as general director, 116
Gaubert, Philippe, 105
Geissmar, Berta, 100, 109, 111, 153
George V, King of England, 123, 156–157
George, Prime Minister David Lloyd, 25
Gerard, Rolf, 270
Gering, Marion, 173
Gigli, Beniamino, 58, 66, 75, 93, 95, 115
Glyndebourne Opera Festival, 249–250
Gobbi, Tito, 232

Goebbels, Joseph, 160
Golde, Walter, 71
Göring, Hermann, 131, 154, 159–160
Gould, Walter, 234
Graarud, Gunnar, 102–103
Grable, Betty, 278
Gradman, Peter, 8–9, 12, 15–16
Gramophone Company, The, 18
Grayson, Kathryn, 217
Grenzebach, Ernst, 58, 122, 308
Guggenheim, Mrs. Robert, 277
Gwenn, Edmund, 20

Hacker, Karl, 40, 49–51, 54, 79, 84–85,
    97, 105, 121, 150–151, 155, 296
Hacker, Maria ("Mutti"), 40, 49–50, 53–
    54, 79, 84–85, 97, 105, 121, 150–
    151, 169, 172, 179, 196–197, 238,
    272, 277, 283, 296
Halasz, László, 249
Hamburg Stadttheater, 77, 80–81, 86–88,
    92, 97, 146, 268
  Melchior debut, 73
  Melchior's last performance, 104–105
Hamilton, David, 304
Hamilton, George, 304
Hamilton, Helle Nielsen, 304, 323
Hansen, Hans, 89, 138, 268, 297, 326
Hansen, Holger, 22
Harewood, Earl of, 158
Hartmann, Carl, 139
Hawkins, Osie, 193, 267
Heger, Robert, 94, 123
Hegermann-Lindencrone, Knud, 8, 158,
    309–311
Heifetz, Jascha, 119, 164
Helena Victoria, Princess, 76, 159
Helm, Anny, 99–100
Henningsen, Gerda, 91–92, 169
Herold, Vilhelm, 94, 169
  trains Melchior as Heldentenor, 13–16
Hersholt, Jean, 197
Hey, Julius, 13
Heylbut, Rose, 4, 7
Hines, Jerome, 276
Hirzel, Max, 156–157
Hitler, Adolf, 4, 104, 155, 168, 222–223
  attitudes on opera, 109, 162
  first hears Melchior, 52–53
  influence on operatic events and careers,
    93, 103, 109–110, 124, 131, 154,
    159–160, 167, 249
  moves to Wahnfried, 52, 161
  writes Mein Kampf, 10
HMV (His Master's Voice) Records, 106–
    107, 139, 158, 160, 169, 231
Hommel, Lauritz Lebrecht, 1, 2
  Melchior named for, 111
Honoré, Arne, 88

Hoover, Herbert, 198
Hope Associates, 129, 164, 175, 207, 217,
    265. See also Hope, Constance;
    Behrens, Edith
Hope, Constance, 76, 131, 164–165, 176,
    179–180, 208–209, 212, 318
  becomes Melchior's publicist, 129
  influence on Melchior's career, 132, 163,
    207, 229
  role in quarrel between Melchior and
    Flagstad, 139
Hopf, Hans, 315
Horne, Marilyn, 230
Hösslin, Franz von, 80
Huehn, Julius, 177, 189, 193
Hunting. See Melchior, Lauritz: hunting
Hüsch, Gerhard, 163
Hye-Knudsen, Johann, 94, 123

Ibbs and Tillett, 22, 35
Ingrid, Queen of Denmark, 309, 324
  as Crown Princess, 150
Institute for the Blind, 5
Insull, Samuel, 118
Iturbi, Amparo, 299
Ivogün, Maria, 58

Jagel, Frederick, 75
Janssen, Herbert, 58, 107, 124, 127, 161,
    183, 193–194, 202, 276, 314
Jenkins, Timothy, 316
Jensen, Frøken Kristine, 3–4, 6–8, 16, 25,
    28
  Frøken Jensens Kogebog, 3
Jensen, Thomas, 308, 310–311
Jeritza, Maria, 65–67, 72–73
Jerndorff, Peter, 8–9
Jerusalem, Siegfried, 330
Jessner, Irene, 204, 267
Johansen, Henry, 134, 153, 174, 188, 253,
    261
  political accusations, 252–253
Johnson, Edward, 139, 141–142, 146, 147,
    148, 151, 185, 188, 189, 202, 203,
    204, 230, 240, 250, 252, 256, 259,
    261, 262, 265, 266–267, 270
  becomes manager of Metropolitan, 142–
    143
  cancels Ring, 247–248
  engages McArthur, 183–184, 262
  McArthur/Leinsdorf controversy, 175–
    177
  Metropolitan becomes independent,
    176–177
  non-Wagner roles for Melchior, 97, 143,
    326
  Parsifal Grail Scene controversy, 246

Johnson, Edward (*continued*)
  rehearsal policy, 227, 251
  replaced by Bing, 249
Johnson, Van, 215, 218–219
Jolson, Al, 211
Judson, Arthur, 60, 63
Juilliard Foundation, 142
Juilliard School, 141, 314

Kahn, Otto, 61, 87, 115, 134
Kaiser, Kay, 235
189 Kaiserallee, 105, 120
Kappel, Gertrude, 89–90, 96, 134, 146
Kappel, Vagn, 310
Kauffmann, Ambassador Henrik, 187
Kierkegaard, Søren, 326
Kinsky, Roberto, 194
Kipnis, Alexander, 58, 71, 80, 93, 127,
  177, 314, 316
Kirchhoff, Walter, 75, 87, 93, 122
Kittel, Professor Karl, 30–31, 35, 46, 101,
  134
Kleiber, Erich, 94, 146
Klemperer, Otto, 113
Klindworth, Karl, 33
Knudsen, Aage Cornelius, 16
Knudsen, Tom, 276, 302
Konetzni, Anny, 113, 134
Korn Kobblers' Band, 258
Krause, Jørgen and Inge, 242, 295, 297
Kullmann, Charles, 241, 246

La Guardia, Mayor Fiorello, 144, 150,
  177, 201
Lakes, Gary, 316
Lamperti, G. B., 141
Lamprecht, Lilly, 10
Lange-Müller, Peter, 14
Larsen, Dorothy, 47–48, 308, 311
Larsén-Todsen, Nanny, 70, 80, 86, 89,
  94, 111, 146
Lassie, 277
Laubenthal, Rudolf, 67, 69, 75, 77, 93,
  106, 122
Laufkötter, Karl, 54, 88, 115, 148–149,
  172, 197, 283, 295, 302
Laufkötter, Hilde, 115, 148, 172, 283,
  295, 299, 301, 316
Laughton, Charles, 20–21
Lawrence, Marjorie, 145, 150, 188, 191
Lee, Gypsy Rose, 280
Lehmann, Captain Ernst, 114–115
Lehmann, Lilli, 33, 47, 68, 132, 195
Lehmann, Lotte, 78, 85, 97, 126–128, 131,
  135, 137–139, 151, 156, 160, 164,
  188, 189, 191, 203–205, 207, 213,
  228, 296–297, 306, 314, 318, 324–
  325
  and Constance Hope, 129

attitude toward Bing, 292
  commercials, 165
  Covent Garden debut, 23, 40
  family escapes from Austria, 161
  leaves Germany, 160
  Metropolitan debut, 127
  recitals with Melchior, 162–163
Leider, Frida, 6–37, 40, 42, 59, 64, 78–
  80, 82, 93, 97, 102, 106–107, 109,
  112–113, 119, 122, 126–127, 129,
  132–133, 135, 137, 146, 159–160,
  225, 243, 272, 296, 308, 313, 321,
  324. *See also* Deman, Rudolf
  Bayreuth debut, 86–87
  Covent Garden debut, 41
  forced by Göring to leave Metropolitan,
  131–132, 134
  Metropolitan debut, 117–119
  Nazi persecution, 161–162, 224
Leigh, W. Colston, 263
Leinsdorf, Erich, 175–177, 180–181, 184,
  190, 194, 202, 238, 253
Lert, Ernst, 145
Levine, Marks, 184, 252
Lewis, Earle, 184
Liebling, Viva, 180
Lillian Nordica Association, The, 191
Lillie, Beatrice, 20
Lindbergh, Charles, 154
List, Emmanuel, 134, 147, 150, 159–160
Liszt, Franz, 30
Ljungberg, Göta, 41
Longstreet, Stephen, 272
Lorenz, Max, 58, 87, 122, 140, 160, 241,
  254, 271, 308, 313
Loria, Gaetano, 125–126
Los Angeles Dodgers, 29
Lubin, Germaine, 167, 184
Ludendorff, General Erich Friedrich
  Wilhelm von, 37, 49
Ludwig, King of Bavaria, 32
Lunddahl, Thora, 4, 22
Luxury Liner, 232, 240
Lyons Opera, 123

MacDonald, Jeannette, 218, 276
Magdeburg Opera, 59–60
Mahler, Gustav, 13, 26, 29, 31, 38
Maison, René, 138, 189
Manski, Dorothée, 144, 162
Marconi, Guglielmo, 18–19, 194
Marek, Daniel, 293
Marie Louise, Princess, 76, 159
Markham, Mary, 285, 299–305
  divorce from Melchior, 304
Marlborough House, 23, 112
Märta, Crown Princess, 254
Martinelli, Giovanni, 93, 96, 115, 125,
  142, 175, 228–229, 252

Martini, Nino, 218, 228
Martino, Juan Emilio, 194
Mary, Queen of England, 20, 123, 156, 157
Maurel, Victor, 125
Maxwell, Elsa, 107, 209–210, 253
Mayer, Louis B., 217
McArthur, Edwin, 136, 138–139, 174–175
  controversy with Leinsdorf, 175–177
  engaged by Metropolitan, 183–184, 262
Medals. *See* Melchior, Lauritz: medals and awards
Meister, Hannelore, 179
Melba, Nellie, 18, 22, 259
Melchior, Agnes (Agge), 1, 3, 4, 120, 221, 298
Melchior, Birte, 91, 97, 104, 105, 121, 156, 178, 237, 306, 307, 324
  birth, 21, 91
  estrangement from father, 298
  left in Denmark during World War II, 170–172
  marriage and birth of sor., 221
  on her parents' divorce, 53
  on hunting, 122
  on Inger, 11, 53–54
  on Kleinchen, 28, 53, 91–92
  on Mary Markham, 301
  on Melchior, 18, 306
  on her relationship with Melchior, 26, 91
  sent away to school, 91–92
Melchior, Bøchman, 22
Melchior, Bodil, 1–5, 9, 94, 120, 221, 297, 298, 302
Melchior, Ellen Marie, 1, 3, 120
Melchior, Henrik Emil (grandfather), 2
Melchior, Henrik Emil (brother), 1, 6
  death, 76, 221
Melchior, Ib Jørgen, 18, 75, 91, 97, 105, 121, 141, 156, 178–179, 221, 227, 293, 300, 303–307, 319–320, 323–324, 326
  birth, 13
  estrangement from father, 172–174, 298, 299, 301
  Kleinchen interferes with professional life, 173
  marriage with Cleo Baldon, 301–302
  on divorce of father and mother, 53–54
  on Lauritz, 172, 322
  on hunting, 121
  on Kleinchen, 28, 53
  on relationship with Lauritz, 26, 91–92, 173–174, 308
  reconciliation with Lauritz, 174, 301–302
  sent away to school, 92
Melchior, Inger Thora Nathansen (Holst-Rasmussen), 10, 12, 16–18, 21, 22–28, 23, 39–40, 53–55, 170, 178, 208, 298
  death, 91, 298
  marries Lauritz, 10–11
  meets Lauritz, 10–11
Melchior, Jack, 324
Melchior, Jørgen Conradt, 1–7, 11, 22, 25, 53, 152, 305
  death, 54
Melchior, Julie Sophie Møller, 1–3
Melchior, Knud, 1
Melchior, Lauritz
  American citizenship, 187, 204, 222, 243, 276
  antiques, 84–85, 105, 155
  birth, childhood, 1–5
  card-playing, 54–55, 61, 69, 74, 82, 118, 121, 138–139, 151, 153, 183, 267, 295, 305
  charity/voluntary pay cuts/benefits, 115, 143, 186–187, 199, 204–205, 220–223, 253, 272, 276
  commercials, 164–165, 208, 233, 235, 258, 282, 300
  Danish attitude toward, 241–245, 312, 325, 326
  death, 304, 321, 323–327
  divorce from Inger, 53–54, 91, 208
  divorce from Mary Markham, 304
  dramatic ability, 8, 10, 14, 15, 44, 46, 67–69, 80, 90, 102, 106–107, 137, 144–149, 159, 184, 192, 226, 237, 254, 289, 329. *See also* Bayreuth style
  efforts to popularize good music, 129–131, 164, 194, 205, 207–209, 212–214, 217–218, 220–221, 226, 230–232, 235, 245, 258, 266, 274–280. *See also* Melchior, Lauritz [musical comedy/Broadway; film career; Lauritz Melchior Show, The; nightclubs; radio work; television work; variety shows]; Palace Theater
  escape from Germany, 168–169
  fees, 41, 56, 66, 75, 78, 87, 90, 92–94, 97, 104, 106–107, 112–113, 115, 142, 157, 162–163, 178, 187, 214–216, 232, 246, 262, 276, 281–282, 288, 289. *See also* Melchior, Maria: financial negotiator for Lauritz' career
  film career, 160, 173, 212, 215–220, 222, 227, 229, 231–237, 240, 246–248, 255, 260, 274, 288–289, 309, 326. See also *Luxury Liner; The Stars Are Singing; This Time for Keeps; Thrill of a Romance; Two Sisters from Boston*
  first trip to America, 61
  Freemasonry, 16, 84, 213, 265, 292, 324
  helps Jewish friends, 155, 172
  homes. *See* Ansonia, Hotel; Chossewitz;

Melchior, Lauritz (*continued*)
  Viking, The; Essex House; 189
    Kaiserallee; 31 Nørregade; 17
    Rothenbaum Chaussee
  hunting, 8, 54, 74, 97, 115, 120–122,
    151, 153–154, 168, 174, 189, 198,
    207, 234, 235, 237, 243, 244–246,
    260–261, 272, 278, 280, 293–294,
    297, 301–303, 305, 320–322
  Lauritz Melchior Foundation, The, 131,
    313–316
  Lauritz Melchior Show, The, 231, 282–
    289, 295
  marriage to Inger, 11
  marriage to Kleinchen, 53–54, 208
  marriage to Mary Markham, 300–302
  medals and awards, 49, 83, 94, 103,
    105, 123, 154, 156, 159, 187, 201,
    204, 213, 220, 222–224, 232, 241,
    243, 276, 292, 302, 306–308
  musical comedy/Broadway, 257, 280–
    282. See also *Arabian Nights;* Palace
    Theater
  nicknames: Big Noise, The, 203; David,
    49; Greatest Parsifal, The, 51;
    Himself, 85; Lalle Menkør, 3;
    Tristanissimo, 101; tusind tak, 108;
    Wagnerian Caruso, The, 199
  nightclubs, 282–289. *See also* Lauritz
    Melchior Show, The non-
    Wagnerian roles controversy, 96–97,
    125–127, 132, 143–144, 193–194,
    326
  on recital singing, 163
  on roles and acting, 4, 15, 34, 42, 47–
    48, 69–71, 81, 88, 101–102, 126,
    159, 317, 321
  on singing, 7–8, 14, 24, 24*fn*, 25–26,
    43–44, 51, 74, 96–97, 102, 126,
    195–196, 238–239, 283, 314, 317–
    318, 321–322, 330
  on Wagner's music and style, 31, 35,
    47–48, 51, 130, 306, 324
  Parsifal Grail Scene controversy, 245–
    246
  radio work, 73, 132, 137, 164, 191, 209–
    215, 217, 220–221, 224, 227–231,
    235–236, 240, 242, 260, 262, 272,
    275, 282, 309, 326
  first male singer to broadcast on radio,
    18–19
  recordings, 19, 56, 72, 106–107, 133,
    157–158, 160, 164, 169, 174, 191,
    193–194, 224, 231, 275, 296, 306,
    309, 313, 324, 328–329
  refuses to sing in German houses, 104–
    105, 110–111, 122
  rehearsal attitude, perceived laziness, 40,
    47–48, 52, 57, 64–66, 77, 119, 122,
    143, 227, 238–239, 257, 326, 330

  retirement from Met, 254–255, 259–
    269, 271–276, 313, 319, 325–326
  rhythmic difficulty, 36, 38, 68, 100–
    101, 228, 237, 256–257, 287, 310,
    326
  stamina, 70, 194–195, 205, 239, 327,
    329–330
  television work, 173, 233, 274–275, 282,
    289, 292
  25th anniversary, 257, 265–266, 268,
    272–274, 276, 325
  variety shows, 278–279, 282
  vocal aging, 44, 205–206, 219, 227, 248,
    293, 310
  vocal suitability to Wagner, 15–16, 35,
    59, 67–69, 80, 88, 146, 148, 149,
    160, 181, 192, 329
  vocal training. *See* Bahr-Mildenburg,
    Anna; Bang, Poul; Beigel, Victor;
    Frey, Freitag; Grenzebach, Ernst;
    Mühlen, Raymond von zur; Rosati,
    Enrico
  vocal warm-up, 35, 35*fn*, 66, 288
  young singers, advice to and help for,
    131, 204, 313–318
Melchior, Leif Lauritz Ib, 172
Melchior, Maria Anna Katharina
    ("Kleinchen"), 3, 28, 40, 42, 49–55,
    58, 60–61, 66–67, 69–71, 73, 78–79,
    81–82, 85, 89–90, 93–94, 97–98,
    103, 105, 107–108, 110, 113, 117,
    119, 122–123, 128, 131–132, 139,
    148, 150–151, 154–157, 161–162,
    167–169, 181–182, 187, 190–191,
    193, 196–197, 200–202, 204, 215–
    216, 218, 221–224, 233, 238–239,
    242, 245, 251–252, 254–262, 264,
    267–268, 276, 280–281, 286–289,
    304, 306, 309, 321
  acting career, 27, 40, 54, 164, 179, 208
  business acuity, 61, 76, 84, 95–96, 112,
    113, 140, 141, 153, 196, 214, 276,
    277, 282, 285–286, 288, 297–298
  death, 208, 294–301, 303
  financial negotiator for Lauritz' career,
    75, 93, 106, 142–143, 214
  frugality, 151, 286, 289
  jewelry, 169, 255, 277–278, 284–285,
    299, 301
  management of Lauritz' career, 55–56,
    71, 74, 75, 76, 78, 86, 92–93, 124,
    138, 196, 245, 256, 275–276, 283–
    284, 288, 289, 295, 297, 329
  marriage, 53–54, 128, 208
  meets Melchior, 27
  meets Melchior (publicity version), 178–
    179, 208
Meister, Hannelore, as, 179
Melchior's children, 91–92, 169–174,
    295, 298, 301

publicity, 129, 164–166, 179, 180, 186, 196, 207, 212, 213, 214, 218, 233, 241, 243, 248, 255, 269, 272, 295, 297
Melchiorianer Association, 221, 242
Melchiors Borger -og Realskole, 2–4, 6, 8
Melton, James, 217, 247
Meneghini, Giovanni Battista, 274
Mennin, Peter, 316
Merrill, Robert, 203, 230, 275–276, 280
Metropolitan on tour, 63, 75, 89–90, 94, 101, 138, 164, 181, 183–185, 188, 190–191, 202, 205, 238, 247–248, 256, 261, 275
Metropolitan Opera, 56–58, 61–77, 85, 87, 89–90, 92–97, 101, 111, 112, 115–120, 122, 127, 129, 131–149, 153, 161, 163–167, 172, 175–178, 180, 183–186, 188–192, 196, 202–204, 206, 211, 212, 215, 216, 218–220, 226–228, 230, 231, 232, 234–241, 245–248, 249–253, 254–276, 279–281, 291, 292, 295, 313, 314, 325–326, 327, 328, 329. See also Bing, Rudolf; Gatti-Casazza, Giulio; Johnson, Edward; Ziegler, Edward
new opera house, 116–117, 318–319
"Save the Met" evenings, 119–120
Metropolitan Opera Club, 232
Metropolitan Opera Guild, 142, 146, 177, 318
Milanov, Zinka, 246
Miller, Ann, 289
Molinari, Bernardino, 125
Moor, Charles, 157
Moore, Grace, 138
Morgenstierne, Wilhelm, 253–254, 309
Moscona, Nicola, 204
Mottl, Felix, 33
Muck, Karl, 52, 86, 99, 103–104, 109, 114
Mühlen, Raymond von zur, 23
Munich Opera, 26
Munsel, Patrice, 203
Muratore, Lucien, 125

Nathansen, Knud, 156, 170–171
Nathansen, Ludwig, 9
Nathansen, Thora, 9
National Association of Teachers of Singing, 320
National Educational Television, 292
Nazis, Nazism, 33–34, 37, 52, 103, 108–110, 114, 122, 154–156, 159–162, 169–171, 181, 183, 186–188, 216, 222, 235, 253
NBC Concert Service, 140
NBC Radio (National Broadcasting Company), 115, 137, 258, 272
Newton, Wayne, 302

New York City Opera, 217
New York Singing Teachers Association, 141
Nielsen, Hans Henrik Melchior, 221
Nielsen, Helle. See Hamilton, Helle
Nilsson, Birgit, 136, 220, 291–292, 314, 316
Nixon, Richard, 198, 292, 324
Nordica, Lillian, 191, 286
31 Nørregade, 2, 118
Norwegian Musicians Association, 252
Norwegian Opera Association, 252
Novotna, Jarmila, 276
Nuremberg Stadttheater, 39

O'Connell, Charles, 75–76, 174
Odeon Records, 154
O'Hara, Maureen, 182
Olczewska, Maria, 41, 85, 107, 118, 127
O'Malley, Peter, 293
O'Malley, Walter, 293, 302, 305, 324
Onegin, Sigrid, 78, 93
One Shot Antelope Club, 198
Ormandy, Eugene, 164
Osborne, Conrad L., on Melchior, 43–44, 101, 192
Oslo Opera, 17, 189

Palace Theater, 280–282
Pampanini, Rosetta, 126
Paris Opéra, 93, 105, 115, 123, 131, 145–146
Paris Wagner Festival, 97, 197, 122, 159–160
Park, William, 107
Pasternak, Joe, 215, 276
Patti, Adelina, 238
Paul VI, Pope, 307
Pavarotti, Luciano, 136, 214, 230
Peerce, Jan, 246, 261
Pelletier, Wilfred, 181
Pen Club, 20
Perlea, Jonel, 260–261
Pettina, Irra, 280
Pickford, Mary, 20
Pilinszky, Sigismund, 110
Pinza, Ezio, 93, 143, 164, 257, 280, 287
Pistor, Gotthelf, 81, 86, 134, 224
Pollak, Egon, 88, 94, 100, 146
Polydor Records, 154
Pons, Lily, 119, 156, 164, 218, 227–228, 246, 261
Ponselle, Carmela, 280
Ponselle, Rosa, 91, 143, 280, 288, 296
Post, Die, 114
Powell, Jane, 302
Promenade Concerts, 16–17, 19, 20, 22

Quisling, Vidkun, 252, 254

Rabinowitz, Harry, 223–234
Radio appearances. *See* Allen, Fred;
    Chamber Music Society of Lower
    Basin Street; NBC Radio; Duffy's
    Tavern; Sinatra, Frank; We the
    People
Ralf, Oskar, 203
Ralf, Torsten, 203, 234, 236, 238, 246,
    254
Raymond, Gene, 276
RCA Victor Records, 75, 164, 193, 231,
    313
Reagan, Ronald, 198
Reiner, Fritz, 100, 131, 164, 276
Resnik, Regina, 257–258
Reszke Academy, de, 125
Reszke, Jean de, 12–13, 24, 24*fn*, 40, 51,
    58, 135, 148, 273
Rethberg, Elisabeth, 143, 147, 150, 159,
    162
Rickenbacker, Eddie, 213
Ricketts, Charles, 42
Riedel, Karl, 65, 193
Riisbro, Klaus, 265, 298–301, 319–324
Roberts, Michael, 282
Robinson, Edward G., 21
Robinson, Francis, 27
Ronald, Sir Landon, 25
Roosevelt, Franklin Delano, 167, 182–183,
    210
Roosevelt, Eleanor, 182–183
Roosevelt, Theodore, 198
Rosati, Enrico, 58, 95–96
Rose, Billy, 240
Roth, George, 282, 287
17 Rothenbaum Chaussee, 84
Rothschild, Baroness Eugènie, 107
Rothschild, Baron Maurice, 94, 107
Rouché, Jacques, 93, 97
Royal Guard, Danish. *See* Danish Royal
    Guard
Royal Danish Guards Outside Denmark.
    See Danish Royal Guards Outside
    Denmark
Royal Opera, Danish. *See* Danish Royal
    Opera
Rüdel, Hugo, 114
Ruffo, Titta, 75
Russell, John, 316

Sachse, Leopold, 88–89
Sadlowski, Ted, 282
St. Leger, Frank, 249
Salter, Jack, 192
Salter, Norbert, 56
Sandemose, Aksel, 241

San Francisco Opera, 97, 126–127, 132,
    139, 146, 162, 202, 234, 254, 320
Santas Elias, Señora, 113
Sarnoff, David, 172
Sayão, Bidu, 246
La Scala Opera, 166
Schalk, Franz, 26, 128, 146
Schech, Marianne, 158
Schillings, Max von, 59, 94, 100
Schoenberg, Arnold, 131
Schorr, Anna, 54, 71, 95, 151
Schorr, Friedrich, 41, 54, 65, 75, 78–79,
    86, 89, 93, 95, 97, 104, 115, 127,
    134, 143, 147, 150–151, 162, 176,
    192, 313
Schultz, George, 198
Schumann, Elisabeth, 85, 107, 127
Schumann-Heink, Ernestine, 70
Schwarzkopf, Elisabeth, 58
Sebastian, Georg, 94, 146
Seider, August, 254
Seidl, Anton, 130
Seyfert, Otto, 182–183, 234
Shore, Dinah, 211
Sidney, Lillian Burnes, 216
Sills, Beverly, 217
Simon, Erich, 56, 87, 92, 134
Sinatra, Frank, 209–210, 214–218, 230,
    232
Singher, Martial, 105–106
Singing Vikings, The, 279, 282
Sitwell, Edith, 20
Skelton, Red, 182
Slezak, Leo, 15, 17, 128, 143
Slezak, Walter, 180, 276, 324
Sloan, George, 177, 220, 240, 270
Smith, Betty, 76, 295, 300, 314–315, 324–
    325
Solti, Sir Georg, 8, 158
Spring, Alexander, 108
Stambog, 2, 91, 302
Stars Are Singing, The, 288–289. *See also*
    Melchior, Lauritz: film career
Stassen, Franz, 57–58
Steber, Eleanor, 260–261, 276
Steinberg, William, 202
Steinharter, Dr. Rudolf, 172, 174
Steinharter, Dr. Stefan, 172
Stellman, Maxine, 246
Stenhus Boarding School, 92
Stephens, Percy Rector, 141
Stiedry, Fritz, 101, 236, 238–239
Stockhausen, Julius, 23
Stokowski, Leopold, 67, 293
Strasfogel, Alma, 76, 152, 193, 197, 291–
    292
Strasfogel, Ignace, 76, 101, 199–201, 233,
    291–292, 316
Strauss, Richard, 15–17, 26, 40
Sullivan, Ed, 173

Supervia, Conchita, 156
Svanholm, Set, 13, 158, 203, 228, 234, 236–239, 241, 246, 248, 254, 268, 310, 315
Svendsen, Otte, 321
Swarthout, Gladys, 218, 228, 255
Szell, George, 314
Szigeti, Joseph, 73

Tagliavini, Ferruccio, 246, 261
Talley, Marian, 66–67
Taubman, Leo, 172
Taucher, Kurt, 67, 75, 77, 122
Teatro Colón (Buenos Aires), 101, 112–114, 146, 199, 201
Teatro del Liceo (Barcelona), 88–89, 92, 94, 101, 146
Tebaldi, Renata, 213
Tegner, Marianne, 83, 319–320, 323
Te Kanawa, Kiri, 230
Telephone Hour, The, 235. See also Melchior, Lauritz: radio work; television work
Television appearances. See Melchior, Lauritz: television work
Tetrazzini, Luisa, 280
Théâtre Champs-Elysées, 94
Théatre Royal de la Monnaie, 123, 133, 146
Thebom, Blanche, 258
This Time for Keeps, 231. See also Melchior, Lauritz: film career
Thomas, Jess, 316
Thorborg, Kerstin, 147, 150, 158, 161, 204
Thrill of a Romance, 215–219, 222. See also Melchior, Lauritz: film career
Tibbett, Lawrence, 75, 143, 153, 198, 228, 249
Tietjen, Heinz, 108, 110, 134, 161–162, 265
Toscanini, Arturo, 94, 98–101, 103, 104, 109–110, 114, 146, 191
Town Hall, 205
Traubel, Helen, 175, 188, 189–192, 202, 203, 236, 238, 254, 257, 258, 260, 261, 264, 267, 268
    first appearance at Metropolitan, 190
    first Wagnerian role, 190
    humor, 193
    Melchior on Traubel, 190
    nightclub career, 274–275, 280
    Traubel on Melchior, 193
Travers, Henry, 219
Trost, Olaf, 18
Truman, Harry, 258, 276
Truman, Margaret, 258, 267, 280
Trunk, Richard, 28, 51, 60
Tucker, Richard, 203, 261, 276

Tunney, Gene, 20
Two Sisters from Boston, 231–232, 237. See also Melchior, Lauritz: film career

Urlus, Jacques, 40

Valente, Val, 282
Varnay, Astrid, 188–189, 203, 204, 246
Verrett, Shirley, 229
Vickers, Jon, 59
Victor Talking Machine Company, 106
Vienna Staatsoper, 107, 123, 141, 146, 161
    audition with Schalk, 26
Viking, The, 18, 196–197, 198, 202, 241, 243, 254, 256, 272, 276, 277–278, 283, 298, 299, 300–305, 307, 319, 320, 323, 324
Villa Wahnfried, 29, 30–31, 33–34, 46, 52, 99, 104, 108, 109, 111, 124
Vinay, Ramon, 318
Visconti, Luchino, 46
Voice of Firestone, The. See Firestone Hour, The
Votipka, Thelma, 246
Votto, Antonino, 126

Wagner, Charles, 176
Wagner, Cosima, 31, 35, 37, 39, 47, 48, 52, 70, 80, 83, 86, 108, 110, 111, 216, 226, 256, 268, 329. See also Bayreuth Festival; Bayreuth style
    anti-Semitism, 33
    auditions Melchior, 28–31
    establishes "Bayreuth style," 29, 32–33
    changes Wagner scores, 99
    codifies eye movements, 46
    death, 103
    gives authority to Siegfried, 30
    marries Wagner, 30
    on acting, 46
    on cutting Tristan, 130
    on singing, 51
Wagner, Friedelind, 34, 48, 108, 111
Wagner, Martin, 282, 288
Wagner, Richard, 27, 29, 30, 31, 34, 48, 83, 86, 98, 99, 100, 102, 104, 108, 256, 326
    marries Cosima, 30
    philosophy of theater, 32–33, 34–35, 68, 130, 331
    design of Festspielhaus, 45
    on orchestra's role in music dramas, 109
Wagner, Siegfried ("Fidi"), 31, 32, 35, 37, 38, 39, 41, 46, 48, 51, 52, 57, 78, 80, 83, 101, 103, 108, 109, 111, 114, 124, 226, 256, 329. See also Bayreuth style; Wagner, Cosima

Wagner Society of New York, 129
Wagner, Verena, 34, 48
Wagner, Wieland, 29, 34, 226, 227, 312
Wagner, Winifred, 37, 49, 109, 111, 134,
      162. *See also* Bayreuth Festival;
      Bayreuth style; Hitler
   anti-Semitism, 33–34
   marries Siegfried, 33
   Nazism, 33–34, 52, 103, 110
   takes over festival, 29, 104, 108
Wagner, Wolfgang, 29, 34, 226, 316, 327
Walbom, Millie, 8
Waldrop, Gideon, 316
Wallis, Duchess of Windsor, 277
Walpole, Hugh, 31, 39, 42, 49–51, 52, 60,
      73, 78, 120, 157
   death, 199
   end of active role in Melchior career,
      55–56
   finances and promotes Melchior career,
      19–27, 35–36, 41, 134, 313
   meets Melchior, 19
   relationship with Lauritz and Kleinchen,
      49
Walska, Gana, 93
Walter, Bruno, 39, 40–41, 60, 72, 85, 94,
      123, 146, 157, 160, 276
Warren, Leonard, 203, 260, 276
Webster, Margaret, 270
Wedel, Mogens, 47, 226, 308, 311, 320
Weigert, Hermann, 189
Weinberger, Caspar, 198

Wemmer, Alan, 282
We the People, 212. *See also* Melchior,
      Lauritz: radio work
Whitehill, Clarence, 90
Wiedemann, Poul, 171
Williams, Edwards, 282, 283
Williams, Esther, 215, 218
Windgassen, Wolfgang, 38, 315
Windheim, Marek, 120, 144, 162
Windsor, Duchess of. *See* Wallis, Duchess
      of Windsor
Witherspoon, Herbert, 141–142, 143, 145,
      269, 329
Wolff Agency, 56. *See also* Simon, Erich
Wolff, Clairchen (Mrs. Fritz), 74–75, 105,
      224, 308
Wolff, Fritz, 74–75, 81, 86, 87, 104, 105,
      224. *See also* Wolff, Clairchen
Wolff, Werner, 94
Wood, Sir Henry, 16–17, 19, 131
Woolf, Virginia, 199
Woolworth, Jessie, 277
World's Fair Wagnerian Festival, 149–150

Zenatello, Giovanni, 133
Ziegler, Edward, 57, 63, 74, 87, 117, 119,
      134, 139, 141, 162, 164, 184, 190
Zukunfstmusik, 32
Zwicki and Stagel Company, 9, 10
Zwicki, Willi, 9